Exploring Writing
Paragraphs and Essays

THIRD EDITION

John Langan
Atlantic Cape Community College

Connect
Learn
Succeed™

Mc
Graw
Hill

The McGraw·Hill Companies

Connect
Learn
Succeed™

EXPLORING WRITING: PARAGRAPHS AND ESSAYS, THIRD EDITION
Published by McGraw-Hill, a business unit of The McGraw-Hill Companies, Inc., 1221 Avenue
of the Americas, New York, NY 10020. Copyright © 2013 by The McGraw-Hill Companies, Inc.
All rights reserved. Printed in the United States of America. Previous editions © 2010 and 2008.
No part of this publication may be reproduced or distributed in any form or by any means, or
stored in a database or retrieval system, without the prior written consent of The McGraw-Hill
Companies, Inc., including, but not limited to, in any network or other electronic storage or
transmission, or broadcast for distance learning.

Some ancillaries, including electronic and print components, may not be available to customers
outside the United States.

This book is printed on acid-free paper.

67890 RMN/RMN 109876

ISBN 978-0-07-353333-9
MHID 0-07-353333-5

ISBN 978-0-07-741128-2 (Annotated Instructor's Edition)
MHID 0-07-741128-5

Vice President & General Manager, HSSL: *Michael Ryan*
Managing Director: *David Patterson*
Director: *Paul Banks*
Executive Brand Manager: *Kelly Villella-Canton*
Senior Marketing Manager: *Jaclyn Elkins*
Director of Development: *Dawn Groundwater*
Development Editor: *Merryl Maleska Wilbur*
Senior Project Manager: *Lisa A. Bruflodt*
Cover Designer: *Preston Thomas*
Photo Research: *David A. Tietz/Editorial Image, LLC.*
Cover Image: *From left to right:—journal: ©Jupiterimages/Gettyimages—woman on laptop: ©David
Freudenthal/STOCK4B/Gettyimages—man at laptop: ©Rob Lewine/Gettyimages*
Buyer: *Laura Fuller*
Compositor: *MPS Limited*
Typeface: *11/13.5 Palatino*
Printer: *RR Donnelley*

All credits appearing on page or at the end of the book are considered to be an extension of the
copyright page.

Library of Congress Cataloging-in-Publication Data

Langan, John, 1942-
    Exploring writing : paragraphs and essays / John Langan.—3rd ed.
        p. cm.
    Includes bibliographical references and index.
    ISBN-13: 978-0-07-353333-9 (acid-free paper)
    ISBN-10: 0-07-353333-5 (acid-free paper)
    1. English language—Paragraphs—Problems, exercises, etc. 2. English language—
Rhetoric—Problems, exercises, etc. 3. Report writing—Problems, exercises, etc. I. Title.

PE1439.L36 2012
808'.042076—dc23

                                                                        2012033283

www.mhhe.com

John Langan has taught reading and writing at Atlantic Cape Community College near Atlantic City, New Jersey, for more than twenty-five years. The author of a popular series of college textbooks on both writing and reading, John enjoys the challenge of developing materials that teach skills in an especially clear and lively way. Before teaching, he earned advanced degrees in writing at Rutgers University and in reading at Rowan University. He also spent a year writing fiction that, he says, "is now at the back of a drawer waiting to be discovered and acclaimed posthumously." While in school, he supported himself by working as a truck driver, a machinist, a battery assembler, a hospital attendant, and an apple packer. John now lives with his wife, Judith Nadell, near Philadelphia. In addition to his wife and Philly sports teams, his passions include reading and turning on nonreaders to the pleasure and power of books. Through Townsend Press, his educational publishing company, he has developed the nonprofit "Townsend Library"—a collection of more than one hundred new and classic stories that appeal to readers of any age.

BRIEF CONTENTS

CONTENTS

PART FIVE Handbook of Sentence Skills 392

SECTION I Grammar 394

CONNECT Writing 2.0 Personalized Learning Plan CORRELATION GUIDE

UNIT	TOPIC IN PERSONALIZED LEARNING PLAN
Writing Clear Sentences	Subjects and Verbs
Fixing Common Problems	Fragments Run-Ons Verb Forms Subject-Verb Agreement Verb Tense Adjectives and Adverbs Pronoun Case Pronoun Agreement Pronoun Reference Misplaced and Dangling Modifiers

21. Subjects and Verbs 395

SECTION II Mechanics   469

CONNECT Writing 2.0 Personalized Learning Plan CORRELATION GUIDE

UNIT	TOPIC IN PERSONALIZED LEARNING PLAN
Addressing Mechanics	Capitalization Abbreviations Numbers

SECTION III Punctuation   484

CONNECT Reading 2.0 Personalized Reading Plan
CORRELATION GUIDE

UNIT	TOPIC IN PERSONALIZED LEARNING PLAN
Punctuating Correctly	Commas Apostrophes End Punctuation Quotation Marks Colons and Semicolons Parentheses Dashes Hyphens

SECTION IV Word Use   512

CONNECT Reading 2.0 Personalized Reading Plan CORRELATION GUIDE

UNIT	TOPIC IN PERSONALIZED LEARNING PLAN
Using Words Effectively	Misspelled Words
	Commonly Confused Words
	Omitted Words
	Slang
	Euphemisms
	Clichés
	Sexist Words
	Biased Words
	Pretentious Words
	Wordy Phrases
	Empty Words
	Redundant Words
	Repetitive Words
	Unnecessary Passive Verbs

Note: Some selections are cross-listed because they illustrate more than one rhetorical method of development.

CAUSE AND/OR EFFECT

COMPARISON AND/OR CONTRAST

DEFINITION

DIVISION-CLASSIFICATION

ARGUMENTATION

Preface

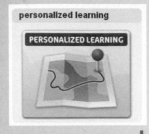

Exploring Personalized Learning

Exploring Writing emphasizes personalized learning. Powered by *Connect Writing*, students gain access to our groundbreaking personalized learning plan, which helps students become aware of what they already know and what they need to practice. A self-study tool, its cutting-edge, continually adaptive technology and exclusive time-management features make students more productive, keep them on track, and give them the writing skills needed for all their college courses.

With a baseline adaptive diagnostic that assesses student proficiencies in five core areas of grammar and mechanics, students can generate a unique learning plan tailored to address their specific needs in the allotted time. Students receive a personalized program of writing lessons, videos, animations, and interactive exercises to improve their skills and are offered immediate feedback on their work. With an engine that incorporates metacognitive learning theory and provides ongoing diagnosis for every learning objective, the personal learning plan continually adapts with each student interaction, while built-in time management tools ensure that students achieve their course goals. This personalized, constantly assessing and adapting online environment increases student readiness, motivation, and confidence, and allows classroom instruction to focus on thoughtful and critical writing processes.

Personalized learning plan icons, like the one above, are integrated throughout the chapters. The detailed Table of Contents also contains a Connect Writing 2.0 Personalized Learning Plan Correlation Guide for Part Three. It lists related individual learning topics in the Connect personalized learning plan.

Exploring Personal, Academic, and Workplace Writing

Exploring Writing is flexible. Throughout *Paragraphs and Essays*, students are exposed to examples of writing that reflect the three key realms of their lives—personal, academic, and workplace. They will find the models, activities, and examples for any writing situation. Parts Two and Three, for example, include new sample paragraphs reflecting academic and workplace writing while continuing to offer familiar as well as updated personal writing examples. This variety provides great flexibility in the kinds of assignments you prefer to give. Icons identifying personal, academic, and workplace writing are integrated throughout the chapters.

Exploring and Mastering the Four Bases: Unity, Support, Coherence, Sentence Skills

Exploring Writing emphasizes writing skills and process. By referring to a set of four skills for effective writing, *Exploring Writing* encourages new writers to see writing as a skill that can be learned and a process that must be explored. The four skills, or bases, for effective writing are as follows:

- **Unity:** Discover a clearly stated point or topic sentence, and make sure that all other information in the paragraph or essay supports that point.

- **Support:** Support the points with specific evidence, and plenty of it.

- **Coherence:** Organize and connect supporting evidence so that paragraphs and essays transition smoothly from one bit of supporting information to the next.

- **Sentence skills:** Revise and edit so that sentences are error-free for clearer and more effective communication.

The four bases are essential to effective writing, whether it be a narrative paragraph, a cover letter for a job application, or an essay assignment.

UNITY

Discover a clearly stated point, or topic sentence, and make sure all the other information in the paragraph or essay is in support of that point.

SUPPORT

Support points with specific evidence, and plenty of it.

COHERENCE

Organize and connect supporting evidence so that paragraphs and essays transition smoothly from one bit of supporting information to the next.

SENTENCE SKILLS

Revise and edit so that sentences are error-free for clearer and more effective communication.

In addition to incorporating the personalized learning plan, maintaining the four bases framework, and continuing to build in many familiar personal writing examples, *Exploring Writing: Paragraphs and Essays 3/e* includes the following chapter-by-chapter changes:

Part One: Writing Skills and Process
- New sample paragraphs that reflect academic and workplace writing
- Revised writing samples to eliminate use of second-person

Part Two: Basic Principles of Effective Writing
- New sample paragraphs that reflect academic and workplace writing
- Revised writing samples to eliminate use of second-person

Part Three: Paragraph Development
- Updated personal writing examples
- New sample paragraphs that reflect academic and workplace writing
- New Activities and Writing Assignments that reflect academic and workplace writing
- Revised writing samples to eliminate use of second-person

Part Four: Essay Development

Chapter 15: Introduction to Essay Development
- Revised presentation of the term "essay," including explanation of "thesis" and coverage of essays with more than three supporting paragraphs
- New explanation of the role of mixed modes in essay writing
- New explanation about limited use of second-person in writing

Chapter 16: Writing the Essay
- Coverage of essays with more than three supporting paragraphs
- Updated, revised full-length sample essay
- Revised writing samples to eliminate use of second-person

Chapter 17: Introductions, Conclusions, and Titles
- Revised treatment of the use of questions in essay structuring
- New Activities and Writing Assignments that reflect academic and workplace writing
- Inclusion of multiple across-chapter cross-references to related topics

Chapter 18: Patterns of Essay Development

- Chapter overhauled
- New introductory text for each pattern with explanation of how multiple modes function together in one essay
- All nine sample essays now emphasize one pattern or mode, but include other modes as well to better reflect real writing
- Revised essay questions, with inclusion of Main Idea, Author's Purpose, and Mixed Modes questions for each essay
- New directions for reading, analyzing, and interacting with each essay
- New sample essays and Writing Assignments that reflect academic and workplace writing
- Revised writing samples to eliminate use of second-person
- Inclusion of multiple across-chapter cross-references to related topics

Chapter 20: Writing a Research Paper

- Updated formatting for sample student paper to better represent academic expectations

Part Five: Handbook of Sentence Skills

- Grammar activities and exercises rewritten to incorporate academic and workplace-related themes
- Review Tests reworked to incorporate academic and workplace-related themes
- Revised material frequently focused on one issue so that it reads as a unified passage rather than a set of disconnected statements
- Improved coverage of certain key grammar topics, such as subordinating words and verb forms
- Targeted instruction on e-mail writing and etiquette
- Inclusion of multiple across-chapter cross-references to related topics

Part Six: Readings for Writers

- Readings updated to include four new selections by diverse and well-respected authors:

    "Superman and Me" by Sherman Alexie
    "Straw into Gold: The Metamorphosis of the Everyday" by Sandra Cisneros
    "Mother Tongue" by Amy Tan
    "Advice to Youth" by Mark Twain

- Each new reading accompanied by a new full set of questions and assignments
- All assignments reflect either personal, academic, or workplace-related themes

Appendixes

- New appendix presents formal e-mail model, along with guidelines for writing e-mails
- New appendix provides lists of most common transition words and phrases

Book-Specific Supplements for Instructors

The Annotated Instructor's Edition (ISBN 007-741128-5) consists of the student text, complete with answers to all activities and tests.

The Online Learning Center (www.mhhe.com/langan) offers a number of instructional materials including an instructor's manual, test bank, and PowerPoint® slides that may be tailored to course needs.

Connect Writing 2.0

Described in more detail inside the cover, this online site provides a personalized learning plan that continually diagnoses and adapts lessons and questions to students' strengths and weaknesses within the five core areas of grammar and mechanics.

Additionally, it offers digital tools developed by composition experts that support and engage your students with a variety of course activities, including: group assignments, discussion board assignments, web-based assignments, blog assignments, writing assignments with peer review and commenting.

Connect LMS Integration

Connect Writing integrates with your local Learning Management System (Blackboard, Desire2Learn, and others.)

McGraw-Hill Campus™ is a new one-stop teaching and learning experience available to users of any learning management system. This complimentary integration allows faculty and students to enjoy single sign-on (SSO) access to all McGraw-Hill Higher Education materials and synchronized grade-book with our award-winning McGraw-Hill *Connect* platform. McGraw-Hill Campus provides faculty with instant access to all McGraw-Hill Higher Education teaching materials (eTextbooks, test banks, PowerPoint slides, animations and learning objects, and so on), allowing them to browse, search, and use any instructor ancillary content in our vast library at no additional cost to the instructor or students. Students enjoy SSO access to a variety of free (quizzes, flash cards, narrated presentations, and so on) and subscription-based products (McGraw-Hill *Connect*). With this integration enabled, faculty and students will never need to create another account to access McGraw-Hill products and services. For more information on McGraw-Hill Campus please visit our Web site at "http://www.mhcampus.com" or contact your local McGraw-Hill representative to find out more about installations on your campus.

Create the Perfect Course Materials with Create™

create   Your courses evolve over time, shouldn't your course material?

With McGraw-Hill Create™, you can easily arrange your book to align with the syllabus, eliminate chapters you do not assign, combine material from other content sources, and quickly upload content you have written, such as your course syllabus or teaching notes to enhance the value of course materials for your students. By visiting www.mcgrawhillcreate .com, you may select content by discipline or collection, including chapters from 4,000 textbooks, 5,500 articles, 25,000 cases, and 11,000 readings. You control the net price of the book as you build it and have the opportunity to choose format: color, black and white, and eBook. When you build a CREATE book, you'll receive a complimentary print review copy in 3 to 5 business days or a complimentary electronic review copy (eComp) via e-mail in about one hour.

Go to www.mcgrawhillcreate.com and register today!

Customize *Exploring Writing* in Create™ with Bonus Content

In addition to reordering and eliminating chapters in *Exploring Writing: Paragraphs and Essays,* adding your own materials, or adding chapters from other McGraw-Hill textbooks, you may customize the readings in Part Six by eliminating or adding readings from other Langan titles or from other McGraw-Hill collections such as *The Ideal Reader* (800 readings by author, genre, mode, theme, and discipline), *Annual Editions* (5,500 articles from journals and periodicals), *Traditions* (readings in the humanities), *Sustainability* (readings with an environment focus), and *American History and World Civilization Documents* (primary sources including maps, charts, letters, memoirs, and essays).

Bonus Content also includes an Appendix on Writing Résumés and Cover Letters and more.

McGraw-Hill Create™ ExpressBooks facilitate customizing your book more quickly and easily. To quickly view the possibilities for customizing your book, visit www.mcgrawhillcreate.com and enter "Exploring Writing" under the Find Content tab. Once you select the current edition of your chosen Exploring Writing book, click on the "View Related ExpressBooks" button or ExpressBooks tab to see options. ExpressBooks contain a combination of pre-selected chapters, articles, cases, or readings that serve as a starting point to help you quickly and easily build your own text. These helpful templates are built using content available on Create and organized in ways that match various course outlines. We understand that you have a unique perspective. Use McGraw-Hill Create ExpressBooks to build the book you've only imagined!

Tegrity

Tegrity Campus is a service that makes class time available all the time by automatically capturing every lecture in a searchable format for students to review when they study and complete assignments. With a simple one-click start and stop process, users capture all computer screens and corresponding audio. Students replay any part of any class with easy-to-use browser-based viewing on a PC or Mac. Educators know that the more students can see, hear, and experience class resources, the better they learn. With Tegrity Campus, students quickly recall key moments by using Tegrity Campus's unique search feature. This search helps students efficiently find what they need, when they need it, across an entire semester of class recordings. Help turn all your students' study time into learning moments immediately supported by your lecture.

CourseSmart®

This text is available as an eTextbook at www. CourseSmart.com. At CourseSmart your students can take advantage of significant savings off the cost of a print textbook, reduce their impact on the environment, and gain access to powerful Web tools for learning. CourseSmart eTextbooks can be viewed online or downloaded to a computer. The eTextbooks allow students to do full text searches, add highlighting and notes, and share notes with classmates. CourseSmart has the largest selection of eTextbooks available anywhere. Visit www.CourseSmart.com to learn more and to try a sample chapter.

ACKNOWLEDGMENTS

Without the contributions and diligence of Zoe L. Albright of Metropolitan Community College—Longview, this edition would not have come to fruition. The quality of *Exploring Writing* is a testament to the suggestions and insights from instructors around the country. Many thanks to all of those who helped improve this project.

Steven R. Acree, *College of the Desert*

Marty Ambrose, *Edison State College*

James M. Andres, *Harper College*

Marcia Backos, *Bryant & Stratton College*

Elizabeth Barnes, *Daytona Beach Community College—Daytona Beach*

Michalle Barnett, *Gulf Coast Community College*

Carolyn Barr, *Broward College*

Elizabeth Bass, *Camden County College*

Elaine Bassett, *Troy University*

Glenda Bell, *University of Arkansas Community College at Batesville*

Victoria S. Berardi-Rogers, *Northwestern Community College*

Manette Berlinger, *Queensborough Community College*

Jennifer Black, *McLennan Community College*

Christian Blum, *Bryant and Stratton College*

Kathleen S. Britton, *Florence-Darlington Technical College*

Marta Brown, *Community College of Denver*

Shanti Bruce, *Nova Southeastern University*

Jennifer Bubb, *Illinois Valley Community College*

Alexandra C. Campbell-Forte, *Germanna Community College*

Jessica Carroll, *Miami Dade College—Wolfson*

Patti Casey, *Tyler Junior College*

Helen Chester, *Milwaukee Area Technical College*

Cathy Clements, *State Fair Community College*

Patricia Colella, *Bunker Hill Community College*

Donna-Marie Colonna, *Sandhills Community College*

Linda Austin Crawford, *McLennan Community College*

Dena DeCastro, *Clark College*

Beverly F. Dile, *Elizabethtown Community and Technical College*

Carrie Dorsey, *Northern Virginia Community College*

Thomas Dow, *Moraine Valley Community College*

Michelle Downey, *Florence-Darlington Technical College*

Joyce Anne Dvorak, *Metropolitan Community College—Longview*

Kevin Dye, *Chemeketa Community College*

Marie Eckstrom, *Rio Hondo College*

Claudia Edwards, *Piedmont Technical College*

Amy England, *University of Cincinnati*

Susan Ertel, *Dixie State College of Utah*

Lori Farr, *Oklahoma City Community College*

Karen Feldman, *Seminole Community College*

Jim Fields, *Iowa Western Community College*

Alexander Fitzner, *Pellissippi State Technical Community College*

Karen Fleming, *Sinclair Community College*

Deborah Fontaine, *Okaloosa-Walton College*

Billy Fontenot, *Louisiana State University—Eunice*

H. L. Ford, *Pellissippi State Technical Community College*

Jaquelyn Gaiters-Jordan, *Pikes Peak Community College*

Valerie Gray, *Harrisburg Area Community College*

Jennifer Green, *Southern University at Shreveport*

Roxanne Hannon-Odom, *Bishop State Community College*

Linda H. Hasty, *Motlow State Community College*

Dawn Hayward, *Delaware County Community College*

Angela Hebert, *Hudson County Community College*

Catherine Higdon, *Tarrant County College—South Campus*

Rita Higgins, *Essex County College*

Desha S. Hill, *Tyler Junior College*

Lee Nell W. Hill, *Tyler Junior College*

Elizabeth Holton, *Frederick Community College*

Sharyn L. Hunter, *Sinclair Community College*

Michael Jaffe, *El Camino College*

Kaushalya Jagasia, *Illinois Valley Community College*

Leslie Johnston, *Pulaski Technical College*

Leigh Jonaitis, *Bergen Community College*

Billy Jones, *Miami Dade College—Kendall*

Julie Kelly, *St. Johns River State College*

Heather Kichner, *Lorain County Community College*

Laura Kingston, *South Seattle Community College*

Trudy Krisher, *Sinclair Community College*

Dianne Krob, *Rose State College*

Kristin Le Veness, *Nassau Community College*

Amy Lerman, *Mesa Community College*

Keming Liu, *Medgar Evers College*

Paulette Longmore, *Essex County College*

Breanna Lutterbie, *Germanna Community College*

Suzanne Lynch, *Hillsborough Community College*

Teri Maddox, *Jackson State Community College*

Jeanette Maurice, *Illinois Valley Community College*

Linda McCloud, *Broward College*

Diane McDonald, *Montgomery County Community College—Blue Bell*

Sarah McFarland, *Northwestern State University*

Candace C. Mesa, *Dixie State College*

Theresa Mohamed, *Onondaga Community College*

Susan Monroe, *Housatonic Community College*

Christopher Morelock, *Walters State Community College*

Lori Renae Morrow, *Rose State College*

Steven Mullis, *Central Piedmont Community College*

Julie Nichols, *Okaloosa-Walton College*

Julie Odell, *Community College of Philadelphia*

Ellen Olmstead, *Montgomery College*

Kelly Ormsby, *Cleveland State Community College*

Robin Ozz, *Phoenix College*

Jay Peterson, *Atlantic Cape Community College*

Susie Peyton, *Marshall Community and Technical College*

Tracy Peyton, *Pensacola Junior College*

Jacklyn R. Pierce, *Lake-Sumter Community College*

Lydia Postell, *Dalton State College*

Teresa Prosser, *Sinclair Community College*

Danielle Reites, *Lake-Sumter Community College*

Charles A. Riley II, *Baruch College, City University of New York*

Michael Roberts, *Fresno City College*

Dawnielle B. Robinson-Walker, *Metropolitan Community College—Longview*

Patty Rogers, *Angelina College*

Stephanie Sabourin, *Montgomery College—Takoma Park/Silver Spring*

Jamie Sadler, *Richmond Community College*

Jim Sayers, *University of New Mexico—Gallup Campus*

Joseph Scherer, *Community College of Allegheny—South*

Anna Schmidt, *Lonestar College—CyFair*

Caroline Seefchak, *Edison State College*

Linda Shief, *Wake Technical Community College*

Lori Smalley, *Greenville Technical College*

Anne Smith, *Northwest Mississippi Community College*

Hank Smith, *Gulf Coast Community College*

James R. Sodon, *St. Louis Community College—Florissant Valley*

Crystal Stallman, *Hawkeye Community College*

James Suderman, *Okaloosa-Walton College*

Holly Susi, *Community College of Rhode Island—Flanagan*

Karen Taylor, *Belmont Technical College*

Lisa Telesca, *Citrus College*

Douglas Texter, *Minneapolis Community and Technical College*

Caryl Terrell-Bamiro, *Chandler-Gilbert Community College*

Connie Kendall Theado, *University of Cincinnati*

Sharisse Turner, *Tallahassee Community College*

Christine Tutlewski, *University of Wisconsin—Parkside*

Kathryn Y. Tyndall, *Wake Technical Community College*

Cynthia VanSickle, *McHenry County College*

Maria Villar-Smith, *Miami Dade College—Wolfson*

Nikka Vrieze, *Rochester Community and Technical College*

Ross Wagner, *Greenville Technical College*

Mark Walls, *Jackson State Community College*

Arthur Wellborn, *McLennan Community College*

Stephen Wells, *Community College of Allegheny—South*

Marjorie-Anne Wikoff, *St. Petersburg College*

Sheila Wiley, *Santa Barbara City College*

Debbie Wilke, *Daytona State College*

Kelli Wilkes, *Valdosta Technical College*

Jim Wilkins-Luton, *Clark College*

Julia Williams, *Harrison College*

Jeff Wheeler, *Long Beach City College*

Mary Joyce Whiteside, *El Paso Community College*

Shonda Wilson, *Suffolk County Community College*

Mary Katherine Winkler, *Blue Ridge Community College*

Xuewei Wu, *Century Community and Technical College*

Deborah Yaden, *Richland Community College*

William Young, *University of South Alabama*

Betsy Zuegg, *Quinsigamond Community College*

Exploring Writing

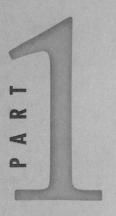

Writing:
Skills and Process

PART ONE WILL

- introduce you to the basic principles of effective writing

- present writing as both a skill and a process of discovery

- explain and illustrate the sequence of steps in writing an effective paragraph, including:

  - prewriting

  - revising

  - editing

- ask you to write a paragraph

EXPLORING WRITING PROMPT:

This part of the text explains writing as an invaluable tool in college and beyond. Focus on one of your favorite activities— playing basketball, cooking, watching movies, listening to music alone in your room, or just taking a walk, for example. Then, pretend that you have been asked to explain the reasons you enjoy this activity to the other students in your writing class. Now, on a piece of paper or on a computer, write the answers to the following questions:

1. Would you rather stand up in front of the class and explain these reasons in person, or would you rather explain them in a written note or letter?

2. What advantages might speaking have over writing in this example? What advantages might there be in writing your reasons in a note or letter?

3. Which method would you find harder? Why?

4. What are the differences between speaking about this topic and writing about it?

An Introduction to Writing

RESPONDING TO IMAGES

College offers many different challenges for students. In order to be a successful student, you should know your individual strengths and weaknesses. Take some time to think about your strengths and weaknesses as a student. Later in this chapter you will be asked to write a paragraph on this topic.

The experience I had writing my first college essay helped shape this book. I received a C– for the essay. Scrawled beside the grade was the comment "Not badly written, but ill-conceived." I remember going to the instructor after class, asking about his comment as well as the word *Log* that he had added in the margin at various spots. "What are all these logs you put in my paper?" I asked, trying to make a joke of it. He looked at me a little wonderingly. "Logic, Mr. Langan," he answered, "logic." He went on to explain that I had not thought out my paper clearly. There were actually two ideas rather than one in my thesis, one supporting paragraph had nothing to do with either idea, another paragraph lacked a topic sentence, and so on. I've never forgotten his last words: "If you don't think clearly," he said, "you won't write clearly."

I was speechless, and I felt confused and angry. I didn't like being told that I didn't know how to think. I went back to my room and read over my paper several times. Eventually, I decided that my instructor was right. "No more logs," I said to myself. "I'm going to get these logs out of my papers."

My instructor's advice was invaluable. I learned that clear, disciplined thinking is the key to effective writing. *Exploring Writing: Paragraphs and Essays* develops this idea by breaking down the writing process into a series of four logical, easily followed steps. These steps, combined with practical advice about prewriting and revision, will help you write strong papers.

Here are the four steps in a nutshell:

1. Discover a clearly stated point.

2. Provide logical, detailed support for your point.

3. Organize and connect your supporting material.

4. Revise and edit so that your sentences are effective and errorfree.

Part 2 of this book explains each of these steps in detail and provides many practice materials to help you master them.

Point and Support

An Important Difference between Writing and Talking

In everyday conversation, you make all kinds of points or assertions. You say, for example, "My boss is a hard person to work for"; "It's not safe to walk in our neighborhood after dark"; or "Poor study habits keep getting me into trouble." Your points concern personal matters as well as, at times, outside issues: "That trade will be a disaster for the team"; "*CSI* is the most entertaining drama on TV"; "Students are better off working for a year before attending college."

The people you are talking with do not always challenge you to give reasons for your statements. They may know why you feel as you do, or they may already agree with you, or they simply may not want to put you on the spot; and so they do not always ask "Why?" But the people who read what you write may not know you, agree with you, or feel in any way obliged to you. If you want to communicate effectively with readers, you must provide solid evidence for any point you make. An important difference, then, between writing and talking is this: *In writing, any idea that you advance must be supported with specific reasons or details.*

Think of your readers as reasonable people. They will not take your views on faith, but they are willing to consider what you say as long as you support it. Therefore, remember to support with specific evidence any point that you make.

Point and Support in a Paragraph

In conversation, you might say to a friend who has suggested a movie, "No, thanks. Going to the movies is just too much of a hassle. Parking, people, everything." From shared past experiences, your friend may know what you are talking about so that you will not have to explain your statement. But in writing, your point would have to be backed up with specific reasons and details.

Below is a paragraph, written by a student named Diane Woods, on why moviegoing is a nuisance. A *paragraph* is a short paper of 150 to 200 words. It usually consists of an opening point called a *topic sentence* followed by a series of sentences that support that point.

The Hazards of Moviegoing

Although I love movies, I have found that there are drawbacks to moviegoing. One problem is just the inconvenience of it all. To get to the theater, I have to drive for at least fifteen minutes, or more if traffic is bad. It can take forever to find a parking spot, and then I have to walk across a huge parking lot to the theater. There I encounter long lines, sold-out shows, and ever-increasing prices. And I hate sitting with my feet sticking to the floor because of other people's spilled snacks. Another problem is my lack of self-control at the theater. I often stuff myself with unhealthy calorie-laden snacks. My choices might include a bucket of popcorn dripping with butter, a box of Junior Mints, a large Coke, or all three. Finally, the worst problem is some of the other moviegoers. As kids run up and down the aisle, teenagers laugh and shout at the screen. People of all ages drop soda cups and popcorn tubs, cough and burp, and talk on their cell phones. All in all, I would rather stay home and wait to see the latest movies On Demand in the comfort of my own living room.

Notice what the supporting evidence does here. It provides you, the reader, with a basis for understanding *why* the writer makes the point that is made. Through this specific evidence, the writer has explained and successfully communicated the idea that moviegoing can be a nuisance.

The evidence that supports the point in a paragraph often consists of a series of reasons followed by examples and details that support the reasons. That is true of the paragraph above: three reasons are provided, with examples and details that back up those reasons. Supporting evidence in a paper can also consist of anecdotes, personal experiences, facts, studies, statistics, and the opinions of experts.

ACTIVITY 1

The paragraph on moviegoing, like almost any piece of effective writing, has two essential parts: (1) a point is advanced, and (2) that point is then supported. Taking a minute to outline the paragraph will help you understand these basic parts clearly. Add the words needed to complete the outline of the paragraph.

Point: There are drawbacks to moviegoing.

Support:

1. _____
   a. Fifteen-minute drive to theater
   b. _____
   c. Long lines, sold-out shows, and increasing prices
   d. _____

2. Lack of self-control
   a. Often stuff myself with unhealthy snacks
   b. Might have popcorn, candy, soda, or all three

3. _____
   a. _____
   b. _____
   c. People of all ages make noise.

ACTIVITY 2

An excellent way to get a feel for the paragraph is to write one. Your instructor may ask you to do that now. The only guidelines you need to follow are the ones described here. There is an advantage to writing a paragraph right away, at a point where you have had almost no instruction. This first paragraph will give a quick sense of your needs as a writer and will provide a baseline—a standard of comparison that you and your instructor can use to measure your writing progress during the semester.

Here, then, is your topic: The opening photo of this chapter asked you to think about your strengths and weaknesses as a student. Select one of your strengths or weaknesses and write a paragraph on why you believe it to be a strength or weakness. Provide three reasons why you consider it a strength or weakness, and give plenty of details to develop each of your three reasons.

Notice that the sample paragraph, "The Hazards of Moviegoing," has the same format your paragraph should have. You should do what this writer has done:

- State a point in the first sentence.

- Give three reasons to support the point.

- Introduce each reason clearly with signal words (such as *First of all*, *Second*, and *Finally*).

- Provide details that develop each of the three reasons.

Knowing Your Purpose and Audience

The three most common purposes of writing are to inform, to persuade, and to entertain. Each is described briefly below.

- To **inform**—to give information about a subject. Authors who are writing to inform want to provide facts that will explain or teach something to readers. For example, an informative paragraph about sandwiches might begin, "Eating food between two slices of bread—a sandwich—is a practice that has its origins in eighteenth-century England."

- To **persuade**—to convince the reader to agree with the author's point of view on a subject. Authors who are writing to persuade may give facts, but their main goal is to argue or prove a point to readers. A persuasive paragraph about sandwiches might begin, "There are good reasons why every sandwich should be made with whole grain bread."

- To **entertain**—to amuse and delight; to appeal to the reader's senses and imagination. Authors write to entertain in various ways, through fiction and nonfiction. An entertaining paragraph about sandwiches might begin, "What I wanted was a midnight snack, but what I got was better—the biggest, most magical sandwich in the entire world."

Much of the writing assigned in this book will involve some form of argumentation or persuasion. You will advance a point or thesis and then support it in a variety of ways. To some extent, also, you will write papers to inform—to provide readers with information about a particular subject. And since, in practice, writing often combines purposes, you might find yourself at times providing vivid or humorous details in order to entertain your readers as well.

Various writing activities throughout this book—in particular the "Beyond the Classroom" writing assignments and "A Writer's Template: Across Disciplines"—will ask you to think about your purpose and audience. For the rest of your writing, your audience will be primarily your instructor and sometimes other students. Your instructor is really a symbol of the larger audience you should see yourself writing for—an audience of educated adults who expect you to present your ideas in a clear, direct, organized way. If you can learn to write to persuade or inform such a general audience, you will have accomplished a great deal.

Benefits of Paragraph Writing

Paragraph writing offers at least three benefits. First of all, mastering the structure of the paragraph will help make you a better writer. For other courses, you'll often do writing that will be variations on the paragraph form—for example, exam answers, summaries, response papers, and brief reports. In addition, paragraphs serve as the basic building blocks of essays, the most common form of writing in college. The basic structure of the traditional paragraph, with its emphasis on a clear point and well-organized, logical support, will help you write effective essays and almost every kind of paper that you will have to do.

Second, the discipline of writing a paragraph will strengthen your skills as a reader and listener. You'll become more critically aware of other writers' and speakers' ideas and the evidence they provide—or fail to provide—to support those ideas.

Most important, paragraph writing will make you a stronger thinker. Writing a solidly reasoned paragraph requires mental discipline and close attention to a set of logical rules. Creating a paragraph in which there is an overall topic sentence supported by well-reasoned, convincing evidence is more challenging than writing a free-form or expressive paper. Such a paragraph obliges you to carefully sort out, think through, and organize your ideas. You'll learn to discover and express just what your ideas are and to develop those ideas in a sound and logical way. Traditional paragraph writing, in short, will train your mind to think clearly, and that ability will prove to be of value in every phase of your life.

Writing as a Skill

A sure way to ruin your chances of learning how to write competently is to believe that writing is a "natural gift" rather than a learned skill. People with such an attitude think that they are the only ones for whom writing is unbearably difficult. They feel that everyone else finds writing easy or at least tolerable. Such people typically say, "I'm not any good at writing" or "English was not one of my good subjects." They imply that they simply do not have a talent for writing, while others do. The result of this attitude is that people try to avoid writing, and when they do write, they don't try their best. Their attitude becomes a self-fulfilling prophecy: Their writing fails chiefly because they have brainwashed themselves into thinking that they don't have the "natural talent" needed to write. Unless their attitude changes, they probably will not learn how to write effectively.

A realistic attitude about writing must build on the idea that *writing is a skill*. It is a skill like driving, typing, or cooking, and like any skill, it can be learned. If you have the determination to learn, this book will give you the extensive practice needed to develop your writing skills.

Many people find it difficult to do the intense, active thinking that clear writing demands. (Perhaps television has made us all so passive that the active thinking necessary in both writing and reading now seems harder than ever.) It is frightening to sit down before a blank sheet of paper or a computer screen and know that, an hour later, nothing on it may be worth keeping. It is frustrating to discover how much of a challenge it is to transfer thoughts and feelings from one's head into words. It is upsetting to find that an apparently simple writing subject often turns out to be complicated. But writing is not an automatic process: we will not get something for nothing—and we should not expect to. For almost everyone, competent writing comes from plain hard work—from determination, sweat, and head-on battle. The good news is that the skill of writing can be mastered, and if you are ready to work, you will learn what you need to know.

| ACTIVITY 3 | To get a sense of just how you regard writing, read the following statements. Put a check (✓) beside those statements with which you agree. This activity is not a test, so try to be as honest as possible. |

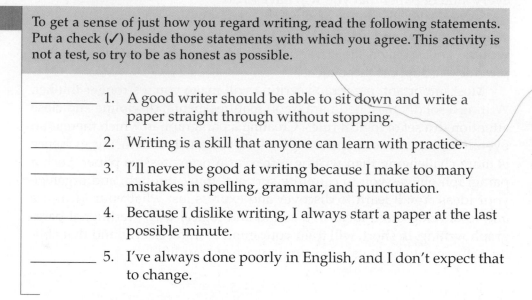

_____ 1. A good writer should be able to sit down and write a paper straight through without stopping.

_____ 2. Writing is a skill that anyone can learn with practice.

_____ 3. I'll never be good at writing because I make too many mistakes in spelling, grammar, and punctuation.

_____ 4. Because I dislike writing, I always start a paper at the last possible minute.

_____ 5. I've always done poorly in English, and I don't expect that to change.

Now read the following comments about the five statements. The comments will help you see if your attitude is hurting or helping your efforts to become a better writer.

Comments

- **A good writer should be able to sit down and write a paper straight through without stopping.**

    Statement 1 is not true. Writing is, in fact, a process. It is done not in one easy step but in a series of steps, and seldom at one sitting. If you cannot do a paper all at once, that simply means you are like most of the other people on the planet. It is harmful to carry around the false idea that writing should be easy.

- **Writing is a skill that anyone can learn with practice.**

    Statement 2 is absolutely true. Writing is a skill, like driving or cooking, that you can master with hard work. If you want to learn to write, you can. It is as simple as that. If you believe this, you are ready to learn how to become a competent writer.

    Some people hold the false belief that writing is a natural gift, which some have and others do not. Because of this belief, they never make a truly honest effort to learn to write—and so they never learn.

- **I'll never be good at writing because I make too many mistakes in spelling, grammar, and punctuation.**

    The first concern in good writing should be content—what you have to say. Your ideas and feelings are what matter most. You should not worry about spelling, grammar, or punctuation while working on content.

    Unfortunately, some people are so self-conscious about making mistakes that they do not focus on what they want to say. They need to realize that a paper is best done in stages, and that applying the rules can and should wait until a later stage in the writing process. Through review and practice, you will eventually learn how to follow the rules with confidence.

- **Because I dislike writing, I always start a paper at the last possible minute.**

    This habit is all too common. You feel you are going to do poorly, and then behave in a way that ensures you *will* do poorly! Your attitude is so negative that you defeat yourself—not even allowing enough time to really try.

    Again, what you need to realize is that writing is a process. Because it is done in steps, you don't have to get it right all at once. If you allow yourself enough time, you'll find a way to make a paper come together.

- **I've always done poorly in English, and I don't expect that to change.**

    How you may have performed in the *past* does not control how you can perform in the *present*. Even if you did poorly in English in high school, it is in your power to make English one of your best subjects in college. If you believe writing can be learned and then work hard at it, you *will* become a better writer.

    In conclusion, your attitude is crucial. If you believe you are a poor writer and always will be, chances are you will not improve. If you realize you can become a better writer, chances are you *will* improve. Depending on how you allow yourself to think, you can be your own best friend or your own worst enemy.

Writing as a Process of Discovery

In addition to believing that writing is a natural gift, many people believe, mistakenly, that writing should flow in a simple, straight line from the writer's head onto the written page. But writing is seldom an easy, one-step journey in which a finished paper comes out in a first draft. The truth is that *writing is a process of discovery* involving a series of steps, and those steps are very often a zigzag journey. Look at the following illustrations of the writing process:

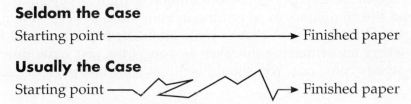

Seldom the Case

Starting point ⟶ Finished paper

Usually the Case

Starting point ⟶ Finished paper

Very often, writers do not discover just what they want to write about until they explore their thoughts in writing. For example, Diane Woods, the author of the paragraph on moviegoing, had been assigned to write about some annoyance in everyday life. She did not know what annoyance she would choose; instead, she just began writing about annoyances in general, in order to discover a topic. One of those annoyances was traffic, which seemed promising, so she began putting down ideas and details that came to her about traffic. One detail was the traffic she had to deal with in going to the movies. That made her think of the traffic in the parking lot at the theater complex. At that point, she realized that moviegoing itself was an annoyance. She switched direction in midstream and began writing down ideas and details about moviegoing.

As Diane wrote, she realized how much other moviegoers annoyed her, and she began thinking that other movie patrons might be her main idea in a paper. But when she was writing about patrons who loudly drop popcorn tubs onto the floor, she realized how much all the snacks at the concession stand tempted her. She changed direction again, thinking now that maybe she could talk about patrons and tempting snacks. She kept writing, just putting down more and more details about her movie experiences, still not having figured out exactly how she would fit both patrons and snacks into the paragraph. Even though her paragraph had not quite jelled, she was not worried, because she knew that if she kept writing, it would eventually come together.

The point is that writing is often a process of continuing discovery; as you write, you may suddenly switch direction or double back. You may be working on a topic sentence and realize suddenly that it could be your concluding thought. Or you may be developing a supporting idea and then decide that it should be the main point of your paper. Chapter 2 will treat the writing process more directly. What is important to remember here is that writers frequently do not know their exact destination as they begin to write. Very often they discover the direction and shape of a paper during the process of writing.

in a writer's words

"I fill notebooks with ideas, and I may take six to eight months writing about a situation that interests me. My ideas get better as time goes on."
—Ross Macdonald

Keeping a Journal

Because writing is a skill, it makes sense that the more you practice writing, the better you will write. One excellent way to get practice in writing, even before you begin composing formal paragraphs, is to keep a daily or almost daily journal. Writing a journal will help you develop the habit of thinking on paper and will show you how ideas can be discovered in the process of writing. A journal can make writing a familiar part of your life and can serve as a continuing source of ideas for papers.

At some point during the day—perhaps during a study period after your last class of the day, or right before dinner, or right before going to bed—spend fifteen minutes or so writing in your journal. Keep in mind that you do not have to plan what to write about, or be in the mood to write, or worry about making mistakes as you write; just write down whatever words come out. You should write at least one page in each session.

You may want to use a notebook that you can easily carry with you for on-the-spot writing. Or you may decide to write on loose-leaf paper that can be transferred later to a journal folder on your desk. Many students elect to keep their journals on their home computer or laptop. No matter how you proceed, be sure to date all entries.

Your instructor may ask you to make journal entries a specific number of times a week, for a specific number of weeks. He or she may have you turn in your journal every so often for review and feedback. If you are keeping the journal on your own, try to make entries three to five times a week every week of the semester. Your journal can serve as a sourcebook of ideas for possible papers. More important, keeping a journal will help you develop the habit of thinking on paper or at the computer, and it can help you make writing a familiar part of your life.

ACTIVITY 4

Following is an excerpt from one student's journal. As you read, look for a general point and supporting material that could be the basis for an interesting paper.

September 6

My first sociology class was tonight. The parking lot was jammed when I got there. I thought I was going to be late for class. A guard had us park on a field next to the regular lot. When I got to the room, it had the usual painted construction. Every school I have ever been in since first grade seems to be made of cinder block. The students all sat there without saying anything, waiting for the instructor to arrive. I think they were all a bit nervous like me. I hoped there wasn't going to be a ton of work in the course. I think I was also afraid of looking foolish somehow. This goes back to grade school, when I wasn't a very good student and teachers sometimes embarrassed me in class. I didn't like grade school, and I hated high school. Now here I am six years later—in college, of all places. Who would have thought I would end up here? The instructor appeared—a woman who I think was a bit nervous herself. I think I like her. Her name is Barbara Hanlin. She says we should call her Barbara. We got right into it, but it was

continued

interesting stuff. I like the fact that she asks questions but then she lets you volunteer. I always hated it when teachers would call on you whether you wanted to answer or not. I also like the fact that she answers the questions and doesn't just leave you hanging. She takes the time to write important ideas on the board. I also like the way she laughs. This class may be OK.

1. If the writer of the journal entry above was looking for ideas for a paragraph, he could probably find several in this single entry. For example, he might write a story about the roundabout way he apparently wound up in college. See if you can find in the entry an idea that might be the basis for an interesting paragraph, and write your point in the space below.

   _____

2. Take fifteen minutes now to write a journal entry on this day in your life. Just start writing about anything that you have seen, said, heard, thought, or felt today, and let your thoughts take you wherever they may.

Tips on Using a Computer

- If you are using your school's computer center, allow yourself plenty of time. You may have to wait for a computer or printer to be free. In addition, you may need several sessions at the computer and printer to complete your paper.

- Every word-processing program allows you to "save" your writing by hitting one or more keys. Save your work frequently as you work on a draft. Work that is saved is preserved by the computer. Work that is not saved is lost when the file you are working on is closed, when the computer is turned off—or if there's a power or system failure.

- Keep your work in two places—the hard drive or CD you are working on and a backup CD or Zip disk. At the end of each session with the computer, copy your work onto the backup CD or Zip disk. Then if the hard drive or working CD becomes damaged, you'll have the backup copy.

- Print out your work at least at the end of every session. Then you'll not only have your most recent draft to work on away from the computer; you'll also have a copy in case something should happen to your CDs.

- Work in single spacing so you can see as much of your writing on the screen at one time as possible. Just before you print out your work, change to double spacing.

- Before making major changes in a paper, create a copy of your file. For example, if your file is titled "Movies," create a file called "Movies 2." Then make all your changes in that file. If the changes don't work out, you can always go back to the original file.

Ways to Use a Computer at Each Stage of the Writing Process

Following are some ways to make computer use a part of your writing. Note that the sections that follow correspond to the stages of the writing process described in Chapter 2, pages 20–34.

Prewriting

If you're a fast typist, many kinds of prewriting will go well on the computer. With freewriting in particular, you can get ideas onto the screen almost as quickly as they occur to you. A passing thought that could be productive is not likely to get lost. You may even find it helpful, when freewriting, to dim the screen of your monitor so that you can't see what you're typing. If you temporarily can't see the screen, you won't have to worry about grammar or spelling or typing errors (none of which matter in prewriting); instead, you can concentrate on getting down as many ideas and details as possible about your subject.

After any initial freewriting, questioning, and list-making on a computer, it's often very helpful to print out a hard copy of what you've done. With a clean printout in front of you, you'll be able to see everything at once and revise and expand your work with handwritten comments in the margins of the paper.

If you have prepared a list of items, you may be able to turn that list into an outline right on the screen. Delete the ideas you feel should not be in your paper (move them to the bottom of your document in case you change your mind), and add any new ideas that occur to you. Then use the cut and paste functions to shuffle the supporting ideas around until you find the best order for your paper.

Word processing also makes it easy for you to experiment with the wording of the point of your paper. You can try a number of versions in a short time. After you have decided on the version that works best, you can easily delete the other versions—or simply move them to a temporary "leftover" section at the end of the paper.

Writing Your First Draft

Some people like to write out a first draft by hand and then type it into the computer for revision. If you do this, you may find yourself making some changes and improvements as you type your handwritten draft. And once you have a draft on the screen, or printed out, you will find it much easier to revise than a handwritten draft.

in a writer's words

"The computer is the most liberating because it is the fastest: I can sneak up on myself and write things that I would never dare to say or write it out longhand or if I had to say it publicly."
—Russell Banks

If you feel comfortable composing directly on the screen, you can benefit from the computer's special features. For example, if you have written an anecdote in your freewriting that you plan to use in your paper, simply copy the story from your freewriting file and insert it where it fits in your paper. You can refine it then or later. Or if you discover while typing that a sentence is out of place, cut it out from where it is and paste it wherever you wish. And if while writing you realize that an earlier sentence can be expanded, just move your cursor back to that point and type in the added material.

Revising

It is during revision that the virtues of word processing really shine. All substituting, adding, deleting, and rearranging can be done easily within an existing file. All changes instantly take their proper places within the paper, not scribbled above the line or squeezed into the margin. You can concentrate on each change you want to make, because you never have to type from scratch or work on a messy draft. You can carefully go through your paper to check that all your supporting evidence is relevant and to add new support here and there where needed. Anything you decide to eliminate can be deleted in a keystroke. Anything you add can be inserted precisely where you choose. If you change your mind, all you have to do is delete or cut and paste. Then you can sweep through the paper focusing on other changes: improving word choice, increasing sentence variety, eliminating wordiness, and so on.

You will find it convenient to print out a hard copy of your file at various points throughout the revision. You can then revise in longhand—adding, crossing out, and indicating changes—and later quickly make those changes in the document.

Editing and Proofreading

Editing and proofreading also benefit richly from word processing. Instead of crossing out or whiting out mistakes, or rewriting an entire paper to correct numerous errors, you can make all necessary changes within the most recent draft. If you find editing or proofreading on the screen hard on your eyes, print out a copy. Mark any corrections on that copy, and then transfer them to the final draft.

If the word-processing program you're using includes spelling and grammar checks, by all means use them. The spell-check function tells you when a word is not in the computer's dictionary. Keep in mind, however, that the spell-check cannot tell you how to spell a name correctly or when you have mistakenly used, for example, *their* instead of *there.* To a spell-check, *Thank ewe four the complement* is as correct as *Thank you for the compliment.* Also use the grammar check with caution, as it may mark things wrong that are OK. In addition, any errors it doesn't uncover are still your responsibility.

A word-processed paper, with its clean appearance and attractive formatting, looks so good that you may think it is in better shape than it really is. Do not be fooled by your paper's appearance. Take sufficient time to review your grammar, punctuation, and spelling carefully.

Even after you hand in your paper, save the computer file. Your teacher may ask you to do some revising, and then the file will save you from having to type the paper from scratch.

Answering the following questions will help you evaluate your attitude about writing.	ACTIVITY 5

1. How much practice were you given writing compositions in high school?

    _____ Much   _____ Some   _____ Little

2. How much feedback (positive or negative comments) from teachers were you given on your compositions?

    _____ Much   _____ Some   _____ Little

3. How did your teachers seem to regard your writing?

    _____ Good   _____ Fair   _____ Poor

4. Do you feel that some people simply have a gift for writing and others do not?

    _____ Yes   _____ Sometimes   _____ No

5. When do you start writing a paper?

    _____ Several days before it is due

    _____ About a day before it is due

    _____ At the last possible minute

Many people who answer *Little* to questions 1 and 2 often answer *Poor, Yes,* and *At the last possible minute* to questions 3, 4, and 5. On the other hand, people who answer *Much* or *Some* to questions 1 and 2 also tend to have more favorable responses to the other questions. The point is that people with little practice in the skill of writing often have understandably negative feelings about their writing ability. They need not have such feelings, however, because writing is a skill that they can learn with practice.

6. Did you learn to write traditional paragraphs in high school?

    _____ Yes   _____ No

7. If so, did your teacher explain to you the benefits of writing such essays?

    _____ Yes, very clearly

    _____ Maybe, but not that I remember

    _____ No

If you answered *Maybe* or *No* to question 7, you may not be looking forward to taking the course in which you are using this book. It will be worth your while to read and consider again (on page 9) the enormous benefits that can come from practice in writing traditional paragraphs.

8. In your own words, explain what it means to say that writing is often a zigzag journey rather than a straight-line journey.

_____

_____

_____

_____

_____

REFLECTIVE ACTIVITY

1. Read the journal entry on a day in your life (Activity 4, pages 13–14). What does it tell you about your ability to generate ideas that might later be used as topics for more complete and more formal writing?

2. You read that writing is a process of discovery, a series of steps. You also learned that going through the process will be like a zigzag journey. How is this different from the way you thought about writing before?

The Writing Process

RESPONDING TO IMAGES

Everyone approaches writing differently. Some people dive right in. Others wait until the last minute. How would you describe your approach? Think about the steps you follow when asked to write for school. Keep in mind that there is no one right way to get started.

Chapter 1 introduced you to the paragraph form and some basics of writing. This chapter will explain and illustrate the sequence of steps in writing an effective paragraph. In particular, the chapter will focus on prewriting and revising—strategies that can help with every paper that you write.

For many people, writing is a process that involves the following steps:

1. Discovering a point—often through prewriting

2. Developing solid support for the point—often through more prewriting

3. Organizing the supporting material, making an outline, and writing it out in a first draft

4. Revising and then editing carefully to ensure an effective, error-free paper

Learning this sequence will help give you confidence when the time comes to write. You'll know that you can use prewriting as a way to think on paper (or on the screen) and to discover gradually just what ideas you want to develop. You'll understand that there are four clear-cut goals to aim for in your writing—unity, support, organization, and error-free sentences. You'll realize that you can revise a paper until it is strong and effective. And you'll be able to edit a paper so that your sentences are clear and errorfree.

Prewriting

Like many people, you may have trouble getting started writing. A mental block may develop when you sit down before a blank sheet of paper. You may not be able to think of an interesting topic sentence. Or you may have trouble coming up with relevant details to support a possible topic sentence. And even after starting a paper, you may hit snags—moments when you wonder, "What else can I say?" or "Where do I go next?"

The following pages describe five prewriting techniques that will help you think about and develop a topic and get words on paper: (1) freewriting, (2) questioning, (3) making a list, (4) diagramming, and (5) preparing a scratch outline. These techniques help you think about and create material, and they are a central part of the writing process.

Technique 1: Freewriting

Freewriting means jotting down in rough sentences or phrases everything that comes to mind about a possible topic. See if you can write nonstop for ten minutes or more. Do not worry about spelling or punctuating correctly, about erasing mistakes, about organizing material, or about finding exact words. Instead, explore an idea by putting down whatever pops into your head. If you get stuck for words, repeat yourself until more words come. There is no need to feel inhibited, since mistakes *do not count* and you do not have to hand in your freewriting.

Freewriting will limber up your writing muscles and make you familiar with the act of writing. It is a way to break through mental blocks about writing. Since you do not have to worry about mistakes, you can focus on discovering what you want to say about a subject. Your initial ideas and impressions will often become clearer after you have gotten them down on paper, and they may lead to other impressions and ideas. Through continued practice in freewriting, you will develop the habit of thinking as you write. And you will learn a technique that is a helpful way to get started on almost any paper.

Freewriting: A Student Model

Diane Woods's paragraph "The Hazards of Moviegoing" on page 6 was developed in response to an assignment to write about some annoyance in everyday life. Diane began by doing some general freewriting and thinking about things that annoy her. At first, she was stuck for words; she had writer's block, a common experience for writers. However, Diane pushed through and just kept putting words on the page. Even writing "stuck, stuck, stuck!" helped her stay focused, and eventually, good ideas began to emerge. Here is her freewriting:

There are lots of things I get annoyed by. One of them that comes to mind is politishans, in fact I am so annoyed by them that I don't want to say anything about them. the last thing I want is to write about them. Stuck, stuck, stuck!.. what else annoys me?? (besides this assignment)—now I'm whining again. That's annoying. OK—Another thing that bothers me are people who keep complaining about everything. If you're having trouble, do something about it just don't keep complaining and just talking. I am really annoyed by traffic. There are too many cars in our block and its not surprising. Everyone has a car, the parents have cars and the parents are just too induljent and the kids have cars, and theyre all coming and going all the time and often driving too fast. Speeding up and down the street. We need a speed limit sign but here I am back with politiks again. I am really bothered when I have to drive to the movie theater all the congestion along the way plus there are just so many cars there at the mall. No space even though the parking lot is huge it just fills up with cars.

continued

> *Movies are a bother anyway because the people can be annoying who are sitting there in the theater with you, talking on their cell phones and dropping popcorn tubs and acting like they're at home when they're not.*

At this point, Diane read over her notes and, as she later commented, "I realized that I had several potential topics. I said to myself, 'What point can I make that I can cover in a paragraph? What do I have the most information about?' I decided that maybe I could narrow my topic down to the annoyances involved in going to the movies. I figured I would have more details for that topic." Diane then did more focused freewriting to accumulate details for a paragraph on problems with moviegoing:

> *I really find it annoying to go see movies anymore. Even though I love films, Traffic to Cinema Six is awful. I hate looking for a parking place, the lot isn't big enough for the theaters and other stores. You just keep driving to find a parking space and hoping someone will pull out and no one else will pull in ahead of you. Then you don't want there to be a long line and to wind up in one of the first rows with this huge screen right in front of you. Then I'm in the theater with the smell of popcorn all around. Sitting there smelling it trying to ignore it and just wanting to pour a whole bucket of popcorn with melted butter down my throat. I can't stop thinking about the choclate bars either. I love the stuff but I don't need it. The people who are there sometimes drive me nuts. Talking and laughing, kids running around, packs of teens hollaring, who can listen to the movie? And I might run into my old boyfriend—the last thing I need. Also sitting thru all the previews and commercals. If I arrive late enough to miss that junk the movie may be selled out.*

Notice that there are errors in spelling, grammar, and punctuation in Diane's freewriting. Diane is not worried about such matters, nor should she be. At this stage, she just wants to do some thinking on paper and get some material down on the page. She knows that this is a good first step, a good way of getting started, and that she will then be able to go on and shape the material.

You should take the same approach when freewriting: explore your topic without worrying at all about being "correct." Figuring out what you want to say and getting raw material down on the page should be your primary focus at this early stage of the writing process.

ACTIVITY 1

a. To get a sense of the freewriting process, take a sheet of paper and freewrite about some of the everyday annoyances in your life. See how much material you can accumulate in ten minutes. And remember not to worry about "mistakes"; you're just thinking on paper.

b. Read over the material that you generated and decide which annoyance you have the most information about. Then do more focused freewriting on that specific annoyance.

Technique 2: Questioning

In *questioning,* you generate ideas and details by asking questions about your subject. Such questions include *Who? What? Where? When? Why?* and *How?* Ask as many questions as you can think of.

Here are some questions that Diane Woods might have asked while developing her paragraph.

Questioning: A Student Model

Questions	Answers
Why don't I like to go to a movie?	*Just too many problems involved.*
What annoys me about going to the movies?	*Everything! Getting to the theater, waiting for the movie to start, eating snacks that I shouldn't be eating, and putting up with others during the movie.*

continued

When is going to the movies a problem?	*Could be any time—when a movie is popular, the theater is too crowded; when traffic is bad, the trip is a drag.*
Where are problems with moviegoing?	*On the highway, in the parking lot, at the concession stand, in the theater itself.*
Who creates the problems?	*I do by wanting to eat too much. The patrons do by creating disturbances. The theater owners do by not having enough parking space and showing too many commercials.*
How can I deal with the problem?	*I can stay home and watch movies on DVD or cable TV.*

> **TIP**   Asking questions can be an effective way of getting yourself to think about a topic from different angles. The questions can help you generate details about a topic.

ACTIVITY 2

To get a sense of the questioning process, use a sheet of paper to ask yourself and answer a series of questions about a specific recent experience you've had involving your everyday annoyance. What happened? Why did the situation annoy you? How did you respond? See how many details you can accumulate in ten minutes. And remember again not to be concerned about "mistakes," because you are just thinking on paper.

Technique 3: Making a List

In *making a list*, also known as *brainstorming*, you collect ideas and details that relate to your subject. Pile these items up, one after another, without trying to sort out major details from minor ones, or trying to put the details in any special order. Your goal is just to make a list of everything about your subject that occurs to you.

After Diane did her freewriting about moviegoing, she made up the following list of details.

Making a List: A Student Model

Traffic is bad between my house and theater

Noisy patrons

Don't want to run into Jeremy

Hard to be on a diet

Kids running in aisles

I'm crowded into seats between strangers who push me off armrests

Not enough parking

Parking lot needs to be expanded

Too many previews

Can't pause or fast-forward as you can with a DVD

Long lines

High ticket prices

Too many temptatons at snack stand

Commercials for food on the screen

Can prepare healthy snacks for myself at home

Tubs of popcorn with butter

Huge choclate bars

Candy has always been my downfall

Movie may be sold out

People talking on their cell phones

People coughing and sneezing

Icky stuff on floor

Teenagers yelling and showing off

One detail led to another as Diane expanded her list. Slowly but surely more details emerged, some of which she could use in developing her paragraph. By the time she was done with her list, she was ready to plan an outline of her paragraph and then to write her first draft.

ACTIVITY 3 To get a sense of list-making, list on a sheet of paper all the details that you can think of about your particular everyday annoyance.

Technique 4: Clustering

Clustering, also known as *diagramming* or *mapping,* is another strategy that can be used to generate material for a paper. This method is helpful for people who like to do their thinking in a visual way. In clustering, you use lines, boxes, arrows, and circles to show relationships among the ideas and details that occur to you.

Begin by stating your subject in a few words in the center of a blank sheet of paper. Then, as ideas and details come to you, put them in boxes or circles around the subject and draw lines to connect them to each other and to the subject. Put minor ideas or details in smaller boxes or circles, and use connecting lines to show how they relate as well.

Keep in mind that there is no right or wrong way of clustering or diagramming. It is a way to think on paper about how various ideas and details relate to one another. Below is an example of what Diane might have done to develop her ideas.

Clustering: A Student Model

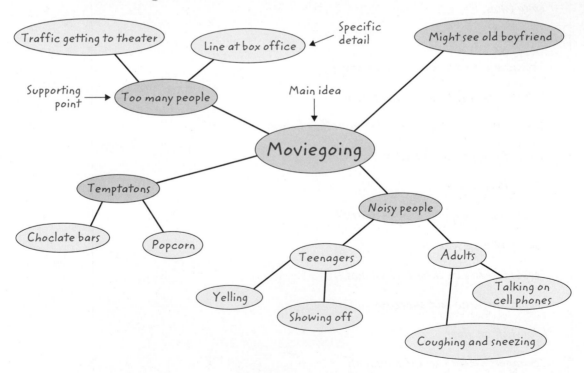

TIP In addition to helping generate material, clustering often suggests ways to organize ideas and details.

> Use clustering (diagramming) to organize the list of details that you created for the previous activity (page 26).

ACTIVITY 4

Technique 5: Preparing a Scratch Outline

A *scratch outline* is an excellent sequel to the first four prewriting techniques. A scratch outline often follows freewriting, questioning, list-making, or diagramming; or it may gradually emerge in the midst of these strategies. In fact, trying to make a scratch outline is a good way to see if you need to do more prewriting. If you cannot come up with a solid outline, then you know you need to do more prewriting to clarify and support your main point.

In a scratch outline, you think carefully about the point you are making, the supporting items for that point, and the order in which you will arrange those items. The scratch outline is a plan or blueprint to help you achieve a unified, supported, well-organized composition.

Scratch Outline: A Student Model

As Diane was working on her list of details, she suddenly realized what the plan of her paragraph could be. She could organize many of her details into one of three supporting groups: (1) annoyances in going out; (2) too many tempting snacks; and (3) other people. She then went back to the list, crossed out items that she now saw did not fit, and numbered the items according to the group where they fit. Here is what Diane did with her list:

1	Traffic is bad between my house and the theater
3	Noisy patrons
	~~Don't want to run into Jeremy~~
2	Hard to be on a diet
3	Kids running in aisles
3	I'm crowded into seats between strangers who push me off armrests
1	Not enough parking
1	Parking lot needs to be expanded
1	Too many previews
	~~Can't pause or fast forward as you can with a DVD~~
1	Long lines
1	High ticket prices
2	Too many temptatons at snack stand
	~~Commercials for food on the screen~~

continued

> 2   Can prepare healthy snacks for myself at home
>
> 2   Tubs of popcorn with butter
>
> 2   Huge choclate bars
>
> ~~Candy has always been my downfall~~
>
> 1   Movie may be sold out
>
> 3   People talking on their cell phones
>
> 3   People coughing and sneezing
>
> 1   Icky stuff on floor
>
> 2   Teenagers yelling and showing off

Under the list, Diane was now able to prepare her scratch outline:

> Going to the movies offers some real problems.
>
> 1.   Inconvenience of going out
>
> 2.   Tempting snacks
>
> 3.   Other moviegoers

After all her prewriting, Diane was pleased. She knew that she had a promising paragraph—one with a clear point and solid support. She saw that she could organize the material into a paragraph with a topic sentence, supporting points, and vivid details. She was now ready to write the first draft of her paragraph, using her outline as a guide.

> TIP   Chances are that if you do enough prewriting and thinking on paper, you will eventually discover the point and support of your paragraph.

ACTIVITY 5   Create a scratch outline that could serve as a guide if you were to write a paragraph about your particular annoyance.

Writing a First Draft

When you write a first draft, be prepared to put in additional thoughts and details that did not emerge during prewriting. And don't worry if you hit a snag. Just leave a blank space or add a comment such as "Do later" and press on to finish the paragraph. Also, don't worry yet about grammar, punctuation, or spelling. You don't want to take time correcting words or sentences that you may decide to remove later. Instead, make it your goal to state your main idea clearly and develop the content of your paragraph with plenty of specific details.

Writing a First Draft: A Student Model

Here is Diane's first draft:

~~Although I love movies, there are just too many problems involved in going to the movies.~~ Although I love movies, I've found that there are drawbacks to moviegoing. One problem is just the inconveneince of it all. To get to the theater you have to drive for at least 15 minutes, or more if traffic is bad. Because of a nearby supermarket and restaurants, it can take forever to find a parking spot and then I have to walk across a huge parking lot to the theater. There I deal with lines that are long, sold-out shows, and ever-increasing prices. I hate sitting with my feet sticking to the floor because of other people's spilled snacks. Another problem is my lack of self-control, I often stuff myself with ~~snacks~~ unhealthy, calorie-laden snacks. My choices might include a bucket of popcorn, a box of junior mints, a giant soda, or all three. My friends are as bad as I am. The worst problem is some of the other moviegoers. Little kids run up and down the aisle. Teenagers laugh and shout at the screen. Other people drop food and soda cups on the floor. They are also talking a lot and doing other stuff—bms! I would rather stay home and wait to see the latest movies On Demand in the comfort of my own living room.

> **TIP**   After Diane finished the first draft, she was able to put it aside until the next day. You will benefit as well if you can allow some time between finishing a draft and starting to revise.

ACTIVITY 6

See if you can fill in the missing words in the following explanation of Diane's first draft.

1. Diane presents her _____ in the first sentence and then crosses it out and revises it right away to make it read smoothly and clearly.

2. There are some misspellings—for example, _____. Diane doesn't worry about spelling at this point. She just wants to get down as much of the substance of her paragraph as possible.

3. There are various punctuation errors, especially the run-on near the (beginning, middle, end) of the paragraph. Again, Diane is focusing on content; she knows she can attend to punctuation and grammar later.

4. Notice that she continues to accumulate specific supporting details as she writes the draft. For example, she crosses out and replaces "snacks" with the more specific _____.

5. Near the end of her draft, Diane can't think of added details to insert so she simply puts the letters "_____" at that point to remind herself to "be more specific" in the next draft. She then goes on to finish her first draft.

ACTIVITY 7

Use the prewriting that you generated in this chapter to write a paragraph about a particular annoyance in everyday life. Provide three reasons why you consider your topic an annoyance, and give plenty of details to support each of your three reasons.

Revising

Revising is as much a stage in the writing process as prewriting, outlining, and doing the first draft. *Revising* means rewriting a paper, building on what has already been done, in order to make it stronger. One writer has said about revision, "It's like cleaning house—getting rid of all the junk and putting things in the right order." But it is not just "straightening up"; instead, you must be ready to roll up your sleeves and do whatever is needed to create an effective paper. Too many students think that the first draft *is* the paper. They start to become writers when they realize that revising a rough draft three or four times is often at the heart of the writing process.

Here are some quick hints that can help make revision easier. First, set your first draft aside for a while. A few hours will do, but a day or two would be better. You can then come back to the draft with a fresh, more objective point of view. Second, work from typed or printed text. You'll be able to see the paper more impartially in this way than if you were just looking at your own familiar handwriting. Next, read your draft aloud. Hearing how your writing sounds will help you pick up problems with meaning as well as with style. Finally, as you do all these things, add your thoughts and changes above the lines or in the margins of your paper. Your written comments can serve as a guide when you work on the next draft.

There are three stages to the revision process:

- Revising content

- Revising sentences

- Editing

in a writer's words

"It would be crazy to begin revising immediately after finishing the first draft, and counter to the way the mind likes to create. You're exhausted. You deserve a vacation."

—Kenneth Atchity

Revising Content

To evaluate and revise the content of your paragraph, ask these questions:

1. Is my paragraph **unified**?

    - Do I have a clear, single point in the first sentence of the paragraph?

    - Does all my evidence truly support and back up my main idea?

2. Is my paragraph **supported**?

    - Are there separate supporting points for the main idea?

    - Do I have *specific* evidence for each supporting point?

    - Is there *plenty of* specific evidence for the supporting point?

3. Is my paragraph **organized**?

    - Do I have a clear method of organizing my paragraph?

    - Do I use transitions and other connecting words?

Chapters 3 and 4 will give you practice in achieving **unity, support,** and **organization** in your writing.

Revising Sentences

To evaluate and revise sentences in your paragraph, ask yourself:

1. Do I use parallelism to balance my words and ideas?

2. Do I have a consistent point of view?

3. Do I use specific words?

4. Do I use active verbs?

5. Do I use words effectively by avoiding slang, clichés, pretentious language, and wordiness?

6. Do I vary my sentences?

Chapter 4 will give you practice in revising sentences.

Editing

After you have revised your paragraph for content and style, you are ready to *edit*—check for and correct—errors in grammar, punctuation, and spelling. Students often find it hard to edit their writing carefully. They have put so much, or so little, work into their writing that it's almost painful for them to look at it one more time. You may simply have to *will* yourself to perform this important closing step in the writing process. Remember that eliminating sentence-skills mistakes will improve an average paragraph and help ensure a strong grade on a good paper. Further, as you get into the habit of checking your work, you will also get into the habit of using the sentence skills consistently. They are an integral part of clear and effective writing.

Chapter 4 and Part 5 of this book will serve as a guide while you are editing your paragraphs for mistakes in **sentence skills.**

An Illustration of the Revising and Editing Processes

Revising with a Second Draft: A Student Model

Since Diane Woods was using a word-processing program on a computer, she was able to print out a double-spaced version of her paragraph about movies, leaving her plenty of room for revisions. Here is her revised paragraph:

Although I love movies, I've found that there are drawbacks to moviegoing. One problem is just the inconveneince of it all. To get to the theater ~~you~~ *I* have to drive for at least 15 minutes, or more if traffic is bad. ~~Because of a nearby supermarket and restaurants,~~ *I* it can take forever to find a parking spot and then I have to walk across a huge parking lot to the theater. There I deal with *long lines* ~~lines that are long~~, sold-out shows, and ever-incresing prices. I hate sitting with my feet sticking to the floor because of other people's spilled snacks. Another problem is my lack of self-control, I often stuff myself with unhealthy, calorie-laden snacks. My choices might include a bucket of popcorn, *dripping with butter* a box of junior mints, a *large coke* ~~giant soda~~, or all three. ~~My friends are as bad as I am.~~ *Finally* The worst problem is some of the other moviegoers. *As* ~~L~~ittle kids run up and down the aisle/ *T*eenagers laugh and shout at the screen. ~~Other people~~ *People of all ages* drop *popcorn tubs* ~~food~~ and soda cups and talk on their cell phones. I would rather stay home and wait to see the latest movies On Demand in the comfort of my own living room.

Diane made her changes in longhand as she worked on the second draft. As you will see when you complete the activity below, her revision serves to make the paragraph more unified, better supported, and better organized.

ACTIVITY 8	Fill in the missing words.

1. To achieve better organization, Diane sets off the third supporting point with the word "_____."

2. In the interest of (unity, support, coherence) _____, Diane crosses out the sentence "_____." She realizes this sentence is not a relevant detail, but really another topic.

3. To add more (unity, support, coherence) _____, Diane changes "giant soda" to "_____"; she changes "food" to "_____"; and she adds "_____" after "bucket of popcorn."

4. To eliminate wordiness, she removes the words "_____ _____" from the fourth sentence.

5. In the interest of parallelism, Diane changes "lines that are long" to "_____."

6. For greater sentence variety, Diane combines two short sentences, beginning the first sentences with the subordinating word "_____."

7. To create a consistent point of view, Diane changes "you have to drive" to "_____."

8. Finally, Diane replaces the somewhat vague "other people" with the more precise "_____."

Editing: A Student Model

After typing into her word-processing file all the changes in her second draft, Diane printed out another clean draft of the paragraph. The paragraph required almost no more revision, so Diane turned her attention mostly to editing changes, illustrated below.

> Although I love movies, I've found that there are drawbacks to
> moviegoing. One problem is just the ~~inconveince~~ *inconvenience* of it all. To get to
> the theater, I have to drive for at least ~~15~~ *fifteen* minutes, or more if traffic is
> bad. It can take forever to find a parking spot, and then I have to walk
> across a huge parking lot to the theater. There I deal with long lines,
> sold-out shows, and ~~ever-incresing~~ *ever-increasing* prices. I hate sitting with my feet
> sticking to the floor because of other people's spilled snacks. Another
> problem is my lack of self-control; I often stuff myself with unhealthy,
> calorie-laden snacks. My choices might include a bucket of popcorn
> dripping with butter, a box of *J*unior *M*ints, a large *C*oke, or all three.
> Finally, the worst problem is some of the other moviegoers. As little kids

continued

> run up and down the aisle, teenagers laugh and shout at the screen.
> People of all ages drop popcorn tubs and soda cups *, cough and burp,* and talk on their
> cell phones. I would rather stay home and wait to see the latest movies
> On Demand in the comfort of my own living room.

Once again, Diane makes her changes in longhand right on the printout of her paragraph. To note these changes, complete the activity below.

| ACTIVITY 9 | Fill in the missing words. |

1. As part of her editing, Diane checked and corrected the _____ of two words, *inconvenience* and *ever-increasing.*

2. She added _____ to set off an introductory phrase ("To get to the theater") and an introductory word ("Finally") and also to connect the two complete thoughts in the fourth sentence.

3. She realized that "junior mints" is a brand name and added _____ _____ to make it "Junior Mints."

4. She realized that a number like "15" should be _____ as "fifteen."

5. And since revision can occur at any stage in the writing process, including editing, she makes one of her details more vivid by adding the descriptive words "_____."

| ACTIVITY 10 | Write a paragraph about the everyday annoyance you've been prewriting about throughout this chapter. Draft your work, and then revise and edit it, using the guidelines on the previous pages. You might want to work with a partner to revise and edit even more effectively. |

Using Peer Review

In addition to having your instructor as an audience for your writing, you will benefit from having another student in your class as an audience. On the day a paper is due, or on a day when you are writing papers in class, your instructor may ask you to pair up with another student. That student will read your paper, and you will read his or her paper.

Ideally, read the other paper aloud while your peer listens. If that is not practical, read it in a whisper while your peer looks on. As you read, both you and your peer should look and listen for spots where the paper does not read smoothly and clearly. Check or circle the trouble spots where your reading snags.

Your peer should then read your paper, marking possible trouble spots. Then each of you should do three things.

1. Identification

At the top of a separate sheet of paper, write the title and author of the paper you have read. Under it, write your name as the reader of the paper.

2. Scratch Outline

"X-ray" the paper for its inner logic by making up a scratch outline. The scratch outline need be no more than twenty words or so, but it should show clearly the logical foundation on which the paragraph or essay is built. It should identify and summarize the overall point of the paper and the three areas of support for the point.

Your outline can look like this:

Point: _____

Support:

(1)_____

(2)_____

(3)_____

For example, here is a scratch outline of the paragraph on moviegoing on page 6:

Point: _____

Support:

(1) _____

(2) _____

(3) _____

3. Comments

Under the outline, write a heading, "Comments." Here is what you should comment on:

- Look at the spots where your reading of the paper snagged. Are words missing or misspelled? Is there a lack of parallel structure? Are there mistakes with punctuation? Is the meaning of a sentence confused? Try to figure out what the problems are and suggest ways to fix them.

- Are there spots in the paragraph or essay where you see problems with *unity, support,* or *organization?* (You'll find it helpful to refer to the checklist on page 31.) If so, offer comments. For example, you might say, "More details are needed," or, "Some of the supporting details don't really back up your point."

- Finally, note something you really liked about the paper, such as good use of transitions or an especially realistic or vivid specific detail.

After you have completed your evaluation of the paper, give it to your peer. Your instructor may give you the option of rewriting a paper in light of the feedback you get. Whether or not you rewrite, be sure to hand in the peer-evaluation form with your paper.

You now have a good overview of the writing process, from prewriting to first draft to revising to editing. The chapters in Part Two will deepen your sense of the four goals of effective writing: unity, support, organization or coherence, and sentence skills.

Review Activities

To reinforce much of the information about the writing process that you have learned in this chapter, you can now work through the following activities:

- Taking a writing inventory
- Prewriting
- Outlining
- Revising

Taking a Writing Inventory

REVIEW ACTIVITY 1   Answer the questions below to evaluate your approach to the writing process. Think about the writing you have done for other classes. This activity is not a test, so try to be as honest as possible. Becoming aware of your writing habits will help you realize changes that may be helpful.

1. When you start work on a paragraph, do you typically do any prewriting?

    _____ Yes   _____ Sometimes   _____ No

2. If so, which prewriting techniques do you use?

    _____ Freewriting   _____ Diagramming

    _____ Questioning   _____ Scratch outline

    _____ List-making   _____ Other (please describe on the lines below)

    _____

    _____

3. Which prewriting technique or techniques work best for you, or which do you think will work best for you?

    _____

    _____

    _____

4. Many students say they find it helpful to handwrite a first draft and then type that draft on a computer. They then print out the draft and

revise it by hand. Describe the way you proceed in drafting and revising a paragraph.

_____

_____

_____

5. After you write the first draft of a paragraph, do you have time to set it aside for a while so that you can come back to it with a fresh eye?

_____ Yes   _____ No

6. How many drafts of a paragraph do you typically write? _____

7. When you revise, are you aware that you should be working toward a paragraph that is unified, solidly supported, and clearly organized? Has this chapter given you a better sense that unity, support, and organization are goals to aim for?

_____

_____

_____

8. Do you revise a paragraph for the clarity and quality of its sentences as well as for its content?

_____ Yes   _____ No

9. Do you typically do any editing of the almost-final draft of a paragraph, or do you tend to "hope for the best" and hand it in without careful checking?

_____ Edit   _____ Hope for the best

10. What (if any) information has this chapter given you about *prewriting* that you will try to apply in your writing?

_____

_____

_____

11. What (if any) information has this chapter given you about *revising* that you will try to apply in your writing?

_____

_____

_____

12. What (if any) information has this chapter given you about *editing* that you will try to apply in your writing?

_____

_____

_____

Prewriting

On the following pages are examples of how the five prewriting techniques could be used to develop the topic "Problems of Combining Work and College." Identify each technique by writing F (for freewriting), Q (for questioning), L (for list-making), C (for clustering), or SO (for the scratch outline) in the answer space.

_____   Never enough time
Miss campus parties
Had to study (only two free hours a night)
Give up activities with friends
No time to rewrite papers
Can't stay at school to hang out with or talk to friends
Friends don't call me to go out anymore
Sunday no longer relaxed day—have to study
Missing sleep I should be getting
Grades aren't as good as they could be
Can't watch favorite TV shows
Really need the extra money
Tired when I sit down to study at 9 o'clock

_____   *What* are some of the problems of combining work and school?

Schoolwork suffers because I don't have time to study or rewrite papers. I've had to give up things I enjoy, like sleep and touch football. I can't get into the social life at college, because I have to work right after class.

How have these problems changed my life?

My grades aren't as good as they were when I didn't work. Some of my friends have stopped calling me. My relationship with a girl I liked fell apart because I couldn't spend much time with her. I miss TV.

What do I do in a typical day?

I get up at 7 to make an 8 A.M. class. I have classes till 1:30, and then I drive to the supermarket where I work. I work till 7 P.M., and then I drive home and eat dinner. After I take a shower and relax for a half hour, it's about 9. This gives me only a couple of hours to study—read textbooks, do math exercises, write essays. My eyes start to close well before I go to bed at 11.

Why do I keep up this schedule?

I can't afford to go to school without working, and I need a degree to get the accounting job I want. If I invest my time now, I'll have a better future.

_____ Juggling a job and college has created major difficulties in my life.
1. Little time for studying
    a. Not reading textbooks
    b. No rewriting papers
    c. Little studying for tests
2. Little time for enjoying social side of college
    a. During school
    b. After school
3. No time for personal pleasures
    a. Favorite TV shows
    b. Sunday football games
    c. Sleeping late

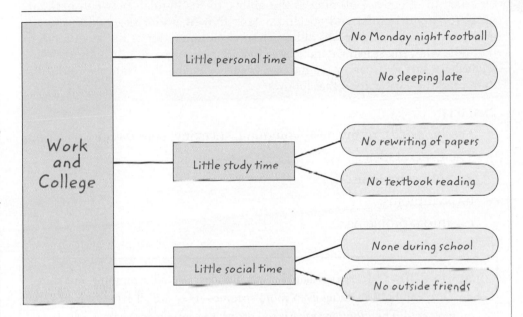

_____ It's hard working and going to school at the same time. I never realized how much I'd have to give up. I won't be quitting my job because I need the money. And the people are friendly at the place where I work. I've had to give up a lot more than I thought. We used to play touch football games every Sunday. They were fun and we'd go out for drinks afterwards. Sundays now are for catch-up work with my courses. I have to catch up because I don't get home every day until 7, I have to eat dinner first before studying. Sometimes I'm so hungry I just eat cookies or chips. Anyway, by the time I take a shower it's 9 P.M. or later and I'm already feeling tired. I've been up since 7 A.M. Sometimes I write an English paper in twenty minutes and don't even read it over. I feel that I'm missing out on a lot in college. The other day some people I like were sitting in the cafeteria listening to music and talking. I would have given anything to stay and not have to go to work. I almost called in sick. I used to get invited to parties, I don't much anymore. My friends know I'm not going to be able to make it, so they don't bother. I can't sleep late on weekends or watch TV during the week.

Outlining

As already mentioned (see page 27), outlining is central to writing a good paragraph. An outline lets you see, plan out, and work on the bare bones of a paper, without the distraction of cluttered words and sentences. It develops your ability to think clearly and logically. Outlining provides a quick check on whether your paper will be *unified.* It also suggests right at the start whether your paper will be adequately *supported.* And it shows you how to plan a paper that is *well organized.*

The following series of exercises will help you develop the outlining skills so important to planning and writing a solid paragraph.

REVIEW ACTIVITY 3

One key to effective outlining is the ability to distinguish between general ideas (or main points) and specific details that fit under those ideas. Read each group of specific details below. Then circle the letter of the general idea that tells what the specific details have in common. Note that the general idea should not be too broad or too narrow. Begin by trying the example item, and then read the explanation that follows.

EXAMPLE

Specific details: runny nose, coughing, sneezing, sore throat

The general idea is:

a. cold symptoms.

b. symptoms.

c. throat problems.

EXPLANATION: It is true that the specific ideas are all symptoms, but they have in common something even more specific—they are all symptoms of the common cold. Therefore, answer *b* is too broad; the correct answer is *a*. Answer *c* is too narrow because it doesn't cover all the specific ideas; it covers only the final item in the list ("sore throat").

 Remember that the general idea is the main point.

1. *Specific details:* leaking toilet, no hot water, broken window, roaches
    The general idea is:
    a. problems.
    b. kitchen problems.
    c. apartment problems.

2. *Specific details:* count to ten, take a deep breath, go for a walk
    The general idea is:
    a. actions.
    b. ways to calm down.
    c. ways to calm down just before a test.

3. *Specific details:* Mark Twain, Kate Chopin, Nathaniel Hawthorne, Toni Morrison

   The general idea is:

   a. famous people.

   b. authors.

   c. American authors.

4. *Specific details:* going to bed earlier, eating healthier foods, reading for half an hour each day, trying to be nicer to my mother

   The general idea is:

   a. resolutions.

   b. problems.

   c. solutions.

5. *Specific details:* money problems, family problems, relationship problems, health problems

   The general idea is:

   a. poor grades.

   b. causes of poor grades.

   c. effects of poor grades.

REVIEW ACTIVITY 4

In each of the following items, specific ideas (details) are given but a general idea is unstated. Fill in each blank with a general heading that accurately describes the list provided.

EXAMPLE

General idea: Household Chores

Specific ideas:
washing dishes
preparing meals
taking out trash
dusting furniture

1. General idea: _____
   Specific ideas:
   convenient work hours
   short travel time to job
   good pay
   considerate boss

2. General idea: _____
   Specific ideas:
   greed
   cowardice
   selfishness
   dishonesty

3. General idea: _____
   Specific ideas:
   the invitations
   get the bride's gown
   rent the tuxedos
   hire a photographer

4. *General idea:* _____
    Specific ideas: "Your cologne stinks."
                        "You look terrible."
                        "You've got no common sense."
                        "Your writing sucks."

5. *General idea:* _____
    Specific ideas: "I love your hair."
                        "You look great in red."
                        "You're so smart."
                        "Your writing is outstanding."

REVIEW ACTIVITY 5   Major and minor ideas are mixed together in the two paragraphs outlined below. Put the ideas in logical order by filling in the outlines.

1. *Topic sentence:* People can be classified by how they treat their cars.
    Seldom wax or vacuum car
    Keep every mechanical item in top shape
    Protective owners
    Ignore needed maintenance
    Indifferent owners
    Wash and polish car every week
    Never wash, wax, or vacuum car
    Abusive owners
    Inspect and service car only when required by state law

    (1) _____
        a. _____
        b. _____

    (2) _____
        a. _____
        b. _____

    (3) _____
        a. _____
        b. _____

2. *Topic sentence:* Living with an elderly parent has many benefits.
    Advantages for elderly person
    Live-in caretaker
    Learn about the past
    Advantages for adult children
    Serve useful role in family

Help with household tasks
Advantages for grandchildren
Stay active and interested in young people
More attention from adults

(1) _____

    a. _____

    b. _____

(2) _____

    a. _____

    b. _____

(3) _____

    a. _____

    b. _____

REVIEW ACTIVITY 6

Again, major and minor ideas are mixed together. In addition, in each outline one of the three major ideas is missing and must be added. Put the ideas in logical order by filling in the outlines that follow (summarizing as needed) and adding a third major idea.

1. *Topic sentence:* Extending the school day would have several advantages.

    Help children academically

    Parents know children are safe at the school

    More time to spend on basics

    Less pressure to cover subjects quickly

    More time for extras like art, music, and sports

    Help working parents

    More convenient to pick up children at 4 or 5 P.M.

    Teachers' salaries would be raised

    (1) _____

        a. _____

        b. _____

    (2) _____

        a. _____

        b. _____

    (3) _____

        a. _____

        b. _____

2. *Topic sentence:* By following certain hints about food, exercise, and smoking, people can increase their chances of dying young

Don't ever walk if there is a ride available

Choose foods such as bacon and lunch meats that are laced with nitrites and other preservatives

Be very selective about what foods are eaten

Keep smoking, even if it causes coughing or shortness of breath

Don't play an outdoor sport; open a beer instead and head for a La-Z-Boy recliner

Resist the urge to exercise

Choose foods from one of four essential groups: fat, starch, sugar, and grease

Smoke on a regular basis

(1) _____

   a. _____

   b. _____

(2) _____

   a. _____

   b. _____

(3) _____

   a. _____

   b. _____

REVIEW ACTIVITY 7

Read the following two paragraphs. Then outline each one in the space provided. Write out the topic sentence in each case and summarize in a few words the supporting points and details that fit under the topic sentence.

1.

Why I'm a Stay-at-Home Baseball Fan

I'd much rather stay at home and watch ball games on television than go to the ballpark. First, it's cheaper to watch a game at home. I don't have to spend twenty-five dollars for a ticket and another ten dollars for a parking space. If I want some refreshments, I can have what's already in the refrigerator instead of shelling out another six dollars for a limp, lukewarm hot dog and a watery Coke. Also, it's more comfortable at home. I avoid a bumper-to bumper drive to the ballpark and pushy crowds who want to go through the same gate I do. I can lie quietly on my living-room sofa instead of sitting on a hard stadium seat with noisy people all around me. Most of all, watching a game on television is more informative. Not only do I see all the plays that I might miss from my twenty-five-dollar seat, but I see some of them two and three times in instant replay. In addition, I get each play explained to me in glorious detail. If I were at the ballpark, I wouldn't know that the pitch our third baseman hit was a high and inside slider or that his grand-slam home run was a record-setting seventh in his career. The other fans can spend their money; put up with traffic, crowds, and hard seats; and guess at the plays. I'll take my baseball lying down—at home.

Topic sentence: _____

_____

(1) _____

    a. _____

    b. _____

(2) _____

    a. _____

    b. _____

(3) _____

    a. _____

    b. _____

2.

Good Employees

Employers are always looking for great employees who are conscientious, focused, and analytical. First, conscientious employees are people who take pride in their work and want to do their best. These employees make sure they contribute the best work possible and meet set deadlines. If they run into a problem, they first try to solve the problem on their own, but if they cannot solve the problem, they seek the help necessary to complete the task. Second, focused employees are people who don't waste time. They arrive on time and use the time at work to do work. They don't unnecessarily talk to their friends or family on the phone, they don't surf the Internet for amusing YouTube videos, and they don't stand around chatting with other employees for long periods of time. Finally, analytical employees are people who see a problem and work to solve the problem. They strive to make things better. If they see a better way that something could be done, they try to implement it. Employees who have these three qualities will always be in demand.

Topic Sentence: _____

_____

(1) _____

    a. _____

    b. _____

(2) _____

    a. _____

    b. _____

(3) _____

    a. _____

    b. _____

Revising

REVIEW ACTIVITY 8

Listed in the box below are five stages in the process of composing a paragraph titled "Dangerous Places."

1. Prewriting (list)

2. Prewriting (freewriting, questioning list, and scratch outline)

3. First draft

4. Revising (second draft)

5. Revising (final draft)

The five stages appear in scrambled order below and on the next page. Write the number 1 in the blank space in front of the first stage of development and number the remaining stages in sequence.

_____ There are some places where I never feel safe. For example, public rest rooms. The dirt and graffiti dirt on the floors and the graffiti scrawled on the walls make the room seem dangerous create a sense of danger. I'm also afraid in parking lots. Late at night, I don't like walking in the lot After class, I don't like the parking lot. When I leave my night class or the shopping mall late the walk to the car is scary. Most parking lots have large lights which make me feel at least a little better. I feel least safe in our laundry room. . . . It is a depressing place . . . Bars on the windows, . . . pipes making noises, . . . cement steps the only way out. . . .

_____   Dangerous Places

Highways
Cars—especially parking lots
Feel frightened in our laundry room
Big crowds—concerts, movies
Closed-in places
Bus and train stations
Airplane
Elevators and escalators

_____   **Dangerous Places**

There are some places where I never feel completely safe. For example, I seldom feel safe in public rest rooms. I worry that I'll suddenly be alone there and that someone will come in to attack me. The ugly graffiti often scrawled on the walls, along with the grime and dirt in the room and crumpled tissues and paper towels on the floor, add to my sense of unease and danger. I also feel unsafe in large, dark parking lots. When I leave my night class a little late, or I am one of the few leaving the mall at 10 P.M., I dread the walk to my car. I am afraid that someone may be lurking behind another car, ready to attack me. And I fear that my car will not start, leaving me stuck in the dark parking lot. The place where I feel least safe is the basement laundry room in our apartment building. No matter what time I do my laundry, I seem to be the only person there. The windows are barred, and the only exit is a steep flight of cement steps. While I'm folding the clothes, I feel trapped. If anyone unfriendly came down those steps, I would have nowhere to go. The pipes in the room make sudden gurgles, clanks, and hisses, adding to my unsettledness. Places like public rest rooms, dark parking lots, and the basement laundry room give me the shivers.

_____   There are some places where I never feel completely safe. For example, I never feel safe in public rest rooms. If I'm alone there, I worry that someone will come in to rob and attack me. The dirt on the floors and the graffiti scrawled on the walls create a sense of danger. I feel unsafe in large, dark parking lots. When I leave my night class a little late or I leave the mall at 10 P.M., the walk to the car is scary. I'm afraid that someone may be behind a car. Also that my car won't start. Another place I don't feel safe is the basement laundry room in our apartment building. No matter when I do the laundry, I'm the only person there. The windows are barred and there are steep steps. I feel trapped when I fold the clothes. The pipes in the room make frightening noises such as hisses and clanks. Our laundry room and other places give me the shivers.

_____   Some places seem dangerous and unsafe to me. For example, last night I stayed till 10:15 after night class and walked out to parking lot alone. Very scary. Also, other places I go to every day, such as places in my apartment building. Also frightened by big crowds and public rest rooms.

Why was the parking lot scary?

Dark
Only a few cars
No one else in lot
Could be someone behind a car
Cold

What places in my building scare me?

Laundry room (especially)
Elevators
Lobby at night sometimes
Outside walkway at night

2 Parking lots
3 Laundry room
1 Public rest rooms

REVIEW ACTIVITY 9   The author of "Dangerous Places" in Review Activity 8 made a number of editing changes between the second draft and the final draft. Compare the two drafts and, in the spaces provided below, identify five of the changes.

1. _____

2. _____

3. _____

4. _____

5. _____

EXPLORING WRITING ONLINE

In this chapter, you learned how to cluster or diagram your ideas. Use your favorite search engine, such as Google, to discover other ways to visually organize your ideas. Do a search for the words "graphic organizers" to find the many different types of printable organizers available. Find at least three that you would like to use during prewriting.

As a college student, you will be asked to write in many of your classes. The writing that you do in these classes will often involve making a point and supporting that point with reasons and details. Keep this in mind when you read the first draft of the paragraph below written by Jennifer for an introductory sociology course, and then answer the questions that follow.

What Do Sociologists Do?

Sociologists are scientists who study people in groups and look at what happens in those groups. They may look at ethnic groups and the things that people in those groups do. They may look at groups defined by age and how people in those groups behave. They may look at families and study what happens in those families.

Collaborative Activity

Jennifer, the writer of the above paragraph, provided three reasons to support her opening point, but not much else. With a classmate, together complete the outline below by providing two specific supporting details for each of Jennifer's three reasons.

Title: What Do Sociologists Do?

Topic sentence: Sociologists are scientists who study people in groups and look at what happens in those groups.

1. They may look at ethnic groups and the things that people in those groups do.

    a. _____

    _____

    b. _____

    _____

2. They may look at groups defined by age and how people in those groups behave.

    a. _____

    _____

    b. _____

3. They may look at families and study what happens in those families.

   a. _____

     _____

   b. _____

Explore Writing Further

Using your outline, revise Jennifer's paragraph.

PART 2

Basic Principles of Effective Writing

PART TWO SHOWS YOU HOW TO

- begin a paper by a point of some kind

- provide specific evidence to support that point

- write a paragraph

- organize specific evidence by using a clear method of organization

- connect the specific evidence by using transitions and other connecting words

- revise so that your sentences flow smoothly and clearly

- edit so that your sentences are errorfree

- evaluate a paragraph for unity, support, coherence, and sentence skills

EXPLORING WRITING PROMPT:

So much of what we do involves communication. In addition to talking, we spend a lot of time writing. We may not write essays, but we send off e-mails and text messages, jot down notes, and write up lists. Take a few minutes to think about how you use writing in everyday life. You may be asked to write down your ideas or share them with others.

The First and Second Steps in Writing

RESPONDING TO IMAGES

There are many different reasons for going to college. Maybe you are fulfilling a dream of yours or maybe you are studying for a specific career. What are your reasons? Take a few minutes to write nonstop, make a list, or draw a diagram of your ideas. In this chapter you will read two separate paragraphs detailing each of the writers' reasons for being in college, and later you will be asked to write a paragraph of your own on this topic.

Chapter 2 emphasized how prewriting and revising can help you become an effective writer. This chapter will focus on the first two steps in writing an effective paragraph:

1. Begin with a point.

2. Support the point with specific evidence.

Chapter 4 will then look at the third and fourth steps in writing:

3. Organize and connect the specific evidence.

4. Write clear, error-free sentences.

Four Steps	Four Bases
1. If you make one point and stick to that point,	➡ your writing will have *unity*.
2. If you back up the point with specific evidence,	➡ your writing will have *support*.
3. If you organize and connect the specific evidence,	➡ your writing will have *coherence*.
4. If you write clear, error-free sentences,	➡ your writing will demonstrate effective *sentence skills*.

Step 1: Begin with a Point

Your first step in writing is to decide what point you want to make and to write that point in a single sentence. The point is commonly known as a *topic sentence*. As a guide to yourself and to the reader, put that point in the first sentence of your paragraph. Everything else in the paragraph should then develop and support in specific ways the single point given in the first sentence.

ACTIVITY 1

Read the two student paragraphs below about families today. Which paragraph clearly supports a single point? Which paragraph rambles on in many directions, introducing a number of ideas but developing none of them?

PARAGRAPH A

Changes in the Family

The demands of modern society in recent years have changed family life. First of all, today's parents spend much less time with their children. Several generations ago, most parents were able to pick their children up from school. Now parents work longer hours, and their children attend an after-school program, stay with a neighbor or older sibling, or go home

Academic

continued

to an empty house. Another change is that families no longer eat together. In the past, Mom would be home and fix a full dinner—salad, pot roast, potatoes and vegetables, with homemade cake or pie to top it off. Dinner today is more likely to be takeout food or frozen dinners eaten at home, or fast food eaten out, with different members of the family eating at different times. Finally, television and the Internet have taken the place of family conversation and togetherness. Back when there were traditional meals, family members would have a chance to eat together at the dining room table, talk with each other, and share events of the day in a leisurely manner. Now, families are more likely to be looking at the TV or browsing the Internet than talking to each other. Clearly, modern life is a challenge to family life.

PARAGRAPH B

The Family

Family togetherness is very important. However, today's mothers spend much less time at home than their mothers did, for several reasons. Most fathers are also home much less than they used to be. In previous times, families had to work together running a farm. Now children are left at other places or are home alone much of the time. Some families do find ways to spend more time together despite the demands of work. Another problem is that with parents gone so much of the day, nobody is at home to prepare wholesome meals for the family to eat together. The meals Grandma used to make would include pot roast and fried chicken, mashed potatoes, salad, vegetables, and delicious homemade desserts. Today's takeout foods and frozen meals can provide good nutrition. Some menu choices offer nothing but high-fat and high-sodium choices. People can supplement prepared foods by eating sufficient vegetables and fruit. Finally, television and the Internet are also big obstacles to togetherness. It sometimes seems that people are constantly watching TV or browsing the Internet and never talking to each other. Even when parents have friends over, it is often to watch something on TV. TV and the Internet must be used wisely to achieve family togetherness.

Complete the following statement: Paragraph _____ is effective because it makes a clear, single point in the first sentence and goes on in the remaining sentences to support that single point.

Paragraph A starts with a point—that demands of modern society in recent years have changed family life—and then supports that idea with examples about parents' work hours, families' eating habits, television, and the Internet.

Paragraph B, on the other hand, does not make and support a single point. At first we think the point of the paragraph may be that "family togetherness is very important." But there is no supporting evidence showing how important family togetherness is. In the second sentence, we read that "today's mothers spend much less time at home than their mothers did, for several reasons." Now we think for a moment that this may be the main point and that the author will go on to list and explain some of those reasons. But the paragraph then goes on to comment on fathers, families in previous times, and families who find ways to spend time together. Any one of those ideas could be the focus of the paragraph, but none is. The paragraph ends with yet another idea that does not support any previous point and that itself could be the point of a paragraph: "TV and the Internet must be used wisely to achieve family togetherness." No single idea in this paragraph is developed, and the result for the reader is confusion.

In summary, while paragraph A is unified, paragraph B shows a complete lack of unity.

Identifying Common Errors in Topic Sentences

When writing a point, or topic sentence, people sometimes make mistakes that undermine their chances of producing an effective paragraph. One mistake is to substitute an announcement of the topic for a true topic sentence. Other mistakes include writing statements that are too broad or too narrow. Following are examples of all three errors, along with contrasting examples of effective topic sentences.

Announcement

My car is the concern of this paragraph

The statement above is a simple announcement of a subject, rather than a topic sentence expressing an idea about the subject.

Statement That Is Too Broad

Many people have problems with their cars.

The statement is too broad to be supported adequately with specific details in a single paragraph.

Statement That Is Too Narrow

My car is a Ford Focus.

The statement above is too narrow to be expanded into a paragraph. Such a narrow statement is sometimes called a *dead-end statement* because there is no place to go with it. It is a simple fact that does not need or call for any support.

Effective Topic Sentence

I hate my car.

The statement above expresses an opinion that could be supported in a paragraph. The writer could offer a series of specific supporting reasons, examples, and details to make it clear why he or she hates the car.

Here are additional examples:

Announcements

The subject of this paper will be my apartment.
I want to talk about increases in the divorce rate.

Statements That Are Too Broad

The places where people live have definite effects on their lives.
Many people have trouble getting along with others.

Statements That Are Too Narrow

I have no hot water in my apartment at night.
Almost one of every two marriages ends in divorce.

Effective Topic Sentences

My apartment is a terrible place to live.
The divorce rate is increasing for several reasons.

ACTIVITY 2	For each pair of sentences below, write A beside the sentence that only *announces* a topic. Write OK beside the sentence that *advances an idea* about the topic.

1. _____ a.   This paper will deal with flunking math.

   _____ b.   I flunked math last semester for several reasons.

2. _____ a.   I am going to write about my job as a gas station attendant.

   _____ b.   Working as a gas station attendant was the worst job I ever had.

3. _____ a.   Obscene phone calls are the subject of this paragraph.

   _____ b.   People should know what to do when they receive an obscene phone call.

4. _____ a.   In several ways, my college library is inconvenient to use.

   _____ b.   This paragraph will deal with the college library.

5. _____ a.   My paper will discuss the topic of procrastinating.

   _____ b.   The following steps will help you stop procrastinating.

ACTIVITY 3	For each pair of sentences below, write TN beside the statement that is *too narrow* to be developed into a paragraph. Write OK beside the statement in each pair that could be developed into a paragraph.

1. _____ a.   Employers notice how applicants dress for a job interview.

   _____ b.   First impressions are important in a job interview.

2. _____ a.   Sophia plans to audition for *American Idol*.

   _____ b.   Sophia is destined for stardom.

3. _____ a.   Jerome left college to serve in the U.S. Army, but now he is back to earn a degree in computer programming.

   _____ b.   Some people "stop out" of college, and then they return more determined.

4. _____ a.   There are many different attractions at Walt Disney World.

   _____ b.   Water park enthusiasts can enjoy Typhoon Lagoon and Blizzard Beach.

5. _____ a.   My daughter Celia has the potential to become a college athlete.

   _____ b.   Celia holds the state track record for the 400-meter dash.

	ACTIVITY 4

For each pair of sentences below, write TB beside the statement that is *too broad* to be supported adequately in a short paper. Write OK beside the statement that makes a limited point.

1. _____ a.   Professional football is a dangerous sport.

   _____ b.   Professional sports are violent.

2. _____ a.   Married life is the best way of living.

   _____ b.   Teenage marriages often end in divorce for several reasons.

3. _____ a.   Aspirin can have several harmful side effects.

   _____ b.   Drugs are dangerous.

4. _____ a.   School has always been challenging.

   _____ b.   I have struggled in school for several reasons.

5. _____ a.   Computers are changing our society.

   _____ b.   Using computers to teach schoolchildren is a mistake.

Understanding the Two Parts of a Topic Sentence

As stated earlier, the point that opens a paragraph is often called a *topic sentence.* When you look closely at a point, or topic sentence, you can see that it is made up of two parts:

1. The *limited topic*

2. The writer's idea about or attitude toward the limited topic

The writer's idea or attitude is usually expressed in one or more *key words.* All the details in a paragraph should support the idea expressed in the key words. In each of the topic sentences below, a single line appears under the topic and a double line under the idea about the topic (expressed in a key word or key words):

My girlfriend is very aggressive.

Highway accidents are often caused by absentmindedness.

The kitchen is the most widely used room in my house.

Voting should be required by law in the United States.

My pickup truck is the most reliable vehicle I have ever owned.

In the first sentence, the topic is *girlfriend*, and the key word that expresses the writer's idea about his topic is that his girlfriend is *aggressive*. In the second sentence, the topic is *highway accidents*, and the key word that determines the focus of the paragraph is that such accidents are often caused by *absentmindedness*. Notice each topic and key word or key words in the other three sentences as well.

ACTIVITY 5	For each point below, draw a single line under the topic and a double line under the idea about the topic.

1. Billboards should be abolished.

2. My boss is an ambitious person.

3. Politicians are often self-serving.

4. The apartment needed repairs.

5. Television commercials lack originality.

6. My parents have rigid racial attitudes.

7. The middle child is often a neglected member of the family.

8. The language in many movies today is inappropriate for children.

9. Doctors are often insensitive.

10. People today are more energy-conscious than ever before.

11. My car is a temperamental machine.

12. My friend Debbie, who is only nineteen, is extremely mature.

13. Looking for a job can be a degrading experience.

14. The daily life of students is filled with conflicts.

15. Regulations in the school cafeteria should be strictly enforced.

16. The national speed limit should be raised.

17. Our vacation turned out to be a disaster.

18. The city's traffic-light system has both benefits and drawbacks.

19. Insects serve many useful purposes.

20. Serious depression often has several warning signs.

Selecting a Topic Sentence

Remember that a paragraph is made up of a topic sentence and a group of related sentences developing the topic sentence. It is also helpful to remember that the topic sentence is a *general* statement. The other sentences provide specific support for the general statement.

> Each group of sentences below could be written as a short paragraph. Circle the letter of the topic sentence in each case. To find the topic sentence, ask yourself, "Which is a general statement supported by the specific details in the other three statements?"
>
> Begin by trying the example item below. First circle the letter of the sentence you think expresses the main idea. Then read the explanation.

ACTIVITY 6

EXAMPLE

   a. By no longer carrying matches or a lighter, people can cut down on impulse smoking.

   b. People who sit in no-smoking areas will smoke less.

   c. There are ways to behave that will help people smoke less.

   d. By keeping personal records of where and when smoking occurs, people can identify the most tempting situations and avoid them.

> EXPLANATION: Sentence *a* explains one way to smoke less. Sentences *b* and *d* also provide specific ways to smoke less. In sentence *c*, however, no one specific way is explained. The words *ways to behave that will make people smoke less* refer only generally to such methods. Therefore, sentence *c* is the topic sentence; it expresses the author's main idea. The other sentences support that idea by providing examples.

1. a. "I couldn't study because I forgot to bring my textbook home."

    b. "I couldn't do my homework because my printer ran out of toner."

    c. Students give instructors some common excuses.

    d. "I couldn't come to class because I had a migraine headache."

2. a. Its brakes are badly worn.

    b. My old car is ready for the salvage yard.

    c. Its floor has rusted through, and water splashes on my feet when the highway is wet.

    d. My mechanic says its engine is too old to be repaired, and the car isn't worth the cost of a new engine.

3. a. The last time I ate at the restaurant, I got food poisoning and was sick for two days.

    b. The city inspector found roaches and mice in the restaurant's kitchen.

    c. The restaurant on 23rd street is a health hazard and ought to be closed down.

    d. The toilets in the restaurant often back up, and the sinks have only a trickle of water.

4. a. Part-time employees can be easily laid off.

    b. Most part-time employees do not receive fringe benefits.

    c. A part-time employee earns 25 to 40 percent less than a full-time employee.

    d. Part-time employment has several disadvantages.

5. a. In early colleges, students were mostly white males.

    b. Colleges of two centuries ago were quite different from today's schools.

    c. All students in early colleges had to take the same courses.

    d. The entire student body at early schools consisted of only a few dozen people.

Writing a Topic Sentence I

ACTIVITY 7

The following activity will give you practice in writing an accurate point. Often you will start with a general topic or a general idea of what you want to write about. You may, for example, want to write a paragraph about some aspect of school life. To come up with a point about school life, begin by limiting your topic. One way to do this is to make a list of all the limited topics you can think of that fit under the general topic. Each of the general topics below is followed by a series of limited topics. Make a point out of *one* of the limited topics in each group.

> **HINT** To create a topic sentence, ask yourself, "What point do I want to make about _____ (*my limited topic*)?"

EXAMPLE

Recreation

- Movies
- Dancing
- TV shows
- Reading
- Sports parks

    Your point: <u>Sports parks today have some truly exciting games.</u>

1. Your school

- Instructor
- Cafeteria

- Specific course
- Particular room or building
- Particular policy (attendance, grading, etc.)
- Classmate

Your point: _____

_____

2. Job

- Pay
- Boss
- Working conditions
- Duties
- Coworkers
- Customers or clients

Your point: _____

_____

3. Money

- Budgets
- Credit cards
- Dealing with a bank
- School expenses
- Ways to get it
- Ways to save it

Your point: _____

_____

4. Cars

- First car
- Driver's test
- Road conditions
- Accident
- Mandatory speed limit
- Safety problems

Your point: _____

_____

5. Sports

- A team's chances
- At your school

- Women's team
- Recreational versus spectator
- Favorite team
- Outstanding athlete

Your point: _____

_____

Writing a Topic Sentence II

ACTIVITY 8

The following activity will give you practice in writing an accurate point, or topic sentence—one that is neither too broad nor too narrow for the supporting material in a paragraph. Sometimes you will construct your topic sentence after you have decided which details you want to discuss. An added value of this activity is that it shows you how to write a topic sentence that will exactly match the details provided in the outline.

1. Topic sentence: _____

_____

   a. They should study the hardest subjects first when their minds are most alert.
   b. They should form study groups and meet regularly at the library.
   c. They should ask teachers for help when they don't understand something.
   d. They should reward themselves when they do well.

2. Topic sentence: _____

_____

   a. My mom always said, "Do unto others as you would have them do unto you."
   b. She believed that everyone should be treated with respect and kindness.
   c. When my brother got caught up in the wrong crowd, she had him promise her that he would never hurt anyone.
   d. At my mom's funeral, so many people talked about how she had helped them.

3. Topic sentence: _____

_____

   a. My friends recommended that I try the new Thai restaurant.
   b. The waiter was friendly and explained the daily lunch specials.
   c. The Evil Jungle Prince was the best red curry I had ever eaten.
   d. I plan to take my family to that restaurant for dinner.

4. Topic sentence: _____

_____

   a. In elementary school, my favorite subject was morning recess.

   b. All I remember about junior high was playing volleyball in P.E. class.

   c. In high school, I kept my grades up so that I could stay on the basketball team.

   d. Before my knee injury, I had hoped to go to college on an athletic scholarship.

5. Topic sentence: _____

_____

   a. People who skip breakfast usually snack a lot.

   b. People who eat breakfast feel less grouchy.

   c. People who eat breakfast are more alert mentally.

   d. Breakfast can help people lose—not gain—weight.

Step 2: Support the Point with Specific Evidence

The first essential step in writing effectively is to start with a clearly stated point. The second basic step is to support that point with specific evidence. Consider the supported point that you read at the beginning of the chapter (p. 55):

Point

The demands of modern society in recent years have changed family life.

Support

(1) Parents
   (a) Today's parents spend much less time with their children
   (b) Most work longer hours now, leaving children at an after-school program, or with a neighbor, or in an empty house

(2) Eating habits
   (a) Formerly full homemade meals, eaten together
   (b) Now prepared foods at home or fast food out, eaten separately

(3) Television and the Internet
   (a) Watching TV or browsing the Internet instead of conversing

The supporting evidence is needed so that we can *see and understand for ourselves* that the writer's point is sound. The author of "Changes in the Family" has supplied specific supporting examples of how changes in our society have weakened family life. The paragraph has provided the evidence that is needed for us to understand and agree with the writer's point.

Now consider the following paragraph:

Good-Bye, Tony

I have decided not to go out with Tony anymore. First of all, he was late for our first date. He said that he would be at my house by 8:30, but he did not arrive until 9:30. Second, he was bossy. He told me that it would be too late to go to the new Jack Black comedy that I wanted to see, and that we would go instead to a new action film with Will Smith. I told him that I didn't like violent movies, but he said that I could shut my eyes during the bloody parts. Only because it was a first date did I let him have his way. Finally, he was abrupt. After the movie, rather than suggest a bite to eat or a drink, he drove right out to a back road near Oakcrest High School to meet his friends. What he did a half hour later angered me most of all. He cut his finger on a bracelet I was wearing and immediately said we had to go right home. He was afraid the scratch would get infected if he didn't put Neosporin and a Band-Aid on it. When he dropped me off, I said, "Good-bye, Tony," in a friendly enough way, but in my head I thought, "Good-bye *forever*, Tony."

The author's point is that she has decided not to go out with Tony anymore. See if you can summarize in the spaces below the three reasons she gives to support her decision:

Reason 1: _____

Reason 2: _____

Reason 3: _____

Notice what the supporting details in this paragraph do. They provide you, the reader, with a basis for understanding why the writer made the decision she did. Through specific evidence, the writer has explained and communicated her point successfully. The evidence that supports the point in a paragraph often consists of a series of reasons introduced by signal words (the author here uses *First of all*, *Second*, and *Finally*) and followed by examples and details that support the reasons. That is true of the sample paragraph above: three reasons are provided, followed by examples and details that back up those reasons.

The Point as an "Umbrella" Idea

You may find it helpful to think of the point as an "umbrella" idea. Under the writer's point fits all of the other material of the paragraph. That other material is made up of specific supporting details—evidence such as examples, reasons, or facts. The diagram to the left shows the relationship for the paragraph "Good-Bye, Tony."

Both of the paragraphs that follow resulted from an assignment to "Write a paper that details your reasons for being in college." Both writers make the point that they have various reasons for attending college. Which paragraph then goes on to provide plenty of specific evidence to back up its point? Which paragraph is vague and repetitive and lacks the concrete details needed to show us exactly why the author decided to attend college?

ACTIVITY 9

HINT Imagine that you've been asked to make a short film based on each paragraph. Which one suggests specific pictures, locations, words, and scenes you could shoot?

PARAGRAPH A

Personal

Reasons for Going to College

I decided to attend college for various reasons. One reason is self-respect. For a long time now, I have had little self-respect. I spent a lot of time doing nothing, just hanging around or getting into trouble, and eventually I began to feel bad about it. Going to college is a way to start feeling better about myself. By accomplishing things, I will improve my self-image. Another reason for going to college is that things happened in my life that made me think about a change. When I lost my job, I realized I would have to do something in life, so I thought about school. I was in a rut and needed to get out of it but did not know how. But when something happens that is out of your control, then you have to make some kind of decision. The most important reason for college, though, is to fulfill my dream. I know I need an education, and I want to take the courses I need to reach the position that I think I can handle. Only by challenging myself can I get what I want. Going to college will help me fulfill this goal. These are the main reasons why I am attending college.

PARAGRAPH B

Personal

Why I'm in School

There are several reasons I'm in school. First of all, my father's attitude made me want to succeed in school. One night last year, after I had come in at 3 A.M., my father said, "Jake, you're a loser. When I look at my son, all I see is a good-for-nothing loser." I was angry, but I knew my father was right in a way. I had spent the last two years working at odd jobs at a convenience store and gas station, while experimenting with all kinds of drugs with my friends. That night, though, I decided I would prove my

continued

father wrong. I would go to college and be a success. Another reason I'm in college is my girlfriend's encouragement. Marie has already been in school for a year, and she is doing well in her computer courses. Marie helped me fill out my application and register for courses. She even lent me two hundred dollars for textbooks. On her day off, she lets me use her car so I don't have to take the bus. The main reason I am in college is to fulfill a personal goal: for the first time in my life, I want to finish something. For example, I quit high school in the eleventh grade. Then I enrolled in a government job-training program, but I dropped out after six months. I tried to get a G.E.D., but I started missing classes and eventually gave up. Now I am in a special program where I will earn my G.E.D. by completing a series of five courses. I am determined to accomplish this goal and to then go on and work for a degree in hotel management.

Complete the following statement: Paragraph _____ provides clear, vividly detailed reasons why the writer decided to attend college.

Paragraph B is the one that solidly backs up its point. The writer gives us specific reasons he is in school. On the basis of such evidence, we can clearly understand his opening point. The writer of paragraph A offers only vague, general reasons for being in school. We do not get specific examples of how the writer was "getting into trouble," what events occurred that forced the decision, or even what kind of job he or she wants to qualify for. We sense that the feeling expressed is sincere; but without particular examples we cannot really see why the writer decided to attend college.

Reinforcing Point and Support

You have now learned the two most important steps in writing effectively: making a point and supporting that point. Take a few minutes now to do the following activity. It will strengthen your ability to recognize a *point* and the *support* for that point.

ACTIVITY 10	In the following groups, one statement is the general point and the other statements are specific support for the point. Identify each point with a P and each statement of support with an S.

EXAMPLE

_____S_____   A city bus pass costs less than a tank of gas.

_____S_____   Brewing coffee at home is cheaper than buying coffee at Starbucks.

_____S_____   Coupons help reduce the grocery bill.

_____P_____   There are several ways to cut down on daily expenses.

> **EXPLANATION:** The point—that daily spending can be reduced—is strongly supported by the three specific ways stated.

1. _____ A person with depression might have sleep problems.

   _____ A person with depression might withdraw from friends.

   _____ Depression can affect a person's life in negative ways.

   _____ A person with depression might feel hopeless all the time.

2. _____ Kim takes online classes, which fit into her busy schedule.

   _____ Kim is able to juggle the demands of school, family, and work.

   _____ Kim taught her kids how to help around the home.

   _____ Kim's supervisor gives her a flexible work schedule.

3. _____ There are serious consequences to plagiarism.

   _____ A student can fail a class for turning in someone else's work.

   _____ Some schools award a grade of FD for academic dishonesty.

   _____ Some schools expel students who plagiarize.

4. _____ Artificial sweeteners provide an alternative to refined sugar.

   _____ Regular exercise helps regulate a person's blood sugar level.

   _____ Blood sugar meters are sold over the counter at pharmacies.

   _____ Diabetes can be managed successfully.

5. _____ Keisha was promoted to shift manager at work.

   _____ Mel received a two-year scholarship from the Rotary Club.

   _____ Keisha and Mel considered themselves fortunate.

   _____ Keisha and Mel were able to find an affordable apartment.

6. _____ Never give out personal information over the phone.

   _____ Shred all bank and credit card statements.

   _____ When using an ATM, remember to take the receipt.

   _____ Everyone should take precautions to avoid identity theft.

7. _____ White Castle sells microwavable hamburgers and cheeseburgers.

   _____ Hooters sells frozen Buffalo-style chicken strips.

   _____ Restaurant chains are selling their products in frozen food sections of supermarkets.

   _____ T.G.I. Friday's sells its popular appetizers, such as potato skins and onion rings.

8. _____ People take personal phone calls during meetings.

   _____ Workplace etiquette is sorely lacking.

_____ People "borrow" coworkers' supplies without asking first.

_____ People leave their dirty dishes in the workplace kitchen.

9. _____ Ms. Lee is an outstanding teacher.

_____ She always asks if students have questions.

_____ She promptly answers e-mail and phone messages.

_____ She adds humor to her class lectures.

10. _____ I am able to do my homework while on my way to school.

_____ I am able to take a nap between school and work.

_____ I am able to play my GameBoy DS on the way home.

_____ I prefer to use the city's public transportation.

11. _____ The musical group The Who performs all the theme songs for the *CSI* shows.

_____ The theme song for *CSI: Vegas* is "Who Are You."

_____ The theme song for *CSI: Miami* is "Won't Get Fooled Again."

_____ The theme song for *CSI: New York* is "Baba O'Riley."

12. _____ Mars has a rocky surface.

_____ Mercury has a rocky surface.

_____ Venus has a rocky surface.

_____ In addition to Earth, three planets in our solar system have rocky surfaces.

13. _____ Some courses have a prerequisite grade of C or better.

_____ Some employers look at a student's grade point average (GPA).

_____ Students should understand the importance of grades.

_____ Students who transfer need to meet that school's minimum GPA.

14. _____ He rearranged his work schedule so he could drop off and pick up his daughter from day care.

_____ He takes online classes to reduce his commuting time to and from school.

_____ Kyong Li takes his parenting responsibilities seriously.

_____ He is working toward an associate degree so he can better support his family.

15. _____ College students depend on technology to assist them in their learning.

_____ Professors may make class lectures available as podcasts.

_____ Campus classes may have an online component.

_____ Students often communicate with professors and class-mates through e-mail.

The Importance of *Specific* Details

The point that opens a paper is a general statement. The evidence that supports a point is made up of specific details, reasons, examples, and facts.

Specific details have two key functions. First of all, details *excite the reader's interest*. They make writing a pleasure to read, for we all enjoy learning particulars about other people—what they do and think and feel. Second, details *support and explain a writer's point;* they give the evidence needed for us to see and understand a general idea. For example, the writer of "Good-Bye, Tony" provides details that make vividly clear her decision not to see Tony anymore. She specifies the exact time Tony was supposed to arrive (8:30) and when he actually arrived (9:30). She mentions the kind of film she wanted to see (a new Jack Black movie) and the one that Tony took her to instead (a violent movie). She tells us what she may have wanted to do after the movie (have a bite to eat or a drink) and what Tony did instead (met up with his friends); she even specifies the exact location of the place Tony took her (a back road near Oakcrest High School).

The writer of "Why I'm in School" provides equally vivid details. He gives clear reasons for being in school (his father's attitude, his girlfriend's encouragement, and his wish to fulfill a personal goal) and backs up each reason with specific details. His details give us many sharp pictures. For instance, we hear the exact words his father spoke: "Jake, you're a loser." He tells us exactly how he was spending his time ("working at odd jobs at a convenience store and gas station while experimenting with all kinds of drugs with my friends"). He describes how his girlfriend helped him (filling out the college application, lending money and her car). Finally, instead of stating generally that "a person has to make some kind of decision," as the writer of "Reasons for Going to College" does, he specifies that he has a strong desire to finish college because he dropped out of many schools and programs in the past: high school, a job-training program, and a G.E.D. course.

In both "Good-Bye, Tony" and "Why I'm in School," then, the vivid, exact details capture our interest and enable us to share in the writer's experience. We see people's actions and hear their words; the details provide pictures that make each of us feel "I am there." The particulars also allow us to understand each writer's point clearly. We are shown exactly why the first writer has decided not to see Tony anymore and exactly why the second writer is attending college.

Recognizing Specific Details

ACTIVITY 11

Each of the five points below is followed by two attempts at support (*a* and *b*). Write S (for *specific*) in the space next to the one that succeeds in providing specific support for the point. Write X in the space next to the one that lacks supporting details.

1. My two-year-old son was in a stubborn mood today.

_____ a. When I asked him to do something, he gave me nothing but trouble. He seemed determined to make things difficult for me, for he had his mind made up.

_____ b. When I asked him to stop playing in the yard and come indoors, he looked me squarely in the eye and shouted "No!" and then spelled it out, "N . . . O!"

2. The prices in the amusement park were outrageously high.

_____ a. The food seemed to cost twice as much as it would in a supermarket and was sometimes of poor quality. The rides also cost a lot, and so I had to tell the children that they were limited to a certain number of them.

_____ b. The cost of the log flume, a ride that lasts roughly three minutes, was ten dollars a person. Then I had to pay four dollars for an eight-ounce cup of Coke and six dollars for a hot dog.

3. My brother-in-law is accident prone.

_____ a. Once he tried to open a tube of Krazy Glue with his teeth. When the cap came loose, glue squirted out and sealed his lips shut. They had to be pried open in a hospital emergency room.

_____ b. Even when he does seemingly simple jobs, he seems to get into trouble. This can lead to hilarious, but sometimes dangerous, results. Things never seem to go right for him, and he often needs the help of others to get out of one predicament or another.

4. The so-called "bargains" at the yard sale were junk.

_____ a. The tables were filled with useless stuff no one could possibly want. They were the kinds of things that should be thrown away, not sold.

_____ b. The "bargains" included two headless dolls, blankets filled with holes, scorched potholders, and a plastic Christmas tree with several branches missing.

5. The key to success in college is organization.

_____ a. Knowing what you're doing, when you have to do it, and so on is a big help for a student. A system is crucial in achieving an ordered approach to study. Otherwise, things become very disorganized, and it is not long before grades will begin to drop.

_____ b. Organized students never forget paper or exam dates, which are marked on a calendar above their desks. And instead of having to cram for exams, they study their clear, neat classroom and textbook notes on a daily basis.

EXPLANATION: The specific support for point 1 is answer *b*. The writer does not just tell us that the little boy was stubborn but provides an example that shows us. In particular, the detail of the son's spelling out "N . . . O!" makes

continued

his stubbornness vividly real for the reader. For point 2, answer *b* gives specific prices (ten dollars for a ride, four dollars for a Coke, and six dollars for a hot dog) to support the idea that the amusement park was expensive. For point 3, answer *a* vividly backs up the idea that the brother-in-law is accident-prone by detailing an accident with Krazy Glue. Point 4 is supported by answer *b*, which lists specific examples of useless items that were offered for sale—from headless dolls to a broken plastic Christmas tree. We cannot help agreeing with the writer's point that the items were not bargains but junk. Point 5 is backed up by answer *b*, which identifies two specific strategies of organized students: they mark important dates on calendars above their desks, and they take careful notes and study them on a daily basis.

In each of the five cases, the specific evidence enables us to *see for ourselves* that the writer's point is valid.

Follow the directions for Activity 11.

ACTIVITY 12

1. The house has been neglected by its owners.

    _____ a. As soon as I looked at the house from the outside, I could tell that repairs need to be made. The roof is badly in need of attention. But it is very obvious that other outside parts of the house also are badly in need of care.

    _____ b. The roof is missing a number of shingles. The house's paint is peeling and spotted with mold. Two windows have been covered with plywood.

2. Students have practical uses for computers.

    _____ a. Students stay in touch with friends by e-mail. They often shop over the Internet. They do all their research online.

    _____ b. Students have an easier way now to communicate with their friends. They can also save time now: they have no need to go out and buy things but can do it at home. Also, getting information they need for papers no longer requires spending time in the library.

3. Rico knew very little about cooking when he got his first apartment.

    _____ a. He had to live on whatever he had in the freezer for a while. He was not any good in the kitchen and had to learn very slowly. More often than not, he would learn how to cook something only by making mistakes first.

    _____ b. He lived on frozen macaroni and cheese dinners for three weeks. His idea of cooking an egg was to put a whole egg in the microwave, where it exploded. Then he tried to make a grilled cheese sandwich by putting slices of cheese and bread in a toaster.

4. Speaking before a group is a problem for many people.

_____ a. They become uncomfortable even at the thought of speaking in public. They will go to almost any length to avoid speaking to a group. If they are forced to do it, they can feel so anxious that they actually develop physical symptoms.

_____ b. Stage fright, stammering, and blushing are frequent reactions. Some people will pretend to be ill to avoid speaking publicly. When asked to rank their worst fears, people often list public speaking as even worse than death.

5. Small children can have as much fun with ordinary household items as with costly toys.

_____ a. A large sheet thrown over a card table makes a great hideout or playhouse. Banging pot covers together makes a tremendous crash that kids love. Also, kids like to make long, winding fences out of wooden clothespins.

_____ b. Kids can make musical instruments out of practically anything. The result is a lot of noise and fun. They can easily create their own play areas as well by using a little imagination. There is simply no need to have to spend a lot of money on playthings.

Providing Supporting Evidence

ACTIVITY 13

Working in groups of two or three, provide three details that logically support each of the following points, or topic sentences. Your details can be drawn from your own experience, or they can be invented. In each case, the details should show in a specific way what the point expresses in only a general way. You may state your details briefly in phrases, or as complete sentences.

EXAMPLE

Each holiday season, several "hot" items are on kids' wish lists.

1. One year, every preschooler wanted a Tickle Me Elmo doll.

2. Kids always want the most up-to-date video game console.

3. Electronic toys are popular among both girls and boys.

1. Everyone has a cure for the common cold.

a. _____

b. _____

c. _____

2. Nothing can take the place of home cooking.

a. _____

b. _____

c. _____

3. We can help save our environment in small but powerful ways.

a. _____

b. _____

c. _____

4. I could never understand the wisdom of my father until I became one.

a. _____

_____

b. _____

_____

c. _____

_____

5. People should look for certain qualities when selecting a doctor.

a. _____

b. _____

c. _____

The Importance of *Adequate* Details

One of the most common and most serious problems in students' writing is inadequate development. You must provide *enough* specific details to support fully the point you are making. You could not, for example, submit a paragraph about your brother-in-law being clumsy and provide only a single short example. You would have to add several other examples or provide an extended example of your brother-in-law's clumsiness. Without such additional support, your paragraph would be underdeveloped.

At times, students try to disguise an undersupported point by using repetition and wordy generalities. You saw this, for example, in paragraph A ("Reasons for Going to College") on page 67. Be prepared to do the plain hard work needed to ensure that each of your paragraphs has full, solid support.

The following paragraphs were written on the same topic, and each has a clear opening point. Which one is adequately developed? Which one has few particulars and uses mostly vague, general, wordy sentences to conceal the fact that it is starved for specific details?	**ACTIVITY 14**

PARAGRAPH A

Abuse of Public Parks

Some people abuse public parks. Instead of using the park for recreation, they go there, for instance, to clean their cars. Park caretakers regularly have to pick up the contents of dumped ashtrays and car litter bags. Certain juveniles visit parks with cans of spray paint to deface buildings, fences, fountains, and statues. Other offenders are those who dig up and cart away park flowers, shrubs, and trees. One couple were even arrested for stealing park sod, which they were using to fill in their lawn. Perhaps the most widespread offenders are the people who use park tables and benches and fireplaces but do not clean up afterward. Picnic tables are littered with trash, including crumpled bags, paper plates smeared with ketchup, and paper cups half-filled with stale soda. On the ground are empty beer bottles, dented soda cans, and sharp metal bottle caps. Parks are made for people, and yet—ironically—their worst enemy is "people pollution."

PARAGRAPH B

Mistreatment of Public Parks

Some people mistreat public parks. Their behavior is evident in many ways, and the catalog of abuses could go on almost without stopping. Different kinds of debris are left by people who have used the park as a place for attending to their cars. They are not the only individuals who mistreat public parks, which should be used with respect for the common good of all. Many young people come to the park and abuse it, and their offenses can occur in any season of the year. The reason for their inconsiderate behavior is known only to themselves. Other visitors lack personal cleanliness in their personal habits when they come to the park, and the park suffers because of it. Such people seem to have the attitude that someone else should clean up after them. It is an undeniable fact that people are the most dangerous thing that parks must contend with.

Complete the following statement: Paragraph _____ provides an adequate number of specific details to support its point.

Paragraph A offers a series of detailed examples of how people abuse parks. Paragraph B, on the other hand, is underdeveloped. Paragraph B speaks only of "different kinds of debris," while paragraph A refers specifically to "dumped ashtrays and car litter bags"; paragraph B talks in a general way of young people abusing the park, while paragraph A supplies such particulars as "cans of spray paint" and defacing "buildings, fences, fountains, and statues." And there is no equivalent in paragraph B for the specifics in paragraph A about people who steal park property and litter park grounds. In summary, paragraph B lacks the full, detailed support needed to develop its opening point convincingly.

REFLECTIVE ACTIVITY

To check your understanding of the chapter so far, see if you can answer the following questions.

1. It has been observed: "To write well, the first thing you must do is decide what nail you want to drive home." What is meant by *nail?*

    _____

2. How do you "drive home the nail" in the paragraph?

    _____

    _____

3. What are the two reasons for using specific details in your writing?

    a. _____

    b. _____

4. Look back at the paragraph you wrote on page 34 about an everyday annoyance. How could you further "drive home the nail"? In other words, what could you do to improve that paragraph?

Identifying Adequate Supporting Evidence

ACTIVITY 15

Two of the following paragraphs provide sufficient details to support their topic sentences convincingly. Write AD, for *adequate development*, beside those paragraphs. There are also three paragraphs that, for the most part, use vague, general, or wordy sentences as a substitute for concrete details. Write U, for *underdeveloped*, beside those paragraphs.

_____ 1.

Academic

Social Saving

The power of the group is often stronger than the power of the individual. This is demonstrated by the blossoming of online group coupon sites like LivingSocial, Groupon, and Dealster. By exercising group buying power, users are able to save money on food, clothing, and entertainment. Most sites offer discounts of at least 50 percent for consumers. Other sites like CauseOn (Portland), DealBug (Kansas City), Scoop St. (New York), and Group Swoop (San Francisco) are set in one area. These are good sites not just for people who live in the area, but also for savvy travelers. In

continued

preparation for a visit to San Francisco, travelers can subscribe to Group Swoop and purchase coupons to be used during the vacation. CauseOn and DealBug are not only social group coupons, but a portion of each of the proceeds goes to local charities—often chosen by the customer from a list of provided options.

_____ 2.

The Dangers of Being Charitable

People need to be aware of the hazards of charity and helping those in need because giving often starts small, but soon takes over and becomes a lifestyle. Charity usually begins with a minor donation of change to the local firefighters' boot drive. The philanthropist feels good for a while, but then that feeling fades. The next time the patron drops change in the boot, it isn't enough—that helpful feeling just isn't there, so she begins to purchase large quantities of bottled water and ready-to-eat foods, and drives around delivering food and water to the homeless. The feeling of doing good returns, but then, a disaster happens—earthquake in Haiti, floods in Pakistan, tornadoes in the Midwest—and the donor fumbles to reclaim that gratifying feeling. Just sending monetary donations doesn't seem to be enough. Just sending food, clothing, and products doesn't seem to be enough. The philanthropist starts charity drives to raise awareness and support, and the humanitarian feeling settles back in. Unfortunately, the feeling still doesn't last and the withdrawal begins to set in. The giver frantically begins to research more and more ways to get involved, chasing that altruistic feeling that has become so elusive. Soon, the donor is spending time at local soup kitchens, adopting needy families, and opening doors to those who have no place to live. Like an addict, the philanthropist is no longer a free agent, but a servant to humanitarian causes.

_____ 3.

Attitudes toward Food

As children, we form attitudes toward food that are not easily changed. In some families, food is love. Not all families are like this, but some children grow up with this attitude. Some families think of food as something precious and not to be wasted. The attitudes children pick up about food are hard to change in adulthood. Some families celebrate

continued

with food. If a child learns an attitude, it is hard to break this later.
Someone once said: "As the twig is bent, so grows the tree." Children
are very impressionable, and they can't really think for themselves when
they are small. Children learn from the parent figures in their lives, and
later from their peers. Some families have healthy attitudes about food.
It is important for adults to teach their children these healthy attitudes.
Otherwise, the children may have weight problems when they are adults.

_____ 4.

Qualities in a Friend

There are several qualities I look for in a friend. A friend should give
support and security. A friend should also be fun to be around. Friends can
have faults, like anyone else, and sometimes it is hard to overlook them.
But a friend can't be dropped because he or she has faults. A friend should
stick around, even in bad times. There is a saying that "a friend in need is
a friend indeed." I believe this means that there are good friends and fair-
weather friends. The second type is not a true friend. He or she is the kind
of person who runs when there's trouble. Friends don't always last a lifetime.
Someone who is believed to be a best friend may lose contact if they move
to a different area or go around with a different group of people. A friend
should be generous and understanding. Friends do not have to be exactly
like each other. Sometimes friends are opposites, but they still like each other
and get along. Since I am a very quiet person, I can't say that I have many
friends. But these are the qualities I believe a friend should have.

_____ 5.

Learning Outside the Classroom

Colleges should require that all students take a service learning course.
Service learning not only combines classroom study and community
service, but it introduces students to hands-on training and helps create a
sense of well-being in students. Students in biology classes often take part
in waterway clean-up projects. These students not only gain a sense of
contributing to their community and helping improve the environment, but
they also get to study the local plants and wildlife and learn just how humans
positively and negatively impact the ecosystems. Students in theater classes
can expand their knowledge about costumes, set design, and lighting

continued

while they participate in community theater programs. Additionally, students can learn how the theater programs can enhance individuals through better social, communication, and problem-solving skills. This, in turn, improves local communities through cross-generational participation. Students in education classes can volunteer at local schools, offering services like free tutoring, aiding teachers, and campus clean-up programs. Not only will this volunteer work have a positive impact on the schools' communities, but it will introduce future teachers to ways of improving the environments they will be working in. Students who are in English composition classes can participate in local adult literacy programs, helping tutor adults in reading and writing. Not only will these students gain a sense of purpose, but they will be increasing their knowledge of reading and writing skills. Service learning improves both classroom learning and lifelong learning and should be a requirement for every college graduate.

Adding Details to Complete a Paragraph

ACTIVITY 16   Each of the following paragraphs needs specific details to back up its supporting points. In the spaces provided, add a sentence or two of realistic details for each supporting point. The more specific you are, the more convincing your details are likely to be.

1.
A Pushover Instructor

We knew after the first few classes that the instructor was a pushover. First of all, he didn't seem able to control the class.

_____

_____

_____

In addition, he made some course requirements easier when a few students complained.

_____

_____

_____

Finally, he gave the easiest quiz we had ever taken.

_____

_____

_____

2.

Helping a Parent in College

There are several ways a family can help a parent who is attending college. First, family members can take over some of the household chores that the parent usually does.

_____

_____

Also, family members can make sure that the student has some quiet study time.

_____

_____

Last, families can take an interest in the student's problems and accomplishments.

_____

_____

Writing a Paragraph

You know now that an effective paragraph does two essential things: (1) it makes a point, and (2) it provides specific details to support that point. You have considered a number of paragraphs that are effective because they follow these two basic steps or ineffective because they fail to follow them.

The following writing assignments will give you practice in writing a paragraph of your own. Choose one of the three assignments below, and follow carefully the guidelines provided.

DEVELOPING AND SUPPORTING A POINT

WRITING ASSIGNMENT 1

Turn back to Activity 13 on page 74 and select the point for which you have the best supporting details. Develop that point into a paragraph by following these steps:

a. If necessary, rewrite the point so that the first sentence is more specific or suits your purpose more exactly. For example, you might want to rewrite the second point so that it includes a specific time and place: "Dinner at the Union Building Cafeteria was terrible yesterday."

b. Provide several sentences of information to develop each of your three supporting details fully. Make sure that all the information in your paragraph truly supports your point.

c. Use the words *first of all, second,* and *finally* to introduce your three supporting details.

d. Conclude your paragraph with a sentence that refers to your opening point. This last sentence "rounds off" the paragraph and lets the reader know that your discussion is complete. For example, the paragraph "Changes in the Family" on pages 55–56 begins with. The demands of modern society in recent years have changed family life. It closes with a statement that refers to, and echoes, the opening point: "Clearly, modern life is a challenge to family life."

e. Supply a title based on your point. For instance, point 3 on page 75 might have the title "Ways to Save the Environment."

Use the following list to check your paragraph for each of the above items:

Yes   No

☐   ☐   Do you begin with a point?

☐   ☐   Do you provide relevant, specific details that support the point?

☐   ☐   Do you use the words *first of all, second*, and *finally* to introduce your three supporting details?

☐   ☐   Do you have a closing sentence?

☐   ☐   Do you have a title based on your point?

☐   ☐   Are your sentences clear and free of obvious errors?

WRITING ASSIGNMENT 2

EXPLAINING YOUR DECISION

In this chapter you have read two paragraphs (pages 67–68) on reasons for being in college. The writing prompt at the opening of this chapter (p. 54) asked you to consider your own reasons for being in college and to write nonstop, make a list, or draw a diagram of your ideas. For this assignment, look back at the ideas you wrote down in response to the chapter opening writing prompt and write a paragraph describing your reasons for being in college. You might also want to look at the following list of common reasons students give for going to school. Write a check mark next to each reason that applies to you. Using this list and the ideas you have written down, select your three most important reasons for being in school and generate specific supporting details for each reason.

Before starting, reread paragraph B on pages 67–68. *You must provide comparable specific details of your own.* Make your paragraph truly personal; do not fall back on vague generalities like those in paragraph A on page 67. As you work on your paragraph, use the checklist for Assignment 1 as a guide.

*Apply in
My Case*   **Reasons Students Go to College**

_____   To have some fun before getting a job

_____   To prepare for a specific career

_____ To please their families

_____ To educate and enrich themselves

_____ To be with friends who are going to college

_____ To take advantage of an opportunity they didn't have before

_____ To find a husband or wife

_____ To see if college has anything to offer them

_____ To do more with their lives than they've done so far

_____ To take advantage of Veterans Administration benefits or other special funding

_____ To earn the status that they feel comes with a college degree

_____ To get a new start in life

_____ Other:

> ## in a writer's words
>
> *"Write what you want to read. The person you know best in the world is you. Listen to yourself. If you are excited by what you are writing, you have a much better chance of putting that excitement over to a reader."*
>
> —Robin McKinley

IDENTIFYING GOALS

Write a paragraph about your goals for the coming year. First, list a series of realistic goals, major and minor, that you would like to accomplish between today and one year from today. Your goals can be personal, academic, and/or career related. Next, organize your list by using clustering or a scratch outline. Use the checklist for Writing Assignment 1 as a guide while you are working on the paragraph.

WRITING ASSIGNMENT 3

Personal

EXPLORING WRITING ONLINE

Go to your school's Web site. What can you learn about your school from its Web Site? Which details might appeal to a student who is considering attending your school? Using specific details from the Web site, write a paragraph explaining why this student should attend your school.

Transitions

Look at the following items. Then check (✓) the one that is easier to read and understand.

_____ Our landlord repainted our apartment. He replaced the dishwasher.

_____ Our landlord repainted our apartment. Also, he replaced the dishwasher.

You probably found the second item easier to understand. The word *also* makes it clear that the writer is adding a second way the landlord has been of help. *Transitions*, or *transition words*, are signal words that help readers follow the direction of the writer's thought. They show the relationship between ideas, connecting one thought to the next. They are "bridge" words, carrying the reader across from one idea to the next.

Two major types of transitions are of particular help when you write: words that show *time* and words that show *addition*.

Words That Show Time

Check (✓) the item that is easier to read and understand.

1. _____ a. I had blood work done. I went to the doctor.

   _____ b. I had blood work done. Then I went to the doctor.

The word *Then* in the second item makes clear the relationship between the sentences. After having blood work done, the writer goes to the doctor. *Then* and words like it are time words, carrying the reader from one idea to the next.

I had blood work done. _____ I went to the doctor.

Here are some more pairs of sentences. Check (✓) the item in each pair that contains a time word and so is easier to read and understand.

2. _____ a. Every week my uncle studies the food ads to see which stores have the best specials. He clips all the coupons.

   _____ b. Every week my uncle studies the food ads to see which stores have the best specials. Next, he clips all the coupons.

3. _____ a. Carmen took a very long shower. There was no hot water left for anyone else in the house.

   _____ b. Carmen took a very long shower. After that, there was no hot water left for anyone else in the house.

In the pair of sentences about the uncle, the word *Next* helps make the relationship between the two sentences clear. The uncle studies ads, and then he clips coupons. In the second pair of sentences, the word *after* makes the relationship clear: after Carmen's long shower, there was no hot water left for anyone else.

Time words tell us *when* something happened in relation to when something else happened. They help writers organize and make clear the order of events, stages, and steps in a process. Below are some common words that show time.

Time Words		
before	next	later
first	as	after
second	when	finally
third	while	then

Fill in each blank with the appropriate time transition from the box. Use each transition once.

ACTIVITY 4

then	first	after	as	later

A Victory for Big Brother

In one of the most terrifying scenes in all of literature, George Orwell in his classic novel *1984* describes how a government known as Big Brother destroys a couple's love. The couple, Winston and Julia, fall in love and meet secretly, knowing the government would not approve. _____ informers turn them in, a government agent named O'Brien takes steps to end their love. _____ he straps Winston down and explains that he has discovered Winston's worst fear.

_____ he sets a cage with two giant, starving sewer rats on the table next to Winston. He says that when he presses a lever, the door of the cage will slide up, and the rats will shoot out like bullets and bore straight into Winston's face. _____ Winston's eyes dart back and forth, revealing his terror, O'Brien places his hand on the lever. Winston knows that the only way out is for Julia to take his place. Suddenly, he hears his own voice screaming, "Do it to Julia! Not me! Julia!" Orwell does not describe Julia's interrogation, but when Julia and Winston see each other _____, they realize that each has betrayed the other. Their love is gone. Big Brother has won.

Words That Show Addition

Check (✓) the item that is easier to read and understand.

1. _____   a. A drinking problem can destroy a person's life. It can tear a family apart.

   _____   b. A drinking problem can destroy a person's life. In addition, it can tear a family apart.

2. _____   a. One way to lose friends is always to talk and never to listen. A way to end friendships is to borrow money and never pay it back.

   _____   b. One way to lose friends is always to talk and never to listen. Another way to end friendships is to borrow money and never pay it back.

In the pair of sentences about a drinking problem, the words *In addition* help make the relationship between the two sentences clear. The author is describing two effects of a drinking problem: it can destroy a life and a family. *In addition* and words like it are known as addition words. In the pair of sentences about losing friends, you probably found the second item easier to understand. The word *Another* is an addition word that makes it clear that the writer is describing a second way to lose friends.

Addition words signal added ideas. They help writers organize information and present it clearly to readers.

Some common words that show addition follow.

Paperback books cost less than hardbacks.  , they are easier to carry.

Addition Words		
one	to begin with	in addition
first	another	next
first of all	second	last (of all)
for one thing	also	finally

ACTIVITY 5   **Fill in each blank with the appropriate addition transition from the box. Use each transition once.**

in	finally	second	first

Social Not-Working

The workplace environment is being affected by social networking sites such as Facebook. _____, most people don't consider

continued

it a negative habit to check Facebook during the work day, but it is actually stealing. People who constantly check Facebook when they should be working are stealing time from the company. If, for example, "Sam" gets paid ten dollars an hour and he spends one hour a week looking at Facebook, he is being paid for one hour that he is not working. In other words, he is stealing ten dollars a week from the company. Over the course of a year, that could add up to over $500. _____, people who check Facebook during the work day and are using company computers are misusing company equipment. Although it might seem harmless, this use of company equipment is no different from driving a company car or using company furniture; maintenance, service, and upgrades cost money and must be budgeted. Taking a company car on a personal trip or borrowing company furniture to decorate a house are not allowed; most companies don't allow personal use of company computers either. _____, many company computers contain private and sensitive material that could be compromised if an employee is on a social networking site. _____, people who check Facebook during work hours can lose focus on their work, causing delays and poor performance. If something exciting or terrible is posted, it could affect the attitude of the employee, which in turn could affect how that employee functions the rest of the day. Although people like to stay connected with each other during the day, company employees need to limit their use of social networking sites to private equipment during lunch hours, breaks, or nonworking hours.

Other Kinds of Transitions

In the following box are other common transitional words, grouped according to the kind of signal they give readers. In the paragraphs you write, you will most often use addition signals (words like *first, also, another,* and *finally*), but all of the following signals are helpful to know as well.

> **Other Common Transitional Words**
>
> *Space signals:* next to, across, on the opposite side, to the left, to the right, in front, in back, above, below, behind, nearby
>
> *Change-of-direction signals:* but, however, yet, in contrast, otherwise, still, on the contrary, on the other hand
>
> *Illustration signals:* for example, for instance, specifically, as an illustration, once, such as
>
> *Conclusion signals:* therefore, consequently, thus, then, as a result, in summary, to conclude, last of all, finally

ACTIVITY 6

1. Underline the three *space* signals in the following paragraph:

    Standing in the burned-out shell of my living room was a shocking experience. Above my head were charred beams, all that remained of our ceiling. In front of me, where our television and stereo had once stood, were twisted pieces of metal and chunks of blackened glass. Strangely, some items seemed little damaged by the fire. For example, I could see the TV remote and a dusty DVD under the rubble. I walked through the gritty ashes until I came to what was left of our sofa. Behind the sofa had been a wall of family photographs. Now, the wall and the pictures were gone. I found only a waterlogged scrap of my wedding picture.

2. Underline the four *change-of-direction* signals in the following paragraph:

    In some ways, train travel is superior to air travel. People always marvel at the speed with which airplanes can zip from one end of the country to another. Trains, on the other hand, definitely take longer. But sometimes longer can be better. Traveling across the country by train allows people to experience the trip more completely. They get to see the cities and towns, mountains and prairies that too often pass by unnoticed when they fly. Another advantage of train travel is comfort. Traveling by plane means wedging adult-sized bodies into narrow seats, bumping knees on the back of the seat, and having to pay five dollars for a tiny bag of pretzels. In contrast, the seats on most trains are spacious and comfortable, permitting even the longest-legged traveler to stretch out and watch the scenery just outside the window. And when train travelers grow hungry, they can get up and stroll to the dining car, where they can order anything from a simple snack to a gourmet meal. There's no question that train travel is definitely slow and old-fashioned compared with air travel. However, in many ways it is much more civilized.

3. Underline the three *illustration* signals in the following selection:

Status symbols are all around us. The cars we drive, for instance, say something about who we are and how successful we have been. The auto makers depend on this perception of automobiles, designing their commercials to show older, well-established people driving luxury sedans and young, fun-loving people driving to the beach in sports cars. Clothing, too, has always been a status symbol. Specifically, schoolchildren are often rated by their classmates according to the brand names of their clothing. Another example of a status symbol is the cell phone. This device, not so long ago considered a novelty, is now used by almost everyone. Being without a cell phone today is like being without a land line in the 1990s.

4. Underline the *conclusion* signal in the following paragraph:

A hundred years ago, miners used to bring caged canaries down into the mines with them to act as warning signals. If the bird died, the miners knew that the oxygen was running out. The smaller animal would be affected much more quickly than the miners. In the same way, animals are acting as warning signals to us today. Baby birds die before they can hatch because pesticides in the environment cause the adults to lay eggs with paper-thin shells. Fish die when lakes are contaminated with acid rain or poisonous mercury. The dangers in our environment will eventually affect all life on earth, including humans. Therefore, we must pay attention to these early warning signals. If we don't, we will be as foolish as a miner who ignored a dead canary —and we will die.

Fill in each blank with the appropriate transition from the box. Use each transition once.

ACTIVITY 7

> *Addition transitions:* first of all, second, finally
> *Time transition:* when
> *Illustration transition:* once
> *Change-of-direction transition:* however
> *Conclusion transition:* as a result

Joining an International Club

One of the best things I've done in college is to join the International Students Club. _____, the club has helped me become friendly with a diverse group of people, including other students who share my Dominican heritage. At any time in my

continued

apartment, I can hear someone from Pakistan chatting about music to someone from Sweden, or someone from Russia talking about politics to someone from Uganda. _____, I made fried sweet plantains for three students from China. They had never tasted such a dish before, but they liked it. A _____ benefit of the club is that it's helped me realize how similar people are. _____ the whole club first assembled, we wound up having a conversation about dating and sex that included the perspectives of fifteen countries and six continents! It was clear we all shared the feeling that sex was fascinating. The talk lasted for hours, with many different people describing the wildest or funniest experience they had had with the opposite sex. Only a few students, particularly those from the United States and Japan, seemed bashful. _____, the club has reminded me about the dangers of stereotyping. Before I joined the club, my only direct experience with people from China was ordering meals in the local Chinese restaurant. _____, I believed that most Chinese people ate lots of rice and worked in restaurants. In the club, _____, I met Chinese people who were soccer players, English majors, and math teachers. I've also seen Jewish and Muslim students—people who I thought would never get along—drop their preconceived notions and become friends. Even more than my classes, the club has been an eye-opener for me.

Other Connecting Words

In addition to transitions, three other kinds of connecting words help tie together the specific evidence in a paragraph: *repeated words, pronouns,* and *synonyms.* Each will be discussed in turn.

Repeated Words

Many of us have been taught by English instructors—correctly so—not to repeat ourselves in our writing. On the other hand, repeating key words can help tie ideas together. In the paragraph that follows, the word *retirement* is repeated to remind readers of the key idea on which the discussion is centered. Underline the word the five times it appears.

Oddly enough, retirement can pose more problems for the spouse than for the retired person. For a person who has been accustomed to a demanding job, retirement can mean frustration and a feeling of uselessness. This feeling will put pressure on the spouse to provide challenges at home equal to those of the workplace. Often, these tasks will disrupt the spouse's well-established routine. Another problem arising from retirement is filling up all those empty hours. The spouse may find himself or herself in the role of social director or tour guide, expected to come up with a new form of amusement every day. Without sufficient challenges or leisure activities, a person can become irritable and take out the resulting boredom and frustration of retirement on the marriage partner. It is no wonder that many of these partners wish their spouses would come out of retirement and do something—anything—just to get out of the house.

Pronouns

Pronouns (*he, she, it, you, they, this, that,* and others) are another way to connect ideas as you develop a paper. Using pronouns to take the place of other words or ideas can help you avoid needless repetition. (Be sure, though, to use pronouns with care in order to avoid the unclear or inconsistent pronoun references described in Chapters 28 and 29 of this book.) Underline the eight pronouns in the passage below, noting at the same time the words that the pronouns refer to.

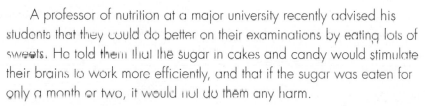

A professor of nutrition at a major university recently advised his students that they could do better on their examinations by eating lots of sweets. He told them that the sugar in cakes and candy would stimulate their brains to work more efficiently, and that if the sugar was eaten for only a month or two, it would not do them any harm.

Synonyms

Using synonyms—words that are alike in meaning—can also help move the reader from one thought to the next. In addition, the use of synonyms increases variety and interest by avoiding needless repetition of the same words. Underline the three words or phrases used as synonyms for *false ideas* in the following passage.

There are many false ideas about suicide. One wrong idea is that a person who talks about suicide never follows through. The truth is that about three out of every four people who commit suicide notify one or more other persons ahead of time. Another misconception is that a person who commits suicide is poor or downtrodden. Actually, poverty appears to be a deterrent to suicide rather than a predisposing factor. A third myth about suicide is that people bent on suicide will eventually take their lives one way or another, whether or not the most obvious means of suicide is removed from their reach. In fact, since an attempt at suicide is a kind of cry for help, removing a convenient means of taking one's life, such as a gun, shows people bent on suicide that someone cares enough about them to try to prevent it.

| ACTIVITY 8 | This activity will give you practice in identifying connecting words that are used to help tie ideas together. |

REPEATED WORDS:

In the space provided, write the repeated words.

1. We absorb radiation from many sources in our environment. Our television sets and microwave ovens, among other things, give off low-level radiation.

_____

2. Many researchers believe that people have weight set-points their bodies try to maintain. This may explain why many dieters return to their original weight.

_____

3. At the end of the concert, thousands of fans held up cell phones in the darkened arena. The sea of cell phones signaled that the fans wanted an encore.

_____

4. Establishing credit is important for everyone. A good credit history is often necessary when applying for a loan or charge account.

_____

SYNONYMS:

In the space provided, write in the synonym for the underlined word.

5. I checked my car's tires, oil, water, and belts before the trip. But the ungrateful machine sputtered and died about fifty miles from home.

_____

6. Women's clothes, in general, use less material than do men's clothes. Yet women's garments usually cost more than men's.

_____

7. The temperance movement in this country sought to ban alcohol. Drinking liquor, movement leaders said, led to violence, poverty, prostitution, and insanity.

_____

8. For me, apathy quickly sets in when the weather becomes hot and sticky. This listlessness disappears when the humidity decreases.

_____

PRONOUNS:

In the space provided, write in the word referred to by the underlined pronoun.

9. At the turn of the twentieth century, bananas were still an oddity in the United States. Some people even attempted to eat <u>them</u> with the peel on.

_____

10. Canning vegetables is easy and economical. <u>It</u> can also be very dangerous.

_____

11. There are a number of signs that appear when students are under stress. For example, <u>they</u> start to have trouble studying, eating, and even sleeping.

_____

REFLECTIVE ACTIVITY

1. Look over the paragraph you wrote in response to Writing Assignment 1, 2, or 3 in Chapter 3 (pages 81–83). Is the paragraph organized well? If not, rewrite it using time or emphatic order as explained on pages 85–88.

2. Is your paragraph easy to follow? If not, see if adding transitions and connective words as explained on pages 90–98 will help.

Step 4: Write Clear, Error-Free Sentences

Up to now this book has emphasized the first three steps in writing an effective paragraph: making a point, supporting the point, and organizing and connecting the evidence. This section will focus on the fourth step: writing clear, error-free sentences. You'll learn how to revise a paragraph so that your sentences flow smoothly and clearly. Then you'll review how to edit a paragraph for mistakes in grammar, punctuation, and spelling.

Revising Sentences

The following strategies will help you to revise your sentences effectively.

- Use parallelism.
- Use a consistent point of view.
- Use specific words.
- Use concise wording.
- Vary your sentences.

in a writer's words

"When I was seven, I said to my mother, may I close my door? And she said yes, but why do you want to close your door? And I said because I want to think. And when I was eleven, I said to my mother, may I lock my door? And she said yes, but why do you want to lock your door? And I said because I want to write."—**Dorothy West**

Use Parallelism

Words in a pair or a series should have a parallel structure. By balancing the items in a pair or a series so that they have the same kind of structure, you will make a sentence clearer and easier to read. Notice how the parallel sentences that follow read more smoothly than the nonparallel ones.

Nonparallel (Not Balanced)	**Parallel (Balanced)**
I resolved to lose weight, to study more, and *watching* less TV.	I resolved to lose weight, to study more, and to watch less TV. (A balanced series of *to* verbs: *to lose, to study, to watch*)
A consumer group rates my car as noisy, expensive, and *not having much safety.*	A consumer group rates my car as noisy, expensive, and unsafe. (A balanced series of descriptive words: *noisy, expensive, unsafe*)
Lola likes wearing soft sweaters, eating exotic foods, and *to bathe* in scented bath oil.	Lola likes wearing soft sweaters, eating exotic foods, and bathing in scented bath oil. (A balanced series of -ing words: *wearing, eating, bathing*)
Single life offers more freedom of choice; *more security is offered by marriage.*	Single life offers more freedom of choice; marriage offers more security. (Balanced verbs and word order: *single life offers . . . ; marriage offers . . .*)

You need not worry about balanced sentences when writing first drafts. But when you rewrite, you should try to put matching words and ideas into matching structures. Such parallelism will improve your writing style.

ACTIVITY 9

Cross out the unbalanced part of each sentence. In the space provided, revise the unbalanced part so that it matches the other item or items in the sentence. The first one is done for you as an example.

1. Our professor warned us that he would give surprise tests, ~~the assignment of term papers~~, and allow no makeup exams.
   assign term papers

2. Making a big dinner is a lot more fun than to clean up after it.

3. The street-corner preacher stopped people walking by was asking them questions, and handed them a pamphlet.

4. My teenage daughter enjoys shopping for new clothes, to try different cosmetics, and reading beauty magazines.

5. Many of today's action movies have attractive actors, fantastic special effects, and dialogue that is silly.

_____

6. While you're downtown, please pick up the dry cleaning, return the library books, and the car needs washing too.

_____

7. I want a job that pays high wages, provides a complete benefits package, and offering opportunities for promotion.

_____

8. As the elderly woman climbed the long staircase, she breathed hard and was grabbing the railing tightly.

_____

9. I fell into bed at the end of the hard day, grateful for the sheets that were clean, soft pillow, and cozy blanket.

_____

10. Ray's wide smile, clear blue eyes, and expressing himself earnestly all make him seem honest, even though he is not.

_____

Cross out the unbalanced part of each sentence. In the space provided, revise the unbalanced part so that it matches the other item or items in the sentence.   **ACTIVITY 10**

1. The preschool teacher asked the children to put away their art supplies and that their hands needed to be washed for lunch.

_____

2. Boring lectures, labs that are long, and mindless homework make college uninteresting.

_____

3. The vending machines on campus offer oily chips that shouldn't be eaten, sugary beverages I shouldn't drink, and stale cookies I don't like.

_____

4. My new apartment has new appliances, storage that are plentiful, and a spacious bedroom.

_____

5. The badly maintained sales showroom needs the displays replaced, the outlets rewired, and cleaning the carpet.

_____

6. I edited my paper for comma splices, sentence fragments, and there were comma mistakes.

_____

7. Rob does not want to spend two hours a day commuting to work, but employment nearby is something he cannot find.

_____

8. Watching DVD movies, buttered popcorn that I eat, and drinking Diet Coke make up my Friday night routine.

_____

9. Raising a two-year-old, a child that is four years old, and a twelve-year-old makes life extremely hectic.

_____

10. The Elton John AIDS Foundation is a global organization that not only educates people about HIV/AIDS prevention but also providing health services to people living with this disease.

_____

Use a Consistent Point of View

Consistency with Verbs Do not shift verb tenses unnecessarily. If you begin writing a paper in the present tense, don't shift suddenly to the past. If you begin in the past, don't shift without reason to the present. Notice the inconsistent verb tenses in the following example:

> The shoplifter *walked* quickly toward the front of the store. When a clerk *shouts* at him, he *started* to run.

The verbs must be consistently in the present tense:

> The shoplifter *walks* quickly toward the front of the store. When a clerk *shouts* at him, he *starts* to run.

Or the verbs must be consistently in the past tense:

> The shoplifter *walked* quickly toward the front of the store. When a clerk *shouted* at him, he *started* to run.

ACTIVITY 11

Change verbs as needed in the following passage so that they are consistently in the past tense. Cross out each incorrect verb and write the correct form above it, as shown in the example. You will need to make nine corrections.

Late one rainy night, Mei Ling woke to the sound of steady dripping.
                                                          splashed
When she got out of bed to investigate, a drop of cold water ~~splashes~~

onto her arm. She looks up just in time to see another drop form on the

ceiling, hang suspended for a moment, and fall to the carpet. Stumbling

to the kitchen, Mei Ling reaches deep into one of the cabinets and lifts out a large roasting pan. As she did so, pot lids and baking tins clattered out and crash onto the counter. Mei Ling ignored them, stumbled back to the bedroom, and places the pan on the floor under the drip. But a minute after sliding her icy feet under the covers, Mei Ling realized she is in trouble. The sound of each drop hitting the metal pan echoed like a gunshot in the quiet room. Mei Ling feels like crying, but she finally thought of a solution. She got out of bed and returns a minute later with a thick bath towel. She lined the pan with the towel and crawls back into bed.

Consistency with Pronouns Pronouns should not shift point of view unnecessarily. When writing a paper, be consistent in your use of first-, second-, or third-person pronouns.

Type of Pronoun	Singular	Plural
First-person pronouns	I (my, mine, me)	we (our, ours, us)
Second-person pronouns	you (your, yours)	you (your, yours)
Third-person pronouns	he (his, him)	they (their, them)
	she (her)	
	it (its)	

TIP Any person, place, or thing, as well as any indefinite pronoun like *one*, *anyone*, *someone*, and so on (page 444), is a third-person word.

For instance, if you start writing in the third person *she*, don't jump suddenly to the second person *you*. Or if you are writing in the first person *I*, don't shift unexpectedly to *one*. Look at the following examples.

Inconsistent	**Consistent**
I enjoy movies like *The Return of the Vampire* that frighten *you*. (A very common mistake people make is to let *you* slip into their writing after they start with another pronoun.)	I enjoy movies like *The Return of the Vampire* that frighten me.
As soon as a person walks into Helen's apartment, *you* can tell that Helen owns a cat. (Again, *you* is a shift in point of view.)	As soon as a person walks into Helen's apartment, *he or she* can tell that Helen owns a cat. (See also the note on *his or her* references on pages 444–445.)

ACTIVITY 12

Cross out the inconsistent pronouns in the following sentences and revise by writing the correct form of the pronoun above each crossed-out word.

EXAMPLE

> I like solving math problems, for ~~you~~ can always find the correct answer.

1. My grades are so low that one may be placed on academic probation.

2. Wanting a more attractive smile, Jenna asked her dentist if teeth whitening could really do you any good.

3. I drink green tea every day because you want to experience its many health benefits.

4. As we entered the café, you could smell the delicious aroma of freshly roasted coffee beans.

5. I hate going to the doctor because you always am told to eat less and exercise more.

6. In my workplace, every employee is encouraged to express your opinion.

7. The Furtado twins are fraternal, but most people cannot tell her apart.

8. As we listened to Mika give her speech, you could hear the nervousness in her voice.

9. Gavin refuses to quit smoking, even though he knows that smoking is not good for you.

10. I love playing *Guitar Hero* on my PlayStation, for you have always wanted to be a rock star.

Use Specific Words

To be an effective writer, you must use specific words rather than general words. Specific words create pictures in the reader's mind. They help capture interest and make your meaning clear. Compare the following sentences:

General	**Specific**
The boy came down the street.	Theo ran down 125th Street.
A bird appeared on the grass.	A blue jay swooped down onto the frost-covered lawn.
She stopped the car.	Jackie slammed on the brakes of her Camry.

The specific sentences create clear pictures in our minds. The details *show* us exactly what has happened.

Here are four ways to make your sentences specific.

1. Use exact names.

   She loves her *car.*

   Renée loves her *Honda.*

2. Use lively verbs.

The garbage truck *went* down Front Street.

The garbage truck *rumbled* down Front Street.

3. Use descriptive words (modifiers) before nouns.

A girl peeked out the window.

A *chubby six-year-old* girl peeked out the *dirty kitchen* window.

4. Use words that relate to the five senses: sight, hearing, taste, smell, and touch.

That woman is a karate expert.
That *tiny, silver-haired* woman is a karate expert. (*Sight*)

When the dryer stopped, a signal sounded.
When the *whooshing* dryer stopped, a *loud buzzer* sounded. (*Hearing*)

Terence offered me an orange slice.
Terence offered me a *sweet, juicy* orange slice. (*Taste*)

The real estate agent opened the door of the closet.
The real estate agent opened the door of the *cedar-scented* closet.
(*Smell*)

I pulled the blanket around me to fight off the wind.
I pulled the *fluffy* blanket around me to fight off the *chilling* wind.
(*Touch*)

| This activity will give you practice in replacing vague, indefinite words with sharp, specific words. Add three or more specific words to replace the general word or words underlined in each sentence. Make changes in the wording of a sentence as necessary. | **ACTIVITY 13** |

EXAMPLE

My bathroom cabinet contains <u>many drugs</u>.

My bathroom cabinet contains aspirin, antibiotics, tranquilizers,

and codeine cough medicine.

1. At the shopping center, we visited several stores.

   _____

   _____

2. Sunday is my day to take care of chores.

   _____

   _____

3. Lauren enjoys various activities in her spare time.

   _____

   _____

4. I spent most of my afternoon doing homework.

   _____

   _____

5. We returned home from vacation to discover that several pests had invaded the house.

   _____

   _____

ACTIVITY 14

With the help of the methods described on pages 104–105 and summarized below, add specific details to the sentences that follow. Note the examples.

- Use exact names.
- Use lively verbs.
- Use descriptive words (modifiers) before nouns.
- Use words that relate to the senses—sight, hearing, taste, smell, touch.

EXAMPLES

The person got out of the car.
The elderly man painfully lifted himself out of the white Buick station wagon.

   _____

The fans enjoyed the victory.
Many of the fifty-thousand fans stood, waved banners, and cheered wildly

when Barnes scored the winning touchdown.

1. The crowd grew restless.

   _____

   _____

2. I relaxed.

   _____

   _____

3. The room was cluttered.

   _____

   _____

4. The child threw the object.

   _____

5. The driver was angry.

   _____

   _____

Use Concise Wording

Wordiness—using more words than necessary to express a meaning—is often a sign of lazy or careless writing. Your readers may resent the extra time and energy they must spend when you have not done the work needed to make your writing direct and concise.

Here are examples of wordy sentences:

Anne is of the opinion that the death penalty should be allowed.

I would like to say that my subject in this paper will be the kind of generous person that my father was.

Omitting needless words improves the sentences:

Anne supports the death penalty.

My father was a generous person.

The following box lists some wordy expressions that could be reduced to single words.

Wordy Form	Short Form
a large number of	many
a period of a week	a week
arrive at an agreement	agree
at an earlier point in time	before
at the present time	now
big in size	big
owing to the fact that	because
during the time that	while
five in number	five
for the reason that	because
good benefit	benefit
in every instance	always
in my own opinion	I think
in the event that	if
in the near future	soon
in this day and age	today
is able to	can
large in size	large
plan ahead for the future	plan
postponed until later	postponed
red in color	red
return back	return

| ACTIVITY 15 | Rewrite the following sentences, omitting needless words. |

1. After a lot of careful thinking, I have arrived at the conclusion that drunken drivers should receive jail terms.

   _____

   _____

2. The movie that I went to last night, which was fairly interesting, I must say, was enjoyed by me and my girlfriend.

   _____

   _____

3. Ben finally made up his mind after a lot of indecisions and decided to look for a new job.

   _____

   _____

4. Due to inclement weather conditions of wind and rain, we have decided not to proceed with the athletic competition about to take place on the baseball diamond.

   _____

   _____

5. Beyond a doubt, the only two things you can rely or depend on would be the fact that death comes to everyone and also that the government will tax your yearly income.

   _____

   _____

| ACTIVITY 16 | Rewrite the following sentences, omitting needless words. |

1. There is this one worker at the warehouse who rarely if ever arrives on time.

   _____

   _____

2. Judging by the looks of things, it seems to me that no one studied for the quiz.

   _____

   _____

3. Seeing as how gas prices are increasing in every instance, in the very near future I will ride my bike everywhere.

   _____

   _____

4. In this day and age it is almost a certainty that someone you know will experience the crime of identity theft.

_____

5. In my personal opinion it is correct to say that organic chemistry is the most difficult course in the science curriculum.

_____

_____

Vary Your Sentences

One aspect of effective writing is to vary your sentences. If every sentence follows the same pattern, writing may become monotonous. This chapter explains four ways you can create variety and interest in your writing style. The first two ways involve coordination and subordination—important techniques for achieving different kinds of emphasis.

The following are four methods you can use to make your sentences more varied and more sophisticated:

1. Add a second complete thought (coordination).

2. Add a dependent thought (subordination).

3. Begin with a special opening word or phrase.

4. Place adjectives or verbs in a series.

Revise by Adding a Second Complete Thought When you add a second complete thought to a simple sentence, the result is a *compound* (or *double*) sentence. The two complete statements in a compound sentence are usually connected by a comma plus a joining, or *coordinating*, word (*and, but, for, or, nor, so, yet*).

Use a compound sentence when you want to give equal weight to two closely related ideas. The technique of showing that ideas have equal importance is called *coordination*. Following are some compound sentences. Each contains two ideas that the writer regards as equal in importance.

Bill has stopped smoking cigarettes, but he is now addicted to chewing gum.

I repeatedly failed the math quizzes, so I decided to drop the course.

Darrell turned all the lights off, and then he locked the office door.

Combine the following pairs of simple sentences into compound sentences. Use a comma and a logical joining word (*and, but, for, so*) to connect each pair. If you are not sure what *and, but, for,* and *so* mean, turn to pages 417–419.

ACTIVITY 17

EXAMPLE

- The cars crept along slowly.
- Visibility was poor in the heavy fog.
  The cars crept along slowly, for visibility was poor in the heavy fog.

_____

1. • Lee thought she would never master the computer.

    • In two weeks she was using it comfortably.

    _____

    _____

2. • Vandals smashed the car's headlights.

    • They slashed the tires as well.

    _____

    _____

3. • I married at age seventeen.

    • I never got a chance to live on my own.

    _____

    _____

4. • A volcano erupts.

    • It sends tons of ash into the air.

    • This creates flaming orange sunsets.

    _____

    _____

5. • The phone rings late at night.

    • We answer it fearfully.

    • It could bring tragic news.

    _____

    _____

Revise by Adding a Dependent Thought When you add a dependent thought to a simple sentence, the result is a complex sentence.* A dependent thought begins with a word or phrase like one of the following:

Dependent Words		
after	if, even if	when, whenever
although, though	in order that	where, wherever
as	since	whether
because	that, so that	which, whichever
before	unless	while
even though	until	who, whoever
how	what, whatever	whose

*The two parts of a complex sentence are sometimes called an *independent clause* and a *dependent clause*. A *clause* is simply a word group that contains a subject and a verb. An independent clause expresses a complete thought and can stand alone. A dependent clause does not express a complete thought in itself and "depends on" the independent clause to complete its meaning. Dependent clauses always begin with a dependent, or subordinating, word.

A *complex* sentence is used to emphasize one idea over another. Look at the following complex sentence:

Although I lowered the thermostat, my heating bill remained high.

The idea that the writer wants to emphasize here—*my heating bill remained high*—is expressed as a complete thought. The less important idea—*Although I lowered my thermostat*—is subordinated to this complete thought. The technique of giving one idea less emphasis than another is called *subordination.*

Following are other examples of complex sentences. In each case, the part starting with the dependent word is the less emphasized part of the sentence.

Even though I was tired, I stayed up to watch the horror movie.

Before I take a bath, I check for spiders in the tub.

When Vera feels nervous, she pulls on her earlobe.

Use logical subordinating words to combine the following pairs of simple sentences into sentences that contain a dependent thought. Place a comma after a dependent statement when it starts the sentence.

ACTIVITY 18

EXAMPLE

- Our team lost.
- We were not invited to the tournament.
  Because our team lost, we were not invited to the tournament.

_____

1. • I receive my degree in June.
   • I will begin to apply for jobs.

   _____

   _____

2. • Robyn doesn't enjoy cooking.
   • She often eats at fast-food restaurants.

   _____

   _____

3. • I sent several letters of complaint.
   • The electric company never corrected my bill.

   _____

   _____

4. • Neil felt his car begin to skid.
   • He took his foot off the gas pedal.

   _____

   _____

5. • The final exam covered sixteen chapters.

   • The students complained.

   _____

   _____

ACTIVITY 19

Using coordination, subordination, or both, combine each of the following groups of simple sentences into two longer sentences. Omit repeated words. Various combinations are possible, so for each group, try to find the combination that flows most smoothly and clearly. Work in pairs to complete this activity.

1. • Lynn pretended not to overhear her coworkers.

   • She couldn't stop listening.

   • She felt deeply embarrassed.

   • They were criticizing her work.

   _____

   _____

   _____

2. • Nigel got home from the shopping mall.

   • He discovered that his rented tuxedo did not fit.

   • The jacket sleeves covered his hands.

   • The pants cuffs hung over his shoes.

   _____

   _____

   _____

3. • The boys waited for the bus.

   • The wind shook the flimsy shelter.

   • They shivered with cold.

   • They were wearing thin jackets.

   _____

   _____

   _____

4. • The engine almost started.

   • Then it died.

   • I realized no help would come.

   • I was on a lonely road.

   • It was very late.

   _____

   _____

5. • Justin was leaving the store.

   • The shoplifting alarm went off.

   • He had not stolen anything.

   • The clerk had forgotten to remove the magnetic tag.

   • The tag was on a shirt Justin had bought.

   _____

   _____

   _____

Revise by Beginning with a Special Opening Word or Phrase Among the special openers that can be used to start sentences are (1) *-ed* words, (2) *-ing* words, (3) *-ly* words, (4) *to* word groups, and (5) prepositional phrases. Here are examples of all five kinds of openers:

-ed word
Tired from a long day of work, Sharon fell asleep on the sofa.

-ing word
Using a thick towel, Mel dried his hair quickly.

-ly word
Reluctantly, I agreed to rewrite the paper.

to word group
To get to the church on time, you must leave now.

Prepositional phrase
With Fred's help, Monika planted the evergreen shrubs.

| Combine the simple sentences into one sentence by using the opener shown in the margin and omitting repeated words. Use a comma to set off the opener from the rest of the sentence. | **ACTIVITY 20** |

EXAMPLE

   • Jen found her car keys.

   • She searched through her purse.   *-ing* word

   Searching through her purse, Jen found her car keys. _____

   _____

1. • Raj studied for the anthropology exam.   *–ed* word

   • He was determined to do well.

   _____

   _____

-ing word | 2. • The soldier volunteered for another tour of duty.

• She knew the danger involved.

_____

_____

–ly word | 3. • I entered the online sweepstakes contest.

• I was optimistic.

_____

_____

to word group | 4. • Gina worked out daily at the gym.

• She wanted to build muscle and lose fat.

_____

_____

Prepositional phrase | 5. • Rick and I sought counseling.

• We hoped to save our relationship.

_____

_____

| **ACTIVITY 21** | Combine the simple sentences into one sentence by using the opener shown in the margin and omitting repeated words. Use a comma to set off the opener from the rest of the sentence. |

-ed word | 1. • We were exhausted from four hours of hiking.

• We decided to stop for the day.

_____

_____

-ing word | 2. • Gus was staring out the window.

• He didn't hear the instructor call on him.

_____

_____

-ly word | 3. • Nobody saw the thieves steal our bikes.

• This was unfortunate.

_____

_____

to word group | 4. • Wayne rented a limousine for the night.

• He wanted to make a good impression.

_____

_____

5. • Joanne logs into Facebook to chat with her friends.

   • She does this during her lunch breaks.

   Prepositional phrase

   _____

Revise by Placing Adjectives or Verbs in a Series Various parts of a sentence may be placed in a series. Among these parts are adjectives (descriptive words) and verbs. Here are examples of both in a series.

Adjectives
The *black, smeary* newsprint rubbed off on my *new butcher-block* table.

Verbs
The quarterback *fumbled* the ball, *recovered* it, and *sighed* with relief.

Combine the simple sentences in each group into one sentence by using adjectives or verbs in a series and by omitting repeated words. In most cases, use a comma between the adjectives or verbs in a series.

ACTIVITY 22

EXAMPLE

   • Before Christmas, I made fruitcakes.

   • I decorated the house.

   • I wrapped dozens of toys.
     Before Christmas, I made fruitcakes, decorated the house, and wrapped
     dozens of toys.

1. • Before going to bed, I locked all the doors.

   • I activated the burglar alarm.

   • I slipped a kitchen knife under my mattress.

   _____

   _____

2. • Jasmine picked sweater hairs off her coat.

   • The hairs were fuzzy.

   • The hairs were white.

   • The coat was brown.

   • The coat was suede.

   _____

   _____

3. • The contact lens fell onto the floor.

    • The contact lens was thin.

    • The contact lens was slippery.

    • The floor was dirty.

    • The floor was tiled.

_____

_____

ACTIVITY 23

Combine the simple sentences in each group into one sentence by using adjectives or verbs in a series and by omitting repeated words. In most cases, use a comma between the adjectives or verbs in a series.

1. Jackie carefully looked into her rear view mirror before leaving the driveway.

    She locked her car door.

    She strapped on her seat belt.

_____

_____

2. I downloaded several games to my laptop.

    The games were free.

    The games require role playing.

    The laptop is new.

    The laptop is a Dell.

_____

_____

3. Steve picked up the phone.

    He cleared his throat.

    He dialed Angelina's number.

    He cleared his throat again.

    He hung up before the first ring.

_____

_____

4. The applicant entered the room.

    She was confident.

    She was applying for a job.

The room was large.

The room was designated for the interview.

_____

_____

5. The pasta was served with a sauce.

The pasta was freshly made.

The pasta was linguini.

The sauce was pesto.

The sauce was topped with roasted pine nuts.

_____

_____

Editing Sentences

After revising sentences in a paragraph so that they flow smoothly and clearly, you need to edit the paragraph for mistakes in grammar, punctuation, mechanics, usage, and spelling. Even if a paragraph is otherwise well-written, it will make an unfavorable impression on readers if it contains such mistakes. To edit a paragraph, check it against the agreed-upon rules or conventions of written English—simply called *sentence skills* in this book. Here are the most common of these conventions:

1. Write complete sentences rather than fragments.

2. Do not write run-ons.

3. Use verb forms correctly.

4. Make sure that subject, verbs, and pronouns agree.

5. Eliminate faulty modifiers.

6. Use pronoun forms correctly.

7. Use capital letters where needed.

8. Use the following marks of punctuation correctly: apostrophe, quotation marks, comma, semicolon, colon, hyphen, dash, parentheses.

9. Use correct manuscript form.

10. Eliminate slang, clichés, and pretentious words.

11. Check for possible spelling errors.

12. Eliminate careless errors.

These sentence skills are treated in detail in Part 5 of this book, and they can be referred to easily as needed. The list of sentence skills on the inside back cover includes chapter references and the list of correction symbols on pages 562–563 includes page references so that you can turn quickly to any skill you want to check.

HINT   Here are some hints that can help you edit the next-to-final draft of a paper for sentence-skills mistakes:

1. Have at hand two essential tools: a good dictionary (see page 513) and a grammar handbook (you can use the one in this book on pages 394–563).
2. Use a sheet of paper to cover your paragraph so that you will expose only one sentence at a time. Look for errors in grammar, spelling, and typing. It may help to read each sentence out loud. If a sentence does not read clearly and smoothly, chances are something is wrong.
3. Pay special attention to the kinds of errors you tend to make. For example, if you tend to write run-ons or fragments, be especially on the lookout for those errors.
4. Try to work on a printed draft, where you'll be able to see your writing more objectively than you can on a handwritten page; use a pen with colored ink so that your corrections will stand out.

A Note on Proofreading

Proofreading means checking the final, edited draft of your paragraph closely for typos and other careless errors. A helpful strategy is to read your paper backward, from the last sentence to the first. This helps keep you from getting caught up in the flow of the paper and missing small mistakes. Here are six helpful proofing symbols:

Proofing Symbol	Meaning	Example
∧	insert missing letter or word	bel*i*eve
ℒ	omit	in the ~~the~~ meantime
∽	reverse order of words or letters	once a upon time
#	add space	alltogether #
‿	close up space	foot ball
cap, lc	Add a capital (or a lowercase) letter	My persian Cat

If you make too many corrections, type in the corrections and reprint the page.

ACTIVITY 24

Academic

In the spaces at the bottom of this paragraph, write the numbers of the ten word groups that contain fragments or run-ons. Then, in the spaces between the lines, edit by making the necessary corrections. One is done for you as an example.

> [1]Two groups of researchers have concluded that "getting cold" has little to do with "catching a cold." [2]When the experiment

continued

was done for the first time. **3**Researchers exposed more than four hundred people to the cold virus. **4**Then divided those people into three groups. **5**One group, wearing winter coats, sat around in ten-degree temperatures. The second group was placed in sixty-degree temperatures. **6**With the third group staying in a room. **7**Where it was eighty degrees. **8**The number of people who actually caught colds was the same. **9**In each group. **10**Other researchers repeated this experiment ten years later. **11**This time they kept some subjects cozy and warm. they submerged others in a tank filled with water. **12**Whose temperature had been lowered to seventy-five degrees. **13**They made others sit around in their underwear in forty-degree temperatures. **14**The results were the same. the subjects got sick at the same rate. Proving that people who get cold do not always get colds.

1. _____   2. _____   3. _____   4. _____   5. _____

6. _____   7. _____   8. _____   9. _____   10. _____

EXPLORING WRITING ONLINE

Visit one of these Web sites and read a news article of your choice. As you read the article, think about how the writer uses transition words to organize and connect evidence. Then, on a separate sheet of paper, list those transition words.

CNN.com: http://www.cnn.com

ABC News: http://www.abcnews.go.com

FoxNews.com: http://www.foxnews.com

MSNBC: http://www.msnbc.msn.com

Four Bases for Revising Writing

ABSOLUTE ON ICE.

NEARLY 50% OF AUTOMOBILE FATALITIES ARE LINKED TO ALCOHOL • 10% OF NORTH AMERICANS ARE ALCOHOLICS
A TEENAGER SEES 100,000 ALCOHOL ADS BEFORE REACHING LEGAL DRINKING AGE

RESPONDING TO IMAGES

Write a paragraph about this "spoof ad," answering the following questions: What statement is it trying to make? Do you agree with this statement? Remember to support your topic sentence with specific evidence.

In the preceding chapters, you learned four essential steps in writing an effective paragraph. The box below shows how these steps lead to four standards, or bases, you can use in revising a paragraph.

Four Steps ⟶	Four Bases
1. If you make one point and stick to that point,	➡ your writing will have *unity*.
2. If you back up the point with specific evidence,	➡ your writing will have *support*.
3. If you organize and connect the specific evidence,	➡ your writing will have *coherence*.
4. If you write clear, error-free sentences,	➡ your writing will demonstrate effective *sentence skills*.

This chapter will discuss the four bases—unity, support, coherence, and sentence skills—and will show how these four bases can be used to evaluate and revise a paragraph.

Base 1: Unity

Understanding Unity

The following two paragraphs were written by students on the topic "Why Students Drop Out of College." Read them and decide which one makes its point more clearly and effectively, and why.

PARAGRAPH A

Why Students Drop Out

Students drop out of college for many reasons. First of all, some students are bored in school. These students may enter college expecting nonstop fun or a series of fascinating courses. When they find out that college is often routine, they quickly lose interest. They do not want to take dull required courses or spend their nights studying, and so they drop out. Students also drop out of college because the work is harder than they thought it would be. These students may have made decent grades in high school simply by showing up for class. In college, however, they may have to prepare for two-hour exams, write fifteen-page term papers, or make detailed presentations to a class. The hard work comes as a shock, and students give up. Perhaps the most common reason students drop out is that they are having personal or emotional problems. Younger students,

continued

especially, may be attending college at an age when they are also feeling confused, lonely, or depressed. These students may have problems with roommates, family, boyfriends, or girlfriends. They become too unhappy to deal with both hard academic work and emotional troubles. For many types of students, dropping out seems to be the only solution they can imagine.

PARAGRAPH B

Student Dropouts

There are three main reasons students drop out of college. Some students, for one thing, are not really sure they want to be in school and lack the desire to do the work. When exams come up, or when a course requires a difficult project or term paper, these students will not do the required studying or research. Eventually, they may drop out because their grades are so poor they are about to flunk out anyway. Such students sometimes come back to school later with a completely different attitude about school. Other students drop out for financial reasons. The pressures of paying tuition, buying textbooks, and possibly having to support themselves can be overwhelming. These students can often be helped by the school because financial aid is available, and some schools offer work-study programs. Finally, students drop out because they have personal problems. They cannot concentrate on their courses because they are unhappy at home, they are lonely, or they are having trouble with boyfriends or girlfriends, or their husbands or wives. Instructors should suggest that such troubled students see counselors or join support groups. If instructors would take a more personal interest in their students, more students would make it through troubled times.

ACTIVITY 1

Fill in the blanks: Paragraph _____ makes its point more clearly and effectively because _____

_____

_____

EXPLANATION: Paragraph A is more effective because it is *unified*. All the details in paragraph A are *on target*; they support and develop the single point expressed in the first sentence—that there are many reasons students drop out of college.

continued

On the other hand, paragraph B contains some details irrelevant to the opening point—that there are three main reasons students drop out. These details should be omitted in the interest of paragraph unity. Go back to paragraph B and cross out the sections that are off target—the sections that do not support the opening idea.

You should have crossed out the following sections: "Such students sometimes . . . attitude about school"; "These students can often . . . work-study programs"; and "Instructors should suggest . . . through troubled times."

The difference between these two paragraphs leads us to the first base, or standard, of effective writing: *unity*. To achieve unity is to have all the details in your paper related to the single point expressed in the topic sentence, the first sentence. Each time you think of something to put in, ask yourself whether it relates to your main point. If if does not, leave it out. For example, if you were writing about a certain job as the worst job you ever had and then spent a couple of sentences talking about the interesting people that you met there, you would be missing the first and most essential base of good writing.

Checking for Unity

To check a paragraph for unity, ask yourself these questions:

1. Is there a clear, single point in the first sentence of the paragraph?

2. Does all the evidence support the opening point?

Evaluating Scratch Outlines for Unity

The best time to check a paragraph for unity is at the outline stage. A scratch outline, as explained on page 27, is one of the best techniques for getting started with a paragraph.

Look at the following scratch outline that one student prepared and then corrected for unity:

I had a depressing weekend.

1. Hay fever bothered me

2. Had to pay seventy-seven-dollar car bill

3. ~~Felt bad~~

4. Boyfriend and I had a fight

5. ~~Did poorly in my math test today as a result~~

6. My mother yelled at me unfairly

Four reasons support the opening statement that the writer was depressed over the weekend. The writer crossed out "Felt bad" because it was not a reason for her depression. (Saying that she felt bad is only another way of saying that she was depressed.) She also crossed out the item about the math test because the point she is supporting is that she was depressed over the weekend.

| ACTIVITY 2 | In each scratch outline, cross out the two items that do not support the opening point. These items must be omitted in order to achieve paragraph unity. |

1. Overweight dogs are more likely to develop health problems.
   a. These dogs can develop arthritis.
   b. They can develop diabetes.
   c. Owners shouldn't feed their dogs table scraps.
   d. Heart disease is another problem.
   e. Overweight cats are also at risk.

2. The community shelter provides needed services.
   a. Emergency housing is available.
   b. The food bank is located two blocks away.
   c. Medical care is offered at no charge.
   d. Receives funding from the government.
   e. Substance abuse counseling is offered.

3. My husband Tom takes several medications.
   a. He takes pills for hypertension.
   b. He takes insulin for type 2 diabetes.
   c. His doctor wants him to exercise more.
   d. He takes pills for high cholesterol.
   e. He started eating oatmeal for breakfast.

4. Teens have many opportunities to volunteer.
   a. They can help at animal shelters.
   b. They don't know how to help.
   c. They can start a recycling project.
   d. They can write letters to soldiers.
   e. They don't have time to volunteer.

5. Jena planned an affordable birthday party for her daughter.
   a. She held the party in the city's beautiful garden pavilion.
   b. Her daughter's best friend came down with chickenpox.
   c. She baked cupcakes and had guests decorate them.
   d. She bought an overpriced cake last year.
   e. She planned old-fashioned games.

Evaluating Paragraphs for Unity

<table>
<tr><td>

Each of the following three paragraphs contains sentences that are off target—sentences that do not support the opening point—and so the paragraphs are not unified. In the interest of paragraph unity, such sentences must be omitted.

Cross out the irrelevant sentences and write the numbers of those sentences in the spaces provided. The number of spaces will tell you the number of irrelevant sentences in each paragraph.

</td><td>**ACTIVITY 3**</td></tr>
</table>

HINT   As you read each paragraph, underline the opening point so you can better detect which details support that point, and which do not.

1.

Other Uses for Cars

¹Many people who own a car manage to turn the vehicle into a trash can, a clothes closet, or a storage room. ²People who use their cars as trash cans are easily recognized. ³Empty snack bags, hamburger wrappers, pizza cartons, soda cans, and doughnut boxes litter the floor. ⁴On the seats are old scratched CDs, blackened fruit skins, crumpled receipts, crushed cigarette packs, and used tissues. ⁵At least the trash stays in the car, instead of adding to the litter on our highways. ⁶Other people use a car as a clothes closet. ⁷The car contains several pairs of shoes, pants, or shorts, along with a suit or dress that's been hanging on the car's clothes hanger for over a year. ⁸Sweaty, smelly gym clothes will also find a place in the car, a fact passengers quickly discover. ⁹The world would be better off if people showed more consideration of others. ¹⁰Finally, some people use a car as a spare garage or basement. ¹¹In the backseats or trunks of these cars are bags of fertilizer, beach chairs, old textbooks, chainsaws, or window screens that have been there for months. ¹²The trunk may also contain an extra spare tire, a dented hubcap, an empty gallon container of window washer fluid, and old stereo equipment. ¹³If apartments offered more storage space, probably fewer people would resort to using their cars for such storage purposes. ¹⁴All in all, people get a lot more use out of their cars than simply the miles they travel on the road.

The numbers of the irrelevant sentences: _____   _____   _____

2.

Yoga

¹Many people start practicing yoga because they think it will help them lose weight, but they get more than just weight loss. ²For starters, the poses, or *asanas*, are specifically designed to stretch and bend different

---

in a writer's words

"What lasts in the reader's mind is not the phrase but the effect the phrase created: laughter, tears, pain, joy. If the phrase is not affecting the reader, what's it doing there? Make it do its job or cut it without mercy or remorse."

—Isaac Asimov

continued

parts of the body to increase blood flow and flexibility. [3]This helps avoid injuries, stiff joints, arthritis, and other ailments that are brought on because of poor circulation. [4]Another benefit that people discover is that they gain better daily focus. [5]Many people struggle with concentration during the day, which affects work and relationships. [6]Many of the *asanas* require very specific movements and positions. [7]Inverted positions are really difficult to do. [8]Moving into the proper stances takes practice, concentration, and patience. [9]The first time getting into the proper pose can be frustrating; however, yoga emphasizes that people listen to their bodies. [10]Some days the body might easily move into a beautiful *utkatasana* (chair pose), and other days it might be very difficult to hold the position. [11]It is often difficult to do positions right after eating a large meal. [12]With patience and focus, the *utkatasana* becomes a position that works the muscles while stimulating the heart without causing aggravation. [13]People who practice yoga also find that they gain better overall health. [14]Many inverted poses like the *salamba sarvangasana* (supported shoulder stand) require strength and stillness. [15]While in a position like this, the blood flows better to the brain, helping nourish the brain and all the glands contained within the upper portion of the body. [16]Such positions also stimulate the thyroid and digestive system and offer better peace of mind because they require meditation and deep breathing, especially when the pose is held for several minutes. [17]People often feel better, have a stronger sense of self, and feel peaceful after a yoga session.

The numbers of the irrelevant sentences: _____   _____   _____

3.

Health Inspection Report: Main Street Grill

[1]The following is a summary of the May 2013 report that recommends Main Street Grill be closed immediately:

[2]The entry of the restaurant is in need of dire repair. [3]Several windows are broken, the front steps are missing a handrail, and the door does not close properly, allowing flies freedom to enter the establishment. [4]The color of the door was a very ugly blue. [5]The flowers in the flower boxes and the grass needed watering. [6]Immediately inside the entryway, sections of flooring are missing, but have been temporarily covered with loose boards. [7]The interior of the restaurant does not appear to have been cleaned in several years. [8]Layers of dust and grease were visible on the lighting fixtures and window sills. [9]The floor, where it wasn't broken, was a dingy gray that upon further inspection should have been white. [10]The kitchen contains several nonworking appliances. [11]Fifteen extension cords were being used to connect appliances to one outlet. [12]Foods were not being stored at the proper temperatures. [13]Tests showed meats

continued

at 105 degrees Fahrenheit and showed milk at 52 degrees Fahrenheit. [14]The meals that the kitchen staff were preparing were burgers and fries, even though the restaurant does not have these meals on the menu. [15]Workers were not wearing hair nets, nor did any of them wash their hands during the inspection. [16]This is the third time that Main Street Grill has failed a health inspection; no improvements have been made since the last visit. [17]The restaurant must be closed immediately.

The number of irrelevant sentences: _____   _____   _____

Base 2: Support

Understanding Support

The following student paragraphs were written on the topic "A Quality of Some Person You Know." Both are unified, but one communicates more clearly and effectively. Which one, and why?

PARAGRAPH A

My Quick-Tempered Father

My father is easily angered by normal everyday mistakes. For example, one day my father told me to wash the car and cut the grass. I did not hear exactly what he said, and so I asked him to repeat it. Then he became hysterical and shouted, "Can't you hear?" Another time he asked my mother to go to the store and buy groceries with a fifty-dollar bill, and he told her to spend no more than twenty dollars. She spent twenty-two dollars. As soon as he found out, he immediately took the change from her and told her not to go anywhere else for him; he did not speak to her the rest of the day. My father even gives my older brothers a hard time with his irritable moods. One day he told them to be home from their dates by midnight; they came home at 12:15. He informed them that they were grounded for three weeks. To my father, making a simple mistake is like committing a crime.

Personal

PARAGRAPH B

My Generous Grandfather

My grandfather is the most generous person I know. He gave up a life of his own in order to give his children everything they wanted. Not only did he give up many years of his life to raise his children properly, but he

continued

is now sacrificing many more years to his grandchildren. His generosity is also evident in his relationship with his neighbors, his friends, and the members of his church. He has been responsible for many good deeds and has always been there to help all the people around him in times of trouble. Everyone knows that he will gladly lend a helping hand. He is so generous that you almost have to feel sorry for him. If one day he suddenly became selfish, it would be earthshaking. That's my grandfather.

ACTIVITY 4

Fill in the blanks: Paragraph ___ makes its point more clearly and effectively because _____

_____

_____

EXPLANATION: Paragraph A is more effective, because it offers specific examples that show us the father in action. We see for ourselves why the writer describes the father as quick-tempered.

Paragraph B, on the other hand, gives us no specific evidence. The writer of paragraph B tells us repeatedly that the grandfather is generous but never shows us examples of that generosity. Just how, for instance, did the grandfather sacrifice his life for his children and grandchildren? Did he hold two jobs so that his son could go to college, or so that his daughter could have her own car? Does he give up time with his wife and friends to travel every day to his daughter's house to babysit, go to the store, and help with the dishes? Does he wear threadbare suits and coats and eat frozen dinners and other inexpensive meals (with no desserts) so that he can give money to his children and toys to his grandchildren? We want to see and judge for ourselves whether the writer is making a valid point about the grandfather, but without specific details we cannot do so. In fact, we have almost no picture of him at all.

Consideration of these two paragraphs leads us to the second base of effective writing: *support*. After realizing the importance of specific supporting details, one student writer revised a paper she had done on a restaurant job as the worst job she ever had. In the revised paper, instead of talking about "unsanitary conditions in the kitchen," she referred to such specifics as "green mold on the bacon" and "ants in the potato salad." All your papers should include many vivid details!

Checking for Support

To check a paragraph for support, ask yourself these questions:

1. Is there *specific* evidence to support the opening point?

2. Is there *enough* specific evidence?

Evaluating Paragraphs for Support

> The three paragraphs that follow lack sufficient supporting details. In each paragraph, identify the spot or spots where more specific details are needed.

ACTIVITY 5

1.

Chicken: Our Best Friend

¹Chicken is the best-selling meat today for a number of good reasons. ²First of all, its reasonable cost puts it within everyone's reach. ³Chicken is popular, too, because it can be prepared in so many different ways. ⁴It can, for example, be cooked by itself, in spaghetti sauce, or with noodles and gravy. ⁵It can be baked, boiled, broiled, or fried. ⁶Chicken is also convenient. ⁷Last and most important, chicken has a high nutritional value. ⁸Four ounces of chicken contain twenty-eight grams of protein, which is almost half the recommended daily dietary allowance.

Fill in the blanks: The first spot where supporting details are needed occurs after sentence number _____. The second spot occurs after sentence number _____.

2.

Controversial Adventures

¹*The Adventures of Huckleberry Finn* by Mark Twain has been causing controversy since it was first written. ²When first printed in 1885, Twain's book was considered as nothing more than garbage with absolutely no moral or literary value. ³In fact, the Concord Public Library refused to shelve the book after the library committee met and agreed that "it contain[ed] but little humor . . . of a very coarse type . . . being more suited to the slums than to intelligent, respectable people." ⁴Later, many claimed that the book glamorized juvenile delinquency. ⁵Huckleberry Finn is a runaway who engages in many questionable activities while harboring a fugitive. ⁶Since the 1960s, however, most people have been offended by the language in *Huckleberry Finn*. ⁷Regardless of the controversy, *The Adventures of Huckleberry Finn* will continue to be read by future generations.

Fill in the blank: The point where details are needed occurs after sentence number _____.

3.

> ### Being on TV
>
> [1]People act a little strangely when a television camera comes their way. [2]Some people behave as if a crazy puppeteer were pulling their strings. [3]Their arms jerk wildly about, and they begin jumping up and down for no apparent reason. [4]Often they accompany their body movements with loud screams, squeals, and yelps. [5]Another group of people engage in an activity known as the cover-up. [6]They will be calmly watching a sports game or other televised event when they realize the camera is focused on them. [7]The camera operator can't resist zooming in for a close-up of these people. [8]Then there are those who practice their funny faces on the unsuspecting public. [9]They take advantage of the television time to show off their talents, hoping to get that big break that will carry them to stardom. [10]Finally, there are those who pretend they are above reacting for the camera. [11]They wipe an expression from their faces and appear to be interested in something else. [12]Yet if the camera stays on them long enough, they will slyly check to see if they are still being watched. [13]Everybody's behavior seems to be slightly strange in front of a TV camera.

Fill in the blanks: The first spot where supporting details are needed occurs after sentence number _____. The second spot occurs after sentence number _____.

Base 3: Coherence

Understanding Coherence

The following two paragraphs were written on the topic "The Best or Worst Job You Ever Had." Both are unified and both are supported. However, one communicates more clearly and effectively. Which one, and why?

PARAGRAPH A

> ### Pantry Helper
>
> My worst job was as a pantry helper in one of San Diego's well-known restaurants. I had an assistant from three to six in the afternoon who did little but stand around and eat the whole time she was there. She would listen for the sound of the back door opening, which was a sure sign the boss was coming in. The boss would testily say to me, "You've got a lot of things to do here, Alice. Try to get a move on." I would come in at two o'clock to relieve the woman on the morning shift. If her day was busy, that meant I would have to prepare salads, slice meat and cheese, and so on. Orders for sandwiches and cold platters would come in and have to be prepared. The

continued

worst thing about the job was that the heat in the kitchen, combined with my nerves, would give me an upset stomach by seven o'clock almost every night. I might be going to the storeroom to get some supplies, and one of the waitresses would tell me she wanted a bacon, lettuce, and tomato sandwich on white toast. I would put the toast in and head for the supply room, and a waitress would holler out that her customer was in a hurry. Green flies would come in through the torn screen in the kitchen window and sting me. I was getting paid only $5.05 an hour. At five o'clock, when the dinner rush began, I would be dead tired. Roaches scurried in all directions whenever I moved a box or picked up a head of lettuce to cut.

PARAGRAPH B

My Worst Job

The worst job I ever had was as a waiter at the Westside Inn. First of all, many of the people I waited on were rude. When a baked potato was hard inside or a salad was flat or their steak wasn't just the way they wanted it, they blamed me, rather than the kitchen. Or they would ask me to light their cigarettes, or chase flies from their tables, or even take their children to the bathroom. Also, I had to contend not only with the customers but with the kitchen staff as well. The cooks and busboys were often undependable and surly. If I didn't treat them just right, I would wind up having to apologize to customers because their meals came late or their water glasses weren't filled. Another reason I didn't like the job was that I was always moving. Because of the constant line at the door, as soon as one group left, another would take its place. I usually had only a twenty-minute lunch break and another ten-minute break in almost nine hours of work. I think I could have put up with the job if I had been able to pause and rest more often. The last and most important reason I hated the job was my boss. She played favorites, giving some of the waiters and waitresses the best-tipping repeat customers and preferences on holidays. She would hover around during my break to make sure I didn't take a second more than the allotted time. And even when I helped out by working through a break, she never had an appreciative word but would just tell me not to be late for work the next day.

Fill in the blanks: Paragraph _____ makes its point more clearly and effectively because _____

_____

_____.

ACTIVITY 6

> EXPLANATION: Paragraph B is more effective because the material is organized clearly and logically. Using emphatic order, the writer gives us a list of four reasons why the job was so bad: rude customers, an unreliable kitchen staff, constant motion, and—most of all—an unfair boss. Further, the writer includes transitional words that act as signposts, making movement from one idea to the next easy to follow. The major transitions are *First of all, Also, Another reason,* and *The last and most important reason.*
>
> While paragraph A is unified and supported, the writer does not have any clear and consistent way of organizing the material. Partly, emphatic order is used, but this is not made clear by transitions or by saving the most important reason for last. Partly, time order is used, but it moves inconsistently from two to seven to five o'clock.

These two paragraphs lead us to the third base of effective writing: *coherence.* The supporting ideas and sentences in a composition must be organized so that they cohere, or "stick together." As has already been mentioned, key techniques for tying material together are a clear method of organization (such as time order or emphatic order), transitions, and other connecting words.

Checking for Coherence

To check a paragraph for coherence, ask yourself these questions:

1. Does the paragraph have a clear method of organization?

2. Are transitions and other connecting words used to tie the material together?

Evaluating Paragraphs for Coherence

ACTIVITY 7   Answer the questions about coherence that follow the paragraph below.

Apartment Hunting

¹Apartment hunting is a several-step process. ²Visit and carefully inspect the most promising apartments. ³Check each place for signs of unwanted guests such as roaches or mice. ⁴Make sure that light switches and appliances work and that there are enough electrical outlets. ⁵Turn faucets on and off and flush the toilet to be sure that the plumbing works smoothly. ⁶Talk to the landlord for a bit to get a sense of him or her as a person. ⁷If a problem develops after you move in, you want to know that a decent and capable person will be there to handle the matter. ⁸Find out what's available that matches your interests. ⁹Your town newspaper and local real estate offices can provide you with a list of apartments for rent. ¹⁰Family and friends may be able to give you leads. ¹¹And your school

continued

may have a housing office that keeps a list of approved apartments for rent. ^{12}Decide just what you need. ^{13}If you can afford no more than $700 a month, you need to find a place that will cost no more than that. ^{14}If you want a location that's close to work or school, you must take that factor into account. ^{15}If you plan to cook, you want a place with a workable kitchen. ^{16}By taking these steps, you should be ready to select the apartment that is best for you.

a. The paragraph should use time order. Write 1 before the step that should come first, 2 before the intermediate step, and 3 before the final step.

_____ Visit and carefully inspect the most promising apartments.

_____ Decide just what you need.

_____ Find out what's available that matches your interests.

b. Before which of the three steps could the transitional words *The first step is to* be added? _____

c. Before which step could the transitional words *After you have decided what you are looking for, the next step is to* be added? _____

d. Before which step could the transitional words *The final step* be added? _____

e. To whom does the pronoun *him or her* in sentence 6 refer to?

_____

f. What is a synonym for *landlord* in sentence 7? _____

g. What is a synonym for *apartment* in sentence 13? _____

Revising Paragraphs for Coherence

The two paragraphs in this section begin with a clear point, but in each case the supporting material that follows the point is not coherent. Read each paragraph and the comments that follow it on how to organize and connect the supporting material. Then do the activity for the paragraph.

PARAGRAPH 1

A Difficult Period

Since I arrived in the Bay Area in midsummer, I have had the most difficult period of my life. I had to look for an apartment. I found only one place that I could afford, but the landlord said I could not move in until it was painted. When I first arrived in San Francisco, my thoughts were to stay with my father and stepmother. I had to set out looking for a job so

continued

that I could afford my own place, for I soon realized that my stepmother was not at all happy having me live with them. A three-week search led to a job shampooing rugs for a housecleaning company. I painted the apartment myself, and at least that problem was ended. I was in a hurry to get settled because I was starting school at the University of San Francisco in September. A transportation problem developed because my stepmother insisted that I return my father's bike, which I was using at first to get to school. I had to rely on a bus that often arrived late, with the result that I missed some classes and was late for others. I had already had a problem with registration in early September. My counselor had made a mistake with my classes, and I had to register all over again. This meant that I was one week late for class. Now I'm riding to school with a classmate and no longer have to depend on the bus. My life is starting to order itself, but I must admit that at first I thought it was hopeless to stay here.

COMMENTS ON PARAGRAPH 1

The writer of this paragraph has provided a good deal of specific evidence to support the opening point. The evidence, however, needs to be organized. Before starting the paragraph, the writer should have decided to arrange the details by using time order. He or she could then have listed in a scratch outline the exact sequence of events that made for such a difficult period.

ACTIVITY 8

Here is a list of the various events described by the writer of paragraph 1. Number the events in the correct time sequence by writing 1 in front of the first event that occurred, 2 in front of the second event, and so on.

Since I arrived in the Bay Area in midsummer, I have had the most difficult period of my life.

_____ I had to search for an apartment I could afford.

_____ I had to find a job so that I could afford my own place.

_____ My stepmother objected to my living with her and my father.

_____ I had to paint the apartment before I could move in.

_____ I had to find an alternative to unreliable bus transportation.

_____ I had to register again for my college courses because of a counselor's mistake.

Your instructor may now have you rewrite the paragraph on separate paper. If so, be sure to use time signals such as *first, next, then, during, when, after,* and *now* to help guide your reader from one event to the next.

PARAGRAPH 2

Childhood Cruelty

When I was in grade school, my classmates and I found a number of excuses for being cruel to a boy named Andy Poppovian. Sometimes Andy gave off a strong body odor, and we knew that several days had passed since he had taken a bath. Andy was very slow in speaking, as well as very careless in personal hygiene. The teacher would call on him during a math or grammar drill. He would sit there silently for so long before answering that she sometimes said, "Are you awake, Andy?" Andy had long fingernails that he never seemed to cut, with black dirt caked under them. We called him "Poppy," or we accented the first syllable in his name and mispronounced the rest of it and said to him, "How are you today, POP-o-van?" His name was funny. Other times we called him "Popeye," and we would shout at him. "Where's your spinach today, Popeye?" Andy always had sand in the corners of his eyes. When we played tag at recess, Andy was always "it" or the first one who was caught. He was so physically slow that five guys could dance around him and he wouldn't be able to touch any of them. Even when we tried to hold a regular conversation with him about sports or a teacher, he was so slow in responding to a question that we got bored talking with him. Andy's hair was always uncombed, and it was often full of white flakes of dandruff. Only when Andy died suddenly of spinal meningitis in seventh grade did some of us begin to realize and regret our cruelty toward him.

COMMENTS ON PARAGRAPH 2

The writer of this paragraph provides a number of specifics that support the opening point. However, the supporting material has not been organized clearly. Before writing this paragraph, the author should have (1) decided to arrange the supporting evidence by using emphatic order and (2) listed in an outline the reasons for the cruelty to Andy Poppovian and the supporting details for each reason. The writer could also have determined which reason to use in the emphatic final position of the paragraph.

Create a clear outline for paragraph 2 by filling in the scheme below. The outline is partially completed.	**ACTIVITY 9**

When I was in grade school, my classmates and I found a number of excuses for being cruel to a boy named Andy Poppovian.

1. Funny name _____   Reason

   a. _____   Details

   b. _____

   c. _____

Reason

Details

2. Physically slow _____

    a. _____

    b. Five guys could dance around him _____

Reason

Details

3. _____

    a. _____

    b. In regular conversation _____

Reason

Details

4. _____

    a. _____

    b. Sand in eyes _____

    c. _____

    d. _____

Your instructor may have you rewrite the paragraph on separate paper. If so, be sure to introduce each of the four reasons with transitions such as *First, Second, Another reason,* and *Finally.* You may also want to use repeated words, pronouns, and synonyms to help tie your sentences together.

Base 4: Sentence Skills

Understanding Sentence Skills

Two versions of a paragraph are given below. Both are unified, supported, and organized, but one version communicates more clearly and effectively. Which one, and why?

PARAGRAPH A

Falling Asleep Anywhere

¹There are times when people are so tired that they fall asleep almost anywhere. ²For example, there is a lot of sleeping on the bus or train on the way home from work in the evenings. ³A man will be reading the newspaper, and seconds later it appears as if he is trying to eat it. ⁴Or he will fall asleep on the shoulder of the stranger sitting next to him. ⁵Another place where unplanned naps go on is the lecture hall. ⁶In some classes, a student will start snoring so loudly that the professor has to ask another student to shake the sleeper awake. ⁷A more embarrassing situation occurs when a student leans on one elbow and starts drifting off to sleep. ⁸The weight of the head pushes the elbow off the desk, and this momentum carries the rest of the body along. ⁹The student wakes up on the floor with no memory of getting there. ¹⁰The worst place to fall asleep is at the wheel of a car. ¹¹Police reports are full of accidents that occur when people lose consciousness and go off the road. ¹²If the drivers are lucky, they are not seriously hurt. ¹³One woman's car, for instance, went into a river. ¹⁴She woke up in four feet of water and thought it was raining. ¹⁵When people are really tired, nothing will stop them from falling asleep—no matter where they are.

PARAGRAPH B

"Falling Asleep Anywhere"

[1]There are times when people are so tired that they fall asleep almost anywhere. [2]For example, on the bus or train on the way home from work. [3]A man will be reading the newspaper, seconds later it appears as if he is trying to eat it. [4]Or he will fall asleep on the shoulder of the stranger sitting next to him. [5]Another place where unplanned naps go on are in the lecture hall. [6]In some classes, a student will start snoring so loudly that the professor has to ask another student to shake the sleeper awake. [7]A more embarrassing situation occurs when a student leans on one elbow and starting to drift off to sleep. [8]The weight of the head push the elbow off the desk, and this momentum carries the rest of the body along. [9]The student wakes up on the floor with no memory of getting there. [10]The worst time to fall asleep is when driving a car. [11]Police reports are full of accidents that occur when people conk out and go off the road. [12]If the drivers are lucky they are not seriously hurt. [13]One womans car, for instance, went into a river. [14]She woke up in four feet of water. [15]And thought it was raining. [16]When people are really tired, nothing will stop them from falling asleep—no matter where they are.

Fill in the blanks: Paragraph ___ makes its point more clearly and effectively

because _____ .

_____

_____

ACTIVITY 10

> **EXPLANATION:** Paragraph A is more effective because it incorporates *sentence skills*, the fourth base of competent writing.

ACTIVITY 11

See if you can identify the ten sentence-skills mistakes in paragraph B. Do this, first of all, by going back and underlining the ten spots in paragraph B that differ in wording or punctuation from paragraph A. Then try to identify the ten sentence-skills mistakes by circling what you feel is the correct answer in each of the ten statements on the following page.

HINT Comparing paragraph B with the correct version may help you guess correct answers even if you are not familiar with the names of certain skills.

1. The title should not be set off with
   a. capital letters.
   b. quotation marks.
2. In word group 2, there is a
   a. missing comma.
   b. missing apostrophe.
   c. sentence fragment.
   d. dangling modifier.
3. In word group 3, there is a
   a. run-on.
   b. sentence fragment.
   c. mistake in subject–verb agreement.
   d. mistake involving an irregular verb.
4. In word group 5, there is a
   a. sentence fragment.
   b. spelling error.
   c. run-on.
   d. mistake in subject–verb agreement.
5. In word group 7, there is a
   a. misplaced modifier.
   b. dangling modifier.
   c. mistake in parallelism.
   d. run-on.

6. In word group 8, there is a(n)
   a. incorrect subject–verb agreement.
   b. run-on.
   c. comma mistake.
   d. missing capital letter.
7. In word group 11, there is a
   a. mistake involving an irregular verb.
   b. sentence fragment.
   c. slang phrase.
   d. mistake in subject–verb agreement.
8. In word group 12, there is a
   a. missing apostrophe.
   b. missing comma.
   c. mistake involving an irregular verb.
   d. sentence fragment.
9. In word group 13, there is a
   a. mistake in parallelism.
   b. mistake involving an irregular verb.
   c. missing apostrophe.
   d. missing capital letter.
10. In word group 15, there is a
   a. missing quotation mark.
   b. mistake involving an irregular verb.
   c. sentence fragment.
   d. mistake in pronoun point of view.

You should have chosen the following answers:

1. b   2. c   3. a   4. d   5. c
6. a   7. c   8. b   9. c   10. c

Part 5 of this book explains these and other sentence skills. You should review all the skills carefully. Doing so will ensure that you know the most important rules of grammar, punctuation, and usage—rules needed to write clear, error-free sentences.

Checking for Sentence Skills

Sentence skills and the other bases of effective writing are summarized in the following chart and on the inside back cover of the book.

A SUMMARY OF THE FOUR BASES OF EFFECTIVE WRITING

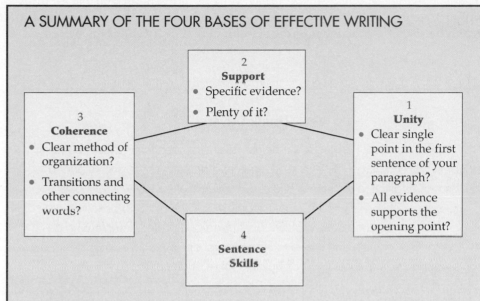

- Fragments eliminated? (page 403)
- Run-ons eliminated? (415)
- Correct verb forms? (426, 439)
- Subject and verb agreement? (434)
- Faulty parallelism and faulty modifiers eliminated? (100, 459)
- Faulty pronouns eliminated? (443, 448)
- Capital letters used correctly? (471)
- Punctuation marks where needed?

  (a) Apostrophe (485)   (d) Semicolon; colon (506)

  (b) Quotation marks (491)   (e) Hyphen; dash (507–508)

  (c) Comma (498)   (f) Parentheses (507)

- Correct paper format? (470)
- Needless words eliminated? (107)
- Effective word choices? (526)
- Possible spelling errors checked? (513)
- Careless errors eliminated through proofreading? (16, 31–34, 117–118)
- Sentences varied? (109–117)

Evaluating Paragraphs for All Four Bases: Unity, Support, Coherence, and Sentence Skills

In this activity, you will evaluate paragraphs in terms of all four bases: unity, support, coherence, and sentence skills. Evaluative comments follow each paragraph below. Circle the letter of the statement that best applies in each case.

1.

Drunk Drivers

People caught driving while drunk—even first offenders—should be jailed. Drunk driving, first of all, is more dangerous than carrying around a loaded gun. In addition, a jail term would show drivers that society will no longer tolerate such careless and dangerous behavior. Finally, severe penalties might encourage solutions to the problem of drinking and driving. People who go out for a good time and intend to have several drinks would always designate one person, who would stay completely sober, as the driver.

a. The paragraph is not unified.
b. The paragraph is not adequately supported.
c. The paragraph is not well organized.
d. The paragraph does not show a command of sentence skills.
e. The paragraph is well written in terms of the four bases.

2.

Pop-Up Restaurants

Foodies don't just like to eat. They live to have that next outstanding food experience. And modern technology has provided a new way to link foodies and chefs. Lacking the funds to open their own establishments, chefs worldwide are beginning to follow Chef Ludo Lefebvre's. Lead in creating dining experiences at different locations and using technology to spread the word. Former executive chef at the famous L'Orangerie in Los Angeles. Seeking establishments that they can use for a limited period—anywhere from 72 hours to three weeks—chefs set up house in these locations and create original and creative meals. But how do the foodies find out? Twitter, Facebook, e-mail, blogs. All of these outlets for advertising are free to the chef, but far more effective than mainstream advertising, in fact, according to National Public Radio, whenever Chef Lefebvre announces his next location, "within seven hours, all reservations are snapped up." Finding that next great restaurant no longer requires a perusal through the yellow pages. But a faithful following on Twitter.

a. The paragraph is not unified.

b. The paragraph is not adequately supported.

c. The paragraph is not well organized.

d. The paragraph does not show a command of sentence skills.

e. The paragraph is well written in terms of the four bases.

3.

Preparing for a Disaster

Every household should prepare for a natural disaster. They should find out where the evacuation centers are in their neighborhood and know how to get to those places. They should decide how they will communicate with each other in the event of a disaster. Some families set up a "phone tree" in which each person calls a specific family member. First, members of a household should put together an emergency survival kit. This kit should include nonperishable food, bottled water, clothing, first aid supplies, medications, candles, matches, a radio, a flashlight, and extra batteries. When a disaster strikes, there is little time to prepare, so people should get ready now.

a. The paragraph is not unified.

b. The paragraph is not adequately supported.

c. The paragraph is not well organized.

d. The paragraph does not show a command of sentence skills.

e. The paragraph is well written in terms of the four bases.

4.

Linguists Beware!

Entertainment in the twenty-first century has been a catalyst for the invention of new words. J.K. Rowling's fantasy world of *Harry Potter* introduced millions of readers to "Muggles, Mudbloods, and Quidditch," and when the books became movies, millions more laid claim to the language of Harry Potter. James Cameron's screen sensation, *Avatar*, introduced viewers to the Na'vi tribe and its made-up language. Additionally, Cameron's movie is credited for the term "Pandora Effect," a feeling of being confused, wistful, and disappointed all at the same time. Furthermore, viewers of *Inception* now regularly "check their totems" to determine the reality of situations. Like movies, TV has affected language. In 2010, the word "Gleeks," referring to those who watch *Glee*, became a mainstream term. Snooki and her friends introduced viewers of *Jersey Shore* to the problem of "tanorexia" (not being tan enough) and being "Snookied" (punched in the face). *The "A" List* introduced its viewers to a "mantrum" (tantrum by a man). Of course,

continued

no TV viewing is complete without a good old fashioned Zitcom (a comedy for a teenage audience) with teenage characters. The Internet, with its endless entertainment possibilities, has given rise to "Mouse Potatoes" who become so glued to the latest online sensations, they often slip into "Internet comas." As entertainment continues to influence the development of language, maybe one day "Shatner commas" and their odd, purposeless positions will become mainstream and the fear of overusing commas will be "refudiated," just "like, like Valley Girls."

a. The paragraph is not unified.

b. The paragraph is not adequately supported.

c. The paragraph is not well organized.

d. The paragraph does not show a command of sentence skills.

e. The paragraph is well written in terms of the four bases.

5.

Velcro: Sticky Results

Velcro has ruined the world. Before Velcro was invented, children had to learn to tie shoes, but now they only have to stick one strap onto another. Learning to tie shoes is a problem-solving activity and can be hard, but sticking one strap to another is easy. There are two popular ways to learn to tie shoes: the bunny ears or the squirrel and the tree. The bunny ears method is probably the most popular. Problem-solving activities are important because they teach critical thinking. Without critical-thinking skills, people often have a hard time getting through college. College classes can be very difficult if students don't study properly. Getting a college degree is really important because it means a better job and better future.

a. The paragraph is not unified.

b. The paragraph is not adequately supported.

c. The paragraph is not well organized.

d. The paragraph does not show a command of sentence skills.

e. The paragraph is well written in terms of the four bases.

REFLECTIVE ACTIVITY

1. Look back at the paragraph that you wrote in Chapter 3 (see pages 81–83). Does your paragraph cover all four bases of effective writing?

2. Afterward, you and your classmates, perhaps working in small groups, should read your paragraphs aloud. Pay attention to spots where you see problems with unity, support, coherence, and sentence skills.

EXPLORING WRITING ONLINE

Visit one of these Web sites to read a movie review of your choice. As you read the movie review, look at how the critic uses specific categories—such as plot, actors, and special effects—to evaluate the movie. Then use the four bases of effective writing to evaluate the movie review itself for unity, support, coherence, and sentence skills.

Movie Review Query Engine: **www.mrqe.com**

FilmCritic.com: **www.filmcritic.com**

RottenTomatoes.com: **www.rottentomatoes.com/critics/**

In college, you may want to ask your classmates to give you feedback on your writing, and you may want to help them with their writing. As you are reading the following paragraph written by Jakeem for a geology class, think about what advice you would offer him as he prepares to write his final draft. Does his paragraph cover all four bases of effective writing? To be sure, use the checklist that follows.

Types of Natural Resources

¹Natural resources can be classified as either renewable or nonrenewable. ²On the one hand, coal, oil, and gas are nonrenewable. ³They take millions of years to form. ⁴Some scientists predicts that we will run out of oil and gas in fifty to a hundred years. ⁵Coal is more plentiful. ⁶As a result, they may last for hundreds of years. ⁷On the other hand, resources such as wood and water are renewable because they can be grown or recycled naturally.

A WRITER'S CHECKLIST

Unity

✔ Is there a clear topic sentence in this paragraph? _____

✔ Does all the material work to support the topic sentence? _____

Support

✔ Does Jakeem provide specific evidence to support his topic sentence? _____

✔ Are there enough supporting details? _____ If not, where would you recommend adding more supporting details? _____

Coherence

✔ Does Jakeem use transitions and other connective devices? _____ List them here:

_____

Sentence Skills

✔ Is there a fragment in the paragraph? _____

Is there a problem with subject and verb agreement in the paragraph?

_____

✔ Can you find any other sentence skills mistakes, as listed on the back inside cover of the book? If you can find a mistake, what type of mistake is it?

_____

 ## Collaborative Activity
Work together as a group or class to make an outline of Jakeem's paragraph. Looking at the outline, can you think of any additional supporting details that could be added to make this paragraph more effective?

PART THREE GIVES YOU PRACTICE

- providing a series of examples to support a point

- telling a story that illustrates or explains a point

- describing a person, place, or thing by using words rich in sensory details

- explaining how to do or make something or how something works

- explaining the causes or effects of something

- explaining how things are similar or different

- illustrating the meaning of something with a series of examples or a story

- breaking one thing down into parts or sorting a group of things into categories according to a single principle

- arguing a position and defending it with a series of solid reasons

EXPLORING WRITING PROMPT:

In our everyday lives, we write to inform, persuade, and entertain. Think about the last time you wrote something—what was the purpose of that message? What did you hope to accomplish? Take a few minutes to freewrite about how you've used your writing recently.

Exemplification

RESPONDING TO IMAGES

Most of us have gone on a diet or intended to do so. Are we as a nation obsessed with losing weight? Write a paragraph in which you answer this question. To support your point, use examples from what you have seen on TV, read in magazines and on Web sites, and experienced in your own life.

In our daily conversations, we often provide *examples*—that is, details, particulars, specific instances—to explain statements that we make. Consider the several statements and supporting examples in the box that follows:

Statement	Examples
Wal-Mart was crowded today.	There were at least four carts waiting at each of the checkout counters, and it took me forty-five minutes to get through a line.
The new shirt I bought is poorly made.	When I washed it, the colors began to fade, one button cracked and another fell off, a shoulder seam opened, and the sleeves shrank almost two inches.
My son Peter is unreliable.	If I depend on him to turn off a pot of beans in ten minutes, the family is likely to eat burned beans. If I ask him to turn down the thermostat before he goes to bed, the heat is likely to stay on all night.

In each case, the examples help us *see for ourselves* the truth of the statement that has been made. In paragraphs, too, explanatory examples help the audience fully understand a point. Lively, specific examples also add interest to a paper.

In this chapter, you will be asked to provide a series of examples to support a topic sentence. Providing examples to support a point is one of the most common and simplest methods of paragraph development. First read the paragraphs, they both use examples to develop their points. Then answer the questions that follow.

Paragraphs to Consider

World Cup Traveling Woes

¹Every four years, the world's largest sporting event, the FIFA World Cup, takes place, and when it does, tourists need to be aware of the changes that overcome the football-crazed countries. ²Countries like England and Spain, which don't have many World Cup Championship wins, witness their citizens temporarily leaving their jobs and homes to fly all over the world, cheering on their teams to hopeful victories. ³Although it may not seem like a big problem, this can often lead to limited services, flight cost increases, and crowded airports. ⁴Other countries that didn't make it into the tournament have citizens who become focused on cheering for befriended countries and cheering against rival countries, often causing crowding in the streets. ⁵During the 2010 World Cup tournament, the Czech Republic and Austria were busy watching how neighboring Germany's standing was affected, leading to very crowded streets and bars during each match that affected Germany's standing. ⁶This severely affected tourists' abilities to get around town during these time periods. ⁷Countries like Germany, which has

continued

been in the top four eleven time, (four as a unified country), also set up large Jumbotrons in city squares, pub parking lots, and in front of historic castles to provide all citizens the opportunity to watch their countries represented on the field. ⁸Although these mass viewings can be quite an experience for tourists, they can make it extremely difficult to visit the castles, museums, and sites that are on the planned itineraries. ⁹The large TV screens are often ugly and don't fit in with the surrounding architecture. ¹⁰Finally, countries like Italy, which has won the cup four times, become so focused during matches that businesses will close down or just refuse to serve customers until the match is over. ¹¹Regardless of how much tourists are willing to pay, they are not going to be able to make their purchase or visit the site while the match is on. ¹²Tourists who are traveling during the World Cup have two choices: join in the festivities with the locals or be met with closed amenities and refused service for the duration of the matches.

Office Politics

¹Office politics is a destructive game played by several types of people. ²For instance, two supervisors may get into a conflict over how to do a certain job. ³Instead of working out an agreement like adults, they carry on a power struggle that turns the poor employees under them into human Ping-Pong balls being swatted between two angry players. ⁴Another common example of office politics is the ambitious worker who takes credit for other people's ideas. ⁵He or she will chat in a "friendly" fashion with inexperienced employees, getting their ideas about how to run the office more smoothly. ⁶Within minutes, Mr. or Ms. Idea-Stealer is having a closed-door session with the boss and getting promotion points for his or her "wonderful creativity." ⁷Yet another illustration of office politics is the spy. ⁸This employee acts very buddy-buddy with other workers, often dropping little comments about things he or she doesn't like in the workplace. ⁹The spy encourages people to talk about their problems at work, how they don't like their boss, the pay, and the working conditions. ¹⁰Then the spy goes straight back and repeats all he or she has heard to the boss, and the employees get blamed for their "poor attitude." ¹¹A final example of office politics is people who gossip. ¹²Too often, office politics can turn a perfectly fine work situation into a stressful one.

QUESTIONS

About Unity

1. Which sentence in "World Cup Traveling Woes" is irrelevant to the point that tourists should be aware of the changes in countries during the World Cup? _____

About Support

2. In "World Cup Traveling Woes," what are some of the specific examples of changes tourists should be aware of?

   _____

3. After which sentence in "Office Politics" are specific details needed?

   _____

About Coherence

4. What are the four transition words or phrases that are used to introduce each new example in "Office Politics"?

   _____   _____   _____   _____

5. Which paragraph clearly uses emphatic order to organize its details, saving for last what the writer regards as the most important example?

   _____

Developing an Exemplification Paragraph

Development through Prewriting

Backing up your statements with clear, specific illustrations is the key to a successful exemplification paragraph. When Charlene, the writer of "Office Politics," was assigned an exemplification paragraph, she at first did not know what to write about.

Then her teacher made a suggestion. "Imagine yourself having lunch with some friends," the teacher said. "You're telling them *how* you feel about something and *why*. Maybe you're saying, 'I am so mad at my boyfriend!' or 'My new apartment is really great.' You wouldn't stop there—you'd continue by saying what your boyfriend does that is annoying, or in what way your apartment is nice. In other words, you'd be making a general point and backing it up with examples. That's what you need to do in this paper."

That night, Charlene was on the phone with her brother. She was complaining about the office where she worked. "Suddenly I realized what I was doing," Charlene said. "I was making a statement—I hate the politics in my office—and giving examples of those politics. I knew what I could write about!"

Charlene began preparing to write her paragraph by freewriting. She gave herself ten minutes to write down everything she could think of on the subject of politics in her office. This is what she wrote:

> Of all the places I've ever worked this one is the worst that way. Cant trust anybody there—everybody's playing some sort of game. Worst one of all is Bradley and the way he pretends to be friendly with people. Gets

continued

them to complain about Ms. Bennett and Mr. Hankins and then runs back to them and reports everything. He should realize that people are catching on to his game and figureing out what a jerk he is. Melissa steals people's ideas and then takes credit for them. Anything to get brownie points. She's always out for herself first you can tell. Then there's all the gossip that goes on. You think you're in a soap opera or something, and its kind of fun in a way but it also is very distracting people always talking about each other and worrying about what they say about you. And people talk about our bosses a lot. Nobody knows why Ms. Bennett and Mr. Hankins hate each other so much but they each want the workers on their sides. You do something one boss's way, but then the other boss appears and is angry that you're not doing it another way. You dont know what to do at times to keep people happy.

Charlene read over her freewriting and then spent some time asking questions about her paragraph. "Exactly what do I want my point to be?" she asked. "And exactly how am I going to support that point?" Keeping those points in mind, she worked on several scratch outlines and wound up with the following:

Office politics are ruining the office.

1. Bradley reports people's complaints.

2. Melissa steals ideas.

3. People gossip.

4. Ms. Bennett and Mr. Hankins make workers choose sides.

Working from this outline, she then wrote the following first draft:

My office is being ruined by office politics. It seems like everybody is trying to play some sort of game to get ahead and don't care what it does to anybody else. One example is Bradley. Although he pretends to

continued

be friendly with people he isn't sincere. What he is trying to do is get them to complain about their bosses. Once they do, he goes back to the bosses and tells them what's been said and gets the worker in trouble. I've seen the same kind of thing happen at two other offices where I've worked. Melissa is another example of someone who plays office politics games. She steals other people's ideas and takes the credit for them. I had a good idea once on how to reduce office memos. I told her we ought to use e-mail to send office memos instead of typing them on paper. She went to Ms. Bennett and pretended the idea was hers. I guess I was partly to blame for not acting on the idea myself. And Ms. Bennett and Mr. Hankins hate each other and try to get us to take sides in their conflict. Then there is all the gossip that goes on. People do a lot of backbiting, and you have to be very careful about your behavior or people will start talking about you. All in all, office politics is really a problem where I work.

Development through Revising

After completing her first draft, Charlene put it aside until the next day. When she reread it, this was her response:

> "I think the paragraph would be stronger if I made it about office politics in general instead of just politics in my office. The things I was writing about happen in many offices, not just in mine. And our instructor wants us to try some third-person writing. Also, I need to make better use of transitions to help the reader follow as I move from one example to another."

With these thoughts in mind, Charlene began revising her paper, and after several drafts she produced the paragraph that appears on page 150.

Writing an Exemplification Paragraph

DESCRIBING AN INDIVIDUAL

Write an exemplification paragraph about one quality of a person you know well. The person might be a member of your family, a friend, a roommate, a boss or supervisor, a neighbor, an instructor, or someone else. Here is a list of descriptions that you might consider choosing

WRITING ASSIGNMENT 1

Personal

from. Feel free to choose another description that does not appear here.

Honest	Hardworking	Jealous
Bad-tempered	Supportive	Materialistic
Ambitious	Suspicious	Sarcastic
Prejudiced	Open-minded	Self-centered
Considerate	Lazy	Spineless
Argumentative	Independent	Good-humored
Softhearted	Stubborn	Cooperative
Energetic	Flirtatious	Self-disciplined
Patient	Irresponsible	Sentimental
Reliable	Stingy	Defensive
Generous	Trustworthy	Dishonest
Persistent	Aggressive	Insensitive
Shy	Courageous	Unpretentious
Sloppy	Compulsive	Tidy

Prewriting

a. Select the individual you will write about and the quality of this person that you will focus on. For example, you might choose a self-disciplined cousin. Her quality of self-discipline will then be the point of your paragraph.

b. Decide if you want your paragraph to be informative, persuasive, or entertaining. Here are some questions to consider: Do you want your readers to understand the person better? Do you want to convince your readers to agree with you? Do you want to amuse them by providing humorous details? Keep in mind that your paragraph can combine purposes.

c. Make a list of examples that will support your point. A list for the self-disciplined cousin might look like this:

Exercises every day for forty-five minutes

Never lets herself watch TV until homework is done

Keeps herself on a strict budget

Organizes her school papers in color-coordinated notebooks

Eats no more than one dessert every week

Balances her checkbook the day her statement arrives

d. Read over your list and see how you might group the items into categories. The list above, for example, could be broken into three categories: schoolwork, fitness, and money.

Exercises every day for forty-five minutes (fitness)

Never lets herself watch TV until homework is done (schoolwork)

Keeps herself on a strict budget (money)

Organizes her school papers in color-coordinated notebooks (schoolwork)

Eats no more than one dessert every week (fitness)

Balances her checkbook the day her bank statement arrives (money)

e. Prepare an outline made up of the details you've generated, with those details grouped into appropriate categories.

1. <u>Self-disciplined about fitness</u>

   A. Exercises every day for forty-five minutes

   B. Eats no more than one dessert every week

2. <u>Self-disciplined about schoolwork</u>

   A. Never lets herself watch TV until homework is done

   B. Organizes her school papers in color-coordinated notebooks

3. <u>Self-disciplined about money</u>

   A. Keeps herself on a strict budget

   B. Balances her checkbook the day her bank statement arrives

f. Write the topic sentence of your paragraph. You should include the name of the person you're writing about, your relationship to that person, and the specific quality you are focusing on. For example, you might write, "Keisha, a schoolmate of mine, is very flirtatious," or "Stubbornness is Uncle Carl's outstanding characteristic." And a topic sentence for the paragraph about the self-disciplined cousin might be "My cousin Mari is extremely self-disciplined."

   Remember to focus on only *one* characteristic. Also remember to focus on a *specific* quality, not a vague, general quality. For instance, "My English instructor is a nice person" is too general.

g. Now you have a topic sentence and an outline and are ready to write the first draft of your paragraph. Remember, as you flesh out the examples, your goal is not just to *tell* us about the person but to *show* us the person by detailing his or her words, actions, or both.

Revising: Peer Review

It's hard to criticize your own work honestly, especially just after you've finished writing. If at all possible, put your paragraph away for a day or so and then return to it. Better yet, wait a day and then read it aloud to a friend or classmate whose judgment you trust and ask that person to comment on your work using the checklist on the next page as a guide.

in a writer's words

"Don't tell me the moon is shining; show me the glint of light on broken glass."
—Anton Chekhov

EXEMPLIFICATION CHECKLIST: THE FOUR BASES

UNITY

✔ Does the topic sentence clearly state whom you are writing about, what that person's relationship is to you, and what quality of that person you are going to focus on?

✔ Do the examples provided truly show that your subject has the quality you are writing about?

SUPPORT

✔ Have you provided enough specific details to solidly support your point that your subject has a certain quality?

COHERENCE

✔ Have you organized the details in your paragraph into several clearly defined categories?

✔ Have you used transitional words such as *also, in addition, for example,* and *for instance* to help the reader follow your train of thought?

SENTENCE SKILLS

✔ Is there a consistent point of view throughout the paragraph?

✔ Does the paragraph contain specific rather than general words?

✔ Have you avoided wordiness and used concise wording?

✔ Are your sentences varied?

✔ Has the paragraph been checked for spelling and other sentence skills, as listed on the inside back cover of the book?

Continue revising your work until you and your reader can answer "yes" to all the checklist questions.

WRITING ASSIGNMENT 2

SUPPORTING A STATEMENT

Write a paragraph that uses examples to develop one of the following statements or a related statement of your own.

1. The daily life of a college student is filled with conflicts.

2. The Internet cannot always be a trusted source of information.

3. Every student needs to have good computer skills in college.

4. Students attend college for various reasons.

5. One of my instructors, _____, has some good (*or* unusual) teaching techniques.

6. Travel is a great way to broaden someone's way of thinking.

7. Colleges have resources to help students succeed.

8. Apple and Microsoft should offer their products for free.

9. Dating in the workplace can be difficult.

10. Some students at _____ do not care about learning (*or are* overly concerned about grades).

Be sure to choose examples that truly support your topic sentence. They should be relevant facts, statistics, personal experiences, or incidents you have heard or read about. Organize your paragraph by listing several examples that support your point. Save the most vivid, most convincing, or most important example for last.

PLANNING YOUR FUTURE

WRITING ASSIGNMENT 3

Write a paragraph that tells what you are majoring in and what you plan to do in your chosen field. In your paragraph you should include details that explain how you decided to enter this field and major influences on your decision. In order to provide added interest to your paragraph, you may want to refer to Chapter 7, "Narration," to read how to incorporate anecdotes into your support. Your topic sentence should include what it is you are majoring in and what you plan to go into.

> "I am studying to get a B.S. in Civil Engineering, so I can become a highway designer."

> "I am going to college to get a bachelor's degree in nursing because I want to become an emergency room nurse."

EXPLAINING POOR CHOICES

WRITING ASSIGNMENT 4

As the cartoon suggests, the diet of many Americans is not healthy. We eat too much junk food and consume far too much cholesterol. Write a paragraph with a topic sentence like one of the following:

> The diet of the average American is unhealthy.

> The diet of many American families is unhealthy.

> Many schoolchildren in America do not have a healthy diet.

Using strategies described in Chapter 20, "Writing a Research Paper" (pages 367–389), research the topic with keywords such as "unhealthy American diets." Combine information you find with your own observations to provide a series of examples that support your point.

REFLECTIVE ACTIVITY

1. Review the exemplification paragraph you wrote for Writing Assignment 2 on pages 156–157. Do you have a clear topic sentence? What is the point you are making in this sentence?

2. Now that you are rereading the paragraph, do you find that it is easy to follow? In other words, have you maintained unity and coherence? What might you add to improve unity and coherence, as explained in this chapter?

3. Check the paragraph's sentences. Are the words they contain specific and clear, or are they general and vague? What can you do to add more specific detail?

4. Are you being wordy? Are there words you can remove without changing the meaning of the paragraph or reducing its effectiveness?

BEYOND THE CLASSROOM

Exemplification

Beyond the classroom, you will find yourself and others providing specific examples to illustrate a point that you have made. A supervisor who is working on a promotion recommendation for a loyal and diligent employee might cite examples of that employee's ability to solve problems or of her willingness to cooperate with others in a team effort. A plant manager might issue safety instructions that list examples of the kinds of behavior or work habits that cause injuries. A doctor might use examples to warn a patient about the various side effects he or she could experience after taking a drug.

For this writing assignment, you will write an exemplification paragraph with a specific purpose and for a specific audience.

Imagine that you are working as a certified nursing assistant in a hospital. A patient will go home in a few days, and you need to provide his or her family with follow-up instructions. Some areas you might consider are diet, medications, and hygiene. What point do you want to emphasize, and what examples will you use to help the patient's family understand the importance of proper care at home? Write your instructions in a paragraph.

EXPLORING WRITING ONLINE

Visit *This Day in History* at http://www.history.com/this-day-in-history.do to find out what happened on the day you were born. As you learn more about these events in history, think about how you would describe this day to someone. Then write a paragraph in which you make a point about this day and provide three examples. For example, your topic sentence might say, "Famous people were born on March 6."

Narration

RESPONDING TO IMAGES

When we watch an athlete win, we share in that person's victory. Look at this photo and write a paragraph about a time you experienced triumph in sports or some other area. How did the experience make you feel? In telling your story, be sure to provide vivid details so that your readers can see and understand why you felt the way you did.

At times we make a statement clear by relating in detail something that has happened. In the story we tell, we present the details in the order in which they happened. A person might say, for example, "I was embarrassed yesterday," and then go on to illustrate the statement with the following narrative:

> I was hurrying across campus to get to a class. It had rained heavily all morning, so I was hopscotching my way around puddles in the pathway. I called to two friends ahead to wait for me, and right before I caught up to them, I came to a large puddle that covered the entire path. I had to make a quick choice of either stepping into the puddle or trying to jump over it. I jumped, wanting to seem cool, since my friends were watching, but didn't clear the puddle. Water splashed everywhere, drenching my shoe, sock, and pants cuff, and spraying the pants of my friends as well. "Well done, Dave!" they said. My embarrassment was all the greater because I had tried to look so casual.

The speaker's details have made his moment of embarrassment vivid and real for us, and we can see and understand just why he felt as he did.

In this section, you will be asked to tell a story that illustrates or explains some point. The paragraphs below present narrative experiences that support a point. Read them and then answer the questions that follow.

Paragraphs to Consider

Heartbreak

[1]Emily and I had gotten engaged in August, just before she left for college at Penn State. [2]A week before Thanksgiving, I drove up to see her as a surprise. [3]When I knocked on the door of her dorm room, she was indeed surprised, but not in a pleasant way. [4]She introduced me to her roommate, who looked uncomfortable and quickly left. [5]I asked Emily how classes were going, and at the same time I tugged on the sleeve of my heavy sweater in order to pull it off. [6]As I was slipping it over my head, I noticed a large photo on the wall—of Emily and a tall guy laughing together. [7]It was decorated with paper flowers and a yellow ribbon, and on the ribbon was written "Emily and Blake." [8]"What's going on?" I said. [9]I stood there stunned and then felt anger that grew rapidly. [10]"Who is Blake?" I asked. [11]Emily laughed nervously and said, "What do you want to hear about—my classes or Blake?" [12]I don't really remember what she then told me, except that Blake was a sophomore computer science major. [13]I felt a terrible pain in the pit of my stomach, and I wanted to rest my head on someone's shoulder and cry. [14]I wanted to tear down the sign and run out, but I did nothing. [15]Clumsily I pulled on my sweater again. [16]My knees felt weak, and I barely had control of my body.

continued

[17]I opened the room door, and suddenly more than anything I wanted to slam the door shut so hard that the dorm walls would collapse. [18]Instead, I managed to close the door quietly. [19]I walked away understanding what was meant by a broken heart.

Losing My Father

[1]Although my father died ten years ago, I felt that he'd been lost to me four years earlier. [2]Dad had been diagnosed with Alzheimer's disease, an illness that destroys the memory. [3]He couldn't work any longer, but in his own home he got along pretty well. [4]I lived hundreds of miles away and wasn't able to see my parents often. [5]So when my first child was a few weeks old, I flew home with the baby to visit them. [6]After Mom met us at the airport, we picked up Dad and went to their favorite local restaurant. [7]Dad was quiet, but kind and gentle as always, and he seemed glad to see me and his new little grandson. [8]Everyone went to bed early. [9]In the morning, Mom left for work. [10]I puttered happily around in my old bedroom. [11]I heard Dad shuffling around in the kitchen, making coffee. [12]Eventually I realized that he was pacing back and forth at the foot of the stairs as if he were uneasy. [13]I called down to him, "Everything all right there? [14]I'll be down in a minute." [15]"Fine!" he called back, with forced-sounding cheerfulness. [16]Then he stopped pacing and called up to me, "I must be getting old and forgetful. [17]When did you get here?" [18]I was surprised, but made myself answer calmly. [19]"Yesterday afternoon. [20]Remember, Mom met us at the airport, and then we went to The Skillet for dinner." [21]"Oh, yes," he said. [22]"I had roast beef." [23]I began to relax. [24]But then he continued, hesitantly, "And … who are you?" [25]My breath stopped as if I'd been punched in the stomach. [26]When I could steady my voice, I answered, "I'm Laura; I'm your daughter. [27]I'm here with my baby son, Max." [28]"Oh," is all he said. [29]"Oh." [30]And he wandered into the living room and sat down. [31]In a few minutes I joined him and found him staring blankly out the window. [32]He was a polite host, asking if I wanted anything to eat, and if the room was too cold. [33]I answered with an aching heart, mourning for his loss and for mine.

Personal

in a writer's words

"*The idea is to write it so that people hear it and it slides right through the brain and goes straight to the heart.*"
—Maya Angelo

About Unity

1. Which paragraph lacks a topic sentence?

_____

Write a topic sentence for the paragraph.

_____

_____

QUESTIONS

About Support

2. What is for you the best (most real and vivid) detail or image in the paragraph "Heartbreak"?

   _____

   _____

3. What is the best detail or image in "Losing My Father"?

   _____

   _____

About Coherence

4. Do the two paragraphs use time order or emphatic order to organize details?

   _____

Developing a Narrative Paragraph

Development through Prewriting

Gary's instructor was helping her students think of topics for their narrative paragraphs. "A narrative is simply a story that illustrates a point," she said. "That point is often about an emotion you felt. Looking at a list of emotions may help you think of a topic. Ask yourself what incident in your life has made you feel any of these emotions."

The instructor then jotted these feelings on the board:

Anger	Thankfulness
Embarrassment	Loneliness
Jealousy	Sadness
Amusement	Terror
Confusion	Relief

As Gary looked over the list, he thought of several experiences in his life. "The word 'angry' made me think about a time when I was a kid. My brother took my skateboard without permission and left it in the park, where it got stolen. 'Amused' made me think of when I watched my roommate, who claimed he spoke Spanish, try to bargain with a street vendor in Mexico. He got so flustered that he ended up paying even more than the vendor had originally asked for. When I got to 'sad,' though, I thought about when I visited Emily and found out she was dating someone else. 'Sad' wasn't a strong enough word, though—I was heartbroken. So I decided to write about heartbreak."

Gary's first step was to do some freewriting. Without worrying about spelling or grammar, he simply wrote down everything that came into his mind concerning his visit with Emily. Here is what he came up with:

I hadn't expected to see Emily until Christmas. We'd got engaged just before she went off to college. The drive to penn state took ten hours each way and that seemed like to much driving for just a weekend visit. But I realized I had a long weekend over thanksgiving I decided to surprise her. I think down deep I knew something was wrong. She had sounded sort of cool on the phone and she hadn't been writing as often. I guess I wanted to convince myself that everything was OK. We'd been dating since we were 16 and I couldn't imagine not being with her. When I knocked at her dorm door I remember how she was smiling when she opened the door. Her expresion changed to one of surprise. Not happy surprise. I hugged her and she sort of hugged me back but like you'd hug your brother. Another girl was in the room. Emily said, "This is Eva," and Eva shot out of the room like I had a disease. Everything seemed wrong and confused. I started taking off my sweater and then I saw it. On a bulletin board was this photo of Emily with Blake, the guy she had been messing around with. They broke up about a year later, but by then I never wanted to see Emily again. I couldn't believe Emily would start seeing somebody else when we were planing to get married. It had even been her idea to get engaged. Before she left for college. Later on I realized that wasn't the first dishonest thing she'd done. I got out of there as quick as I could.

Development through Revising

Gary knew that the first, freewritten version of his paragraph needed work. Here are the comments he made after he reread it the following day:

"Although my point is supposed to be that my visit to Emily was heartbreaking, I didn't really get that across. I need to say more about how the experience felt.

"I've included some information that doesn't really support my point. For instance, what happened to Emily and Blake later isn't important here. Also, I think I spend too much time explaining the circumstances of the visit. I need to get more quickly to the point where I arrived at Emily's dorm.

   "I think I should include more dialogue, too. That would make the reader feel more like a witness to what really happened."

With this self-critique in mind, Gary revised his paragraph until he had produced the version that appears on page 160–161.

Writing a Narrative Paragraph

OBSERVING EVENTS

WRITING ASSIGNMENT 1

Narrate a real-life event you have witnessed. Listed below are some places where interesting personal interactions often happen. Think of an event that you saw happen at one of these places, or visit one of them and take notes on an incident to write about.

   The traffic court or small-claims court in your area

   The dinner table at your or someone else's home

   A waiting line at a supermarket, unemployment office, ticket counter, movie theater, or cafeteria

   A doctor's office

   An audience at a movie, concert, or sports event

   A classroom

   A restaurant

   A student lounge

Prewriting

a. Decide what point you will make about the incident. What one word or phrase characterizes the scene you witnessed? Your narration of the incident will emphasize that characteristic.

b. Write your topic sentence. The topic sentence should state where the incident happened as well as your point about it. Here are some possibilities:

   I witnessed a *heartwarming* incident at Taco Bell yesterday.

   Two fans at last week's baseball game got into a *hilarious* argument.

   The scene at our family dinner table Monday was one of complete *confusion*.

   A *painful* dispute went on in Atlantic County small-claims court yesterday.

c. Use the questioning technique to remind yourself of details that will make your narrative come alive. Ask yourself questions like these and write down your answers:

   Whom was I observing?

   How were they dressed?

What were their facial expressions like?

What tones of voice did they use?

What did I hear them say?

d. Drawing details from the notes you have written, write the first draft of your paragraph. Remember to use time signals such as *then, after that, during, meanwhile*, and *finally* to connect one sentence to another.

Revising: Peer Review

After you have put your paragraph away for a day, read it to a friend or classmate who will give you honest feedback. You and your reader should consider these questions:

NARRATION CHECKLIST: THE FOUR BASES

UNITY

✔ Does the topic sentence make a general point about the incident?

SUPPORT

✔ Do descriptions of the appearance, tone of voice, and expressions of the people involved paint a clear picture of the incident?

COHERENCE

✔ Is the sequence of events made clear by transitional words, such as *first, later*, and *then*?

SENTENCE SKILLS

✔ Have you used a consistent point of view throughout the paragraph?

✔ Have you used specific rather than general words?

✔ Have you avoided wordiness and used concise wording?

✔ Are the sentences varied?

✔ Has the paragraph been checked for spelling and other sentence skills, as listed on the inside back cover of the book?

Continue revising your work until you and your reader can answer "yes" to all these questions.

EXPLAINING AN INCIDENT

WRITING ASSIGNMENT 2

In a story, something happens. The cartoon on the next page, for example, is a little story about a man feeling much older than his friends because he's out of touch with technology. For this assignment, tell a story about something that happened to you.

Make sure that your story has a point, expressed in the first sentence of the paragraph. If necessary, tailor your narrative to fit your purpose. Use

"George," www.george-comics.com. © 2009 John Norton. Reprinted by permission of John Norton.

time order to organize your details (*first* this happened; *then* this; *after* that, this; *next*, this; and so on). Concentrate on providing as many specific details as possible so that the reader can really share your experience. Try to make it as vivid for the reader as it was for you when you first experienced it.

Choose one of the topics below. Whichever topic you choose, remember that your story must illustrate or support a point stated in the first sentence of your paragraph.

a. Think of a time when you achieved a personal goal. Some ideas might include being accepted into college, gaining employment at your dream job, or purchasing your first home. Tell the story of why this was an important goal and how you achieved it.

b. Think of a time when you disagreed with someone else's decision and decided to speak up against it. Some ideas might include a time a teacher gave you a grade you disagreed with, when a city implemented a new law you didn't like, or a neighbor painted his or her house in an unbearable color. In your story, explain how the decision was made, why you disagreed with it, how you stood up against it, and why it was important for you.

c. Think of a time when you stood up for yourself and/or your beliefs. Some ideas might be supporting a political candidate you like by canvassing neighborhoods, rallying support for someone being persecuted, or participating in an organized protest. In your story show why it was important for you to make the stand and how it affected you afterward.

d. Think of a time when you taught a skill, idea, or subject to another person. Some ideas might be teaching a child how to read or write, explaining a religious belief to a new church parishioner, or teaching a friend about a class you are taking. Tell the story of what you taught, how you taught it, and why it needed to be taught.

WRITING ASSIGNMENT 3

SUGGESTING A SOLUTION

Write a one-paragraph e-mail to your boss describing how something at the company could be done better. In your paragraph identify the problem, support it with a story that demonstrates the problem, and then suggest a possible solution. You must explain why your solution will work, so you will want to read Chapter 14, "Argument," to help you create a persuasive tone for both your story and solution. Keep in mind that writing to a boss requires formal language and detailed support. A formal e-mail also requires proper formatting that includes the sender, addressee, date, and subject matter. A sample has been provided for you in Appendixes; refer to this e-mail for proper formatting.

Beyond the classroom, there are many instances where narrative writing would be used. For example, a lifeguard might need to provide a narrative account of a swimming accident that he or she witnessed, or a sports reporter might need to narrate the key events of a sporting event.

For this writing assignment, you will write a narrative paragraph with a specific purpose and for a specific audience. You have two options.

Option 1

Imagine that you are a law enforcement officer at the scene of an accident or crime. You spoke to an eyewitness who saw the event, and now you must write up this person's statement. Write a paragraph in which you recount his or her story, presenting details in the order in which they happened. Begin your paragraph with a clear topic sentence that states whom you interviewed and what that person witnessed.

Option 2

Alternatively, imagine that you saw the accident or crime. The law enforcement officer has asked you to write a witness statement.

REFLECTIVE ACTIVITY

Review the essay that you wrote for Writing Assignment 1. Can you include additional descriptions to make your story more interesting? Can you add more details to support your story's topic sentence? Refer to Chapter 6 for information on examples and Chapter 8 for information on description.

EXPLORING WRITING ONLINE

Visit one of these Web sites to watch a movie trailer of your choice. As you watch the clip, think about what the movie's main point is. Then write a narration paragraph in which you state the movie's main point and include relevant details from the trailer.

Movie.com: http://movies.com/movietrailers

ComingSoon.net: www.comingsoon.net/trailers/

The Internet Movie Database: www.imdb.com/Sections/Trailers/

Description

RESPONDING TO IMAGES

Imagine that you have subscribed to an online dating service, such as Match.com, Zoosk, eHarmony, or OutTime.com. Write a paragraph in which you describe yourself. Your goal is to give interested members of the dating service a good idea of who you are.

When you describe something or someone, you give your readers a picture in words. To make this "word picture" as vivid and real as possible, you must observe and record specific details that appeal to your readers' senses (sight, hearing, taste, smell, and touch). More than any other type of writing, a descriptive paragraph needs sharp, colorful details.

Here is a description in which only the sense of sight is used:

A rug covers the living-room floor.

In contrast, here is a description rich in sense impressions:

A thick, reddish-brown shag rug is laid wall to wall across the living-room floor. The long, curled fibers of the shag seem to whisper as you walk through them in your bare feet, and when you squeeze your toes into the deep covering, the soft fibers push back at you with a spongy resilience.

Sense impressions include sight (*thick, reddish-brown shag rug; laid wall to wall; walk through them in your bare feet; squeeze your toes into the deep covering; push back*), hearing (*whisper*), and touch (*bare feet, soft fibers, spongy resilience*). The sharp, vivid images provided by the sensory details give us a clear picture of the rug and enable us to share the writer's experience.

In this section, you will be asked to describe a person, place, or thing for your readers by using words rich in sensory details. To prepare for the assignment, first read the two paragraphs ahead and then answer the questions that follow.

in a writer's words

"You can take for granted that people know more or less what a street, a shop, a beach, a sky, an oak tree look like. Tell them what makes this one different."
—Neil Gaiman

Paragraphs to Consider

A Depressing Place

¹The pet shop in the mall is a depressing place. ²A display window attracts passersby who stare at the prisoners penned inside. ³In the right-hand side of the window, two puppies press their forepaws against the glass and attempt to lick the human hands that press from the outside. ⁴A cardboard barrier separates the dogs from several black-and-white kittens piled together in the opposite end of the window. ⁵Inside the shop, rows of wire cages line one wall from top to bottom. ⁶At first, it is hard to tell whether a bird, hamster, gerbil, cat, or dog is locked inside each cage. ⁷Only an occasional movement or a clawing, shuffling sound tells visitors that living creatures are inside. ⁸Running down the center of the store is a line of large wooden perches that look like coatracks. ⁹When customers pass by, the parrots and mynahs chained to these perches flutter their clipped wings in a useless attempt to escape. ¹⁰At the end of this center aisle is a large plastic tub of dirty, stagnant-looking water containing a few motionless turtles. ¹¹The shelves against the left-hand wall are packed with all kinds of pet-related items. ¹²The smell inside the entire shop is an unpleasant mixture of strong chemical deodorizers, urine-soaked newspapers, and musty sawdust. ¹³Because so

continued

many animals are crammed together, the normally pleasant, slightly milky smell of the puppies and kittens is sour and strong. ¹⁴The droppings inside the uncleaned birdcages give off a dry, stinging odor. ¹⁵ Visitors hurry out of the shop, anxious to feel fresh air and sunlight. ¹⁶The animals stay on.

House for Sale!

¹The wide porch encourages visitors to come into this awe-inspiring Craftsman-style home that was built in 2012 and is filled with details and characteristics that every new home owner should have. ²Upon opening the front door, buyers will be greeted by a two-story foyer that opens into a formal dining room, featuring a boxed ceiling and hard-wood wainscoting. ³Off the dining room is the eat-in kitchen that boasts double-ovens, professional-grade appliances, a combined built-in buffet and wine cabinet, antiqued ceiling, and large oak table. ⁴The kitchen opens into the cozy living room, which is accentuated by large French doors and a magnificent stone fireplace. ⁵The master suite is also located on the main floor across from a uniquely designed half-bath. ⁶A lot of people like having the master suite on the main level. ⁷Bathrooms boast high ceilings and vibrantly warm colors that maintain the magnificence of this home. ⁸The highlight of the home is the upstairs "kid zone." ⁹A large playroom is the centerpiece, and the children's rooms all lead off this area. ¹⁰Each of the rooms has been decorated to satisfy the whimsy of every child. ¹¹With lofts, hidden rooms, and undersea adventure murals, this child-focused area is a masterpiece of creativity and originality. ¹²Not to be missed, the lower level of the house includes a home office, bar, media room equipped with a 70" television, and an additional play area for the children. ¹³A final unique feature of this home is the carriage house located over the detached three-car garage and accessed through a beautifully designed breezeway, overlooking a little fountain bubbling in the backyard. ¹⁴Boasting the same quality cabinetry and appliances that the main home has, the carriage house's one-bedroom apartment is a perfect getaway for guests and a perfect complement to the home.

QUESTIONS

About Unity

1. Which sentence in the paragraph about the house should be omitted in the interest of paragraph unity? (*Write the sentence number here.*)

_____

About Support

2. Label as *sight, touch, hearing,* or *smell* all the sensory details in the following sentences taken from the two paragraphs. The first sentence is done for you as an example.

                 sight   *hearing*

  a. Only an occasional movement, or a clawing, shuffling sound tells

      visitors that living creatures are inside.

b.   Because so many animals are crammed together, the normally pleasant, slightly milky smell of the puppies and kittens is sour and strong.

c.   A final unique feature of this home is the carriage house located over the three-car garage and accessed through a beautifully designed breezeway, overlooking a little fountain bubbling in the backyard.

3.   After which sentence in "A Depressing Place" are specific details needed? _____

About Coherence

4.   The writer of "House for Sale!" organizes the details by observing the house in an orderly fashion. Which of the house's features is described first? _____ Which of the house's features is described last? _____ Check the method of spatial organization that best describes the paragraph:

_____ Exterior to interior

_____ Near to far

_____ Top to bottom

Developing a Descriptive Paragraph

Development through Prewriting

When Victor was assigned a descriptive paragraph, he thought at first of describing his own office at work. He began by making a list of details he noticed while looking around the office:

adjustable black chair	computer
beige desk	pictures of Marie and kids on desk
piles of papers	desk calendar

But Victor quickly became bored. Here is how he describes what happened next:

"As I wrote down what I saw in my office, I was thinking, 'What a drag.' I gave up and worked on something else. Later that evening I told my wife that I was going to write a boring paragraph about my boring office. She started laughing at me. I said, 'What's so funny?' and she said, 'You're so certain that a writing assignment has to be boring that you deliberately chose a subject that bores you. How about writing about something you care about?' At first I was annoyed, but then I realized she was right. When I hear 'assignment' I automatically think 'pain in the neck' and just want to get it over with."

Victor's attitude is not uncommon. Many students who are not experienced writers don't take the time to find a topic that interests them. They grab the one closest at hand and force themselves to write about it just for the sake of completing the assignment. Like Victor, they ensure that they (and probably their instructors as well) will be bored with the task.

In Victor's case, he decided that this assignment would be different. That evening as he talked with his son, Mike, he remembered a visit the two had made to a mall a few days earlier. Mike had asked Victor to take him to the pet store. Victor had found the store a very unpleasant place. "As I remembered the store, I recalled a lot of descriptive details—sounds, smells, sights," Victor said. "I realized not only that it would be easier to describe a place like that than my bland, boring office, but that I would actually find it an interesting challenge to make a reader see it through my words. For me to realize writing could be enjoyable was a real shock!"

Now that Victor had his subject, he began making a list of details about the pet shop. Here is what he wrote:

Sawdust, animal droppings on floor

Unhappy-looking puppies and kittens

Dead fish floating in tanks

Screech of birds

Chained parrots

Tanks full of dirty water

Strong urine smell

No place for animals to play

Bored-looking clerks

Animals scratching cages for attention

As he looked over his list of details, the word that came to mind was "depressing." He decided his topic sentence would be "The pet store in the mall is depressing." He then wrote this first draft:

The pet store in the mall is depressing. There are sawdust and animal droppings all over the floor. Sad-looking puppies and kittens scratch on their cages for attention. Dead fish and motionless turtles float in tanks of stagnant water. The loud screeching of birds is everywhere, and parrots with clipped wings try to escape when customers walk too

---

continued

> *near. Everywhere there is the smell of animal urine that has soaked the*
>
> *sawdust and newspapers. The clerks, who should be cleaning the cages,*
>
> *stand around talking to each other and ignoring the animals.*

Development through Revising

The next day Victor's instructor asked to see the students' first drafts. This is what she wrote in response to Victor's:

> This is a very good beginning. You have provided some strong details that appeal to the reader's senses of smell, hearing, and sight.
>
> In your next draft, organize your paragraph by using spatial order. In other words, describe the room in some logical physical order—maybe from left to right, or from the front of the store to its back.. Such an organization mirrors the way a visitor might move through the store.
>
> I encourage you to become even more specific in your details. For instance, in what way did the puppies and kittens seem sad? As you work on each sentence, ask yourself if you can add more descriptive details to paint a more vivid picture in words.

In response to his teacher's suggestion about a spatial method of organization, Victor rewrote the paragraph, beginning with the display window that attracts visitors, then going on to the store's right-hand wall, the center aisle, and the left-hand wall. He ended the paragraph with a sentence that brought the reader back outside the shop. Thinking about the shop in this way enabled Victor to remember and add a number of new specific details as well. He then wrote the version of "A Depressing Place" that appears on pages 169–170.

Writing a Descriptive Paragraph

WRITING A CHARACTERIZATION

Write a paragraph describing a specific person. Select a dominant impression of the person, and use only details that will convey that impression. You might want to write about someone who falls into one of these categories.

TV or movie personality	Coworker
Instructor	Clergyman or clergywoman
Employer	Police officer
Child	Store owner or manager
Older person	Bartender
Close friend	Politician
Rival	Neighbor

WRITING ASSIGNMENT 1

Academic

Prewriting

a. Reread the paragraph about the pet shop that appears earlier in this chapter. Note the dominant impression that the writer wanted to convey: that the pet shop is a depressing place. Having decided to focus on that impression, the writer included only details that contributed to his point. Profiling a person requires similar unity; instead of trying to tell everything about that person, you should focus on one dominant aspect of your subject's appearance, personality, or behavior.

Once you have chosen the person you will write about and the impression you plan to portray, put that information into a topic sentence. Here are some examples of topic sentences that mention a particular person and the dominant impression of that person:

Kate gives the impression of being permanently nervous.

The old man was as faded and brittle as a dying leaf.

The child was an angelic little figure.

Our high school principal resembled a cartoon character.

The TV newscaster seems as synthetic as a piece of Styrofoam.

Our neighbor is a fussy person.

The rock singer seemed to be plugged into some special kind of energy source.

The drug addict looked as lifeless as a corpse.

My friend Jeffrey is a slow, deliberate person.

The owner of that grocery store seems burdened with troubles.

b. Make a list of the person's qualities that support your topic sentence. Write quickly; don't worry if you find yourself writing down something that doesn't quite fit. You can always edit the list later. For now, just write down all the details that occur to you that support the dominant impression you want to convey. Include details that involve as many senses as possible (sight, sound, hearing, touch, smell). For instance, here's a list one writer jotted down to support the sentence "Our high school principal resembled a cartoon character":

tall with long spindly legs and arms

wore an eye-patch even though his vision was perfect

carried a briefcase

dashed everywhere, leaving a cloud of dust behind him

had a red moustache and a head of thick red curls

made a sound like a hyena when he laughed

wore lots of purple and smelled like patchouli

c. Edit your list, striking out details that don't support your topic sentence and adding others that do. The author of the paragraph on the high school principal crossed out one detail from the original list and added a new one:

tall with long spindly legs and arms

wore an eye-patch even though his vision was perfect

~~carried a briefcase~~

dashed everywhere, leaving a cloud of dust behind him

had a red moustache and a head of thick red curls

made a sound like a hyena when he laughed

wore lots of purple and smelled like patchouli

had a huge forehead and exaggerated features

d. Decide on a spatial order of organization. In the example above, the writer ultimately decided to describe the principal from head to toe.

e. Make a scratch outline for your paragraph, based on the organization you have chosen.

f. Then proceed to write a first draft of your paragraph.

Revising: Peer Review

Put your paragraph away for a day or so if at all possible. When you return to it, read the paragraph aloud—ideally to a friend or classmate whose judgment you trust. Then ask that person to comment on your draft, using the following checklist as a guide:

DESCRIPTION CHECKLIST: THE FOUR BASES

UNITY

✔ Does the topic sentence clearly state the dominant impression of the subject?

✔ If you left out the key words in your topic sentence (the words that state your dominant impression), would a reader know what idea fits there?

✔ Does every detail support your topic sentence?

SUPPORT

✔ Are the details you have included specific rather than vague and general?

COHERENCE

✔ Have you used a logical spatial organization that helps the reader follow your description?

SENTENCE SKILLS

✔ Have you used a consistent point of view throughout your paragraph?

✔ Have you avoided wordiness and used concise wording?

✔ Are the sentences varied?

✔ Has the paragraph been checked for spelling and other sentence skills, as listed on the inside back cover of the book?

Continue revising your work until you and your reader can answer "yes" to all these questions.

WRITING ASSIGNMENT 2

WRITING ABOUT MUSIC

As the picture shown here suggests, artists take great care to create an image that reflects their music. From the clothes they wear during concerts to the design of their album covers to their official Web sites, artists pay attention to every detail. In this assignment, you are to choose a music group that you enjoy and using details like

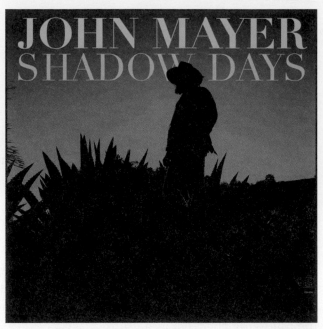

those above, explain to your reader what type of music the group plays, why you relate to the music, how the music makes you feel, and when you most like to listen to that group. For added detail and interest, you may want to incorporate short stories to support your descriptive details. The purpose of this assignment is to help your reader gain a full understanding of the experience he or she would have by listening to this music group.

WRITING ASSIGNMENT 3

MARKETING A PRODUCT

Imagine that you work for a marketing firm and have to create an advertising campaign. Choose an object that you would like to sell, and then write a paragraph describing that object, how it is used, and why it would make a good purchase. Include as many sensory details as possible that will emotionally connect the buyer to the product. Once you decide on the impression you want to convey, compose a topic sentence like the one below that summarizes the details:

> Every household should not be without the amazing, all-purpose, environmentally friendly, lawn care system known as "The Goat."

Remember to provide colorful, detailed descriptions to help your readers picture the image you are writing about. Note the contrast in the two items below:

Lacks rich descriptive details: Our lawn looked really nice after it had been cut.

Includes rich descriptive details: After using "The Goat" for the first time, our lawn was only one-inch high and had a beautiful dark green color from all the natural fertilizer.

Profiling a Place

Personal

Visit a place you have never gone to before and write a paragraph describing it. You may want to visit:

A restaurant

A classroom, a laboratory, an office, a workroom, or some other room in your school

A kind of store you ordinarily don't visit: for example, a hardware store, toy store, record shop, sports shop, or a particular men's or women's clothing store

A bus terminal, train station, or airport

A place of worship

A park, vacant lot, or street corner

You may want to jot down details about the place while you are there or very soon after you leave. Again, decide on a dominant impression you want to convey of the place, and use only those details that will support that impression. Follow the notes on "Prewriting" and "Revising" for Writing Assignment 1.

REFLECTIVE ACTIVITY

1. Chapters 7 and 8 cover methods for narration and description, two types of writing that are related. Read each of the paragraphs you wrote for those chapters (the assignments appear on pages 164–167 and 173–177).

2. What do these paragraphs have in common? Does description appear in the narrative paragraph? Does narration appear in the descriptive paragraph? If not, find a way to include descriptive details in the narrative paragraph and narrative details in the descriptive paragraph.

BEYOND THE CLASSROOM

Description

Work

Beyond the classroom, there are many circumstances that call for descriptive writing. For example, a journalist may need to use vivid, descriptive details to give his or her readers a clear mental picture of an event.

For this writing assignment, you will write a description paragraph with a specific purpose and for a specific audience. You have two options.

Option 1
Imagine that you are an interior designer. A new affordable-housing complex is going to be built, and you have been asked by the developers to create the layout for a sample studio apartment. Write a paragraph describing your design, telling what it would include and how

continued

it would be arranged. You might list all the relevant needs you can think of, such as storage space, appropriate lighting, and a separate kitchen. Then put all the parts together to describe the floor plan. Use a spatial order in your paragraph to help the developers "see" the apartment. Begin your topic sentence with the words, "My design for the studio apartment offers. . . ".

Option 2

As an alternative, write a paragraph describing your design for a public space. You might want to focus on a restaurant, coffee shop, night club, convenience store, preschool, playground, skate park, fitness center, or any public area of your choice.

EXPLORING WRITING ONLINE

Visit the United States National Park Service at http://www.nps.gov/ and find a park that is either located near you or one that you have always wanted to visit. Read the section dedicated to that park and view the pictures and web-cams. Using the visual aids, write a description of the park from the perspective of a parks employee who is trying to bring in more visitors.

Process

RESPONDING TO IMAGES

Every four years, a president and a vice president are elected in the United States. Each state, however, determines its own voting process. Some use paper ballots; others use electronic devices. Some provide absentee and early voting. Write a paragraph in which you explain how the voting process works—or how you think it should work—in your state.

Every day we perform many activities that are *processes*—that is, series of steps carried out in a definite order. Many of these processes are familiar and automatic: for example, tying shoelaces, changing bed linen, using a vending machine, and starting a car. We are thus seldom aware of the sequence of steps making up each activity. In other cases, such as when we are asked for directions to a particular place, or when we try to read and follow the directions for a new game, we may be painfully conscious of the whole series of steps involved in the process.

In this section, you will be asked to write a process paragraph—one that explains clearly how to do or make something. To prepare for this assignment, you should first read the student process paragraphs below and then respond to the questions that follow.

> **TIP**   In process writing, you are often giving instruction to the reader, and so the pronoun *you* can appropriately be used. One of the model paragraphs here uses *you*—as indeed does much of this book, which gives instruction on how to write effectively. As a general rule, though, do not use *you* in your writing.

Paragraphs to Consider

My First Time Voting

1I took this more seriously than anything else I had done in my life until then. 2I read up on the candidates and tried to see both sides of every argument. 3I categorized how each candidate responded to my own views, especially in terms of education, the environment, and world affairs. 4But there were other preparations to think about. 5I made sure I had registered and that all the information on my card was accurate. 6I also located my local precinct weeks before, to make sure I knew how to get there on Election Day. 7I listened to the debates and the political analyses on television. 8I discussed with my college professors and peers, all the while constructing my own arguments. 9When Election Day finally came, I arrived at the location early. 10Once I approached the identification table, an older woman searched for my name and verified my identity with my driver's license. 11Once she located me on the roll, I was given instructions and a ballot. 12Next, I was escorted to my booth. 13I took a deep breath and began reading every line carefully and punching in my selections. 14Before I knew it, I had gone through all the questions. 15I reviewed all of my selections one more time before I cast my vote. 16I've always wanted to do what was right. 17I did very well in school and sports, and always made my parents proud. 18After exiting the voting booth, a sticker was placed on my blouse. 19It read, "I voted today." 20I proudly wore that sticker all day. 21I had voted, and no matter the outcome of the election, I truly felt like an American that day.

Dealing with Verbal Abuse

¹If you are living with a significant other who abuses you verbally with criticism, complaints, and insults, you should take steps to change your situation. ²First, realize that you are not to blame for his or her abusive behavior. ³This may be difficult for you to believe. ⁴Years of verbal abuse have probably convinced you that you're responsible for everything that's wrong with your relationship. ⁵But that is a lie. ⁶If your partner is verbally abusive, it is his or her responsibility to learn why he or she chooses to deal with his problems by saying nasty things. ⁷Perhaps he observed his father treating his mother that same way. ⁸Maybe she never learned any more positive ways to deal with negative emotions, like anger, fear, or disappointment. ⁹Steps two and three need to be done one right after the other. ¹⁰Step two is for you to announce that you will no longer tolerate being verbally abused. ¹¹State that you are a person who deserves respect and civil behavior, and that you will accept no less. ¹²Next, offer to go with your partner to talk to a counselor who will help both of you learn new ways to communicate. ¹³While he or she learns to express feelings without attacking you, you can learn to stand up for yourself and express your feelings clearly. ¹⁴If the significant other refuses to take responsibility for changing his or her abusive behavior, then you must consider step four: to leave. ¹⁵You were not put here on earth to have your self-concept demolished by serving as someone else's verbal punching bag.

QUESTIONS

About Unity

1. Which paragraph lacks an opening topic sentence?

   _____

2. Which two sentences in "My First Time Voting" should be eliminated in the interest of paragraph unity? (*Write the sentence numbers here.*)

   _____   _____

About Support

3. Summarize the four steps in the process of dealing with verbal abuse.

   a. _____

   b. _____

   c. _____

   d. _____

About Coherence

4. Do these paragraphs use time order or emphatic order?

   _____

Developing a Process Paragraph

Development through Prewriting

To be successful, a process paragraph must explain clearly each step of an activity. The key to preparing to write such a paragraph is thinking through the activity as though you're doing it for the first time. Selma is the author of "Dealing with Verbal Abuse." As she considered possible topics for her paper, she soon focused on a situation in her own life: living with an abusive partner. Selma had not known how to change her situation. But with the help of a counselor, she realized there were steps she could take—a process she could follow. She carried out that process and finally left her abusive partner. Remembering this, Selma decided to write about how to deal with abuse.

She began by making a list of the steps she followed in coping with her own abusive relationship. This is what she wrote:

Tell him or her you won't accept any more abuse.

Open your own checking account.

Apply for credit cards in your own name.

Offer to go with your partner to counseling.

Realize you're not to blame.

Learn to stand up for yourself.

Go into counseling yourself if he or she won't do it.

Call the police if he or she ever becomes violent.

Leave if your partner refuses to change.

Next, she numbered the steps in the order in which she had performed them. She crossed out some items she realized weren't really part of the process of dealing with verbal abuse.

---

2   Tell him or her you won't accept any more abuse.

~~Open your own checking account.~~

~~Apply for credit cards in your own name.~~

3   Offer to go with your partner to counseling.

1   Realize you're not to blame.

5   Learn to stand up for yourself.

---

continued

4   Go into counseling yourself if he or she won't do it.

~~Call the police if he ever becomes violent.~~

6   Leave if your partner refuses to change.

Then Selma grouped her items into four steps. Those steps were (1) realize you're not to blame; (2) tell the abuser you won't accept more abuse; (3) get into counseling, preferably with him or her; and (4) if necessary, leave.

Selma was ready to write her first draft. Here it is:

Some people think that "abuse" has to mean getting punched and kicked, but that's not so. Verbal abuse can be as painful inside as physical abuse is on the outside. It can make you feel worthless and sad. I know because I lived with a verbally abusive man for years. Finally I found the courage to deal with the situation. Here is what I did. With the help of friends, I finally figured out that I wasn't to blame. I thought it was my fault because that's what he always told me—that if I wasn't so stupid, he wouldn't criticize and insult me. When I told him I wanted him to stop insulting and criticizing me, he just laughed at me and told me I was a crybaby. One of my friends suggested a counselor, and I asked Harry to go talk to him with me. We went together once but Harry wouldn't go back. He said he didn't need anyone to tell him how to treat his woman. I wasn't that surprised because Harry grew up with a father who treated his mother like dirt and his mom just accepts it to this day. Even after Harry refused to go see the counselor, though, I kept going. The counselor helped me see that I couldn't make Harry change, but I was still free to make my own choices. If I didn't want to live my life being Harry's verbal punching bag, and if he didn't want to change, then I would have to. I told Harry that I wasn't going to live that way anymore. I told him if he wanted to work together on better ways to communicate, I'd work with him. But otherwise, I would leave. He gave me his usual talk about "Oh, you know I don't really mean half the stuff I say when I'm mad." I said that wasn't a good enough

continued

excuse, and that I did mean what I was saying. He got mad all over again and called me every name in the book. I stuck around for a little while after that but then realized "This is it. I can stay here and take this or I can do what I know is right for me." So I left. It was a really hard decision but it was the right one. Harry may be angry at me forever but I know now that his anger and his verbal abuse are his problem, not mine.

Development through Revising

After Selma had written her first draft, she showed it to a classmate for her comments. Here is what the classmate wrote in response:

> In order for this to be a good process essay, I think you need to do a couple of things.
>
> First, although the essay is based on what you went through, I think it's too much about your own experience. I'd suggest you take yourself out of it and just write about how any person could deal with any verbally abusive situation. Otherwise this paper is about you and Harry, not the process.
>
> Second, you need a clear topic sentence that tells the reader what process you're going to explain.
>
> Third, I'd use transitions like "first" and "next" to make the steps in the process clearer. I think the steps are all there, but they get lost in all the details about you and Harry.

When Selma reread her first draft, she agreed with her classmate's suggestions. She then wrote the version of "Dealing with Verbal Abuse" that appears on page 181.

Writing a Process Paragraph

WRITING ASSIGNMENT 1

EXPLAINING HOW

Write a paragraph about one of the following processes. For this assignment, many of the topics are so broad that entire books have been written about them. A big part of your task, then, will be to narrow the topic down enough so that it can be covered in one paragraph. Then you'll have to invent your own steps for the process. In addition, you'll need to make decisions about how many steps to include and the order in which to present them.

- How to encourage someone's forgiveness
- How to gather information on a company in preparation for a job interview
- How to get along with a professor
- How to get over a broken relationship

- How to improve a course you have taken
- How to improve the place where you work
- How to make someone happy
- How to procrastinate
- How to properly/improperly answer a phone at a place of business
- How to properly/improperly write an e-mail to a boss or professor
- How to show appreciation to others

Prewriting

a. Choose a topic that appeals to you.

b. Decide if you want your paragraph to be informative, persuasive, or entertaining. Here are some questions to consider: Do you want your readers to understand this process better? Do you want to convince your readers to agree with your steps? Do you want to amuse them by providing humorous details? Keep in mind that your paragraph can combine purposes.

c. Ask yourself, "How can I make this broad, general topic narrow enough to be covered in a particular paragraph?" A logical way to proceed would be to think of a particular time you have gone through this process.

d. Make a list of as many different items as you can think of that concern your topic. Don't worry about repeating yourself, about putting the items in order, about whether details are major or minor, or about spelling. Simply make a list of everything about your topic that occurs to you. Here, for instance, is a list of items generated by a student writing about decorating her apartment on a budget:

Bought towels and used them as wall hangings

Trimmed overgrown shrubs in front yard

Used old mayonnaise jars for vases to hold flowers picked in the yard

Found an old oriental rug at a yard sale

Painted mismatched kitchen chairs in bright colors

Kept dishes washed and put away

Bought a slipcover for a battered couch

Used energy-saver lightbulbs

Hung colored sheets over the windows

e. Next, decide what order you will present your items in and number them. (As in the example of "decorating an apartment," there may not be an order that the steps *must* be done in. If that is the case, you'll need to make a decision about a sequence that makes sense, or that you followed yourself.) As you number your items, strike out items that do not fit in the list and add others that you think of, like this:

6 Bought towels and used them as wall hangings

~~Trimmed overgrown shrubs in front yard~~

7   Used old mayonnaise jars for vases to hold flowers picked in the yard

4   Found an old oriental rug at a yard sale

2   Painted mismatched kitchen chairs in bright colors

   ~~Kept dishes washed and put away~~

1   Bought a slipcover for a battered couch

8   Used energy-saver lightbulbs

5   Hung colored sheets over the windows

3   Built bookshelves out of cinder blocks and boards

f.   Referring to your list of steps, write the first draft of your paper. Add additional steps as they occur to you.

Revising: Peer Review

If you can, put your first draft away for a day or so and then return to it. Read it out loud to yourself or, better yet, to a friend or classmate who will give you honest feedback. Ask that person to comment on your work using the checklist below as a guide.

PROCESS CHECKLIST: THE FOUR BASES

UNITY

✔ Have you included a clear topic sentence that tells what process you will be describing?

✔ Does the rest of the paragraph support your topic sentence?

SUPPORT

✔ Have you included all the essential information so that anyone reading your paragraph could follow the same process?

COHERENCE

✔ Have you made the sequence of steps easy to follow by using transitions like *first*, *second*, *then*, *next*, *during*, and *finally*?

SENTENCE SKILLS

✔ Have you used a consistent point of view throughout your paragraph?

✔ Have you used specific rather than general words?

✔ Have you avoided wordiness and used concise wording?

✔ Are your sentences varied?

✔ Has the paragraph been checked for spelling and other sentence skills, as listed on the inside back cover of the book?

Continue revising your work until you and your reader can answer "yes" to all these questions.

WRITING ABOUT WEIGHT GAIN

Every year, people are bombarded by advertisements promising incredible weight loss with very little effort. In this assignment, you are going to take the opposite view and write a paragraph describing how to gain weight. As the author, you could have a humorous tone and include steps like "eating until there is no food left in the fridge," or you could have a more serious tone and include steps like "ignoring the sensation of being full."

ANALYZING YOUR JOB PERFORMANCE

Many employers require their employees to be reviewed each year. This often includes a self-evaluation of the employees' work over the past year. In this assignment, you are going to pretend that you are being required to assess your work over the course of the past year, focusing specifically on a new skill or task that you learned. Write a paragraph in which you discuss the steps involved in learning the new skill or task. It may be that your company introduced a new e-mail system and you had to learn how to use it, or it may be that you were promoted to a new position and had to learn some specific tasks related to that position.

REFLECTIVE ACTIVITY

Reread the process paragraph that you wrote for Writing Assignment 1 (pages 184–186). Have you explained your process enough that anyone reading your paragraph could understand each step? Can you add additional details and descriptions (Chapter 8) to make your process more clear? Is your process convincing (Chapter 14)? Could your process be enhanced by anecdotes (Chapter 7)?

**BEYOND THE
CLASSROOM**

Process

Beyond the classroom, there are many instances where process writing is used. For example, a salesperson may need to explain to a customer how to install computer software or set up the wiring for a new TV.

For this writing assignment, you will write a process paragraph with a specific purpose and for a specific audience. You have two options.

Option 1

Imagine that you have a job helping out at a day-care center. The director, who is pleased with your work and wants to give you more responsibility, has put you in charge of a group activity (for example, an alphabet lesson, a playground game, or an art project). Before you actually begin the activity, the director wants to see a summary of how

continued

What caused Todd to drop out of school? Why are soap operas so popular? Why does our football team do so poorly each year? How has retirement affected Mom and Dad? What effects does divorce have on children? Every day we ask such questions and look for answers. We realize that situations have causes and also effects—good or bad. By examining causes and effects, we seek to understand and explain things.

In this section, you will be asked to do some detective work by examining the causes of something or the effects of something. First read the two paragraphs that follow and answer the questions about them. Both paragraphs support their opening points by explaining a series of causes or a series of effects.

Paragraphs to Consider

Treatment of American Indians

¹Two major policies, the Indian Removal Act of 1830 and the Dawes Severalty Act of 1887, had profound and lasting effects on American Indians. ²In 1830, President Andrew Jackson signed the act that authorized the United States government to transfer eastern American Indians like the Cherokee into unclaimed western territories. ³After several years of court battles, what followed was one of the most heartbreaking events in early American history—The Trail of Tears. ⁴Thousands of Cherokee men, women, and children were forced to march more than a thousand miles to Oklahoma. ⁵Estimates say that at least four thousand died on the journey. ⁶Then, in 1887, the Dawes Act allowed the United States government the right to divide reservation lands among individual American Indians and their families. ⁷In other words, it gave plots of land to those who were willing to sign a registry, anglicize their name, and renounce allegiance to their tribe. ⁸Reservations were broken up, tribes fought among themselves, and the unity that was central to tribes' survival disappeared. ⁹Today, there are about three hundred reservations in the United States, but there are over five hundred recognized tribes. ¹⁰Most reservations are located in the western portion of the United States in areas that often lack natural resources, and many have high rates of poverty and unemployment.

Why I Stopped Smoking

¹For one thing, I realized that my cigarette smoke bothered others, irritating people's eyes and causing them to cough and sneeze. ²They also had to put up with my stinking smoker's breath. ³Also, cigarettes are a messy habit. ⁴Our house was littered with ashtrays piled high with butts, matchsticks, and ashes, and the children were always knocking them over. ⁵Cigarettes are expensive, and I estimated that the carton a week that I

continued

was smoking cost me about $2,000 a year. ^{6}Another reason I stopped was because I felt exploited. ^{7}I hated the thought of wealthy, greedy corporations making money off my sweat and blood. ^{8}The rich may keep getting richer, but—at least as regards cigarettes—with no thanks to me. ^{9}Cigarettes were also inconvenient. ^{10}Whenever I smoked, I would have to drink something to wet my dry throat, and that meant I had to keep going to the bathroom all the time. ^{11}I sometimes seemed to spend whole weekends doing nothing but smoking, drinking, and going to the bathroom. ^{12}Most of all I resolved to stop smoking when the message about cigarettes being harmful to health finally got through to me. ^{13}I'd known they could hurt the smoker—in fact, a heavy smoker I know from work is in Eagleville Hospital now with lung cancer. ^{14}But when I realized what secondhand smoke could do to my wife and children, causing them bronchial problems and even increasing their risk of cancer, it really bothered me.

About Unity

QUESTIONS

1. Which of the above paragraphs lacks a topic sentence?

   _____

About Support

2. What pieces of evidence does the author use to support the point that the Indian Removal Act and Dawes Severalty Act had lasting effects on American Indians?

   _____

   _____

   _____

   _____

3. How many separate causes are given in "Why I Stopped Smoking"?
   _____ four   _____ five   _____ six   seven _____

About Coherence

4. Which sentences in "Treatment of American Indians" contain transition words or phrases? (Write the sentence numbers here.)

   _____

Developing a Cause-and-Effect Paragraph

Development through Prewriting

In order to write a good cause-and-effect paragraph, you must clearly define an effect (*what* happened) and the contributing causes (*why* it happened). In addition, you will need to provide details that support the causes and effects you're writing about.

Jerome is the student author of "Why I Stopped Smoking." As soon as the topic occurred to him, he knew he had his *effect* (he had stopped smoking). His next task was to come up with a list of *causes* (reasons he had stopped). He decided to make a list of all the reasons for his quitting smoking that he could think of. This is what he came up with:

Annoyed others   Bad for health

Messy   Expensive

Taking his list, Jerome then jotted down details that supported each of those reasons:

<u>Annoyed others</u>

Bad breath

Irritates eyes

Makes other people cough

People hate the smell

<u>Messy</u>

Ashtrays, ashes, butts everywhere

Messes up my car interior

<u>Bad for health</u>

Marco in hospital with lung cancer

Secondhand smoke dangerous to family

My morning cough

<u>Expensive</u>

Carton a week costs more than $2,000 a year

Tobacco companies getting rich off me

Jerome then had an effect and four causes with details to support them. On the basis of this list, he wrote a first draft:

My smoking annoyed other people, making them cough and burning their eyes. I bothered them with my smoker's breath. Nonsmokers usually hate

continued

the smell of cigarettes and I got embarrassed when nonsmokers visited

my house. I saw them wrinkle their noses in disgust at the smell. It is

a messy habit. My house was full of loaded ashtrays that the kids were

always knocking over. My car was messy too. The price of cigarettes keeps

going up and I was spending too much on smokes. When I see things

in the paper about tobacco companies and their huge profits it made

me mad. A guy from work, Marco, who has smoked for years, is in the

hospital now with lung cancer. It doesn't look as though he's going to

make it. Secondhand smoke is bad for people too and I worried it would

hurt my wife and kids. Also I realized I was coughing once in a while.

Development through Revising

The next day, Jerome traded first drafts with his classmate Roger. This is what Roger had to say about Jerome's work:

> The biggest criticism I have is that you haven't used many transitions to tie your sentences together. Without them, the paragraph sounds like a list, not a unified piece of writing.
>
> Is one of your reasons more important than the others? If so, it would be good if you indicated that.
>
> You could add a little more detail in several places. For instance, how could secondhand smoke hurt your family? And how much were you spending on cigarettes?

As Jerome read his own paper, he realized he wanted to add one more reason to his paragraph: the inconvenience to himself. "Maybe it sounds silly to write about always getting drinks and going to the bathroom, but that's one of the ways that smoking takes over your life that you never think about when you start," he said. Jerome decided that the most important reason for quitting was health—both his family's and his own. Using Roger's comments and his own new idea, he produced the paragraph that appears on pages 190–191.

Writing a Cause-and-Effect Paragraph

GIVING PRAISE

WRITING ASSIGNMENT 1

Personal

Most of us find it easy to criticize other people, but we may find it harder to give compliments. In this assignment, you will be asked to write a one-paragraph letter praising someone. The letter may be to a person you know (for instance, a parent, relative, or friend); to a public figure (an actor, politician, religious leader, sports star, and so on); or to a company or organization (for example, a newspaper, a government agency, a store where you shop, or the manufacturer of a product you own).

Prewriting

a. The fact that you are writing this letter indicates that its recipient has had an *effect* on you: you like, admire, or appreciate the person or organization. Your job will be to put into words the *causes,* or reasons, for this good feeling. Begin by making a list of reasons for your admiration. Here, for example, are a few reasons a person might praise an automobile manufacturer:

> My car is dependable.
>
> The price was reasonable.
>
> I received prompt action on a complaint.
>
> The car is well designed.
>
> The car dealer was honest and friendly.
>
> The car has needed little maintenance.

Reasons for admiring a parent might include these:

> You are patient with me.
>
> You are fair.
>
> You have a great sense of humor.
>
> You encourage me in several ways.
>
> I know you have made sacrifices for me.

Develop your own list of reasons for admiring the person or organization you've chosen.

b. Now that you have a list of reasons, you need details to back up each reason. Jot down as many supporting details as you can for each reason. Here is what the writer of a letter to the car manufacturer might do:

<u>My car is dependable.</u>

Started during last winter's coldest days when neighbors' cars wouldn't start

Has never stranded me anywhere

<u>The price was reasonable.</u>

Costs less than other cars in its class

Came standard with more options than other cars of the same price

<u>I received prompt action on a complaint.</u>

When I complained about rattle in door, manufacturer arranged for a part to be replaced at no charge

<u>The car is well designed.</u>

Controls are easy to reach

Dashboard gauges are easy to read

in a writer's words

"Write freely and as rapidly as possible and throw the whole thing on paper. Never correct or rewrite until the whole thing is down. Rewrite in process is usually found to be an excuse for not going on."
—John Steinbeck

<u>The car dealer was honest and friendly.</u>

No pressure, no fake "special deal only today"

<u>The car has needed little maintenance.</u>

Haven't done anything but regular tune-ups and oil changes

c. Next, select from your list the three or four reasons that you can best support with effective details. These will make up the body of your letter.

d. Now number these three or four reasons by order of importance (1 as most important). Save your most important point for last.

e. For your topic sentence, make the positive statement you wish to support. For example, the writer of the letter to the car manufacturer might begin like this: "I am a very satisfied owner of a 2009 Camry."

f. Now combine your topic sentence, reasons, and supporting details, and write a draft of your letter.

Revising: Peer Review

If possible, put your letter aside for a day. Then read it aloud to a friend or classmate. As you and he or she listen to your words, you should both use the following checklist as a guide:

CAUSE AND EFFECT CHECKLIST: THE FOUR BASES

UNITY

✔ Is the topic sentence a positive statement that is supported by the details?

✔ Does the rest of your letter directly support the topic sentence?

SUPPORT

✔ Does the letter clearly state several different reasons for liking and admiring the person or organization?

✔ Is each of those reasons supported with specific evidence?

COHERENCE

✔ Are the sentences linked together with transitional words and phrases?

SENTENCE SKILLS

✔ Have you avoided wordiness and used concise wording?

✔ Are your sentences varied?

✔ Has the paragraph been checked for spelling and other sentence skills, as listed on the inside back cover of the book?

Continue revising your work until you and your reader can answer "yes" to all these questions.

WRITING ASSIGNMENT 2

Academic

WRITING ABOUT ADDICTION

What does this poster suggest? Look at the image and write a paragraph about a particular addiction or risky behavior. You might write about someone you know who is addicted to soda, shopping, watching TV, online gambling, or thrill seeking. In your paragraph, discuss several possible reasons for this addiction, or discuss several effects on the person's life. To create a persuasive tone to your paragraph, refer to Chapter 14, "Argument," and to add support using stories, refer to Chapter 7, "Narration."

Here are some sample topic sentences for this assignment:

My cousin is addicted to overeating, and her addiction is harming her in a number of ways.

There were at least three reasons why I became addicted to cigarettes.

WRITING ASSIGNMENT 3

Academic

ANALYZING AN EVENT

Investigate the reasons behind a current news event. For example, you may want to discover the causes of one of the following:

A civilian protest against a governmental decision

A new law, policy, or tax

A traffic accident, a fire, a plane crash, or some other disaster

The popularity of a new phone, car, or other gadget

Research the reasons for the event by reading current newspapers (especially big-city dailies that are covering the story in detail) or weekly news magazines (such as *Time* and *Newsweek*), watching television shows and specials, or consulting an Internet news source.

Decide on the major cause or causes of the event and their specific effects. Then write a paragraph explaining in detail the causes and effects. To avoid any possible plagiarism, you may want to read Chapter 20 to help you properly incorporate your research material. Below is a sample topic sentence for this assignment.

The rape and murder that occurred recently on Willow Street have caused much fear and caution throughout the neighborhood.

Note how this topic sentence uses general words (*fear, caution*) that can summarize specific supporting details. Support for the word *caution,* for example, might include specific ways in which people in the neighborhood are doing a better job of protecting themselves.

REFLECTIVE ACTIVITY

Reread the cause-and-effect paragraph you chose to write. Did your paragraph need only causes, effects, or both? Could you strengthen your paper by adding a mix of causes and effects or by focusing on one or the other? Would your paragraph benefit from added details like anecdotes (Chapter 7), some comparisons (Chapter 11), or more persuasive language (Chapter 14)? Choose what types of evidence will create a stronger paragraph and make the necessary revisions.

BEYOND THE CLASSROOM
Cause and Effect

Beyond the classroom, there are many instances where cause-and-effect writing would be used. For example, a nutritionist may have to explain to a patient the dietary causes of hypertension, or a pharmacist may have to explain the effects that a particular drug has on someone with diabetes.

For this writing assignment, you will write a cause-and-effect paragraph with a specific purpose and for a specific audience. You have two options.

Option 1

Assume that your boss has asked you to prepare a report about an issue that is affecting your career field. In your report, you should write what has caused this issue. For instance, nurses might be affected by a rise in workloads because of a lack of qualified nurses, budget cuts, or an increase in patients.

Option 2

Alternatively, think about the effects that this issue might have on your career field. Write a report to your boss indicating what the impact of this issue will be on you. For instance, nurses who have bigger workloads may be suffering exhaustion that leads to mistakes being made on the job.

EXPLORING WRITING ONLINE

Visit *The Why Files* at http://whyfiles.org/ and find an article to read. Then write a short paragraph that summarizes the causes and effects examined in your article. (For example, an article about Haiti's devastating 2010 earthquake might attempt to explain what caused so many buildings to collapse.)

Comparison or Contrast

RESPONDING TO IMAGES

Before you make a household purchase, you might compare brands, models, prices, and features. You might even look at consumer ratings. Write a paragraph in which you compare two products, such as two child car seats, two TVs, or two video game consoles. Think about the categories that you use to help you make your decision.

Comparison and contrast are two everyday thought processes. When we *compare* two things, we show how they are similar; when we *contrast* two things, we show how they are different. We might compare or contrast two brand-name products (for example, Nike versus Adidas running shoes), two television shows, two instructors, two jobs, two friends, or two courses of action we could take in a given situation. The purpose of comparing or contrasting is to understand each of the two things more clearly and, at times, to make judgments about them.

In this chapter, you will be asked to write a paragraph that compares or contrasts. First, however, you must learn the two common methods of developing a comparison or contrast paragraph. Read the two paragraphs that follow and try to explain the difference in the two methods of development.

Paragraphs to Consider

My Senior Prom

¹My senior prom was nothing like what I expected it to be. ²From the start of my senior year, I had pictured putting on a sleek silvery slip dress that my aunt would make and that would cost more than $500 in any store. ³No one else would have a gown as attractive as mine. ⁴I imagined my boyfriend coming to the door with a lovely deep-red corsage, and I pictured myself happily inhaling its perfume all evening long. ⁵I saw us setting off for the evening in his brother's BMW convertible. ⁶We would make a flourish as we swept in and out of a series of parties before the prom. ⁷Our evening would be capped by a delicious shrimp dinner at the prom and by dancing close together into the early morning hours. ⁸The prom was held on May 15, 2005, at the Pony Club on Black Horse Pike. ⁹However, because of an illness in her family, my aunt had no time to finish my gown and I had to buy the only dress I could find in my size at such short notice. ¹⁰Not only was it ugly, but it was my least favorite color, pink. ¹¹My corsage of red roses looked terrible on my pink gown, and I do not remember its having any scent. ¹²My boyfriend's brother was out of town, and I stepped outside and saw the stripped-down Chevy that he used at the races on weekends. ¹³We went to one party where I drank a lot of wine that made me sleepy and upset my stomach. ¹⁴After we arrived at the prom, I did not have much more to eat than a roll and some celery sticks. ¹⁵Worst of all, we left early without dancing because my boyfriend and I had had a fight several days before, and at the time we did not really want to be with each other.

Keys to Success in College

¹College is very different from high school, and in order to succeed, students should practice good organizational skills that aren't commonly needed in high school. ²First of all, instead of going to class every day,

continued

students may attend college classes only one day a week, three days a week, or even at night. ³With this flexibility, students need to schedule blocks of study time in order to make sure they are getting their work done on time because it can be very tempting not to study until the last minute. ⁴In high school, students are in class for at least six hours a day, and teachers often schedule time in class to work on assignments. ⁵Conversely, in college, students may spend as little as two hours a day in class, and professors rarely allow in-class time to work on assignments. ⁶In high school, students may need to spend an hour or two each evening on homework, but in college, students are expected to work on homework for at least two hours for each hour they are in class. ⁷High school teachers and college professors have very different attitudes toward students' social lives. ⁸High school teachers often accommodate students' activities like prom, sports, and school plays by assigning less homework, so students can participate in the activities. ⁹On the other hand, college professors aren't concerned about activities outside of the classroom; regardless of students' schedules, they must complete the assignments on time. ¹⁰Finally, in high school, teachers don't always use syllabi with course schedules, and they spend a lot of time reminding students about due dates. ¹¹College professors, however, hand out the syllabi at the beginning of the semester and expect students to complete the assignments by the due dates with few or no reminders. ¹²Students who are new to college may find it difficult at first, but with good organization and planning, students can succeed.

Complete this comment: The difference in the methods of contrast in the two paragraphs is that

_____

_____

_____

Compare your answer with the following explanation of the two methods of development used in comparison or contrast paragraphs.

Methods of Development

There are two common methods, or formats, of development in a comparison or contrast paper. One format presents the details *one side at a time*. The other presents the details *point by point*. Each format is explained next.

One Side at a Time

Look at the outline of "My Senior Prom":

Topic sentence: My senior prom was nothing like what I had expected it to be.

A. Expectations (first half of paragraph)

   1. Dress (expensive, silver)

   2. Corsage (deep red, fragrant)

   3. Car (BMW convertible)

   4. Parties (many)

   5. Dinner (shrimp)

   6. Dancing (all night)

B. Reality (second half of paragraph)

   1. Dress (ugly, pink)

   2. Corsage (wrong color, no scent)

   3. Car (stripped-down Chevy)

   4. Parties (only one)

   5. Dinner (roll and celery)

   6. Dancing (none because of quarrel)

When you use the one-side-at-a-time method, follow the same order of points of contrast or comparison for each side, as in the outline above. For example, both the first half of the paragraph and the second half begin with the same idea: what dress would be worn. Then both sides go on to the corsage, the car, and so on.

Point by Point

Now look at the outline of "Keys to Success in College":

Topic sentence: College is very different from high school, and in order to succeed students should practice good organizational skills that aren't commonly needed in high school.

A. Class schedules

   1. High school students go to school every day.

   2. College students have varied schedules.

   3. High school students go to school at least six hours a day.

   4. College students may be in class as little as two hours a day.

B. Homework

   1. High school students may have only an hour or two of homework.

   2. College students need to spend at least two hours on homework for each hour of class.

C. Attitudes toward social activities

   1. High school teachers accommodate student activities by adjusting assignments and homework.

2. College professors expect students to meet assignment deadlines regardless of extracurricular activities.

D. Syllabus and deadline reminders

1. High school teachers don't always use syllabi with schedules and they remind students of due dates.

2. College professors hand out syllabi with due dates at the beginning of the semester and rarely remind students of the deadlines.

The outline shows how the two experiences are contrasted point by point. First, the writer contrasts the schedule differences between high school and college. Next, the writer contrasts the homework differences between high school and college. Then the writer contrasts the attitudes between high school teachers and college professors. Finally, the writer contrasts how teachers and college professors tell students about due dates.

When you begin a comparison or contrast paper, you should decide right away which format you are going to use: one side at a time or point by point. An outline is an essential step in helping you decide which format will be more workable for your topic. Keep in mind, however, that an outline is just a guide, not a permanent commitment. If you later feel that you've chosen the wrong format, you can reshape your outline to the other format.

| ACTIVITY 1 | Complete the partial outlines provided for the two paragraphs that follow. |

1.

Reorganization Summary Report for Smith Family

In order to instill a sense of calm inside the main floor of the Smith home, the team from Organize It! reorganized, discarded, and repurposed items within the home. Before the reorganization took place, the owners' home was confined, dark, and crowded. The kitchen counters were covered with appliances and nonperishable food items. Many of the drawers were stuffed and didn't close properly. Several cupboards contained both food items and dishes. The living room had two couches, three chairs, and four tables crammed around a large television. The floor space of the living room was eaten up by toys, DVDs, and books. The dining room contained a table and four chairs, but all surface space, including the floor, was covered in toys, projects, and outdated mail. The final room of the main floor, the bathroom, was overfilled with towels, soap products, and toilet paper. After the organization team worked for three days, the differences were obvious. Many of the appliances in the kitchen were no longer working, so they were properly discarded, opening space on the counters. Cupboards were organized by purpose—food was with food, dishes with dishes, and glasses with glasses. Organization was created in the drawers by using dividers and baskets. Nonworking and duplicate items were discarded and multiple items were sorted; some were kept and others were donated.

---

continued

Similar organization occurred in the living and dining areas. All items were pulled out of the rooms and then sorted into keep, donate, and discard. The furniture in the living room was rearranged to provide more space, and a specific area was set aside for a play area. Toys were sorted and stored in large baskets to provide easy access and easy cleanup. DVDs and books were organized and put into a new bookcase. One of the tables from the living room was repurposed into a desk in the dining room. On this desk, several baskets were placed to help the owner organize mail and keep track of bills. The bathroom went through a similar process as all items were removed; only necessary items like spare rolls of toilet paper and a couple of extra hand towels were put back. Afterward, the team demonstrated how the owners could work to maintain the new sense of calm on the main level and create the same sense of calm on the upper levels.

Topic sentence: In order to instill a sense of calm inside the main floor of the Smith home, the team from Organize It! reorganized, discarded, and repurposed items within the home.

   a. Before the reorganization

      (1) _____

      (2) _____

      (3) _____

      (4) _____

   b. After the reorganization

      (1) _____

          _____

      (2) _____

      (3) _____

          _____

      (4) _____

Complete the following statement: Paragraph 1 uses the _____ method of development.

2.

Good and Bad Horror Movies

    A good horror movie is easily distinguishable from a bad one. A good horror movie, first of all, has both male and female victims. Both sexes suffer terrible fates at the hands of monsters and maniacs.

continued

Therefore, everyone in the audience has a chance to identify with the victim. Bad horror movies, on the other hand, tend to concentrate on women, especially half-dressed ones. These movies are obviously prejudiced against half the human race. Second, a good horror movie inspires compassion for its characters. For example, the audience will feel sympathy for the victims in the horror classics about the Wolfman, played by Lon Chaney, Jr., and also for the Wolfman himself, who is shown to be a sad victim of fate. In contrast, a bad horror movie encourages feelings of aggression and violence in viewers. For instance, in the *Halloween* films, the murders are seen from the murderer's point of view. The effect is that the audience stalks the victims along with the killer and feels the same thrill he does. Finally, every good horror movie has a sense of humor. In *Alien*, as a crew member is coughing and choking just before the horrible thing bursts out of his chest, a colleague chides him, "The food ain't *that* bad, man." Humor provides relief from the horror and makes the characters more human. A bad horror movie, though, is humorless and boring. One murder is piled on top of another, and the characters are just cardboard figures. Bad horror movies may provide cheap thrills, but the good ones touch our emotions and live forever.

Topic sentence: **A good horror movie is easily distinguished from a bad one.**

    a. Kinds of victims

        (1) _____

        (2) _____

    b. Effect on audience

        (1) _____

        (2) _____

    c. Tone

        (1) _____

        (2) _____

Complete the following statement: Paragraph 2 uses the _____ method of development.

Additional Paragraph to Consider

Read this additional paragraph of comparison or contrast and then answer the questions that follow.

My Broken Dream

¹When I became a police officer in my town, the job was not as I had dreamed it would be. ²I began to dream about being a police officer at about age ten. ³I could picture myself wearing a handsome blue uniform with an impressive-looking badge on my chest. ⁴I could also picture myself driving a powerful patrol car through town and seeing everyone stare at me with envy. ⁵But most of all, I dreamed of wearing a gun and using all the equipment that "TV cops" use. ⁶My favorite "TV cop" is Elliot Stabler on *Law and Order SVU.* ⁷I knew everyone would be proud of me. ⁸I could almost hear the guys on the block saying, "Boy, Steve made it big. ⁹Did you hear he's a cop?" ¹⁰I dreamed of leading an exciting life, solving big crimes, and meeting lots of people. ¹¹I knew that if I became a cop, everyone in town would look up to me. ¹²However, when I actually did become a police officer, I soon found out that the reality was different. ¹³My first disappointment came when I was sworn in and handed a well-used, baggy uniform. ¹⁴My disappointment continued when I was given a badge that looked like something pulled out of a Cracker Jack box. ¹⁵I was assigned a beat-up old junker and told that it would be my patrol car. ¹⁶It had a striking resemblance to a car that had lost in a demolition derby at a stock-car raceway. ¹⁷Disappointment seemed to continue. ¹⁸I soon found out that I was not the envy of all my friends. ¹⁹My job was not as exciting as I had dreamed it would be, either. ²⁰Instead of solving robberies and murders every day, I found that I spent a great deal of time comforting a local resident because a neighborhood dog had watered his favorite bush.

About Unity

1. Which sentence in "My Broken Dream" should be eliminated in the interest of paragraph unity? (*Write the sentence number here.*) _____

About Support

2. After which sentence are supporting details needed? _____

About Coherence

3. What method of development (one side at a time or point by point) is used in "My Broken Dream"?

QUESTIONS

Developing a Comparison or Contrast Paragraph

Development through Prewriting

Gayle, the author of "My Senior Prom," had little trouble thinking of a topic for her comparison or contrast paragraph.

"My instructor said, 'You might compare or contrast two individuals, jobs you've had, or places you've lived,'" Gayle said. "Then he added, 'Or you might compare or contrast your expectations of a situation with the reality.' I immediately thought of my prom—boy, were my expectations different from the reality! I had thought it would be the high point of my senior year, but instead it was a total disaster."

Because she is a person who likes to think visually, Gayle started her preparations for her paragraph by clustering. She found this a helpful way to "see" the relationships between the points she was developing. Her diagram is shown here:

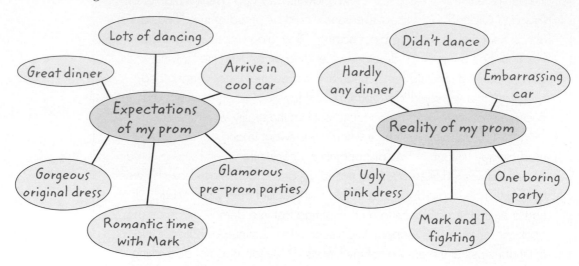

Taking a detail first from the "Expectations" part of the diagram, then one from the "Reality" portion, then another from "Expectations," and so on, Gayle began to write her paragraph using a point-by-point format:

> My senior prom was nothing like what I expected. First of all, I expected to be wearing a beautiful dress that my aunt would make for me. But because she couldn't finish it in time, I had to buy an ugly one at the last minute. Second, I thought I'd have a wonderful romantic evening with my boyfriend. But we'd been fighting that week and by the time the prom came around we were barely speaking. I thought we'd have a great time stopping in at lots of parties before the prom, but we went to only one and I left with an upset stomach.

Gayle stopped here, because she wasn't satisfied with the way the paragraph was developing. "I wanted the reader to picture the way I had imagined my prom, and I didn't like interrupting that picture with the reality of

the evening. So I decided to try the one-side-at-a-time approach instead."
Here is Gayle's first draft:

> My senior prom was nothing like what I expected. I imagined myself wearing a beautiful, expensive-looking dress that my aunt would make. I thought my boyfriend and I would have a wonderful romantic evening together. We'd dance all through the night and we would cruise around in my boyfriend's brother's hot car. We would stop in at a lot of fun pre-prom parties, I thought, and we'd have a delicious shrimp dinner at the prom itself. But instead my uncle had a gallbladder attack that the doctor thought might be a heart attack and my aunt went to the hospital with him instead of finishing my dress. I had to go to the mall at the last minute and buy an ugly dress that nobody else had wanted. Mark and I had been fighting all week. Because he's in track and has a part-time job too we don't have much time together and still he wants to go out on Saturdays with his guy friends. So by the night of the prom we were hardly speaking to each other. We went to only one party before the prom and I left it feeling sick. And the restaurant was so crowded and noisy that I hardly got anything to eat. Because we were angry at each other, we didn't dance at all. And instead of his brother's luxury car, we had to use a stripped-down racing car.

Development through Revising

Gayle's instructor reviewed her first draft. Here are his comments:

> All this is very promising, but some of your details are out of order—for example, you mention the pre-prom parties after the dance itself. Be sure to follow the evening's sequence of events.
>
> More descriptive details are needed! For instance, what was your "beautiful" dress supposed to look like, and what did the "ugly" one you ended up with look like?
>
> You include some unnecessary information: for example, the details of your uncle's illness. Everything in your paragraph should support your topic sentence.

Following her instructor's suggestions (and remembering a few more details she wanted to include), Gayle created the outline on pages 200–201, and then she wrote the version of her paragraph that appears on page 199.

Writing a Comparison or Contrast Paragraph

LOOKING AT LIFE

Write a paragraph in which you compare or contrast your life in the real world with your life in an imagined "perfect world." If the purpose of your writing is to inform, your paragraph will be serious. If your purpose is to entertain, your paragraph will be humorous.

Prewriting

a. As your "real life" and "ideal life" are too broad for a paragraph, choose three specific areas to focus on. You might select any of the areas below, or think of a specific area yourself.

Work	Friends
Money	Possessions
Romance	Housing
Physical location	Talents
Personal appearance	

b. Write the name of one of your three areas (for example, "Work"), across the top of a page. Divide the page into two columns. Label one column "real world" and the other "perfect world." Under "real world," write down as many details as you can think of describing your real-life work situation. Under "perfect world," write down details describing what your perfect work life would be like. Repeat the process on separate pages for your other two major areas.

c. Write a topic sentence for your paragraph. Here's an example: "In my perfect world, my life would be quite different in the areas of work, money, and housing."

d. Decide which approach you will take: one side at a time or point by point.

e. Write a scratch outline that reflects the format you have selected. The outline for a point-by-point format would look like this:

Topic sentence: In my perfect world, my life would be quite different in the areas of work, money, and housing.

1. Work
   a. Real-life work
   b. Perfect-world work
2. Money
   a. Real-life money
   b. Perfect-world money
3. Housing
   a. Real-life housing
   b. Perfect-world housing

The outline for a one-side-at-a-time format would look like this:

Topic sentence: In my perfect world, my life would be quite different in the areas of work, money, and housing.

1. Real life
   a. Work
   b. Money
   c. Housing
2. Perfect world
   a. Work
   b. Money
   c. Housing

f. Drawing from the three pages of details you generated in step *b*, complete your outline by jotting down your strongest supporting details for each point.

g. Write the first draft of your paragraph.

Revising: Peer Review

Reread your paragraph, and then show it to a friend or classmate who will give you honest feedback. You should both review it with these questions in mind:

COMPARISON OR CONTRAST CHECKLIST: THE FOUR BASES

UNITY

✔ Does the paragraph have a clearly stated topic sentence that states the main idea, identifies the two things being compared or contrasted, and identifies the three points of comparison or contrast?

✔ Is the rest of your paragraph on target in support of your topic sentence?

SUPPORT

✔ Does the paragraph provide specific details that describe both the "real-life" situation and the "perfect world" situation?

COHERENCE

✔ Does the paragraph follow a consistent format: point by point or one side at a time?

SENTENCE SKILLS

✔ Is there a consistent point of view throughout the paragraph?

✔ Does the paragraph contain specific rather than general words?

✔ Have you avoided wordiness and used concise wording?

✔ Are your sentences varied?

✔ Has the paragraph been checked for spelling and other sentence skills, as listed on the inside back cover of the book?

Continue revising your work until you and your reader can answer "yes" to all these questions.

WRITING ASSIGNMENT 2

CONSIDERING ALTERNATIVES

Write a comparison or contrast paragraph on one of the topics listed below. Once you choose a topic, you will need to decide if you want to emphasize comparisons, contrasting details, or a mixture of both. Some of these topics may require you to use research (Chapter 20) or incorporate other modes of writing like description (Chapter 8) and exemplification (Chapter 6).

Here is an example of a possible topic sentence for a paper that contrasts a dream vacation and a real vacation:

> I have always wanted to take a luxury cruise around the world, but my budget only allows road trips through my home state.

- A used car versus a new one
- An ad on television versus an ad for the same product in a magazine
- Different ways to lose weight
- News in a newspaper versus news on the Internet
- *People* versus *OK!* (or any other two popular magazines)
- People who love their jobs versus people who hate their jobs
- Two historical events
- Two or more stages in a person's life
- Two poems, two short stories, or two books
- Two political candidates
- Working parents versus stay-at-home parents

WRITING ASSIGNMENT 3

ANALYZING FAVORITE FOODS

Dave Zinczenko uses comparison and contrast in his popular weight-loss book, *Eat This, Not That!* by comparing two food items—cheeseburgers, pizza, or chicken meals, for example—and then contrasting calories and grams of fat.

Write a paragraph in which you compare two food items that are familiar to you, and then contrast at least two qualities that both items share. Zinczenko focuses on calories and fat, but you can focus on flavor, spiciness, authenticity, or whatever qualities seem appropriate. Here are some suggestions:

Grandma's fried chicken and KFC fried chicken

homemade burritos and Taco Bell burritos

organic strawberries and nonorganic strawberries

New York–style pizza and Chicago-style pizza

chocolate ice cream and chocolate frozen yogurt

Book Design by George Karabotsos, used with permission.

Beyond the classroom, you will find yourself and others comparing and contrasting people, places, and things. Sales representatives contrast their products with those of competitors. Historians compare and contrast events, circumstances, and problems that have occurred in different ages. Politicians contrast their voting records with those of their opponents during election campaigns. Consumer advocates compare and contrast different makes or brands of a product to help consumers make appropriate decisions. Automotive engineers use contrast to explain the workings of two different fuel or braking systems.

For this writing assignment, you will write a comparison or contrast paragraph with a specific purpose and for a specific audience.

Imagine that you are living in an apartment building in which new tenants are making life unpleasant for you. Write a letter of complaint to your landlord comparing and contrasting life before and after these neighbors arrived. You might want to focus on one or more of the following:

Noise

Guests

Trash

Safety hazards

Parking situation

BEYOND THE CLASSROOM

Comparison or Contrast

Personal

EXPLORING WRITING ONLINE

Visit two networking sites, such as LinkedIn at http://www.linkedin.com and *Facebook* at http://www.facebook.com. Click on the "About" link to find out more about each site. Then write a paragraph in which you compare or contrast each site's unique purpose and audience.

Definition

RESPONDING TO IMAGES

What are some words that come to mind as you look at this photo of the astronauts on the Columbia Space Shuttle Mission STS-107? Write a paragraph in which you define one of those words. For example, you may look at the photograph and think bravery, danger, or exploration.

In talking with other people, we sometimes offer informal definitions to explain just what we mean by a particular term. Suppose, for example, we say to a friend, "Keith can be so clingy." We might then expand on our idea of "clingy" by saying, "You know, a clingy person needs to be with someone every single minute. If Keith's best friend makes plans that don't include him, he becomes hurt. And when he dates someone, he calls her several times a day and gets upset if she even goes to the grocery store without him. He hangs on to people too tightly." In a written definition, we make clear in a more complete and formal way our own personal understanding of a term. Such a definition typically starts with one meaning of a term. The meaning is then illustrated with a series of examples or a story.

In this section, you will be asked to write a paragraph that begins with a one-sentence definition; that sentence will be the topic sentence. The two student papers below are both examples of definition paragraphs. Read them and then answer the questions that follow.

Paragraphs to Consider

Disillusionment

[1]Disillusionment is the feeling we have when one of our most cherished beliefs is stolen from us. [2]I learned about disillusionment firsthand the day Mr. Keller, our eighth-grade teacher, handed out the grades for our class biology projects. [3]I had worked hard to assemble what I thought was the best insect collection any school had ever seen. [4]For weeks, I had set up homemade traps around our house, in the woods, and in vacant lots. [5]At night, I would stretch a white sheet between two trees, shine a lantern on it, and collect the night-flying insects that gathered there. [6]With my own money, I had bought killing jars, insect pins, gummed labels, and display boxes. [7]I carefully arranged related insects together, with labels listing each scientific name and the place and date of capture. [8]Slowly and painfully, I wrote and typed the report that accompanied my project at the school science fair. [9]In contrast, my friend Eddie did almost nothing for his project. [10]He had his father, a psychologist, build an impressive maze complete with live rats and a sign that read, "You are the trainer." [11]A person could lift a little plastic door, send a rat running through the maze, and then hit a button to release a pellet of rat food as a reward. [12]This exhibit turned out to be the most popular one at the fair. [13]I felt sure that our teacher would know that Eddie could not have built it, and I was certain that my hard work would be recognized and rewarded. [14]Then the grades were finally handed out, and I was crushed. [15]Eddie had gotten an A+, but my grade was a B. [16]I suddenly realized that honesty and hard work don't always pay off in the end. [17]The idea that life is not fair, that sometimes it pays to cheat, hit me with such force that I felt sick. [18]I will never forget that moment.

Classroom Ringmasters

¹Elementary teachers should not be self-important experts, but enthusiastic ringmasters. ²Like ringmasters in circuses, teachers need to organize, introduce, and guide, but instead of circus acts and performers, teachers work with information and students. ³Many ringmasters participate in the planning and organizing of the show; if they weren't involved, performers wouldn't know their cues, stagehands wouldn't know when to set up, and the show would not become a unified experience. ⁴Teachers are also in charge of planning and organizing their lessons, but some teachers fail to do this and, like a bad circus, create a disjointed and choppy experience. ⁵My sixth-grade language arts teacher rarely had any plan for what was going to occur each day. ⁶As a result, our class spent many days repeating lessons or skipping over information, which led to frustration and poor learning. ⁷I hated the reading selections that we were assigned for language arts. ⁸Another job of circus ringmasters is to introduce the acts that are coming up. ⁹Teachers also prepare students for and introduce students to new information. ¹⁰For a new math unit on subtraction, a second-grade teacher brought in clusters of grapes. ¹¹She passed out filled bowls to the students and had them count the individual grapes. ¹²Once they knew how many grapes they had, the teacher invited the students to eat some of the grapes. ¹³She then had the students count up their new totals. ¹⁴Within a very short period, the students were excited about the new topic of subtraction and already had a strong understanding of what it meant, as well as a nice snack. ¹⁵Like a good ringmaster, a good teacher has to make sure that each "act" runs smoothly into another without any major breaks, overlaps, or mishaps. ¹⁶My son's first-grade teacher was the ultimate ringmaster. ¹⁷He was full of enthusiasm for his subject, and students responded. ¹⁸It was hard for six-year-olds not to get excited about spelling when the teacher was standing on his desk leading the class in a spelling cheer. ¹⁹But like a good ringmaster, the teacher never let the lesson get out of hand; instead, he transitioned the students from spelling cheers to quiet reading time with the precision of a veteran director. ²⁰There are many types of teachers, but the best recognize that their jobs are to keep the show running, not be the star of the show.

QUESTIONS

About Unity

1. Which sentence in "Classroom Ringmasters" should be omitted in the interest of paragraph unity? (*Write the sentence number here.*)
   _____

About Support

2. Which paragraph develops its definitions through a series of short narrative examples?

_____

_____

3. Which paragraph develops its definition through a single extended example?

_____

About Coherence

4. Which paragraph uses time order to organize its details?

_____

Developing a Definition Paragraph

Development through Prewriting

When Harry, the author of "Disillusionment," started working on his assignment, he did not know what he wanted to write about. He looked around the house for inspiration. His two-year-old twins racing around the room made him think about defining "energy." The fat cat asleep on a sunny windowsill suggested that he might write about "laziness" or "relaxation." Still not sure of a topic, he looked over his notes from that day's class. His instructor had jotted a list of terms on the blackboard, saying, "Maybe you could focus on what one of these words has meant in your own life." Harry looked over the words he had copied down: _honesty, willpower, faith, betrayal, disillusionment_—"When I got to the word 'disillusionment,' the eighth-grade science fair flashed into my mind," Harry said. "That was a bitter experience that definitely taught me what disillusionment was all about."

Because the science fair had occurred many years before, Harry had to work to remember it well. He decided to try the technique of questioning himself to come up with the details of what had happened. Here are the questions Harry asked himself and the answers he wrote:

> _When did I learn about disillusionment?_
>
> _When I was in eighth grade_
>
> _Where did it happen?_
>
> _At the school science fair_
>
> _Who was involved?_
>
> _Me, Eddie Loomis and his father, and Mr. Keller_

continued

in a writer's words

"New writers are often told, 'Write what you know.' I would broaden that by saying, 'Write what you know emotionally.'"

—Marjorie Franco

What happened?

I had worked very hard on my insect collection. Eddie had done almost nothing but he had a rat maze that his father had built. I got a B on my project while Eddie got an A+.

Why was the experience so disillusioning?

I thought my hard work would be rewarded. I was sure Mr. Keller would recognize that I had put far more effort into my project than Eddie had. When Eddie won, I learned that cheating can pay off and that honest work isn't always rewarded.

How did I react?

I felt sick to my stomach. I wanted to confront Mr. Keller and Eddie and make them see how unfair the grades were. But I knew I'd just look like a poor loser, so I didn't do anything.

On the basis of this experience, how would I define "disillusionment"?

It's finding out that something you really believed in isn't true.

Drawing from the ideas generated by his self-questioning, Harry wrote the following draft of his paragraph:

Disillusionment is finding out that one of your most important beliefs isn't true. I learned about disillusionment at my eighth-grade science fair. I had worked very hard on my project, an insect collection. I was sure it would get an A. I had worked so hard on it, even spending nights outside making sure it was very good. My friend Eddie also did a project, but he barely worked on his at all. Instead, he had his father build a maze for a rat to run through. The trainer lifted a little plastic door to let the rat into the maze, and if it completed the maze, the trainer could release a pellet of food for it to eat. It was a nice project, but the point is that Eddie hadn't made it. He just made things like the banner that hung over it. Mr. Keller was our science teacher. He gave Eddie an A+ and me just a B. So that really taught me about disillusionment.

Development through Revising

The next day, Harry's teacher divided the class into peer-review groups of three. The groups reviewed each member's paragraph. Harry was grouped with Curtis and Jocelyn. After reading through Harry's paper several times, the group had the following discussion:

> Jocelyn: "My first reaction is that I want to know more about your project. You give details about Eddie's, but not many about your own. What was so good about it? You need to show us, not just tell us. Also, you said that you worked very hard, but you didn't show us how hard."
>
> Harry: "Yeah. I remember my project clearly, but I guess the reader has to know what it was like and how much effort went into it."
>
> Curtis: "I like your topic sentence, but when I finished the paragraph I wasn't sure what 'important belief' you'd learned wasn't true. What would you say that belief was?"
>
> Harry: "I'd believed that honest hard work would always be rewarded. I found out that it doesn't always happen that way, and that cheating can actually win."
>
> Curtis: "I think you need to include that in your paragraph."
>
> Jocelyn: "I'd like to read how you felt or reacted after you saw your grade, too. If you don't explain that, the paragraph ends sort of abruptly."

Harry agreed with his classmates' suggestions. After he had gone through several revisions, he produced the version that appears on page 213.

Writing a Definition Paragraph

PORTRAYING A PERSON

WRITING ASSIGNMENT 1

Write a paragraph that defines one of the following terms. Each term refers to a certain kind of person.

Artist	Geek	Pessimist
Beauty	Genius	Philanthropist
Bubba	Good neighbor	Pushover
Charmer	Good sport	Romantic
Con-artist	Idealist	Self-promoter
Control freak	Intellect	Showoff
Coward	Introvert	Slacker
Darwin Award winner	Know-it-all	Snob
Fair-weather friend	Leader	Trustworthy
Feminist	Manipulator	Workaholic
Flirt	Optimist	
Friend-padder	Pack rat	

Prewriting

a.   Write a topic sentence for your definition paragraph. This is a two-part process:

- *First,* place the term in a class, or category. For example, if you are writing about a certain kind of person, the general category is *person.* If you are describing a type of friend, the general category is *friend.*

- *Second,* describe what you consider the special feature or features that set your term apart from other members of its class. For instance, say what *kind* of person you are writing about or what *type* of friend.

In the following topic sentence, try to identify three things: the term being defined, the class it belongs to, and the special feature that sets the term apart from other members of the class.

A chocoholic is a person who craves chocolate.

The term being defined is *chocoholic.* The category it belongs to is *person.* The words that set *chocoholic* apart from any other person are *craves chocolate.*

Below is another example of a topic sentence for this assignment. It is a definition of *whiner.* The class, or category, is underlined: A whiner is a type of person. The words that set the term *whiner* apart from other members of the class are double-underlined.

A whiner is a <u>person</u> who <u><u>feels wronged by life.</u></u>

In the following sample topic sentences, underline the class and double-underline the special features.

A clotheshorse is a person who needs new clothes to be happy.

The class clown is a student who gets attention through silly behavior.

A worrywart is a person who sees danger everywhere.

b.   Develop your definition by using one of the following methods:

Examples. Give several examples that support your topic sentence.

Extended example. Use one longer example to support your topic sentence.

Contrast. Support your topic sentence by contrasting what your term *is* with what it is *not.* For instance, you may want to define a *fair-weather friend* by contrasting his or her actions with those of a true friend.

c.   Once you have created a topic sentence and decided how to develop your paragraph, make a scratch outline. If you are using a contrast method of development, remember to present the details one side at a time or point by point (see pages 200–204).

d.   Write a first draft of your paragraph.

Revising: Peer Review

Before revising, have a friend or classmate read your paragraph. Together, you should respond to the questions in the checklist on the next page:

DEFINITION CHECKLIST: THE FOUR BASES

UNITY

✔ Does the topic sentence (1) place your term in a class and (2) name some special features that set it apart from its class?

✔ Is the rest of the paragraph on target in support of the topic sentence?

SUPPORT

✔ Have you made a clear choice to develop the topic sentence through either several examples, one extended example, or contrast?

COHERENCE

✔ If you have chosen to illustrate your topic through contrast, have you consistently followed either a point-by-point or a one-side at-a-time format?

✔ Have you used appropriate transitions (*another, in addition, in contrast, for example*) to tie your thoughts together?

SENTENCE SKILLS

✔ Have you used a consistent point of view throughout the paragraph?

✔ Have you used specific rather than general words?

✔ Have you avoided wordiness and used concise wording?

✔ Are your sentences varied?

✔ Has the paragraph been checked for spelling and other sentence skills, as listed on the inside back cover of the book?

Continue revising your work until you and your reader can answer "yes" to all these questions.

DESCRIBING IN FIVE

WRITING ASSIGNMENT 2

Many times during job interviews, people are asked to describe themselves in five adjectives; in essence, they are being asked to define themselves. For this assignment, you are to pretend that you are preparing for a job interview and write a paragraph that answers the question, "What five adjectives would you use to describe yourself and why?"

As a guide in writing your paragraph, use the suggestions for "Prewriting" and "Revising" in Writing Assignment 1. Also, to add support and detail to your paragraph, you will need to offer examples that demonstrate your definition of the adjectives you are using to describe yourself. Read Chapter 7, "Narration," for ways to incorporate stories as part of your definition. Read Chapter 8, "Description," for ways to improve your specific details to better support your definition. Read Chapter 14, "Argument," for ways to create a persuasive tone to help you convince your audience that the adjectives you have chosen really do define you.

Here are some sample topic sentences:

- I will make a great nurse because I am honest, compassionate, intelligent, independent, and confident.

- The five words that describe me are dedicated, funny, bold, logical, and thoughtful.

- Good teachers should be intelligent, creative, compassionate, funny, and understanding, which are five words that describe me.

WRITING ASSIGNMENT 3

Academic

EXPLORING STRESS

Since stress affects all of us to some degree—in the workplace (as shown in the cartoon here), in school, in our families, and in our everyday lives—it is a useful term to explore. Write a paragraph defining *stress*. Organize your paragraph in one of these ways:

- Use a series of examples (see pages 148–158) of stress.

- Use narration (see pages 159–167) to provide one longer example of stress: Create a hypothetical person (or use a real person) and show how this person's typical morning or day illustrates your definition of *stress*.

Using strategies described in Chapter 20 (pages 367–391), do some research on stress. Your reading will help you think about how to proceed with the paper.

© Mike Baldwin/Cornered

"You win some, you lose some. Don't worry about it. No one's keeping score."

Reprinted by permission of CartoonStock. Ltd.
www.CartoonStock.com.

HINT

Do not simply write a series of general, abstract sentences that repeat and reword your definition. If you concentrate on providing specific support, you will avoid the common trap of getting lost in a maze of generalities.

Make sure your paragraph is set firmly on the four bases: unity, support, coherence, and sentence skills. Edit the next-to-final draft of the paragraph carefully for sentence-skills errors, including spelling.

BEYOND THE CLASSROOM

Definition

Work

Beyond the classroom, there are many instances where definition writing would be used. For example, a restaurant manager may have to define the job requirements for a newly hired food server, or a zookeeper may need to provide a descriptive definition of an animal for the signage of a new exhibit. Attorneys often define legal terms or complicated legal procedures to clients, and computer technicians

continued

and instructors sometimes need to explain terms such as *flash drive* or *spyware*. A health professional might have to explain CAT or open MRI to a patient, and an investment counselor or banker might be asked to define terms like *hedge fund* or *ARM* (*adjustable-rate mortgage*).

For this writing assignment, you will write a definition paragraph with a specific purpose and for a specific audience.

Imagine that one of your coworkers has just quit, creating a new job opening. Since you have been working there for a while, your boss has asked you to write a description of the position. That description—a detailed definition of the job—will be sent to employment agencies. These agencies will be responsible for interviewing candidates. Choose any position you know about, and write a paragraph defining it. First state the purpose of the job, and then list its duties and responsibilities. Finally, describe the qualifications for the position. Below is a sample topic sentence for this assignment:

> Purchasing clerk is a position in which someone provides a variety of services to suppliers and contractors.

In a paragraph with this topic sentence, the writer would go on to list and describe the various services the purchasing clerk must provide.

EXPLORING WRITING ONLINE

Think of a word used as slang that has a separate formal meaning (for example *chill*, *sweet*, *tight*, *cheesy*, etc.). Visit http://www.urbandictionary.com to look at the slang definitions and uses. Then, visit http://www.dictionary.com and find the word's formal meaning. Write a paragraph that discusses the differences in meanings, when they would be used, and how listeners know the difference. Review Chapter 11, "Comparison or Contrast," to help organize your paragraph.

Division-Classification

RESPONDING TO IMAGES

Modern technology allows us to communicate in so many ways. In the span of a few minutes, we might make a call to the babysitter, send a text message to our friend, and e-mail our teacher about a quiz. Write a paragraph in which you classify three different means of communication and explain how each one is used.

If you were doing the laundry, you might begin by separating the clothing into piles. You would then put all the whites in one pile and all the colors in another. Or you might classify the laundry not according to color, but according to fabric—putting all cottons in one pile, polyesters in another, and so on. *Classifying* is the process of taking many things and separating them into categories. We generally classify to better manage or understand many things. Librarians classify books into groups (novels, travel, health, etc.) to make them easier to find. A scientist sheds light on the world by classifying all living things into two main groups: animals and plants.

Dividing, in contrast, is taking one thing and breaking it down into parts. We often divide, or analyze, to better understand, teach, or evaluate something. For instance, a tinkerer might take apart a clock to see how it works; a science text might divide a tree into its parts to explain their functions. A music reviewer may analyze the elements of a band's performance—for example, the skill of the various players, rapport with the audience, selections, and so on.

In short, if you are classifying, you are sorting *numbers of things* into categories. If you are dividing, you are breaking *one thing* into parts. It all depends on your purpose—you might classify flowers into various types or divide a single flower into its parts.

In this section, you will be asked to write a paragraph in which you classify a group of things into categories according to a single principle. To prepare for this assignment, first read the paragraphs below, and then work through the questions and the activity that follows.

Paragraphs to Consider

Three Little Dumplings

[1]First, there are the light, fluffy dumplings that are found in England and the United States. [2]These dumplings are generally half-boiled or half-steamed and usually incorporated into soups and stews. [3]In the United States, the most well-known dish is "Chicken and Dumplings." [4]Jamaica has a fluffy dumpling. [5]The second type of dumpling is the filled pocket of pasta. [6]Italy's ravioli and tortellini are often filled with cheeses, vegetables, fish, and/or meats, depending on the region. [7]Preparation also varies from region to region; pastas can be boiled, baked, fried, or poached. [8]Chinese potstickers are similar to ravioli and tortellini as they are also both steamed and then fried until they "stick to the pot." [9]In Latin America, empanadas are often filled with pork, chicken, cheese, and vegetables. [10]Although they are larger than ravioli or potstickers, they contain many of the same basic ingredients. [11]The third type of dumpling is the sweet dessert dumpling. [12]In countries like Poland, the sweet filled pierogi are often boiled and then fried and served with butter or sour cream. [13]In Germany and Hungary, sweet dumplings are wrapped around plums or apricots. [14]In Japan, kushi-dango are small sweet dumplings made out of rice flour, skewered on a stick, and then grilled. [15]Attempting to taste every type of dumpling in the world will be a treat for the taste buds.

Three Kinds of Dogs

¹A city walker will notice that most dogs fall into one of three categories. ²First there are the big dogs, which are generally harmless and often downright friendly. ³They walk along peacefully with their masters, their tongues hanging out and big goofy grins on their faces. ⁴Apparently they know they're too big to have anything to worry about, so why not be nice? ⁵Second are the spunky medium-sized dogs. ⁶When they see a stranger approaching, they go on alert. ⁷They prick up their ears, they raise their hackles, and they may growl a little deep in their throats. ⁸"I could tear you up," they seem to be saying, "but I won't if you behave yourself." ⁹Unless the walker leaps for their master's throat, these dogs usually won't do anything more than threaten. ¹⁰The third category is made up of the shivering neurotic little yappers whose shrill barks could shatter glass and whose needle-like little teeth are eager to sink into a friendly outstretched hand. ¹¹Walkers always wonder about these dogs— don't they know that people who really wanted to could squash them under their feet like bugs? ¹²Apparently not, because of all the dogs a walker meets, these provide the most irritation. ¹³Such dogs are only one of the potential hazards that the city walker encounters.

QUESTIONS

About Unity

1. Which paragraph lacks a topic sentence?

_____

2. Which sentence in "Three Kinds of Dogs" should be eliminated in the interest of paragraph unity? (*Write the sentence number here.*) _____

About Support

3. Which of the examples in "Three Little Dumplings" lacks specific details?

_____

About Coherence

4. Which sentences in "Three Kinds of Dogs" contain transition words or phrases? (*Write the sentence numbers here.*)

_____   _____   _____

ACTIVITY 1

This activity will sharpen your sense of the classifying process. In each of the ten groups, cross out the one item that has not been classified on the same basis as the other three. Also, indicate in the space provided the single principle of classification used for the remaining three items. Note the examples.

EXAMPLES

Water
a. Cold
b. ~~Lake~~
c. Hot
d. Lukewarm
Unifying principle:
Temperatures

Household pests
a. ~~Mice~~
b. Ants
c. Roaches
d. Flies
Unifying principle:
Insects

1. Eyes
   a. Blue
   b. Nearsighted
   c. Brown
   d. Hazel
   Unifying principle:

5. Books
   a. Novels
   b. Biographies
   c. Boring
   d. Short stories
   Unifying principle:

2. Mattresses
   a. Double
   b. Twin
   c. Queen
   d. Firm
   Unifying principle:

6. Wallets
   a. Leather
   b. Plastic
   c. Stolen
   d. Fabric
   Unifying principle:

3. Zoo animals
   a. Flamingo
   b. Peacock
   c. Polar bear
   d. Ostrich
   Unifying principle:

7. Newspaper
   a. Wrapping garbage
   b. Editorials
   c. Making paper planes
   d. Covering floor while painting
   Unifying principle:

4. Vacation
   a. Summer
   b. Holiday
   c. Seashore
   d. Weekend
   Unifying principle:

8. Students
   a. First-year
   b. Transfer
   c. Junior
   d. Sophomore
   Unifying principle:

9. Exercise
   a. Running
   b. Swimming
   c. Gymnastics
   d. Fatigue
   Unifying principle:

   _____

10. Leftovers
    a. Cold chicken
    b. Feed to dog
    c. Reheat
    d. Use in a stew
    Unifying principle:

    _____

Developing a Division-Classification Paragraph

Development through Prewriting

Marcus walked home from campus to his apartment, thinking about the assignment to write a division-classification paragraph. As he strolled along his familiar route, his observations made him think of several possibilities. "First I thought of writing about the businesses in my neighborhood, dividing them into the ones run by Hispanics, Asians, and African-Americans," he said. "When I stopped in at my favorite coffee shop, I thought about dividing the people who hang out there. There is a group of old men who meet to drink coffee and play cards, and there are students like me, but there didn't seem to be a third category and I wasn't sure two was enough. As I continued walking home, though, I saw Mr. Enriquez and his big golden retriever, and a woman with two nervous little dogs that acted as if they wanted to eat me, and the newsstand guy with his mutt that's always guarding the place, and I thought 'Dogs! I can classify types of dogs.'"

But how would he classify them? Thinking further, Marcus realized that he thought of dogs as having certain personalities depending on their size. "I know there are exceptions, of course, but since this was going to be a lighthearted, even comical paragraph, I thought it would be OK if I exaggerated a bit." He wrote down his three categories:

> Big dogs
>
> Medium-sized dogs
>
> Small dogs

Under each division, then, he wrote down as many characteristics as he could think of:

Big dogs	good-natured
calm	dumb
friendly	lazy

continued

small dogs	_Medium-sized dogs_
nervous	_spunky_
trembling	_energetic_
noisy	_ready to fight_
yappy	_protective_
snappy	_friendly if they know you_
annoying	

Marcus then wrote a topic sentence: "Dogs seem to fall into three categories." Using that topic sentence and the scratch outline he'd just produced, he wrote the following paragraph:

Most dogs seem to fall into three categories. First there are the big dumb friendly dogs. They give the impression of being sweet but not real bright. One example of this kind of dog is Lucy. She's a golden retriever belonging to a man in my neighborhood. Lucy goes everywhere with Mr. Enriquez. She doesn't even need a leash but just follows him. Dogs like Lucy never bother anybody. She just lies at Mr. Enriquez's feet when he stops to talk to anyone. The guy who runs the corner newsstand I pass every day has a spunky medium-sized dog. Once the dog knows you he's friendly and even playful. But he's always on the lookout for a stranger who might mean trouble. For a dog who's not very big he can make himself look pretty fierce if he wants to. Then there are my least favorite kind of dogs. Little nervous yappy ones. My aunt used to have a Chihuahua like that. It knew me for nine years and still went crazy shaking and yipping at me every time we met. She loved that dog but I can't imagine why. If I had a dog it would definitely come from category 1 or 2.

Development through Revising

Marcus traded his first draft with a fellow student, Rachel, and asked her to give him feedback. Here are the comments Rachel wrote on his paper:

This is a change in point of view—you haven't been using "you" before.

Is this the beginning of a second category? That's not clear.

Not a complete sentence.

Another change in point of view—you've gone from writing in the third person to "you" to "me."

> Most dogs seem to fall into one of three categories. First there are the big dumb friendly dogs. They give the impression of being sweet but not real bright. One example of this kind of dog is Lucy, a golden retriever belonging to a man in my neighborhood. Lucy goes everywhere with Mr. Enriquez. She doesn't even need a leash but just follows him everywhere. Lucy never bothers you. She just lies at Mr. Enriquez's feet when he stops to talk to anyone. The guy who runs the corner newsstand I pass every day has a spunky medium-sized dog. Once the dog knows you he's friendly and even playful. But he's always on the lookout for a stranger who might mean trouble. For a dog who's not very big he can make himself look pretty fierce if he wants to scare you. Then there are my least favorite kind of dogs. Little nervous yappy ones. My aunt used to have a Chihuahua like that. It knew me for nine years and still went crazy shaking and yipping at me every time we met. She loved that dog but I can't imagine why. If I had a dog it would definitely come from category 1 or 2.

Rachel also provided Marcus with the following helpful feedback:

Marcus—I think you need to make your three categories clearer. Your first one is OK—"big dogs," which you say are friendly—but categories 2 and 3 aren't stated as clearly.

It's distracting to have your point of view change from third person to "you" to "me."

Since you're trying to divide and classify all dogs, I'm not sure it's a good idea to talk only about three individual dogs. This way it sounds as if you're just describing those three dogs instead of putting them into three groups.

When Marcus considered Rachel's comments and reread his paragraph, he agreed with what she had written. "I realized it was too much about three particular dogs and not enough about the categories of dogs," he said. "I decided to revise it and focus on the three classes of dogs."

Marcus then wrote the version that appears on page 224.

Writing a Division-Classification Paragraph

ORGANIZING IDEAS

Write a classification paragraph on one of the following topics:

Attitudes toward life	Houseguests
Commercials	Reasons for attending college
Employers	Ways to get a new job
Jobs	Types of political candidates
First dates	Ways to save money
Parents	Ways to protect/destroy the environment
Neighbors	Types of characters in a favorite novel, TV show, or movie
Preferred Pandora stations	

Prewriting

a. Decide if you want your paragraph to be informative, persuasive, or entertaining. Here are some questions to consider: Do you want your readers to understand your topic and categories better? Do you want to convince your readers to agree with your method of classification? Do you want to amuse them by providing humorous details for each category? Keep in mind that your paragraph can combine purposes.

b. Classify members of the group you are considering writing about into three categories. Remember: *You must use a single principle of division when you create your three categories.* For example, if your topic is "school courses" and you classify them into easy, moderate, and challenging, your basis for classification is "degree of difficulty." It would not make sense to have as a fourth type "foreign language" (the basis of such a categorization would be "subject matter") or "early morning" (the basis of that classification would be "time of day the classes meet"). You *could* categorize school courses on the basis of subject matter or time of day they meet, for almost any subject can be classified in more than one way. In a single paper, however, you must choose *one* basis for classification and stick to it.

c. Once you have a satisfactory three-part division, spend at least five minutes freewriting about each of your three points. Don't be concerned yet with grammar, spelling, or organization. Just write whatever comes into your mind about each of the three points.

d. Expand your topic into a fully stated topic sentence.

e. At this point, you have all three elements of your paragraph: the topic sentence, the three main points, and the details needed to support each point. Now weave them all together in one paragraph.

Revising: Peer Review

Do not attempt to revise your paragraph right away. Put it away for a while, if possible until the next day. When you reread it, try to be as critical of it as you would be if someone else had written it. Have a friend or classmate read your paragraph as well, and as you both go over your work, refer to the questions in the following checklist:

DIVISION-CLASSIFICATION CHECKLIST: THE FOUR BASES

UNITY

✔ Have you divided or classified your topic into three distinct parts?

✔ Is each of those parts based on the same principle of division?

SUPPORT

✔ Have you provided effective details to back up each of your three points?

✔ Have each of the three parts been given approximately equal weight? In other words, have you spent about the same amount of time discussing each part?

COHERENCE

✔ Are there appropriate transitions and other connective devices weaving the paragraph together?

SENTENCE SKILLS

✔ Have you used a consistent point of view throughout the paragraph?

✔ Are there specific rather than general words?

✔ Has wordiness been avoided and concise wording used?

✔ Are your sentences varied?

✔ Has the paragraph been checked for spelling and other sentences skills, as listed on the inside back cover of the book?

Continue revising your work until you and your reader can answer "yes" to all these questions.

WRITING ASSIGNMENT 2

Personal

ANALYZING CLASSMATES

There are many ways you could classify your fellow students. Pick out one of your courses and write a paragraph in which you classify the students in that class according to one underlying principle. You may wish to choose one of the classification principles below.

Attitude toward the class	Punctuality
Participation in the class	Attendance

Method of taking notes in class   Level of confidence

Performance during oral reports,
speeches, presentations, lab sessions

If you decide, for instance, to classify students according to their attitude toward class, you might come up with these three categories:

Students actually interested in learning the material

Students who know they need to learn the material, but don't want to overdo it

Students who find the class a good opportunity to catch up with lost sleep

Of course, you may use any other principle of classification that seems appropriate. Follow the steps listed under "Prewriting" and "Revising" for Writing Assignment 1.

REVIEWING A RESTAURANT

WRITING ASSIGNMENT 3

Personal

When we go to a restaurant, we probably hope that the service will be helpful, the atmosphere will be pleasant, and the food will be tasty. But as the cartoon shown here suggests, restaurants that are good in all three respects may be hard to find. Write a review of a restaurant, analyzing its (1) service, (2) atmosphere, and (3) food. Visit a restaurant for this assignment, or draw on an experience you have had recently. Freewrite or make a list of observations about such elements as:

I said well done!

why thank you!

Reprinted by permission from Brad Fitzpatrick and Fitzillo Incorporated

Quantity of food you receive   Attitude of the servers

Taste of the food   Efficiency of the servers

Temperature of the food   Décor

Freshness of the ingredients   Level of cleanliness

How the food is presented (garnishes, dishes, and so on)   Noise level and music, if any

Feel free to write about details other than those listed above. Just be sure each detail fits into one of your three categories: food, service, or atmosphere.

For your topic sentence, rate the restaurant by giving it from one to five stars, on the basis of your overall impression. Include the restaurant's name and location in your topic sentence. Here are some examples:

Guido's, an Italian restaurant downtown, deserves three stars.

The McDonald's on Route 70 merits a four-star rating.

The Circle Diner in Westfield barely earns a one-star rating.

REFLECTIVE ACTIVITY

1. Reread the paragraph you wrote for Writing Assignment 1. Does your paragraph contain enough detail to support the main point made in your topic sentence? Is all of the information in the paragraph directly related to the topic sentence?

2. Can you think of a way to incorporate another mode of writing, like narration (Chapter 7) or argument (Chapter 14)? If so, revise the paragraph to incorporate the added support by using an additional mode(s) of writing.

BEYOND THE CLASSROOM

Division-Classification

Beyond the classroom, you will find yourself and others dividing or classifying objects and concepts. Scientists classify plants and animals in order to study them more effectively. Medical researchers use this method to organize information about related diseases or drugs. Educators sometimes classify students into groups based on placement-test scores in order to design and deliver effective programs of study. Psychiatrists use classification to organize information about various emotional disorders, and marketing researchers use classification to determine which age, ethnic, or income group might be more interested in a product than another group.

For this writing assignment, you will write a division or classification paragraph with a specific purpose and for a specific audience.

Imagine that you are a travel agent and several clients have asked you for suggestions about affordable family vacations. Write a paragraph classifying vacations for families into three or more types—for example, vacations in amusement parks, on cruises, at resorts, or in the outdoors. For each type, include an explanation with one or more examples. Keep in mind that all these suggestions should be affordable.

EXPLORING WRITING ONLINE

Visit an online music store and browse through the categories of music. You may want to visit the *iTunes Store* at http://www.apple.com/itunes/store/ or go to the music department at *Amazon.com*. Then design your own site selling something similar (you can be as creative as you like). Provide at least five different categories of your "product" and explain what makes each category different.

Argument

RESPONDING TO IMAGES

An alarming number of high school and college athletes use steroids and other drugs to improve their performance on the court and in the field. Write a paragraph in which you argue whether random testing of such drugs should be allowed. Include at least three separate reasons to support your position.

The ability to advance sound, compelling arguments is an important skill in everyday life. We can use argument to get an extension on a term paper, obtain a favor from a friend, or convince an employer that we are the right person for a job. Understanding argumentation based on clear, logical reasoning can also help us see through the sometimes faulty arguments advanced by advertisers, editors, politicians, and others who try to bring us over to their side.

In this section, you will be asked to argue a position and defend it with a series of solid reasons. In a general way, you are doing the same thing with all the paragraph assignments in the book: making a point and then supporting it. The difference here is that an argument advances a *debatable* point, a point that at least some of your readers will not be inclined to accept, so you must consider their objections. To prepare for this assignment, first read about five strategies you can use in advancing an argument and work through the accompanying activities. Then read two student paragraphs and work through the questions that follow.

Strategies for Arguments

Because an argument assumes *debate,* you have to work especially hard to convince readers of the validity of your position. Here are five strategies to help you deal with readers whose viewpoints may differ from yours.

Use Tactful, Courteous Language

In an argument paragraph, you are attempting to persuade readers to see the merit of your viewpoint. It is important, then, not to anger them by referring to them or their opinions in rude terms. Don't write, "People who talk on the phone while driving are stupid." Also, stay away from sweeping statements like "Everyone knows that Internet dating is dangerous." Also, keep the focus on the issue you are discussing, not on the people involved in the debate. Don't write, "My opponents say that vaccines don't cause autism." Instead, write, "Supporters of vaccines say that vaccines don't cause autism," which suggests that those who don't agree with you are still reasonable people who are willing to consider differing opinions.

Point Out Common Ground

Another way to persuade readers to consider your opinion is to point out common ground—opinions that you share. Find points on which people on all sides of the argument can agree. Perhaps you are arguing that soda machines should be banned in schools. Before going into detail about your proposal, remind readers who oppose such a ban that you and they share certain goals: the importance of proper nutrition and a lower obesity rate for children and teens. Readers will be more receptive to your idea once they have considered the ways in which you and they think alike.

Acknowledge Differing Viewpoints

Don't simply ignore viewpoints that conflict with yours. Instead, acknowledge other viewpoints. Readers are more likely to consider your point of view if you indicate a willingness to consider theirs. One effective technique is to cite the opposing viewpoint in your topic sentence. For example, you might say, "Although some students believe that studying a foreign language is a waste of time, two years of foreign-language study should be required of all college graduates." In the first part, you acknowledge the other side's point of view; in the second, you state your opinion, suggesting that yours is the stronger viewpoint. Another effective technique is to include a separate sentence before your topic sentence to acknowledge the opposing viewpoint. If you oppose workplace discrimination, you might first say, "Some employers believe that male employees shouldn't wear earrings."

When Appropriate, Grant the Merits of Differing Viewpoints

Sometimes an opposing viewpoint contains a point whose validity you cannot deny. The strongest strategy, then, is to admit that the point is a good one. Admit the merit of one aspect of the other argument while making it clear that you still believe your argument to be stronger overall. Suppose that you oppose mandatory curbside recycling. You might start with a statement admitting that the other side has a valid point, but you could quickly follow this admission with a statement making your own viewpoint clear: "Granted, recycling reduces landfill waste and conserves natural resources, but mandatory curbside recycling will cost taxpayers too much and, therefore, curbside recycling should be voluntary."

Rebut Differing Viewpoints

Sometimes simply acknowledging a differing viewpoint and presenting your own may not be enough. When you are dealing with an issue that your readers feel strongly about, you may need to rebut an opposing viewpoint by pointing out problems with that viewpoint. You can use this strategy at any point in your paragraph. Imagine, for instance, that you oppose a sex offender registry, but you know that many supporters believe that a registry reduces crimes of this nature. You might rebut that point by citing that only offenders who comply with the law register, so the registry offers a false sense of security.

ACTIVITY 1

The box below summarizes the five strategies for arguments. Read the statements that follow it, and in the space provided, write the letter of the kind of strategy used in each case.

A. Use Tactful, Courteous Language
B. Point Out Common Ground
C. Acknowledge Differing Viewpoints
D. Grant the Merits of Differing Viewpoints
E. Rebut Differing Viewpoints

_____   1.   While homeless shelters provide temporary relief, the government needs to provide needy families with more affordable housing, job training, and subsidized child care.

_____   2.   Granted, students who are self-motivated can excel in online classes, but students who don't have time-management skills shouldn't take these classes.

_____   3.   Supporters of closed or confidential adoption value the privacy of the birth mother.

_____   4.   We all want what is best for our children and believe that they should be protected.

_____   5.   College students, already financially strapped, would have trouble paying the proposed tuition increase to cover the cost of the new athletic building.

ACTIVITY 2

This activity will give you practice in stating a clear position and acknowledging an opposing viewpoint. In each item, you will see a statement and then a question related to that statement. Write *two* answers to each question. Your first will answer "yes" to the question and briefly explain why. The other will answer "no" to the question and also state why.

HINT   Use words such as *should* (*not*), *must* (*not*), and *ought* (*not*) to make your position clear.

EXAMPLE

Cigarette smoking has been proven to be harmful. Should it therefore be made illegal?

"Yes": Because smoking has been shown to have so many harmful health effects, the sale of cigarettes should be made illegal.

"No": Although smoking has been linked to various health problems, adults should have the right to make their own decision about whether or not to smoke. Smoking, therefore, should not be made illegal.

1.   Animals feel pain when they are killed for food. Is eating animals therefore immoral?

"Yes": _____

_____

"No": _____

_____

2. Professional boxing often leads to serious injury. Should this sport be outlawed?

"Yes": _____

_____

"No": _____

_____

3. The obesity rate among children and teenagers is rising. Should schools ban the sale of soda and junk food?

"Yes": _____

_____

_____

"No": _____

_____

_____

4. Some teenagers commit violent crimes, such as rape and murder. Should they be tried in court as adults?

"Yes": _____

_____

"No": _____

_____

5. Studies show that boys and girls learn differently. Should single-sex education be encouraged?

"Yes": _____

_____

"No": _____

_____

Paragraphs to Consider

Mandatory Attendance Isn't the Answer

[1]Teachers want students to learn, and students want this, too. [2]They both know that one of the best places to learn is the classroom. [3]In college, however, class attendance shouldn't be mandatory. [4]First of all, mandatory attendance has its flaws. [5]Even if students are in class, they may not be learning. [6]A student may be so tired from pulling a double shift at work that he dozes off in class, and another student may be preoccupied because her daughter is sick. [7]Some teachers are too nice, so they don't enforce the attendance policy. [8]If a student begs or gives a sob story, a teacher might make an exception. [9]Teachers sometimes forget to take attendance, so those who weren't in class get a free pass, which is unfair. [10]Another reason attendance shouldn't be mandatory is because college students have valid reasons for their absences. [11]Many students have jobs, and sometimes a boss may be inflexible about a work schedule. [12]Plus, students often cannot afford to miss work. [13]Many students have a family, which is just as important as school. [14]A child might be sick, or a babysitter might cancel at the last minute, causing a student to miss class. [15]Students might also miss class because they are sick and don't want to make anyone else sick. [16]The most important reason against a mandatory attendance is that college students are responsible for their own learning. [17]Although some students may be recent high school graduates, in college they are considered adults. [18]If students miss class, they can catch up by asking classmates for lecture notes or emailing instructors about their absence. [19]When a student simply "blows off" class, that student should accept the consequences. [20]Some supporters of mandatory attendance worry that students will think that class is optional if attendance is no longer required. [21]However, teachers can emphasize its importance and promote attendance by having in-class activities that can't be made up later. [22]For all these reasons, mandatory attendance has no place in college.

Bring Back Public Humiliation!

[1]Society has gotten lazy about manners, and in order to get people back on track, public humiliation should be reinstated. [2]One offense that many people are guilty of is forgetting to say "please" or "thank you." [3]Using words like "please" and "thank you" shows gratitude to others for their actions, but omitting these words shows a lack of concern for how others may feel. [4]Those who are found guilty of this offense should be required to

continued

stand outside of the location where they committed the offense and wear a board that announces, "I don't know how to use 'please' and 'thank you.' Please help me practice." ⁵They should be required to do this exercise for one hour per offense. ⁶In order to be good parents, people should teach their children to use "please" and "thank you." ⁷Another offense that many people are guilty of is talking on cell phones at inappropriate times. ⁸When people are found guilty, they should be subjected to *The Scarlet Letter* punishment and be forced to wear a large letter "R" for one month. ⁹This letter would alert others that the person is guilty of being rude. ¹⁰Restaurants could refuse service to or have a special section for people bearing the letter "R"; stores could force people with the letter "R" to use one specific check-out line. ¹¹In this way, people in general would know that the offender had treated others disrespectfully. ¹²A final rude offense that many people are guilty of is aggressive driving like tailgating, cutting off other cars, or failing to stay in one lane. ¹³People who are found guilty should be required to turn in their car for a period of a month and drive a punishment car. ¹⁴Punishment cars would be painted in obnoxious colors and announce that the driver had "committed rudeness." ¹⁵Using public humiliation to deter social misbehavior has a long history of working and should be brought back in full force before society's rudeness gets out of hand.

About Unity

1. Which sentence in "Bring Back Public Humiliation!" should be eliminated in the interest of paragraph unity? (*Write the sentence number here.*) _____

About Support

2. How many reasons are given to support the topic sentence in each paragraph?

   a. In "Mandatory Attendance Isn't the Answer" ____ one ____ two ____ three ____ four

   b. In "Bring Back Public Humiliation!" ____ one ____ two ____ three ____ four

3. Which sentences in "Mandatory Attendance Isn't the Answer" point out common ground? _____ and _____

4. Which paragraph rebuts differing viewpoints? _____
   _____

About Coherence

5. What transition words or phrases are used to introduce the three reasons listed in "Mandatory Attendance Isn't the Answer"?

   _____   _____   _____

QUESTIONS

Developing an Argument Paragraph

Development through Prewriting

Yolanda is the author of "Mandatory Attendance Isn't the Answer." She was stumped when her instructor told her to choose a topic for the argument paragraph. She first thought of topics that she thought she *should* write about—death penalty, abortion, gun control, cloning, medical marijuana, drinking age, mercy killing—but worried that she wouldn't have enough evidence. Yolanda also worried that her topic wouldn't be good enough because, as she said, she "just didn't feel it."

She decided on her topic after her classmate Nate said, "Think of an issue that gets you all riled up, one that makes you clench your jaw just thinking about it." That morning, her classmate Zach slept through most of class but received credit for being there, yet the week before Yolanda missed class to take her daughter to the doctor's and, as a result, lost points for attendance. "That's so unfair," she told Nate. "Attendance shouldn't be mandatory. We're in college after all, not high school."

Yolanda began by making a list of all the negative aspects of mandatory attendance. This is what she came up with:

college students are adults!

college is not high school

we're responsible for our own learning

we should accept the consequences

teachers should make classes more fun

valid reasons for missing classes

work conflicts

family is just as important

not want to make others sick

mandatory classroom participation doesn't work

able to catch up

not always learning even if in class

some teachers are too nice and don't enforce the policy

Prof. Cummins is too strict about everything

some teachers forget to take attendance

teachers have different tardiness rules

After Yolanda wrote her list, she thought about how she could organize her ideas. She came up with three supporting reasons: (1) flaws in the current policy, (2) valid reasons for absences, and (3) students' own responsibility. She went back to her list, struck out items that didn't fit, and numbered items according to her three reasons:

3 college students are adults!

3 college is not high school

3 we're responsible for our own learning

3 we should accept the consequences

~~teachers should make classes more fun~~

2 valid reasons for missing classes

2 work conflicts

2 family is just as important

2 not want to make others sick

~~mandatory classroom participation doesn't work~~

3 able to catch up

1 not always learning even if in class

1 some teachers are ~~too nice~~ and don't enforce the policy

~~Prof. Cummins is too strict about everything~~

1 some teachers forget to take attendance

~~teachers have different tardiness rules~~

Yolanda then prepared a scratch outline:

Class attendance shouldn't be mandatory in college.

1.   Mandatory attendance has its flaws.

2.   Students have valid reasons for their absences.

3.   Students are responsible for their own learning.

Yolanda knew that some of her readers might not share her opinions, so she needed to consider their viewpoints. She jotted down three reasons in favor of mandatory attendance, and then thought about how she might address those points:

> recent high school graduates are used to this being the policy
>
> (they're not in high school anymore)
>
> students will think that class is optional (need to promote, not require, attendance) ~~Rewards those who regularly attend class~~
>
> (this point is weak)

Using the material she created, Yolanda wrote the following first draft of her paragraph:

> In my own opinion, class attendance shouldn't be mandatory in college. First, mandatory attendance has its flaws. Even if students are in class, they may not be learning. Some teachers are too nice, so they don't enforce the attendance policy. If a student begs or gives a sob story, a teacher might make an exception. Teachers sometimes forget to take attendance, so those who weren't in class get a free pass. I think that that's so unfair! Second, college students have valid reasons for their absences. Many students have jobs. Many students in this day and age also have a family. A student might also miss class because he or she is sick and doesn't want to make anyone else sick. Third, I'm against a mandatory attendance policy because we are responsible for our own learning. Although some students may be used to such a policy having just come from high school, college students are adults. If a student misses class, he or she should be able to catch up by asking a classmate for the lecture notes or emailing the instructor. When a student simply blows off class, that student should accept the consequences. My opponents worry that students will think that class is optional if attendance is no longer required. However, teachers can emphasize its importance and promote attendance by having in-class activities that can't be made up later.

Development through Revising

Yolanda's instructor asked her to pair up with another student, so she turned to her classmate Nate. He read her paper aloud while she listened. As Nate read, they listened for spots where her paper didn't read clearly. Then Nate wrote several comments on Yolanda's draft:

> Given how many times *I've* been absent, you know I support your position! Seriously, I like how you consider other viewpoints but don't let those points weaken yours. In fact, this strategy makes your argument stronger. Also, you found a topic that you care about, and this shows. As a reader, I know exactly what your position is.
>
> Okay, you know I hate pointing out what's wrong, but I want to help you, so here goes. You use transitions—*first, second, third*—but I'm wondering why you organized your ideas in this way. I'm thinking that the last point is the most important. Also, I found myself wanting to see more details about work and family. There's so much more you could say. You could also end on a stronger note by adding one last sentence.
>
> If you still want to revise your paragraph, think about what our instructor said regarding point of view and concise wording.

With these comments in mind, Yolanda revised her paragraph until she produced the version that appears on page 238.

RESPONDING TO IMAGES

Images can make effective arguments as well. What visual argument does the poster shown here make?

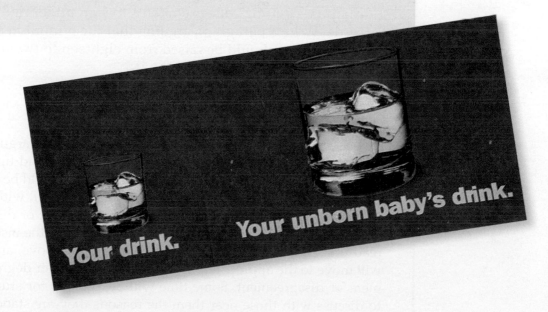

Writing an Argument Paragraph

Academic

Arguing Your Opinion

Choose one of the topics below and follow the directions. The purpose is to take a strong stand, and you must support your claim with at least three reasons.

- Write a letter to the editor arguing against or supporting the banning of a specific book like *To Kill a Mockingbird, Slaughterhouse Five, The Adventures of Huckleberry Finn,* or a book of your choosing.

- Your college has just announced that the grading scale is going to be changed from a 10-point scale (79–89, 90–100) to a 7-point scale (85–92, 93–100). Write a paragraph in which you support or oppose this decision.

- Your local school district is going to require all students to wear school uniforms. Write a paragraph (either as a student attending or as a parent) in which you support or oppose this decision.

- As you are applying for a new job, your potential employer requests to see your social networking profiles. Write a letter expressing why you don't think this is a valid way to check a potential employee's background.

- As you are starting your new job, you are informed that you get eight days of holiday and vacation time a year. Write a paragraph explaining why you should get more holidays and longer vacations.

- Since the current age for a person to get his or her own credit card is eighteen, many credit card companies canvas college campuses getting college students to sign up for multiple cards. Write a paragraph arguing that the minimum age for a credit card should be raised from eighteen to twenty-one years.

PREWRITING

a. As a useful exercise to help you begin developing your argument, your instructor might give class members a chance to "stand up" for what they believe in. One side of the front of the room should be designated *strong agreement* and the other side *strong disagreement,* with an imaginary line representing varying degrees of agreement or disagreement in between. As the class stands in front of the room, the instructor will read one value statement at a time from the list above, and students will move to the appropriate spot, depending on their degree of agreement or disagreement. Some time will be allowed for students, first, to discuss with those near them the reasons they are standing where they are; and, second, to state to those at the other end of the scale the reasons for their position.

b. Begin your paragraph by writing a sentence that expresses your attitude toward one of the value statements above, for example, "I feel that the minimum age to apply for a credit card should be raised from eighteen to twenty-one years."

c. Outline the reason or reasons you hold the opinion that you do. Your support may be based on your own experience, the experience of someone you know, or logic. For example, an outline of a paragraph based on one student's logic looked like this:

> I feel that the minimum age to apply for a credit card should be raised from eighteen to twenty-one years for the following reasons:
>
> 1. Eighteen-year-olds may be inexperienced handling their finances.
>
> 2. Eighteen-year-olds may not have the income to make credit card payments.
>
> 3. Most of all, given that so many young adults are in financial debt, they should avoid ruining their credit history.

Another outline, based on experience, proceeded as follows:

> The experiences of a twenty-one-year-old I know show that the minimum age to apply for a credit card should be raised from eighteen to twenty-one years.
>
> 1. At eighteen, this person had a credit card but did not even have a checking account.
>
> 2. At eighteen, this person was earning minimum wage at a part-time, temporary job and was unable to make monthly credit card payments.
>
> 3. This person didn't realize until he was twenty-one that a few missed payments would ruin his credit history.

d. Write a first draft of your paragraph, providing specific details to back up each point in your outline.

Revising: Peer Review

Put your paragraph away for a while, ideally at least a day. Ask a friend or classmate whose judgment you trust to read and critique it. Your reader should consider each of these questions as he or she reads:

ARGUMENT CHECKLIST: THE FOUR BASES

UNITY

✔ Does the topic sentence clearly state your opinion on a controversial subject?

SUPPORT

✔ Does the paragraph include at least three separate and distinct reasons that support the argument?

✔ Is each of the three reasons backed up by specific, relevant evidence?

COHERENCE

✔ Has the most powerful reason been saved for last?

SENTENCE SKILLS

✔ Is there a consistent point of view throughout the paragraph?

✔ Have you used specific rather than general words?

✔ Have you avoided wordiness and used concise wording?

✔ Are sentences varied?

✔ Has the paragraph been checked for spelling and other sentence skills, as listed on the inside back cover of the book?

Continue revising your work until you and your reader can answer "yes" to all these questions.

WRITING ASSIGNMENT 2

REQUIRING CIVIL SERVICE

Currently, when high school students in America graduate, they have the option of continuing their education or working, in contrast to countries like Switzerland and Israel that require either military or civilian service for a minimum period of time. Some countries, like Austria, allow conscientious objectors to participate in a civilian corps instead of military service. In this assignment, you are to argue that all high school graduates must participate in AmeriCorps for a minimum of twelve months. Your argument will require you to visit the AmeriCorps Web site (http://www.americorps.gov) to learn about the three different programs and their projects and benefits. Use the following, or something similar, for your topic sentence:

> Upon graduating from high school, all American students should be required to participate in AmeriCorps for a minimum period of twelve months, after which they can enter college, enter the working force, or re-enter AmeriCorps.

For each reason you advance, include at least one persuasive example. Support can be presented as fact (Chapter 20), as anecdotes (Chapter 7), as contrasts (Chapter 11), and/or as processes (Chapter 9). After deciding on your points of support, arrange them in a brief outline, saving your strongest point for last. In your paragraph, introduce each of your reasons with an additional transition, such as *first of all, another, also,* and *finally.*

USING RESEARCH FOR SUPPORT

WRITING ASSIGNMENT 3

Write a paragraph in which you use research findings to help support one of the points below.

- Cigarettes should be illegal.

- Any person convicted of drunken driving should be required to spend time in jail.

- Drivers should not be permitted to text while driving.

- High schools should (or should not) pass out birth control devices and information to students.

- Schools should be in session year round.

- Advertising should not be permitted on young children's TV shows.

- All college students should be required to take four years of a foreign language.

- All students (K–12) and all college students should be required to take a physical education course every day.

- To save money, all high schools should require every student to take at least four online courses.

Chapter 20, "Writing a Research Paper" (pages 367–391), will show you how to use keywords and the Internet to think about your topic and do research. See if you can organize your paragraph in the form of three separate and distinct reasons that support the topic. Put these reasons into a scratch outline and use it as a guide in writing your paragraph.

REFLECTIVE ACTIVITY

1. Exchange argument paragraphs with a classmate. Ask him or her to explain whether your paragraph is convincing. If not, ask your partner to offer suggestions to strengthen it. Do the same for him or her.

2. Think about the suggestions your partner has made. Do you agree with all of them? Are there any that you might reject?

BEYOND THE CLASSROOM

Argument

Personal

Beyond the classroom, you will find yourself taking a stand on an issue and providing solid evidence to support that position. Attorneys use arguments in courts, both criminal and civil. Legislators, meeting in bodies such as city councils, state assemblies, and the U.S. Congress, argue for the passage of bills and resolutions. Advertisers use argumentative techniques to get consumers to buy products or use services. Fundraisers use argumentation to persuade people to donate to charities, building funds, and other worthy causes.

For this writing assignment, you will write an argument paragraph with a specific purpose and for a specific audience. Imagine that, for various reasons, you experienced financial hardship and had to use your credit card to help you "make ends meet." Now you are having a difficult time making minimum monthly payments. Write a letter to the credit card company in which you explain your situation and negotiate a new payment plan. Be sure to address any doubts that the company may have about your ability to honor the agreement.

EXPLORING WRITING ONLINE

Visit the *US Newspaper List* at http://www.usnpl.com and click on the link to your state. From the listing, select a newspaper in your area, and then scroll to that paper's Opinion or Op-Ed section. Read one of the articles posted and write a paragraph in which you identify the author's main point and supporting reasons.

As you are reading the following paragraph written by John for a city planning class, think about what advice you would offer him as he prepares to write his final draft. Does his paragraph cover all four bases of effective writing? To be sure, review each question in the checklist that follows and write your answers in the lines provided.

The Job of City Planners

[1]City planners advise local governments on ways to improve communities. [2]For example, in South Florida, city planners are working to improve existing communities. [3]The population of the area is expected to increase from 5.5 million to 7.5 million by 2020. [4]This growth is headed to the west, where there is still open land, but western growth creates a costly need for new roads and threatens the ecological system of the Florida Everglades. [5]As a result, city planners are trying to lure people back into the older, more developed eastern section of the region by funneling growth in that direction and away from the western section. [6]City planners also plan and develop new communities. [7]These communities, called new cities or new towns, include both places to live and places to work.

A WRITER'S CHECKLIST

Unity

✔ Does the writer give a clear, direct topic sentence stating the main point of the paragraph? _____

✔ Is all the material on target in support of the topic sentence? _____

_____

Support

✔ Does John provide specific evidence to support his topic sentence? _____

✔ Are there enough supporting details? _____

Coherence

✔ Does the writer use transitions and other connective devices? _____ List them here:

_____   _____

Sentence Skills

✔ Are sentences varied? _____

✔ Can you find any other sentence skills mistakes, as listed on the back inside cover of the book? If you can find a mistake, what type of mistake is it?

_____

Collaborative Activity

In your group or class, make an outline of John's paragraph. Looking at the outline, can you think of any additional supporting details that could be added to make this paragraph more effective?

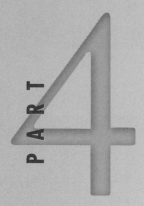

PART 4

Essay Development

PART FOUR SHOWS YOU HOW TO

- differentiate between an essay and a paragraph

- structure a traditional essay

- determine your point of view

- do a personal review

PART FOUR ALSO GIVES YOU PRACTICE

- beginning an essay with a point, or thesis

- revising essays for unity, support, coherence, and sentence skills

- writing introductory and concluding paragraphs

- developing nine different patterns of essay development

- taking essay exams

- writing a summary

- writing a report

- writing a research paper

EXPLORING WRITING PROMPT:

In college, you will be asked to write essays. In Part 4, you will learn how to write them, but before you start, take a few minutes to explore what you think—and how you feel—about the essay. Freewrite, brainstorm, or diagram your thoughts on this topic.

Introduction to Essay Development

RESPONDING TO IMAGES

Everyone knows how to fix a sandwich. No matter what we use for its filling—a hamburger patty, egg salad, peanut butter and jelly, cold cuts—we always start with two pieces of bread. An essay is like a sandwich in that it has a "top" and "bottom" bun; namely, an introduction and a conclusion. Think about how else a sandwich resembles an essay. Using this food metaphor, what are paragraphs and transitions?

What Is an Essay?

Differences between an Essay and a Paragraph

An essay is simply a paper of several paragraphs, rather than one paragraph, that supports a single point. In an essay, subjects can and should be treated more fully than they would in a single-paragraph paper. Unlike paragraphs that are usually developed using one mode of writing, like description, essays are usually developed using several modes of writing to support the single point.

The main idea or point developed in an essay is called the *thesis statement* or *thesis sentence* (rather than, as in a paragraph, the *topic sentence*). The thesis statement appears in the introductory paragraph, and it is then developed in the supporting paragraphs that follow. A concluding paragraph closes the essay.

Structure of the Traditional Essay

A Model Essay

The following model will help you understand the form of an essay. Diane Woods, the writer of the paragraph on moviegoing in Chapter 1 (page 6), later decided to develop her subject more fully. Here is the essay that resulted.

The Hazards of Moviegoing

I am a movie fanatic. My friends count on me to know movie trivia (who was the pigtailed little girl in *E.T.: The Extra-Terrestrial*? Drew Barrymore) and to remember every big Oscar awarded since I was in grade school (Best picture 1994? *Forrest Gump*). My friends, though, have stopped asking me if I want to go out to the movies. While I love movies as much as ever, the inconvenience of going out, the temptations of the theater, and the behavior of some patrons are reasons for me to wait and rent the DVD.

To begin with, I just don't enjoy the general hassle of the evening. Since small local movie theaters are a thing of the past, I have to drive for fifteen minutes to get to the nearest multiplex. The parking lot is shared with several restaurants and a supermarket, so it's always jammed. I have to drive around at a snail's pace until I spot another driver backing out. Then it's time to stand in an endless line, with the constant threat that tickets for the show I want will sell out. If we do get tickets, the theater will be so crowded that I won't be able to sit with my friends, or we'll have to sit in a front row gaping up at a giant screen. I have to shell out a ridiculous amount of money—up to $10—for a ticket. That entitles me to sit while my shoes seal themselves to a sticky floor coated with spilled soda, bubble gum, and crushed Raisinets.

Introductory paragraph

First supporting paragraph

continued

Second supporting paragraph

Second, the theater offers tempting snacks that I really don't need. Like most of us, I have to battle an expanding waistline. At home I do pretty well by simply not buying stuff that is bad for me. I can make do with snacks like celery and carrot sticks because there is no ice cream in the freezer. Going to the theater, however, is like spending my evening in a Seven-Eleven that's been equipped with a movie screen and comfortable seats. As I try to persuade myself to just have a diet Coke, the smell of fresh popcorn dripping with butter soon overcomes me. Chocolate bars the size of small automobiles seem to jump into my hands. I risk putting on the pounds as I chew enormous mouthfuls of Junior Mints. By the time I leave the theater, I feel disgusted with myself.

Third supporting paragraph

Many of the other patrons are even more of a problem than the concession stand. Little kids race up and down the aisles, usually in giggling packs. Teenagers try to impress their friends by talking back to the screen, whistling, and making what they consider to be hilarious noises. Adults act as if they were at home in their own living room. They comment loudly on the ages of the stars and reveal plot twists that are supposed to be a secret until the film's end. And people of all ages create distractions. They crinkle candy wrappers, stick gum on their seats, and drop popcorn tubs or cups of crushed ice and soda on the floor. They also cough and burp, talk on their cell phones, file out for repeated trips to the rest rooms or concession stands, and elbow me out of the armrest on either side of my seat.

Concluding paragraph

After arriving home from the movies one night, I decided that I was not going to be a moviegoer anymore. I was tired of the problems involved in getting to the theater, resisting unhealthy snacks, and dealing with the patrons. The next day, I arranged to have Movies on Demand installed as part of my cable TV service, and I also got a membership at my local video store. I may now see movies a bit later than other people, but I'll be more relaxed watching box office hits in the comfort of my own living room.

Parts of an Essay

"The Hazards of Moviegoing" is a good example of the standard short essay you will write in college English. It is a composition of over five hundred words that consists of an introduction, conclusion, and body. The introduction and conclusion are usually only one paragraph each, and the body of the essay is at least three paragraphs, but can often be more.

Introductory Paragraph

The introductory paragraph of an essay should start with several sentences that attract the reader's interest. It should then advance the central idea, or *thesis*, that will be developed in the essay. The thesis often includes a *plan of development*—a "preview" of the major points that will support the thesis. These supporting points should be listed in the order in which they will appear in the essay. Such a thesis might assert, "Winter is my favorite season because I like the weather, the holidays, and the sports," leading to an essay that has a paragraph about weather, followed by a paragraph about the holidays, and so forth. In some cases, however, the plan of development is omitted. For example, a thesis that claims, "Education can be a key to socioeconomic security" doesn't state how the essay will be developed, but still advances a central idea.

1. In "The Hazards of Moviegoing," which sentence or sentences are used to attract the reader's interest?

   a. First sentence

   b. First two sentences

   c. First three sentences

2. In which sentence is the thesis of the essay presented?

   a. Third sentence

   b. Fourth sentence

3. Does the thesis include a plan of development?

   a. Yes

   b. No

4. Write the words in the thesis that announce the three major supporting points in the essay:

   a. _____

   b. _____

   c. _____

ACTIVITY 1

Body: Supporting Paragraphs

Many essays have three supporting points, developed at length over three separate paragraphs. However, more developed essays require four or more body paragraphs to support the thesis. This is very common in essays with thesis statements that omit a plan of development. Each of the supporting paragraphs should begin with a *topic sentence* that states the point to be detailed in that paragraph. Just as a thesis provides a focus for the entire essay, the topic sentence provides a focus for a supporting paragraph.

1. What is the topic sentence for the first supporting paragraph of the model essay?

   _____

   _____

ACTIVITY 2

2. The first topic sentence is then supported by the following details (fill in the missing details):

   a. Have to drive fifteen minutes

   b. _____

   c. Endless ticket line

      d. _____

      e. _____

      f. Sticky floor

3. What is the topic sentence for the second supporting paragraph of the essay?

    _____

    _____

4. The second topic sentence is then supported by the following details:

    a. At home, only snacks are celery and carrot sticks.

    b. Theater is like a Seven-Eleven with seats.

      (1) fresh popcorn

      (2) _____

      (3) _____

5. What is the topic sentence for the third supporting paragraph of the essay?

    _____

    _____

6. The third topic sentence is then supported by the following details:

    a. _____

    b. _____

    c. Adults talk loudly and reveal plot twists.

    d. People of all ages create distractions.

Concluding Paragraph

The concluding paragraph often summarizes the essay by briefly restating the thesis and, at times, the main supporting points. In addition, the writer often presents a concluding thought about the subject of the paper.

ACTIVITY 3

1. Which two sentences in the concluding paragraph restate the thesis and supporting points of the essay?

    a. First and second

    b. Second and third

    c. Third and fourth

2. Which sentence in the concluding paragraph contains the final thought of the essay?

    a. Second

    b. Third

    c. Fourth

Diagram of an Essay

Introductory Paragraph

| Introduction |
| Thesis statement |
| Plan of development |
| Points 1,2,3 |

The *introduction* attracts the reader's interest.

The *thesis statement* (or *thesis sentence*) states the main idea advanced in the paper.

The *plan of development* is a list of points that support the thesis. The points are presented in the order in which they will be developed in the paper.

} Introduction

First Supporting Paragraph

| Topic sentence (point 1) |
| Specific evidence |

The *topic sentence* advances the first supporting point for the thesis, and the *specific evidence* in the rest of the paragraph develops that first point.

Second Supporting Paragraph

| Topic sentence (point 2) |
| Specific evidence |

The *topic sentence* advances the second supporting point for the thesis, and the *specific evidence* in the rest of the paragraph develops that second point.

} Body

Third Supporting Paragraph

| Topic sentence (point 3) |
| Specific evidence |

The *topic sentence* advances the third supporting point for the thesis, and the *specific evidence* in the rest of the paragraph develops that third point.

Concluding Paragraph

| Summary, |
| conclusion, |
| or both |

A *summary* is a brief restatement of the thesis and its main points. A *conclusion* is a final thought or two stemming from the subject of the paper.

} Conclusion

Identifying the Parts of an Essay

ACTIVITY 4 Each cluster below contains one topic, one thesis statement, and two supporting sentences. In the space provided, label each item as follows:

> **T**   topic
> **TH** thesis statement
> **S**   supporting sentence

GROUP 1

_____ a. People listen to audiobooks while doing other tasks, such as commuting or exercising.

_____ b. Audiobooks are more convenient than printed books for several reasons.

_____ c. Listeners hear a dramatization of a printed book by the actual author or an actor.

_____ d. Audiobooks

GROUP 2

_____ a. A radiologic technology degree allows a person to work in medical settings where x-rays, CT scans, MRIs, sonograms, and other diagnostic imaging are needed.

_____ b. There are many career opportunities for those in the medical sciences.

_____ c. Medical sciences

_____ d. A person who obtains a degree in phlebotomy is able to work as a clinical laboratory technician.

GROUP 3

_____ a. Study skills

_____ b. Time management is essential when juggling deadlines and other responsibilities.

_____ c. Strong study skills are needed if a student wants to be successful in college.

_____ d. Notetaking provides a student with the opportunity to review information later.

GROUP 4

_____   a.   Shingles

_____   b.   People should be aware of the symptoms of shingles, a neurological disease.

_____   c.   Burning pain is one of the first symptoms of shingles.

_____   d.   Painful skin rash and blisters often follow the burning pain.

GROUP 5

_____   a.   Dogs should be trained at an early age.

_____   b.   A puppy can be housebroken as soon as he or she is brought home.

_____   c.   Dogs

_____   d.   A puppy should be trained not to bite or "mouth" people, especially children.

ACTIVITY 5

This activity will sharpen your sense of the parts of an essay. "Coping with Old Age" has no indentations starting new paragraphs. Read this essay carefully, and then double-underline the thesis and single-underline the topic sentence for each of the three supporting paragraphs and the first sentence of the conclusion. Write the numbers of those sentences in the spaces provided at the end.

Personal

Coping with Old Age

¹I recently read about an area of the former Soviet Union where many people live to be well over a hundred years old. ²Being 115 or even 125 isn't considered unusual there, and these old people continue to do productive work right up until they die. ³The United States, however, isn't such a healthy place for older people. ⁴Since I retired from my job, I've had to cope with the physical, mental, and emotional stresses of being "old." ⁵For one thing, I've had to adjust to physical changes. ⁶Now that I'm over sixty-five, the trusty body that carried me around for years has turned traitor. ⁷Aside from the deepening wrinkles on my face and neck, and the wiry gray hairs that have replaced my brown hair, I face more frightening changes. ⁸I don't have the energy I used to. ⁹My eyes get tired. ¹⁰Once in a while, I miss something that's said to me. ¹¹My once faithful feet seem to have lost their comfortable soles, and I sometimes feel I'm walking on marbles. ¹²In order to fight against this slow decay, I exercise whenever I can. ¹³I walk, I stretch, and I climb stairs. ¹⁴I battle constantly to keep as fit as possible. ¹⁵I'm also trying to cope with mental changes. ¹⁶My mind was once as quick and sure as a champion gymnast. ¹⁷I never found it difficult to memorize answers in school or to remember the names of people I met.

continued

18Now, I occasionally have to search my mind for the name of a close neighbor or favorite television show. 19Because my mind needs exercise, too, I challenge it as much as I can. 20Taking a college course like this English class, for example, forces me to concentrate. 21The mental gymnast may be a little slow and out of shape, but he can still do a back flip or turn a somersault when he has to. 22 Finally, I must deal with the emotional impact of being old. 23Our society typecasts old people. 24We're supposed to be unattractive, senile, useless leftovers. 25We're supposed to be the crazy drivers and the cranky customers. 26At first, I was angry and frustrated that I was considered old at all. 27And I knew that people were wrong to stereotype me. 28Then I got depressed. 29I even started to think that maybe I was a cast-off, one of those old animals that slow down the rest of the herd. 30But I have now decided to rebel against these negative feelings. 31I try to have friends of all ages and to keep up with what's going on in the world. 32I try to remember that I'm still the same person who sat at a first-grade desk, who fell in love, who comforted a child, who got a raise at work. 33I'm not "just" an old person. 34 Coping with the changes of old age has become my latest full-time job. 35Even though it's a job I never applied for, and one for which I had no experience, I'm trying to do the best I can.

Thesis statement in "Coping with Old Age": _____

Topic sentence of first supporting paragraph: _____

Topic sentence of second supporting paragraph: _____

Topic sentence of third supporting paragraph: _____

Topic sentence of the conclusion: _____

Important Considerations in Essay Development

Determining Your Point of View

When you write, you can take any of three approaches, or points of view: first person, second person, or third person.

First-Person Approach

In the first-person approach—a strongly individualized point of view—you draw on your own experience and speak to your audience in your own voice, using pronouns like *I, me, mine, we, our,* and *us.*

The first-person approach is most common in narrative essays based on personal experience. It also suits other essays where most of the evidence presented consists of personal observation.

Here is a first-person supporting paragraph from an essay on camping:

> First of all, I like comfort when I'm camping. My Airstream motor home, with its completely equipped kitchen, shower stall, toilet, double bed, and television, resembles a mobile motel room. I can sleep on a real mattress, clean sheets, and fluffy pillows. Next to my bed are devices that make me feel at home: a radio, an alarm clock, and a TV remote-control unit. Unlike the poor campers huddled in tents, I don't have to worry about cold, rain, heat, or annoying insects. After a hot shower, I can slide into my best nightgown, sit comfortably on my down-filled quilt, and read the latest mystery novel while a thunderstorm booms outside.

Second-Person Approach

In the second-person approach, the writer speaks directly to the reader, using the pronoun *you*. The second-person approach is considered appropriate for giving direct instructions and explanations to the reader. That is why *you* is used throughout this book.

You should plan to use the second-person approach only when writing a process essay, though a better approach would be third-person. As a general rule, never use the word *you* in writing. (If doing so has been a common mistake in your writing, you should review the rule about pronoun point of view on page 103.)

Third-Person Approach

The third-person approach is by far the most common point of view in academic writing. In the third person, the writer includes no direct references to the reader (*you*) or the self (*I, me*). Third person gets its name from the stance it suggests—that of an outsider or "third person" observing and reporting on matters of public rather than private importance. In this approach, you draw on information that you have gotten through observation, thinking, or reading.

Here is the paragraph on camping, recast in the third person. Note the third-person pronouns *their, them,* and *they,* which all refer to *campers* in the first sentence.

> First of all, modern campers bring complete bedrooms with them. Winnebagos, Airstream motor homes, and Fleetwood recreational vehicles lumber into America's campgrounds every summer like mobile motel rooms. All the comforts of home are provided inside. Campers sleep on real mattresses with clean sheets and fluffy pillows. Next to their beds are the same gadgets that litter their night tables at home—radios, alarm clocks, and TV remote-control units. It's not necessary for them to worry about annoyances like cold, heat, rain, or buzzing insects, either. They can sit comfortably in bed and read the latest mystery novels while a thunderstorm booms outside.

Doing a Personal Review

1. While you're writing and revising an essay, you should be constantly evaluating it in terms of *unity*, *support*, and *organization*. Use the essay checklist below as a guide.

2. After you've finished the next-to-final draft of an essay, check it for the *sentence skills* listed on the inside back cover. It may also help to read the paper out loud. If a given sentence does not sound right—that is, if it does not read clearly and smoothly—chances are something is wrong. Then revise or edit as needed until your paper is error-free.

ESSAY CHECKLIST: THE FOUR BASES

UNITY

✔ Clearly stated thesis in the introductory paragraph of the essay?

✔ All the supporting paragraphs on target in backing up the thesis?

SUPPORT

✔ At least three separate supporting points for the thesis?

✔ *Specific* evidence for each of the separate supporting points?

✔ *Plenty* of specific evidence for each supporting point?

COHERENCE

✔ Clear method of organization?

✔ Transitions and other connecting words?

✔ Effective introduction and conclusion?

SENTENCE SKILLS

✔ Clear, error-free sentences? (Use the checklist on the inside back cover of this book.)

Writing the Essay

RESPONDING TO IMAGES

In April 2011, a massive EF-4 tornado tore through Alabama, leaving 1500 injured and 65 dead. This photo, showing college students assisting the clean-up in Pleasant Grove, Alabama a week after the tornado, evokes many emotions, even if you were not one of the thousands who experienced its devastation firsthand. Write an essay about a tragedy you experienced in your own life. What was the experience like and how did it change you — for better or worse?

The four steps in writing an effective essay are the same steps you have been using to write effective paragraphs:

1. Begin with a point, or thesis.

2. Support the thesis with specific evidence.

3. Organize and connect the specific evidence.

4. Write clear, error-free sentences.

Much of this chapter, then, will be familiar, as we walk through how these steps can be applied to writing the essay as well.

Step 1: Begin with a Point, or Thesis

You already know from your work on the paragraph that your first step in writing is to discover what point you want to make and to write that point out as a single sentence. There are two reasons for doing this. You want to know right from the start if you have a clear and workable thesis. Also, you will be able to use the thesis as a guide while writing your essay. At any stage you can ask yourself, "Does this support my thesis?" With the thesis as a guide, the danger of drifting away from the point of the essay is greatly reduced.

Understanding Thesis Statements

In Chapter 15, you learned that effective essays center around a thesis, or main point, that a writer wishes to express. This central idea is usually presented as a *thesis statement* in an essay's introductory paragraph.

Just like the topic sentence of a paragraph, a good thesis statement does two things. First, it tells readers an essay's *topic*. Second, it presents the writer's *attitude, opinion, idea,* or *point* about that topic. For example, look at the following thesis statement:

Owning a pet has several important benefits.

In this thesis statement, the topic is *owning a pet;* the writer's main point is that owning a pet *has several important benefits.*

Writing a Good Thesis I

Now that you know how thesis statements work, you can prepare to begin writing your own. To start, you need a topic that is neither too broad nor too narrow. Suppose, for example, that an instructor asks you to write a paper on marriage. Such a subject is too broad to cover in a five-hundred-word essay. You would have to write a book to support adequately any point you might make about the general subject of marriage. What you need to do, then, is limit your subject. Narrow it down until you have a thesis that you can deal with specifically in about five hundred words. In the box that follows are (1) several general subjects, (2) a limited version of each general subject, and (3) a thesis statement about each limited subject.

General Subject	Limited Subject	Thesis
Marriage	Honeymoon	A honeymoon is perhaps the worst way to begin a marriage.
Family	Older sister	My older sister helped me overcome my shyness.
Television	TV preachers	TV evangelists use sales techniques to promote their messages.
Children	Disciplining of children	My husband and I have several effective ways of disciplining our children.
Sports	Players' salaries	Players' high salaries are bad for the game, for the fans, and for the values our children are developing.

ACTIVITY 1

Sometimes a subject must go through several stages of limiting before it is narrow enough to write about. Below are four lists reflecting several stages that writers went through in moving from a general subject to a narrow thesis statement. Number the stages in each list from 1 to 5, with 1 marking the broadest stage and 5 marking the thesis.

LIST 1

_____ Teachers

_____ Education

_____ Math teacher

_____ My high school math teacher was incompetent.

_____ High school math teacher

LIST 2

_____ Bicycles

_____ Dangers of bike riding

_____ Recreation

_____ Recreational vehicles

_____ Bike riding in the city is a dangerous activity.

LIST 3

_____ Retail companies

_____ Supermarkets

_____ Dealing with customers

_____ Working in a supermarket

_____ I've learned how to handle unpleasant supermarket customers.

LIST 4

_____ Camping

_____ First camping trip

_____ Summer vacation

_____ My first camping trip was a disastrous experience.

_____ Vacations

Later in this chapter you will get more practice in narrowing general subjects to thesis statements.

Writing a Good Thesis II

When writing thesis statements, you want to avoid making the same mistakes we discussed when writing topic sentences for your paragraphs. One mistake is to simply announce the subject rather than state a true thesis. A second mistake is to write a thesis that is too broad, and a third is to write a thesis that is too narrow. An additional mistake is to write a thesis containing more than one idea. The following activities will give you practice in avoiding such mistakes and writing good thesis statements.

Write Statements, Not Announcements

ACTIVITY 2	Write A beside each sentence that is an announcement rather than a thesis statement. Write OK beside the statement in each pair that is a clear, limited point that could be developed in an essay.

1. _____ a. This essay will discuss the fitness classes offered at my gym.

   _____ b. My gym offers spinning, kick boxing, and yoga classes.

2. _____ a. I learned the hard way that online gambling is very addictive.

   _____ b. My thesis in this paper is the very addictive nature of online gambling.

3. _____ a. The Korean *jeon*, the French crêpe, and the American hotcake are variations of the pancake.

   _____ b. Variations of the pancake is the subject of this paper.

4. _____ a. This paper will be about the toys my cat prefers.

   _____ b. My cat snubs store-bought toys in favor of toilet paper rolls, twist ties, and paper bags.

5. _____ a. My concern here is to discuss the rising fuel costs in the U.S. today.

   _____ b. There are several possible explanations for the rising fuel costs in the U.S. today.

Avoid Statements That Are Too Broad

ACTIVITY 3	Write TB beside each statement that is too broad to be developed in an essay. Write OK beside the statement in each pair that is a clear, limited point.

1. _____ a. In many ways, sports are an important part of American life.

   _____ b. Widespread gambling has changed professional football for the worse.

2. _____ a. Modern life makes people suspicious and unfriendly.

   _____ b. A frightening experience in my neighborhood has caused me to be a much more cautious person in several ways.

3. _____ a. Toy ads on television teach children to be greedy, competitive, and snobbish.

   _____ b. Advertising has bad effects on all of society.

4. _____ a. Learning new skills can be difficult and frustrating.

   _____ b. Learning to write takes work, patience, and a sense of humor.

5. _____ a. I didn't get along with my family, so I did many foolish things.

   _____ b. Running away from home taught me that my parents weren't as terrible as I thought.

Avoid Statements That Are Too Narrow

Write TN beside each statement that is too narrow to be developed in an essay. Write OK beside the statement in each pair that is a clear, limited point.

ACTIVITY 4

1. _____ a. I had squash, tomatoes, and corn in my garden last summer.

   _____ b. Vegetable gardening can be a frustrating hobby.

2. _____ a. The main road into our town is lined with billboards.

   _____ b. For several reasons, billboards should be abolished.

3. _____ a. There are now more single-parent households in our country than ever before.

   _____ b. Organization is the key to being a successful single parent.

4. _____ a. My first job taught me that I had several bad work habits.

   _____ b. Because I was late for work yesterday, I lost an hour's pay and was called in to see the boss.

5. _____ a. Americans abuse alcohol because it has become such an important part of their personal and public celebrations.

   _____ b. Consumption of wine, beer, and hard liquor increases in the United States every year.

Make Sure Statements Develop Only One Idea

Here are three statements that contain more than one idea:

One of the most serious problems affecting young people today is bullying, and it is time more kids learned the value of helping others.

Studying with others has several benefits, but it also has drawbacks and can be difficult to schedule.

Teachers have played an important role in my life, but they were not as important as my parents.

In this group, each statement contains more than one idea. For instance, "One of the most serious problems affecting young people today is bullying, and it is time more kids learned the value of helping others" clearly has two separate ideas ("One of the most serious problems affecting young people today is bullying" *and* "it is time more kids learned the value of helping others"). The reader is asked to focus on two separate points, each of which more logically belongs in an essay of its own. Remember, the point of an essay is to communicate a *single* main idea to readers. To be as clear as possible, then, try to limit your thesis statement to the single key idea you want your readers to know. Revised thesis statements based on each of the examples above are as follows:

One of the most serious problems affecting young people today is bullying.

Studying with others has several benefits.

Teachers have played an important role in my life.

ACTIVITY 5	Complete the following thesis statements by adding a third supporting point that will parallel the two already provided. You might first want to revisit the section on parallelism in Chapter 4 (page 100) to make sure you understand parallel form.

1. Because I never took college preparatory courses in high school, I entered college deficient in mathematics, study skills, and _____.

2. A good salesperson needs to like people, to be aggressive, and _____ _____.

3. Rather than blame myself for failing the course, I blamed the instructor, my adviser, and even _____.

4. Anyone who buys an old house planning to fix it up should be prepared to put in a lot of time, hard work, and _____.

5. Our old car eats gas, makes funny noises, and _____ _____.

6. My mother, my boss, and my _____ are three people who are very important in my life right now.

7. Getting married too young was a mistake because we hadn't finished our education, we weren't ready for children, and _____ _____.

8. Some restaurant patrons seem to leave their honesty, their cleanliness,

   and their _____ at home.

9. During my first semester at college, I had to learn how to manage my

   time, my diet, and _____.

10. Three experiences I wish I could forget are the time I fell off a ladder,

    the time I tried to fix my parents' lawn mower, and _____

    _____.

ACTIVITY 6

Working with a partner, write a thesis for each group of supporting statements. This activity will give you practice in writing an effective essay thesis—one that is neither too broad nor too narrow. It will also help you understand the logical relationship between a thesis and its supporting details.

1. Thesis: _____.

   a. My first car was a rebellious-looking one that matched the way I felt and acted as a teenager.

   b. My next car reflected my more mature and practical adult self.

   c. My latest car seems to tell me that I'm aging; it shows my growing concern with comfort and safety.

2. Thesis: _____.

   a. All the course credits that are accumulated can be transferred to a four-year school.

   b. Going to a two-year college can save a great deal of money in tuition and other fees.

   c. If the college is nearby, there are also significant savings in everyday living expenses.

3. Thesis: _____.

   a. First, I tried simply avoiding the snacks aisle of the supermarket.

   b. Then I started limiting myself to only one serving of any given snack.

   c. Finally, in desperation, I began keeping the bags of snacks in a padlocked cupboard.

4. Thesis: _____.

   a. The holiday can be very frightening for little children.

   b. Children can be struck by cars while wearing vision-obstructing masks and dark costumes.

   c. There are always incidents involving deadly treats: fruits, cookies, and candies that contain razor blades or even poison.

5. Thesis: _____.

    a. First of all, I was a typical "type A" personality: anxious, impatient, and hard-driving.

    b. I also had a family history of relatives with heart trouble.

    c. My unhealthy lifestyle, though, was probably the major factor.

The following activity will give you practice in distinguishing general from limited subjects and in writing a thesis.

ACTIVITY 7

Here is a list of ten general subjects. Working in pairs with a fellow classmate, limit five of the subjects. Then write a thesis statement about each of the five limited subjects.

HINT To create a thesis statement for a limited subject, ask yourself, "What point do I want to make about _____ (*my limited subject*)?"

GENERAL SUBJECT	LIMITED SUBJECT
1. Pets	_____
2. Teenagers	_____
3. Internet	_____
4. Work	_____
5. College	_____
6. Doctors	_____
7. Vacations	_____
8. Cooking	_____
9. Money	_____
10. Shopping	_____

Thesis statements for five of the limited subjects:

_____

_____

_____

_____

_____

_____

_____

_____

_____

_____

_____

_____

Step 2: Support the Thesis with Specific Evidence

The first essential step in writing a successful essay is to formulate a clearly stated thesis. The second basic step is to support the thesis with specific reasons or details, just as you would support the topic sentence of your paragraph.

To ensure that your essay will have adequate support, you may find an informal outline very helpful. Write down a brief version of your thesis idea, and then work out and jot down three or more points that will support the thesis.

Here is the scratch outline that was prepared by the author of the essay on moviegoing in Chapter 15:

> *Moviegoing is a problem.*
>
> 1. *Inconvenience of going out.*
>
> 2. *Tempting snacks*
>
> 3. *Other moviegoers*

A scratch outline like this one looks simple, but developing it often requires a great deal of careful thinking. The time spent on developing a logical outline is invaluable, though. Once you have planned the steps that logically support your thesis, you will be in an excellent position to go on to write an effective essay.

Activities in this section will give you practice in the crucial skill of planning an essay clearly.

| Following are ten informal outlines. Complete any five of them by adding a third logical supporting point (*c*) that will parallel the two already provided (*a* and *b*). | **ACTIVITY 8** |

1. College registration can be a confusing process.

   a. Some classes fill quickly.

   b. Several placement tests are needed.

   c. _____

2. People seek out comfort food at roadside diners.

   a. Meatloaf sandwich

   b. Baked macaroni and cheese

   c. _____

3. White lies are socially acceptable.

   a. Avoid hurting a person's feelings

   b. Avoid facing consequences

   c. _____

4. Back-to-school shopping can be expensive.

   a. Backpack

   b. Textbooks

   c. _____

5. Big-box stores such as Wal-Mart have everything shoppers need.

   a. Supermarket

   b. Pharmacy

   c. _____

6. Mike moved to Southern California to enjoy water sports.

   a. He surfs.

   b. He scuba dives.

   c. _____

7. A cell phone can be customized to fit the owner.

   a. Ringtone

   b. Wallpaper

   c. _____

8. Technology makes handling finances so much easier.

   a. Automatic bill payments

   b. Online banking services

   c. _____

9. My boss has three qualities I admire.

   a. Shrewdness

   b. Intelligence

   c. _____

10. Traveling by air is stressful.

   a. Security restrictions

   b. Delayed flights

   c. _____

The Importance of *Specific* Details

Just as a thesis must be developed with at least three supporting points, each supporting point must be developed with specific details.

All too often, the body paragraphs in essays contain only vague generalities, rather than the specific supporting details that are needed to engage and convince a reader. Here is what one of the paragraphs in "The Hazards of Moviegoing" (see Chapter 15) would have looked like if the writer had not detailed her supporting evidence vividly:

> Some of the other patrons are even more of a problem than the theater itself. Many people in the theater often show themselves to be inconsiderate. They make noises and create disturbances at their seats. Included are people in every age group, from the young to the old. Some act as if they were at home in their own living room watching the TV set. And people are often messy, so that you're constantly aware of all the food they're eating. People are also always moving around near you, creating a disturbance and interrupting your enjoyment of the movie.

The following box contrasts the vague support in the preceding paragraph with the specific support in the essay.

Vague Support	Specific Support
1. Many people in the theater show themselves to be inconsiderate. They make noises and create disturbances at their seats. Included are people in every age group, from the young to the old. Some act as if they were at home in their own living room watching the TV set.	1. Little kids race up and down the aisles, usually in giggling packs. Teenagers try to impress their friends by talking back to the screen, whistling, and making what they consider to be hilarious noises. Adults act as if they were at home in their own living room and comment loudly on the ages of the stars or why movies aren't as good anymore.
2. And people are often messy, so that you're constantly aware of all the food they're eating.	2. And people of all ages crinkle candy wrappers, stick gum on their seats, and drop popcorn tubs or cups of crushed ice and soda on the floor.
3. People are also always moving around near you, creating a disturbance and interrupting your enjoyment of the movie.	3. They also cough and burp, talk on their cell phones, file out for repeated trips to the rest rooms or concession stand, and elbow you out of the armrest on either side of your seat.

The effective paragraph from the essay provides details that make vividly clear the statement that patrons are a problem in the theater. The writer specifies the exact age groups (little kids, teenagers, and adults) and the offenses of each (giggling, talking and whistling, and loud comments). She specifies the various food excesses (crinkled wrappers, gum on seats, dropped popcorn and soda containers). Finally, she provides concrete details that enable us to see and hear other disturbances (coughs and burps, talking on cell phones, constant trips to rest rooms, jostling for elbow room). The ineffective paragraph asks us to guess about these details; the effective paragraph describes the details in a specific and lively way.

In the strong paragraph, then, sharp details capture our interest and enable us to share the writer's experience. They provide pictures that make each of us feel, "I am there." The particulars also enable us to understand clearly the writer's point that patrons are a problem. Aim to make your own writing equally convincing by providing detailed support.

The Importance of *Adequate* Details

You must provide *enough* specific details to fully support the point in a body paragraph of an essay. You could not, for example, include a paragraph about a friend's unreliability and provide only a one- or two-sentence example. You know from your previous work on writing paragraphs that you would have to extend the example or add several other examples showing your friend as an unreliable person. Without such additional support, your paragraph would be underdeveloped.

ACTIVITY 9 	Take a few minutes to write a paragraph supporting the point "My _____ is (are) a mess." You might write about your backpack, your bedroom, your desk, your finances, your personal life, even your life as a whole. If you want, be humorous. Afterward, you and your classmates, working in small groups, should read your paragraphs aloud. The best-received paragraphs are almost sure to be those with plenty of specific details.

Adding Details to Complete an Essay

ACTIVITY 10	The following essay needs specific details to back up the ideas in the supporting paragraphs. Using the spaces provided, add a sentence or two of clear, convincing details for each supporting idea. This activity will give you practice at supplying specific details and an initial feel for writing an essay.

Introduction

Life Off-Line

When my family's Internet provider had some mechanical problems that interrupted our service for a week, my parents, my sister, and I thought we would never make it. Getting through long evenings without streaming movies, e-mails, Twitter updates, and Internet searches seemed impossible. We soon realized, though, that living off-line for a while was a stroke of good fortune. It became easy for each of us to enjoy some activities alone, to complete some postponed chores, and to spend rewarding time with each other and friends.

First of all, now that we were disconnected, we found plenty of hours for personal interests. We all read more that week than we had read during the six months before. _____

_____

_____

We each also enjoyed some hobbies we had ignored for ages. _____

_____

_____

In addition, my sister and I both stopped procrastinating with our homework. _____

_____

_____

First supporting paragraph

Second, we did chores that had been hanging over our heads for too long. There were many jobs around the house that had needed attention for some time. _____

_____

_____

We had a chance to do some long-postponed shopping. _____

_____

_____

Also, each of us did some paperwork that was long overdue. _____

_____

_____

Second supporting paragraph

Finally, and probably most important, we spent time with each other. Instead of just being in the same room together while we stared at different screens, we actually talked for many pleasant hours. _____

_____

_____

Third supporting paragraph

continued

Moreover, for the first time in years my family played some card games and board games together. _____

_____

_____

Because we couldn't keep up with everyone electronically, we had some family friends over one evening and spent an enjoyable time with them.

_____

_____

_____

Conclusion

    Once our Internet provider got the problems fixed, we were not prepared to go back to our previous ways. We had gained a sense of how our online activities had not only taken over our lives, but had interrupted our family's life. We still spend time streaming movies, gaming, e-mailing, and tweeting, but we make sure to spend at least two evenings a week focusing on each other. As a result, we have found that we can enjoy our virtual lives and still have time left over for our real lives!

Step 3: Organize and Connect the Specific Evidence

As you are generating the specific details needed to support a thesis, you should be thinking about ways to organize and connect those details. All the details in your essay must *cohere*, or stick together, so that your reader will be able to move smoothly from one bit of supporting information to the next. This section shows you how to organize and connect supporting details by using (1) common methods of organization, (2) transitions, and (3) other connecting words.

Common Methods of Organization

You are already familiar with the two common methods used to organize the supporting material in an essay: *time order* and *emphatic order*.

    As you'll recall *time*, or *chronological, order* simply means that details are listed as they occur in time. *First* this is done; *next* this; *then* this; *after* that, this; and so on. Here is an outline of an essay in which time order is used:

> To exercise successfully, a person should follow a simple plan consisting of arranging time, making preparations, and warming up properly.
>
> 1. The first thing that should be done is to set aside a regular hour for exercise.
>
> 2. Next, preparations for the exercise session should be made.
>
> 3. Finally, a series of warm-up activities should be completed.

Thesis

Fill in the missing words: The topic sentences in the essay use the words _____ , _____ , and _____ to help show time order.

Emphatic order is a way to put *emphasis* on the most interesting or important detail by placing it in the last part of a paragraph or in the final supporting paragraph of an essay. *Finally, last of all,* and *most important* are typical words or phrases showing emphasis. Here is an outline of an essay that uses emphatic order:

> Celebrities lead very stressful lives.
>
> 1. For one thing, celebrities don't have the privacy an ordinary person does.
>
> 2. In addition, celebrities are under constant pressure.
>
> 3. Most important, celebrities must deal with the stress of being in constant danger.

Thesis

Fill in the missing words: The topic sentences in the essay use the words _____ , _____ , and _____ to help show emphatic order.

Some essays use a combination of time order and emphatic order. For example, the essay on moviegoing in Chapter 15 includes time order: the writer first describes getting to the theater, then the theater itself, and finally the behavior of patrons during the movie. At the same time, the writer uses emphatic order, ending with the most important reason for her dislike of moviegoing: "Some of the other patrons are even more of a problem than the theater itself."

Transitions

Transitional Words

Transitions signal the direction of a writer's thought. They are like the road signs that guide travelers. In the box that follows are some common transitions you have already been using in writing your paragraphs. They are grouped according to the kind of signal they give to readers. Note that certain words provide more than one kind of signal.

Addition signal: one, first of all, second, the third reason, also, next, another, and, in addition, moreover, furthermore, finally, last of all

Time signals: first, then, next, after, as, before, while, meanwhile, soon, now, during, finally

Space signals: next to, across, on the opposite side, to the left, to the right, above, below, near, nearby

Change-of-direction signals: but, however, yet, in contrast, although, otherwise, still, on the contrary, on the other hand

Illustration signals: for example, for instance, specifically, as an illustration, once, such as

Conclusion signals: therefore, consequently, thus, then, as a result, in summary, to conclude, last of all, finally

---

| ACTIVITY 11 | Work together with a fellow classmate to complete the following activity. |

1. Underline the three *addition* signals in the following selection:

To create the time a student needs to pass each semester, he or she should incorporate different types of courses. Mixing course types allows students to access different parts of their brains to avoid overload. One way a student can mix courses is to take a course that keeps him or her active—for example, a physical education course. Hours of studying can be exhausting, but exercise has been shown to be a positive cure. After studying anatomy facts like the muscular system, a student could work out those very muscles, creating a hands-on review. Another way a student can mix courses is to take a literature course during the same semester as a math course. Math homework can often be repetitive and lengthy, but breaking it up by reading a story about growing up during the Industrial Age can offer the mental break needed. A final way a student can add variety to his or her schedule is to take a "fun" course each semester. For one student, a fun course might be a photography course, but for another student computer programming would be more fun. Fun courses are not necessarily easy, but they are courses that a student chooses based upon his or her personal interest.

2. Underline the four *time* signals in the following selection:

After a person has acquired the job of TV sports reporter, it is important to begin working on the details of his or her image, so viewers connect. First, it is important that a new sports reporter invests in two or three versatile suit jackets. They should be made from fabrics that are neutral in color, so the reporter can mix-and-match a variety of shirts and ties. The best colors would be basic neutrals like black, navy, and beige. Next, a new sports reporter should invest in a variety of ties. Everyday ties should include basic stripes and muted patterns. However, since a reporter is on TV daily, it is also important to have one or two unique ties that viewers will enjoy seeing occasionally. It is also good to have a few holiday ties that will bring smiles to the viewers. Finally, it is important that a new sportscaster create a personality that viewers will respond to. Supporting the home team is always important, and a good reporter will find ways to describe both wins and losses in a positive manner. His or her tone should always show that despite the home team's performance, the fans will remain loyal.

3.   Underline the three *space* signals in the following selection:

The vegetable bin of my refrigerator contained an assortment of weird-looking items. Next to a shriveled, white-coated lemon were two oranges covered with blue fuzz. To the right of the oranges was a bunch of carrots that had begun to sprout points, spikes, knobs, and tendrils. The carrots drooped into U shapes as I picked them up with the tips of my fingers. Near the carrots was a net bag of onions; each onion had sent curling shoots through the net until the whole thing resembled a mass of green spaghetti. The most horrible item, though, was a head of lettuce that had turned into a pool of brown goo. It had seeped out of its bag and coated the bin with a sticky, evil-smelling liquid.

4.   Underline the two *change-of-direction* signals in the following selection:

Taking small children on vacation, for instance, sounds like a wonderful experience for the entire family. But vacations can be scary or emotionally overwhelming times for children. When children are taken away from their usual routine and brought to an unfamiliar place, they can become very frightened. That strange bed in the motel room or the unusual noises in Grandma's spare bedroom may cause nightmares. On vacations, too, children usually clamor to do as many things in one day as they can and to stay up past their usual bedtime. And, since it is vacation time, parents may decide to give in to the children's demands. A parental attitude like this, however, can lead to problems. After a sixteen-hour day of touring the amusement park, eating in a restaurant, and seeing a movie, children can experience sensory and emotional overload. They become cranky, unhappy, or even rebellious and angry.

5.   Underline the two *illustration* signals in the following selection:

Supermarkets also use psychology to encourage people to buy. For example, in most supermarkets, the milk and the bread are either at opposite ends of the store or located far away from the first aisle. Even if shoppers have stopped at the market only for staples like these, they must pass hundreds of items in order to reach them. The odds are that instead of leaving with just a quart of milk, they will leave with additional purchases as well. Special displays, such as a pyramid of canned green beans in an aisle and a large end display of cartons of paper towels, also increase sales. Because shoppers assume that these items are a good buy, they may pick them up. However, the items may not even be on sale! Store managers know that customers are automatically attracted to a display like this, and they will use it to move an overstocked product.

6. Underline the two *conclusion* signals in the following selection:

Finally, my grandmother was extremely thrifty. She was one of those people who hoard pieces of used aluminum foil after carefully scraping off the cake icing or beef gravy. She had a drawer full of old eyeglasses that dated back at least thirty years. The lens prescriptions were no longer accurate, but Gran couldn't bear to throw away "a good pair of glasses." She kept them "just in case," but we could never figure out what situation would involve a desperate need for a dozen pairs of old eyeglasses. We never realized the true extent of Gran's thriftiness, though, until after she died. Her house was to be sold, and therefore we cleaned out its dusty attic. In one corner was a cardboard box filled with two- and three-inch pieces of string. The box was labeled, in Gran's spidery hand, "String too short to be saved."

Transitional Sentences

Transitional, or *linking, sentences* are used between paragraphs to help tie together the supporting paragraphs in an essay. They enable the reader to move smoothly from the idea in one paragraph to the idea in the next paragraph.

Here is the linking sentence used in the essay on moviegoing:

> Many of the other patrons are even more of a problem than the concession stand.

The words *concession stand* remind us of the point of the first supporting paragraph, while *Many of the other patrons* presents the point to be developed in the second supporting paragraph.

ACTIVITY 12

Following are brief sentence outlines from two essays. In each outline, the second and third topic sentences serve as transitional, or linking, sentences. Each reminds us of the point in the preceding paragraph and announces the point to be developed in the current paragraph. Working in groups of two or three, use the spaces provided to add the words needed to complete the second and third topic sentences.

Thesis 1

In order to set up an in-home day-care center, a person must be sure the house conforms to state regulations, the necessary legal permits are in place, and services are advertised in the right places.

First supporting paragraph

First of all, a potential operator of an in-home day-care center must make sure the house conforms to state regulations....

After making certain that _____

_____,

the potential operator must obtain _____. . . .

Second supporting paragraph

Finally, once the necessary _____

the potential operator can begin to _____.

Third supporting paragraph

Cheaper cost, greater comfort, and superior electronic technology make watching football at home more enjoyable than attending a game at the stadium.

Thesis 2

Personal

For one thing, watching the game on TV eliminates the cost of attending the game. . . .

First supporting paragraph

In addition to saving me money, watching the game at home is more _____ than sitting in a stadium. . . .

Second supporting paragraph

Even more important than _____ and _____, though, is the _____ that makes a televised game better than the "real thing." . . .

Third supporting paragraph

Other Connecting Words

In addition to transitions, there are three other kinds of connecting words that help tie together the specific evidence in a paper: *repeated words, pronouns,* and *synonyms.* For a description of each, revisit pages 96–98.

Identifying Transitions and Other Connecting Words

The following items use connecting words to help tie ideas together. The connecting words you are to identify are set off in italics. In the space, write T for *transition,* RW for *repeated word,* S for *synonym,* or P for *pronoun.*

ACTIVITY 13

_____ 1. The family watched helplessly as the firefighters rushed into their home. Their *house* was engulfed in flames.

_____ 2. Sanjay's dream is to become a computer software engineer. *That* is why he is going to college.

_____ 3. Fiji is located between New Caledonia and Tonga. *Nearby* in the Pacific Ocean is Samoa.

_____ 4. Jimmy donated his Air Jordans to the Nike Reuse-A-Shoe Program. His *shoes* will be recycled to build the turf for play-grounds and basketball courts.

_____ 5. Grant's daughter Anna was adopted from an orphanage in Sichuan Province, China. At seven years of age, *she* is now eager to have a younger sibling.

_____ 6. Barbara is taking classes to learn American Sign Language. Once she masters this *language*, she wants to become an interpreter.

_____ 7. Alden completed his ten weeks of basic training for the Army National Guard. After *he* was done, he said that he felt like a changed person.

_____ 8. The nurse advised his patient to prepare a living will before the surgery. *He* also told his patient that everything would be okay.

_____ 9. My son is constantly sending his friends text messages. *On the other hand*, I know very little about "txt talk."

_____ 10. The Levi's that I bought are a relaxed fit. When I wear these jeans, I feel *relaxed*.

_____ 11. I'm so lucky that my apartment has a full-sized washer and dryer. These *appliances* are fairly new.

_____ 12. During deforestation, trees are cut down. *As a result*, more carbon dioxide remains in the air.

_____ 13. Grace works part time as an accounting clerk. She plans to earn an *accounting* degree so that she can secure a full-time job.

_____ 14. During the winter, I constantly remind my kids to put on a jacket before going out. Predictably, they find themselves needing an additional layer of *clothing*.

_____ 15. The library is located near the admissions office. *On the opposite side* of campus, there is a computer lab and a tutoring center.

Step 4: Write Clear, Error-Free Sentences

You have now seen how the first three goals in effective writing, unity, support, and coherence, can be applied to writing the essay. This section focuses on the fourth goal of writing effectively: sentence skills. When writing essays, you should continue to revise your sentences using the following strategies:

- parallelism
- a consistent point of view
- specific words
- concise words
- varied sentences

An additional strategy, which will be discussed below, is to use active verbs.

Use Active Verbs

When the subject of a sentence performs the action of the verb, the verb is in the *active voice*. When the subject of a sentence receives the action of a verb, the verb is in the *passive voice*.

The passive form of a verb consists of a form of the verb *to be (am, is, are, was, were)* plus the past participle of the main verb (which is usually the same as its past tense form). Look at the following active and passive forms.

Passive	**Active**
The computer was *turned on* by Hakim.	Hakim *turned on* the computer.
The car's air conditioner *was fixed* by the mechanic.	The mechanic *fixed* the car's air conditioner.

In general, active verbs are more effective than passive verbs. Active verbs give your writing a simpler and more vigorous style.

ACTIVITY 14

Revise the following sentences, changing verbs from the passive to the active voice and making any other word changes necessary.

EXAMPLE

Fruits and vegetables are painted often by artists.

Artists often paint fruits and vegetables.

1. Many unhealthy foods are included in the typical American diet.

2. The family picnic was invaded by hundreds of biting ants.

3. Antibiotics are used by doctors to treat many infections.

4. The fatal traffic accident was caused by a drunk driver.

5. Final grades will be determined by the instructor on the basis of class performance.

_____

Practice in Revising Sentences

You are already aware that practice in *editing* sentences is best undertaken after you have worked through the sentence skills in Part Five. The focus in this section, then, will be a review on revising sentences—using a variety of methods to ensure that your sentences flow smoothly and are clear and interesting. You will work through the following series of Review Activities:

1. Using parallelism

2. Using a consistent point of view

3. Using specific words

4. Using active verbs

5. Using concise words

6. Varying your sentences

Using Parallelism

REVIEW ACTIVITY 1

Cross out the unbalanced part of each sentence. In the space provided, revise the unbalanced part so that it matches the other item or items in the sentence.

EXAMPLE

Microwavable pizza is convenient, cheap, and it tastes good.

tasty _____

1. Before I do my homework, I need to prepare dinner, bathing the kids, and pay bills.

   _____

2. Features I look for in a computer are the speed of the processor, RAM memory, and hard drive space.

   _____

3. "Txt talk" includes slang, emoticons, and abbreviating words.

   _____

4. On the weekends, Kurt enjoys playing basketball, TV, and hanging out with his friends.

   _____

5. My ideal mate would be attractive, wealthy, and have a great personality.

   _____

Using a Consistent Point of View

Change verbs as needed in the following selection so that they are consistently in the past tense. Cross out each incorrect verb and write the correct form above it, as shown in the example. You will need to make ten corrections.

Personal

My uncle's shopping trip last Thursday was discouraging to him. First of all, he had to drive around for fifteen minutes until he ~~finds~~ *found* a parking space. There was a half-price special on paper products in the supermarket, and every spot is taken. Then, when he finally got inside, many of the items on his list were not where he expected. For example, the pickles he wanted are not on the same shelf as all the other pickles. Instead, they were in a refrigerated case next to the bacon. And the granola was not on the cereal shelves but in the health-food section. Shopping thus proceeds slowly. About halfway through his list, he knew there would not be time to cook dinner and decides to pick up a barbecued chicken. The chicken, he learned, was available at the end of the store he had already passed. So he parks his shopping cart in an aisle, gets the chicken, and came back. After adding half a dozen more items to his cart, he suddenly realizes it contained someone else's food. So he retraced his steps, found his own cart, transfers the groceries, and continued to shop. Later, when he began loading items onto the checkout counter, he notices that the barbecued chicken was missing. He must have left it in the other cart, certainly gone by now. Feeling totally defeated, he returned to the deli counter and says to the clerk, "Give me another chicken. I lost the first one." My uncle told me that when he saw the look on the clerk's face, he felt as if he'd flunked Food Shopping.

Using Specific Words

Revise the following sentences, changing vague, indefinite words into sharp, specific ones.

EXAMPLE

My roommate Marcelo listens to a *variety of music*.

. . . hip-hop, heavy metal, and reggae.

1. When my marriage broke up, I felt *various emotions*.

    _____

    _____

    _____

2. The *food choices* in the cafeteria were unappetizing.

    _____

    _____

    _____

3. *Bugs* invaded our kitchen and pantry this summer.

    _____

    _____

    _____

4. All last week, *the weather was terrible*.

    _____

    _____

    _____

5. In the car accident, our teacher suffered *a number of injuries*.

    _____

    _____

    _____

Using Active Verbs

REVIEW ACTIVITY 4   Revise the following sentences, changing verbs from the passive to the active voice and making any other necessary word changes.

EXAMPLE

Soccer is played by children all over the world.

Children all over the world play soccer.

1. The pizza restaurant was closed by the health inspector.

    _____

2. Huge stacks of donated books were sorted by the workers in the library.

_____

3. My computer was infected by a virus.

_____

4. Gasoline prices will not be increased by oil companies this winter.

_____

5. High-powered bombs were dropped by our airplanes onto enemy bases.

_____

6. An additional charge was placed on our phone bill by the telephone company.

_____

7. The community center was damaged by a group of vandals.

_____

8. Stress is relieved by physical activity, meditation, and relaxation.

_____

9. Taxes will be raised by the federal government to pay for highway improvements.

_____

10. Studies show that violent behavior among young children is increased by watching violent TV programs.

_____

_____

Using Concise Words

Revise the following sentences, omitting needless words.	**REVIEW ACTIVITY 5**

EXAMPLE

The ground beef patties that are manufactured at Wendy's are square in size.

The burgers at Wendy's are square.

1. Gio at this point in time does not know the answer owing to the fact that he was not in attendance at class last week.

_____

2. The oval in shape pendant that I chose holds a large in size and blue in color sapphire stone.

_____

3. You are informed that your line of credit has been increased due to the fact that you made payments by the deadlines.

_____

_____

4. Professor Lee is of the opinion that students enrolled in his class should turn off their cellular phone devices before the beginning of a class session.

_____

5. Alberta has a personal preference for a writing instrument that is a pencil over a writing instrument that is a pen, which, in her honest and humble opinion, is preferable because her handwritten mistakes can be removed with a rubber eraser.

_____

_____

Varying Your Sentences

REVIEW ACTIVITY 6   Combine each of the following groups of simple sentences into one longer sentence. Omit repeated words. Various combinations are often possible, so try to find a combination in each group that flows most smoothly and clearly.

EXAMPLE

The technician arrived at the scene.
The technician worked for a crime lab.
The technician needed to dust for fingerprints.

The crime lab technician arrived at the scene to dust for fingerprints.

1. Sophie had repaired her broken watchband with a paper clip.
The clip snapped.
The watch slid off her wrist.

_____

_____

2. The physical therapist watched.
Julie tried to stand on her weakened legs.
They crumpled under her.

_____

_____

3. There were parking spaces on the street.
   Richie pulled into an expensive garage.
   He did not want to risk damage to his new car.

   _____

   _____

4. The truck was speeding.
   The truck was brown.
   The truck skidded on some ice.
   The truck almost hit a police officer.
   The police officer was startled.
   The police officer was young.

   _____

   _____

5. The rainstorm flooded our basement.
   The rainstorm was sudden.
   The rainstorm was terrible.
   It knocked slates off the roof.
   It uprooted a young tree.

   _____

   _____

Revising Essays for All Four Bases: Unity, Support, Coherence, and Sentence Skills

ACTIVITY 15

In this activity, you will evaluate and revise two essays in terms of all four bases: unity, support, coherence, and sentence skills. Comments follow each supporting paragraph. Circle the letter of the *one* statement that applies in each case.

Chiggers

Essay 1

1

I had lived my whole life not knowing what chiggers are. I thought they were probably a type of insect Humphrey Bogart encountered in *The African Queen*. I never had any real reason to care, until one day last summer. Within twenty-four hours, I had vividly experienced what chigger bites are, learned how to treat them, and learned how to prevent them.

2

First of all, I learned that chiggers are the larvae of tiny mites found in the woods and that their bites are always multiple and cause intense itching. A beautiful summer day seemed perfect for a walk in the woods. I am definitely not a city person, for I couldn't stand to be surrounded by people, noise, and concrete. As I walked through the ferns and pines, I noticed what appeared to be a dusting of reddish seeds or pollen on

continued

my slacks. Looking more closely, I realized that each speck was a tiny insect. I casually brushed off a few and gave them no further thought. I woke up the next morning feeling like a victim staked to an anthill by an enemy wise in the ways of torture. Most of my body was speckled with measlelike bumps that at the slightest touch burned and itched like a mosquito bite raised to the twentieth power. When antiseptics and calamine lotion failed to help, I raced to my doctor for emergency aid.

a. Paragraph 2 contains an irrelevant sentence.

b. Paragraph 2 lacks supporting details at one key spot.

c. Time order in paragraph 2 is confused.

d. Paragraph 2 contains two run-ons.

3

Healing the bites of chiggers, as the doctor diagnosed them to be, is not a simple procedure. It seems that there is really no wonder drug or commercial product to help. The victim must rely on a harsh and primitive home remedy and mostly wait out the course of the painful bites. First, the doctor explained, the skin must be bathed carefully in alcohol. An antihistamine spray applied several hours later will soothe the intense itching and help prevent infection. Before using the spray, I had to saturate each bite with gasoline or nail polish remover to kill any remaining chiggers. A few days after the treatment, the bites finally healed. Although I was still in pain, and desperate for relief, I followed the doctor's instructions. I carefully applied gasoline to the bites and walked around for an hour smelling like a filling station.

a. Paragraph 3 contains an irrelevant sentence.

b. Paragraph 3 lacks supporting details at one key spot.

c. Time order in paragraph 3 is confused.

d. Paragraph 3 contains one fragment.

4

Most important of all, I learned what to do to prevent getting chigger bites in the future. Mainly, of course, stay out of the woods in the summertime. But if the temptation is too great on an especially beautiful day, I'll be sure to wear the right type of clothing, like a long-sleeved shirt, long pants, knee socks, and closed shoes. In addition, I'll cover myself with clouds of superstrength insect repellent. I will then shower thoroughly as soon as I get home, I also will probably burn all my clothes if I notice even one suspicious red speck.

a. Paragraph 4 contains an irrelevant sentence.

b. Paragraph 4 lacks supporting details at one key spot.

c. Paragraph 4 lacks transitional words.

d. Paragraph 4 contains a run-on and a fragment.

> I will never forget my lessons on the cause, cure, and prevention of chigger bites. I'd gladly accept the challenge of rattlesnakes and scorpions in the wilds of the West but will never again confront a siege of chiggers in the pinewoods.

5

The Hazards of Being an Only Child

> Many people who have grown up in multichild families think that being an only child is the best of all possible worlds. They point to such benefits as the only child's annual new wardrobe and the lack of competition for parental love. But single-child status isn't as good as people say it is. Instead of having everything they want, only children are sometimes denied certain basic human needs.
>
> Only children lack companionship. An only child can have trouble making friends, since he or she isn't used to being around other children. Often, the only child comes home to an empty house; both parents are working, and there are no brothers or sisters to play with or to talk to about the day. At dinner, the single child can't tell jokes, giggle, or throw food while the adults discuss boring adult subjects. An only child always has his or her own room but never has anyone to whisper to half the night when sleep doesn't come. Some only children thrive on this isolation and channel their energies into creative activities like writing or drawing. Owing to this lack of companionship, an only child sometimes lacks the social ease and self-confidence that come from being part of a close-knit group of contemporaries.

Essay 2

1

2

a. Paragraph 2 contains an irrelevant sentence.

b. Paragraph 2 lacks supporting details at one key spot.

c. Paragraph 2 lacks transitional words.

d. Paragraph 2 contains one fragment and one run-on.

> Second, only children lack privacy. An only child is automatically the center of parental concern. There's never any doubt about which child tried to sneak in after midnight on a weekday. And who will get the lecture the next morning. Also, whenever an only child gives in to a bad mood, runs into his or her room, and slams the door, the door will

3

continued

open thirty seconds later, revealing an anxious parent. Parents of only children sometimes don't even understand the child's need for privacy. For example, they may not understand why a teenager wants a lock on the door or a personal telephone. After all, the parents think, there are only the three of us, there's no need for secrets.

a. Paragraph 3 contains an irrelevant sentence.

b. Paragraph 3 lacks supporting details at one key spot.

c. Paragraph 3 lacks transitional words.

d. Paragraph 3 contains one fragment and one run-on.

4   Most important, only children lack power. They get all the love; but if something goes wrong, they also get all the punishment. When a bottle of perfume is knocked to the floor or the television is left on all night, there's no little sister or brother to blame it on. Moreover, an only child has no recourse when asking for a privilege of some kind, such as permission to stay out late or to take an overnight trip with friends. There are no other siblings to point to and say, "You let them do it. Why won't you let me?" With no allies their own age, only children are always outnumbered, two to one. An only child hasn't a chance of influencing any major family decisions, either.

a. Paragraph 4 contains an irrelevant sentence.

b. Paragraph 4 lacks supporting details at one key spot.

c. Paragraph 4 lacks transitional words.

d. Paragraph 4 contains one fragment and one run-on.

5   Being an only child isn't as special as some people think. It's no fun being without friends, without privacy, and without power in one's own home. But the child who can triumph over these hardships grows up self-reliant and strong. Perhaps for this reason alone, the hazards are worth it.

Introductions, Conclusions, and Titles

RESPONDING TO IMAGES

What would you and your family or friends do without electronic media or online access? In the previous chapter, you helped complete one student's essay in response to a similar question. How would your own essay about life without electronic media and/or online access be different? Take some time to brainstorm, and then prepare a scratch outline before writing your first draft.

A well-organized essay also needs a strong introductory paragraph, an effective concluding paragraph, and a good title.

Introductory Paragraph

Functions of the Introduction

A well-written introductory paragraph performs four important roles:

1. It attracts the reader's interest, encouraging him or her to continue reading the essay.

2. It supplies any background information that the reader may need to understand the essay.

3. It presents a thesis statement. This clear, direct statement of the main idea of the essay usually appears near the end of the introductory paragraph.

4. It indicates a plan of development. In this "preview," the major supporting points for the thesis are listed in the order in which they will be presented. In some cases, the thesis and plan of development appear in the same sentence. However, writers sometimes choose not to describe the plan of development.

Common Methods of Introduction

Here are some common methods of introduction. Use any one method, or a combination of methods, to introduce your subject to the reader in an interesting way.

1. **Begin with a broad, general statement of your topic and narrow it down to your thesis statement.** Broad, general statements ease the reader into your thesis statement by first introducing the topic. In the example below, the writer talks generally about diets and then narrows down to comments on a specific diet.

> Bookstore shelves today are crammed with dozens of different diet books. The American public seems willing to try any sort of diet, especially the ones that promise instant, miraculous results. And authors are more than willing to invent new fad diets to cash in on this craze. Unfortunately, some of these fad diets are ineffective or even unsafe. One of the worst fad diets is the "Palm Beach" plan. It is impractical, doesn't achieve the results it claims, and is a sure route to poor nutrition.

2. **Start with an idea or a situation that is the opposite of the one you will develop.** This approach works because your readers will be surprised, and then intrigued, by the contrast between the opening idea and the thesis that follows it.

When I decided to return to school at age thirty-five, I wasn't at all worried about my ability to do the work. After all, I was a grown woman who had raised a family, not a confused teenager fresh out of high school. But when I started classes, I realized that those "confused teenagers" sitting around me were in much better shape for college than I was. They still had all their classroom skills in bright, shiny condition, while mine had grown rusty from disuse. I had to learn how to locate information in a library, how to write a report, and even how to speak up in class discussions.

3. **Explain the importance of your topic to the reader.** If you can convince your readers that the subject in some way applies to them, or is something they should know more about, they will want to keep reading.

Diseases like scarlet fever and whooping cough used to kill more young children than any other cause. Today, however, child mortality due to disease has been almost completely eliminated by medical science. Instead, car accidents are the number-one killer of our children. And most of the children fatally injured in car accidents were not protected by car seats, belts, or restraints of any kind. Several steps must be taken to reduce the serious dangers car accidents pose to our children.

4. **Use an incident or a brief story.** Stories are naturally interesting. They appeal to a reader's curiosity. In your introduction, an anecdote will grab the reader's attention right away. The story should be brief and should be related to your main idea. The incident in the story can be something that happened to you, something you have heard about, or something you have read about in a newspaper, magazine, or online.

Early Sunday morning the young mother dressed her little girl warmly and gave her a candy bar, a picture book, and a well-worn stuffed rabbit. Together, they drove downtown to a Methodist church. There the mother told the little girl to wait on the stone steps until children began arriving for Sunday school. Then the young mother drove off, abandoning her five-year-old because she couldn't cope with being a parent anymore. This incident is one of thousands of cases of child neglect and abuse that occur annually. Perhaps the automatic right to become a parent should no longer exist. Would-be parents should be forced to apply for parental licenses for which they would have to meet three important conditions.

5. **Use a quotation.** A quotation can be something you have read in a book or an article. It can also be something that you have heard: a popular saying or proverb ("Never give advice to a friend"), a current or recent advertising slogan ("Just do it"), or a favorite expression used by friends or family ("My father always says ..."). Using a quotation in your introductory paragraph lets you add someone else's voice to your own.

> "Fish and visitors," wrote Benjamin Franklin, "begin to smell after three days." Last summer, when my sister and her family came to spend their two week vacation with us, I became convinced that Franklin was right. After only three days of my family's visit, I was thoroughly sick of my brother-in-law's corny jokes, my sister's endless complaints about her boss, and their children's constant invasions of our privacy.

ACTIVITY 1

The box below summarizes the five kinds of introduction. Read the introductions that follow it and, in the space provided, write the letter of the kind of introduction used in each case.

A. General to narrow	D. Incident or story
B. Starting with an opposite	E. Quotation
C. Stating importance of topic	

_____ 1. The ad, in full color on a glossy magazine page, shows a beautiful kitchen with gleaming counters. In the foreground, on one of the counters, stands a shiny new food processor. Usually, a feminine hand is touching it lovingly. Around the main picture are other, smaller shots. They show mounds of perfectly sliced onion rings, thin rounds of juicy tomatoes, heaps of matchstick-sized potatoes, and piles of golden, evenly grated cheese. The ad copy tells the reader how wonderful, how easy, food preparation will be with a processor. Don't believe it. My processor turned out to be expensive, difficult to operate, and very limited in its use.

_____ 2. My father stubbornly says, "You *can* often tell a book by its cover," and when it comes to certain paperbacks, he's right. Whenever a person is browsing in the drugstore or supermarket and he or she sees a paperback featuring an attractive young woman in a low-cut dress fleeing from a handsome dark figure in a shadowy castle, it is obvious what the book will be about. Every romance novel has the same elements: an innocent heroine, an exotic setting, and a cruel but fascinating hero.

_____ 3. Americans are incredibly lazy. Instead of cooking a simple, nourishing meal, we pop a frozen dinner into the microwave. Instead of studying a daily newspaper, we are content with the capsule summaries on the network news. Worst of all, instead of walking even a few blocks to the local convenience store, we jump into our cars. This dependence on the automobile, even for short trips, has robbed us of a valuable experience—walking. If we drove less and walked more, we would save money, become healthier, and discover fascinating things about our surroundings.

Concluding Paragraph

A concluding paragraph is your chance to remind the reader of your thesis idea and bring the paper to a natural and graceful end.

Common Methods of Conclusion

You may use any one of the methods below, or a combination of methods, to round off your paper.

1. **End with a summary and final thought.** When army instructors train new recruits, each of their lessons follows a three-step formula:

   a. Tell them what you're going to tell them.

   b. Tell them.

   c. Tell them what you've told them.

   An essay that ends with a summary is not very different. After you have stated your thesis ("Tell them what you're going to tell them") and supported it ("Tell them"), you restate the thesis and supporting points ("Tell them what you've told them"). However, don't use the exact wording you used before. Here is a summary conclusion:

> Catalog shopping at home, then, has several advantages. Such shopping is convenient, saves money, and saves time. It is not surprising that growing numbers of devoted catalog shoppers are welcoming those full-color mail brochures that offer everything from turnip seeds to televisions.

Note that the summary is accompanied by a final comment that "rounds off" the paper and brings the discussion to a close. This combination of a summary and a final thought is the most common method of concluding an essay.

2. **Include a thought-provoking quotation.** A well-chosen quotation can be effective in re-emphasizing your point. Here is an example:

> Rude behavior has become commonplace and needs to stop. People no longer treat each other with the respect and courtesy they should. People talk on their cell phones at inappropriate times and places. Cutting off other drivers in order to save mere seconds happens more and more often. As the Dalai Lama said, "Love and kindness are the very basis of society. If we lose these feelings, society will face tremendous difficulties; the survival of humanity will be endangered."

3. **End with a prediction or recommendation.** Predictions and recommendations appeal to the reader to continue thinking about the essay.

A prediction states what may happen in the future:

> If people stopped to think before acquiring pets, there would be fewer instances of cruelty to animals. Many times, it is the people who adopt pets without considering the expense and responsibility involved who mistreat and neglect their animals. Pets are living creatures. They do not deserve to be treated as carelessly as one would treat a stuffed toy.

A recommendation suggests what should be done about a situation or problem:

> Stereotypes such as the helpless homemaker, harried executive, and dotty grandparent are insulting enough to begin with. In magazine ads or television commercials, they become even more insulting. Now these unfortunate characters are not just being laughed at; they are being turned into peddlers to sell products to an unsuspecting public. Consumers should boycott companies whose advertising continues to use such stereotypes.

ACTIVITY 2

In the space provided, note how each concluding paragraph ends: with a summary and final thought (write S in the space), with a prediction or recommendation (write P/R), or with a quotation (write Q).

_____ 1. Even though tens of thousands of people die each year in the United States from lung cancer, there are steps that can be taken to reduce risk factors. Smokers should stop smoking. People should avoid being around smokers, ask those smoking to stop, or leave if others are smoking. Life is too valuable to have it ended by this disease.

_____ 2. My father spent thirty years smoking three packs of cigarettes a day, a habit that he thought was more harmful to his wallet than to his lungs. According to the American Society of Addiction Medicine, "[n]icotine dependence is the most common form of chemical dependence in the United States . . . and [in 1989] caused more than 400,000 premature deaths in the United States." My father was one of them.

_____ 3. Lung cancer, then, can spread to the esophagus, the trachea, and the heart. Although an operation to remove the tumor is often unlikely, there are treatments available to control its spread. More research, however, is needed to find a cure.

Identifying Introductions and Conclusions

The following box lists five common kinds of introductions and three common kinds of conclusions. Read the three pairs of introductory and concluding paragraphs that follow. Then, in the space provided, write the letter of the kind of introduction and conclusion used in each paragraph.

ACTIVITY 3

Introductions	Conclusions
A. General to narrow	F. Summary and final thought
B. Starting with an opposite	G. Quotation
C. Stating importance of topic	H. Prediction or recommendation
D. Incident or story	
E. Quotation	

PAIR I

_____ Shortly before Easter, our local elementary school sponsored a fund-raising event at which classroom pets and their babies—hamsters, guinea pigs, and chicks—were available for adoption. Afterward, as I was driving home, I saw a hand drop a baby hamster out of the car ahead of me. I couldn't avoid running over the tiny creature. One of the parents had taken the pet, regretted the decision, and decided to get rid of it. Such people have never stopped to consider the several real obligations involved in owning a pet.

_____ A pet cannot be thrown onto a trash heap when it is no longer wanted or tossed into a closet if it begins to bore its owner. A pet, like us, is a living thing that needs attention and care. Would-be owners, therefore, should think seriously about their responsibilities before they acquire a pet.

PAIR 2

Academic

_____ In 2011, the school board sent out a letter laying out all the changes that were going to occur for the future school year. In an effort to cut costs, music classes, physical education classes, art classes, and honors classes were no longer going to be offered. When Franklin D. Roosevelt was president, he stated that "[t]he school is the last expenditure upon which America should be willing to economize." Despite the budget crisis that the school district faces, FDR's words must be heeded and a better plan must be made in order not to put the education of our students at risk.

Personal

_____ Cutting classes like music and physical education is a mistake. We must not put our students at risk by taking away the very classes that create culture and focus on the health of the population. If we continue to cut funding from education, we are ensuring that our future is going to be bleak.

PAIR 3

Personal

_____ "Few things are harder to put up with," said Mark Twain, "than the annoyance of a good example." Twain obviously knew the problems faced by siblings cursed with older brothers or sisters who are models of perfection. All our lives, my older sister Shelley and I have been compared. Unfortunately, in competition with my sister's virtues, my looks, talents, and accomplishments always ended up on the losing side.

Personal

_____ Although I always lost in the sibling contests of looks, talents, and accomplishments, Shelley and I have somehow managed not to turn into deadly enemies. Feeling like the "dud" of the family, in fact, helped me to develop a drive to succeed and a sense of humor. In our sibling rivalry, we both managed to win.

Titles

A title is usually a very brief summary of what your essay is about. It is often no more than several words. You may find it easier to write the title *after* you have completed your essay.

Following are the introductory paragraphs for two of the essays in this text, along with the titles of the essays.

Introductory Paragraph

I'm not just a consumer—I'm a victim. If I order a product, it is sure to arrive in the wrong color, size, or quantity. If I hire people to do repairs, they never arrive on the day scheduled. If I owe a bill, the computer is bound to overcharge me. Therefore, in self-defense, I have developed the following consumer's guide to complaining effectively.

Title: How to Complain

Introductory Paragraph

> Schools divide people into categories. From first grade on up, students are labeled "advanced" or "deprived" or "remedial" or "antisocial." Students pigeonhole their fellow students, too. We've all known the "brain," the "jock," the "dummy," and the "teacher's pet." In most cases, these narrow labels are misleading and inaccurate. But there is one label for a certain type of college student that says it all: "zombie."

Title: Student Zombies

Note that you should not underline the title, put quotation marks around it, boldface it, or increase the font size. On the other hand, you should capitalize the first letter of all but the small connecting words in the title. Also, you should skip a space between the title and the first line of the text. (See "Manuscript Form," page 470.)

| Write an appropriate title for each of the introductory paragraphs that follow. | **ACTIVITY 4** |

1. It is a terrible time to be a teenager or even a teenager's parent. Television, magazines, and newspapers are all full of frightening stories about teenagers and families. They say that America's families are falling apart, that kids do not care about anything, and that parents have trouble doing anything about it. However, not all teens and families are lost and without values. While they struggle with problems, successful families are doing what they have always done: finding ways to protect and nurture their children. Families are fighting against the influence of the media, against the loss of quality family time, and against the loss of community.

   Title: _____

2. Some of my friends can't believe that my car still runs. Others laugh when they see it parked outside the house and ask if it's an antique. They aren't being fair to my twenty-year-old Toyota Corolla. In fact, my "antique" has opened my eyes to the rewards of owning an old car.

   Title: _____

3. Regular exercise is something like the weather—we all talk about it, but we tend not to do anything about it. Exercise classes on television and exercise programs on videos and CDs—as well as instructions in books, magazines, and pamphlets—now make it easy to have a low-cost personal exercise program without leaving home. However, for success in exercise, we should follow a simple plan consisting of arranging time, making preparations, and starting off at a sensible place.

   Title: _____

in a writer's words

"It's important to try to write when you are in the wrong mood or the weather is wrong. Even if you don't succeed you'll be developing a muscle that may do it later on."

—John Ashbery

Essay Writing Assignments

> **HINT** Keep the points below in mind when writing an essay on any of the topics that follow.
>
> 1. Your first step must be to plan your essay. Prepare both a scratch outline and a more detailed outline.
>
> 2. While writing your essay, use the checklist on page 264 to make sure that your essay touches all four bases of effective writing.
>
> 3. Each essay will require support that incorporates different modes of writing. The appropriate chapters are listed in each assignment. You will want to review those chapters as necessary.
>
> 4. Don't forget to give your essay a title.

WRITING ASSIGNMENT 1

Personal

ANALYZING YOUR HOME

Write an essay on the advantages or disadvantages (not both) of the house or apartment where you live. In your introductory paragraph, briefly describe the place you plan to write about. End the paragraph with your thesis statement and a plan of development. Here are some suggestions for thesis statements:

> The best features of my apartment are its large windows, roomy closets, and great location.
>
> The drawbacks of my house are its unreliable oil burner, tiny kitchen, and old-fashioned bathroom.
>
> An inquisitive landlord, sloppy neighbors, and platoons of cockroaches came along with our rented house.
>
> My apartment has several advantages, including friendly neighbors, lots of storage space, and a good security system.

Depending on your chosen plan, you will want to incorporate support that includes anecdotes (Chapter 7), vivid descriptions of the home (Chapter 8), and/or a tone that persuades your reader to agree with you (Chapter 14).

WRITING ASSIGNMENT 2

Personal

RECALLING A MISTAKE

Write an essay about the biggest mistake you made within the past year. Describe the mistake and show how its effects have convinced you that it was the wrong thing to do. For instance, if you write about "taking a full-time job while going to school" as your biggest mistake, show the problems it caused. (You might discuss such matters as low grades, constant exhaustion, and poor performance at work.)

To get started, make a list of all the things you did last year that, with hindsight, now seem to be mistakes. Then pick out the action that has had the most serious consequences for you and that you can discuss in detail. Make a brief outline to guide you as you write, as in the example below.

Thesis: Buying a used car to commute to school was the worst mistake of last year.

1. Unreliable—late for class or missed class
2. Expenses for insurance, repairs
3. Led to an accident

Good support will include narration (Chapter 7), effects (Chapter 10), and argument (Chapter 14).

DESCRIBING DEMANDS IN LIFE

College demands a lot. You must attend classes, take notes, read textbooks, study for quizzes, write papers—the list goes on. In addition to school, you probably have other demands in your life. What are those demands? Write an essay that focuses on three demands that compete for your time. To help you get started, here is a list of demands common to college students:

Job	Health conditions
Housing	Other family members
Children	Financial debt
Transportation	Living expenses
Spouse or significant other	Hobbies and leisure activities

In your thesis statement, let your readers know what your three demands are and how they affect your life. Each of these demands should be developed in a separate paragraph. Each paragraph should have its own detailed examples. To create a strong essay, you will want to review Chapter 14, "Argument"; Chapter 13, "Division-Classification"; Chapter 10, "Cause and Effect"; and Chapter 6, "Exemplification."

WRITING ASSIGNMENT 3

Personal

SELLING (OR NOT) THE SINGLE LIFE

Write an essay on the advantages or drawbacks of single life. To get started, make a list of all the advantages and drawbacks you can think of.

Advantages might include:

Fewer expenses

Fewer responsibilities

More personal freedom

More opportunities to move or travel

Drawbacks might include:

Parental disapproval

Being alone at social events

WRITING ASSIGNMENT 4

Academic

No companion for shopping, movies, and so on

Sadness at holiday time

After you make up two lists, select the thesis for which you feel you have more supporting material. Then organize your material into a scratch outline. Be sure to include an introduction, a clear topic sentence for each supporting paragraph, and a conclusion. Alternatively, write an essay on the advantages or drawbacks of married life. Follow the directions given above.

Good support should include exemplification (Chapter 6) and argument (Chapter 14).

WRITING ASSIGNMENT 5

Academic

ANALYZING LIVES

Write an essay that claims that students' lives are much more difficult than professors' lives (or vice versa). You will need to speak with both professors and students and ask questions like:

Daily life: What does a typical day look like for you? What are your responsibilities? Do you have time each day just for yourself?

Academic life: How much time do you spend preparing for class? How much time do you spend in class? How much time do you spend grading (professors only)?

Social life: How much time do you spend participating in social activities?

Personal life: Do you work outside of your academic life? Do you have added responsibilities you haven't addressed?

Once you have gathered information, you will want to write an essay that asserts one group has a tougher life than the other. One way to organize your essay would be creating a paragraph for each of the categories; another way to organize it would be to write all the information that supports the thesis about one group and then follow with information about the other group. You will want to review Chapter 11, "Comparison or Contrast"; Chapter 14, "Argument"; and Chapter 20, "Writing a Research Paper" to help create a persuasive and effective essay.

WRITING ASSIGNMENT 6

Personal

EXAMINING THE EFFECTS OF ADVERSITY

We all experience adversity. Some believe that adversity—hardship, misfortune, bad luck, or suffering—makes a person stronger. Others believe that hardship wears a person down. What do you believe? Think about an adversity that you lived through and how that experience affected your life. Here are several categories to consider:

Relationships	Peer pressure
Employment	Finances
Physical health	Discrimination
Education	Housing
Mental health	

Then, write an essay on the effects—positive or negative—that this adversity has had on you. In your introduction, describe your adversity. Each of your body paragraphs should explain how this experience affected you in a specific way. You will need to review Chapter 7, "Narration"; Chapter 8, "Description"; and Chapter 10, "Cause and Effect."

EVALUATING A FILM OR TELEVISION SHOW

WRITING ASSIGNMENT 7

Academic

Write an essay about a television show or movie you have seen very recently. The thesis of your essay will be that the show (or movie) has both good and bad features. (If you are writing about a TV series, be sure that you evaluate only one episode.)

In your first supporting paragraph, briefly summarize the show or movie. Don't get bogged down in small details here; just describe the major characters briefly and give the highlights of the action.

In your second supporting paragraph, explain what you feel are the best features of the show or movie. Listed below are some examples of good features you might write about.

Suspenseful, ingenious, or realistic plot

Good acting

Good scenery or special effects

Surprise ending

Good music

Believable characters

In your third supporting paragraph, explain what you feel are the worst features of the show or movie. Here are some possibilities:

Far-fetched, confusing, or dull plot

Poor special effects

Bad acting

Cardboard characters

Unrealistic dialogue

Remember to cover only a few features in each paragraph; do not try to include everything. You will want to review Chapter 8, "Description" and Chapter 14, "Argument" to help you create a persuasive and detailed essay.

DESCRIBING YOUR CHARACTERISTICS

WRITING ASSIGNMENT 8

Personal

It has been said that the older we get, the more we see our parents in ourselves. Indeed, our temperament and many of our habits (good and bad) and beliefs can often be traced to one of our parents.

Write a paragraph in which you describe three characteristics you have "inherited" from a parent. You might want to think about your topic by asking yourself a series of questions: "How am I like my mother (or

"I said your son doesn't listen well in class..."

Reprinted by permission of CartoonStock, Ltd. www.CartoonStock.com.

father)?"; "When and where am I like her (or him)?"; "Why am I like her (or him)?"

One student who wrote such a paper used the following thesis statement: "Although I hate to admit it, I know that in several ways I'm just like my mom." She then went on to describe how she works too hard, worries too much, and judges other people too harshly. Another student wrote, "I resemble my father in my love of TV sports, my habit of putting things off, and my reluctance to show my feelings."

Be sure to include examples and support for each of the characteristics you mention. For ideas of types of support you will want to include, review Chapter 7, "Narration"; Chapter 8, "Description"; and Chapter 11, "Comparison or Contrast."

REFLECTIVE ACTIVITY

1. Reread an essay you wrote in response to one of the writing assignments in this chapter. Did you use any of the five common methods for writing introductions explained on pages 296–298? If so, which one(s)? If not, which of those method(s) might you include when you rewrite this essay?

2. Do the same for the conclusion of your essay. Methods for writing conclusions appear on pages 299–301.

3. Reread the essay yet again and consider the various methods for writing introductions and conclusions once more. Would methods other than the ones you chose have been useful as well? Explain.

Patterns of Essay Development

RESPONDING TO IMAGES

These two recruiting posters are from the United States Navy. The first was used in 1917 and the second is from today. Think about different ways to write about these posters. What is the main point of each poster, and how would you support that point with examples? How would you compare or contrast the posters? How would you describe them? Using a specific pattern of development, write an essay about these posters.

The nine different patterns of paragraph writing you learned in Part 3—*exemplification, narration, description, process, cause and effect, comparison or contrast, definition, division-classification,* and *argument*—can also be used to write essays. Because essays are much longer works than paragraphs, it is common that multiple patterns are incorporated to fully support the thesis statement. A history student may need to employ exemplification, cause and effect, and argument in a class paper. A scientist preparing a report may need to employ description, definition, and argument to defend his or her hypothesis. A real estate agent may employ description and narration to write about a house for sale. Everyday writing involves determining which patterns to use and how best to organize them to effectively support your purpose. The rest of this chapter will show you how.

Developing an Essay with Emphasis on Exemplification

Considering Purpose and Audience

If you make a statement and someone says to you, "Prove it," what do you do? Most likely, if you can, you will provide an example or two to support your claim. An essay that emphasizes exemplification has the same purpose: to use specific instances or actual cases to convince an audience that a particular point is true.

In an essay that emphasizes exemplification, you support it by *illustrating* it with examples. These examples may range from facts that you have researched to personal accounts. If, for instance, you decide to write an essay that claims capital punishment is immoral, you might cite several cases in which an innocent person was executed. Keep in mind that your examples should connect clearly to your main point so that readers will see the truth of your claim.

The number of examples you choose to include in your essay may vary depending, in part, on your audience. For a group already opposed to the death penalty, you would not need detailed examples to support your belief that capital punishment is immoral. However, if you were writing to a group undecided about capital punishment, you would need more instances to get your point across—and even then, some would not believe you. Still, when used well, examples make writing more persuasive, increasing the chances readers will understand and believe your point.

Student Essay to Consider

Directions for Reading the Essay: As you read the following essay, circle areas that strike you as interesting or especially descriptive, underline areas that seem to be out of place or need work, place stars by any areas where you think additional information could be added, and mark the different modes of writing within this essay. Finally, respond to the claim made within the essay. Do you agree with the author about Americans' state of mind?

Altered States

Most Americans are not alcoholics. Most do not cruise seedy city streets looking to score crack cocaine or heroin. Relatively few try to con their doctors into prescribing unneeded mood-altering medications. And yet, many Americans are traveling through life with their minds slightly out of kilter. In its attempt to cope with modern life, the human mind seems to have evolved some defense strategies. Confronted with inventions like television, the shopping center, and the Internet, the mind will slip—all by itself—into an altered state.

Never in the history of humanity have people been expected to sit passively for hours, staring at moving pictures emanating from an electronic box. Since too much exposure to flickering images of police officers, detectives, and talk-show hosts can be dangerous to human sanity, the mind automatically goes into a state of TV hypnosis. The eyes see the sitcom or the dog-food commercial, but the mind goes into a holding pattern. None of the televised images or sounds actually enters the brain. This is why, when questioned, people cannot remember commercials they have seen five seconds before or why the TV cops are chasing a certain suspect. In this hypnotic, trancelike state, the mind resembles an armored armadillo. It rolls up in self-defense, letting the stream of televised information pass by harmlessly.

If the TV watcher arises from the couch and goes to a shopping mall, he or she will again cope by slipping into an altered state. In the mall, the mind is bombarded with the sights, smells, and sounds of dozens of stores, restaurants, and movie theaters competing for its attention. There are hundreds of questions to be answered. Should I start with the upper or lower mall level? Which stores should I look in? Should I bother with the sweater sale at Macy's? Should I eat fried chicken or try the healthier-sounding pita wrap? Where is my car parked? To combat this mental overload, the mind goes into a state resembling the whiteout experienced by mountain climbers trapped in a blinding snowstorm. Suddenly, everything looks the same. The shopper is unsure where to go next and cannot remember what he or she came for in the first place. The mind enters this state deliberately so that the shopper has no choice but to leave. Some kids can be in a shopping mall for hours, but they are exceptions to the rule.

But no part of everyday life so quickly triggers the mind's protective shutdown mode as that favorite pastime of the new millennium: online surfing. A computer user sits down with the intention of briefly checking his or her e-mail or looking up a fact for a research paper. But once tapped into the immense storehouse of information, entertainment, and seemingly intimate personal connections that the Internet offers, the user loses all sense of time and priorities. Prospects flood the mind: Should I explore the rise of Nazi Germany? Play a trivia game? Hear the life story of a lonely

1

2

3

4

continued

stranger in Duluth? With a mind dazed with information overload, the user numbly hits one key after another, leaping from topic to topic, from distraction to distraction. Hours fly by as he or she sits hunched over the terminal, unable to account for the time that has passed.

These poor victims are merely trying to cope with the mind-numbing inventions of modern life and are not responsible for their glazed eyes and robotic motions. People need to be aware of them and treat them with kindness and understanding. Going out of the way to bring these coma sufferers back to real life is the job of all those who have managed to avoid the side effects of television, shopping, and the Internet; otherwise, humanity will suffer.

5

QUESTIONS

About the Main Idea and Author's Purpose

1. In your own words, write the main idea of the essay.

    _____

    _____

2. What is the author's purpose, and how can you determine this?

    _____

    _____

    _____

About Unity

3. Which sentence in paragraph 3 of "Altered States" should be omitted in the interest of paragraph unity? (Write the opening words.)

    _____

About Support

4. What three pieces of evidence does the writer offer to support the statement that the Internet is an "immense storehouse of information, entertainment, and seemingly intimate personal connections"?

    _____

    _____

    _____

About Coherence

5. What sentence indicates that the author has used emphatic order, saving his most important point for last? (Write the opening words.)

    _____

6. Which sentence in paragraph 1 begins with a change-of-direction signal phrase? (Write the opening words.)

_____

7. Which sentence in paragraph 2 begins with an illustration signal phrase? (Write the opening words.)

_____

About Mixed Modes

8. What are the different types of modes the author employed to create such a fluid and interesting essay?

_____

About the Introduction and Conclusion

9. Which sentence in paragraph 5 begins with a concluding signal word? (Write the opening words.)

_____

10. Which statement best describes the concluding paragraph?
    a. It contains a prediction.
    b. It combines a summary with a recommendation of how to treat people in an altered state.
    c. It refers to the point made in the introduction about alcohol and drugs.
    d. It contains thought-provoking questions about altered states.

Writing an Essay with Emphasis on Exemplification

RESPONDING TO STATEMENTS

Write an essay that uses examples to develop one of the following statements.

WRITING ASSIGNMENT 1

Personal

I would do anything for/to _____.

There are many terrible jobs that people do, but the worst is _____
_____.

I wouldn't _____ even if someone paid me a million dollars.

Be sure to choose examples that support your topic sentence. They should include relevant personal experiences (Chapter 7), examples you have read about (Chapter 20), and as many descriptive details as possible (Chapter 8). Organize your paragraph so you save your most vivid, most convincing, or most important example for last.

WRITING ASSIGNMENT 2

RESPONDING TO A READING

Write an essay that is based on an outside reading. It might be a selection recommended by your instructor, or it might be a piece by one of the following authors, all of whom have written short stories, books, or essays that should be available in your college library.

Willa Cather	Nelson Mandela
Winston Churchill	Toni Morrison
Sandra Cisneros	George Orwell
Annie Dillard	Katherine Ann Porter
Ralph Waldo Emerson	John Steinbeck
F. Scott Fitzgerald	Amy Tan
Ellen Goodman	Deborah Tannen
Thomas Jefferson	Calvin Trillin
Maxine Hong Kingston	Kurt Vonnegut
Jhumpa Lahiri	Marie Winn
Sinclair Lewis	Walt Whitman

Base your essay on an idea in the selection you have chosen, and provide examples to back up your idea. You will want to review Chapter 6, "Exemplification" and Chapter 8, "Description" to help you provide the best examples for your essay. You will also want to review Chapter 20, "Writing a Research Paper" to help you use quotations and summaries from your chosen work to establish solid support for your thesis.

BEYOND THE CLASSROOM

Exemplification

In this essay that emphasizes exemplification, you will write with a specific purpose and for a specific audience.

EXPLAINING A DECISION   Often when students are applying for grants or scholarships, they have to write an essay that demonstrates why they should receive the funds. Assume that you are writing an essay to receive a scholarship for "students who are new to college." The decision to receive the funds is based on your honesty about your reasons for attending college and your hopes of what a college degree will get you. You will want to incorporate stories and examples to support your claims. You will want to review Chapter 6, "Exemplification"; Chapter 7, "Narration"; and Chapter 8, "Description."

Developing an Essay with Emphasis on Narration

Considering Purpose and Audience

In an essay that emphasizes narration you make a point and incorporate one central story or several brief stories as support. Colorful details and interesting events that build up to a point make these essays enjoyable for readers and writers alike.

Life requires recalling events for different purposes. Students tell stories to teachers explaining why they didn't get their homework done. Witnesses recall events to police officers and juries. Boards and committees have to keep detailed minutes of all meetings. All of these examples require people to remember the events in order, provide details that affect meaning and understanding, and relay the information to others in a clear and coherent manner.

Unlike a narrative paragraph that only focuses on telling a story, an essay that emphasizes narration may also contain description, argument, cause and effect, and/or research. As you have seen in the paragraph development sections, different modes require different forms of writing, so it is important to use the specific modes and writing techniques where and when needed. The purpose of your essay will determine what events should be told, what events should be eliminated, and what strategies should be employed when writing.

Student Essay to Consider

Directions for Reading the Essay: As you read the following essay, circle areas that strike you as interesting or especially descriptive, underline areas that seem to be out of place or need work, place stars by any areas you think additional information could be added, and mark the different modes of writing within this essay. This essay remarks about several novels the student read; if you are familiar with any of the books, decide if you agree with the author's opinion. If you aren't familiar with the books, do the author's descriptions make you want to read any of the books? Be prepared to explain your decision.

Summer Read-a-thons

1   I remember when I was growing up that I spent many sunny afternoons in my backyard. I was fortunate to have a carefree happy mother who enjoyed reading and helped books come alive. We would spread out a blanket on the long green grass and have read-a-thons together. Reading became a doorway into a new and exciting world that I have often chosen to enter. I fell in love with reading in my yard, where my kind mother helped me find my imagination, learn about the world, and learn more about myself.

2   At first my mother would bribe me with candy and popcorn, enticing me onto the reading blanket, but soon I would gladly assemble near her ready for the adventures to begin. She would ask me what book I wanted to hear for the day. Did I want to listen to a story of a little mouse that lived in a hotel and snuck around at night, flying through the hallways on his *real* toy-sized motorcycle? Or perhaps I would prefer finding myself in the middle of the Salem witch trials running for my life with Kit Tyler from *The Witch of Blackbird Pond*?

3   My mom would help me think about new ideas through books. We would read a story together and then discuss deep topics about

continued

what symbolism we found. My brother often liked to be part of these conversations. One of my favorite discussions we had sparked from the book *Mrs. Frisby and the Rats of Nimh.* It's about Mrs. Frisby, a mother field mouse and her determination to protect her children, especially her young, ill son. She needs additional help from some neighbors who happen to be rats. The other animals had previously been afraid of the rats on this farm because they have strange ways and do strange things. Mrs. Frisby learns not to judge only by appearance. One young rat is especially notable as he gives his life for his fellow rats because it is the right thing to do. He became a hero of mine. As a young child I learned about service and sacrifice from this simple, yet beautifully told story of rats and mice. I learned not to be as judgmental, and my imagination grew abundantly.

As I grew older, I developed a love for novels, biographies, and historical fiction. I especially enjoyed reading about World War II. In the book *The Hiding Place,* by Corrie ten Boom, I felt as if I knew Corrie and her sister Betsie, and was alongside them as they helped hide Jews from the Gestapo. They had tremendous courage and became symbols of bravery and tenacity. I learned much from these young girls as I read about the Nazis taking all of their possessions, locking them into a concentration camp, and enduring the indignities that they suffered. If I am ever feeling sorry for myself or that the world is out to get me, I think about Corrie ten Boom and her story, and I am humbled and grateful for my simple life.

4

Like the previous books, Catherine Clinton's book also inspired me. In *Harriet Tubman: The Road to Freedom,* a book about the Underground Railroad during the Civil War era, Harriet helps to free 300 slaves and guides them north to safety. I was in awe of the miracles that happened in her quest. No one was captured; again and again she found families to hide fleeing slaves. I found myself wishing I could meet her and talk with her about how she became so daring, so willing to sacrifice her own life for others. An enjoyment of history developed from these books, and I couldn't get enough of them. I wanted to immerse myself in them and learn about other leaders throughout history, what made them strong, what made them act! Harriet Tubman's story inspired me to do more, to not be as selfish, and to be more understanding of different cultures and different beliefs. I learned that it is good to have a strong opinion, but I should listen to others, and be compassionate in my judgments.

5

I am thankful my mother loves to read, and that she had the insight to hold those summer read-a-thons to help me develop a deep love of reading that has stayed with me throughout my life. I still think back to those summer days beside her in my yard, and the contentment I felt, hearing her laughter and gaining strength from her soft-spoken voice. I remember the encouragement she gave me, telling me that I could do anything I put my mind to, and that I was smart and capable. I am grateful my mother brought reading to life, and I discovered a part of me that I hadn't realized was there to find.

6

About the Main Idea and Author's Purpose

1. In your own words, write the main idea of the essay.

   _____

   _____

   _____

2. What is the author's purpose and how can you determine this?

   _____

   _____

   _____

About Unity

3. Which sentence in paragraph 3 should be omitted and why?

   _____

   _____

   _____

About Support

4. The author uses a variety of descriptive words to help create strong images in the reader's mind. List some of the words and phrases and explain why you chose these specific examples.

   _____

   _____

   _____

   _____

About Coherence

5. Which paragraph could be enhanced with stronger transitional words?

   _____

   _____

   _____

About Mixed Modes

6. What are the different types of modes the author employed in her paragraphs to create such a fluid and interesting essay?

   _____

   _____

About the Introduction and Conclusion

7.   What technique does the author use in her conclusion? Explain your
     answer.

     _____

     _____

     _____

     _____

Writing an Essay with Emphasis on Narration

RECALLING AN IMPORTANT LEARNING MOMENT

WRITING ASSIGNMENT 1

In this assignment, you should recall a significant learning moment. This learning moment might be learning to read and/or write, learning to read and/or write music, teaching a child to read, or recalling a teacher who made a positive or negative impact. You will want to review Chapter 7, "Narration" and Chapter 8, "Description." If you choose to focus on someone who had a positive or negative impact on your learning, you should also review Chapter 10, "Cause and Effect."

WRITING YOUR OBITUARY

WRITING ASSIGNMENT 2

In the poem "The Dash," Linda Ellis asks, "Would you be proud of the things they said about how you spent your dash?" (the period between the dates of your birth and death). Many of us live in the here and now, not contemplating what our obituary will say when we die. Think about what your obituary might say if you were to die tomorrow. Then think about what you would like your obituary to say after you have lived a long life. What would you like to change? Write an essay detailing what you would like your obituary to say about you after you have lived a long and happy "dash." You will want to review Chapter 7, "Narration"; Chapter 8, "Description"; and Chapter 10, "Cause and Effect."

BEYOND THE CLASSROOM

Narration

In this essay that emphasizes narration, you will write with a specific purpose and for a specific audience.

BECOMING A TRAVEL WRITER   In this assignment, you should pretend to be a travel writer and write about your hometown, making it sound like the ultimate destination. As many travel writers do, you will want to incorporate short vignettes, or stories, to demonstrate the excitement of visiting your hometown. You will want to review Chapter 7, "Narration"; Chapter 8, "Description"; and Chapter 14, "Argument."

Developing an Essay with Emphasis on Description

Considering Purpose and Audience

The main purpose of an essay with an emphasis on description is to make readers see—or hear, taste, smell, or feel—what you are writing about. Vivid details are the key to good descriptions, enabling your audience to picture and, in a way, experience what you describe.

Unlike a descriptive paragraph that focuses only on describing the topic, an essay that emphasizes description may also contain cause and effect, comparison or contrast, or narration. As you start to think about your own essay, choose a topic that will allow you to write descriptions that appeal strongly to at least one of your senses.

As you have seen in the paragraph development sections, different modes require different forms of writing, so it is important to use the specific modes and writing techniques where and when needed. The purpose of your essay will determine what events should be told, what events should be eliminated, and what strategies should be employed when writing. If your topic is a familiar one you can assume your audience already understands the general idea. However, if you are presenting something new or unfamiliar to your readers—perhaps a description of one of your relatives or a place where you've lived—you must provide background information.

Student Essay to Consider

Directions for Reading the Essay: As you read the following essay, circle areas that strike you as interesting or especially descriptive, underline areas that seem to be out of place or need work, place stars by any areas where you think additional information could be added, and mark the different modes of writing within this essay. Additionally, think about why the grandmother would have given her granddaughter the picture and whether or not it made a true difference for the granddaughter. Use words and images from the essay to support your opinion.

Family Portrait

1 My grandmother, who is ninety years old, recently sent me a photograph of herself that I had never seen before. While cleaning out the attic of her Florida home, she came across a studio portrait she had taken about a year before she married my grandfather. This picture of my grandmother as a twenty-year-old girl and the story behind it have fascinated me from the moment I began to consider it.

2 The young woman in the picture has a face that resembles my own in many ways. Her face is a bit more oval than mine, but the softly waving brown hair around it is identical. The small, straight nose is the same model I was born with. My grandmother's mouth is closed, yet there is just the slightest hint of a smile on her full lips. I know that

---

continued

if she had smiled, she would have shown the same wide grin and down-curving "smile lines" that appear in my own snapshots. The most haunting feature in the photo, however, is my grandmother's eyes. They are an exact duplicate of my own large, dark-brown ones. Her brows are plucked into thin lines, which are like two pencil strokes added to highlight those fine, luminous eyes.

I've also carefully studied the clothing and jewelry in the photograph. Although the photo was taken seventy years ago, my grandmother is wearing a blouse and skirt that could easily be worn today. The blouse is made of heavy eggshell-colored satin and reflects the light in its folds and hollows. It has a turned-down cowl collar and smocking on the shoulders and below the collar. The smocking (tiny rows of gathered material) looks hand-done. The skirt, which covers my grandmother's calves, is straight and made of light wool or flannel. My grandmother is wearing silver drop earrings. They are about two inches long and roughly shield-shaped. On her left wrist is a matching bracelet. My grandmother can't find this bracelet now, despite the fact that we spent hours searching through the attic for it. On the third finger of her left hand is a ring with a large, square-cut stone.

3

The story behind the picture is as interesting to me as the young woman it captures. Grandma, who was earning twenty-five dollars a week as a file clerk, decided to give her boyfriend (my grandfather) a picture of herself. She spent almost two weeks' salary on the skirt and blouse, which she bought at a fancy department store downtown. She borrowed the earrings and bracelet from her older sister, my Great-Aunt Dorothy. The ring she wore was a present from another young man she was dating at the time. Grandma spent another chunk of her salary to pay the portrait photographer for the hand-tinted print in old-fashioned tones of brown and tan. Just before giving the picture to my grandfather, she scrawled at the lower left, "Sincerely, Gloria."

4

When I study this picture, I react in many ways. I think about the trouble that Grandma went to in order to impress the young man who was to be my grandfather. I laugh when I look at the ring, which was probably worn to make my grandfather jealous. I smile at the serious, formal inscription my grandmother used at this stage of the budding relationship. Sometimes, I am filled with a mixture of pleasure and sadness when I look at this frozen long-ago moment. It is a moment of beauty, of love, and—in a way—of my own past.

5

QUESTIONS

About the Main Idea and Author's Purpose

1. In your own words, write the main idea of the essay.

_____

_____

_____

2. What is the author's purpose and how can you determine this?

_____

_____

About Unity

3. Which of the following sentences from paragraph 3 of "Family Portrait" should be omitted in the interest of paragraph unity?
   a. Although the photo was taken seventy years ago, my grandmother is wearing a blouse and skirt that could easily be worn today.
   b. It has a turned-down cowl collar and smocking on the shoulders and below the collar.
   c. My grandmother can't find this bracelet now, despite the fact that we spent hours searching the attic for it.
   d. On the third finger of her left hand is a ring with a large, square-cut stone.

About Support

4. How many separate items of clothing and jewelry are described in paragraph 3?
   a. four
   b. five
   c. seven

5. Label as sight, touch, hearing, or smell all the sensory details in the following sentences taken from the essay.
   a. "The blouse is made of heavy eggshell-colored satin and reflects the light in its folds and hollows."
   b. "Her brows are plucked into thin lines, which are like two pencil strokes added to highlight those fine, luminous eyes."

About Coherence

6. Which method of organization does paragraph 2 use?
   a. Time order
   b. Emphatic order

7. Which sentence in paragraph 2 suggests the method of organization? (_Write the opening words._)

_____

About Mixed Modes

8. What are the different types of modes the author employed in the paragraphs to create such an interesting essay?

_____

About the Introduction and Conclusion

9. Which statement best describes the introduction?

    a. It starts with an idea that is the opposite of the one that is developed.

    b. It explains the importance of the topic to its readers

    c. It begins with a general statement of the topic and narrows it down to a thesis statement.

    d. It begins with an anecdote.

Writing an Essay with Emphasis on Description

RECALLING AN IMPORTANT EXPERIENCE

WRITING ASSIGNMENT 1

Personal

In this assignment, you will write an essay that describes an experience that has significantly affected you. You will want to use specific details in addition to examples that support your purpose. You will want to review Chapter 6, "Exemplification"; Chapter 8, "Description"; and Chapter 10, "Cause and Effect."

WRITING A BIOGRAPHY

WRITING ASSIGNMENT 2

Academic

In this assignment, you should choose a person whom you would like to know more about. A good biographical profile will include information that is relevant to your purpose, which should describe why you think this person is important enough to profile. As you interview your person, you will want to take careful notes to ensure the material you write is accurate and to allow you to use direct quotes where needed. Your purpose will determine the information you need to include. You may need to write about your person's childhood, education, and/or work, or you may only need to focus on one specific aspect of his or her life. You will want to review Chapter 7, "Narration"; Chapter 8, "Description"; and Chapter 20, "Writing a Research Paper."

REACTING TO A WORK OF ART

WRITING ASSIGNMENT 3

Academic

In this assignment, you will be required to choose a piece of art, like the *Mona Lisa* or Michelangelo's *David*, and explain why it is significant. You will need to describe the work so the reader fully understands what the piece looks like, and you will need to argue the work's importance. You will want to review Chapter 8, "Description" and Chapter 14, "Argument." If you need to research information about your chosen work of art, you will need to review Chapter 20, "Writing a Research Paper."

In this essay that emphasizes description, you will write with a specific purpose and for a specific audience.

DESIGNING A BROCHURE   Imagine that you work at your city's visitor's bureau and need to create a brochure for tourists describing your city's top attractions and "selling" your city as a top tourist destination. You will want to consider which sites should be highlighted, which hotels would offer different levels of accommodation, and why your city is the best choice. You will want to review Chapter 8, "Description" and Chapter 14, "Argument."

BEYOND THE CLASSROOM

Description

Work

Developing an Essay with Emphasis on Process

Considering Purpose and Audience

Glance at a newsstand and you'll see magazine cover stories with titles such as "How to Impress Your Boss," "How to Add Romance to Your Life," or "How to Dress Like a Movie Star." These articles promise to give readers directions or information they can follow, and they are popular versions of essays that emphasize process.

In general, essays that emphasize process will explain the steps involved in a particular action, process, or event. Some of these essays focus on giving readers actual instructions, others focus on giving readers information, and still others focus on persuading readers. The type of essay you write depends on the specific topic and purpose you choose.

No matter what your main purpose, keep your audience in mind as you work. As with any essay, select a topic that will interest readers. A group of college students, for example, might be interested in reading an essay that explains how and why to get financial aid but bored by an essay on how and why to plan for retirement. In addition, consider how much your readers already know about your topic. An audience unfamiliar with financial aid may need background information and definitions in order to understand your essay. Finally, be sure that your organization is very logically organized so your readers can easily follow your ideas, thus supporting your purpose.

Student Essay to Consider

Directions for Reading the Essay: As you read the following essay, circle areas that strike you as interesting or especially descriptive, underline areas that seem to be out of place or need work, place stars by any areas where you think additional information could be added, and mark the different modes of writing within this essay. Finally, respond to the claim made within the essay. Do you agree or disagree with the author? Could the author have used better examples to support his or her claim? Be prepared to explain your opinion.

About Mixed Modes

7. What are the different types of modes the author employed in the paragraphs to create such a fluid and interesting essay?

About the Introduction and Conclusion

8. Which statement best describes the introduction?
   a. It begins with a couple of general points about the topic and narrows down to the thesis.
   b. It explains the importance of daily exercise to the reader.

Writing an Essay with Emphasis on Process

SHARING YOUR EXPERTISE

Everyone is an expert at something. Using your personal experiences and insights, write an essay with an emphasis on process. If you are a parent, you might write about how you taught your children to read. If you work as a sales representative, you might write about how monthly sales quotas are met. If you are a recovering addict, you might write about how the twelve-step recovery process works. As a college student, you might write about how the registration process works at your school. Each of these topics will require you to incorporate several modes of writing, such as narration (Chapter 7) and description (Chapter 8).

THINKING AS A SCIENTIST

The scientific method is a process that all scientists use. In this essay, you are to research the scientific method; then, using this method, write about an experiment. Possible experiments that could be described are dropping Mentos candies into Coca-Cola bottles, creating non-Newtonian oobleck, or turning needles into magnets. This essay will require you to read Chapter 20, "Writing a Research Paper"; Chapter 8, "Description"; and Chapter 9, "Process."

BEYOND THE CLASSROOM

Process

In this essay that emphasizes process, you will write with a specific purpose and for a specific audience.

PREPARING A HANDOUT Imagine that you are a job recruiter working at an employment agency. Your supervisor has asked you to help new clients understand the job-seeking process. You decide to create a handout on how to prepare for a job interview. What would be the first step that a job seeker should consider? What would be the next step? What about the final step? Select three steps and develop each in a separate paragraph. Some areas you might consider are these: dressing appropriately, arriving on time, offering a firm handshake, maintaining eye contact, staying positive throughout the interview, bringing a sense of humor, and being honest at all times. You will want to review Chapter 6, "Exemplification" and Chapter 9, "Process."

Developing an Essay with Emphasis on Cause and/or Effect

Considering Purpose and Audience

The main purpose of an essay that emphasizes cause and/or effect is to support your purpose by using examples that explain (1) the causes of a particular event or situation; (2) the effects of an event or a situation; or, more rarely, (3) a combination of both.

The type of essay you write will depend on the topic you choose and the main point you wish to communicate. If, for example, your purpose is to profile a special person who has had a great impact on you, your essay would emphasize the effects of that person. However, if your purpose is to exemplify why you moved out of your family home, your essay would focus on the causes of your decision.

As with all essays, try to pick a topic that will appeal to your audience of readers. An essay on the negative effects of steroids and other drugs on professional athletes may be especially interesting to an audience of sports fans. On the other hand, this same topic might not be as appealing to people who dislike sports. In addition to selecting a lively topic, be sure to make your main point clear so that your audience can follow the cause-effect relationship you've chosen to develop. In the above instance, you might even announce specific causes or effects by signaling them to readers: "One effect drug use has on athletes is to . . . ."

Student Essay to Consider

Directions for Reading the Essay: As you read the following essay, circle areas that strike you as interesting or especially descriptive, underline areas that seem to be out of place or need work, place stars by any areas where you think additional information could be added, and mark the different modes of writing within this essay. Additionally, think about the student's experience with college and your own experience. What types of comparisons can you make? Be prepared to share your findings.

The Challenges of Going Back to School

1   When I first decided to go back to school, I wasn't sure about my ability to do the work. When I was in high school, I was a pretty good student. But then I met Jonathan. Everything changed after that. My studies were no longer my main focus, and my relationship became my reason for living. By the end of senior year, I was pregnant. I didn't attend my senior prom, and Jonathan and I were quickly married off by our parents. Well, now it was fifteen years later, and I was back at school. Little did I know that returning to school after a long period would bring me so many challenges.

2   First of all, my writing skills had really deteriorated. As a result of not having used my grammar skills in fifteen years, I tested into a

continued

developmental writing class. I was so ashamed and even frustrated when I couldn't recognize a fragment, use commas correctly, or fix a dangling modifier. My essays started off terribly, but eventually, with a lot of hard work and effort, the grades started to improve. My favorite essay assignment involved attending a campus rally and writing about it.

3

Second, math classes were another challenge for me. As a housewife and young mother, I had to keep a pretty tight budget with groceries and expenses. I thought I had maintained my basic math skills in check. Was I wrong! That's when it really hit me. I thought about how much I loved being with my children when they were young, and how many important lessons I learned while being home. But I also realized that I should have listened to my parents and friends and continued with my education much sooner. The choices I had made back in high school came suddenly crashing before me.

4

Socially I felt awkward as well. I didn't seem to have the leisure time some of my classmates had to socialize and study in groups. I once tried to study with a group in my American History class, but the time the group met conflicted with my part-time job I had taken to pay for my classes. I found myself studying mostly on my own. Jonathan was a great support, but he couldn't help me with some of my homework. After much trial and tribulation, I completed all my coursework, including my paralegal courses, and was ready to start my new life.

5

Going back to school after so many years proved to be an enormous challenge. I am now working as a paralegal and feel that my life is back on track. I'm even thinking about applying for law school. I don't want to rush things, though. I am presently enjoying my job and learning many things about the law and society. My experience with going back to school changed my view of myself and my personal goals. I learned that decisions carry many consequences, and that I should look at all my options before I make an important, life-altering decision.

QUESTIONS

About the Main Idea and Author's Purpose

1. In your own words, write the main idea of the essay.

   _____

   _____

2. What is the author's purpose, and how can you determine this?

   _____

   _____

   _____

   _____

About Unity

3. Which sentence in paragraph 2 should be omitted in the interest of paragraph unity? (Write the opening words.)

About Support

4. After which sentence in paragraph 3 is more support needed?

About Coherence

5. What are the two transition words or phrases that signal two major points of support for the thesis?

Mixed Modes

6. What are the different types of modes the author employed in her paragraphs to create such an interesting essay?

About the Introduction and Conclusion

7. Which sentence best describes the opening paragraph?
    a. It begins with a general statement of the topic and narrows it down to a thesis statement.
    b. It uses an incident or brief story.
    c. It explains the importance of the topic to the reader.
    d. It starts with an idea that is the opposite of the one then developed.

8. Which method is used in the conclusion?
    a. Summary and final thoughts
    b. Recommendation
    c. Thought-provoking quotation

Writing an Essay with Emphasis on Cause and/or Effect

CONSIDERING THE STATE OF THE HUMAN RACE

WRITING ASSIGNMENT 1

If friendly aliens from a highly developed civilization decided to visit our planet, they would encounter a contradictory race of beings—us. We humans would have reasons to feel both proud and ashamed of the kind of society the aliens would encounter. Write an essay explaining whether you would be proud or ashamed of the state of the human race today. Good support may include narration (Chapter 7), description (Chapter 8), cause and effect (Chapter 10), argument (Chapter 14), and possibly some research (Chapter 20).

WRITING ASSIGNMENT 2

ANALYZING A FAMOUS FIGURE

Write an essay about an author, a musician, or an actor who has had a positive or negative influence on society. To develop your idea, use reasons that demonstrate the effects of your chosen subject's actions. You may want to refer to Chapter 6, "Exemplification"; Chapter 10, "Cause and Effect"; and Chapter 14, "Argument." If you use ideas other than your own, refer to Chapter 20, "Writing a Research Paper" for proper documentation and citation.

BEYOND THE CLASSROOM

Cause-and-Effect

In this essay that emphasizes cause and/or effect, you will write with a specific purpose and for a specific audience.

REVIEWING AN EMPLOYEE Imagine that you are a retail store manager and must write a quarterly performance report for one of your employees. Not only is this person a top seller, but he or she has a positive attitude and shows leadership qualities. Write an essay in which you focus on how this person has brought about three positive changes in the company. Each change should be developed in a separate paragraph.

Although much of your essay will focus on the effects (Chapter 10) this person has had on the company, it should also incorporate examples (Chapter 6) and anecdotes (Chapter 7) that support the thesis.

Developing an Essay with Emphasis on Comparison and/or Contrast

Considering Purpose and Audience

The purpose of an essay that emphasizes comparison and/or contrast is to make a point by including examples that show how distinct items or people are either similar or different. Whether you choose to use comparison or contrast depends on the specific point you want to convey to readers. As you think about your own essay, ask yourself what type of essay would benefit from this type of support. Then determine whether you want to focus on the differences between the items or their similarities. You may even decide that you want to do both. If, say, you choose to persuade your reader that he or she should purchase a specific type of computer, you may include paragraphs on the similarities and differences between Mac and PC computers. Once you determine your purpose, be sure you keep your readers in mind when planning your essay as your audience will determine your tone and needed background information, definitions, and examples.

Unlike a comparison or contrast paragraph that focuses only on the similarities or differences of two or more subjects, an essay that emphasizes comparison and/or contrast may also contain description, narration, persuasion, and/or research. As you have seen in the paragraph development sections, different modes require different forms of writing, so it is important to look at your essay as a mix, using the specific modes and writing techniques where and when needed.

Student Essay to Consider

Directions for Reading the Essay: As you read the following essay, circle areas that strike you as interesting or especially descriptive, underline areas that seem to be out of place or need work, place stars by any areas where you think additional information could be added, and mark the different modes of writing within this essay. Additionally, compare the author's study habits, both in high school and college, to your own study habits, and be prepared to discuss them.

Studying: Then and Now

1   One June day, I staggered into a high school classroom to take my final exam in United States History IV. I had made my usual desperate effort to cram the night before, with the usual dismal results—I had gotten only to page seventy-five of a four-hundred-page textbook. My study habits in high school, obviously, were a mess. But in college, I've made an attempt to reform my note taking, studying, and test-taking skills.

2   As I took notes in high school classes, I often lost interest and began doodling, drawing Martians, or seeing what my signature would look like if I married the cute guy in the second row. Now, however, I try not to let my mind wander, and I pull my thoughts back into focus when they begin to go fuzzy. In high school, my notes often looked like something written in hieroglyphics. In college, I've learned to use a semiprint writing style that makes my notes understandable. When I would look over my high school notes, I couldn't understand them. There would be a word like "Reconstruction," then a big blank, then the word "important." Weeks later, I had no idea what Reconstruction was or why it was important. I've since learned to write down connecting ideas, even if I have to take the time to do it after class. Taking notes is one thing I've really learned to do better since high school days.

3   Ordinary studying during the term is another area where I've made changes. In high school, I let reading assignments go. I told myself that I'd have no trouble catching up on two hundred pages during a fifteen-minute ride to school. College courses have taught me to keep pace with the work. Otherwise, I feel as though I'm sinking into a quicksand of unread material. When I finally read the high school assignment, my eyes would run over the words but my brain would be plotting how to get the car for Saturday night. Now, I use several techniques that force me to really concentrate on my reading.

4   In addition to learning how to cope with daily work, I've also learned to handle study sessions for big tests. My all-night study sessions in high school were experiments in self-torture. Around 2:00 A.M., my mind, like a soaked sponge, simply stopped absorbing things. Now, I space out exam study sessions over several days. That way, the night before can be devoted to an overall review rather than raw memorizing. Most important,

continued

though, I've changed my attitude toward tests. In high school, I thought tests were mysterious things with completely unpredictable questions. Now, I ask instructors about the kinds of questions that will be on the exam, and I try to anticipate which areas or facts instructors are likely to ask about. These practices really work, and for me they've taken much of the fear and mystery out of tests.

Since I've reformed, note-taking and studying are not as tough as they once were. And I am beginning to reap the benefits. As time goes on, my college test sheets are going to look much different from the red-marked tests of my high school days.

5

QUESTIONS

About the Main Idea and Author's Purpose

1. In your own words, write the main idea of the essay.

   _____

   _____

2. What is the author's purpose, and how can you determine this?

   _____

   _____

About Unity

3. In which supporting paragraph in "Studying: Then and Now" is the topic sentence at the end rather than at the beginning, where it generally belongs in student essays?

   _____

About Support

4. Which sentence in paragraph 3 needs to be followed by more supporting details? (Write the opening words.)

   _____

About Coherence

5. What method of development does the author use?

   _____

About Mixed Modes

6. What are the different types of modes the author employed to support her purpose?

   _____

About the Introduction and Conclusion

7. Which sentence best describes the opening paragraph?

a. It begins with a broad statement that narrows down to the thesis.

b. It explains the importance of the topic to the reader.

c. It uses an incident or a brief story.

RESPONDING TO IMAGES

Is there such a thing as a "typical family"? The Pritchetts, a true modern family, resemble what many families of the twenty-first century now look like. What is your idea of a typical family? Write an essay comparing or contrasting your own family with your concept of a typical family.

Writing an Essay with Emphasis on Comparison and/or Contrast

ANALYZING ATTITUDES

Write an essay in which you analyze two attitudes on a controversial subject. You may want to contrast your views with those of someone else, or contrast the way you felt about the subject in the past with the way you feel now. You will want to review Chapter 11, "Comparison or Contrast"; additionally, if you choose the first option, you may need to do research, so you will need to read Chapter 20, "Writing a Research Paper" in order to properly document and cite your information.

WRITING ASSIGNMENT 1

COMPARING VIEWPOINTS

Emily Dickinson is known for her poems about solitude. Write an essay that compares or contrasts Dickinson's view about solitude in two of the poems. Then discuss how your view of solitude is either similar to or different from that which is presented by the poems. To create good support, you will want to review Chapter 11, "Comparison or Contrast" and Chapter 6, "Exemplification." You may also want to review Chapter 12, "Definition" as this assignment may require you to compare your definition of solitude to Emily Dickinson's definition. Finally, if you use direct quotes or paraphrases of Dickinson's poems, you should review Chapter 20, "Writing a Research Paper" for proper citation and documentation.

WRITING ASSIGNMENT 2

In this essay that emphasizes comparison and/or contrast, you will write with a specific purpose and for a specific audience.

REQUESTING A PROMOTION   Assume that there is a desirable job opening at your workplace. Write a letter in which you persuade your boss that you are the ideal candidate for this position. To support your point, you will want to compare your abilities with those of the ideal candidate for this position. Use the point-by-point method, discussing each desired qualification and then describing how well you measure up to it. Use the requirements of a job you are familiar with, ideally a job you would really like to apply for someday. Additional support should be given through actual examples (Chapter 6, "Exemplification" and Chapter 7, "Narration") of your abilities.

Developing an Essay with Emphasis on Definition

Considering Purpose and Audience

When you write an essay that emphasizes definition, your main purpose is to explain to readers your understanding of a key term or concept, while your secondary purpose is to persuade them that your definition is a legitimate one. Keep in mind that when you present a definition in your essay, you should not simply repeat a word's dictionary meaning. Instead, you should convey what a particular term means to you through persuasive examples. For example, if you were to write about the term "patriotism," you might begin by presenting your definition of the word. You might say patriotism means turning out for Fourth of July parades, displaying the flag, or supporting the government. Or perhaps you think patriotism is about becoming politically active and questioning government policy. Whatever definition you choose, be sure to provide specific instances so that readers can fully understand your meaning of the term. For example, in writing an essay on patriotism, you might describe three people whom you see as truly patriotic. Writing about each person will help ensure that readers see and understand the term as you do.

As with other essay forms, keep your audience in mind. If, for instance, you were proposing a new definition of "patriotism," an audience of war veterans might require different examples than would an audience of college students.

Student Essay to Consider

Directions for Reading the Essay: As you read the following essay, circle areas that strike you as interesting or especially descriptive, underline areas that seem to be out of place or need work, place stars by any areas where you think additional information could be added, and mark the different modes of writing within this essay. Do you agree or disagree with these labels? Can you think of a label the author left out? Be prepared to discuss your ideas.

Student Zombies

Schools divide people into categories. From first grade on up, students are labeled "advanced" or "deprived" or "remedial" or "antisocial." Students pigeonhole their fellow students, too. We've all known the "brain," the "jock," the "dummy," and the "teacher's pet." In most cases, these narrow labels are misleading and inaccurate. But there is one label for a certain type of college student that says it all: "zombie."

Zombies are the living dead. Most of us haven't known a lot of real zombies personally, but we do know how they act. We have horror movies to guide us. The special effects in horror movies are much better these days. Over the years, we've learned from the movies that zombies stalk around graveyards, their eyes glued open by Hollywood makeup artists, bumping like cheap toy robots into living people. Zombie students in college do just about the same thing. They stalk around campus, eyes glazed, staring off into space. When they do manage to wander into a classroom, they sit down mechanically and contemplate the ceiling. Zombie students rarely eat, talk, laugh, or toss Frisbees on campus lawns. Instead, they vanish when class is dismissed and return only when some mysterious zombie signal summons them back into a classroom. The signal may not occur for weeks.

Zombies are controlled by some mysterious force. According to legend, real zombies are corpses that have been brought back to life to do the bidding of a voodoo master. Student zombies, too, seem directed by a strange power. They continue to attend school although they have no apparent desire to do so. They show no interest in college-related activities like tests, grades, papers, and projects. And yet some inner force compels them to wander through the halls of higher education.

An awful fate awaits all zombies unless something happens to break the spell they're under. In the movies, zombies are often shot, stabbed, drowned, electrocuted, and run over by large vehicles, all to no avail. Finally the hero or heroine realizes that a counterspell is needed. Once that spell is cast, with the appropriate props of chicken feet, human hair, and bats' eyeballs, the zombie-corpse can return peacefully to its coffin. The only hope for a student zombie to change is for him or her to undergo a similarly traumatic experience.

All college students know that it's not necessary to see *Night of the Living Dead* or *Land of the Dead* in order to see zombies in action—or nonaction. They can forget the campus film series or the late-late show. All they need to do is just sit in a classroom and wait. They know what they're looking for—the students who walk in without books or papers and sit in the very last row of seats. The ones with iPods plugged into their ears don't count as zombies—that's a whole different category of "student." *Day of the Living Dead* is showing every day at a college nearby.

1

2

3

4

5

QUESTIONS

About the Main Idea and Author's Purpose

1. In your own words, write the main idea of the essay.

   College students are no different from Zombies

2. What is the author's purpose, and how can you determine this?

   Compare and contrast students like Zombies

About Unity

3. Which sentence in paragraph 2 of "Student Zombies" should be omitted in the interest of paragraph unity? (Write the opening words.)

   The special effects in horror

4. What sentence in the final paragraph introduces a new topic and so should be eliminated? (Write the opening words.)

   The ones with iPods unplugged into their ears

About Support

5. After which sentence in paragraph 4 is more support needed? (Write the opening words.)

   The only hope

About Coherence

6. Which sentence in paragraph 2 begins with a change-of-direction transitional word? (Write the opening words.)

   Instead, they vanish

About Mixed Modes

7. What are the different types of modes the author employed in the paragraphs to create such an entertaining and interesting essay?

About the Introduction and Conclusion

8. Which method of introduction is used in the opening paragraph? (Circle the letter of the answer.)

   a. Anecdote

   b. Idea that is the opposite of the one to be developed

   c. Quotation

   d. Broad, general statement narrowing to a thesis

Writing an Essay with Emphasis on Definition

DEFENDING A BOOK

Each year, the Young Adult Library Services Association puts out a list of the best books for young adults. The decisions are made by a committee. Pretend you are on the committee and you need to defend your choice of book. You will need to define what you think makes a great book, and then demonstrate how this book fits your definition. You will want to review Chapter 12, "Definition" and Chapter 14, "Argument" to help you present a solid essay that persuades the committee to include your book on the list. You may also need to review Chapter 20, "Writing a Research Paper" if you decide to visit the YALSA Web site, http://www.ala.org/yalsa/booklistsawards/booklistsbook, and/or incorporate direct quotations or summaries of your book.

WRITING ASSIGNMENT 1

Personal

DEFENDING A THEORY

Famous philosophers like Aristotle, Plato, and Friedrich Nietzsche spent their lives thinking about and trying to solve some of life's most difficult questions. In this assignment, you are to research a philosopher and learn about his or her most famous theory/theories. You could study Epicurus and his theory of happiness or G. E. Moore and his theory of truth. Then, you are to write an essay that explains why you agree or disagree with the ideas you have studied and why.

If your idea of happiness differs from that of Epicurus, give examples of the differences, or if your idea of truth is the same as that of Moore, explain why you have come to that idea. This essay will require you to define the term or theory (Chapter 12), compare or contrast your definition to the philosopher's definition (Chapter 11), and persuade your audience to believe why your definition is the correct one (Chapter 14).

WRITING ASSIGNMENT 2

Academic

In this essay that emphasizes definition, you will write with a specific purpose and for a specific audience.

PROMOTING A HEALTHY LIFESTYLE You work in a doctor's office and have been asked to write a brochure that will be placed in the waiting room. The brochure is intended to tell patients what a healthy lifestyle is. Write an essay that defines "healthy lifestyle" for your readers, using examples whenever appropriate. Your definition might focus on both mental and physical health and might include eating, sleeping, exercise, and recreational habits. You may want to look at Chapter 6, "Exemplification"; Chapter 7, "Narration"; and Chapter 12, "Definition" for help in developing solid support for your essay.

BEYOND THE CLASSROOM

Definition

Work

Developing an Essay with Emphasis on Division and Classification

Considering Purpose and Audience

When writing an essay that emphasizes division and classification, your purpose is to present your audience with your own unique way of dividing and classifying particular topics. In order to write a successful essay, you will need to first choose a topic that interests readers and lends itself to support that can be divided and classified. Once you pick your topic and decide on the support you will use, you will then have to come up with your own unique sorting system—one that readers will be able to understand.

For example, if your essay focuses on types of clothing, there are a number of ways to sort this topic into categories. You could divide clothing by the function it serves: shirts and jackets (to cover the upper body), pants and skirts (for the lower body), and shoes and socks (for the feet). Or you could divide clothes according to the materials they are made from: animal products, plant products, and synthetic materials. A more interesting, and potentially humorous, way to divide clothes is by fashion: clothes that are stylish, clothes that are going out of style, and clothes that are so unattractive that they never were in style. Notice that in all three of these cases, the broad topic of clothing has been divided into categories according to a particular principle (function, materials, and fashion).

Unlike a classification and division paragraph that focuses only on presenting the categories, an essay that emphasizes classification and division may also contain description and/or narration. As you have read in the paragraph development sections, different modes require different forms of writing, so it is important to use the specific modes and writing techniques where and when needed. Also, depending on the different categories that you include, you may need to research more information. Your audience and the purpose of your essay will determine the kinds of categorizations you will establish, if research is required, where extra description may be needed, and what strategies should be employed while writing.

Student Essay to Consider

Directions for Reading the Essay: As you read the following essay, circle areas that strike you as interesting or especially descriptive, underline areas that seem to be out of place or need work, place stars by any areas where you think additional information could be added, and mark the different modes of writing within this essay. Additionally, do you think the examples support the purpose of the essay, or should the author have chosen different examples? Be prepared to explain your opinion.

Don't Judge a Person . . .

Knowing what is on a person's iPod has become so popular, Web sites and forums are dedicated to answering just that question. On YouTube, people have posted videos creatively sharing what is on their

1

continued

iPods. In magazines, celebrities are often asked what is on their iPod, and the article that follows then dissects the celebrity's personality based upon his or her music choices. Unfortunately, people are often judged by the type of music they listen to, but stereotyping people according to their music often creates an incorrect picture.

2

One example of music listeners who are frequently mislabeled is rap music fans. Rap music is often stereotyped as angry, sexual, and violent. Because of this, people who listen to rap are often labeled as gang members or trouble-makers. There are listeners who like it because it symbolizes gangs and trouble, but many people have much simpler reasons for listening. Some people like to listen to rap because the songs usually have very strong rhythms, which can be hypnotic and fun. Others like to listen to rap because they find it therapeutic; the rappers sing about topics that many of the listeners are experiencing, but don't know how to deal with. When Common, a rapper and poet, was invited to a poetry event at the White House, many people were astonished and upset. Picturing a president listening to rap and inviting that artist to the White House was too much. The president shouldn't be inviting rappers to the White House. Common's performance, however, was not angry, sexual, or violent, and those who heard him praised his performance.

3

Christian music listeners are another group that is often mislabeled. Because of the nature of Christian music, listeners are often labeled as "goody-two-shoes" or naive. Most listeners of Christian music like the fact that it incorporates many genres, including rap, but doesn't usually contain vulgar language or sexually explicit lyrics.

4

A final group of music listeners that is often wrongly stereotyped is country music listeners. These listeners are often labeled as "pickup-driving hunters" and "hicks." However, many country music fans are urbanites who have spent very little time in the country. Other fans of country music like it because, like Christian music, the songs are often less vulgar and racy than other popular forms of music. Despite his sexy, superstar "nonhick" image, Taylor Lautner listens to several types of music, including country.

5

Countless numbers of people are judged or stereotyped by what music they listen to. However, wrapping someone in a label according to the music he or she listens to is often more wrong than right. As the saying goes, "Don't judge a book by its cover," or in this case don't judge a person by his or her iPod.

About the Main Idea and Author's Purpose

QUESTIONS

1. In your own words, write the main idea of the essay.

_____

_____

2. What is the author's purpose, and how can you determine this?

_____

_____

_____

About Unity

3. Which sentence in paragraph 2 of "Don't Judge a Person . . ." should be omitted in the interest of paragraph unity? *(Write the opening words.)*

_____

_____

_____

About Support

4. After which sentence in paragraph 3 is more support needed? (Write the opening words.)

_____

_____

_____

About Coherence

5. List the transitional words used at the beginning of paragraphs 2, 3, and 4.

_____

_____

_____

Mixed Modes

6. What are the different types of modes the author employed in her paragraphs to create such a fluid essay?

_____

_____

_____

About the Introduction and Conclusion

7. What method of introduction is used in the opening paragraph? (Circle the letter of the answer.)

   a. Anecdote

   b. Idea that is the opposite of the one to be developed

   c. Broad, general statement narrowing to a thesis

   d. Quotation

Writing an Essay with Emphasis on Division and Classification

EXAMINING CATEGORIES

Choose one of the following subjects as the basis for an essay that emphasizes division and classification. Once you have chosen a topic, you will want to decide what other modes of writing will help support your purpose and review the relevant chapters. If your essay requires description, review Chapter 8; if it requires comparison or contrast, review Chapter 11. Remember, all essays are a mix of writing modes.

Music	Pet owners	Vacations
Videos	Junk food	Bosses
Catalogs	College courses	Voicemail messages
Fiction	Dating couples	Breakfast foods
Web sites	Shoppers	Parties

GETTING TO KNOW YOUR COLLEGE LIBRARY

The library on your campus is a central part of the learning process. At some point, most classes will require students to use the library for something other than checking their e-mail and Facebook. In this assignment, you will be required to visit your local library and interview a librarian to find out all the resources available. Once you have gathered your information, you will want to classify the types of services offered at your library, supporting the classifications with detailed information. This assignment will require you to review Chapter 6, "Exemplification"; Chapter 8, "Description"; Chapter 13, "Division-Classification"; and Chapter 20, "Writing a Research Paper."

In this essay that emphasizes division or classification, you will write with a specific purpose and for a specific audience.

DESCRIBING THE IDEAL JOB Unsure about your career direction, you have gone to a job counseling center. To help select the work best suited for you, a counselor has asked you to write a detailed description of your "ideal job," which will be used to match you to different types of employment.

To describe your "ideal job," choose three categories from the following list:

Activities done on the job

Skills used on the job

People you work with

Physical environment

Salary and fringe benefits

Opportunities for advancement

continued

In your essay, explain your ideals for each category (Chapter 13, "Division-Classification"). You will also need to use specific examples to illustrate your points like anecdotes (Chapter 7, "Narration") and possibly researched support (Chapter 20, "Writing a Research Paper").

Developing an Essay with Emphasis on Argument

Considering Purpose and Audience

When you write an essay that has an emphasis on argument, your main purpose is to convince readers that your particular view or opinion on an issue or topic is correct. In addition, at times, you may have a second purpose for your essay: to persuade your audience to take some sort of action.

in a writer's words

"Words are, of course, the most powerful drug used by mankind."
—Rudyard Kipling

While consideration of your audience is important for all essay forms, it is absolutely critical to the success of an essay that is persuasive in tone. Depending on the main point you choose, your audience may be firmly opposed to your view or somewhat supportive of it. As you begin planning, consider what your audience already knows and how it feels about the main point of your essay. Say, for example, you want to argue that public schools should require students to wear uniforms. Using this example, ask yourself what opinion your audience holds about school uniforms. What are likely to be their objections to your argument? Why would people not support your main point? What, if anything, are the merits of the opposing point of view? In order to "get inside the head" of your opposition, you might even want to interview a few people you're sure will disagree with you: say, for instance, a student with a very funky personal style who you know would dislike wearing a uniform. By becoming aware of the points of view your audience might have, you will know how to proceed in researching your rebuttal to their arguments. By directly addressing your opposition, you add credibility to your argument and increase the chances that others will be convinced that your main point is valid.

The purpose of your essay will determine what research should be included (Chapter 20), what tone should be taken, and what modes of writing should be used for support. As you have seen in the paragraph development sections, different modes require different forms of writing, so it is important to look at the specific modes and writing techniques where and when needed.

Student Essay to Consider

Directions for Reading the Essay: As you read the following essay, circle areas that strike you as interesting or especially descriptive, underline areas that seem to be out of place or need work, place stars by any areas where you think additional information could be added, and mark the different modes of writing within this essay. Additionally, determine if the examples the author provided are persuasive enough, and if not, what would have offered better support. Be prepared to discuss your opinion.

AAA Gets an A for Service

When many people pack for road trips, they include things like clothes, food, games, more food, and, for some, GPS units. What many people forget to pack is a membership in the American Automobile Association (AAA). AAA offers travel planning, roadside service, and peace of mind. Although more and more people are getting GPS units for their cars, nothing should replace a service like AAA.

Trip planning is one of the services that AAA offers that a GPS unit cannot truly do. Although many people like to plan trips on their own, having a service like AAA can add a whole new dimension to the planning. They offer a service that organizes all the travel, whether road, air, train, or boat. A wonderful product is the TripTik— road trip plans that include navigational directions, roadside interests, fun sites, and restaurants. Although GPS units can offer similar things, not all GPS units can be utilized while the car is being driven, so the driver must pull over in order for the navigator to be able to access the information. A TripTik is paper, so it doesn't require a parked car to override the navigational unit and is easily accessible. Another positive thing about the TripTik is that even if a GPS unit is being used, the navigator can follow along with the TripTik, making suggestions and providing a backup just in case the GPS unit fails. When my husband and I were on a trip, our GPS unit started misreading our location. We were on an interstate in the middle of traffic and were able to continue with the use of the TripTik until it was possible to get our GPS unit reset.

Another great service that AAA offers is a free selection of guidebooks. Travelers can pick up guidebooks for states, regions, and cities. The guidebooks contain everything from information about hotels and restaurants to activities to do in that area. Not only do the guidebooks make finding a last-minute hotel or dinner venue easy, but they can also provide enough background information so that travelers can become their own tour guides. To purchase similar guidebooks at a bookstore would be an annoyance. Although they also contain lists of restaurants, hotels, and activities, GPS units don't have teams of people visiting these venues and rating them on cleanliness, service, quality of food, and value for money. During one trip, we had an unplanned overnight stay. Instead of spending time looking through our GPS hotel listing and possibly staying in a questionable place, we consulted our guidebook and found a great hotel that had been approved by AAA and offered a discounted price for AAA members.

One of the best benefits of AAA is the emergency roadside service. If a car breaks down, the driver can call AAA to get help. AAA will send someone out to change a flat tire, jumpstart the car, or even deliver gas. If the person dispatched to help cannot provide assistance, he or she will call for a tow truck to take the car and its passengers to a nearby garage. Again, like the restaurant and hotel guides, the tow truck will be AAA-approved and

1

2

3

4

continued

should be free to the AAA customer. Additionally, the tow truck will take the car to an approved garage that has proven itself to be honest and reliable. No task is too small for AAA, even retrieving keys locked in the car.

Technology is great and having a GPS unit in a car is a comfort to many drivers. However, one comfort that all drivers should have is the knowledge that they packed their card containing their AAA membership number and the toll-free number that reaches live operators. GPS units may offer navigational security, but they cannot replace the security that AAA provides its members.

5

QUESTIONS

About the Main Idea and Author's Purpose

1. In your own words, write the main idea of the essay.

   _____

   _____

2. What is the author's purpose, and how can you determine this?

   _____

   _____

About Unity

3. Which sentence in paragraph 3 should be omitted in the interest of paragraph unity? (Write the opening words.)

   _____

About Support

4. After which sentence in paragraph 4 is more support needed? (Write the opening words.)

   _____

About Coherence

5. What transition words does the author use at the beginning of each paragraph?

   _____

   _____

   _____

Mixed Modes

6. What are the different types of modes the author employed in her paragraphs to create such a persuasive essay?

   _____

About the Introduction and Conclusion

7.   What method is used in the conclusion?

   a.   Summary and final thoughts

   b.   Recommendation

   c.   Thought-provoking question

Writing an Essay with Emphasis on Argument

SUPPORTING AN ARGUMENT

WRITING ASSIGNMENT 1

Work

Write an essay in which you argue *for* or *against* the statement: "An employer should be able to use information from social networking sites such as *MySpace* and *Facebook* before hiring a job applicant."

   Support and defend your essay by drawing on your reasoning ability and general experience. Use the modes of writing that will best help you support your essay. If you use any research, refer to Chapter 20, "Writing a Research Paper," to help you document and cite your information properly.

WRITING A LETTER TO THE COLLEGE PRESIDENT

WRITING ASSIGNMENT 2

Academic

Write a letter to the president of your college about something that needs to be changed on campus; it could be parking issues, tuition, schedules, fees, and so on. In your letter, explain what the problem is, why it needs to be fixed, and offer a solution. Keeping your audience in mind, you will want to maintain a formal tone and provide solid evidence. Your evidence might include the effects of the problem (Chapter 10), anecdotes of fellow students' experiences (Chapter 7), and/or examples from other colleges that have had the same problem (Chapter 11 and Chapter 20).

BEYOND THE CLASSROOM

Argument

Personal

In this essay that emphasizes argument, you will write with a specific purpose and for a specific audience.

RAISING AWARENESS You care deeply about the issues in your community. As a concerned citizen, you would like to make others aware of a growing problem—for example, a rise in auto thefts, speeding in a school zone, graffiti on the roadways, or illegal dumping. Write a letter to the editor of your local newspaper in which you argue why more should be done to address this problem. Provide convincing reasons to support your position and address any skepticism that readers may have. Good research (Chapter 20) and anecdotes (Chapter 7) will help provide valid reasons to support your position.

Special College Skills

RESPONDING TO IMAGES

Sweaty palms, an increased heart rate, difficulty concentrating—these are signs of test-taking anxiety. Think back to how you felt the last time you took a test. Were you nervous? Take a few minutes to describe how you felt. Next, think about ways you might reduce test-taking anxiety. In this chapter, you will learn how to prepare for and take essay exams.

Taking Essay Exams

Essay exams are perhaps the most common type of writing you will do in school. They include one or more questions to which you must respond in detail, writing your answers in a clear, well-organized manner. Many students have trouble with essay exams because they do not realize there is a sequence to follow that will help them do well on such tests. This section describes five basic steps needed to prepare adequately for an essay test and to take the test. It is assumed, however, that you are already doing two essential things: first, attending class regularly and taking notes on what happens in class; second, reading your textbook and other assignments and taking notes on them. If you are *not* consistently going to class, reading your text, and taking notes in both cases, you are likely to have trouble with essay exams and other tests as well.

To write an effective exam essay, follow these five steps:

Step 1: Anticipate ten probable questions.

Step 2: Prepare and memorize an informal outline answer for each question.

Step 3: Look at the exam carefully and do several things.

Step 4: Prepare a brief, informal outline before writing your essay answer.

Step 5: Write a clear, well-organized essay.

The following pages explain and illustrate these steps.

Step 1: Anticipate Ten Probable Questions

Because exam time is limited, the instructor can give you only a limited number of questions to answer. He or she will, reasonably, focus on questions dealing with the most important areas of the subject. You can probably guess most of them.

Go through your class notes with a colored pen and mark off those areas where your instructor has spent a good deal of time. The more time spent on any one area, the better the chance you will get an essay question on it. If the instructor spent a week talking about present-day changes in the traditional family structure, or the importance of the carbon molecule, or the advantages of capitalism, or key early figures in the development of psychology as a science, you can reasonably expect that you will get a question about the emphasized area.

In both your class notes and your textbooks, pay special attention to definitions and examples and to basic lists of items (enumerations). Enumerations in particular are often a key to essay questions. For instance, if your instructor spoke at length about causes of the Great Depression, effects of water pollution, or advantages of capitalism, you should probably expect a question such as "What were the causes of the Great Depression?" or "What are the effects of water pollution?" or "What are the advantages of capitalism?"

If your instructor has given you a study guide, look there for probable essay questions. (Some instructors choose essay questions from those listed in study guides.) Look for clues to essay questions on any short quizzes that you may have been given. Finally, consider very carefully any review that the instructor provides. Always write down such reviews—your instructor has often made up the test or is making it up at the time of the review and is likely to give you valuable hints about it. Take advantage of them! Note also that if the instructor does not offer to provide a review, do not hesitate to *ask* for one in a friendly way. Essay questions are likely to come from areas the instructor may mention.

An Illustration of Step 1

A psychology class was given one day to prepare for an essay exam on stress— a subject that had been covered in class and comprised a chapter in the textbook for the course. One student, Mark, read carefully through his class notes and the textbook chapter. On the basis of the headings, major enumerations, and definitions he noted, he decided that there were five likely essay questions:

1. What are the common sources of stress?

2. What are the types of conflict?

3. What are the defense mechanisms that people use to cope with stress?

4. What effects can stress have on people?

5. What are the characteristics of a well-adjusted person?

Step 2: Prepare and Memorize an Informal Outline Answer for Each Question

Write out each question you have made up and, under it, list the main points that need to be discussed. Put important supporting information in parentheses after each main point. You now have an informal outline that you can memorize.

Pick out a *key word* in each part, and then create a *catchphrase* to help you remember the key words.

> **TIP** If you have spelling problems, make up a list of words you might have to spell in writing your answers. For example, if you are having a psychology test on the principles of learning, you might want to study such terms as *conditioning, reinforcement, Pavlov, reflex, stimulus,* and so on.

An Illustration of Step 2

After identifying the likely questions on the exam, Mark made up an outline answer for each of the questions. For example, here is the outline answer that he made up for the first question:

Common sources of stress:

1. (Pressure) (internal and external)

2. (Anxiety) (sign of internal conflict)

3. (Frustration) (can't reach desired goal)

4. (Conflict) (three types of approach-avoidance)

   P A F C (People are funny creatures.)

See whether you can complete the following explanation of what Mark has done in preparing for the essay question.

First, Mark wrote down the heading and then numbered the sources of stress under it. Also, in parentheses beside each point he added

_____. Then he circled the four key words, and he wrote

down the first _____ of each word underneath his outline. Mark then used the first letter in each key word to make up a catchphrase that

he could easily remember. Finally, he _____ himself over and over until he could recall all four of the sources of stress that the first letters stood for. He also made sure that he recalled the supporting material that went with each idea.

Step 3: Look at the Exam Carefully and Do Several Things

1. Get an overview of the exam by reading *all* the questions on the test.

2. Note *direction words* (*compare, illustrate, list,* and so on) for each question. Be sure to write the kind of answer that each question requires. For example, if a question says "illustrate," do not "compare." The list on the next page will help clarify the distinctions among various direction words.

3. Budget your time. Write in the margin the number of minutes you should spend for each essay. For example, if you have three essays worth an equal number of points and a one-hour time limit, figure twenty minutes for each essay. Make sure you are not left with only a couple of minutes to do a high-point essay.

4. Start with the easiest question. Getting a good answer down on paper will help build up your confidence and momentum. Number your answers plainly so that your instructor knows what question you are answering first.

An Illustration of Step 3

When Mark received the exam, the question was "Describe the four common sources of stress in our lives." Mark circled the direction word *describe,* which meant he should explain in detail each of the four causes of stress. He also jotted a "30" in the margin when the instructor said that students would have a half hour to write the answer.

Complete the short matching quiz below. It will help you review the meanings of some of the direction words listed on the following page.

1. List _____

2. Contrast _____

a. Tell in detail about something.

b. Give a series of points and number them 1, 2, 3, etc.

3. Define _____   c. Give a condensed account of the main points.
4. Summarize _____   d. Show differences between two things.
5. Describe _____   e. Give the normal meaning of a term.

Direction Words

Term	Meaning
Compare	Show similarities between things.
Contrast	Show differences between things.
Criticize	Give the positive and negative points of a subject as well as evidence for those positions.
Define	Give the formal meaning of a term.
Describe	Tell in detail about something.
Diagram	Make a drawing and label it.
Discuss	Give details and, if relevant, the positive and negative points of a subject as well as evidence for those positions.
Enumerate	List points and number them 1, 2, 3, and so on.
Evaluate	Give the positive and negative points of a subject as well as your judgment about which outweighs the other and why.
Illustrate	Explain by giving examples.
Interpret	Explain the meaning of something.
Justify	Give reasons for something.
List	Give a series of points and number them 1, 2, 3, and so on.
Outline	Give the main points and important secondary points. Put main points at the margin and indent secondary points under the main points. Relationships may also be described with logical symbols, as follows:

1. _____

    a. _____

    b. _____

2. _____

Term	Meaning
Prove	Show to be true by giving facts or reasons.
Relate	Show connections among things.
State	Give the main points.
Summarize	Give a condensed account of the main points.
Trace	Describe the development or history of a subject.

Step 4: Prepare a Brief, Informal Outline before Writing Your Essay Answer

Use the margin of the exam or a separate piece of scratch paper to jot down quickly, as they occur to you, the main points you want to discuss in each answer. Then decide in what order you want to present these points in your response. Write 1 in front of the first item, 2 beside the second, and so on. You now have an informal outline to guide you as you answer your essay question.

If there is a question on the exam that is similar to the questions you anticipated and outlined at home, quickly write down the catchphrase that calls back the content of the outline. Below the catchphrase, write the key words represented by each letter in the catchphrase. The key words, in turn, will remind you of the concepts they represent. If you have prepared properly, this step will take only a minute or so, and you will have before you the guide you need to write a focused, supported, organized answer.

An Illustration of Step 4

Mark immediately wrote down his catchphrase, "People are funny creatures." He next jotted down the first letters in his catchphrase and then the key words that went with each letter. He then filled in several key details and was ready to write his essay answer. Here is what his brief outline looked like:

> People are funny creatures.
>
> P   Pressure (internal and external)
>
> A   Anxiety (internal conflict)
>
> F   Frustration (prevented from reaching goal)
>
> C   Conflict (approach-avoidance)

Step 5: Write a Clear, Well-Organized Essay

If you have followed steps 1 through 4, you have done all the preliminary work needed to write an effective essay. Now, be sure not to ruin your chance of getting a good grade by writing carelessly. Keep in mind the bases of good writing: unity, support, coherence, and clear, error-free sentences.

First, start your essay with a sentence that clearly states what your answer will be about. Then make sure that everything in your paper relates to your opening statement.

Second, though you must obviously take time limitations into account, provide as much support as possible for each of your main points.

Third, use transitions to guide your reader through your answer. Words such as *first, next, then, however,* and *finally* make it easy to follow your thought.

Last, leave time to proofread your essay for sentence-skills mistakes you may have made while you concentrated on writing your answer. Look for words omitted, miswritten, or misspelled (if it is allowed, bring a dictionary with you); look for awkward phrasings or misplaced punctuation marks; and look for whatever else may prevent the reader from understanding your thought. Cross out any mistakes and make your corrections neatly above the errors. If you want to change or add to some point, insert an asterisk at the appropriate spot, put another asterisk at the bottom of the page, and add the corrected material there.

An Illustration of Step 5

Read Mark's answer, reproduced below, and then do the activity that follows.

There are four common sources of stress in our lives. The first one is pressure, which can be internal or external. Internal pressure occurs when a person tries to live up to his or her own goals and standards. This kind of pressure can help (when a person strives to be a better musician, for instance) or hurt (as when someone tries to reach impossible standards of beauty). External pressure occurs when people must compete, deal with rapid change, or cope with outside demands. Another source of stress is anxiety. People who are ~~anxous~~ anxious often don't know why they feel this way. Some psychologists think anxiety comes from some internal conflict, like feeling angry and trying hard to repress this ~~angry feeling~~ anger. A third source of stress is frustration, which occurs when people are prevented from reaching goals or obtaining certain needs. For example, a woman may do poorly on an important exam because she has a bad cold. She feels angry and frustrated because she could not reach her goal of an A or B grade. The most common source of stress is conflict. Conflict results when a person is faced with two incompatible ~~goals~~ desires. The person may want both goals (a demanding career and motherhood, for instance). This is called approach- approach. Or a person may want to avoid both choices (avoidance- avoidance). Or a person may be both attracted to and repelled by a desire (as a woman who wants to marry a gambler). This is approach-avoidance.

ACTIVITY 3

The following sentences comment on Mark's essay. Fill in the missing word or words in each case.

1. Mark begins with a sentence that clearly states what his essay _____. Always begin with such a clear statement!

2. Notice the _____ that Mark made when writing and proof-reading his paper. He neatly crossed out miswritten or unwanted words, and he used insertion signs (^) to add omitted words.

3. The four signal words that Mark used to guide his readers, and himself, through the main points of his answer are _____, _____, _____, and _____.

ACTIVITY 4

1. Make up five questions you might be expected to answer on an essay exam for a course in a social or physical science (such as sociology, psychology, or biology).

2. For each of the five questions, make up an outline answer comparable to the one on anxiety.

3. Finally, write a full essay answer, in complete sentences, to one of the questions. Your outline will serve as your guide.

Be sure to begin your essay with a statement that makes clear the direction of your answer. An example might be "The six major defense mechanisms are defined and illustrated below." If you are explaining in detail the different causes of, reasons for, or characteristics of something, you may want to develop each point in a separate paragraph. For example, if you were answering a question in sociology about the primary functions of the family unit, you could start with the statement "The family unit has three primary functions" and go on to develop and describe each function in a separate paragraph.

You will submit the essay answer to your English instructor, who will evaluate it using the standards for effective writing applied to your other written assignments.

EXPLORING WRITING ONLINE

Using a search engine of your choice, enter the phrase "taking an essay exam" into the search box. Then visit a handful of the sites and choose one to recommend to your class. Write a one-paragraph review of the site to hand in to your instructor. Was it helpful? What advice did it offer?

Writing a Summary

At some point in a course, your instructor may ask you to write a summary of a book, an article, a TV show, or the like. In a *summary* (also referred to as a *précis* or an *abstract*), you reduce material in an original work to its main points and key supporting details. Unlike an outline, however, a summary does not use symbols such as I, A, 1, 2, etc., to indicate the relations among parts of the original material.

A summary may consist of a single word, a phrase, several sentences, or one or more paragraphs. The length of any summary you prepare will depend on your instructor's expectations and the length of the original work. Most often, you will be asked to write a summary consisting of one or more paragraphs.

Writing a summary brings together a number of important reading, study, and writing skills. To condense the original assigned material, you must preview, read, evaluate, organize, and perhaps outline it. Summarizing, then, can be a real aid to understanding; you must "get inside" the material and realize fully what is being said before you can reduce its meaning to a few words.

How to Summarize an Article

To write a summary of an article, follow the steps described below. If the assigned material is a TV show or film, adapt the suggestions accordingly.

1. Take a few minutes to preview the work. You can preview an article in a magazine by taking a quick look at the following:

   a. *Title.* A title often summarizes what an article is about. Think about the title for a minute, and about how it may condense the meaning of the article.

   b. *Subtitle.* A subtitle, if given, is a short summary appearing under or next to the title. For example, in a *Newsweek* article titled "Growing Old, Feeling Young," the following caption appeared: "Not only are Americans living longer, they are staying active longer—and their worst enemy is not nature, but the myths and prejudices about growing old." In short, the subtitle, the caption, or any other words in large print under or next to the title often provide a quick insight into the meaning of an article.

   c. *First and last several paragraphs.* In the first several paragraphs, the author may introduce you to the subject and state the purpose of the article. In the last several paragraphs, the writer may present conclusions or a summary. The previews or summaries can give you a quick overview of what the entire article is about.

   d. *Other items.* Note any heads or subheads that appear in the article. They often provide clues to the article's main points and give an immediate sense of what each section is about. Look carefully at any pictures, charts, or diagrams that accompany the article. Page space in a magazine or journal is limited, and such visual aids are generally used only to illustrate important points in the article. Note any words or phrases set off in *italic type* or **boldface type**; such words have probably been emphasized because they deal with important points in the article.

2. Read the article for all you can understand the first time through. Do not slow down or turn back. Check or otherwise mark main points and key supporting details. Pay special attention to all the items noted in the preview. Also, look for definitions, examples, and enumerations (lists of items), which often indicate key ideas.

You can also identify important points by turning any heads into questions and reading to find the answers to the questions.

3. Go back and reread more carefully the areas you have identified as most important. Also, focus on other key points you may have missed in your first reading.

4. Take notes on the material. Concentrate on getting down the main ideas and the key supporting points.

5. Prepare the first draft of your summary, keeping these points in mind:

   a. Identify at the start of the summary the title and author of the work. Include in parentheses the date of publication. For example, "In 'Leaking with a Vengeance' (*Time*, October 13, 2008), Michael Duffy states. . . ."

   b. Do not write an overly detailed summary. Remember that the purpose of a summary is to reduce the original work to its main points and essential supporting details.

   c. Express the main points and key supporting details in your own words. Do not imitate the style of the original work.

   d. Quote from the material only to illustrate key points. Also, limit your quotations. A one-paragraph summary should not contain more than one or two quoted sentences or phrases.

   e. Preserve the balance and proportion of the original work. If the original devoted 70 percent of its space to one idea and only 30 percent to another, your summary should reflect that emphasis.

   f. Revise your first draft, paying attention to the four bases of effective writing (*unity, support, coherence,* and *sentence skills*) explained in Part 2.

   g. Write the final draft of the paper.

A Model Summary of an Article

Here is a model summary of a magazine article:

> In "How to Heal a Hypochondriac" (*Time,* September 30, 2009), Michael Lemonick reports on research into ways of dealing with hypochondria, a thinking disorder that makes healthy people believe that they are suffering from one or more serious diseases. Not only do hypochondriacs genuinely suffer from their disorder, but they create a significant burden on the health-care system. Research suggests that hypochondriacs fall into three categories: those who have a variant of obsessive-compulsive disorder, those whose hypochondria was triggered by a stressful life event, and those who are hypersensitive to any physical symptoms. Cognitive therapy, in which patients are trained to direct their attention away from their symptoms, and antidepressant medication both seem helpful in treating hypochondria. The most difficult part of treatment is suggesting that a patient suffers from hypochondria without angering or embarrassing him or her.

ACTIVITY 5   Write an essay-length summary of the following article. Include a short introductory paragraph that states the thesis of the article. Then summarize in your three supporting paragraphs the three important areas in which study skills can be useful. Your conclusion might be a single sentence restating the thesis.

Power Learning

Jill had not done as well in high school as she had hoped. Since college involved even more work, it was no surprise that she didn't do better there.   1

The reason for her so-so performance was not a lack of effort. She attended most of her classes and read her textbooks. And she never missed handing in any assignment, even though it often meant staying up late the night before homework was due. Still, she just got by in her classes. Before long, she came to the conclusion that she simply couldn't do any better.   2

Then one day, one of her instructors said something to make her think otherwise. "You can probably build some sort of house by banging a few boards together," he said. "But if you want a sturdy home, you'll have to use the right techniques and tools. Building carefully takes work, but it gets better results. The same can be said of your education. There are no shortcuts, but there are some proven study skills that can really help. If you don't use them, you may end up with a pretty flimsy education."   3

Jill signed up for a study-skills course and found out a crucial fact—that learning how to learn is the key to success in school. There are certain dependable skills that have made the difference between disappointment and success for generations of students. These techniques won't free you from work, but they will make your work far more productive. They include three important areas: time control, classroom note-taking, and textbook study.   4

Time Control

Success in college depends on time control. *Time control* means that you deliberately organize and plan your time, instead of letting it drift by. Planning means that you should never be faced with an overdue term paper or a cram session the night before a test.   5

There are three steps involved in time control. *First,* you should prepare a large monthly calendar. Buy a calendar with a large white block around each date, or make one yourself. At the beginning of the college semester, circle important dates on this calendar. Circle the days on which tests are scheduled; circle the days when papers are due. This calendar can also be used to schedule study plans. At the beginning of the week, you can jot down your plans for each day. An alternative method would be to make plans for each day the night before. On Tuesday night, for example, you might write down "Read Chapter 5 in psychology" in the Wednesday block. Hang this calendar where you will see it every day—your kitchen, bedroom, even your bathroom!   6

continued

The *second step* in time control is to have a weekly study schedule for the semester—a chart that covers all the days of the week and all the waking hours in each day. Below is part of one student's schedule:

7

Time	Mon.	Tue.	Wed.	Thurs.	Fri.	Sat.	
6:00 A.M.							
7:00	Breakfast	Breakfast	Breakfast	Breakfast	Breakfast		
8:00	Math	STUDY	Math	STUDY	Math	Breakfast	
9:00	STUDY	Biology	STUDY	Biology	STUDY	Job	
10:00	Psychology	↓	Psychology	↓	Psychology		
11:00		English		English		↓	
12:00	Lunch		Lunch		Lunch	↓	

On your own schedule, fill in all the fixed hours in each day—hours for meals, classes, job (if any), and travel time. Next, mark time blocks that you can *realistically* use for study each day. Depending on the number of courses you are taking and the demands of these courses, you may want to block off five, ten, or even twenty or more hours of study time a week. Keep in mind that you should not block off time that you do not truly intend to use for study. Otherwise, your schedule will be a meaningless gimmick. Also, remember that you should allow time for "rest and relaxation." You will be happiest, and able to accomplish the most, when you have time for both work and play.

The *third step* in time control is to make a daily or weekly "to do" list. This may be the most valuable time-control method you ever use. On this list, write down the things you need to do for the following day or the following week. If you choose to write a weekly list, do it on Sunday night. If you choose to write a daily list, do it the night before. Here is part of one student's daily list:

8

To Do   Tuesday

*1. Review biology notes before class
*2. Proofread English paper due today
*3. See Dick about game on Friday
*4. Get gas for car
*5. Read next chapter of psychology text

You may use a three- by five-inch notepad or a small spiral-bound notebook for this list. Carry the list around with you during the day. Always concentrate on doing the most important items first. To make the best use of your time, mark high-priority items with an asterisk and give them precedence over low-priority items. For instance, you may find yourself wondering what to do after dinner on Thursday evening. Among the items on your list are "Clean inside of car" and "Review chapter for

continued

math quiz." It is obviously more important for you to review your notes at this point; you can clean out the car some other time. As you complete items on your "to do" list, cross them out. Do not worry about unfinished items. They can be rescheduled. You will still be accomplishing a great deal and making more effective use of your time.

Classroom Note-Taking

One of the most important single things you can do to perform well in a college course is to take effective class notes. The following hints should help you become a better note-taker.

9

First, attend class faithfully. Your alternatives—reading the text, reading someone else's notes, or both—cannot substitute for the class experience of hearing ideas in person as someone presents them to you. Also, in class lectures and discussions, your instructor typically presents and develops the main ideas and facts of the course—the ones you will be expected to know on exams.

10

Another valuable hint is to make use of abbreviations while taking notes. Using abbreviations saves time when you are trying to get down a great deal of information. Abbreviate terms that recur frequently in a lecture and put a key to your abbreviations at the top of your notes. For example, in sociology class, *eth* could stand for *ethnocentrism*; in a psychology class, *STM* could stand for *short-term memory*. (When a lecture is over, you may want to go back and write out the terms you have abbreviated.) Also, use *e* for *example*; *def* for *definition*; *info* for *information*; + for *and*; and so on. If you use the same abbreviations all the time, you will soon develop a kind of personal shorthand that makes taking notes much easier.

11

A third hint for taking notes is to be on the lookout for signals of importance. Write down whatever your instructor puts on the board. If he or she takes the time to put material on the board, it is probably important, and the chances are good that it will come up later on exams. Always write down definitions and enumerations. Enumerations are lists of items. They are signaled in such ways as "The four steps in the process are … "; "There were three reasons for … "; "The two effects were … "; "Five characteristics of … "; and so on. In your notes, always number such enumerations (1, 2, 3, etc.). They will help you understand relationships among ideas and organize the material of the lecture. Watch for emphasis words—words your instructor may use to indicate that something is important. Examples of such words are "This is an important reason … "; "A point that will keep coming up later … "; "The chief cause was … "; "The basic idea here is … "; and so on. Always write down the important statements announced by these and other emphasis words. Finally, if your instructor repeats a point, you can assume that it is important. You might put an *R* for *repeated* in the margin so that later you will know that your instructor stressed it.

12

Next, be sure to write down the instructor's examples and mark them with an *e*. The examples help you understand abstract points. If you do

13

continued

not write them down, you are likely to forget them later, when they are needed to help make sense of an idea.

Also, be sure to write down the connections between ideas. Too many students merely copy terms the instructor puts on the board. They forget that, as time passes, the details that serve as connecting bridges between ideas quickly fade. You should, then, write down the relationships and connections in class. That way you'll have them to help tie together your notes later on.

Review your notes as soon as possible after class. You must make them as clear as possible while they are fresh in your mind. A day later may be too late, because forgetting sets in very quickly. Make sure that punctuation is clear, that all words are readable and correctly spelled, and that unfinished sentences are completed (or at least marked off so that you can check your notes with another student's). Add clarifying or connecting comments wherever necessary. Make sure that important ideas are clearly marked. Improve the organization if necessary so that you can see at a glance main points and relationships among them.

Finally, try in general to get down a written record of each class. You must do this because forgetting begins almost immediately. Studies have shown that within two weeks you are likely to have forgotten 80 percent or more of what you have heard. And in four weeks you are lucky if 5 percent remains! This is so crucial that it bears repeating: To guard against the relentlessness of forgetting, it is absolutely essential that you write down what you hear in class. Later you can concentrate on working to understand fully and to remember the ideas that have been presented in class. And then, the more complete your notes are, the more you are likely to learn.

Textbook Study

In many college courses, success means being able to read and study a textbook skillfully. For many students, unfortunately, textbooks are heavy going. After an hour or two of study, the textbook material is as formless and as hard to understand as ever. But there is a way to attack even the most difficult textbook and make sense of it. Use a sequence in which you preview a chapter, mark it, take notes on it, and then study the notes.

Previewing

Previewing a selection is an important first step to understanding. Taking the time to preview a section or chapter can give you a bird's-eye view of the way the material is organized. You will have a sense of where you are beginning, what you will cover, and where you will end.

There are several steps in previewing a selection. First, study the title. The title is the shortest possible summary of a selection and will often tell you the limits of the material you will cover. For example, the title "FDR and the Supreme Court" tells you to expect a discussion of President Roosevelt's dealings with the Court. You know that you will probably not

14

15

16

17

18

19

continued

encounter any material dealing with FDR's foreign policies or personal life. Next, quickly read over the first and last paragraphs of the selection; these may contain important introductions to, and summaries of, the main ideas. Then briefly examine the headings and subheadings in the selection. Together, the headings and subheadings are a mini-outline of what you are reading. Headings are often main ideas or important concepts in capsule form; subheadings are breakdowns of ideas within main areas. Finally, read the first sentence of some paragraphs, look for words set off in **boldface** or *italics*, and look at pictures or diagrams. After you have previewed a selection in this way, you should have a good general sense of the material to be read.

Marking

You should mark a textbook selection at the same time that you read it through carefully. Use a felt-tip highlighter to shade material that seems important, or use a ballpoint pen and put symbols in the margin next to the material: stars, checks, or NB (*nota bene,* Latin for "note well"). What to mark is not as mysterious as some students believe. You should try to find main ideas by looking for clues: definitions and examples, enumerations, and emphasis words.

20

1. *Definitions and examples:* Definitions are often among the most important ideas in a selection. They are particularly significant in introductory courses in almost any subject area, where much of your learning involves mastering the specialized vocabulary of that subject. In a sense, you are learning the "language" of psychology or business or whatever the subject might be.

21

Most definitions are abstract, and so they usually are followed by one or more examples to help clarify their meaning. Always mark off definitions and at least one example that makes a definition clear to you. In a psychology text, for example, we are told that "rationalization is an attempt to reduce anxiety by deciding that you have not really been frustrated." Several examples follow, among them: "A young man, frustrated because he was rejected when he asked for a date, convinces himself that the girl is not very attractive or interesting."

22

2. *Enumerations:* Enumerations are lists of items (causes, reasons, types, and so on) that are numbered 1, 2, 3, . . . or that could easily be numbered. They are often signaled by addition words. Many of the paragraphs in this book, for instance, use words like *First of all, Another, In addition,* and *Finally* to signal items in a series. Other textbooks also use this very common and effective organizational method.

23

3. *Emphasis words:* Emphasis words tell you that an idea is important. Common emphasis words include phrases such as *a major event, a key feature, the chief factor, important to note, above all,* and *most of all.* Here is an example: "The most significant contemporary use

24

continued

of marketing is its application to nonbusiness areas, such as political parties."

Note-Taking

Next, you should take notes. Go through the chapter a second time, rereading the most important parts. Try to write down the main ideas in a simple outline form. For example, in taking notes on a psychology selection, you might write down the heading "Defense Mechanisms." Below the heading you would define them, number and describe each kind, and give an example of each.   25

Defense Mechanisms

a. *Definition: unconscious attempts to reduce anxiety*

b. *Kinds:*

   (1) *Rationalization: An attempt to reduce anxiety by deciding that you have not really been frustrated.*

   Example: A man turned down for a date decides that the woman was not worth going out with anyway.

   (2) *Projection: Projecting onto other people motives or thoughts of one's own.*

   Example: A wife who wants to have an affair accuses her husband of having one.

Studying Notes

To study your notes, use repeated self-testing. For example, look at the heading "Defense Mechanisms" and say to yourself, "What are the kinds of defense mechanisms?" When you can recite them, then say to yourself, "What is rationalization?" "What is an example of rationalization?" Then ask yourself, "What is projection?" "What is an example of projection?" After you learn each section, review it, and then go on to the next section.   26

Do not simply read your notes; keep looking away and seeing if you can recite them to yourself. This self-testing is the key to effective learning.   27

Summary: Textbook Study

In summary, remember this sequence for dealing with a textbook: preview, mark, take notes, study the notes. Approaching a textbook in this methodical way will give you very positive results. You will no longer feel bogged down in a swamp of words, unable to figure out what you are supposed to know. Instead, you will understand exactly what you have to do, and how to go about doing it.   28

Take a minute now to evaluate your own study habits. Do you practice many of the above skills in order to take effective classroom notes, control your time, and learn from your textbooks? If not, perhaps you should. The skills are not magic, but they are too valuable to ignore. Use them carefully and consistently, and they will make academic success possible for you. Try them, and you won't need convincing.   29

ACTIVITY 6

Write an essay-length summary of a broadcast of the NBC television show *Dateline*. In your first sentence, include the date of the show. For example, "The March 25, 2012, broadcast of NBC's *Dateline* dealt with three subjects most people would find of interest. The first segment of the show centered on . . . ; the second segment examined . . . ; the final segment discussed . . . ". Be sure to use parallel form in describing the three segments of the show. Then summarize each segment in the three supporting paragraphs that follow.

ACTIVITY 7

Write an essay-length summary of a cover story of interest to you in a recent issue of *Time*, *Newsweek*, or *U.S. News & World Report*.

How to Summarize a Book

To write a summary of a book, first preview the book by briefly looking at:

1. *Title.* A title is often the shortest possible summary of what a book is about. Think about the title and how it may summarize the whole book.

2. *Table of contents.* The contents will tell you the number of chapters in the book and the subject of each chapter. Use the contents to get a general sense of how the book is organized. You should also note the number of pages in each chapter. If thirty pages are devoted to one episode or idea and an average of fifteen pages to other episodes or ideas, you should probably give more space in your summary to the contents of the longer chapter.

3. *Preface.* Here you will probably find out why the author wrote the book. Also, the preface may summarize the main ideas developed in the book and may describe briefly how the book is organized.

4. *First and last chapters.* In these chapters, the author may preview or review important ideas and themes developed in the book.

5. *Other items.* Note how the author has used headings and subheadings to organize information in the book. Check the opening and closing paragraphs of each chapter to see if these paragraphs contain introductions or summaries. Look quickly at charts, diagrams, and pictures in the book, since they are probably there to illustrate key points. Note any special features (index, glossary, appendixes) that may appear at the end of the book.

Next, adapt steps 2 through 5 for summarizing an article on pages 354–355.

ACTIVITY 8

Write an essay-length summary of a book you have read.

EXPLORING WRITING ONLINE

Visit one of these TV network Web sites and select one of your favorite TV shows. Watch a video of an entire episode or find an episode that you have already seen, and then read the synopsis or recap of that episode. Next, write a summary of your own.

CBS.com: http://www.cbs.com

ABC.com: http://abc.go.com

NBC.com: http://www.nbc.com

Fox Broadcasting: http://www.fox.com

Writing a Report

Each semester, you will probably be asked by at least one instructor to read a book or an article and write a paper recording your response to the material. In these reports or reaction papers, your instructor will most likely expect you to do two things: *summarize the material* and *detail your reaction to it*. The following pages explain both parts of a report.

Part 1 of a Report: A Summary of the Work

To develop the first part of a report, do the following. (An example follows, on pages 365–366.)

1. Identify the author and title of the work, and include in parentheses the publisher and publication date. With magazines, give the date of publication.

2. Write an informative summary of the material. Condense the content of the work by highlighting its main points and key supporting points. (See pages 353–363 for a complete discussion of summarizing techniques.) Use direct quotations from the work to illustrate important ideas.

Do *not* discuss in great detail any single aspect of the work while neglecting to mention other equally important points. Summarize the material so that the reader gets a general sense of *all* key aspects of the original work. Also, keep the summary objective and factual. Do not include in the first part of the paper your personal reaction to the work; your subjective impression will form the basis of the second part of the paper.

Part 2 of a Report: Your Reaction to the Work

To develop the second part of a report, do the following:

1. Focus on any or all of the following questions. (Check with your instructors to see if they want you to emphasize specific points.)

in a writer's words

"Write what you really think and mean, not what you think you should write and not what you thought you would think and not what you hope it will mean, but what is really authentic and true."

—Susan Orlean

a. How is the assigned work related to ideas and concerns discussed in the course? For example, what points made in the course textbook, class discussions, or lectures are treated more fully in the work?

b. How is the work related to problems in our present-day world?

c. How is the work related to your life, experiences, feelings, and ideas? For instance, what emotions did it arouse in you? Did it increase your understanding of an issue or change your perspective?

2. Evaluate the merit of the work: the importance of its points; its accuracy, completeness, and organization; and so on. You should also indicate here whether you would recommend the work to others, and why.

Points to Keep in Mind When Writing a Report

Here are some important matters to consider as you prepare a report:

1. Apply the four basic standards of effective writing (unity, support, coherence, and clear, error-free sentences).

a. Make sure each major paragraph presents and then develops a single main point. For example, in the model report that follows, a paragraph summarizes the book, and the three paragraphs that follow detail three separate reactions that the student writer had. The student then closes the report with a short concluding paragraph.

b. Support with specific reasons and details any general points or attitudes you express. Statements such as "I agreed with many ideas in this article" and "I found the book very interesting" are meaningless without specific evidence that shows why you feel as you do. Look at the model report to see how the main point or topic sentence of each paragraph is developed by specific supporting evidence.

c. Organize the material in the paper. Follow the basic *plan of organization* already described: an introduction, a summary consisting of one or more paragraphs, a reaction consisting of two or more paragraphs, and a conclusion. Use *transitions* to connect the parts of the paper.

d. Proofread the paper for grammar, mechanics, punctuation, and word use.

2. Document quotations from all works by giving the page number in parentheses after the quoted material (see the model report). You may use quotations in the summary and reaction parts of the paper, but do not rely too much on them. Use them only to emphasize key ideas.

A Model Report

Here is a report written by a student in an introductory sociology course. Look at the paper closely to see how it follows the guidelines for report writing described in this chapter.

A Report on *I Know Why the Caged Bird Sings*

Introductory paragraph

1

In *I Know Why the Caged Bird Sings* (New York: Bantam Books, 1971), Maya Angelou tells the story of her earliest years. Angelou, a dancer, poet, and television producer as well as a writer, has continued her life story in three more volumes of autobiography. *I Know Why the Caged Bird Sings* is the start of Maya Angelou's story; in this book, she writes with crystal clarity about the pains and joys of being black in America.

2

PART 1: SUMMARY
Topic sentence for summary paragraph

I Know Why the Caged Bird Sings covers Maya Angelou's life from age three to age sixteen. We first meet her as a gawky little girl in a white woman's cut-down lavender silk dress. She has forgotten the poem she had memorized for the Easter service, and all she can do is rush out of the church. At this point, Angelou is living in Stamps, Arkansas, with her grandmother and uncle. The town is rigidly segregated: "People in Stamps used to say that the whites in our town were so prejudiced that a Negro couldn't buy vanilla ice cream" (40). Yet Angelou has some good things in her life: her adored older brother Bailey, her success in school, and her pride in her grandmother's quiet strength and importance in the black community. There is laughter, too, as when a preacher is interrupted in midsermon by an overly enthusiastic woman shouting, "Preach it, I say preach it!" The woman, in a frenzied rush of excitement, hits the preacher with her purse; his false teeth fly out of his mouth and land at Angelou's feet. Shortly after this incident, Angelou and her brother are taken by her father to live in California with their mother. Here, at age eight, she is raped by her mother's boyfriend, who is mysteriously murdered after receiving only a suspended sentence for his crime. She returns, silent and withdrawn, to Stamps, where the gloom is broken when a friend of her mother introduces her to the magic of great books. Later, at age thirteen, Angelou returns to California. She learns how to dance. She runs away after a violent family fight and lives for a month in a junkyard. She becomes the first black female to get a job on the San Francisco streetcars. She graduates from high school eight months pregnant. And she survives.

3

PART 2: REACTION
Topic sentence for first reaction paragraph

I was impressed with the vividness of Maya Angelou's writing style. For example, she describes the lazy dullness of her life in Stamps: "Weekdays revolved in a sameness wheel. They turned into themselves so steadily and inevitably that each seemed to be the original of yesterday's rough draft" (93). She also knows how to bring a scene to life, as when she describes her eighth-grade graduation. For months, she has been looking forward to this event, knowing she will be honored for her academic successes. She is even happy with her appearance: her hair has become pretty, and her yellow dress is a miracle of hand-sewing. But the ceremony is spoiled when the speaker—a white man—implies that the only success available to blacks is in athletics. Angelou remembers: "The man's dead words fell like bricks around the auditorium and too many settled in my belly. . . . The proud graduating class of 1940 had dropped their heads" (152). Later, Angelou uses a crystal-clear image to describe her father's mistress

continued

sewing: "She worked the thread through the flowered cloth as if she were sewing the torn ends of her life together" (208). With such vivid details and figures of speech, Maya Angelou re-creates her life for her readers.

Topic sentence for second reaction paragraph

I also reacted strongly to the descriptions of injustices suffered by blacks two generations ago. I was as horrified as the seven-year-old Maya when some "powhitetrash" girls torment her dignified grandmother, calling her "Annie" and mimicking her mannerisms. In another incident, Mrs. Cullinan, Angelou's white employer, decides that Marguerite (Angelou's real name) is too difficult to pronounce and so renames her Mary. This loss of her name—a "hellish horror" (91)—is another humiliation suffered at white hands, and Angelou leaves Mrs. Cullinan's employ soon afterward. Later, Angelou encounters overt discrimination when a white dentist tells her grandmother, "Annie, my policy is I'd rather stick my hand in a dog's mouth than in a nigger's" (160)—and only slightly less obvious prejudice when the streetcar company refuses to accept her application for a conductor's job. We see Angelou over and over as the victim of a white society.

4

Topic sentence for third reaction paragraph

Although I was saddened to read about the injustices, I rejoiced in Angelou's triumphs. Angelou is thrilled when she hears the radio broadcast of Joe Louis's victory over Primo Camera: "A Black boy. Some Black mother's son. He was the strongest man in the world" (114). She weeps with pride when the class valedictorian leads her and her fellow eighth-graders in singing the Negro National Anthem. And there are personal victories, too. One of these comes after her father has gotten drunk in a small Mexican town. Though she has never driven before, she manages to get her father into the car and drives fifty miles through the night as he lies intoxicated in the backseat. Finally, she rejoices in the birth of her son: "He was beautiful and mine. Totally mine. No one had bought him for me" (245). Angelou shows us, through these examples, that she is proud of her race—and of herself.

5

Concluding paragraph

I Know Why the Caged Bird Sings is a remarkable book. Angelou could have been just another casualty of race prejudice. Yet by using her intelligence, sensitivity, and determination, she succeeds in spite of the odds against her. And by writing with such power, she lets us share her defeats and joys. She also teaches us a vital lesson: with strength and persistence, we can all escape our cages—and sing our songs.

6

EXPLORING WRITING ONLINE

Visit the *Rolling Stone* Web site at www.rollingstone.com/reviews and select a review of a CD that you have listened to. Read the review, and then write a report of your own in which you include a summary of the CD, your reaction to the music, and an evaluation of the work. Be sure to end your report with a statement about whether you would recommend the CD to others, and why.

Writing a Research Paper

RESPONDING TO IMAGES

If you were to write a research paper on war, what would you focus on? War itself is too broad a topic to cover in one paper. You would need to select a more limited topic to write about, for example, the effect of war on the economy. Looking at the above photograph of an American soldier, interacting with local people, can you think of some other limited topics you might cover in a research paper?

Step 1: Select a Topic That You Can Readily Research

Researching at a Local Library

First of all, do a subject search of your library's catalog and see whether there are several books on your general topic. For example, if you initially choose the broad topic "parenting," try to find at least three books on being a parent. Make sure that the books are actually available on the library shelves.

Next, go to a *periodicals index* in your library to see if there are a fair number of magazine, newspaper, or journal articles on your subject. You can use the *Readers' Guide to Periodical Literature* (found in just about every library) to locate articles that appear in the back issues of periodicals that your library may keep. But you may find that your library also subscribes to an electronic database such as Academic Search Premier, CQ Researcher, or JSTOR, which will allow you access to articles published in a far greater range of publications. For instance, when Sonya Philips, author of the model research paper "Successful Families," visited her local library, she typed the search term "parenting" into a computer that connected her to Academic Search Premier. In seconds, Academic Search Premier came back with hundreds of "hits"—titles, publication information, and the complete text of articles about parenting.

Researching on the Internet

If you have access to the Internet on a home or library computer you can determine if online resources are available for your topic.

The first step is to go to the subjects section of a library catalog or large online bookseller to find relevant books. (Don't worry—you don't have to buy any books; you're just browsing for information.) Two of the largest online booksellers are Barnes and Noble and Amazon.

"I checked out both Barnes and Noble and Amazon as I began my research," said Sonya Philips. "When I went to their Web sites, I saw that I could search for books by subject, and I knew that I was in business. All I had to do was click on a box titled 'Browse Subjects.'

"Barnes and Noble has a category called 'Parenting and Family,' and when I clicked on that, I got a bunch of subcategories, including one for 'Teenagers.' I clicked on 'Teenagers' and that brought up a list of hundreds of books! I went through the list, and when I got to a book that sounded promising, I just clicked on that title and up like magic came reviews of the book—and sometimes a table of contents and a summary as well! All of this information helped me decide on the dozen or so books I eventually picked out that seemed relevant to my paper. I then went to my local library and found five of those titles on the shelves. Another title was a recent paperback, so I went to a nearby bookstore and bought it." (If you find relevant books in your online search that your local library does not own, ask your research librarian if he or she can obtain them from another library through an interlibrary loan program.)

Next, determine if magazine or newspaper articles on your topic are available online. The simplest way is to use the online search engine Google

(google.com), which allows you to search for information on any topic you like. Sonya relates her experience using Google in this way:

"First I typed in the word 'parenting' in the keyword box," she said. "I got more than eight million hits! So I tried more specific search terms. I tried 'parenting and teenagers' first, but that was still too general. I got several hundred thousand hits and I didn't know where to start reading. So I narrowed my topics even more: 'parenting and teenagers and television' and 'parenting and teenagers and home-schooling.' Those reduced the number of hits a lot. I was still getting thousands, but I could see that some of the very first ones looked really promising. Better yet I found some useful sites, like 'The Television Project,' which is an online resource that doesn't exist anywhere else.

"In order to look just for magazine and newspaper articles, I went directly to the site of some popular publications, such as *Time* (time.com), *Newsweek* (newsweek.com), and *USA Today* (usatoday.com). I was able to search each one for recent articles about parenting. I was able to read and print each article online. Between doing that and using Academic Search Premier, I found plenty of recent material related to my subject."

In summary, then, the first step in doing a research paper is to find out if both books and articles are available on the topic in which you are interested. If they are, pursue your topic. Otherwise, you may have to explore another topic. You cannot write a paper on a topic for which research materials are not available.

Step 2: Limit Your Topic and Make the Purpose of Your Paper Clear

A research paper should *thoroughly* develop a *limited* topic. The paper should be narrow and deep rather than broad and shallow. Therefore, as you read through books and articles, look for ways to limit your general topic.

For instance, as Sonya read through materials on the general topic "parenting," she chose to limit her topic to the particular problems of parents raising children in today's culture. Furthermore, she decided to limit it even more by focusing on what successful parents do to deal with those challenges. To take some other examples, the general topic "drug abuse" might be narrowed to successful drug treatment programs for adolescents. After doing some reading on the worldwide problem of overpopulation, you might decide to limit your paper to the birth-control policies enforced by the Chinese government. The broad subject "death" could be reduced to euthanasia or the unfair pricing practices in some funeral homes. "Divorce" might be limited to its most damaging effects on the children of divorced parents; "stress in everyday life" could be narrowed to methods of reducing stress in the workplace.

The subject headings in your library's catalog and periodicals indexes will give you helpful ideas about how to limit your subject. For example, under the subject heading "Parenting" in the book file were several related headings, such as "moral and ethical considerations of parenting" and "stepparenting." In addition, there was a list of seventy-eight books, including several titles that suggested limited directions for research: parents and discipline, parenting and adolescent girls, how parents can protect their kids from violence, parents' questions about teenagers' development. Under the subject heading "Parenting" in the library's periodicals index were subheadings and titles of many articles that suggested additional limited topics that a research paper might explore: how parents can limit the impact of TV on kids, keeping the lines of communication open between parents and teenagers, how much influence parents can have on kids, secrets to raising a successful teen. The point is that *subject headings and related headings, as well as book and article titles, may be of great help to you in narrowing your topic.* Take advantage of them.

Do not expect to limit your topic and make your purpose clear all at once. You may have to do quite a bit of reading as you work out the limited focus of your paper. Note that many research papers have one of two general purposes. Your purpose might be to make and defend a point of some kind. (For example, your purpose in a paper might be to provide evidence that elected officials should be limited to serving a single term in office.) Or, depending on the course and the instructor, your purpose might simply be to present information about a particular subject. (For instance, you might be asked to write a paper describing the most recent scientific findings about the effect of diet on heart disease.)

Step 3: Gather Information on Your Limited Topic

After you have a good sense of your limited topic, you can begin gathering relevant information. A helpful way to proceed is to sign out the books that you need from your library. In addition, make copies of all relevant articles from magazines, newspapers, or journals. If your library has an online periodicals database, you may be able to print out those articles.

In other words, take the steps needed to get all your key source materials together in one place. You can then sit and work on these materials in a quiet, unhurried way in your home or some other place of study.

Step 4: Plan Your Paper and Take Notes on Your Limited Topic

Preparing a Scratch Outline

As you carefully read through the material you have gathered, think constantly about the specific content and organization of your paper. Begin making decisions about exactly what information you will present and how you will arrange it. Prepare a scratch outline for your paper that shows both its thesis and the areas of support for the thesis. Try to plan at least three areas of support.

Thesis: _____

Support: (1)_____

(2)_____

(3)_____

Following, for example, is the brief outline that Sonya Philips prepared for her paper on successful parenting.

> **Thesis:** There are things parents can do to overcome the negative influences hurting their families.
>
> **Support:** (1) Create quality time with families
> (2) Increase families' sense of community
> (3) Minimize the impact of media and technology

Note-Taking

With a tentative outline in mind, you can begin taking notes on the information that you expect to include in your paper. Write your notes on four-by-six-inch or five-by-eight-inch cards, on sheets of loose-leaf paper, or in a computer file. The notes you take should be in the form of *direct quotations, summaries in your own words,* or both. At times, you may also *paraphrase*—use an equal number of your own words in place of someone else's words. Since most research involves condensing information, you will summarize much more than you will paraphrase. (For more information on summarizing, see pages 353–363.)

A *direct quotation* must be written *exactly* as it appears in the original work. But as long as you don't change the meaning, you may omit words from a quotation if they are not relevant to your point. To show such an omission, use three spaced periods (known as *ellipses*) in place of the deleted words:

We cannot guarantee that bad things will happen, but we can argue that good things are not happening. It is the contention of this report that increasing numbers of young people are left to their own devices at a critical time in their development.	**Original passage**

"We cannot guarantee that bad things will happen, but we can argue that good things are not happening. . . . [I]ncreasing numbers of young people are left to their own devices at a critical time in their development."	**Direct quotation with ellipses**

(Note that there are four dots in the above example; the first dot indicates the period at the end of the sentence. The capital letter in brackets shows that the word was capitalized by the student but did not begin the sentence in the original source.)

In a *summary,* you condense the original material by expressing it in your own words. Summaries may be written as lists, as brief paragraphs, or both. Following is one of Sonya Philips's summary note cards.

Keep in mind the following points about your research notes:

- Write on only one side of each card or sheet of paper.

> *Movie content*
> *Study conducted in 2006 showed that of PG-13 movies, 91 percent had crude language, 89 percent had obscene language, 45 percent had actual or suggested sex. Worrisome because most parents assume PG-13 movies are OK for their kids.*
>
> *Medved and Medved, 62*

- Write only one kind of information, from one source, on any one card or sheet. For example, the sample card above has information on only one idea (movie content) from one source (Medved and Medved).

- At the top of each card or sheet, write a heading that summarizes its content. This will help you organize the different kinds of information that you gather.

- Identify the source and page number at the bottom.

Whether you quote or summarize, be sure to record the exact source and page from which you take each piece of information. In a research paper, you must document all information that is not common knowledge or not a matter of historical record. For example, the birth and death dates of Dr. Martin Luther King, Jr., are established facts and do not need documenting. On the other hand, the average number of hours worked annually today compared with the 1980s is a specialized fact that should be documented. As you read several sources on a subject, you will develop a sense of what authors regard as generally shared or common information and what is more specialized information that must be documented.

A Caution about Plagiarism

If you fail to document information that is not your own, you will be stealing. The formal term is *plagiarizing*—using someone else's work as your own, whether you borrow a single idea, a sentence, or an entire essay.

One example of plagiarism is turning in a friend's paper as if it is one's own. Another example is copying an article found in a magazine, newspaper, journal, or online and turning it in as one's own. By copying someone else's work, you may risk being failed or even expelled. Equally, plagiarism deprives you of what can be a most helpful learning and organization experience—researching and writing about a selected topic in detail.

Keep in mind, too, that while the Internet has made it easier for students to plagiarize, it has also made it riskier. Teachers can easily discover that a student has taken material from an online source by typing a sentence or two from the student's paper into Google; that source is then often quickly identified.

With the possibility of plagiarism in mind, then, be sure to take careful, documented notes during your research. Remember that if you use another person's material, *you must acknowledge your source.* When you cite a source properly, you give credit where it is due, you provide your readers with a way to locate the original material on their own, and you demonstrate that your work has been carefully researched.

ACTIVITY 1

Here are three sets of passages. Each set begins with an original passage followed by notes on the passage. Both notes include a parenthetical citation (24) crediting the original source. But while one note is an acceptable paraphrase/summary, the other is an unacceptable paraphrase/summary in which the sentences and ideas too closely follow the original, using some of the same structure and the same words as the original. Identify the acceptable note with an *A* and the unacceptable note with a *U*.

SET 1: ORIGINAL PASSAGE

The self-confessed television addict often feels he "ought" to do other things—but the fact that he doesn't read and doesn't plant his garden or sew or crochet or play games or have conversations means that those activities are no longer as desirable as television. In a way the heavy viewer's life is as imbalanced by his television "habit" as a drug addict's or an alcoholic's. He is living in a holding pattern, as it were, passing up the activities that lead to growth or development or a sense of accomplishment. This is one reason people talk about their television viewing so ruefully, so apologetically. They are aware that it is an unproductive experience, that almost any other endeavor is more worthwhile by any human measure.
—Marie Winn, from "Television Addiction,"
in *The Plug-In Drug* (Viking Penguin, 2002)

_____ a. Television addicts may feel they should do other things like play games or have conversations. But they pass up activities that might lead to a sense of accomplishment. Their lives are as imbalanced by their television watching as a drug addict's or alcoholic's. Aware of how unproductive television viewing is, they talk about it apologetically (24).

_____ b. TV addicts feel that they ought to spend their time doing more worthwhile activities. But like alcohol or drugs, TV has taken over their lives. The addicts' apologetic tone when they talk about their TV watching indicates that they know they're wasting time on a completely unproductive activity (24).

SET 2: ORIGINAL PASSAGE

Now, however, there is growing evidence that restorative naps are making a comeback. Recognizing that most of their employees are chronically sleep-deprived, some companies have set up nap rooms with reclining chairs, blankets and alarm clocks. If unions are truly interested in worker welfare, they should make such accommodations a standard item in contract negotiations. Workers who take advantage of the opportunity to sleep for twenty minutes or so during the workday report that they can go back to work with renewed enthusiasm and energy. My college roommate, Dr. Linda Himot, a psychiatrist in Pittsburgh, who has a talent for ten-minute catnaps between patients, says these respites help her focus better on each patient's problems, which are not always scintillating. And companies that encourage napping report that it reduces accidents and errors and increases productivity, even if it shortens the workday a bit. Studies have shown that sleepy workers make more mistakes and cause more accidents, and are more susceptible to heart attacks and gastrointestinal disorders.

—Jane Brody, from "New Respect for the Nap" (*New York Times*, 2001)

_____ a. As employers realize that many workers are short on sleep, they are becoming more open to the idea of napping on the job. Some even provide places for workers to stretch out and nap briefly. Companies that allow napping find their employees are more alert and productive, and even suffer fewer physical ailments (24).

_____ b. Naps are becoming more acceptable. Some companies have done such things as set up nap rooms with reclining chairs and blankets. Naps provide workers with renewed enthusiasm and energy. Although naps shorten the workday a bit, they reduce accidents and increase productivity. Sleep-deprived workers are prone to heart attacks and gastrointestinal disorders (24).

SET 3: ORIGINAL PASSAGE

Chances are, you are going to go to work after you complete college. How would you like to earn an extra $950,000 on your job? If this sounds appealing, read on. I'm going to reveal how you can make an extra $2,000 a month between the ages of 25 and 65. Is this hard to do? Actually, it is simple for some, but impossible for others. All you have to do is be born a male and graduate from college. If we compare full-time workers, this is how much more the average male college graduate earns over the course of his career. Hardly any single factor pinpoints gender discrimination better than this total. The pay gap, which shows up at all levels of education, is so great that women who work full-time average only two-thirds (67 percent) of what men are paid. This gap does not occur only in the United States. All industrialized nations have it, although only in Japan is the gap larger than in the United States.

—James Henslin, from *Essentials of Sociology*, Fourth Edition (Allyn and Bacon, 2002)

_____ a. In order to make an extra $2,000 a month between the ages of 25 and 65, you need to be born male and graduate from college. This adds up to an additional $950,000. The pay gap between genders shows up at all levels of education. It is so great that women who work full-time make only two-thirds what men make. The gender gap occurs in all industrialized nations, although only in Japan is it greater than in the U.S. (24).

b. The effect of gender on salary is significant. At all levels of education, a woman who works full-time earns about two-thirds as much as a man who works full-time. For college graduates, this adds up to a difference of $950,000 over the course of a 40-year working life. The gender gap exists in all industrialized nations, but it is greatest in Japan and the U.S. (24).

Step 5: Write the Paper

After you have finished your reading and note-taking, you should have a fairly clear idea of the plan of your paper. Make a *final outline* and use it as a guide to write your first full draft. If your instructor requires an outline as part of your paper, you should prepare either a *topic outline,* which contains your thesis plus supporting words and phrases, or a *sentence outline,* which consists of complete sentences. In the model paper shown on pages 379–388, a topic outline appears on pages 380–381. You will note that roman numerals are used for first-level headings, capital letters for second-level headings, and arabic numbers for third-level headings.

In an *introduction,* include a thesis statement expressing the purpose of your paper and indicate the plan of development that you will follow. The section on writing introductions for an essay (pages 296–299) is also appropriate for the introductory section of the research paper. Notice that the model research paper uses a two-paragraph introduction (pages 381–382).

As you move from *introduction* to *main body* to *conclusion,* strive for unity, support, and coherence so that your paper will be clear and effective. Repeatedly ask, "Does each of my supporting paragraphs develop the thesis of my paper?" Use the checklist on the inside back cover of this book to make sure that your paper follows all four bases of effective writing.

Step 6: Use an Acceptable Format and Method of Documentation

Format

The model paper shows acceptable formats for a research paper, including the style recommended by the Modern Language Association (MLA). Be sure to note carefully the comments and directions that are set in small print in the margins of each page.

Documentation of Sources

You must tell the reader the sources (books, articles, and so on) of borrowed material in your paper. Whether you quote directly or summarize ideas in your own words, you must acknowledge your sources. In the past, you may have used footnotes and a bibliography to cite your sources. Here you will learn a simplified and widely accepted documentation style used by the MLA.

Citation within a Paper

When citing a source, you must mention the author's name and the relevant page number. The author's name may be given either in the sentence you are writing or in parentheses following the sentence. Here are two examples:

> In *The Way We Really Are*, Stephanie Coontz writes, "Right up through the 1940s, ties of work, friendship, neighborhood, ethnicity, extended kin, and voluntary organizations were as important a source of identity for most Americans, and sometimes a more important source of obligation, than marriage and the nuclear family" (37).
>
> "Some . . . are looking for a way to reclaim family closeness in an increasingly fast-paced society. . . . Still others worry about unsavory influences in school—drugs, alcohol, sex, violence" (Kantrowitz and Wingert 66).

There are several points to note about citations within the paper:

- When referring to an author within the parenthetical citation, use only the last name.

- There is no punctuation between the author's name and the page number.

- The parenthetical citation is placed after the borrowed material but before the period at the end of the sentence.

- If you are using more than one work by the same author, include a shortened version of the title within the parenthetical citation. For example, suppose you were using two books by Stephanie Coontz, and you included a second quotation from her book *The Way We Really Are*. Your citation within the text would be

> (Coontz, *Really Are* 39).

Note that a comma separates the author's last name from the abbreviated title and page number.

Citations at the End of a Paper

Your paper should end with a list of "Works Cited" that includes all the sources actually used in the paper. (Don't list any other sources, no matter how many you have read.) Look at the "Works Cited" page in the model research paper (page 388) and note the following points:

- The list is organized alphabetically according to the authors' last names. Entries are not numbered.

- Entries are double-spaced, with no extra space between entries.

- After the first line of each entry, there is a half-inch indentation for each additional line in the entry.

- Use the abbreviation *qtd. in* when citing a quotation from another source. For example, a quotation from Edward Wolff on page 2 of the paper is from a book not by Wolff but by Sylvia Ann Hewlett and Cornel West. The citation is therefore handled as follows:

The economist Edward Wolff explains the loss of time:

> Over a thirty-year time span, parental time has declined 13 percent. The time parents have available for their children has been squeezed by the rapid shift of mothers into the paid labor force, by escalating divorce rates and the subsequent abandonment of children by their fathers, and by an increase in the number of hours required on the job. The average worker is now at work 163 hours a year more than in 1969, which adds up to an extra month of work annually (qtd. in Hewlett and West 48).

Model Entries for a List of "Works Cited"

Model entries of "Works Cited" are given below. Use these entries as a guide when you prepare your own list.

Bryson, Bill. *A Short History of Nearly Everything*. New York: Broadway Books, 2003. Print.

Book by One Author

Note that the author's last name is written first. This is followed by the title of the book with the first word and all major words capitalized. Next comes the place of publication and the name of the publisher and the date. The entry ends with the word "Print," to indicate the medium in which the work was published.

---. *I'm a Stranger Here Myself*. New York: Broadway Books, 2005. Print.

Two or More Entries by the Same Author

If you cite two or more entries by the same author (in the example above, a second book by Bill Bryson is cited) do not repeat the author's name. Instead, begin the line with three hyphens followed by a period. Then give the remaining information as usual. Arrange works by the same author alphabetically by title. The words *A, An,* and *The* are ignored in alphabetizing by title.

Simon, David, and Edward Burns. *The Corner*. New York: Broadway Books, 2000. Print.

Book by Two or More Authors

For a book with two or more authors, give all the authors' names but reverse only the first name.

Kalb, Claudia. "Brave New Babies." *Newsweek* 26 Jan. 2009: 45–52. Print.

Magazine Article

Farrell, Greg. "Online Time Soars at Office." *USA Today* 18 Feb. 2009: A1-2. Print.

Newspaper Article

The final letter and numbers refer to pages 1 and 2 of section A. If the article is not printed on consecutive pages, simply list the first page followed by a plus sign ("+"). In that case, the above example would read "A1+".

"Fouling the Air." Editorial. *New York Times* 23 Aug. 2009: A12. Print.

Editorial

List an editorial as you would any signed or unsigned article, but indicate the nature of the piece by adding *Editorial* after the article's title.

Article in a Professional Journal

Andrews, Elmer. "The Gift and the Craft: An Approach to the Poetry of Seamus Heaney." *Twentieth Century Literature* 31.4 (2000): 368–69. Print.

Selection in an Edited Collection

Paige, Satchel. "Rules for Staying Young." *Baseball: A Literary Anthology.* Ed. Nicholas Dawidoff. New York: Library of America, 2002. 318. Print.

Revised or Later Edition

Henslin, James M. *Essentials of Sociology.* 5th ed. Boston: Allyn, 2004. Print.

The abbreviations *Rev. ed., 2nd ed., 3rd ed.,* and so on, are placed right after the title.

Chapter or Section in a Book by One Author

Krugman, Paul. "The Angry People." *The Great Unraveling.* New York: Norton, 2003. 272–74. Print.

Pamphlet

Funding Your Education 2009–2010. Washington: Department of Education Office of Federal Student Aid. 2009. Print.

Television Program

"Musically Speaking." *60 Minutes.* Report. Lesley Stahl. CBS. 28 Sept. 2009. Television.

Film

The Dark Knight. Dir. Christopher Nolan. Warner Bros. Pictures, 2008. Film.

Sound Recording

Springsteen, Bruce. "The Wrestler." *Working on a Dream.* Columbia Records, 2009. CD.

Videocassette

"Cedric's Journey." *Nightline.* Narr. Ted Koppel. ABC, WABC, New York. 24 June 1998. ABC/FDCH, 1998. Videocassette.

DVD

Superbad. Perf. Michael Cera, Jonah Hill. Dir. Greg Mottola. Columbia Pictures, 2007. DVD. Sony, 2007.

Personal Interview

McClintock, Ann. Personal interview. 23 June 2004.

Article in an Online Magazine

Hobson, Catherine. "Cancer: The Best Tests to Find a Killer." *US News .com* 1 Sept. 2007. Web. 9 Oct. 2008.

The first date (1 Sept. 2007) refers to the issue of the publication in which the article appeared; the second date (9 Oct. 2008) refers to the day when the student researcher accessed the source. Note: Do not include URLs in Web entries.

Article in a Web Site

"Being Chased." *Dreams and Nightmares.* Internet Resources. 2008. Web. 17 Mar. 2009.

No author is given, so the article is cited first, followed by the title of the Web site. The first date (2008) refers to when the material was electronically published, updated, or posted; the second date (17 Mar. 2009) refers to when the student researcher accessed the source. When no date appears in a Web site, write *n.d.* If no publisher's name appears in a Web source, write *N.p.*

> Costa, Stefano. "Music in Dreams and the Emergence of the Self." *Journal of American Psychology* 54.1 (2009): 81–83. *Academic Search Premier.* Web. 3 Mar. 2009.

Article in Reference Database

The first date (2009) refers to when the material was electronically published, updated, or posted; the second date (3 Mar. 2009) refers to when the student researcher accessed the source.

> Graham, Vanessa. "Re: Teenager Problems." Message to Sonya Philips. 12 Apr. 2009. E-mail.

E-mail

ACTIVITY 2

On a separate sheet of paper, convert the information in each of the following references into the correct form for a list of "Works Cited." Use the appropriate model above as a guide.

1. A book by David Anderegg called *Worried All the Time* and published in New York by Free Press in 2003.

2. An article by Susan Page titled "No Experience Necessary" on pages 1A–2A of the September 29, 2007, issue of *USA Today.*

3. A book by Michael W. Passer and Ronald E. Smith titled *Psychology: The Science of Mind and Behavior* and published in a fourth edition by McGraw-Hill in New York in 2008.

4. An article by Mark Miller titled "Parting with a Pet" found on May 16, 2007, in the October 8, 2007, issue of *Newsweek Online.*

5. An article titled "Depression in Teenagers" found on April 24, 2007, on the Web site titled *Troubled Teens*, which is sponsored by the Aspen Education Group.

Model Paper

While the *MLA Handbook* does not require a title page or an outline for a paper, your instructor may ask you to include one or both. Here is a model title page.

Model Title Page

Successful Families:

Fighting for Their Kids

by

Sonya Philips

English 101

Professor Lessing

5 May 2009

The title should begin about one-third of the way down the page. Center the title. Double-space between lines of the title and your name. Also center and double-space the instructor's name and the date.

Model First Page of MLA-Style Paper

Double-space all 4 lines

Double-space between lines. Leave a one-inch margin on all sides.

↑ 1 inch

Papers written in MLA style use the simple format shown below. There is no title page or outline.

↑ 1/2 inch

Philips 1

Sonya Philips

Professor Lessing

English 101

5 May 2009

Successful Families: Fighting for Their Kids

It's a terrible time to be a teenager, or even a teenager's parent. That message is everywhere. Television, magazines, and newspapers are all full of frightening stories about teenagers and families. They say that America's families are falling apart, that kids don't care about anything, and that parents have trouble doing anything....

Model Outline Page

After the title page, number all pages in upper-right corner, a half-inch from the top. Place your name before the page number. Use small roman numerals on outline pages. Use arabic numerals on pages following the outline.

The word *Outline* (without underlining or quotation mark) is centered one inch from the top. Double-space between lines. Leave a one-inch margin on all sides.

Use this format if your instructor asks you to submit an outline of your paper.

Outline

Thesis: Although these are difficult times to be raising teenagers, successful families are finding ways to cope with the challenges.

I. Meeting the challenge of spending quality time together

  A. Barriers to spending quality time

    1. Increased working hours

    2. Rising divorce rates

    3. Women in workforce

  B. Danger of lack of quality time

  C. Ways found to spend time together

    1. Working less and scaling back lifestyle

    2. Home schooling

II. Meeting the challenge of creating sense of community

  A. Lack of traditional community ties

  B. Ways found to create sense of community

    1. Intentional communities

    2. Religious ties

III.   Meeting the challenge of limiting the negative impact of media
and technology

   A.   Negative impact of media and technology

      1.   Creation of environment without protection

      2.   Flood of uncontrolled, inappropriate information

   B.   Ways of controlling media and technology

      1.   Banning TV

      2.   Using technology in beneficial ways

Here is a full model paper. It assumes the writer has included a title page.

Philips 1

Successful Families: Fighting for Their Kids

It's a terrible time to be a teenager or even a teenager's parent.
That message is everywhere. Television, magazines, and newspapers
are all full of frightening stories about teenagers and families. They
say that America's families are falling apart, that kids don't care about
anything, and that parents have trouble doing anything about it.
Bookstores are full of disturbing titles like these: *Parenting Your Out-of-
Control Teenager, Teenage Wasteland, Unhappy Teenagers,* and *Teen
Torment.* These books describe teenage problems that include apathy,
violence, suicide, sexual abuse, depression, loss of values, poor mental
health, crime, gang involvement, and drug and alcohol addiction.

Naturally, caring parents are worried by all this. Their worry
showed in a 2005 national poll in which 76% of parents said that
raising children was "a lot harder" than it was when they were
growing up ("A Lot Easier Said"). But just as most popular TV shows
don't give a realistic view of American teens, these frightening books
and statistics do not provide a complete picture of what's going

Academic

Double-space
between lines of
the text. Leave a
one-inch margin all
the way around the
page. Your name
and page number
should be typed
one-half inch from
the top of the page.

Common
knowledge is not
documented.

This typical
citation shows the
source by giving
the author's last
name or (as here,
if no author is
provided) the
title of the article
(and if relevant,
a page number).
"Works Cited"
then provides full
information about
the source.

Philips 2

on in families today. The fact is that not all teens and families are lost and without values. While they struggle with problems in our culture like everyone else, successful families are doing what they've always done: finding ways to protect and nurture their children. They are fighting the battle for their families in three ways: by fighting against the loss of quality family time, by fighting against the loss of community, and by fighting against the influence of the media.

It's true that these days, parents face more challenges than ever before when it comes to finding quality time to spend with their children. The economist Edward Wolff explains the loss of time:

> Over a thirty-year time span, parental time has declined 13%.
> The time parents have available for their children has been
> squeezed by the rapid shift of mothers into the paid labor force,
> by escalating divorce rates and the subsequent abandonment
> of children by their fathers, and by an increase in the number of
> hours required on the job. The average worker is now at work
> 163 hours a year more than in 1969, which adds up to an
> extra month of work annually (qtd. in Hewlett and West 48).

As a result, more children are at home alone than ever before. And this situation does leave children vulnerable to getting into trouble. Richardson and others, in their study of five thousand eighth-graders in California, found that children who were home alone after school were twice as likely to experiment with drugs and alcohol as children who had a parent (or another adult) home in the after-school hours.

But creative parents still come up with ways to be there for their kids. For some, it's been a matter of cutting back on working hours and living more simply. For example, in her book *The Shelter of Each Other*, Mary Pipher tells the story of a couple with three-year-old twin boys. Eduardo worked sixty-hour weeks at a factory. Sabrina supervised checkers at a K-Mart, cared for the boys, and tried to watch over her mother, who had cancer. Money was tight, especially

---

Thesis, followed by plan of development.

Source is identified by name and area of expertise.

Direct quotations of five typed lines or more are indented ten spaces (or one inch) from the left margin. Quotation marks are not used.

The abbreviation *qtd.* means *quoted*. No comma is used between the author's names and the page number.

When citing a work in general, not part of a work, it is best to include the author's name in the text instead of using a parenthetical citation. No page number is needed, as the citation refers to the findings of the study overall.

Philips 3

since day care was expensive and the parents felt they had to keep the twins stylishly dressed and supplied with new toys. The parents were stressed over money problems, their lack of time together, and especially having so little time with their boys. It bothered them that the twins had begun to cry when their parents picked them up at day care, as if they'd rather stay with the day-care workers. Finally, Sabrina and Eduardo made a difficult decision. Sabrina quit her job, and the couple invited her mother (whose illness was in remission) to live with them. With three adults pooling their resources, Sabrina and Eduardo found that they could manage without Sabrina's salary. The family no longer ate out, and they gave up their cable TV. Their sons loved having their grandmother in the house. Sabrina was able to begin doing relaxed, fun projects with the boys. They planted a garden and built a sandbox together. Sabrina observed, "I learned I could get off the merry-go-round" (195). Other parents have "gotten off the merry-go-round" by working at home, even if it means less money than they had previously.

Only the page number is needed, as the author has already been named in the text.

Some parents even home-school their children as a way to be sure they have plenty of time together. Home schooling used to be thought of as a choice made only by very religious people or back-to-nature radicals. Now, teaching children at home is much less unusual. It's estimated that as many as 2 million American children are being home-schooled. Harvard even has an admissions officer whose job it is to review applications from home-schooled kids. Parents who home-school have different reasons, but according to a cover story in *Newsweek*, "Some . . . are looking for a way to reclaim family closeness in an increasingly fast-paced society. . . . Still others worry about unsavory influences in school—drugs, alcohol, sex, violence" (Kantrowitz and Wingert 66). Home schooling is no guarantee that a child will resist those temptations, but some families do believe it's a great way to promote family closeness. One fifteen-year-old, home-schooled since

When omitting a word or words from a quotation, indicate the deleted word or words by using ellipsis marks, which are three periods (...). In this instance, the fourth period represents the end of the sentence.

Philips 4

kindergarten, explained why he liked the way he'd been raised and educated. He ended by saying, "Another way I'm different is that I love my family. One guy asked me if I'd been brainwashed. I think it's spooky that liking my family is considered crazy" (Pipher 103).

Many parents can't quit their jobs or teach their children at home. But some parents find a second way to nurture their children, through building community ties. They help their children develop a healthy sense of belonging by creating links with positive, constructive people and activities. In the past, community wasn't so hard to find. In *The Way We Really Are*, Stephanie Coontz writes, "Right up through the 1940s, ties of work, friendship, neighborhood, ethnicity, extended kin, and voluntary organizations were as important a source of identity for most Americans, and sometimes a *more* important source of obligation, than marriage and the nuclear family" (37). Even when today's parents were teenagers, neighborhoods were places where kids felt a sense of belonging and responsibility. But today "parents ... mourn the disappearance of neighborhoods where a web of relatives and friends kept a close eye on everyone's kids. And they worry their own children grow up isolated, knowing more about the cast of *Friends* than the people in surrounding homes" (Donahue D1).

One way that some families are trying to build old-fashioned community is through "intentional community" or "cohousing." Begun in Denmark in 1972, the cohousing movement is modeled after the traditional village. It brings together a number of families who live in separate houses but share some common space. For instance, families might share central meeting rooms, dining areas, gardens, day care, workshops, or office space. They might own tools and lawn mowers together, rather than each household having its own. The point is that they treat their neighbors as extended family, not as strangers. As described by the online site *Cohousing.org*, cohousing is "a type

Ellipses show where the student has omitted material from the original source. The quoted material is not capitalized because the student has blended it into a sentence with an introductory phrase.

Philips 5

of collaborative housing that attempts to overcome the alienation of modern subdivisions in which no one knows their neighbors, and there is no sense of community." In its 2009 database, the Intentional Communities Web site estimates that "several thousand" such communities exist in North America.

Other families turn to religion as a source of community. Michael Medved and Diane Medved, authors of *Saving Childhood*, are raising their family in a religious Jewish home. Their children attend Jewish schools, go to synagogue, and follow religious customs. They frequently visit, eat, play with, and are cared for by neighboring Jewish families. The Medveds believe their family is stronger because of their belief "in planting roots—in your home, in your family, in your community. That involves making a commitment, making an investment both physically and emotionally, in your surroundings" (200). Other religious traditions offer families a similar sense of community, purpose, and belonging. Marcus and Tracy Glover are members of the Nation of Islam. They credit the Nation with making their marriage and family strong and breaking a three-generation cycle of single motherhood (Hewlett and West 201–202).

A third way that families are fighting to protect their children is by controlling the impact of the media and technology. Hewlett and West and Pipher use similar words to describe this impact. As they describe growing up today, Hewlett and West write about children living "without a skin" (xiii), and Pipher writes about "houses without walls" (12). These authors mean that today—unlike in the old days when children were protected from the outside world while they were in their homes—the home offers little protection. Even in their own living rooms, all children have to do is to turn on a TV, radio, or computer to be hit with a flood of violence, sick humor, and often weird sexuality. Children are growing up watching shows like *The Osbournes*, a program that celebrated two spoiled, foul-mouthed

Cited material extends from one page to another, so both page numbers are given.

children and their father—a burnt-out rock star slowed by years of carefree drug abuse. A recent article in *Science* magazine offered the most damning link yet between TV watching and antisocial behavior. Reporting on the results of its seventeen-year study that followed viewers from youth to adulthood, *Science* found that the more television a teen watched, the higher the chances he or she would commit violent acts later in life. Of kids who watched an hour or less TV a day, fewer than 6% of teens went on to commit assaults, robberies, or other violent acts as adults. But nearly 28% of teens who watched TV three or more hours a day did commit crimes of violence (Anderson and Bushman 2377–79). Sadly many parents seem to have given up even trying to protect their growing kids against the flood of televised garbage. They are like the mother quoted in *USA Today* as saying, "How can I fight five hundred channels on TV?" (Donahue D1).

Fortunately, some parents are still insisting on control over the information and entertainment that comes into their homes. Some subscribe to "The Television Project," an online educational organization that helps parents "understand how television affects their families and community and proposes alternatives that foster positive emotional, cognitive and spiritual development within families and communities." Others ban TV entirely from their homes. More try to find a way to use TV and other electronics as helpful tools, but not allow them to dominate their homes. One family in Nebraska, the Millers, who home-school their children, described to Mary Pipher their attitude toward TV. They hadn't owned a TV for years, but they bought one so that they could watch the Olympics. The set is now stored in a closet unless a program is on that the family agrees is worthwhile. Some programs the Millers have enjoyed together include the World Cup soccer games, the TV drama *Sarah Plain and Tall*, and an educational TV course in sign language. Pipher

Philips 7

was impressed by the Miller children, and she thought their limited exposure to TV was one reason why. In Pipher's words:

> Calm, happy children and relaxed, confident parents are so rare today. Probably most notable were the long attention spans of the children and their willingness to sit and listen to the grown-ups talk. The family had a manageable amount of information to deal with. They weren't stressed by more information than they could assimilate. The kids weren't overstimulated and edgy. Nor were they sexualized in the way most kids now are. (107)

Pipher's words describe children raised by parents who won't give in to the idea that their children are lost. Such parents structure ways to be present in the home, build family ties to a community, and control the impact of the media in their homes. Through their efforts, they succeed in raising nurtured, grounded, successful children. Such parents acknowledge the challenges of raising kids in today's America, but they are up to the job.

The conclusion provides a summary and restates the thesis.

Works cited should be double-spaced. Titles of books, magazines, and the like should be italicized.

Include the date you accessed a Web source—in the first case, January 4, 2009.

Philips 8

Works Cited

"A Lot Easier Said Than Done: Parents Talk About Raising Children in Today's America." *Public Agenda*. Oct. 2005. Web. 4 Jan. 2009.

Anderson, Craig A., and Brad J. Bushman. "The Effects of Media Violence on Society." *Science*. 29 Mar. 2002: 2377–79. Print.

Coontz, Stephanie. *The Way We Really Are*. New York: Basic Books, 2001. Print.

Dohahue, Deirdre. "Struggling to Raise Good Kids in Toxic Times." *USA Today* 1 Oct. 2008: D1+. Print.

Hewlett, Sylvia Ann, and Cornel West. *The War Against Parents*. Boston: Houghton, 2006. Print.

The Intentional Communities Home Page. Fellowship of Intentional Communities. n.d. Web. 2 Mar. 2009.

Kantrowitz, Barbara, and Pat Wingert. "Learning at Home: Does It Pass the Test?" *Newsweek* 5 Oct. 2008: 64–70. Print.

Louv, Richard. *Childhood's Future*. Boston: Houghton Mifflin, 2000. Print.

Medved, Michael, and Diane Medved. *Saving Childhood*. New York: HarperCollins, 2002. Print.

Pipher, Mary. *The Shelter of Each Other*. New York: Putnam, 2007. Print.

The Television Project Home Page. The Television Project. n.d. Web. 2 Feb. 2009.

"What Is Cohousing?" *Cohousing*. The Cohousing Association of the United States. 10 Sept. 2008. Web. 2 Feb. 2009.

RESPONDING TO IMAGES

Although the student writer of the research paper emphasized the impact of TV on children, she referred to the computer as another source of "violence, sick humor, and often weird sexuality." In your opinion, which do you feel is more dangerous for children when unsupervised, the computer or the TV? Why?

EXPLORING WRITING ONLINE

Visit the *Plagiarism.org* Web site at http://www.plagiarism.org to learn more about what plagiarism is and how to avoid it. Read the section, "Education Tips on Plagiarism Prevention," and then write a paragraph about this issue using a pattern of development, such as cause and effect, comparison and contrast, or argumentation. If you reference the Web site, be sure to avoid plagiarism yourself.

As you are reading the following essay written by Serena for a health and wellness class, think about what advice you would offer her as she prepares to write her final draft. Does her essay cover all four bases of effective writing? To be sure, use the checklist that follows.

The Common Cold

[1]According to the National Center for Health Statistics, "62 million cases of the common cold occur each year and 20 million school days are lost annually in the United States due to the common cold." [2]That's a lot of stuffy noses, sore throats, and coughs. [3]Since the cold is so common, it would make sense that scientists should have found a cure by now. [4]However, common does not mean simple, and the common cold is very complex.

[5]First of all, a cold is caused by a virus, and it's not just one type of virus. [6]More than two hundred viruses cause colds by attacking healthy cells of the nose, throat, or lungs. [7]The virus then gets into the cells and takes control. [8]A single virus makes hundreds or thousands of cold viruses inside each cell. [9]Eventually, the cell bursts open and dies. [10]The viruses, though, escape and attack healthy cells. [11]By now the victim is sneezing and coughing. [12]His or her throat is sore. [13]The virus keeps infecting healthy cells.

[14]Second, only the body can fight cold viruses. [15]Billions of white blood cells travel in the blood. [16]White blood cells make antibodies. [17]These proteins attach themselves to viruses and destroy them.

[18]In addition, there isn't much the victim can do to fight a cold. [19]Antibiotic drugs don't work against viruses. [20]Nose drops and cough medicines only relieve symptoms. [21]Chicken soup seems to help. [22]Vitamin C may help too. [23]A dose of 1,000 milligrams of vitamin C on the first day of a cold may quicken recovery.

[24]Most importantly, people need to be healthy so they don't catch a cold at all. [25]They should eat a well-balanced diet and get eight hours of sleep each day. [26]They should exercise regularly. [27]They should stay away from coughing, sneezing people, because the cold virus spreads through the air. [28]The cold virus can live up to three hours outside the body. [29]That means it can be picked up from touching money, doorknobs, and other people. [30]So people should wash their hands often. [31]Prevention are the best action.

A WRITER'S CHECKLIST

Unity

✔ 1. The thesis statement can be found in sentence number _____.

✔ 2. Why do you think the writer chose to place the thesis statement where she did?

_____

Support

✔ 1. Fill in the supporting points for the thesis statement in the following brief outline:

The common cold is complex and has no cure.

a. _____

b. _____

c. _____

d. _____

✔ 2. Does Serena provide specific evidence for each point? _____

_____

✔ 3. Does Serena properly document her information? _____

_____

Coherence

✔ 1. Has Serena effectively used transitional words? If so, what are those words? If not, where should she include them? _____

_____

✔ 2. Which method of organization did Serena use? _____ How do you know?

_____

Sentence Skills

✔ 1. Has Serena avoided wordiness and used concise wording? _____

✔ 2. Were the sentences varied? _____

_____

✔ 3. Can you find any other sentence skills mistakes, as listed on the inside back cover of the book?

_____

Collaborative Activity

In your group or class, make an outline of Serena's essay. Looking at the outline, can you think of any additional supporting details that could be added to make this essay more effective?

Handbook of Sentence Skills

PART FIVE WILL

- explain the basic skills needed to write clear, error-free sentences

- provide numerous activities so that you can practice these skills enough to make them habits

- contain editing tests at the end of each section to offer additional practice activities

EXPLORING WRITING PROMPT:

College writing requires accuracy and correctness in grammar, mechanics, punctuation, and word use—all of which are covered in Part Five. However, we are seeing more and more examples of incorrect writing in shop windows, on bulletin boards, in posters that advertise concerts or movies, in restaurant menus, or in product advertisements. We also experience non-standard English in music, on television, and in the movies.

Keep a list of such examples in a notebook or in your journal over a seven-day period. You can start with the wooden sign pictured above. What sentence-skills mistake do you notice? Then, find an article online on any popular subject or activity that interests you. Rewrite it correcting errors in grammar, mechanics, punctuation, and especially word use. If possible, condense the article by using fewer words than the original.

Grammar

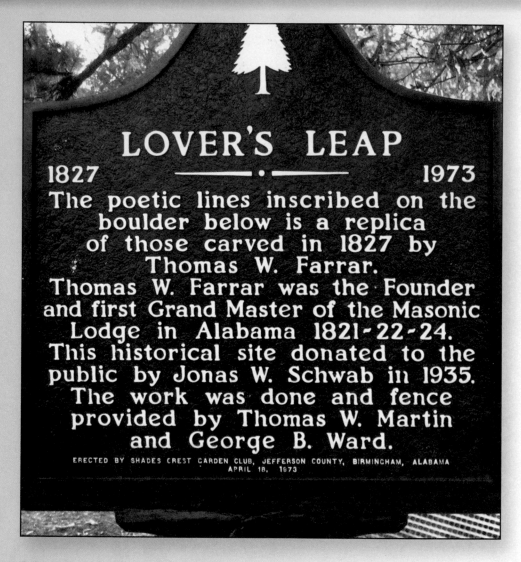

RESPONDING TO IMAGES

Can you find any sentence-skills errors in the Lover's Leap plaque pictured above? What could be done to make the plaque grammatically correct?

Subjects and Verbs

The basic building blocks of English sentences are subjects and verbs. Understanding them is an important first step toward mastering a number of sentence skills.

Every sentence has a subject and a verb. Who or what the sentence speaks about is called the *subject*; what the sentence says about the subject is called the *verb*. In the following sentences, the subject is underlined once and the verb twice.

The boy cried.

That fish smells.

Many people applied for the job.

The show is a documentary.

A Simple Way to Find a Subject

To find a subject, ask *who* or *what* the sentence is about. As shown below, your answer is the subject.

Who is the first sentence about? The boy

What is the second sentence about? That fish

Who is the third sentence about? Many people

What is the fourth sentence about? The show

A Simple Way to Find a Verb

To find a verb, ask what the sentence *says about* the subject. As shown below, your answer is the verb.

What does the first sentence *say about* the boy? He cried.

What does the second sentence *say about* the fish? It smells.

What does the third sentence *say about* the people? They applied.

What does the fourth sentence *say about* that show? It is a documentary.

A second way to find the verb is to put *I, you, we, he, she, it,* or *they* in front of the word you think is a verb. If the result makes sense, you have a verb. For example, you could put *he* in front of *cried* in the first sentence, with the result, *he cried,* making sense. Therefore, you know that *cried* is a verb. You could use the same test with the other three verbs as well.

Finally, it helps to remember that most verbs show action. In the sentences already considered, the three action verbs are *cried, smells,* and *applied.* Certain other verbs, known as *linking verbs,* do not show action. They do, however, give information about the subject. In "The show is a documentary," the linking verb *is* joins the subject (*show*) with a word that identifies or describes it (*documentary*). Other common linking verbs include *am, are, was, were, feel, appear, look, become,* and *seem.*

| ACTIVITY 1 | In each of the following sentences, draw one line under the subject and two lines under the verb. |

1. The children's abandoned toys collected dust in the attic.

2. Long-distance running requires mental and physical discipline.

3. Teresa sprained her ankle while playing beach volleyball.

4. My roommate owes me money for this month's rent.

5. A cockroach scampered across the kitchen floor.

6. The patient's lab results arrived in the mail.

7. My ex-husband called me yesterday.

8. On New Year's Day, my grandmother prepared traditional Japanese *ozoni* soup.

9. Sarah's mother visits her grandchildren every summer.

10. During the winter season, everyone needs a flu shot.

More about Subjects and Verbs

1. A sentence may have more than one verb, more than one subject, or several subjects and verbs.

   The engine coughed and sputtered.

   Broken glass and empty cans littered the parking lot.

   Marta, Nilsa, and Robert met after class and headed downtown.

2. The subject and verb of the sentence never appear within a prepositional phrase. A *prepositional phrase* is simply a group of words that begins with a preposition. Following is a list of the more commonly used prepositions.

Prepositions				
about	before	despite	into	throughout
above	behind	down	like	to
across	below	during	near	toward
after	beneath	except	of	under
against	beside	far	off	underneath
along	between	for	on, onto	until
among	beyond	from	out	up
around	by	in	over	upon
as	concerning	including	since	with
at	considering	inside	through	without

Crossing out prepositional phrases will help you find the subject or subjects of a sentence.

> A stream ~~of cold air~~ seeps in ~~through the space below the door~~.
>
> Specks ~~of dust~~ dance gently ~~in a ray of sunlight~~.
>
> The people ~~in the apartment above ours~~ fight loudly.
>
> The murky waters ~~of the polluted lake~~ spilled ~~over the dam~~.
>
> The amber lights ~~on its sides~~ outlined the tractor-trailer ~~in the hazy dusk~~.

3. Many verbs consist of more than one word. (The extra verbs are called *auxiliary*, or *helping*, verbs.) Here, for example, are some of the many forms of the verb *work*.

Forms of *work*		
work	worked	should work
works	were working	will be working
does work	have worked	can work
is working	had worked	could be working
are working	had been working	must have worked

4. Words like *not, just, never, only,* and *always* are not part of the verb, although they may appear within the verb.

> Ruby has never liked cold weather.
>
> Our boss will not be singing with the choir this year.
>
> The intersection has not always been this dangerous.

5. A verb preceded by *to* is never the verb of a sentence.

At night, my son likes to read under the covers.

Evelyn decided to separate from her husband.

6. An *-ing* word by itself is never the verb of a sentence. (It may be part of the verb, but it must have a helping verb in front of it.)

They going on a trip this weekend.

(not a sentence, because the verb is not complete)

They are going on a trip this weekend. (a sentence)

ACTIVITY 2

Draw a single line under subjects and a double line under verbs. Cross out prepositional phrases as necessary to find the subjects.

1. A thick layer of dust covers the top of our refrigerator.

2. In June, sagging Christmas decorations were still hanging in the windows of the abandoned house.

3. The people in the all night coffee shop seemed weary and lost.

4. Every plant in the dim room bent toward the small window.

5. A glaring headline about the conviction of a local congressman attracted my attention.

6. Two of the biggest stores in the mall are going out of business.

7. The battery tester's tiny red lights suddenly started to flicker.

8. A neighbor of mine does all her work at home and e-mails it to her office.

9. The jar of peppercorns tumbled from the spice shelf and shattered on the floor.

10. The scar in the hollow of Brian's throat is the result of an emergency operation to clear his windpipe.

REVIEW TEST

Draw a single line under the subjects and a double line under the verbs. Note that many sentences have multiple subjects and multiple verbs. Cross out prepositional phrases as necessary to find the subjects.

1. John Muir is known as the "Father of the National Park Service."

2. Muir was born in Scotland, but his family moved to the United States in 1849.

3. As a freshman at the University of Wisconsin, he studied chemistry, but was soon introduced to botany.

4. In 1866, Muir moved to Indianapolis for a job in a factory, and his life was changed forever.

5. As Muir was working on a machine, a tool slipped and struck Muir in the eye.

6. After his remarkable recovery, Muir realized that he should follow his dreams of study and exploration.

7. In 1867, Muir embarked on a 1,000-mile journey from Indianapolis to Florida, where he studied the flora and fauna, met people, and learned about America.

8. After his long walk, Muir sailed to San Francisco and immediately traveled to Yosemite.

9. His experience in Yosemite and Ralph Waldo Emerson's essays on nature inspired Muir.

10. He published articles about his experiences.

11. After Yosemite, Muir traveled to Utah, Alaska, and Mt.Rainier.

12. With the importance of the natural world in mind, Muir convinced President Roosevelt that Yosemite, Mt. Rainier, and the Grand Canyon must be protected.

13. In 1890, 1500 acres of Yosemite were established as preserved land.

14. This paved the way for the creation of over fifty protected parks now within the United States National Park System.

Sentence Sense

What Is Sentence Sense?

As a speaker of English, you already possess the most important of all sentence skills. You have *sentence sense*—an instinctive feel for where a sentence begins, where it ends, and how it can be developed. You learned sentence sense automatically and naturally, as part of learning the English language, and you have practiced it through all the years that you have been speaking English. It is as much a part of you as your ability to speak and understand English is a part of you.

Sentence sense can help you recognize and avoid fragments and run-ons, two of the most common and most serious sentence-skills mistakes in written English. Sentence sense will also help you to properly place commas and spot awkward and unclear phrasing. Many of the following chapters will give you detailed practice using commas correctly, avoiding fragments and run-ons, and creating clarity.

Sentence sense can also assist you in adding variety to your sentences, by helping you determine how many simple sentences, compound sentences, and complex sentences you should use to create a well-developed, coherent paragraph. Too many simple sentences—sentences that contain one independent clause—can create a choppy-sounding paragraph. Adding compound sentences—sentences that contain two or more independent clauses—can take some of the choppiness out of your paragraph. Additionally, complex sentences—sentences that contain one independent clause and one or more dependent clauses—can make your paragraph flow better while adding needed variety. Chapter 4, "The Third and Fourth Steps in Writing," offers additional background information as well as suggestions for creating good compound and complex sentences (pp. 109–111).

You may ask, "If I already have this 'sentence sense,' why do I still make mistakes in punctuating sentences?" One answer could be that your past school experiences in writing were unrewarding or unpleasant. English courses may have been a series of dry writing topics and heavy doses of "correct" grammar and usage, or they may have given no attention at all to sentence skills. For any of these reasons, or perhaps for other reasons, the instinctive sentence skills you practice while speaking may turn off when you start writing. The very act of picking up a pen may shut down your natural system of language abilities and skills.

Turning On Your Sentence Sense

Chances are that you don't *read a paper aloud* after you write it, or you don't do the next best thing: read it "aloud" in your head. But reading aloud is essential to turn on the natural language system within you. By reading aloud, you will be able to hear the points where your sentences begin and end. In addition, you will be able to pick up any trouble spots where your thoughts are not communicated clearly and well.

The activities that follow will help you turn on and rediscover the enormous language power within you. You will be able to see how your built-in sentence sense can guide your writing just as it guides your speaking.

ACTIVITY 1

Each item that follows lacks basic punctuation. There is no period to mark the end of one sentence and no capital letter to mark the start of the next. Read each item aloud (or in your head) so that you "hear" where each sentence begins and ends. Your voice will tend to drop and pause at the point of each sentence break. Draw a light slash mark (/) at every point where you hear a break. Then go back and read the item a second time. If you are now sure of each place where a split occurs, insert a period and change the first small letter after it to a capital. Minor pauses are often marked in English by commas; these are already inserted. Part of item 1 is done for you as an example.

1. I take my dog for a walk on Saturdays in the big park by the lake. I do this very early in the morning before children come to the park. That way I can let my dog run freely. He jumps out the minute I open the car door and soon sees the first innocent squirrel. then he is off like a shot and doesn't stop running for at least half an hour.

2. When Vince first started college, he did not know what major to pursue at first, he wanted to become a computer software engineer, but he struggled in his math classes a counselor suggested that he might think about entering a technical program since he is skilled with his hands for instance, last summer he helped his neighbors renovate their kitchen and bathroom he also assisted in the building of a house through Habitat for Humanity now Vince is considering the carpentry technology program.

3. When I sit down to write, my mind is blank all I can think of is my name, which seems to me the most boring name in the world often I get sleepy and tell myself I should take a short nap other times I start daydreaming about things I want to buy sometimes I decide I should make a telephone call to someone I know the piece of paper in front of me is usually still blank when I leave to watch my favorite television show.

4. One of the biggest regrets of my life is that I never told my father I loved him. I resented the fact that he had never been able to say the words "I love you" to his children even during the long period of my father's illness, I remained silent and unforgiving then one morning

he was dead, with my words left unspoken a guilt I shall never forget tore a hole in my heart. I determined not to hold in my feelings with my daughters they know they are loved, because I both show and tell them this all people, no matter who they are, want to be told that they are loved.

5. A month ago, Christina decided to become a vegetarian she never really liked meat all that much, except for an occasional hamburger or grilled steak she decided to give up meat because she read about the health benefits that a vegetarian lifestyle could provide also, she knew that eating more fruits, vegetables, and grains would be beneficial some of her friends asked if she opposed the killing of animals, which she had not considered everything was going well for Christina and her new lifestyle she began to try new recipes, shop at the local farmers' market, and even feel more energetic then last Saturday she went out to dinner at an Italian restaurant with her friends without thinking, Christina ordered her favorite item on the menu, Shrimp Scampi after she was halfway through her meal, one of her friends said, "Christina, you're eating meat!" she was stunned for she had completely forgotten about being a vegetarian she felt disappointed in herself, especially since there were several vegetarian pasta dishes on the menu one of her friends smiled nonchalantly and said, "Don't worry, Christina, you're a pescatarian—someone who's mostly a vegetarian but occasionally eats fish and seafood." Christina smiled and happily finished her meal.

Summary: Using Sentence Sense

You probably did well in locating the end stops in these selections— proving to yourself that you *do* have sentence sense. This instinctive sense will help you deal with fragments and run-ons, perhaps the two most common sentence-skills mistakes.

Remember the importance of *reading your paper aloud.* By reading aloud, you turn on the natural language skills that come from all your experience of speaking English. The same sentence sense that helps you communicate effectively in speaking will help you communicate effectively in writing.

Fragments

Every sentence must have a subject and a verb and must express a complete thought. A word group that lacks a subject or a verb and does not express a complete thought is a *fragment*. Following are the most common types of fragments that people write:

1. Dependent-word fragments
2. *-ing* and *to* fragments
3. Added-detail fragments
4 Missing-subject fragments

Once you understand what specific kinds of fragments you might write, you should be able to eliminate them from your writing. The following pages explain all four types.

Dependent-Word Fragments

Some word groups that begin with a dependent word are fragments. Following is a list of common dependent words. Whenever you start a sentence with one of these words, you must be careful that a fragment does not result.

Dependent Words		
after	if, even if	when, whenever
although, though	in order that	where, wherever
as	since	whether
because	that, so that	which, whichever
before	unless	while
even though	until	who
how	what, whatever	whose

4. Since getting my college degree is so important

Since getting my college degree is so important, I must work hard.

5. Unless I study

Unless I study, I wouldn't do good on my test.

ACTIVITY 2

Underline the dependent-word fragment in each item. Then rewrite the items, correcting each fragment by attaching it to the sentence that comes before or the sentence that comes after it—whichever sounds more natural. Use a comma after the dependent word group if it starts the sentence.

1. Whenever I spray deodorant. My cat arches her back. She thinks she is hearing a hissing enemy.

   Whenever I spray deodorant, my cat arches her back and she thinks she is hearing a hissing enemy.

2. My father, a salesman, was on the road all week. We had a great time playing football in the house. Until he came home for the weekend.

   My father, a salesman, was on the road all week. We had a great time playing football in the house, until he came home for the weekend.

3. If Kim takes too long saying good-bye to her boyfriend. Her father will start flicking the porch light. Then he will come out with a flashlight.

   If Kim takes too long saying good-bye to her boyfriend, her father will start flicking the porch light, then he will come out with a flash light.

4. Scientists are studying mummified remains. That are thousands of years old. Most of the people were killed by parasites.

   Scientists are studying mummified remains, that are thousands of years old, most people were killed by parasites.

5. After I got to class. I realized my report was still on the kitchen table. I had been working there the night before.

   After I got to class, I realized my report was still on the kitchen table, I had been working there all night.

-ing and to Fragments

When an -ing word appears at or near the start of a word group, a fragment may result. Such fragments often lack a subject and part of the verb. In the items below, underline the word groups that contain -ing words. Each is a fragment.

1. Ellen walked all over the neighborhood yesterday. Trying to find her dog Bo. Several people claimed they had seen him only hours before.

2. We sat back to watch the movie. Not expecting anything special. To our surprise, we clapped, cheered, and cried for the next two hours.

3. I telephoned the balloon store. It being the day before our wedding anniversary. I knew my wife would be surprised to receive a dozen heart-shaped balloons.

People sometimes write *-ing* fragments because they think that the subject of one sentence will work for the next word group as well. Thus, in item 1 the writer thinks that the subject *Ellen* in the opening sentence will also serve as the subject for *Trying to find her dog Bo.* But the subject must actually be in the same sentence.

How to Correct *-ing* Fragments

1. Attach the fragment to the sentence that comes before it or the sentence that comes after it, whichever makes sense. Item 1 could read: "Ellen walked all over the neighborhood yesterday, trying to find her dog Bo."

2. Add a subject and change the *-ing* verb part to the correct form of the verb. Item 2 could read: "We didn't expect anything special."

3. Change *being* to the correct form of the verb be (*am, are, is, was, were*). Item 3 could read: "It was the day before our wedding anniversary."

How to Correct *to* Fragments

When *to* appears at or near the start of a word group, a fragment sometimes results:

At the Chinese restaurant, Tim used chopsticks. To impress his date. He spent one hour eating a small bowl of rice.

The second word group is a fragment and can be corrected by adding it to the preceding sentence:

At the Chinese restaurant, Tim used chopsticks to impress his date.

Underline the *-ing* fragment in each of the following items. Then correct the item by using the method described in parentheses.

ACTIVITY 3

EXAMPLE

Stepping hard on the accelerator. Armon tried to beat the truck to the intersection. He lost by a hood.
(Add the fragment to the sentence that comes after it.)
Stepping hard on the accelerator, Armon tried to beat the truck to the intersection.

1. Marble-sized hailstones fell from the sky. Flattening the young plants in the cornfield. A year's work was lost in an hour.
(Add the fragment to the preceding sentence.)
Marble-sized hailstones fell from the sky flattening the young plants in the cornfield.

2. A noisy fire truck suddenly raced down the street. Coming to a stop at my house. My home security system had sent a false alarm.
(Correct the fragment by adding the subject *it* and changing *coming* to the proper form of the verb, *came*.)

A noisy fire truck suddenly raced down the street. It Came to a stop at my house

3. My phone doesn't ring. Instead, a light on it blinks. The reason for this being that I am partially deaf.
(Correct the fragment by changing *being* to the proper form of the verb, *is*.)

My phone doesn't ring, instead it light on it blinks, the reason is that I am partialy deaf.

ACTIVITY 4

Underline the *-ing* or *to* fragment in each item. Then rewrite each item, correcting the fragment by using one of the three methods described above.

1. Looking at the worm on the table. Shelby groaned. She knew she wouldn't like what the biology teacher said next.

Looking at the worm on the table, Shelby

2. I put a box of baking soda in the freezer. To get rid of the musty smell. However, my ice cubes still taste like old socks.

I put a box of baking soda in the freezer, to get rid

3. Staring at the clock on the far wall. I nervously began my speech. I was afraid to look at any of the people in the room.

4. Jerome sat quietly at his desk. Fantasizing about the upcoming weekend. He might meet the girl of his dreams at Saturday night's party.

5. To get to the bus station from here. You have to walk two blocks out of your way. The sidewalk is torn up because of construction work.

To get to the bus station from here, you

Added-Detail Fragments

Added-detail fragments lack a subject and a verb. They often begin with one of the following words:

also	especially	except	for example
like	including	such as	

Underline the one added-detail fragment in each of the following items:

1. Before a race, I eat starchy foods. Such as bread and spaghetti. The carbohydrates provide quick energy.

2. Bob is taking a night course in auto mechanics. Also, one in plumbing. He wants to save money on household repairs.

3. My son keeps several pets in his room. Including hamsters and mice.

People often write added-detail fragments for much the same reason they write -*ing* fragments. They think the subject and verb in one sentence will serve for the next word group. But the subject and verb must be in *each* word group.

How to Correct Added-Detail Fragments

1. Attach the fragment to the complete thought that precedes it. Item 1 could read: "Before a race, I eat starchy foods such as bread and spaghetti."

2. Add a subject and a verb to the fragment to make it a complete sentence. Item 2 could read: "Bob is taking a night course in auto mechanics. Also, he is taking one in plumbing."

3. Insert the fragment within the preceding sentence. Item 3 could read: "My son keeps several pets, including hamsters and mice, in his room."

Underline the fragment in each of the following items. Then make it a sentence by rewriting it, using the method described in parentheses.

ACTIVITY 5

EXAMPLE

My mother likes watching daytime television shows. Especially old movies and soap operas. She says that daytime television is less violent. (Add the fragment to the preceding sentence.)

My mother likes watching daytime television shows, especially old movies and soap operas.

1. Luis works evenings in a movie theater. He enjoys the fringe benefits. For example, seeing the new movies first.
(Correct the fragment by adding the subject and verb *he sees*.)

_____

_____

2. Bob's fingernails are ragged from years of working as a mechanic. And his fingertips are always black. Like ink pads.
   (Attach the fragment to the preceding sentence.)

   And his fingertips are always black, like ink pads.

3. Electronic devices keep getting smaller. Such as video cameras and cell phones. Some are so tiny they look like toys.
   (Correct the fragment by inserting it in the preceding sentence.)

   Electronic devices keep getting smaller, such as video cameras and cell phones, some electric devices

---

ACTIVITY 6   Underline the added-detail fragment in each item. Then rewrite to correct the fragment. Use one of the three methods described on the previous page.

1. Left-handed students face problems. For example, right-handed desks. Spiral notebooks can also be uncomfortable to use.

   problems, for example

   _____

2. Mrs. Fields always wears her lucky clothes to bingo. Such as a sweater printed with four-leaf clovers. She also carries a rhinestone horseshoe.

   to bingo, such as

   _____

3. Hundreds of moths were swarming around the stadium lights. Like large flecks of snow. However, I knew they couldn't be snow—it was eighty degrees outside.

   the stadium lights, like

   _____

4. Trevor buys and sells paper collectors' items. For instance, comic books and movie posters. He sets up a display at local flea markets and carnivals.

   items, for

   _____

5. I wonder now why I had to learn certain subjects. Such as geometry. No one has ever asked me about the hypotenuse of a triangle.

   subjects, such

Missing-Subject Fragments

In each item below, underline the word group in which the subject is missing:

1. Alicia loved getting wedding presents. <u>But hated writing thank-you notes.</u>

2. Mickey has orange soda and potato chips for breakfast. <u>Then eats more junk food, like root beer and cookies, for lunch.</u>

How to Correct Missing-Subject Fragments

1. Attach the fragment to the preceding sentence. Item 1 could read: "Alicia loved getting wedding presents but hated writing thank-you notes."

2. Add a subject (which can often be a pronoun standing for the subject in the preceding sentence). Item 2 could read: "Then he eats more junk food, like root beer and cookies, for lunch."

Underline the missing-subject fragment in each item. Then rewrite that part of the item needed to correct the fragment. Use one of the two methods of correction described above.

ACTIVITY 7

1. Every other day, Kara runs two miles. <u>Then does fifty sit-ups.</u> She hasn't lost weight, but she looks trimmer and more muscular.

   Every other day, Kara runs two miles, then does fifty sit ups.

2. I like all kinds of fresh pizza. <u>But refuse to eat frozen pizza.</u> The sauce is always dried out, and the crust tastes like leather.

   I like all kinds of fresh pizza, but refuse to eat frozen pizza.

3. Many people are allergic to seafood. They break out in hives when they eat it. <u>And can even have trouble breathing.</u>

   They break out in hives when they eat it, and can even have trouble breathing

4. To distract me, the dentist tugged at a corner of my mouth. <u>Then jabbed a needle into my gums and injected a painkiller.</u> I hardly felt it.

   To distract me, the dentist tugged at a corner of my mouth, then jabbed a needle into my gums

5. Last semester, I took six courses. <u>And worked part-time in a discount drugstore.</u> Now that the term is all over, I don't know how I did it.

   Last semester, I took six courses, and worked.

> **A Review: How to Check for Sentence Fragments**
>
> 1. Read your paper aloud from the *last* sentence to the *first*. You will be better able to see and hear whether each group you read is a complete thought.
>
> 2. If you think a word group may be a fragment, ask yourself: Does this contain a subject and a verb and express a complete thought?
>
> 3. More specifically, be on the lookout for the most common fragments:
>
>   - Dependent-word fragments (starting with words like *after*, *because*, *since*, *when*, and *before*)
>
>   - *-ing* and *to* fragments (*-ing* and *to* at or near the start of a word group)
>
>   - Added-detail fragments (starting with words like *for example*, *such as*, *also*, and *especially*)
>
>   - Missing-subject fragments (a verb is present but not the subject)

REVIEW TEST 1

Each word group in the following student paragraph is numbered. In the space provided, write C if a word group is a complete sentence; write F if it is a fragment. You will find eight fragments in the paragraph.

_C_	1. ¹I'm starting to think that there is no safe place left. ²To ride
_F_	2. a bicycle. ³When I try to ride on the highway, in order to
_C_	3. go to school. ⁴I feel like a rabbit being pursued by predators.
_C_	4. ⁵Drivers whip past me at high speeds. ⁶And try to see how
_C/F_	5. close they can get to my bike without actually killing me.
____	6. ⁷When they pull onto the shoulder of the road or make a
_C_	7. right turn. ⁸Drivers completely ignore my vehicle. ⁹On city
_F_	8. streets, I feel more like a cockroach than a rabbit. ¹⁰Drivers
_C_	9. in the city despise bicycles. ¹¹Regardless of an approaching
_F_	10. bike rider. ¹²Street-side car doors will unexpectedly open.
_C_	11. ¹³Frustrated drivers who are stuck in traffic will make nasty
_C_	12. comments. ¹⁴Or shout out obscene propositions. ¹⁵Even
_C_	13. pedestrians in the city show their disregard for me. ¹⁶While
_F_	14. jaywalking across the street. ¹⁷The pedestrian will treat
_C_	15. me, a law-abiding bicyclist, to a withering look of disdain.
_F_	16. ¹⁸Pedestrians may even cross my path deliberately. ¹⁹As if to

_C_   17. prove their higher position in the pecking order of the city

_C_   18. streets. [20]Today, bicycling can be hazardous to the rider's

_F_   19. health.

_C_   20.

Now (on separate paper) correct the fragments you have found. Attach the fragments to sentences that come before or after them or make whatever other change is needed to turn each fragment into a sentence.

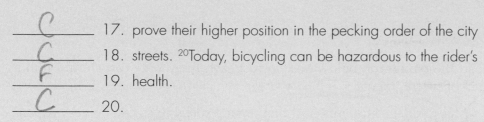

REVIEW TEST 2

Each of the following items includes a fragment. Make whatever changes are needed to turn the fragments into sentences.

EXAMPLE

One of the most popular series of books in the twenty-first century has been the Millennium trilogy. By Stieg Larsson.

1. Larsson was an outspoken Swedish writer and journalist. Who died in 2004 from a heart attack. He was fifty.

2. His books became an instant sensation. In Sweden and by 2010 had sold more than 20 million copies in 41 countries.

3. The first book of the series, *The Girl with the Dragon Tattoo*, is a suspenseful novel about a computer hacker. Lisbeth Salander, and a journalist, Mikael Blomqvist, who work to solve a financial fraud mystery.

4. The second book, *The Girl who Played with Fire*, finds Mikael trying to save Lisbeth. From being arrested for a triple murder.

5. The third book, *The Girl who Kicked the Hornet's Nest*, focuses on Lisbeth's planned revenge against those who tried to kill her. And on Mikael's help in implementing her plan.

6. Unlike many trilogies, the Millennium trilogy does not have a conclusive ending. Because Larsson didn't plan for it to be only a trilogy.

7. He died before he could finish the series. Which he planned to be ten books.

8. It's surprising that it wasn't until 2011 that the first book was made into a movie in America. Since all three books were made into movies in Sweden in 2009.

REVIEW TEST 3

Read the paragraph below and correct each fragment. You should find a total of six fragments.

Many college students find that having social lives can be very expensive. Which means they need to find ways to save money. Most colleges have numerous activities. That are free or cost little. For instance, colleges may have art galleries that are free to visit or free movie nights. Some colleges even bring bands to campus and charge students a nominal fee. Students can also use their local library. To provide free or inexpensive entertainment. Many libraries, both on campus and off, have free programs that include classes, speakers, and activities. Libraries are also filled with books and movies. That can be checked out at no cost to the student. Although eating out is another expense that students often have. There are creative ways to cut dining costs as well. The easiest way to cut costs is not to eat out and instead to invite friends to each bring a dish for an old fashioned pot-luck dinner. If eating out is a must. Many students can take advantage of "all-you-can-eat" buffets and "before 4:00" specials. Part of college life is the social life, but activities, movies, concerts, and dining out can quickly deplete a person's wallet, so saving and planning is essential.

Run-Ons

What Are Run-Ons?

A *run-on* is two complete thoughts that are run together with no adequate sign given to mark the break between them.*

Some run-ons have no punctuation at all to mark the break between the thoughts. Such run-ons are known as *fused sentences:* they are fused, or joined together, as if they were only one thought.

Fused Sentences

The bus stopped suddenly I spilled coffee all over my shirt.

Mario told everyone in the room to be quiet his favorite show was on.

In other run-ons, known as *comma splices,* a comma is used to connect, or "splice" together, the two complete thoughts. However, a comma alone is *not enough* to connect two complete thoughts. Some stronger connection than a comma alone is needed.

Comma Splices

The bus stopped suddenly, I spilled coffee all over my shirt.

Mario told everyone in the room to be quiet, his favorite show was on.

Comma splices are the most common kind of run-on. Students sense that some kind of connection is needed between two thoughts, and so they often put a comma at the dividing point. But the comma alone is *not sufficient.* A stronger, clearer mark is needed between the two complete thoughts.

*Notes:

1. Some instructors regard all run-ons as fused sentences. But for many other instructors, and for our purposes in this book, the term *run-on* applies equally to fused sentences and comma splices. The bottom line is that you do not want either fused sentences or comma splices in your writing.

2. Some instructors refer to each complete thought in a run-on as an *independent clause.* A clause is simply a group of words having a subject and a verb. A clause may be *independent* (expressing a complete thought and able to stand alone) or *dependent* (not expressing a complete thought and not able to stand alone). Using this terminology, we'd say that a run-on is two independent clauses run together with no adequate sign given to mark the break between them.

3. Pages 109–111 in Chapter 4, "The Third and Fourth Steps in Writing," demonstrate how to take simple sentences and make them compound or complex sentences without creating run-ons.

A Warning: Words That Can Lead to Run-Ons

People often write run-ons when the second complete thought begins with one of the following words:

I	we	there	now
you	they	this	then
he, she, it	that	next	

Whenever you use one of these words in writing a paper, remember to be on the alert for run-ons.

How to Correct Run-Ons

Here are three common methods of correcting a run-on:

1. Use a period and a capital letter to break the two complete thoughts into separate sentences:

   The bus stopped suddenly. I spilled coffee all over my shirt.

   Mario told everyone in the room to be quiet. His favorite show was on.

2. Use a comma plus a joining word (*and, but, for, or, nor, so, yet*) to connect the two complete thoughts:

   The bus stopped suddenly, and I spilled coffee all over my shirt.

   Mario told everyone in the room to be quiet, for his favorite show was on.

3. Use a semicolon to connect the two complete thoughts:

   The bus stopped suddenly; I spilled coffee all over my shirt.

   Mario told everyone in the room to be quiet; his favorite show was on.

A fourth method of correcting a run-on is to use *subordination*. The following activities will give you practice in the first three methods. Subordination is described fully on pages 110–111, in the section of the book that deals with sentence variety.

Method 1: Period and a Capital Letter

One way of correcting a run-on is to use a period and a capital letter between the two complete thoughts. Use this method especially if the thoughts are not closely related or if another method would make the sentence too long.

ACTIVITY 1

In each of the following run-ons, locate the point at which one complete thought ends and another begins. Each is a *fused sentence*—that is, each consists of two sentences fused, or joined together, with no punctuation at all between them. Reading each sentence aloud will help you "hear" where a major break or split between the thoughts occurs. At such a point, your voice will probably drop and pause.

Correct the run-on by putting a period at the end of the first thought and a capital letter at the start of the next thought.

EXAMPLE

Bev's clock radio doesn't work anymore. She spilled a glass of soda on it.

1. The men at the door claimed to have paving material left over from another job. they wanted to pave our driveway for a "bargain price."

2. Linh, a paralegal who speaks Vietnamese, helps other people from her country write wills. she assists others by going with them when they have to appear in court.

3. Vicky has her own unique style of dressing. she wore a man's tuxedo with a red bow tie to her cousin's wedding.

4. In the summer, ants are attracted to water. they will often enter a house through the dishwasher.

5. Humans have managed to adapt to any environment. they can survive in Arctic wastes, tropical jungles, and barren deserts.

6. A five-year-old child knows over six thousand words. he or she has also learned more than one thousand rules of grammar.

7. I rummaged around the crowded drawer looking for a pair of scissors, then it suddenly stabbed me in the finger.

8. Squirrels like to jump from trees onto our roof. their footsteps sound like ghosts running around our attic.

9. Today I didn't make good time driving to work. every traffic light along the way was red.

10. Since I got my own notebook computer, I've sent hundreds of e-mails to my friends. I never write letters by hand anymore.

Method 2: Comma and a Joining Word

Another way of correcting a run-on is to use a comma plus a joining word to connect the two complete thoughts. Joining words (also called *conjunctions*) include *and, but, for, or, nor, so,* and *yet.* Here is what the four most common joining words mean:

and   in addition

Teresa works full-time for an accounting firm, and she takes evening classes.

(*And* means *in addition:* Teresa works full-time for an accounting firm; *in addition,* she takes evening classes.)

but   however, on the other hand

I turned to the want ads, but I knew my dream job wouldn't be listed.

and but for, so

(*But* means *however:* I turned to the want ads; *however,* I knew my dream job wouldn't be listed.)

> **for**   because
>
> Lizards become sluggish at night, for they need the sun's warmth to maintain an active body temperature.

(*For* means *because:* Lizards become sluggish at night *because* they need the sun's warmth to maintain an active body temperature.)

> **so**   as a result, therefore
>
> The canoe touched bottom, so Dave pushed it toward deeper water.

(*So* means *as a result:* The canoe touched bottom; *as a result,* Dave pushed it toward deeper water.)

ACTIVITY 2

Insert the joining word (*and, but, for, so*) that logically connects the two thoughts in each sentence.

1. Napoleon may have been a brave general, __but__ he was afraid of cats.

2. The large dog was growling at me, __for and__ there were white bubbles of foam around its mouth.

3. The library had just closed, __so__ I couldn't get any of the reserved books.

4. He checked on the new baby every five minutes, __for__ he was afraid that something would happen to her.

5. Kate thought the milk was fresh, __but__ it broke up into little sour flakes in her coffee.

6. Elephants have no thumbs, __so__ baby elephants suck their trunks.

7. Lonnie heard a noise and looked out the window, __but__ the only thing there was his reflection.

8. Although I like most creatures, I am not fond of snakes, __and__ I like spiders even less.

9. My sister wants to exercise more and use her car less, __so__ she walks to the grocery store.

10. Barry spends hours every day on his computer, __and__ he often has the television on at the same time.

ACTIVITY 3

Add a complete and closely related thought to go with each of the following statements. Use a comma plus the indicated joining word when you write the second thought.

EXAMPLE

for The journalist interviewed the children at my son's school _____
__, for she was writing a story about bullying on campus.__

1. Most reality TV shows are unoriginal, _but they are_ _mostly about the same thing_ | but

2. Ryan enrolled in an online class, _for his job won't_ _give him time off._ | for

3. My mom taught me to respect others, _and don't speak_ _when someone else is talking._ | and

4. The warehouse fire occurred late last night, _so a lot of_ _workers didn't know._ | so

5. Sharla called in sick to work today, _but was seen at the_ _movie._ | but

---

ACTIVITY 4

Correct each run-on with either (1) a period and a capital letter or (2) a comma and a logical joining word. Do not use the same method of correction for every sentence.

Some of the run-ons are fused sentences (there is no punctuation between the two complete thoughts), and some are comma splices (there is only a comma between the two complete thoughts). One sentence is correct.

EXAMPLE

so
There was a strange odor in the house, Tommy called the gas company immediately.

1. I suffer from seasonal allergies, the worst season is spring when all the trees are in bloom.

2. Christmas is a great holiday people decorate their houses so nicely.

3. The children on the bus were very loud, the bus driver often had a headache.

4. The cake baking in the oven smelled wonderful, and my mouth watered at the thought of eating it.

5. The new book by Anita Diamante is extremely interesting one of her best books is *The Red Tent*.

6. Meteorologists have very interesting jobs, they use science to predict the weather.

7. Interviewing for a new job is very stressful, anticipating what questions will be asked is difficult.

8. Many people have problems getting rid of junk, their homes quickly become filled and cluttered.

9. The car stalled on the railroad tracks the train engineer quickly applied the brakes and avoided an accident.

10. John bought a new car from the dealership down the road, we have purchased two cars from that same dealership.

Method 3: Semicolon

A third method of correcting a run-on is to use a semicolon to mark the break between two thoughts. A *semicolon* (;) looks like a period above a comma and is sometimes called a *strong comma*. A semicolon signals more of a pause than a comma alone but not quite the full pause of a period. When it is used to correct run-ons, the semicolon can be used alone or with a transitional word.

Semicolon Alone

Here are some earlier sentences that were connected with a comma plus a joining word. Now they are connected by a semicolon alone. Notice that the semicolon alone—unlike the comma alone—can be used to connect the two complete thoughts in each sentence:

> Lonnie heard a noise and looked out the window; the only thing there was his reflection.

> He checked on the new baby every five minutes; he was afraid something would happen to her.

> Lizards become sluggish at night; they need the sun's warmth to maintain an active body temperature.

> The large dog was growling at me; there were white bubbles of foam around its mouth.

> We knew a power failure had occurred; all the clocks in the building were forty-seven minutes slow.

Using semicolons can add to sentence variety. For some people, however, the semicolon is a confusing punctuation mark. Keep in mind that if you are not comfortable using it, you can and should use one of the first two methods of correcting run-ons.

ACTIVITY 5

Insert a semicolon where the break occurs between the two complete thoughts in each of the following sentences.

EXAMPLE

Neither my dad nor my mom attended college;I plan to be the first person in my family to earn a bachelor's degree.

1. Everyone at the fundraising event brought canned goods the organizers hoped to donate several thousand pounds of food to the local food pantry.

2. The council member was censured for his comments he quickly apologized when he realized that others found his remarks offensive.

3. Sarah took her favorite stuffed animal with her to the hospital she hugged Boo Boo when the nurse stuck the IV needle into Sarah's arm.

4. Someone from the credit card company called this afternoon I am several months behind in my payments.

5. The attorney called her witness to the stand the witness, however, was too nervous to answer questions.

6. Ravi asked me out to dinner we plan to eat sushi at the new Japanese restaurant.

7. The job market in our city has slowed down; many people are being forced to find employment in neighboring areas.

8. Dave thinks that he owns the remote control; he doesn't realize that I removed the batteries from it.

9. Insulin medication was made from beef- and pork-based products until 1982; people with diabetes now use insulin made from genetically altered bacteria.

10. Mari is lactose intolerant; she never eats ice cream or drinks milk.

Semicolon with a Transitional Word

A semicolon can be used with a transitional word and a comma to join two complete thoughts. Here are some examples:

Larry believes in being prepared for emergencies; therefore, he stockpiles canned goods in his basement.

I tried to cash my paycheck; however, I had forgotten to bring identification.

Athletic shoes must fit perfectly; otherwise, wearers may injure their feet or ankles.

A short nap at the end of the day relaxes me; in addition, it gives me the energy to spend the evening on my homework.

Some zoo animals have not learned how to be good parents; as a result, baby animals are sometimes brought up in zoo nurseries and even in private homes.

People use seventeen muscles when they smile; on the other hand, they use forty-three muscles when they frown.

Following is a list of common transitional words (also known as *adverbial conjunctions*), with brief meanings.

Transitional Word	Meaning
however	but
nevertheless	however
on the other hand	however
instead	as a substitute
meanwhile	in the intervening time
otherwise	under other conditions
indeed	in fact
in addition	also, and
also	in addition
moreover	in addition
furthermore	in addition
as a result	thus, therefore

continued

Transitional Word	Meaning
thus	as a result
consequently	as a result
therefore	as a result

ACTIVITY 6

For each sentence, choose a logical transitional word from the box above, and write it in the space provided. Use a semicolon *before* the connector and a comma *after* it.

EXAMPLE

I dread going to parties ___; however,___ my husband loves meeting new people.

1. Jackie suffers from migraine headaches ; *thus* [*therefore*] her doctor has advised her to avoid caffeine and alcohol.

2. Ray's apartment is always neat and clean ; *but* [*on the other hand*] the interior of his car looks like the aftermath of a tornado.

3. I try to attend all my math classes ; *otherwise* I'll get too far behind to pass the weekly quizzes.

4. B. J. was singing Mary J. Blige tunes in the shower ; *meanwhile* his toast was burning in the kitchen.

5. The reporter was tough and experienced ; *moreover* [*however*] even he was stunned by the tragic events.

A Note on Subordination

A fourth method of joining related thoughts is to use subordination. *Subordination* is a way of showing that one thought in a sentence is not as important as another thought. (Subordination is explained in full on pages 110–111.) Below are three earlier sentences, recast so that one idea is subordinated to (made less important than) the other idea. In each case, the subordinate (or less important) thought is underlined. Note that each subordinate clause begins with a dependent word.

Because the library had just closed, I couldn't get any of the reserved books.

When the canoe touched bottom, Dave pushed the craft toward deeper water.

I didn't make good time driving to work today because every traffic light along the way was red.

A Review: How to Check for Run-Ons

1. To see if a sentence is a run-on, read it aloud and listen for a break marking two complete thoughts. Your voice will probably drop and pause at the break.

continued

2. To check an entire paper, read it aloud from the *last* sentence to the *first*. Doing so will help you hear and see each complete thought.

3. Be on the lookout for words that can lead to run-on sentences:

I	he, she, it	they	this	then	now
you	we	there	that	next	

4. Correct run-ons by using one of the following methods:

   Period and a capital letter

   Comma and a joining word (*and, but, for, or, nor, so, yet*)

   Semicolon, alone or with a transitional word

   Subordination

REFLECTIVE ACTIVITY

Re-read any essay you wrote for Chapter 18. Are there any run-ons in your paper? Correct them using what you learned in Chapter 24.

REVIEW TEST 1

Correct each run-on with either (1) a period and a capital letter or (2) a comma (if needed) and the joining word *and, but, for,* or *so.* Do not use the same method of correction for every sentence.

Some of the run-ons are fused sentences (there is no punctuation between the two complete thoughts), and some are comma splices (there is only a comma between the two complete thoughts). One sentence is correct.

1. Our boss expects us to work four hours without a break, he wanders off to a vending machine at least once an hour.

2. The children in the next car were making faces at other drivers, when I made a face back, they giggled and sank out of sight.

3. Chuck bent over and lifted the heavy tray, then he heard an ominous crack in his back.

4. The branches of the tree were bare they made a dark feathery pattern against the orange-pink sunset.

5. In the dark alley, the air smelled like rotten garbage, a large rat crept in the shadows.

ACTIVITY 2

Some verbs in the sentences that follow need -d or -ed endings. Cross out each nonstandard verb form or incorrect tense and write the standard form or correct tense in the space provided.

managed 1. One of my classmates manage to earn a full scholarship to a four-year university.

interviewed 2. The police officer interview several witnesses at the scene of the accident.

realized 3. This morning, Susan realize that she had left her backpack in a carrel at the library.

planted 4. I plant rosemary and basil in the garden last spring.

asked 5. The manager ask the customers for their feedback on the new menu items.

Irregular Verbs

Irregular verbs have irregular forms in past tense and past participle. For example, the past tense of the irregular verb *choose* is *chose*; its past participle is *chosen*.

Almost everyone has some degree of trouble with irregular verbs. When you are unsure about the form of a verb, you can check the following list of irregular verbs. (The present participle is not shown on this list because it is formed simply by adding *-ing* to the base form of the verb.) Or you can check a dictionary, which gives the principal parts of irregular verbs.

A List of Irregular Verbs

Present	Past	Past Participle
arise	arose	arisen
awake	awoke *or* awaked	awoken *or* awaked
be (am, are, is)	was (were)	been
become	became	become
begin	began	begun
bend	bent	bent
bite	bit	bitten
blow	blew	blown
break	broke	broken
bring	brought	brought
build	built	built
burst	burst	burst
buy	bought	bought
catch	caught	caught
choose	chose	chosen
come	came	come
cost	cost	cost
cut	cut	cut
do (does)	did	done

continued

Present	Past	Past Participle
draw	drew	drawn
drink	drank	drunk
drive	drove	driven
eat	ate	eaten
fall	fell	fallen
feed	fed	fed
feel	felt	felt
fight	fought	fought
find	found	found
fly	flew	flown
freeze	froze	frozen
get	got	got *or* gotten
give	gave	given
go (goes)	went	gone
grow	grew	grown
have (has)	had	had
hear	heard	heard
hide	hid	hidden
hold	held	held
hurt	hurt	hurt
keep	kept	kept
know	knew	known
lay	laid	laid
lead	led	led
leave	left	left
lend	lent	lent
let	let	let
lie	lay	lain
light	lit	lit
lose	lost	lost
make	made	made
meet	met	met
pay	paid	paid
ride	rode	ridden
ring	rang	rung
run	ran	run
say	said	said
see	saw	seen
sell	sold	sold
send	sent	sent
shake	shook	shaken
shrink	shrank	shrunk
shut	shut	shut
sing	sang	sung
sit	sat	sat
sleep	slept	slept
speak	spoke	spoken
spend	spent	spent

continued

Present	Past	Past Participle
stand	stood	stood
steal	stole	stolen
stick	stuck	stuck
sting	sting	stung
swear	swore	sworn
swim	swam	swum
take	took	taken
teach	taught	taught
tear	tore	torn
tell	told	told
think	thought	thought
wake	woke *or* waked	woke *or* waked
wear	wore	worn
win	won	won
write	wrote	written

ACTIVITY 3

Cross out the incorrect verb form or tense in each of the following sentences. Then write the correct form or tense of the verb in the space provided.

EXAMPLE

flown   After it had ~~flew~~ into the picture window, the dazed bird huddled on the ground.

worn   1. She had wore her best dress for the party, but it still wasn't fancy enough.

stood   2. As Jane stands in the aisle at the grocery store and stared at the different types of bread, she couldn't choose which one to purchase.

swum   3. Even though my son is eight years old, he has never swam.

grown   4. The children had grew much taller over the course of the summer, so their mother took them shopping for new clothes.

known   5. If I had knew how much I would like Indian food, I would have started eating it much earlier in my life.

rode   6. Peter was afraid of horses, so it was quite a triumph when he finally rides one.

shook   7. After the earthquake shaked the building, the people were relieved that no one was hurt.

brought   8. He was asked to bring chips and salsa to the party, but he brang a vegetable platter instead.

laid   9. The young child was very tired so he lied down to take a nap.

fed   10. Last night, before he went to bed, Tom feeds his pets.

Nonstandard Forms of Three Common Irregular Verbs

People who use nonstandard forms of regular verbs also tend to use nonstandard forms of three common irregular verbs: *be, have,* and *do.* Instead of saying, for example, "My neighbors *are* nice people," a person using a nonstandard form might say, "My neighbors *be* nice people." Instead of saying, "She *doesn't* agree," they might say, "She *don't* agree." Instead of saying, "We *have* tickets," they might say, "We *has* tickets."

The following charts compare the nonstandard and the standard forms of *be, have,* and *do.*

Be

Community Dialect		Standard English	
(Do *not* use in your writing)		(Use for clear communication)	
Present tense			
I be (*or* is)	we be	I am	we are
you be	you be	you are	you are
he, she, it be	they be	he, she, it is	they are
Past tense			
I were	we was	I was	we were
you was	you was	you were	you were
he, she, it were	they was	he, she, it was	they were

Have

Community Dialect		Standard English	
(Do *not* use in your writing)		(Use for clear communication)	
Present tense			
I has	we has	I have	we have
you has	you has	you have	you have
he, she, it have	they has	he, she, it has	they have
Past tense			
I has	we has	I had	we had
you has	you has	you had	you had
he, she, it have	they has	he, she, it had	they had

Do

	Community Dialect		Standard English	
	(Do *not* use in your writing)		(Use for clear communication)	
	Present tense			
	~~I does~~	~~we do~~	I do	we do
	you does	~~you does~~	you do	you do
	~~he, she, it do~~	~~they does~~	he, she, it does	they do
	Past tense			
	~~I done~~	~~we done~~	I did	we did
	you done	~~you done~~	you did	you did
	~~he, she, it done~~	~~they done~~	he, she, it did	they did

> **TIP**   Many people have trouble with one negative form of *do*. They will say, for example, "He don't agree" instead of "He doesn't agree," or they will say "The door *don't* work" instead of "The door doesn't work." Be careful to avoid the common mistake of using *don't* instead of *doesn't*.

ACTIVITY 4

Cross out the nonstandard verb form in each sentence. Then write the standard form of *be*, *have*, or *do* in the space provided.

_is_   1. My cat, Tugger, ~~be~~ the toughest animal I know.

has   2. He ~~have~~ survived many close calls.

was   3. Three years ago, he ~~were~~ caught inside a car's engine.

has   4. He ~~have~~ one ear torn off and lost his sight in one eye.

were   5. We ~~was~~ surprised that he lived through the accident.

was   6. Within weeks, though, he ~~were~~ back to normal.

were   7. Then, last year, we ~~was~~ worried that we would lose Tugger.

were   8. Lumps that ~~was~~ growing on his back turned out to be cancer.

did   9. But the vet ~~done~~ an operation that saved Tugger's life.

has   10. By now, we know that Tugger really ~~do~~ have nine lives.

REVIEW TEST 1

Cross out the incorrect verb form or tense in each sentence. Then write the correct form or tense in the space provided.

were   1. The Declaration of Independence ~~was~~ signed in 1776 and establishes the United States as an independent country.

was   2. George Washington ~~is~~ elected the first president of the United States in 1789.

was   3. The philosophical idea of Manifest Destiny, the belief that the United States should expand across the continent, were popular throughout the 1840s and 1850s.

claimed   4. Between 1861 and 1865, the Civil War claim over 600,000 American lives.

were   5. The Eighteenth Amendment, which was signed in 1919 and prohibits the sale of alcohol, was repealed by the Twenty-First Amendment in 1933.

avoided   6. The United States avoids fighting in World War II until Japan attacked Pearl Harbor on December 7, 1941.

were   7. In 1959, President Eisenhower admit Alaska and Hawaii as the 49th and 50th states.

took   8. As the first man on the moon, Neil A. Armstrong takes "one small step for man, one giant leap for mankind" on July 20, 1969 and established NASA and the United States as leaders in space exploration

became   9. In 1974, President Richard Milhous Nixon becomes the first American president to resign from office.

celebrated   10. The United States celebrate its 200th anniversary in the year 1976.

were   11. Geraldine Ferraro were the first female vice-presidential candidate in 1984; she was followed twenty-four years later, in 2008, by vice-presidential candidate Sarah Palin.

REVIEW TEST 2

Write short sentences that use the tense requested for the following verbs.

EXAMPLE

Past of _grow_ _I grew my own tomatoes last year._

1. Past of _know_ _knew_

2. Present of _take_ _took_

3. Past participle of _give_ _given_

4. Past participle of _write_ _written_

5. Past of _do_ _done_

6. Past of _talk_ _talked_

7. Present of _begin_ _began_

8. Past of _go_ _went_

9. Past participle of _see_ _Seen_

10. Present of _drive_ _drive_

Subject-Verb Agreement

A verb must agree with its subject in number. A *singular subject* (one person or thing) takes a singular verb. A *plural subject* (more than one person or thing) takes a plural verb. Mistakes in subject–verb agreement are sometimes made in the following situations:

1. When words come between the subject and the verb

2. When a verb comes before the subject

3. With compound subjects

4. With indefinite pronouns

Each of these situations is explained in this chapter. Additional information about subjects and verbs can be found in Chapter 21.

Words between Subject and Verb

Words that come between the subject and the verb do not change subject–verb agreement. In the sentence

The sharp <u>fangs</u> in the dog's mouth <u>look</u> scary.

the subject (*fangs*) is plural, and so the verb (*look*) is plural. The words that come between the subject and the verb are a prepositional phrase: *in the dog's mouth*. They do not affect subject–verb agreement. (A list of prepositions can be found on page 397.)

To help find the subject of certain sentences, you should cross out prepositional phrases.

The lumpy <u>salt</u> ~~in the shakers~~ <u>needs</u> to be changed.

An old <u>chair</u> ~~with broken legs~~ <u>has sat</u> in our basement for years.

ACTIVITY 1

Working in groups of two, underline the subject and lightly cross out any words that come between the subject and the verb. Then double-underline the verb in parentheses that you believe is correct.

1. Some <u>members</u> ~~of the parents' association~~ (<u>want</u>, wants) to ban certain books from the school library.

2. Chung's trench <u>coat</u>, with its big lapels and shoulder flaps, (<u>make</u>, makes) him feel ~~like a tough private eye~~.

3. Misconceptions about apes like the gorilla (has, have) turned a relatively peaceful animal into a terrifying monster.

4. The rising cost of necessities like food and shelter (force, forces) many elderly people to live in poverty.

5. In my opinion, a few slices of pepperoni pizza (make, makes) a great evening.

Verb before Subject

A verb agrees with its subject even when the verb comes *before* the subject. Words that may precede the subject include *there, here*, and, in questions, *who, which, what*, and *where*.

Here are some examples of sentences in which the verb appears before the subject:

There are wild dogs in our neighborhood.

In the distance was a billow of black smoke.

Here is the newspaper.

Where are the children's coats?

If you are unsure about the subject, ask *who* or *what* of the verb. With the first example above, you might ask, "*What* are in our neighborhood?" The answer, *wild dogs*, is the subject.

Write the correct form of each verb in the space provided.	ACTIVITY 2

1. There ___are___ dozens of frenzied shoppers waiting for the store to open. (is, are)
2. Here ___are___ the notes from yesterday's anthropology lecture. (is, are)
3. When ___do___ we take our break? (do, does)
4. There ___were___ scraps of yellowing paper stuck between the pages of the cookbook. (was, were)
5. At the very bottom of the grocery list ___was___ an item that meant a trip all the way back to aisle one. (was, were)

Compound Subjects

A *compound subject* is two subjects separated by a joining word, such as *and*. Subjects joined by *and* generally take a plural verb.

A patchwork quilt and a sleeping bag cover my bed in the winter.

Dave and Carrie are a contented couple.

When subjects are joined by *either … or, neither … nor, not only … but also,* the verb agrees with the subject closer to the verb.

> Neither the <u>negotiator</u> nor the union <u>leaders</u> <u>want</u> the strike to continue.

The nearer subject, *leaders,* is plural, and so the verb is plural.

> Neither the union <u>leaders</u> nor the <u>negotiator</u> <u>wants</u> the strike to continue.

In this version, the nearer subject, *negotiator,* is singular, so the verb is singular.

ACTIVITY 3	Write the correct form of the verb in the space provided.

(know, knows)

1. The driver and her passenger __*knows*__ that they are at fault for the auto accident.

(are, is)

2. The coffee and dessert __*are*__ ready to be served.

(encourage, encourages)

3. Not only my teachers, but also my wife __*encourages*__ me to work hard in college.

(was, were)

4. Before the birth of my son, video games and television __*were*__ important to me.

(interest, interests)

5. Neither accounting nor marketing __*interests*__ Mike, but he still plans to major in business.

Indefinite Pronouns

The following words, known as *indefinite pronouns,* always take singular verbs:

(*-one* words)	(*-body* words)	(*-thing* words)	
one	nobody	nothing	each
anyone	anybody	anything	either
everyone	everybody	everything	neither
someone	somebody	something	

> TIP   *Both* always takes a plural verb.

Write the correct form of the verb in the space provided.

1. Neither of those Web sites __*is*__ credible.   (are, is)

2. Somebody in the classroom __*knows*__ who stole my wallet.   (know, knows)

3. Both of the professors you mentioned __*are*__ hard, but you will learn a lot in their classes.   (are, is)

4. One of these DVDs __*needs*__ to be returned to the video rental store by midnight tonight.   (need, needs)

In the space provided, write the correct form of the verb shown in the margin.

1. Tornadoes __*are*__ massive storms characterized by rotating columns of air that create funnels.   (is, are)

2. Almost a third of all the tornadoes in the United States __*occur*__ in Tornado Alley, an area that covers Nebraska, Kansas, Oklahoma, and Texas.   (occurs, occur)

3. The majority of tornadoes __*develop*__ between April and June.   (develops, develop)

4. Tornado watches __*are*__ often issued to alert people that weather conditions could produce tornadoes.   (is, are)

5. If either a storm chaser or radar __*spots*__ a tornado, a warning is issued.   (spots, spot)

6. Storm chasers __*are*__ people who attempt to get close to the tornadoes to film, study, or just experience the storm.   (is, are)

7. When the National Weather Service __*issues*__ tornado warnings, people prepare by seeking safety in basements or shelters.   (issues, issue)

8. Hail, heavy rain, and a greenish black sky __*are*__ signs that a tornado may occur.   (is, are)

9. Tornadoes are measured on the Fujita Scale, which __*rates*__ the storms based on an estimate of the strength of the winds.   (rates, rate)

10. Although the Fujita Scale rates tornadoes from F0 to F6, most meteorologists __*feel*__ an F6 tornado is inconceivable.   (feels, feel)

Cross out the incorrect verb form in each sentence. In addition, underline the subject or subjects that go with the verb. Then write the correct form of the verb in the space provided.

__*are*__   1. Why is Jonathan and his friends cutting their hair so short?

is   2. Neither of my essays for history or economics are well written.

were   3. A digital camera, a cellular phone, and an iPod was on my daughter's wish list.

look   4. The mangoes on the tree looks ripe.

are   5. Here is the midterm report you requested and the copies of the files I duplicated.

prevents   6. The annoying barking from the neighbor's dogs prevent me from studying.

is   7. One of my sports heroes are decathlon winner Bryan Clay, who attributed his success at the Beijing Olympics to discipline and perseverance.

make   8. Three eggs, grated cheese, and chopped ham makes for a hearty omelet.

thinks   9. A person in his or her twenties often think that retirement planning isn't necessary.

has   10. Each of the contestants on the new game show have a chance of winning the million-dollar grand prize.

Additional Information about Verbs

The purpose of this chapter is to provide additional information about verbs. Some people will find the grammatical terms here a helpful reminder of what they've learned earlier, in school, about verbs. For them, the terms will increase their understanding of how verbs function in English. Other people may welcome more detailed information about terms used elsewhere in the text. In either case, remember that the most common mistakes people make with verbs have been treated in previous chapters of the book.

Verb Tense

Verbs tell us the time of an action. The time that a verb shows is usually called *tense*. The most common tenses are the simple present, past, and future. In addition, there are nine tenses that enable us to express more specific ideas about time than we could with the simple tenses alone. Following are the twelve verb tenses and examples of each tense. Read them over to increase your sense of the many different ways of expressing time in English.

Tenses	Examples
Present	I *work*. Tony *works*.
Past	Ellen *worked* on her car.
Future	You *will work* on a new project next week.
Present perfect	He *has worked* on his term paper for a month. They *have worked* out a compromise.
Past perfect	The nurse *had worked* two straight shifts.
Future perfect	Next Monday, I *will have worked* here exactly two years.
Present progressive	I *am working* on my speech for the debate. You *are working* too hard. The tape recorder *is* not *working* properly.
Past progressive	He *was working* in the basement. The contestants *were working* on their talent routines.
Future progressive	My son *will be working* in our store this summer.
Present perfect progressive	Sarah *has been working* late this week.

continued

Tenses	Examples
Past perfect progressive	Until recently, I *had been working* nights.
Future perfect progressive	My mother *will have been working* as a nurse for forty-five years by the time she retires.

ACTIVITY 1   On a separate paper, write twelve sentences using the twelve verb tenses.

Helping Verbs

There are three common verbs that can either stand alone or combine with (and "help") other verbs. Here are the verbs and their forms:

be (am, are, is, was, were, being, been)

have (has, having, had)

do (does, did)

Here are examples of the helping verbs:

Used Alone	**Used as Helping Verbs**
I *was* confident.	I *was becoming* confident.
Lance *has* the answer.	Lance *has remembered* the answer.
My mom *did* a good job raising me.	My mom *did raise* me well.

There are nine helping verbs (traditionally known as *modals*, or *modal auxiliaries*) that are always used in combination with other verbs. Here are the nine verbs and a sentence example of each:

can	I *can study* for my sociology exam this weekend.
could	I *could* not *find* my professor after class.
may	The quiz *may cover* last week's assigned readings.
might	Steve *might attend* the group study session tonight.
shall	I *shall ask* my classmate Arnel to help me with my math homework.
should	She *should know* the answers because she attended the lecture.

continued

will	Tara *will want* to attend the biology field trip to the tidal pools.
would	The person at the counter *would* not *tell* me when the financial aid forms were due.
must	You *must ask* questions when you don't understand.

Note from the examples that these verbs have only one form. They do not, for instance, add an *-s* when used with *he, she, it,* or any one person or thing.

| On separate paper, write nine sentences using the nine helping verbs. | **ACTIVITY 2** |

Verbals

Verbals are words formed from verbs. Verbals, like verbs, often express action. They can add variety to your sentences and vigor to your writing style. The three kinds of verbals are *infinitives, participles,* and *gerunds.*

Additional information about infinitives can be found on page 407. Additional information about participles and gerunds can be found on page 407 and pages 460–461.

Infinitive

An infinitive is *to* plus the base form of the verb.

I love *to dance.*

Lina hopes *to write* for a newspaper.

I asked the children *to clean* the kitchen.

Participle

A participle is a verb form used as an adjective (a descriptive word). The present participle ends in *-ing*. The past participle ends in *-ed* or has an irregular ending.

Peering into the cracked mirror, the *crying* woman wiped her eyes.

The *astounded* man stared at his *winning* lottery ticket.

Swinging a sharp ax, Omar split the *rotted* beam.

Gerund

A gerund is the *-ing* form of a verb used as a noun.

Swimming is the perfect exercise.

Eating junk food is my diet downfall.

Through *doodling,* people express their inner feelings.

ACTIVITY 3

On separate paper, write three sentences using infinitives, three sentences using participles, and three sentences using gerunds. At least three of your sentences must be written about the photograph below.

REFLECTIVE ACTIVITY

Re-read any paragraph you wrote for an assignment in Chapter 7, "Narration," or any essay you wrote for Chapter 18, "Patterns of Essay Development." Do you see any verb problems or subject–verb agreement problems in your paper? If so, correct them using what you learned in Chapters 25–27.

Pronoun Agreement and Reference

Nouns name persons, places, or things. *Pronouns* are words that take the place of nouns. In fact, the word *pronoun* means "for a noun." Pronouns are shortcuts that keep you from unnecessarily repeating words in writing. Here are some examples of pronouns:

> Eddie left *his* camera on the bus.
> (*His* is a pronoun that takes the place of *Eddie's*.)
>
> Elena drank the coffee even though *it* was cold.
> (*It* replaces *coffee*.)
>
> As I turned the newspaper's damp pages, *they* disintegrated in my hands.
> (*They* is a pronoun that takes the place of *pages*.)

This chapter presents rules that will help you avoid two common mistakes people make with pronouns. The rules are:

1. A pronoun must agree in number with the word or words it replaces.

2. A pronoun must refer clearly to the word it replaces.

Pronoun Agreement

A pronoun must agree in number with the word or words it replaces. If the word a pronoun refers to is singular, the pronoun must be singular; if that word is plural, the pronoun must be plural. (Note that the word a pronoun refers to is known as the *antecedent*.)

> Marie showed me *her* antique wedding band.

> Students enrolled in the art class must provide *their* own supplies.

In the first example, the pronoun *her* refers to the singular word *Marie*; in the second example, the pronoun *their* refers to the plural word *Students*.

ACTIVITY 1

Write the appropriate pronoun (*their, they, them, it*) in the blank space in each of the following sentences.

EXAMPLE

I bought a used bicycle and gave ____it____ a new coat of paint.

1. Melinda and Jo bought tickets for the concert, and ____they____ also made reservations for dinner at the new Italian restaurant on Sanchez Avenue.

2. The leftover pizza was cold, but I decided to eat ____it____ for breakfast.

3. The teachers at my college are very committed, for ____they____ often stay after class to help students.

4. Leon's children are coming over on Friday, and then ____their____ mother will pick them up on Sunday night.

5. This morning, Sarah forgot to bring the quarterly sales report, so she caught a cab home before the meeting to get ~~them~~ *it*.

Indefinite Pronouns

The following words, known as *indefinite pronouns*, are always singular.

(*-one* words)	(*-body* words)	
one	nobody	each
anyone	anybody	either
everyone	everybody	neither
someone	somebody	

If a pronoun in a sentence refers to one of these singular words, the pronoun should be singular.

Somebody left (her) bag on the back of a chair.

One of the busboys just called and said (he) would be an hour late.

Everyone in the club must pay (his) dues next week.

Each circled pronoun is singular because it refers to an indefinite pronoun.

There are two important points to remember about indefinite pronouns:

1. In the last example, if everyone in the club was a woman, the pronoun would be *her*. If the club had women and men, the pronoun would be *his or her*:

Everyone in the club must pay his or her dues next week.

Traditionally, writers used *his* to refer to both women and men; however, most writers now use *his or her* to avoid an implied sexual bias. To avoid using *his* or the somewhat awkward *his or her,* a sentence can often be rewritten in the plural:

Club members must pay their dues next week.

2. In informal spoken English, *plural* pronouns are often used with the indefinite pronouns. Many people would probably not say:

Everybody has his or her own opinion about the election.

Instead, they would be likely to say:

Everybody has their own opinion about the election.

Here are other examples:

Everyone in the choir must buy their robes.

Everybody in the line has their ticket ready.

No one in the class remembered to bring their books.

In such cases, the indefinite pronouns are clearly plural in meaning, and using them helps people avoid the awkward *his or her.* In time, the plural pronoun may be accepted in formal speech or writing. Until then, however, you should use the grammatically correct singular form in your writing.

Underline the correct pronoun.	ACTIVITY 2

1. Neither of the potential buyers had really made up (her, their) mind.
2. Not one of the new cashiers knows what (he, they) should be doing.
3. Each of these computers has (its, their) drawbacks.
4. Anyone trying to reduce (his or her, their) salt intake should avoid canned and processed foods.
5. If anybody calls when I'm out, tell (him, them) I'll return in an hour.

Pronoun Reference

A sentence may be confusing and unclear if a pronoun appears to refer to more than one word or does not refer to any specific word. Look at this sentence:

Malia was annoyed when they failed her car for a faulty turn signal.

Who failed her car? There is no specific word that *they* refers to. Be clear:

Malia was annoyed when the inspectors failed her car for a faulty turn signal.

Here are sentences with other faulty pronoun references. Read the explanations of why they are faulty and look carefully at how they are corrected.

Faulty	**Clear**
Peter told Alan that his wife was unhappy. (Whose wife is unhappy: Peter's or Alan's? Be clear.)	Peter told Alan, "My wife is unhappy."
Kia is really a shy person, but she keeps it hidden. (There is no specific word that *it* refers to. It would not make sense to say, "Kia keeps shy hidden.")	Kia is really a shy person, but she keeps her shyness hidden.
Jodie attributed her success to her husband's support, which was generous. (Does *which* mean that Jodie's action was generous or that her husband's support was generous?)	Generously, Jodie attributed her success to her husband's support. *Or:* Jodie attributed her success to her husband's generous support.

ACTIVITY 3

Rewrite each of the following sentences to make clear the vague pronoun reference. Add, change, or omit words as necessary.

EXAMPLE

Amanda's sister picked up her daughter from the babysitter after work.
Amanda's sister picked up Amanda's daughter from the babysitter after work.

1. Lance went down to the shoe store but didn't find one that fit him.
   Lance went down to the shoe store but didn't find a shoes that fit

2. To check out books at the library, they will ask you if you have a valid student identification card.
   the Librarian
   _____

3. Roberto told Calvin that his computer-animated art project was well designed.
   Roberto told Calvin that his computer-animated art
   was well designed.

4. Jiggling her key into the rusty padlock, Susan knew that she had found the right one.
   the right key.

5. Yumiko visited the counseling center because they could help her decide on a major.
   the counselors could help
   her decide on a major.

Cross out the pronoun error in each sentence, and write the correct word(s) on the line following the sentence. Then, in the space provided, write whether the rule being followed is about pronoun agreement or about pronoun reference.

EXAMPLES

Pronoun Agreement Many students begin college without any idea what ~~he or she~~ are going to study. _they_

Pronoun Reference The years pass quickly, and ~~they~~ will soon need to focus on a main interest. _students_

Pronoun Agreement 1. If a person wants to become a high school history teacher, ~~they~~ should major in secondary education. _One_

Pronoun Reference 2. Astronomers are scientists who study the stars; they are often out late at night. _the stars_ _these scientists_

Pronoun Agreement 3. College students wanting to be cryptologists need to study math, and ~~he or she~~ also must be good at solving puzzles and creating and breaking codes. _they_

Pronoun Agreement 4. Anybody who wants to be a firefighter will need to be in top physical condition to pass ~~their~~ physical examination. ~~he/she~~ _his/her_

Pronoun Reference 5. Not all food service workers need college degrees, but ~~they~~ can help with advancement. ~~he/she~~ _the degrees_

Pronoun Agreement 6. A student who wants to study the field of biomedical engineering should be prepared to spend his college years taking chemistry, biology, anatomy, and engineering classes. _his/her_

Pronoun Reference 7. Zoologists work at zoos and aquariums with animals, and they sometimes live in natural habitats to learn more. _the zoologist_

Pronoun Agreement 8. A student who wants to work outdoors could choose to be a fish and game warden, but they should be prepared to major in wildlife management. _he/she_

> **TIP** for Rule 3
>
> Avoid mistakes by mentally adding the "missing" verb at the end of the sentence.

Object Pronouns

Object pronouns (me, him, her, us, them) are the objects of verbs or prepositions. (*Prepositions* are connecting words like *for, at, about, to, before, by, with,* and *of.* See also page 397.)

> Tony helped me. (*Me* is the object of the verb *helped.*)
>
> We took *them* to the college. (*Them* is the object of the verb *took.*)
>
> Leave the children with *us.* (*Us* is the object of the preposition *with.*)
>
> I got in line behind *him.* (*Him* is the object of the preposition *behind.*)

People are sometimes uncertain about what pronoun to use when two objects follow a verb.

Incorrect	**Correct**
I gave a gift to Ray and *she.*	I gave a gift to Ray and *her.*
She came to the movie with Adrianna and *I.*	She came to the movie with Adrianna and *me.*

> **TIP** If you are not sure what pronoun to use, try each pronoun by itself in the sentence. The correct pronoun will be the one that sounds right. For example, "I gave a gift to she" does not sound right; "I gave a gift to her" does.

ACTIVITY 1

Underline the correct subject or object pronoun in each of the following sentences. Then show whether your answer is a subject or object pronoun by circling the S or O in the margin. The first one is done for you as an example.

S (O) 1. The sweaters Mom knitted for Victor and (I, <u>me</u>) are too small.

(S) O 2. The umpire and (he, <u>him</u>) started to argue.

(S) O 3. No one has a quicker temper than (<u>she</u>, her).

(S) (O) 4. Your grades prove that you worked harder than (they, <u>them</u>).

(S) O 5. (<u>We</u>, Us) runners train indoors when the weather turns cold.

(S) O 6. (<u>She</u>, Her) and Sienna never put the cap back on the toothpaste.

(S) (O̶) 7. Chris and (he, him) are the most energetic kids in the first grade.

(S̶) (O) 8. Arguing over clothes is a favorite pastime for my sister and (I, me).

S (O) 9. The rest of (they, them) will be arriving in about ten minutes.

(S̶) (O) 10. The head of the ticket committee asked Maggie and (I, me) to help with sales.

Possessive Pronouns

Here is a list of possessive pronouns:

my, mine	our, ours
your, yours	your, yours
his	their, theirs
her, hers	
its	

Possessive pronouns show ownership or possession.

Adam revved up *his* motorcycle and took off.

The keys are *mine.*

> **TIP** A possessive pronoun *never* uses an apostrophe. (See also page 488.)

Incorrect	**Correct**
That coat is *hers'*.	That coat is *hers*.
The card table is *theirs'*.	The card table is *theirs*.

Cross out the incorrect pronoun form in each of the sentences below. Write the correct form in the space at the left.   **ACTIVITY 2**

EXAMPLE

hers   Those Nintendo games are ~~hers'~~.

its   1. I didn't know that the blender I bought at the garage sale had lost ~~its'~~ blade.

theirs   2. Several strangers at the park asked the couple if the unleashed dog was ~~theirs'~~.

hers   3. Kimi's chemistry professor wondered if the correct answers were indeed ~~hers'~~.

ours   4. The boxes of donated items for the annual food drive are ~~ours'~~.

yours   5. You should tell everyone that the idea was entirely ~~yours'~~.

Demonstrative Pronouns

Demonstrative pronouns point to or single out a person or thing. There are four demonstrative pronouns:

this	these
that	those

Generally speaking, *this* and *these* refer to things close at hand; *that* and *those* refer to things farther away. The four demonstrative pronouns are also commonly used as demonstrative adjectives.

Is anyone using *this* spoon?

I am going to throw away *these* magazines.

I just bought *that* black pickup truck at the curb.

Pick up *those* toys in the corner.

> **TIP**   Do not use *them, this here, that there, these here,* or *those there* to point out. Use only *this, that, these,* or *those*.

ACTIVITY 3   Cross out the incorrect pronoun form of the demonstrative pronoun, and write the correct form in the space provided.

EXAMPLE

Those   ~~Them~~ pizza boxes are empty.

~~These~~ This   1. ~~This~~ here iPod is outdated.

Those   2. Bring ~~them~~ files to the meeting on Monday.

Those   3. The salesperson politely asked ~~them~~ customers if they needed help.

that

~~those~~   4. I baked ~~that~~ there apple pie with Splenda.

those   5. What do ~~them~~ Japanese *kanji* characters on your tattoo mean?

REFLECTIVE ACTIVITY

Re-read any paragraph you wrote for an assignment in Chapter 8, "Description," or any essay you wrote while studying Chapter 18, "Patterns of Essay Development." Ask yourself if you see any pronoun-agreement problems in your writing. Are there any problems with pronoun types as explained in Chapters 28 and 29? If so, correct them using what you learned in those chapters.

REVIEW TEST

Read the paragraph and underline the correct word in the parentheses.

Many people have heard of the Bill & Melinda Gates Foundation, but few know (its, it's) history or (its, their) purposes. In 1975, Bill Gates and Paul Allen founded Microsoft, which was nothing more than two very smart men and (his, their) ideas. By 1986, Microsoft had gone public and Gates was a billionaire. In 1994, (he, him) created the William H. Gates Foundation that focused on health issues around the world. In 1997, (he, him) and (his, his') wife, Melinda, created the Gates Library Foundation to help fund libraries and help provide free Internet access to Americans through library access. In 1999, (they, them) renamed the Gates Library Foundation; it became known as the Gates Learning Foundation. (This, These) broadened (its, it's) focus to include initiatives for helping low-income students prepare and pay for college. In 2000, the William H. Gates Foundation and the Gates Learning Foundation merged to become the Bill & Melinda Gates Foundation. Since 1994, the foundation has provided funds of more than three billion dollars through (its, their) Global Development Program to help create sustainable solutions in poorer countries. Some of (these, them) programs are agricultural development, financial services for the poor, and initiatives for educating about and establishing clean water, good sanitation, and healthful hygiene. The foundation has also funded over fourteen billion dollars in its Global Health Program. (This, This here) program finances initiatives that focus on saving lives in poor countries through vaccinations, neonatal and infant health care, and treatment of illnesses such as HIV/AIDS, malaria, and tuberculosis. A third program, the United States Program, has received almost six billion dollars to continue to fund the programs started by the Gates Learning Foundation. All of (these, those) programs have had an impact on millions of lives through the founders' belief that "every life has equal value."

Adjectives and Adverbs

Adjectives

What Are Adjectives?

Adjectives describe nouns (names of persons, places, or things) or pronouns.

> Yoko is a *wise* woman. (The adjective *wise* describes the noun *woman*.)

> She is also *funny*. (The adjective *funny* describes the pronoun *she*.)

> I'll carry the *heavy* bag of groceries. (The adjective *heavy* describes the noun *bag*.)

> It is *torn*. (The adjective *torn* describes the pronoun *it*.)

Adjectives usually come before the word they describe (as in *wise* woman and *heavy* bag). But they also come after forms of the verb *be* (*is, are, was, were,* and so on). They also follow verbs such as *look, appear, seem, become, sound, taste,* and *smell*.

> That road is *slippery*. (The adjective *slippery* describes the road.)

> The dogs are *noisy*. (The adjective *noisy* describes the dogs.)

> Those customers were *impatient*. (The adjective *impatient* describes the customers.)

> Your room looks *neat*. (The adjective *neat* describes the room.)

RESPONDING TO IMAGES

Describe this artwork using as many specific details as possible. How many adjectives did you use? Circle them.

Using Adjectives to Compare

Adjectives are often used to compare things or people. Use the comparative form of the adjective if two or more people or things are being compared. Use the superlative form of the adjective if three or more people or things are being compared.

For all one-syllable adjectives and some two-syllable adjectives, add *-er* when comparing two things and *-est* when comparing three or more things.

> Phil's beard is *longer* than mine, but Lee's is the *longest*.

> Meg may be the *quieter* of the two sisters; but that's not saying much, since they're the *loudest* girls in school.

For some two-syllable adjectives and all longer adjectives, use *more* when comparing two things and *most* when comparing three or more things.

> Liza Minnelli is *more famous* than her sister; but their mother, Judy Garland, is still the *most famous* member of the family.

> The red letters on the sign are *more noticeable* than the black ones, but the fluorescent letters are the *most noticeable*.

You can usually tell when to use *more* and *most* by the sound of a word. For example, you can probably tell by its sound that "carefuller" would be too awkward to say and that *more careful* is thus correct. But there are many words for which both *-er* or *-est* and *more* or *most* are equally correct. For instance, either "a more fair rule" or "a fairer rule" is correct.

To form negative comparisons, use *less* and *least*.

> During my first dance class, I felt *less graceful* than an injured elephant.

> When the teacher came to our house to complain to my parents, I offered her the *least* comfortable chair in the room.

Points to Remember about Comparing

Point 1

Use only one form of comparison at a time. That is, do not use both an *-er* ending and *more* or both an *-est* ending and *most*:

Incorrect	Correct
My mother's suitcase is always *more heavier* than my father's.	My mother's suitcase is always *heavier* than my father's.
Psycho is still the *most frighteningest* movie I've ever seen.	*Psycho* is still the *most frightening* movie I've ever seen.

Point 2

Learn the irregular forms of the words shown below.

	Comparative (for comparing two things)	Superlative (for comparing three or more things)
bad	worse	worst
good, well	better	best
little (in amount)	less	least
much, many	more	most

Do not use both *more* and an irregular comparative or *most* and an irregular superlative.

Incorrect	Correct
It is *more better* to give than to receive.	It is *better* to give than to receive.
Last night I got the *most worst* headache I ever had.	Last night I got the *worst* headache I ever had.

ACTIVITY 1	Add to each sentence the correct form of the word in the margin.

EXAMPLES

bad — The ____worst____ job I ever had was baby-sitting for spoiled four-year-old twins.

wonderful — The ____most wonderful____ day of my life was when my daughter was born.

good — 1. The __worst__ chocolate cake I ever ate had bananas in it.

young — 2. Aunt Sonja is the __youngest__ of the three sisters.

bad — 3. A rain that freezes is __bad__ than a snowstorm.

unusual — 4. That's the __most unusual__ home I've ever seen—it's shaped like a teapot.

little — 5. Being painfully shy has made Erin the __most__ friendly person I know.

Adverbs

What Are Adverbs?

Adverbs describe verbs, adjectives, or other adverbs. They usually end in *-ly*.

The father *gently* hugged the sick child. (The adverb *gently* describes the verb *hugged*.)

Newborns are *totally* innocent. (The adverb *totally* describes the adjective *innocent*.)

The lecturer spoke so *terribly* fast that I had trouble taking notes. (The adverb *terribly* describes the adverb *fast*.)

A Common Mistake with Adverbs and Adjectives

People often mistakenly use an adjective instead of an adverb after a verb.

Incorrect	Correct
Sam needs a haircut *bad*.	Sam needs a haircut *badly*.
She gets along *easy* with others.	She gets along *easily* with others.
You might have lost the race if you hadn't run so *quick* at the beginning.	You might have lost the race if you hadn't run so *quickly* at the beginning.

Underline the adjective or adverb needed. (Remember that adjectives describe nouns, and adverbs describe verbs and other adverbs.)

1. As Jun Li spoke, the audience listened (attentive, <u>attentively</u>).

2. I added a teaspoon of (<u>dark</u>, darkly) sugar to the teriyaki steak marinade.

3. The couple talked (continuous, <u>continuously</u>) during the movie.

4. The moon shined (<u>bright</u>, brightly) the night that Ron and I went fishing.

5. Our teacher assured us that the pop quiz contained (<u>easy</u>, easily) questions.

Well and *Good*

Two words that are often confused are *well* and *good. Good* is an adjective; it describes nouns. *Well* is usually an adverb; it describes verbs. But *well* (rather than *good*) is used as an adjective when referring to health.

Write *well* or *good* in each of the sentences that follow.

1. If you kids do a ___good___ job of cleaning your bedrooms, I'll take you out for some ice cream.

2. If I organize the office records too ___well___, my bosses may not need me anymore.

3. After eating a pound of peanuts, I didn't feel too ___well___.

4. When Pete got AIDS, he discovered who his ___good___ friends really were.

5. Just because brothers and sisters fight when they're young doesn't mean they won't get along ___well___ as adults.

Review a paragraph you wrote for an assignment in Chapter 8, "Description," or an essay you wrote for Chapter 18, "Patterns of Essay Development." Underline all of the adjectives and adverbs in the paper. Are there any problems with these words? If so, correct them using what you learned in Chapter 30.

REVIEW TEST 1

Underline the correct word in parentheses.

1. The waitress poured (littler, <u>less</u>) coffee into my cup than yours.

2. Humid air seems to make Sam's asthma (<u>more worse</u>, worse).

3. The movie is so interesting that the three hours pass (quick, <u>quickly</u>).

4. The talented boy sang as (confident, <u>confidently</u>) as a seasoned performer.

5. Our band played so (good, <u>well</u>) that a local firm hired us for its annual dinner.

6. Tamika is always (<u>truthful</u>, truthfully), even when it might be better to tell a white lie.

7. The driver stopped the bus (sudden, <u>suddenly</u>) and yelled, "Everybody out!"

8. Shirt and pants in the same color make you look (more thin, <u>thinner</u>) than ones in contrasting colors.

9. Your intentions may have been (<u>good</u>, well), but I'd prefer that you ask before arranging a blind date for me.

10. Our cat likes to sit in the (<u>warmest</u>, most warm) spot in any room—by a fireplace, on a windowsill in the sunshine, or on my lap.

REVIEW TEST 2

There are eight adjective and adverb errors in the following paragraph. Draw a line through each error and above that word, write the correct word(s).

Every year, sightseers to Washington, D.C. visit parts of the Smithsonian Institution, which is the world's ~~larger~~ largest museum complex. It consists of nineteen different museums and galleries, which are ~~real~~ really big, and nine of the most best research facilities in the world. Three extreme popular museums are the National Air and Space Museum, the National Museum of Natural History, and the National Museum of American History. The National Zoo is also under the jurisdiction of the Smithsonian Institution and is home to over 2,000 animals. Like the museums, the zoo is very big and cannot be toured ~~quick~~ quickly, so visitors should plan to spend the entire day. When tourists visit the Smithsonian, they often choose the ~~popularest~~ most popular museums, but this can mean dealing with ~~hugely~~ huge crowds. Those who wish to avoid crowds might want to visit least-known museums like the Postal Museum.

Misplaced and Dangling Modifiers

Misplaced Modifiers

Misplaced modifiers are words that, because of awkward placement, do not describe what the writer intended them to describe. A misplaced modifier can make a sentence confusing or unintentionally funny. To avoid this, place words as close as possible to what they describe.

CHAPTER PREVIEW

Misplaced Modifiers
Dangling Modifiers

Misplaced Words	**Correctly Placed Words**
George couldn't drive to work in his small sports car *with a broken leg*. (The sports car had a broken leg?)	With a broken leg, George couldn't drive to work in his small sports car. (The words describing George are now placed next to *George*.)
The washing machine was sold to us by a charming salesman *with a money-back guarantee*. (The salesman had a money back guarantee?)	The washing machine with a money-back guarantee was sold to us by a charming salesman. (The words describing the washing machine are now placed next to it.)
He *nearly* brushed his teeth for twenty minutes every night. (He came close to brushing his teeth but in fact did not brush them at all?)	He brushed his teeth for nearly twenty minutes every night. (The meaning—that he brushed his teeth for a long time—is now clear.)

> Underline the misplaced word or words in each sentence. Then rewrite the sentence, placing related words together and thereby making the meaning clear.

ACTIVITY 1

EXAMPLES

Sliced cucumbers were placed on my weary eyes <u>that were chilled in the refrigerator.</u>

> Sliced cucumbers that were chilled in the refrigerator were placed on my weary eyes.

Professor Ramirez spoke about the national housing crisis <u>during her lecture.</u>

> During her lecture, Professor Ramirez spoke about the national housing crisis.

1. The tortilla soup was prepared by my mother-in-law <u>on the stove.</u>

   The tortilla soup on the stove, was prepared by my mother-in-law

2. The customer spoke to the branch manager with a service complaint.

The customer spoke to the branch manger about a service comple

3. Victor added a mango to his fruit smoothie, which was grown in his own yard.

Victor added a mango which was grown in his own yard to his fruit smoothie.

4. Emily deposited the money that she would use to pay for her college tuition in the bank.

Emily deposited the money in the bank, that she would use to pay for her college tuition

5. Mari watched the movie on her portable DVD player that her friends recommended.

Marie watched the movie that her friends recomm on her portable DVD player.

6. I nearly sent out two dozen job applications this week alone.

This week alone I sent out two dozen job app—

7. The motivational speaker talked about his former drug addiction speaking from experience.

Speaking from experience the motivational speaker talked about his former drug addiction.

8. I knew that I should avoid the traffic accident on the interstate highway listening to the radio.

Listening to the radio I knew that I should have avoided the traffic accident on the interstate

9. The man asked the pharmacist for cough syrup with a sore throat.

The man with a sore throat asked the pharmacist for cough syrup.

10. I gave a sizable donation to the candidate at the end of the political fundraiser event.

At the end of the political fundraiser event I gave a sizable donation to the candidate.

Dangling Modifiers

A modifier that opens a sentence must be followed immediately by the word it is meant to describe. Otherwise, the modifier is said to be dangling, and the sentence takes on an unintended meaning. For example, in the sentence

While reading the newspaper, my dog sat with me on the front steps.

the unintended meaning is that the *dog* was reading the paper. What the writer meant, of course, was that *he* (or *she*), the writer, was reading the paper. The writer should have said,

While reading the newspaper, *I* sat with my dog on the front steps.

The dangling modifier could also be corrected by placing the subject within the opening word group:

While *I* was reading the newspaper, my dog sat with me on the front steps.

Here are other sentences with dangling modifiers. Read the explanations of why they are dangling, and look carefully at how they are corrected.

Dangling	**Correct**
Shaving in front of the steamy mirror, the razor nicked Ed's chin. (*Who* was shaving in front of the mirror? The answer is not *razor* but *Ed*. The subject *Ed* must be added.)	Shaving in front of the steamy mirror, *Ed* nicked his chin with the razor. *Or:* While *Ed* was shaving in front of the steamy mirror, he nicked his chin with the razor.
While turning over the bacon, hot grease splashed my arm. (*Who* is turning over the bacon? The answer is not *hot grease*, as it unintentionally seems to be, but *I*. The subject *I* must be added.)	While *I* was turning over the bacon, hot grease splashed my arm. *Or:* While turning over the bacon, *I* was splashed by hot grease.
Taking the exam, the room was so stuffy that Keisha almost fainted. (*Who* took the exam? The answer is not the *room* but *Keisha*. The subject Keisha must follow the modifier.)	Taking the exam, *Keisha* found the room so stuffy that she almost fainted. *Or:* When *Keisha* took the exam, the room was so stuffy that she almost fainted.
To impress the interviewer, punctuality is essential. (*Who* is to impress the interviewer? The answer is not *punctuality* but *you*. The subject *you* must be added.)	To impress the interviewer, *you* must be punctual. *Or:* For *you* to impress the interviewer, punctuality is essential.

The examples above show two ways of correcting a dangling modifier. Decide on a logical subject and do one of the following:

1. Place the subject *within* the opening word group:

    While *Ed* was shaving in front of the steamy mirror, he nicked his chin.

> TIP In some cases, an appropriate subordinating word such as *when* must be added and the verb may have to be changed slightly as well.

2. Place the subject right *after* the opening word group:

    Shaving in front of the steamy mirror, *Ed* nicked his chin.

Note: Some instructors might consider the third example on this page a misplaced modifier since the subject of the phrase taking the exam—Keisha—does appear later in the sentence. However, since correcting the error would involve omitting one word (was) and changing additional words (Keisha found the room so stuffy that she), this type of error is classified as a dangling modifier in *Exploring Writing: Paragraphs and Essays*. In general, if a word group is a participial phrase, and if the phrase occurs at the beginning of the sentence but modifies a subject that does not appear until later in the sentence, it is called a dangling rather than a misplaced modifier.

ACTIVITY 2

Look at the opening words in each sentence and ask, *Who?* The subject that answers the question should be nearby in the sentence. If it is not, provide the logical subject by using either method of correction just described.

EXAMPLE

While pitching his tent, a snake bit Parker on the ankle.

While Parker was pitching his tent, a snake bit him on the ankle.

Or: While pitching his tent, Parker was bitten on the ankle by a snake.

1. Dancing on their hind legs, the audience cheered wildly as the elephants paraded by.

   The audience cheered wildly as the elephants paraded by dancing on their hind legs.

2. Last seen wearing dark glasses and a blond wig, the police spokesperson said the suspect was still being sought.

   _____

   _____

3. Pouring out the cereal, a coupon fell into my bowl of milk.

   Pouring out the cereal, into my bowl, a coupon of milk fell into

4. Escorted by dozens of police motorcycles, I knew the limousine carried someone important.

   I knew the limousine carried someone important who was escorted by dozens of police motorcycles.

5. Tired and exasperated, the fight we had was inevitable.

   _____

   _____

6. Packed tightly in a tiny can, Joe had difficulty removing the anchovies.

   _____

   _____

7. Kicked carelessly under the bed, Raquel finally found her sneakers.

   _____

   _____

8. Working at the copy machine, the morning dragged on.

   _____

   _____

REFLECTIVE ACTIVITY

Re-read any paragraph you wrote for an assignment in Chapter 9, "Process," or any essay you wrote while studying Chapter 18, "Patterns of Essay Development." Ask yourself if any of your sentences contain misplaced or dangling modifiers. If so, correct them using what you learned in Chapter 31. In each case, make sure you understand why the correction is much better than the original.

REVIEW TEST 1

Write MM for *misplaced modifier* or C for *correct* in the space provided for each sentence.

___MM___ 1. While in Vegas, I almost spent five hundred dollars at one slot machine.

___C___ 2. While in Vegas, I spent almost five hundred dollars at one slot machine.

___C___ 3. Roberto patiently waited as the meal he ordered was being prepared in the kitchen.

___MM___ 4. Roberto patiently waited as the meal was being prepared in the kitchen he ordered.

___MM___ 5. Kimberly registered for her two summer classes on Monday.

___C___ 6. On Monday, Kimberly registered for her two summer classes.

___MM___ 7. Behind the sofa, the dog hid the biscuit that was given to him by his owner.

___C___ 8. The dog hid the biscuit that was given to him by his owner behind the sofa.

___MM___ 9. I ordered a new hard drive that was refurbished from the Web site.

___C___ 10. I ordered from the Web site a new hard drive that was refurbished.

REVIEW TEST 2

Write DM for *dangling modifier* or C for *correct* in the space provided for each sentence.

___DM___ 1. While riding the bicycle, a vicious-looking German shepherd snapped at Tim's ankles.

___C___ 2. While Tim was riding the bicycle, a vicious-looking German shepherd snapped at his ankles.

_____C_____   3. Afraid to look his father in the eye, Charley kept his head bowed.

_____DM____   4. Afraid to look his father in the eye, Charley's head remained bowed.

_____DM____   5. Boring and silly, I turned the YouTube video off.

_____C_____   6. I turned off the boring and silly YouTube video.

_____DM____   7. Munching leaves from a tall tree, the giraffe fascinated the children.

_____C_____   8. Munching leaves from a tall tree, the children were fascinated by the giraffe.

_____DM____   9. At the age of twelve, several colleges had already accepted the boy genius.

_____C_____   10. At the age of twelve, the boy genius had already been accepted by several colleges.

REVIEW TEST 3

Make the changes needed to correct the misplaced and dangling modifiers in the following sentences.

Academic

1. Willa Cather, author of *O Pioneers*, often wrote about women doing unusual things in her books.

   Willa Cather author of O Pioneers often wrote about women doing unsual things in her books.

2. A disturbing short story, Edgar Allan Poe's "The Fall of the House of Usher," contains the standard features of a Gothic story.

   _____

   _____

3. Kate Chopin wrote about the oppression of women in traditional society in many stories.

   _____

   _____

4. In "And of Clay Are We Created," Isabel Allende writes about how the death of a young girl affects a young man with deep feeling.

   _____

   _____

5. Often reflecting very real situations and violent deaths, Ambrose Bierce wrote many short stories.

   _____

   _____

6. Reading "The Metamorphosis" by Franz Kafka, an unexplained fear of apples and large bugs is caused.

_____

_____

7. F. Scott Fitzgerald is best known for his novel, which takes place in the 1920s, *The Great Gatsby*.

_____

_____

8. Credited as the father of the American short story, "Rip Van Winkle" was written by Washington Irving.

_____

_____

9. Although "The Lottery" by Shirley Jackson was written in 1948, it is influencing other stories still in the twenty-first century.

_____

_____

10. Overlooking the connection and courage her family offers in "Everyday Use," Alice Walker writes about a young woman, Dee, who strives to find her identity.

_____

_____

_____

REVIEW TEST 4

Complete the following sentences. In each case, a logical subject should follow the opening words.

EXAMPLE

Looking through the door's peephole, *I couldn't see who rang the doorbell.*

1. Noticing the light turn yellow, _____

2. Being fragile, _____

3. While washing the car, _____

4. Although very expensive, _____

5. Driving past the cemetery, _____

SECTION I: GRAMMAR EDITING TEST I

Decide which of the following items are fragments or run-ons and which are correct. Place your answers in the spaces at the bottom by writing F for fragment, RO for run-on, and C for correct. Then correct the incorrect items by rewriting them in the margins or between the lines.

---

1. The heart is a muscle. 2. That pumps blood throughout the body. 3. The human heart is about the size of one's closed fist, it is shaped like a pear. 4. Located in the chest. 5. It can be found slightly to the left of the breastbone. 6. The human heart has two compartments. 7. Which are divided into two other chambers. 8. The upper sections are called the atria, the lower ones are called the ventricles. 9. The heart also contains valves. 10. Which control the flow of blood.

---

1. _____   2. _____   3. _____   4. _____   5. _____
6. _____   7. _____   8. _____   9. _____   10. _____

SECTION I: GRAMMAR EDITING TEST II

In the margins or between the lines, rewrite the following paragraphs to correct problems in subject–verb agreement, verb forms, and pronoun agreement and pronoun reference.

Starbucks may has gotten its start in 1971, but coffee and coffee-houses has been around much longer. There are many legends surrounding the beginnings of coffee, including one about an Ethiopian goatherd who found them goats munching on the berries (raw beans) of the local coffee plants, but most believe it was first roasted and brewed in the fifteenth century. Sufi monasteries in Yemen is credited for this discovery. In the 1500s, coffee was very popular in Egypt, Turkey, and Persia. Travelers to these countries discover coffee and bring it to Europe.

continued

People are drinking coffee at home, but the most popular way to drink it was at a coffeehouse. Coffee gains popularity throughout Europe as it was seen as a safe drink that enhanced their abilities to think and reason. In fact, people believe the French Revolution was started at the Café de Foy in 1789. By the nineteenth century, coffeehouses are the place to be and be seen. Many famous writers, musicians, and politicians meets in coffeehouses to exchange ideas and implement new policies. In the twenty-first century, people who purchase coffee and relax in the atmosphere of Starbucks cafés should know that he or she was part of hundreds of years of tradition.

SECTION I: GRAMMAR EDITING TEST III

Rewrite the following e-mail to correct problems with adjectives and adverbs, with misplaced or dangling modifiers, and with pronoun agreement and reference.

From: rose889@gmail.com
Sent: Saturday, August 24, 2013 12:03 PM
To: dodgers69@comcast.net
Subject: your recovery

Dad,

Mom called me on my cell phone late last night, to tell me that you have not been feeling good over the past few days because your medications are making you dizzy and weak. However, the doctor said that by taking your medicines regularly, your condition should improve within weeks. I know that you'll feel a lot better then. Remember that following the doctor's orders close is the only way to recovery. Sticking with the plan, your helath sure will return and you can face the future more confident than ever.

You are lucky that your lungs suffered only minor damage. Smoking cigarettes for that long, serious illnesses could have been contracted. Of course we all pray that you never smoke again. Going back to cigarettes, your current struggle to get healthy will have been for nothing. Remember

continued

that a full recovery never comes quick. However, each day your condition will improve, slow but sure. You will actually feel yourself getting more and more stronger as the months without cigarettes pass. Your sense of smell will return, and foods will taste more better than ever. Your clothes will stop stinking so bad, too. Finally, your urge to have a smoke will become less stronger, and you will wonder what made you start smoking in the first place.

____

Mechanics

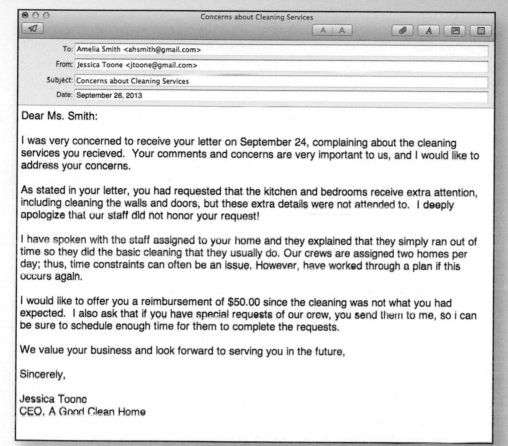

RESPONDING TO IMAGES

People often forget to apply sentence skills to their writing when composing e-mails. The two e-mails pictured here are geared toward different audiences, but both contain sentence-skills mistakes. Do you think such mistakes should be excusable in e-mails? Compare the different audiences, form, and style of each e-mail; then find and correct the three errors in the first e-mail.

Manuscript Form

When you hand in a paper for any course, it will probably be judged first by its format. It is important, then, to make the paper look attractive, neat, and easy to read. Here is a checklist you should use when preparing a paper for an instructor:

____ • Is the paper full-size, 8½ by 11 inches?

____ • Are there wide margins (1 inch) all around the paper? In particular, have you been careful not to crowd the right hand or bottom margin?

____ • If the paper is handwritten, have you

Used a blue or black pen?

Been careful not to overlap letters or to make decorative loops on letters?

Made all your letters distinct, with special attention to a, e, i, o, and u—five letters that people sometimes write illegibly?

Kept all your capital letters clearly distinct from small letters?

____ • Have you centered the title of your paper on the first line of page 1? Have you been careful *not* to put quotation marks around the title and *not* to underline it? Have you been careful *not* to place the title in bold or in a different font type or size? Have you capitalized all the words in the title except short connecting words like *of, for, the, and, in,* and *to*?

____ • Have you included a double-space between the title and the first line of your paper?

____ • Have you indented the first line of each paragraph about five spaces (half an inch) from the left-hand margin?

____ • Have you made commas, periods, and other punctuation marks firm and clear? If you are typing, have you left a space after a period?

____ • If you have broken any words at the end of a line, have you been careful to break only between syllables?

____ • Have you put your name, the date, and other information at the end of the paper (or wherever your instructor has specified)?

Also ask yourself these important questions about the title and the first sentence of your paper:

_____ • Is your title made up of several words that tell what the paper is about? (The title should be just several words, not a complete sentence.)

_____ • Does the first sentence of your paper stand independent of the title? (The reader should *not* have to use the words in the title to make sense of the opening sentence.)

Use the checklist to locate the seven mistakes in format in the following lines from a student paper. Explain the mistakes in the spaces provided. One mistake is described for you as an example.

ACTIVITY 1

	"Being alone"
	This is something that I simply cannot tolerate, and I will predictably
	go to great lengths to prevent it. For example, if I know that

1. Hyphenate only between syllables (predict-ably, not predi-ctably).

2. _____

3. _____

4. _____

5. _____

6. _____

7. _____

Capital Letters

Main Uses of Capital Letters

Capital letters are used with

1. First word in a sentence or direct quotation
2. Names of persons and the word *I*
3. Names of particular places and institutions
4. Names of days of the week, months, and holidays
5. Names of commercial products
6. Titles of books, magazines, newspapers, articles, stories, poems, films, television shows, songs, papers that you write, and the like
7. Names of companies, associations, unions, clubs, religious and political groups, and other organizations

Each use is illustrated in this chapter.

First Word in a Sentence or Direct Quotation

The corner grocery was robbed last night.

The alien said, "Take me to your leader."

"If you need help," said Teri, "call me. I'll be over in no time."

In the third example above, *If* and *I'll* are capitalized because they start new sentences. But *call* is not capitalized, because it is part of the first sentence.

Names and Titles

Names of Persons and the Word I

Last night, I saw a hilarious movie starring Ben Stiller and Jack Black.

Names of Particular Places and Institutions

Although Bill dropped out of Port Charles High School, he eventually earned his degree and got a job with Atlas Realty Company.

But   Use small letters if the specific name is not given.

Although Bill dropped out of high school, he eventually earned his degree and got a job with a real estate company.

Names of Days of the Week, Months, and Holidays

On the last Friday afternoon in May, the day before Memorial Day, my boss is having a barbecue for all the employees.

But   Use small letters for the seasons—summer, fall, winter, spring.

Most people feel more energetic in the spring and fall.

Names of Commercial Products

Keith installed a new Sony stereo into his old Ford Ranger pickup.

But   Use small letters for the *type* of product (stereo, pickup, and so on).

Titles of Books, Magazines, Newspapers, Articles, Stories, Poems, Films, Television Shows, Songs, Papers That You Write, and the Like

We read the book *Hiroshima*, by John Hersey, for our history class.

In the doctor's waiting room, I watched *General Hospital*, read an article in *Reader's Digest*, and leafed through the *Miami Herald*.

Names of Companies, Associations, Unions, Clubs, Religious and Political Groups, and Other Organizations

Joe Naples is a Roman Catholic, but his wife is a Methodist.

The Hilldale Square Dancers' Club has won many competitions.

Brian, a member of Bricklayers Local 431 and the Knights of Columbus, works for Ace Construction.

ACTIVITY 1

Underline the words that need capitals in the following sentences. Then write the capitalized form of each word in the space provided. The number of spaces tells you how many corrections to make in each case.

EXAMPLE

In our biology class, each student must do a report on an article in the magazine *scientific american*.   <u>Scientific</u>   <u>American</u>

1. Meghan's collection of beatles souvenirs includes a pair of tickets from their last concert in candlestick park in San Francisco.

   <u>Candlestick</u>   <u>Park</u>

2. Yumi read in *natural health* magazine that abraham lincoln suffered from severe depression.

   <u>Natural Health</u>   <u>Abraham Lincoln</u>

3. When i have a cold, I use vicks ointment and chew halls lozenges.

   <u>I</u>   <u>Halls</u>   <u>Lozenges</u>

4. Since no man volunteered for the job, the boy scouts in <u>springfield, illinois,</u> have a woman troop leader.

Illinos Spring-field

5. A nature trail for the blind in <u>cape cod</u>, <u>massachusetts</u>, has signs written in Braille that encourage visitors to smell and touch the plants.

Cape   Cod   Massachusetts

6. Some of the most popular items at a restaurant called <u>big river</u> are <u>chilean</u> sea bass and <u>atlantic</u> clam chowder.

Big   River   Chilean   Atlantic

7. My father is a confirmed Dallas <u>cowboys</u> fan, though he lives in <u>boston.</u>

Cowboys   Boston

8. Isabella bought a <u>diet pepsi</u> to wash down her <u>hostess twinkie.</u>

Diet   Peppi   Hostess   Twinkie

9. Vince listened to songs by U2 and Coldplay on his iPod while Donna read an article in *glamour* titled "What Do <u>men</u> Really <u>want?</u>"

Glamour   Men   Want

10. After having her baby, <u>joan</u> received a card from one of her friends that read, "<u>congratulations,</u> we all knew you had it in you."

Joan   Congratulations

Other Uses of Capital Letters

Capital letters are also used with

1. Names that show family relationships
2. Titles of persons when used with their names
3. Specific school courses
4. Languages
5. Geographic locations
6. Historical periods and events
7. Races, nations, and nationalities
8. Opening and closing of a letter

Each use is illustrated on the following pages.

Names That Show Family Relationships

All his life, Father has been addicted to gadgets.

I browsed through Grandmother's collection of old photographs.

Aunt Florence and Uncle Bill bought a mobile home.

But   Do not capitalize words like *mother, father, grandmother, grandfather, uncle, aunt,* and so on when they are preceded by a possessive word (such as *my, your, his, her, our, their*).

> All his life, my father has been addicted to gadgets.

> I browsed through my grandmother's collection of old photographs.

> My aunt and uncle bought a mobile home.

Titles of Persons When Used with Their Names

> I contributed to Senator McCain's campaign fund.

> Is Dr. Gomez on vacation?

> Professor Adams announced that there would be no tests in the course.

But   Use lowercase letters when titles appear by themselves, without specific names.

> I contributed to my senator's campaign fund.

> Is the doctor on vacation?

> The professor announced that there would be no tests in the course.

Specific School Courses

> The college offers evening sections of Introductory Psychology I, Abnormal Psychology, Psychology and Statistics, and Educational Psychology.

But   Use lowercase letters for general subject areas.

> The college offers evening sections of many psychology courses.

Languages

> My grandfather's Polish accent makes his English difficult to understand.

Geographic Locations

> He grew up in the Midwest but moved to the South to look for a better job.

But   Use lowercase letters in directions.

> Head west for five blocks and then turn south on State Street.

Historical Periods and Events

> During the Middle Ages, the Black Death killed over one-quarter of Europe's population.

Races, Nations, and Nationalities

The questionnaire asked if the head of our household was Caucasian, African American, Asian, Latino, or Native American.

Tanya has lived on army bases in Germany, Italy, and Spain.

Denise's beautiful features reflect her Chinese and Mexican parentage.

Opening and Closing of a Letter

Dear Sir: Sincerely yours,

Dear Ms. Henderson: Truly yours,

Capitalize only the first word in a closing.

ACTIVITY 2   Underline the words that need capitals in the following sentences. Then write the capitalized forms of the words in the spaces provided. The number of spaces tells you how many corrections to make in each case.

1. The students at the university of hawaii enjoyed visiting the beach, mount kilauea, and Honolulu.

   University _Hawaii_ _Mount_ _Kilauea_

2. Secretary of state henry kissinger played a major role during president Nixon's years in office.

   State _Henry_ _Kissinger_ _President_ _Of_

3. The students in american indian literature 267 decided that *tracks* by louise erdrich was their favorite book.

   American _Indian_ _Literature_ _Tracks_
   Louise _Erdrich_

4. John and sue are taking a cruise through the panama canal.

   Sue _Panama_ _Canal_

5. Three countries I would like to visit one day are greece, morocco, and india.

   Greece _Morocco_ _India_

Unnecessary Use of Capitals

ACTIVITY 3   Many errors occur when capitalization is used when it is not needed. Underline the incorrectly capitalized words in the following sentences, and write the correct forms in the spaces provided. The number of spaces tells you how many corrections to make in each sentence.

1. George Washington's <u>Forces</u> starved at Valley Forge because Pennsylvania <u>Farmers</u> preferred to sell food to the British for cash.

    forces   farmer

2. The virus damaged the files on my Brother's Dell Computer.

    brother's   computer

3. The Country cheered during the 2008 Summer Olympics when Michael Phelps won a record-breaking eight Gold Medals in Beijing.

    Record - Breaking   Eight

4. In his Book titled *Offbeat Museums*, Saul Rubin tells about various Unusual Museums, such as the Kansas Barbed Wire museum.

    unusual museums book   Museum

5. The theory of relativity, which Einstein developed when he was only twenty-six, led to the invention of the Electron Microscope, Television, and Atomic bomb.

    electron microscope television ,

REVIEW TEST 1

Add or delete capitals where needed in the following sentences.

EXAMPLE

My favorite quote about ~~T~~hinking is from the ~~f~~rench philosopher, Descartes, who stated, "~~i~~ think, therefore ~~i~~ am."

1. In 1841, Ralph Waldo emerson wrote, "what is the hardest task in the world? to think."

2. George bernard shaw, the irish playwright, once wrote, "few people think more than two or three times a year; I have made an International reputation for myself by thinking once a week."

3. The saying, "A man is but the product of his thoughts; what he thinks, he becomes," was written by Mohandas k. Gandhi in *ethical religion*.

4. william james, a nineteenth-century american Philosopher, stated, "a great many people think they are thinking when they are merely rearranging their prejudices."

5. Don Marquis, a Newspaper columnist, challenged people by stating, "if you make people think they're thinking, They'll love you; but if you really make them think, they'll hate you."

6. In "faculties of the mind," the marquis of halifax wrote, "A man may dwell so long upon a thought that it may take him prisoner."

7. In 1854, Henry David Thoreau wrote *walden; or life in the woods*, a book that reflected on life and meaning. In it, he stated, " if i were confined to a corner of a garret all my days, like a spider, the world would be just as large to me while i had my thoughts about me."

8. "great thoughts spring from the heart," was written in the Eighteenth century by Vauvenargues, a french essayist.

9. Samuel Butler, best known for his novel, *the way of all flesh,* once wrote, "all Thinking is . . . a state of unrest tending towards equilibrium."

10. albert schweitzer wrote, "Renunciation of thinking is a Declaration of spiritual bankruptcy."

REVIEW TEST 2

On separate paper, write

1. Seven sentences demonstrating the seven main uses of capital letters.

2. Eight sentences demonstrating the eight other uses of capital letters.

Numbers and Abbreviations

Numbers

Here are three helpful rules for using numbers.

Rule 1

Spell out numbers that take no more than two words. Otherwise, use the numbers themselves.

> In Jody's kitchen is her collection of seventy-two cookbooks.
>
> Jody has a file of 350 recipes.
>
> It will take about two weeks to fix the computer database.
>
> Since a number of people use the database, the company will lose over 150 workdays.
>
> Only twelve students have signed up for the field trip.
>
> Nearly 250 students came to the lecture.

Rule 2

Be consistent when you use a series of numbers. If some numbers in a sentence or paragraph require more than two words, then use numbers for the others, too.

> After the storm, maintenance workers unclogged 46 drains, removed 123 broken tree limbs, and rescued 3 kittens who were stuck in a drainpipe.

Rule 3

Use numbers to show dates, times, addresses, percentages, and chapters of a book.

> The burglary was committed on October 30, 2010, but not discovered until January 2, 2011.
>
> Before I went to bed, I set my alarm for 6:45 A.M. (*But*: Spell out numbers before *o'clock*. For example: I didn't get out of bed until seven o'clock.)
>
> The library is located at 45 West 52nd Street.
>
> When you take the skin off a piece of chicken, you remove about 40 percent of the fat.
>
> The name of the murderer is revealed in Chapter 8 on page 236.

| ACTIVITY 1 | Cross out the mistakes in numbers and write the corrections in the spaces provided. |

1. The Pan-Pacific Festival will begin at ~~four-thirty~~ in front of the park bandstand at ~~ninety-four~~ North ~~Fifty-Third~~ Street.

   _4:30_   _94_   _53ʳᵈ_

2. Christine spent 8 hours writing all 15 pages of her English paper.

   _____   _____

3. My supervisor wants me to finish at least ~~sixty~~ percent of the projects by July fifteen.

   _60_   _15ᵗʰ_

Abbreviations

Using abbreviations can save you time when you take notes. In formal writing, however, you should avoid most abbreviations. Listed below are some of the few abbreviations that are considered acceptable in compositions. Note that a period is used after most abbreviations.

1. Mr., Mrs., Ms., Jr., Sr., Dr. when used with names:

   Mrs. Johnson   Dr. Garcia   Howard Kelley, Jr.

2. Time references:

   A.M. or a.m.   P.M. or p.m.   B.C., A.D.

3. Initials in a person's name:

   J. Edgar Hoover   John F. Kennedy   Samuel L. Jackson

4. Organizations, technical words, and company names known primarily by their initials:

   IBM   UNICEF   ABC   IRS   NBA   FAA

| ACTIVITY 2 | Cross out the words that should not be abbreviated, and correct them in the spaces provided. |

1. I hope to graduate with my ~~deg.~~ by mid ~~Aug.~~, if not sooner.

   degree   _August_

2. Galen needs to make an ~~appt.~~ with Dr. Wong, who is an endocrinologist, in ~~Feb.~~ to monitor his diabetes.

   Appointment   ~~February~~ _February_

3. I want to find an inexpensive ~~apart.~~ near campus with one ~~bdrm.~~ and a separate kitchen.

   Apartment   _bedroom_

REFLECTIVE ACTIVITY

Review a paragraph you wrote for an assignment in Chapter 10, "Cause and Effect," or an essay you wrote while studying Chapter 18, "Patterns of Essay Development." Do you find any errors in mechanics, specifically manuscript form, capitalization, and the use of numbers and abbreviations? If so, correct them according to what you learned in Chapters 32–34.

REVIEW TEST

The following e-mail contains errors in capitalization and the use of numbers and abbreviations. Rewrite the e-mail to correct these errors in the margins or in spaces between the lines. You should make twenty-five corrections in all.

From: Sarah L.

Sent: Saturday, August 24, 2013

To: Prof. Jane Smith

Subject: Spanish 2 Schedule, Weeks 1- three

Hi Prof. Smith:

I wanted to make sure I had our assignments clear for the next
(Spanish) *(September 8th)*
3 weeks in Span. class. By Sept. eight, I am supposed to learn to
(21)
count from 1 to twenty-one and study Chapter One in the textbook.

For the next week of class, I will need to read Chapters 2 and 3, and
(page 63) *(3rd)*
complete the 5 exercises on pg. sixty-three. In the third week of class,
(1:30)
I will need to visit Wash. h.s. from 9:30 am until one-thirty pm each

day. During the visit, each of us in class will work with the

h.s. Span. Class. Is this right?

Thank you.

Sarah leet

SECTION II: MECHANICS EDITING TEST I

The following sentences contain errors in capitalization and in the use of numbers and abbreviations. Rewrite these sentences to correct these errors in the margins or in spaces between lines. You should make twenty-six corrections in all.

Aaron Copland was an important american Composer. Born in new york city on november nineteenth, 1900, he studied music in paris, france, during the early years of the twentieth century. Copland's early works were inspired by jazz. During the great depression of the 1930s and 1940s, however, he turned to folk songs, using themes from this music in works entitled *lincoln portrait, billy the kid,* and his masterpiece *Appalachian spring*. During this period he also wrote scores for films like *Of Mice and Men*, which is based on john steinbeck's novel of the same name. One of Copland's most famous works is " fanfare for the common man," which appears in a symphony he wrote in the nineteen forties. Copland died on dec. the second, 1990, in Tarrytown, N. York, at the age of 90.

SECTION II: MECHANICS EDITING TEST II

The following paragraphs contain errors in capitalization and the use of numbers and abbreviations. Rewrite each paragraph to correct these errors in the margins or in spaces between lines. You should make twenty-four corrections in all.

The metric system, a standard system of measurement, was officially adopted in france in seventeen ninety one. Today it is used in continental europe and in other parts of the World, except for english-speaking Countries. It is also used by the Scientific community around the globe. It is based on the meter, which measures a little more than 36 ins., or about one yard. Another metric unit is the gram. One hundred grams are known as a centigram; one thousand grams

continued

are called a kilogram. These units measure an object's Mass. A gram is very small. In fact, an ounce, a measurement in the english system, equals 28 grams. The liter, another metric unit, measures volume. A liter equals about 1 Eng. quart.

The English system, still in use in Great Britain and the United Sts., has different units. For example, measurements of length include the inch, the foot, and the yd. The inch is equivalent to about two-and-one-half centimeters in the metric system. The English system also includes a furlong, which is two hundred and twenty yards or about two hundred and one meters; it also includes the mile, which is five thousand two hundred and eighty-nine feet—slightly more than one-and-one-half kilometers. finally, the Engl. System measures volume in pints, quarts, and gallons. One gln. is approximately four-and-one-half liters.

SECTION III

Punctuation

RESPONDING TO IMAGES

Can you find the two punctuation errors in the sign pictured here? What should be done to correct them?

Apostrophe

The two main uses of the apostrophe are

1. To show the omission of one or more letters in a contraction
2. To show ownership or possession

Each use is explained in this chapter.

Apostrophe in Contractions

A *contraction* is formed when two words are combined to make one word. An apostrophe is used to show where letters are omitted in forming the contractions. Here are two contractions:

have + not = haven't (the *o* in *not* has been omitted)

I + will = I'll (the *wi* in *will* has been omitted)

Following are some other common contractions:

I + am = I'm	it + is = it's
I + have = I've	it + has = it's
I + had = I'd	is + not = isn't
who + is = who's	could + not = couldn't
do + not = don't	I + would = I'd
did + not = didn't	they + are = they're

Will + not has an unusual contraction: won't.

Write the contractions for the words in parentheses. One is done for you.

1. (Is not) **Isn't** the trigonometry exam scheduled for the last week of December?

2. I (do not) **don't** know (who is) **who's** invited to Dillon's birthday party.

3. (It is) **It's** unfortunate that the classes I need to take (are not) **aren't** offered this semester.

4. Our teacher (can not) _can't_ expect us to know all the answers because (we are) _we're_ still learning the material.

5. (I have) _I've_ a reservation at the Italian restaurant for Saturday night, but I (could not) _couldn't_ get tickets to the concert.

> **TIP** Even though contractions are common in everyday speech and in written dialogue, it is often best to avoid them in formal writing.

Apostrophe to Show Ownership or Possession

To show ownership or possession, we can use such words as *belongs to, possessed by, owned by,* or (most commonly) *of.*

> the umbrella *that belongs to* Mark
>
> the toys *possessed by* children
>
> the DVD player *owned by* the school
>
> the gentleness *of* my father

But the apostrophe plus *s* (if the word does not end in *s*) is often the quickest and easiest way to show possession. Thus we can say

> Mark's umbrella
>
> children's toys
>
> the school's DVD player
>
> my father's gentleness

Points to Remember

1. The *'s* goes with the owner or possessor (in the examples given, *Mark, children, the school, my father*). What follows is the person or thing possessed (in the examples given, *the umbrella, the toys, the DVD player, gentleness*).

2. There should always be a break between the word and *'s*.

    Mark's   not   *Mark's*

    Yes   No

3. An apostrophe plus *s* is used to show possession with a singular word even if the word already ends in *s*: for example, Doris's purse (the purse belonging to Doris).

ACTIVITY 2

Working in pairs with a fellow classmate, rewrite the *italicized* part of each of the sentences below, using 's to show possession. Remember that the 's goes with the owner or possessor.

EXAMPLE

The wing of the bluejay was broken.

The bluejay's wing was broken.

1. *The annoying voice of the comedian* irritated me, so I changed the TV channel.

   The comedian's annoying voice irritated me.

2. *The performance of the quarterback* is inconsistent.

   The quarterback's performance is inconsistent

3. *The thin hand belonging to the old woman* felt as dry as parchment.

   The old woman's thin hand felt as dry as parchment

4. *In the window of the jewelry store* is a sign reading "Ears Pierced While You Wait."

   In the jewelry store's wind a sign reading "Ears Pierced While You Wait"

5. A fly flew into *the mouth of the TV weatherperson.*

   _____

6. *The new denim shirt belonging to Lamont* was as scratchy as sandpaper.

   _____

7. *The hair belonging to Rachel* is usually not green—she colored it for Halloween.

   _____

8. *The bowl of cereal belonging to Dennis* refused to snap, crackle, or pop.

   _____

9. *The Honda owned by Donna* was crammed with boxes and furniture.

   Donna's Honda was crammed w/ boxes and furniture

10. *The previous tenant of the apartment* had painted all the walls bright green.

    The apartment's previous tenant had painted all the walls bright green

ACTIVITY 3

Add 's to each of the following words to make it the possessor or owner of something. Then write sentences using the words. The first one is done for you.

1. rock star ___rock star's_____

   The rock star's limousine pulled up to the curb.

2. Felipe ___*Felipe's*___

Felipe's mother was very ill.

3. pilot ___*pilot's*___

The pilot's ~~mma~~ planes came late

4. neighbor ___*neighbor's*___

The neighbor's dog got loose

5. school ___*school's*___

The school's policy was true

6. soldier ___*soldier's*___

The soldier's eheif was very mean.

Apostrophe versus Possessive Pronouns

Do not use an apostrophe with possessive pronouns. They already show ownership. Possessive pronouns include *his, hers, its, yours, ours,* and *theirs.*

Incorrect	**Correct**
The files are on his' laptop.	The files are on his laptop.
The restored Model T is theirs'.	The restored Model T is theirs.
The decision is yours'.	The decision is yours.
The plaid suitcase is ours'.	The plaid suitcase is ours.
The lion charged its' prey.	The lion charged its prey.

Apostrophe versus Simple Plurals

When you want to make a word plural, just add an *s* at the end of the word. Do not add an apostrophe. For example, the plural of the word *movie* is *movies*, not *movie's* or *movies'*.

Look at this sentence:

Tim coveted his roommate's collection of music downloads and Nintendo Wii games.

The words *downloads* and *games* are simple plurals, meaning more than one download, more than one game. The plural is shown by adding *s* only. On the other hand, the *'s* after *roommate* shows possession—that the roommate owns the downloads and games.

ACTIVITY 4	Insert an apostrophe where needed to show possession in the following sentences. Write *plural* above words where the *s* ending simply means more than one thing.

EXAMPLE

                   plural
Ryan's computer has two viruses.

         Plural
1. Old historic houses are Sams main interest, but he also likes modern houses.

2. Reurbanization districts are popping up all over the country. Johns *[plural]* house is in such a district.

3. Old mansions *[plural]* are often refurbished and used as wedding venues.

4. Jeffs porch has a large swing that the neighbors *[Plural]* kids like to use.

5. Andreas husband collects cars *[plural]* and currently has three classic convertibles and two racecars.

6. Erics home has a private pool, but Micheles family *[plural]* uses the neighbor-hood pool.

7. Jasons car has been hit twice this week, so he is parking in his brothers *[plural]* garage.

8. My best friends cupcakes *[plural]* come in flavors like chocolate raspberry and pink lemonade.

9. Tims shoe collection includes *[plural]* forty pairs of Birkenstocks.

10. The administrative assistants office was broken into and his computers *[plural]* were stolen.

Apostrophe with Plurals Ending in -s

Plurals that end in -s show possession simply by adding the apostrophe, rather than an apostrophe plus s.

the Thompsons' porch

the players' victory

her parents' motor home

the Killers' latest CD

the soldiers' hats

Add an apostrophe where needed.	ACTIVITY 5

1. Several campers' tents collapsed during the storm.

2. The Murrays' phone bills are often over $400 a month.

3. Many buildings' steep steps make it difficult for wheelchair users to gain access.

4. The twins' habit of dressing alike was started by their mother when they were children.

5. At the crowded intersection, several young men rushed out to wash the cars' windshields.

REVIEW TEST

In the paragraph below, underline the words that either need apostrophes or have misused apostrophes. Then, in the spaces between the lines, correct the mistakes. You should make eleven corrections in all.

Spiders silk is an amazing substance! Paul Hillyard says in *The Book of the Spider* (1994), "For an equal [diameter], spider silk is stronger than steel and about as strong as nylon. It is, however much more resilient and can stretch several time's before breaking—it is twice as elastic as nylon and more difficult to break than rubber." Because of it's strength and durability, many scientists are studying spider's dragline silk, a silk that can be extended 30 to 50 percent of it's length before it breaks. The U.S. Army is interested in spider silk to use in product's like bulletproof vests, and medical scientists are interested in creating artificial ligaments and tendons from spider silk. All these study's show that spider silk has the qualities' to be useful, but creating enough has proven difficult. One researcher, however, has been genetically modifying goats to produce the spider silk protein in the goats milk. Once the milk is specially processed, threads of spider silk are created. Researchers' are also studying alfalfa plants ability to produce the silk protein. It's highly likely that one day in the near future, spider silk may be mass produced by nonspider methods.

Quotation Marks

The two main uses of quotation marks are

1. To set off the exact words of a speaker or writer

2. To set off the titles of short works

Each use is explained here.

TIP Quotation marks are also used in research papers to signify direct quotes. See pages 371–376.

Quotation Marks to Set Off the Words of a Speaker or Writer

Use quotation marks to show the exact words of a speaker or writer.

"I feel as though I've been here before," Angie murmured to her husband.
(Quotation marks set off the exact words that Angie spoke to her husband.)

Ben Franklin once wrote, "To lengthen thy life, lessen thy meals."
(Quotation marks set off the exact words that Ben Franklin wrote.)

"Did you know," said the nutrition expert, "that it's healthier to be ten pounds overweight?"
(Two pairs of quotation marks are used to enclose the nutrition expert's exact words.)

The biology professor said, "Ants are a lot like human beings. They farm their own food and raise smaller insects as livestock. And, like humans, ants send armies to war."
(Note that the end quotation marks do not come until the end of the biology professor's speech. Place quotation marks before the first quoted word and after the last quoted word. As long as no interruption occurs in the speech, do not use quotation marks for each new sentence.)

TIP In the four examples above, notice that a comma sets the quoted part off from the rest of the sentence. Also, observe that commas and periods at the end of a quotation always go *inside* quotation marks.

ACTIVITY 1

Complete the following statements, which explain how capital letters, commas, and periods are used in quotations. Refer to the four previous examples as guides.

1. Every quotation begins with a _____ letter.

2. When a quotation is split (as in the sentence about the nutrition expert), the second part does not begin with a capital letter unless it is a _____ sentence.

3. _____ are used to separate the quoted part of a sentence from the rest of the sentence.

4. Commas and periods that come at the end of a quotation go _____ the quotation marks.

The answers are *capital, new, Commas,* and *inside.*

ACTIVITY 2

Place quotation marks around the exact words of a speaker or writer in the sentences that follow.

1. Several people have been credited with saying, The more I see of people, the more I like dogs.

2. Beverly asked, Do you give a discount to senior citizens?

3. This hamburger is raw! cried Leon.

4. The bumper sticker on the rear of the battered old car read, Don't laugh—it's paid for.

5. I know why Robin Hood robbed only the rich, said the comedian. The poor don't have any money.

6. These CDs, proclaimed the television announcer, are not sold in any store.

7. When chefs go to great lengths, the woman at the diet center said, I go to great widths.

8. If I go with you to the dinner party, my friend said, you must promise not to discuss politics.

9. On a tombstone in a Maryland cemetery are the words Here lies an atheist, all dressed up and no place to go.

10. The columnist advised, Be nice to people on your way up because you'll meet them on your way down.

ACTIVITY 3

1. Write a sentence in which you quote a favorite expression of someone you know. In the same sentence, identify the person's relationship to you.

EXAMPLE   My grandfather loves to say, "It can't be as bad as all that."

_____

_____

2. Write a quotation that contains the words *Pablo asked Teresa*. Write a second quotation that includes the words *Teresa replied*.

_____

_____

_____

_____

3. Quote an interesting sentence or two from a book, magazine, or other published work. In the same sentence, identify the title and author of the work.

EXAMPLE   In *The Dilbert Desk Calendar* by Scott Adams, the cartoon character Dilbert says, "I can please only one person per day. Today isn't your day, and tomorrow isn't looking good either."

_____

_____

_____

_____

_____

Indirect Quotations

An indirect quotation is a rewording of someone else's comments rather than a word-for-word direct quotation. The word *that* often signals an indirect quotation.

Direct Quotation	**Indirect Quotation**
The nurse said, "Some babies cannot tolerate cows' milk." (The nurse's exact spoken words are given, so quotation marks are used.)	The nurse said that some babies cannot tolerate cows' milk. (We learn the nurse's words indirectly, so no quotation marks are used.)
Vicky's note to Dan read, "I'll be home by 7:30." (The exact words that Vicky wrote in the note are given, so quotation marks are used.)	Vicky left a note for Dan saying that she would be home by 7:30. (We learn Vicky's words indirectly, so no quotation marks are used.)

ACTIVITY 4

Rewrite the following sentences, changing words as necessary to convert the sentences into direct quotations. The first one has been done for you as an example.

1. Leona asked me if I wanted to study at the library after class.

   <u>Leona asked me, "Do you want to study at the library after class?"</u>

   _____

2. My supervisor said that I should apply for the opening in Seattle.

   _____

   _____

3. Heidi asked if she could order the Catch of the Day without the béarnaise sauce.

   _____

   _____

4. The witness testified in court that she saw the suspect flee the convenience store with a gun.

   _____

   _____

5. Professor Quigley said that he grades on a curve.

   _____

   _____

Quotation Marks to Set Off Titles of Short Works

Titles of short works are usually set off by quotation marks, while titles of long works are italicized. Use quotation marks to set off titles of such short works as articles in books, newspapers, or magazines; chapters in a book; short stories; poems; and songs. But you should italicize titles of books, newspapers, magazines, plays, movies, CDs, and television shows. Following are some examples.

Quotation Marks	**Italics**
the essay "On Self-Respect"	in the book *Slouching Towards Bethlehem*
the article "The Problem of Acid Rain"	in the newspaper the *New York Times*
the article "Living with Inflation"	in the magazine *Newsweek*
the chapter "Chinese Religion"	in the book *Paths of Faith*
the story "Hands"	in the book *Winesburg, Ohio*

the poem "When I Have Fears"   in the book *Complete Poems of John Keats*

the song "Ziggy Stardust"   in the CD *Changes*

                                    the television show *CSI:NY*

                                    the movie *Titanic*

> **TIP** When you are typing a paper, you should always italicize longer works; however, if you are handwriting a paper, you should underline longer works. For example, *The Hunger Games* by Suzanne Collins would be handwritten <u>The Hunger Games</u> by Suzanne Collins.

Use quotation marks as needed. Underline titles that should be italicized. Once you have completed the activity, go over your answers with a partner.

1. My personal trainer told me to read the article Five Ways to Trick Yourself into Eating Less, which appeared in Newsweek.

2. The title of Maya Angelou's autobiography I Know Why the Caged Bird Sings comes from Paul Laurence Dunbar's poem Sympathy.

3. I was so inspired to read the chapter It's About How to Live Your Life in Randy Pausch's book The Last Lecture.

4. Everyone in the class was inspired after reading Beth Johnson's article The Professor Is a Dropout about Guadalupe Quintanilla.

5. The movie The Fellowship of the Ring, which starred Viggo Mortensen as Aragon, was originally cast with Stuart Townsend in that role.

6. The movie Alien has many spin-offs, including an entire film series, novels, comic books, and video games.

7. The history test will cover the chapters The First World War and The Second World War.

8. The American Broadcasting Company's ABC's Wide World of Sports was the longest running sports show on television.

9. Michael Jackson holds the record for the highest selling album, entitled Thriller, with such songs as Beat It and Billie Jean.

10. I am reading the essay Of Our Spiritual Strivings, which was first published in W.E.B. DuBois's The Souls of Black Folk.

Other Uses of Quotation Marks

Quotation marks are also used as follows:

1. To set off special words or phrases from the rest of a sentence:

> In grade school, we were taught a little jingle about the spelling rule "*i* before *e*."

What is the difference between "it's" and "its"?
(In this book, *italics* are often used instead of quotation marks to set off words.)

2. To mark off a quotation within a quotation:

The physics professor said, "For class on Friday, do the problems at the end of the chapter titled 'Work and Energy.'"

Brendan remarked, "Did you know that Humphrey Bogart never actually said, 'Play it again, Sam' in the movie *Casablanca*?"

> **TIP** A quotation within a quotation is indicated by *single* quotation marks, as shown above.

REVIEW TEST 1

Insert quotation marks where needed in the sentences that follow. One sentence is correct; mark that sentence with a *C*.

1. The May 2011 issue of *Diabetes Forecast* included articles such as Kids, I Have Diabetes: How to Talk to Children about Your Disease and Dreaming of a Healthy Tomorrow.

2. An article titled Nat Strand's Amazing Ways highlighted Nat Strand, who was part of a two-woman team to win a million-dollar race around the world.

3. Carolyn Butler wrote about how the winner of CBS's reality show *The Amazing Race* had the added challenge of controlling her diabetes while racing.

4. The race, said Strand, is probably the hardest situation you can imagine for a diabetic.

5. In the article, Butler asked Strand, How do you pack light when you have diabetes—and absolutely no idea where you are going?

6. Strand replied, I had so much [diabetes-related] stuff that I didn't even pack a hairbrush.

7. When asked about the boiled sheep's head she had to eat during one challenge, Strand replied, I just gritted my teeth and hoped that since it was protein, it was low-carb.

8. Later in the article, Strand's teammate Kat Chang remarked, I definitely have a new respect and understanding for diabetes—that it is just so, so so difficult to manage, and it is absolutely 24/7.

9. After describing what the race was like for Strand and discussing the outpouring of support for the diabetic competitor, Butler wrote, In June she [Strand] will lobby members of Congress with the Juvenile Diabetes Research Foundation.

10. Strand ended her interview saying, I'm never going to say diabetes is easy—I'm never going to say it's something I would choose if I had a choice—but it's not a limitation.

Source: *Diabetes Forecast*, May 2011.

Go through the comics section of a newspaper to find a comic strip that amuses you. Be sure to choose a strip in which two or more characters are speaking to each other. Write a full description that will enable people who have not read the comic strip to visualize it clearly and appreciate its humor. Describe the setting and action in each panel, and enclose the words of the speakers in quotation marks.

Comma

Six Main Uses of the Comma

Commas are used mainly as follows:

1. To separate items in a series

2. To set off introductory material

3. On both sides of words that interrupt the flow of thought in a sentence

4. Between two complete thoughts connected by *and, but, for, or, nor, so, yet*

5. To set off a direct quotation from the rest of a sentence

6. For certain everyday material

You may find it helpful to remember that the comma often marks a slight pause or break in a sentence. Read aloud the sentence examples given for each rule, and listen for the minor pauses or breaks that are signaled by commas.

1. Comma between Items in a Series

Use commas to separate items in a series.

> The street vendor sold watches, necklaces, and earrings.

> The pitcher adjusted his cap, pawed the ground, and peered over his shoulder.

> The exercise instructor told us to inhale, exhale, and relax.

> Joe peered into the hot, still-smoking engine.

A. The final comma in a series is optional, but it is often used.

B. A comma is used between two descriptive words in a series only if *and* inserted between the words sounds natural. You could say:

> Joe peered into the hot *and* still-smoking engine.

But notice in the following sentence that the descriptive words do not sound natural when *and* is inserted between them. In such cases, no comma is used.

> Tony wore a pale green tuxedo. (A pale *and* green tuxedo does not sound right, so no comma is used.)

Place commas between items in a series.

1. The nursery was furnished with a convertible crib a changing table and a glider chair.

2. Upon coming home Alyssa threw her keys on the table turned on her computer and checked her e-mail messages.

3. The tourists snapped photos of the forceful awe-inspiring lava cascades that erupted from the mountain.

4. The serene solitary forest is an ideal place to go for a relaxing meditation.

5. The interviewer's friendly open smile made the nervous job applicant suddenly feel at ease.

2. Comma after Introductory Material

Use a comma to set off introductory material.

Just in time, Sherry applied the brakes and avoided a car accident.

Muttering under his breath, Hassan reviewed the terms he had memorized.

In a wolf pack, the dominant male holds his tail higher than the other pack members.

Although he had been first in the checkout line, Damien let an elderly woman go ahead of him.

After the fire, we slogged through the ashes of the burned-out house.

TIP   If the introductory material is brief, the comma is sometimes omitted. In the activities here, however, you should include the comma.

Place commas after introductory material.

1. Entering school this fall John will begin studying to be a lawyer.

2. As the weather was sunny and warm the family decided to go to the beach.

3. Before she went to the store Jane wrote out a list of items she needed to buy.

4. If I had studied better I don't think I would have failed the exam.

5. Although flying is a quicker way to travel some people prefer to drive.

3. Comma around Words That Interrupt the Flow of Thought

Use a comma on both sides of words or phrases that interrupt the flow of thought in a sentence.

> The leather car seat, sticky from the heat, clung to my skin.

> Marty's computer, which his wife got him as a birthday gift, occupies all of his spare time.

> The hallway, dingy and dark, was illuminated by a bare bulb hanging from a wire.

Usually, by reading a sentence aloud, you can "hear" words that interrupt the flow of thought. In cases where you are not sure if certain words are interrupters, remove them from the sentence. If it still makes sense without the words, you know that the words are interrupters and that the information they give is nonessential. *Such nonessential or extra information is set off with commas.*

In the sentence

> Sue Dodd, who goes to yoga class with me, was in a serious car accident.

the words *who goes to yoga class with me* are extra information not needed to identify the subject of the sentence, *Sue Dodd.* Commas go around such nonessential information. On the other hand, in the sentence

> The woman who goes to yoga class with me was in a serious accident.

the words *who goes to yoga class with me* supply essential information—information needed for us to identify the woman being spoken of. If the words were removed from the sentence, we would no longer know exactly who was in the accident: "The woman was in a serious accident." Here is another example:

> *Watership Down,* a novel by Richard Adams, is the most thrilling adventure story I've ever read.

Here the words *a novel by Richard Adams* could be left out, and we would still know the basic meaning of the sentence. Commas are placed around such nonessential material. But in the sentence

> Richard Adams's novel *Watership Down* is the most thrilling adventure story I've ever read.

the title of the novel is essential. Without it the sentence would read, "Richard Adams's novel is the most thrilling adventure story I've ever read." We would not know which of Richard Adams's novels was so thrilling. Commas are not used around the title, because it provides essential information.

Most of the time you will be able to "hear" words that interrupt the flow of thought in a sentence and will not have to think about whether the words are essential or nonessential.

ACTIVITY 3

Use commas to set off interrupting words.

1. A slight breeze hot and damp ruffled the bedroom curtains.

2. The defrosting chickens loosely wrapped in plastic left a pool on the counter.

3. Lenny's wallet which he kept in his front pants pocket was linked to his belt with a metal chain.

4. Mr. Delgado who is an avid Yankees fan remembers the grand days of Mickey Mantle and Yogi Berra.

5. The fleet of tall ships a majestic sight made its way into the harbor.

4. Comma between Complete Thoughts

Use a comma between two complete thoughts connected by *and, but, for, or, nor, so, yet.*

Sam closed all the windows, but the predicted thunderstorm never arrived.

I like wearing comfortable clothing, so I buy oversize shirts and sweaters.

Peggy doesn't envy the skinny models in magazines, for she is happy with her own well-rounded body.

A. The comma is optional when the complete thoughts are short.

The Ferris wheel started and Wilson closed his eyes.

Many people left but the band played on.

I made a wrong turn so I doubled back.

B. Be careful not to use a comma to separate two verbs that belong to one subject. The comma is used in sentences made up of two complete thoughts (two subjects and two verbs). In the sentence

The doctor stared over his bifocals and lectured me about smoking.

there is only one subject (*doctor*) and a double verb (*stared* and *lectured*). No comma is needed. Likewise, the sentence

Dean switched the lamp on and off and then tapped it with his fingers.

has only one subject (*Dean*) and a double verb (*switched* and *tapped*); therefore, no comma is needed.

ACTIVITY 4

Place a comma before a joining word that connects two complete thoughts (two subjects and two verbs). Remember, do *not* place a comma within a sentence that has only one subject and a double verb. (Some items may be correct as given.)

1. Armand left work early to pick up his daughter from school and take her to basketball practice.

2. He can spend hours circling the parking lot looking for a spot near the store or he can easily park a few yards away and get some exercise.

3. Our professor told us that the quiz would cover material we learned since the last exam but the quiz also covered material that we learned before the exam.

4. Kristine was worried that she would lose her sales job so she began taking accounting classes at the local community college.

5. Only a few people attended the game but that did not discourage the players from playing to their utmost and winning the division title.

6. I used last night's leftovers to make a delicious chicken salad sandwich for lunch and prepare a chicken casserole for the freezer.

7. I made an appointment with a personal financial advisor for I need to start planning for retirement.

8. Lance promised that he would teach me how to play Texas Hold'em and I promised that I would help him with his math homework.

9. Claire was worried about her father's health so she made an appointment for him with a doctor at the community clinic.

10. The customer tried on dozens of outfits but walked out of the store without purchasing a single item.

5. Comma with Direct Quotations

Use a comma to set off a direct quotation from the rest of a sentence.

The carnival barker cried, "Step right up and win a prize!"

"Now is the time to yield to temptation," my horoscope read.

"I'm sorry," said the restaurant hostess. "You'll have to wait."

"For my first writing assignment," said Scott, "I have to turn in a five-hundred-word description of a stone."

TIP Commas and periods at the end of a quotation go inside quotation marks. See also page 491.

ACTIVITY 5
Use commas to set off direct quotations from the rest of the sentence.

1. The coach announced "In order to measure your lung capacity you're going to attempt to blow up a plastic bag with one breath."

2. "A grapefruit" said the comedian "is a lemon that had a chance and took advantage of it."

3. My father asked "Did you know that the family moving next door has thirteen children?"

4. "Speak louder" a man in the back row said to the guest speaker. "I paid fifty dollars to hear you talk, not whisper."

5. The zookeeper explained to the visitors "We can't tell the sex of a giant tortoise for almost ten years after its birth."

6. Comma with Everyday Material

Use a comma with certain everyday material.

If you're the last to leave, Paul, please switch off the lights.	**Persons Spoken To**
Fred, I think we're on the wrong road.	
Did you see the playoff game, Lisa?	
June 30, 2012, is the day I make the last payment on my car.	**Dates**
I buy discount children's clothing from Isaac's Baby Wear Factory, Box 900, Chicago, Illinois 60614.	**Addresses**

 TIP No comma is used before a zip code.

Dear Santa,	Sincerely yours,	**Openings and Closings of Letters**
Dear Roberto,	Truly yours,	

TIP In formal letters, a colon is used after the opening:
Dear Sir: *or* Dear Madam: *or* Dear Allan: *or* Dear Ms. Mohr:

The insurance agent sold me a $10,000 term life insurance policy.	**Numbers**

Place commas where needed   **ACTIVITY 6**

1. Would you mind Perlita if I used your name as a reference on this job application?

2. The Pad Thai served at Mekong's Restaurant 5001 South Prince Street is authentic.

3. Approximately 1500 protesters flooded City Hall on September 12 2008 to voice their concern about the proposed educational cuts.

4. The report indicates Kay that 5012 customers purchased extended warranties during the first quarter.

5. The community center's address is 94-1201 Mojave Drive San Jose California 95102.

REVIEW TEST 1

Insert commas where needed. In the space provided below each sentence, summarize briefly the rule that explains the comma or commas used

1. "First impressions" the job recruiter said "are crucial during a job interview."

_____

2. I had wanted to buy roses for Jo on Valentine's Day but the florist said that I should have placed an order at least a month ago.

   _____

3. The motivational speaker ended her presentation by saying "Remember that you can make a difference."

   _____

4. At the age of forty-three John F. Kennedy was the youngest person to be elected to the office of United States President.

   _____

5. The driver who was clearly at fault took his eyes off the road while sending a text message on his BlackBerry.

   _____

6. After two weeks into the semester I still need to buy textbooks for my chemistry astronomy and history classes.

   _____

REVIEW TEST 2

Insert commas where needed. Mark the one sentence that is correct with a C.

1. A person studying art history will have to learn about the many different movements like French Impressionism Art Nouveau Cubism Surrealism and Pop Art.

2. From 1869 to 1890 French Impressionism was very popular.

3. Artists like Claude Monet Camille Pissarro and Paul Gauguin challenged the art world with their painting styles.

4. Edgar Degas a French Impressionist was most famous for his paintings of ballet dancers.

5. The era of Art Nouveau which lasted from 1890 to 1910 was not limited to paintings.

6. Many artists during this period also worked with furniture buildings and jewelry.

7. Rene Lalique a French architect became famous for his Art Nouveau glass.

8. Another movement, Cubism, occurred from 1908 to 1914.

9. Pablo Picasso used to be credited with creating Cubism but now he shares that honor with Georges Braque.

10. From 1920 to 1930 Surrealism was the popular way to paint and this movement was led by Andre Breton.

11. The most famous Surrealist painter Salvador Dali painted *The Persistence of Memory*.

12. Dali like other Surrealist painters painted illogical pictures that were meant to represent images from the subconscious mind.

13. Pop Art a movement characterized by popular culture occurred between 1955 and 1970.

14. Andy Warhol was most famous for his screen prints of Marilyn Monroe his soup cans and his Coca-Cola bottles.

REVIEW TEST 3

In the following passage, there are ten missing commas. Add the commas where needed. The types of mistakes to look for are shown in the box preceding the passage.

> 2 commas missing between items in a series
> 1 comma missing after introductory material
> 4 commas missing around interrupting words
> 2 commas missing between complete thoughts
> 1 comma missing with a direct quotation

Personal

When I was about ten years old I developed several schemes to avoid eating liver, a food I despise. My first scheme involved my little brother. Timmy too young to realize what a horrible food liver is always ate every bit of his portion. On liver nights, I used to sit next to Tim and slide my slab of meat onto his plate when my parents weren't paying attention. This strategy worked until older and wiser Tim decided to reject his liver along with the rest of us. Another liver-disposal method I used was hiding the meat right on the plate. I'd cut the liver into tiny squares half the size of postage stamps and then I would carefully hide the pieces. I'd put them inside the skin of my baked potato beneath some mashed peas, or under a crumpled paper napkin. This strategy worked perfectly only if my mother didn't look too closely as she scraped the dishes. Once she said to me "Do you know you left a lot of liver on your plate?" My best liver trick was to hide the disgusting stuff on a three-inch-wide wooden ledge that ran under our dining-room table. I'd put little pieces of liver on the ledge when Mom wasn't looking; I would sneak the dried-up scraps into the garbage early the next day. Our dog would sometimes smell the liver try to get at it, and bang his head noisily against the bottom of the table. These strategies seemed like a lot of work but I never hesitated to take whatever steps I could. Anything was better than eating a piece of meat that tasted like old socks soaked in mud.

REVIEW TEST 4

On separate paper, write six sentences, one illustrating each of the six main comma rules.

Other Punctuation Marks

Colon (:)

Use the colon at the end of a complete statement to introduce a list, a long quotation, or an explanation.

1. List:

   The store will close at noon on the following dates: November 26, December 24, and December 31.

2. Quotation:

   In his book *Life Lines*, Forrest Church maintains that people should cry more: "Life is difficult. Some people pretend that it is not, that we should be able to breeze through. Yet hardly a week passes in which most of us don't have something worth crying about."

3. Explanation:

   Here's a temporary solution to a dripping faucet: tie a string to it, and let the drops slide down the string to the sink.

ACTIVITY 1

Place colons where needed in the sentences below:

1. Bring these items to registration a ballpoint pen, your student ID card, and a check made out to the college.

2. The road was closed because of an emergency an enormous tree had fallen and blocked both lanes.

3. Willa Cather, the American author, had an insightful comment about plots "There are only two or three human stories, and they go on repeating themselves as fiercely as if they had never happened before."

Semicolon (;)

The main use of the semicolon is to mark a break between two complete thoughts, as explained on pages 420–422. Another use is to mark off items in a series when the items themselves contain commas. Here are some examples:

Maya's children are named Melantha, which means "black flower"; Yonina, which means "dove"; and Cynthia, which means "moon goddess."

My parents' favorite albums are *Rubber Soul,* by the Beatles; *Songs in the Key of Life,* by Stevie Wonder; and *Bridge over Troubled Water,* by Simon and Garfunkel.

ACTIVITY 2

Working in pairs with a classmate, place semicolons where needed in the sentences below.

1. Strange things happen at very low temperatures a rose will shatter like glass.

2. My sister had a profitable summer: by mowing lawns, she earned $125 by washing cars, $85 and by walking the neighbors' dogs, $110.

3. The children who starred in the play were Kari Rosoff, nine years old Flora Junco, twelve years old and Ezra Johnson, three years old.

Dash (—)

A dash signals a pause longer than a comma but not as complete as a period. Use a dash to set off words for dramatic effect:

> I was so exhausted that I fell asleep within seconds—standing up.

> He had many good qualities—sincerity, honesty, and thoughtfulness— yet he had few friends.

> The pardon from the governor finally arrived—too late.

TIPS

a. A dash can be formed on a keyboard by striking the hyphen twice (--). Computer software also has a symbol for the dash. In handwriting, a dash is as long as two letters would be.
b. Be careful not to overuse dashes.

ACTIVITY 3

Place dashes where needed in the following sentences.

1. The women's 5K race held each May in honor of Mother's Day attracts participants of all ages.

2. The stolen car was found abandoned on the freeway minus the car stereo and owner's personal belongings.

3. After months of working on my research paper, I could hope for only one thing an A to reward me for all my hard work.

Parentheses ( )

Parentheses are used to set off extra or incidental information from the rest of a sentence:

> In 1913, the tax on an annual income of $4,000 (a comfortable wage at that time) was one penny.

> Arthur C. Clarke, author of science fiction books (including *2001: A Space Odyssey*), was inspired as a young man by the magazine *Astounding Stories*.

> ### TIP
> Do not use parentheses too often in your writing.

ACTIVITY 4   Working with a partner, add parentheses where needed.

1. President Taft 1909–1913 established many things during his term in office, including a postal savings system.

2. Zachary Taylor was in office for one short year 1849–1850.

3. Franklin D. Roosevelt FDR and John F. Kennedy JFK are often referred to by their initials.

Hyphen (-)

1. Use a hyphen with two or more words that act as a single unit describing a noun.

   The light-footed burglar silently slipped open the sliding glass door.

   While being interviewed on the late-night talk show, the quarterback announced his intention to retire.

   With a needle, Rich punctured the fluid-filled blister on his toe.

2. Use a hyphen to divide a word at the end of a line of writing or typing. When you need to divide a word at the end of a line, divide it between syllables. Use your dictionary to be sure of correct syllable divisions.

   Selena's first year at college was a time filled with numerous new pressures and responsibilities.

> ### TIPS
> a. Do not divide words of one syllable.
> b. Do not divide a word if you can avoid dividing it.

ACTIVITY 5   Place hyphens where needed.

1. The apartment complex was no longer a laughter filled place once the neighborhood children had grown and moved out.

2. Samantha, who is usually a high strung person, decided to start yoga and Zen meditation.

3. My last minute efforts produced a poorly written paper, which I was embarrassed to submit to my professor.

REFLECTIVE ACTIVITY

Look over a paragraph you wrote for an assignment in Chapter 11, "Comparison or Contrast," or an essay you wrote while studying Chapter 18, "Patterns of Essay Development." Do you notice any errors with apostrophes, quotation marks, commas, or other punctuation marks? If so, correct them using what you learned in Chapters 35–38.

REVIEW TEST

At the appropriate spot, place the punctuation mark shown in the margin.

— 1. A bad case of flu, a burglary, the death of an uncle it was not what you would call a pleasant week.

( ) 2. My grandfather who will be ninety in May says that hard work and a glass of wine every day are the secrets of a long life.

: 3. Mark Twain offered this advice to writers "The difference between the right word and the nearly right word is the difference between light-ning and the lightning bug."

- 4. The passengers in the glass bottomed boat stared at the colorful fish in the water below.

( ) 5. Ellen's birthday December 27 falls so close to Christmas that she gets only one set of presents.

, 6. The dog-show winners included Freckles, a springer spaniel King Leo, a German shepherd and Big Guy, a miniature schnauzer.

— 7. I feel I have two chances of winning the lottery slim and none.

- 8. Cold hearted stepmothers are a fixture in many famous fairy tales.

; 9. Some people need absolute quiet in order to study they can't concen-trate with the soft sounds of a radio, air conditioner, or television in the background.

: 10. A critic reviewing a bad play wrote, "I saw the play under the worst possible circumstances the curtain was up."

SECTION III: PUNCTUATION EDITING TEST I

Correct the following paragraphs by adding and/or removing marks of punctuation as needed.

Migraine headache's affect millions of people in the United States. This illness attacks all segments of the population both adults and children. However it is more common in females than in males. Migraine's are so serious a problem that they cause millions of lost work and study hours in factories warehouses offices stores schools and colleges. An essay entitled What Are Migraine Headaches   describes the problem in the following words: an intense throbbing or pounding pain. The pain from migraines is most often unilateral in other words it is on one side of the head.

Nausea, vomiting, dizziness sensitivity to light and even diarrhea are other symptoms that migraines can cause. The most effective remedy is a good night s sleep however there are several drug's that can also help. A migraine patient should also avoid certain foods sharp cheeses red wines and some types of nuts. Smoking also makes things worse so doctors advise staying away from cigarettes, and other tobacco products.

SECTION III: PUNCTUATION EDITING TEST II

Correct the following items by adding and/or removing marks of punctuation as needed.

Bossypants was published in 2011 it contains many funny short stories and essays about the author, Tina Fey. Some of the short storie's, like Peeing in Jars with Boys   "Sarah, Oprah, and Captain Hook, or How to Succeed by Sort of Looking Like Someone Else" and A Childhood Dream, Realized focus on her life during her years at *Saturday Night Live*. Another short story   Young Men's Christian Association   tells about one of her first jobs as a front desk clerk at

continued

the Evanston Illinois YMCA. Her shortest chapter "What Turning Forty Means to Me" is only three sentences long! She even offers advice to her readers Do your thing and don't care if they like it. Although it won't ever be considered a classic piece of literature like Shakespeares *Romeo and Juliet,* it is a book that will create laughter in thousand's of homes.

SECTION

IV

Word Use

LEMON POOPY SEED MUFFIN

$2.29

RESPONDING TO IMAGES

Sometimes making a spelling error or confusing similar words can give your writing a completely different and unintended meaning! What error was made in the sign above and how does it change the sign's meaning?

Spelling Improvement

Poor spelling often results from bad habits developed in the early school years. With work, such habits can be corrected. If you can write your name without misspelling it, there is no reason why you cannot do the same with almost any word in the English language. Following are steps you can take to improve your spelling.

Step 1: Use the Dictionary

Get into the habit of using the dictionary. When you write a paper, allow yourself time to look up the spelling of all those words you are unsure about. Do not overlook the value of this step just because it is such a simple one. By using the dictionary, you can probably make yourself a 95 percent better speller.

Step 2: Keep a Personal Spelling List

Keep a list of words you misspell and study the words regularly. Write the list on the back page of a frequently used notebook or save them in a Word document titled "Personal Spelling List."

To master the words on your personal spelling list, do the following:

1. Write down any hint that will help you remember the spelling of a word. For example, you might want to note that *occasion* is spelled with two *c*'s or that *all right* is two words, not one word.

2. Study a word by looking at it, saying it, and spelling it. You may also want to write out the word one or more times, or "air write" it with your finger in large, exaggerated motions.

3. When you have trouble spelling a long word, try to break the word into syllables and see whether you can spell the syllables. For example, *inadvertent* can be spelled easily if you can hear and spell in turn its four syllables: *in ad ver tent.* The word *consternation* can be spelled easily if you hear and spell its four syllables in turn: *con ster na tion.* Remember, then: Try to see, hear, and spell long words in terms of their syllables.

4. Keep in mind that review and repeated self-testing are keys to effective learning. When you are learning a series of words, go back after studying each new word and review all the preceding ones.

Step 3: Master Commonly Confused Words

Master the meanings and spellings of the commonly confused words on pages 517–525. Your instructor may assign twenty words for you to study at a time and give you a series of quizzes until you have mastered the words.

Step 4: Learn Key Words in Major Subjects

Make up and master lists of words central to the vocabulary of your major subjects. For example, a list of key words in business might include *economics, management, resources, scarcity, capitalism, decentralization, productivity, enterprise,* and so on; in psychology, *behavior, investigation, experimentation, frustration, cognition, stimulus, response, organism,* and so on. Set aside a specific portion of your various course notes to be used only for such lists, and study them using the methods described above for learning words.

Step 5: Study a Basic Word List

Following is a list of 250 English words that are often misspelled. Study their spellings. Your instructor may assign 25 or 50 words for you to study at a time and give you a series of quizzes until you have mastered the entire list.

THE 250 ENGLISH WORDS MOST OFTEN MISSPELLED

absence	breathe	deceit
ache	brilliant	definite
achieve	bureau	deposit
acknowledge	business	dictionary
advice	cafeteria	disastrous
aisle	calendar	disease
all right	candidate	distance
already	category	doctor
amateur	ceiling	doubt
answer	cemetery	efficient
anxious	chief	eighth
appearance	choose	either
appetite	cigarette	emphasize
attempt	citizen	entrance
attendance	college	environment
autumn	column	exaggerate
awful	comfortable	examine
bachelor	committed	existence
balance	completely	familiar
bargain	conceit	fascinate
basically	conscience	February
beautiful	conscious	financial
believe	conversation	foreign
beneficial	cruelty	forty
25 bottom	50 daughter	75 friend

continued

furniture
government
grammar
grieve
guidance
hammer
handkerchief
harass
height
hospital
hundred
husband
imitation
incredible
independent
instant
instead
intelligence
interest
interfere
interrupt
irresistible
January
kindergarten
100 leisure
library
lightning
likely
livelihood
loneliness
loose
magazine
making
maintain
marriage
material
mathematics
medicine
minute
mortgage
muscle
naturally
necessary
neither
nickel
niece
ninety
noise
obedience

125 obstacle
occasion
occur
occurrence
omission
opinion
opportunity
optimist
ounce
outrageous
pageant
pamphlet
people
perform
persistent
physically
picnic
plausible
pleasant
policeman
possible
precede
prefer
preference
prejudice
150 prescription
probably
psychology
pursue
quantity
quarter
quiet
quiz
raise
really
recede
receive
recognize
recommend
reference
region
reign
relieve
religion
representative
resistance
restaurant
rhythm
ridiculous

right
175 safety
said
salary
scarcely
scholastic
science
scissors
secretary
seize
separate
sergeant
several
severely
shriek
siege
similar
sincerely
sophomore
straight
succeed
suppress
telephone
temperature
tenant
tendency
200 tenth
than
theater
though
thousand
through
tomorrow
tongue
tonight
tournament
toward
transferred
trousers
truly
twelfth
unanimous
until
unusual
usage
used
usual
usually
vacuum

continued

valuable	wear	won't
variety	weather	writing
225 vegetable	Wednesday	written
vengeance	weight	wrong
view	weird	yesterday
villain	welcome	yolk
vision	whether	your
visitor	which	250 you're
voice	woman	
Washington	women	

Step 6: Use Electronic Aids

There are several electronic aids that can help your spelling. First, *electronic spell-checks* are pocket-size devices that look much like the pocket calculators you may use in math class. Electronic spellers can be found in almost any electronics store. The checker includes a tiny keyboard. You type out the word the way you think it is spelled, and the checker quickly provides you with the correct spelling of related words. Second, *a computer with a spell-checker* as part of its word-processing program will identify incorrect words and suggest correct spellings. If you know how to write on the computer, you will have little trouble learning how to use the spell-check feature.

Commonly Confused Words

Homonyms

Some words are commonly confused because they have the same sounds but different meanings and spellings; such words are known as *homonyms*. Following are a number of homonyms. Complete the activity for each set of words, and check off and study the words that give you trouble.

all ready   completely prepared

already   previously; before

> I was *all ready* for the test when I learned that my teacher had cancelled class.

> It was *already* May by the time I thought about applying for college.

Fill in the blanks: Sasha was __all ready__ for bed by nine o'clock, and she had __already__ laid out her clothes for the next day.

brake   stop

break   come apart

> The mechanic advised me to add *brake* fluid to my car.

> During a commercial *break*, Marie lay on the floor and did fifty sit-ups.

Fill in the blanks: Tim, a poor driver, would always __brake__ at the last minute and would usually __break__ the speed limit as well.

course   part of a meal; a school subject; direction; progression of time

coarse   rough

> During the *course* of the evening, I had to endure my date's *coarse* behavior.

Fill in the blanks: When the waitress brought the main __course__, I was surprised that the cornmeal used for the hush puppies was so __coarse__.

hear   perceive with the ear

here   in this place

> I can *hear* the performers so well from *here* that I don't want to change my seat.

Fill in the blanks: The chairperson explained that the meeting was being held ___here___ in the auditorium to enable everyone to ___hear___ the debate.

hole	an empty spot
whole	entire

A *hole* in the crumbling brick mortar made a convenient home for a small bird and its *whole* family.

Fill in the blanks: The ___hole___ in Dave's argument wouldn't exist if he put his ___whole___ concentration into his thinking.

its	belonging to it
it's	shortened form of "it is" or "it has"

It's unfortunate that your college is unable to finance all *its* students' tuition.

Fill in the blanks: I withdrew my application because ___it's___ too difficult to start a new job at the end of the semester, even though the job and ___its___ fringe benefits were tempting.

knew	past form of *know*
new	not old

No one *knew* our *new* phone number, but the obscene calls continued.

Fill in the blanks: Even people who ___knew___ Charlie well didn't recognize him with his ___new___ beard.

know	to understand
no	a negative

By the time students complete that course, they *know* two computer languages and have *no* trouble writing their own programs.

Fill in the blanks: Dogs and cats usually ___know___ by the tone of the speaker's voice when they are being told "___No___."

passed	went by; succeeded in; handed to
past	a time before the present; by, as in "I drove past the house"

Travis *passed* up the offer to play basketball with his friends because he remembered his *past* mistakes, which included neglecting his homework.

Fill in the blanks: This ___past___ year, LeMarcus was determined to move up in the company, and thus he was not ___passed___ over for the promotion.

peace	calm
piece	a part

The best *piece* of advice she ever received was to maintain her own inner *peace*.

Fill in the blanks: Upon hearing that _____ of music, my angry mood was gradually replaced by one of _____.

plain	simple
plane	aircraft

The *plain* box contained a very expensive model *plane* kit.

Fill in the blanks: After unsuccessfully trying to overcome her fear, Selena finally admitted the _____ truth: she was terrified of flying in a _____.

principal	main; a person in charge of a school
principle	a law or standard

If the *principal* ingredient in this stew is octopus, I'll abandon my *principle* of trying everything at least once.

Fill in the blanks: Our _____ insists that all students adhere to every

school _____ regarding dress, tardiness, and smoking.

right	correct; opposite of "left"
write	to put words on paper

Our professor was *right* when she said that it's difficult to *write* a research paper without plagiarizing, even unintentionally.

Fill in the blanks: I tried to _____ down the directions correctly, but I obviously didn't record the _____ street address because I am lost now.

than	(thăn)	used in comparisons
then	(thĕn)	at that time

I made more money *then*, but I've never been happier *than* I am now.

Fill in the blanks: When I was in high school, I wanted a racy two-seater convertible more _____ anything else; but _____ my friends pointed out that only one person would be able to ride with me.

their	belonging to them
there	at that place; a neutral word used with verbs like *is*, *are*, *was*, *were*, *have*, and *had*
they're	shortened form of "they are"

The tenants *there* are complaining because *they're* being cheated by *their* landlord.

Fill in the blanks: The tomatoes I planted _____ in the back of the garden are finally ripening, but _____ bright red color will attract hungry raccoons, and I fear _____ going to be eaten.

threw	past form of *throw*
through	from one side to the other; finished

When my daughter was a toddler, she often *threw* a tantrum when she was *through* eating.

Fill in the blanks: As the children moved _____ the museum, one of them _____ a candy wrapper into the display area.

to	verb part, as in *to smile*; toward, as in "I'm going *to* heaven"
too	overly, as in "The pizza was *too* hot"; also, as in "The coffee was hot, *too.*"
two	the number 2

I ran *to* the car *to* roll up the windows. (The first *to* means "toward"; the second *to* is a verb part that goes with *roll.*)

That amusement park is *too* far away; I hear that it's expensive, *too.* (The first *too* means "overly"; the second *too* means "also.")

The *two* players (2 players) jumped up to tap the basketball away.

Fill in the blanks: The _____ of them have been dating for a year, but lately they seem _____ be arguing _____ often to pretend nothing is wrong.

wear	to have on
where	in what place

Where I will *wear* a purple feather boa is not the point; I just want to buy it.

Fill in the blanks: _____ were we going the night I refused to _____ a tie?

weather	atmospheric conditions
whether	if it happens that; in case; if

Although meteorologists are *weather* specialists, even they can't predict *whether* a hurricane will change course.

Fill in the blanks: The gloomy _____ report in the paper this morning ended all discussion of _____ to pack a picnic lunch for later.

| whose | belonging to whom |
| who's | shortened form of "who is" and "who has" |

Tell me *who's* the person *whose* dirty dishes are left in the workroom sink?

Fill in the blanks: The emcee asked the guests, "_____ the person _____ birthday is closest to the guest of honor's?"

| your | belonging to you |
| you're | shortened form of "you are" |

You're confident that *your* grades are high enough to earn you a scholarship next year.

Fill in the blanks: If _____ sure that you can pay the rent, you and _____ family should move into a larger apartment.

Other Words Frequently Confused

Not all frequently confused words are homonyms. Here is a list of other words that people often confuse. Complete the activities for each set of words, and check off and study the words that give you trouble.

| a, an | Both *a* and *an* are used before other words to mean, approximately, "one." |

Generally you should use *an* before words starting with a vowel (*a, e, i, o, u*):

　　　an orange　　an umbrella　　an indication　　an ape　　an effort

Generally you should use *a* before words starting with a consonant (all other letters):

　　　　a genius　　a movie　　a speech　　a study　　a laptop

Fill in the blanks: The morning after the party, I had _____ pounding headache and _____ upset stomach.

| accept | (ăk sĕpt') | to receive; agree to |
| except | (ăk sĕpt') | excluding; but |

I wanted to *accept* the job offer, *except* that I already committed to staying at my current job for another year.

Fill in the blanks: Do you _____ your spouse for who he or she is, or do you say, "I love you _____ for your faults"?

| advice | (ăd vīs') | noun meaning "an opinion" |
| advise | (ăd vīs') | verb meaning "to counsel, to give advice" |

I have learned not to take my sister's *advice* on straightening out my life.

A counselor can *advise* you about the courses you'll need next year.

Fill in the blanks: Karen is so troubled about losing her job that I will

_____ her to seek the _____ of a professional counselor.

| affect | (uh fĕkt´) | verb meaning "to influence" |
| effect | (ĭ fĕkt´) | verb meaning "to cause something"; noun meaning "result" |

The bad weather will definitely *affect* the outcome of the election.

If we can *effect* a change in George's attitude, he may do better in his courses.

One *effect* of the strike will be dwindling supplies in the supermarkets.

Fill in the blanks: Scientists have studied the _____ of large quantities of saccharine on lab animals but have yet to learn how similar amounts

_____ human beings.

| among | implies three or more |
| between | implies only two |

The committee had to choose one person *among* five applicants, not *between* two applicants as previously thought.

Fill in the blanks: _____ you and me, I would rather live by myself

than _____ friends.

| beside | along the side of |
| besides | in addition to |

Besides doing daily inventories, I have to stand *beside* the cashier whenever the store gets crowded.

Fill in the blanks: _____ those books on the table, I plan to use these

magazines stacked _____ me while doing my research paper.

| fewer | used with things that can be counted |
| less | refers to amount, value, or degree |

I've taken *fewer* classes this semester, so I hope to have *less* trouble finding time to study.

Fill in the blanks: This beer advertises that it has _____ calories and

is _____ filling.

| former | refers to the first of two items named |
| latter | refers to the second of two items named |

Sherry enjoys cooking and gardening: the *former* allows her to try new recipes, and the *latter* provides her with fresh vegetables, which she uses in her dishes.

Fill in the blanks: When Nikki learned that she had the flu, she immediately called her shift manager and her history professor. She told the _____ that she would miss work, and she told the _____ that she would miss class.

learn	to gain knowledge
teach	to give knowledge

I can't *learn* a new skill unless someone with lots of patience *teaches* me.

Fill in the blanks: Because she is quick to _____ new things, Mandy has offered to _____ me how to play the latest video games.

loose	(lo͞os)	not fastened; not tight-fitting
lose	(lo͞oz)	to misplace; fail to win

In this strong wind, the house may *lose* some of its *loose* roof shingles.

Fill in the blanks: A _____ wire in the television set was causing us to _____ the picture.

quiet	(kwī′ĭt)	peaceful
quite	(kwīt)	entirely, really; rather

Jennifer seems *quiet* and demure, but she has *quite* a temper at times.

Fill in the blanks: Most people think the library is _____ a good place to study, but I find the extreme _____ distracting.

ACTIVITY 1

These sentences check your understanding of *its, it's; there, their, they're; to, too, two;* and *your, you're.* Underline the two incorrect spellings in each sentence. Then spell the words correctly in the spaces provided.

_____   1. There still complaining about the weather even though
_____   its sunny and warm.

_____   2. The dog ate it's bone while too other dogs watched.
_____

_____   3. Although I told them not to park by the tree, there car
_____   is parked their.

_____   4. "Your going to be late," said his mother. "The carpool is
_____   not going too wait for you."

_____   5. Since your the fastest runner on the team, you're going
_____   two run the anchor leg.

_____ 6. Your clothes are to wild for me, but I think their perfect
_____   for you.

_____ 7. Their were to things I needed to buy at the store, but I
_____   forgot both.

_____ 8. You're aunt has a very nice house, but she has two many
_____   pillows on her furniture, and I couldn't even sit down!

_____ 9. John and Sarah spent to much money on there wedding,
_____   but their honeymoon was a free gift.

_____10. It's to late to return their car since I wrecked it this
_____   afternoon and its totaled!

REVIEW TEST 1

Underline the correct word in the parentheses. Rather than guessing, look
back at the explanations of the words when necessary.

1. I (know, no) that several of the tenants have decided (to, too, two) take
   (their, there, they're) case to court.

2. (Whose, Who's) the author of that book about the (affects, effects) of
   eating (to, too, two) much protein?

3. In our supermarket is a counter (where, wear) (your, you're) welcome
   to sit down and have free coffee and doughnuts.

4. (Its, It's) possible to (loose, lose) friends by constantly giving out unwanted (advice, advise).

5. For a long time, I couldn't (accept, except) the fact that my husband
   wanted a divorce; (then, than) I decided to stop being angry and get on
   with life.

6. I spent the (hole, whole) day browsing (threw, through) the chapters in
   my business textbook, but I didn't really study them.

7. The newly appointed (principal, principle) is (quite, quiet) familiar
   with the problems (hear, here) at our school.

8. I found that our cat had (all ready, already) had her kittens (among,
   between) the weeds (beside, besides) the porch.

9. I (advice, advise) you not to take children to that movie; the special
   (affects, effects) are (to, too, two) frightening.

10. It seems that nobody will ever be able to (learn, teach) Mario to take
    (fewer, less) chances with his car.

On separate paper, write short sentences using the ten words shown below.

1. except

2. it's

3. your

4. among

5. there

6. through

7. whose

8. here

9. whether

10. than

Effective Word Choice

CHAPTER PREVIEW

Slang

Clichés

Inflated Words

Choose your words carefully when you write. Always take the time to think about your word choices rather than simply use the first word that comes to mind. You want to develop the habit of selecting words that are precise and appropriate for your purpose. One way you can show sensitivity to language is by avoiding slang, clichés, and inflated words.

Slang

We often use slang expressions when we talk because they are so vivid and colorful. However, slang is usually out of place in formal writing. Here are some examples of slang:

Mario exercises daily to keep his *six-pack abs*.

Ruthie needs a *triple* from Starbucks if she plans to *pull an all-nighter*.

My sister knows how to *dish it out*, but I can *throw* some *'tude*, too.

The new songs Stefan downloaded are *phat*.

Slang expressions have a number of drawbacks. They go out of date quickly, they become tiresome if used excessively in writing, and they may communicate clearly to some readers but not to others. Also, the use of slang can be an evasion of the specific details that are often needed to make one's meaning clear in writing. For example, in "The new songs Stefan downloaded are phat," the writer has not provided specific details about the songs necessary for us to clearly understand the statement. Was it the artist, the music, or the lyrics that the writer found outstanding? In general, then, you should avoid slang in your writing. If you are in doubt about whether an expression is slang, it may help to check a recently published hardbound dictionary.

ACTIVITY 1	Rewrite the following sentences, replacing the italicized slang words with more formal ones.

EXAMPLE

My neighbor keeps his TV on 24-7, which *drives me up the wall*.

My neighbor keeps his TV on constantly, which irritates me.

1. I *crammed* for my test all night, but I *bombed* it anyway.

_____

_____

_____

2. My mom cooked a meal the other day that was just *sick*!

_____

_____

3. When I first met Nick, I thought he was *dope*, but he turned out to be *a hater* and didn't want me to have other friends.

_____

_____

_____

4. Keira's so busy that she's *IM-ing* her friends rather than giving them *face time*.

_____

_____

_____

5. My friend likes *chillaxin'* after school before she does her *h/w*.

_____

_____

_____

Clichés

A *cliché* is an expression that has been worn out through constant use. Here are some typical clichés:

short but sweet	last but not least
drop in the bucket	work like a dog
had a hard time of it	all work and no play
word to the wise	it goes without saying
it dawned on me	at a loss for words
sigh of relief	taking a big chance
too little, too late	took a turn for the worse
singing the blues	easier said than done
in the nick of time	on top of the world
too close for comfort	time and time again
saw the light	make ends meet

Clichés are common in speech but make your writing seem tired and stale. Also, they are often an evasion of the specific details that you must work to provide in your writing. You should, then, avoid clichés and try to express your meaning in fresh, original ways.

ACTIVITY 2

Underline the cliché in each of the following sentences. Then substitute specific, fresh words for the trite expression.

EXAMPLE

My boyfriend has stuck with me <u>through thick and thin</u>.

through good times and bad

1. As the only girl in an otherwise all-boy family, I got away with murder.

2. When I realized I'd lost my textbook, I knew I was up the creek without a paddle.

3. My suggestion is just a shot in the dark, but it's better than nothing.

4. Janice got more than she bargained for when she offered to help Larry with his math homework.

5. Bob is pushing his luck by driving a car with bald tires.

6. On a hot, sticky midsummer day, iced tea or any frosty drink really hits the spot.

7. Nadia thanks her lucky stars that she was born with brains, beauty, and humility.

8. Anything that involves mathematical ability has always been right up my alley.

9. Your chance of buying a good used car from that dealer is one in a million.

10. Even when we are up to our eyeballs in work, our boss wonders if we have enough to do.

ACTIVITY 3

Write a short paragraph describing the kind of day you had. Try to put as many clichés as possible into it. For example, "I got up at the crack of dawn, ready to take on the world. I grabbed a bite to eat. . . ." Once you are finished, exchange paragraphs with a partner. Each of you should read the other's paragraph aloud. By making yourself aware of clichés in this way, you should lessen the chance that they will appear in your writing.

Inflated Words

Some people feel that they can improve their writing by using fancy, elevated words rather than simple, natural words. They use artificial, stilted language that more often obscures their meaning than communicates it clearly. This frequently occurs when students attempt to use a dictionary or thesaurus, but just pick words at random to replace the simpler words. Using college-level vocabulary is a way to improve your writing, but you must be careful in choosing words. Not only can certain choices sound artificial, but another problem may arise when words are chosen without enough thought. Since many words can act as nouns, verbs, adjectives, and adverbs, using the wrong part of speech often leads to obscured meaning.

Here are some unnatural-sounding sentences:

It was a marvelous gamble to procure some slumber.

We relished the delectable noon-hour repast.

The officer apprehended the imbibed operator of the vehicle.

The female had an affectionate spot in her heart for domesticated canines.

The same thoughts can be expressed more clearly and effectively by using plain, natural language, as below:

It was an excellent chance to get some sleep.

We enjoyed the delicious lunch.

The officer arrested the drunk driver.

The woman had a warm spot in her heart for dogs.

Here are some other inflated words and simpler words that could replace them:

Inflated Words	Simpler Words
amplitude	fullness or abundance
terminate	finish
subsequent to	after
delineate	describe or explain
facilitate	assist or help
moribund	dying or wasting away
manifested	established or shown
to endeavor	to attempt or to try
habituated	accustomed or familiar

ACTIVITY 4

Cross out the inflated words in each sentence. Then substitute clear, simple language for the inflated words.

EXAMPLE

A man dressed in odd ~~attire accosted~~ me on the street.
... clothing stopped ...
_____

1. John utilized Natalie's conceptualization to create a video on YouTube.

   _____

2. My six-year-old daughter plans to facilitate a termination of world hunger.

   _____

3. Leanne aspires to legally change her identification to "Li Ahn."

   _____

4. I enlightened the cashier about the calculation discrepancy on our bill.

   _____

5. Only Jonah comprehended what transpired at the finalization of the movie.

   _____

REVIEW TEST

Certain words are italicized in the following paragraph. These words are either clichés, slang, or inflated. In the space between the lines, replace the italicized words with more effective diction. One italicized phrase is not needed at all; simply cross that one out.

Performance evaluations can be *the worst of times* for both employee and employer. Employers *check out* how the employee has performed over a certain period of time and then *facilitate an interview with* the employee. One of the things employers focus on is improvement. Under areas of improvement, employers write things like: *needs to initiate proper arrival time at work, needs to facilitate excellent group collaboration*, and needs to increase production. Another area that employers focus on is goal setting because this gives an employee something to work toward. Sometimes goal setting might identify skill areas that need improvement, but often it involves something simple like increasing production *by a big percent* or setting up a fifteen-minute break every afternoon. After focusing on the things that employees need to improve, employers will often *chew the fat about* the employee's accomplishments. This is when both the employee and employer have a chance to *revel in* the positive part of the review. Accomplishments that employers like to highlight are things like *working like a dog*, landing large accounts, or overall positive behavior. Although performance evaluations can *generate heart palpitations*, they often help employers and employees *implement changes that attain positive personnel performance.*

Editing Tests

The twelve editing tests in this chapter will give you practice in revising to correct sentence-skills mistakes. Remember that if you don't edit carefully, you run the risk of undermining much of the work you have put into a paper. If readers see too many surface flaws, they may assume that you don't place much value on what you have to say, and they may not give your ideas a fair hearing. Revising to eliminate sentence-skills errors is a basic part of clear, effective writing.

In five of the tests, the spots where errors occur have been underlined; your job is to identify and correct each error. In the rest of the tests, you must locate as well as identify and correct the errors.

EDITING HINTS
Here are hints that can help you edit the next-to-final draft of a paper for sentence-skills mistakes:

1. Have at hand two essential tools: a good dictionary and a sentence-skills handbook (you can use Chapter 4 and Part Five of this book).

2. Use a sheet of paper to cover your essay so that you will expose only one sentence at a time. Look for errors in grammar, spelling, and typing. It may help to read each sentence out loud. If a sentence does not read clearly and smoothly, chances are something is wrong.

3. Pay special attention to the kinds of errors you yourself tend to make. For example, if you tend to write run-ons or fragments, be especially on the lookout for those errors.

4. Proofreading symbols that may be of particular help are the following:

ℓ	omit	draw two ~~two~~ conclusions	ℓ
^	insert missing letter or word	ach*i*eve	
cap, lc	add a capital (or a lowercase) letter	(cap) My english Class (lc)	

EDITING TEST 1

In the spaces at the bottom, write the numbers of the ten word groups that contain fragments or run-ons. Then, in the spaces between the lines and in the margin, edit by making the necessary corrections.

Personal

¹I remember my childhood as being generally happy and can recall experiencing some of the most carefree times of my life. ²But I can also remember, even more vividly, other moments. ³When I was deeply frightened. ⁴As a child, I was truly terrified of the dark and of getting lost. ⁵These fears were very real, they caused me some extremely uncomfortable moments.

⁶Maybe it was the strange way things looked and sounded in my familiar room at night. ⁷That scared me so much. ⁸The streetlight outside or passing car lights would create shadows in my room. ⁹As a result, clothes hung over a chair taking on the shape of an unknown beast.

¹⁰Out of the corner of my eye, I saw curtains move when there was no breeze. ¹¹A tiny creak in the floor would sound a hundred times louder than in daylight, my imagination would take over. ¹²Creating burglars and monsters on the prowl. ¹³Because darkness always made me feel so helpless. ¹⁴I would lie there motionless so that the "enemy" would not discover me.

¹⁵Another of my childhood fears was that I would get lost. ¹⁶Especially on the way home from school. ¹⁷After school, all the buses lined up along the curb, I was terrified that I'd get on the wrong one. ¹⁸Scanning the bus windows for the faces of my friends. ¹⁹I'd also look to make sure that the bus driver was the same one I had had in the morning.

1. _____   3. _____   5. _____   7. _____   9. _____

2. _____   4. _____   6. _____   8. _____   10. _____

EDITING TEST 2

Identify the five mistakes in essay format in the student paper that follows. From the box below, choose the letters that describe the five mistakes and write those letters in the spaces provided.

> a. Title should not be underlined.
> b. Title should not be set off in quotation marks.
> c. There should not be a period at the end of a title.
> d. All major words in a title should be capitalized.
> e. Title should be a phrase, not a complete sentence.
> f. First line of a paper should stand independent of the title.
> g. One line should be skipped between title and first line of the paper.
> h. First line of a paragraph should be indented.
> i. Right-hand margin should not be crowded.
> j. Hyphenation should occur only between syllables.

	"eating in fast-food restaurants"
	Doing so doesn't need to be completely unhealthy. Although
	I often stop at Wendy's or Burger King, I find ways to make
	healthful choices there. For one thing, I order sandwiches
	that are as plain as possible. A broiled hamburger or fish
	sandwich isn't so bad, as long as it isn't covered with melted
	cheese, fatty sauces, bacon, or other extras" that pile on
	the "fat and calories. Another health-conscious choice is to
	skip deep-fat-fried potatoes loaded with salt and heavy with
	cholesterol; instead, I'll order a plain baked potato from
	Wendy's and add just a bit of butter and salt for taste.
	In addition, I take advantage of healthful items on menus.
	For example, most fast-food places now offer green salads
	and low-fat chicken choices. And finally, I order a sensible
	beverage—ice water or a diet soda—instead of soda or
	a milk shake.

1. _____   2. _____   3. _____   4. _____   5. _____

Identify the ten sentence-skills mistakes at the underlined spots in the student paper that follows. From the box below, choose the letter that describes each mistake and write that letter in the space provided. (The same kind of mistake may appear more than once.) Then, in the spaces between the lines, edit and correct each mistake.

a. fragment	d. dangling modifier
b. run-on	e. missing comma
c. inconsistent verb tense	f. spelling mistake

> I had a strange experience last <u>winter, I</u> was shopping for Christmas
> ₁
> presents when I came to a small clothing shop. I was going to pass it
> by, <u>Until I saw a beautiful purple robe on a mannequin in the window.</u>
> ₂
> <u>Stopping to look at it</u>, the mannequin seemed to wink at me. I was
> ₃
> really <u>startled, I</u> looked around to see if anyone else was watching.
> ₄
> Shaking my <u>head</u> I stepped closer to the window. Then I really began
> ₅
> to question my <u>sanity, it</u> looked as if the mannequin moved <u>it's</u> legs
> ₆   ₇
> My face must have shown alarm because the mannequin then <u>smiles</u>.
> ₈
> <u>And even waved her arm.</u> I sighed with <u>relief, it</u> was a human model
> ₉   ₁₀
> after all.

1. _____ 3. _____ 5. _____ 7. _____ 9. _____

2. _____ 4. _____ 6. _____ 8. _____ 10. _____

EDITING TEST 4

Identify the ten sentence-skills mistakes at the underlined spots in the student paper that follows. From the box below, choose the letter that describes each mistake and write that letter in the space provided. (The same kind of mistake may appear more than once.) Then, in the spaces between the lines, edit and correct each mistake.

a. run-on	e. wordiness
b. mistake in subject–verb agreement	f. slang
c. faulty parallelism	g. missing comma
d. missing quotation marks	

It is this writer's opinion that smokers should quit smoking for
          1
the sake of those who are around them. Perhaps the most helpless

creatures that suffer from being near a smoker is unborn babies,
                                                  2   3
according to Dr. Sears, a leading pediatric expert, one study suggests

that the risk of having an undersized baby is doubled if pregnant

women are exposed to cigarette smoke for about two hours a day.

Pregnant women should refrain from smoking and to avoid smoke-
                                                 4
filled rooms. The American Heart Association has stated that passive

smoking is very dangerous, so spouses of smokers are also

in big trouble. They are more likely than spouses of nonsmokers to die
    5
of heart disease and the development of fatal cancers. Office workers
                          6
are a final group that can be harmed by a smoke-filled environment.

The U.S. Surgeon General has said "Workers who smoke are a health
                                7
risk to their coworkers. While it is undoubtedly true that one can argue
                8   9
that smokers have the right to hurt themselves they do not have the
                                            10
right to hurt others. Smokers should abandon their deadly habit for the

health of others at home and at work.

1. _____   3. _____   5. _____   7. _____   9. _____

2. _____   4. _____   6. _____   8. _____   10. _____

Identify the ten sentence-skills mistakes at the underlined spots in the student paper that follows. From the box below, choose the letter that describes each mistake and write that letter in the space provided. (The same kind of mistake may appear more than once.) Then, in the spaces between the lines, edit and correct each mistake.

a. fragment	e. dangling modifier
b. run-on	f. missing comma
c. mistake in subject–verb agreement	g. wordiness
d. misplaced modifier	h. slang

The United States will never be a drug-free <u>society but</u> we
could eliminate many of our drug-related problems by legalizing
drugs. Drugs would be sold by companies and not criminals <u>if they
were legal.</u> The drug trade would then take place like any <u>business

freeing</u> the police and courts to devote their time to other problems.
Lawful drugs would be sold at a fair <u>price, no</u> one would need to steal
in order to buy them. <u>By legalizing drugs,</u> organized crime would lose
one of its major sources of revenue. <u>It goes without saying that we</u>
would, instead, create important tax revenues for the government.
Finally, if drugs <u>was</u> sold through legal outlets, we could reduce drug
problems among our young people. It would be illegal to sell drugs to
people under a certain age. <u>Just as is the case now with alcohol.</u> And
because the profits on drugs would no longer <u>be out of sight,</u> there
would be little incentive for drug pushers to sell to young people.
Decriminalizing drugs, in short, could be a solution. <u>To many of the

problems that result from the illegal drug trade.</u>

1. _____   3. _____   5. _____   7. _____   9. _____

2. _____   4. _____   6. _____   8. _____   10. _____

EDITING TEST 6

Identify the ten sentence-skills mistakes at the underlined spots in the student paper that follows. From the box below, choose the letter that describes each mistake and write that letter in the space provided. (The same kind of mistake may appear more than once.) Then, in the spaces between the lines, edit and correct each mistake.

a. fragment	e. mistake with quotation marks
b. run-on	f. mistake in pronoun point of view
c. mistake in subject–verb agreement	g. spelling error
d. mistake in verb tense	h. missing comma

One reason that I enjoy the commute to school is that the drive gives me <u>uninterupted</u> time to myself. The classes and socializing
₁

at college <u>is</u> great, and so is the time I spend with my family, but
₂

sometimes all this togetherness keeps <u>you</u> from being able to think.
₃

In fact, I look forward to the time I have <u>alone, it</u> gives me a chance
₄

to plan what I'll accomplish in the day ahead. For example, one Tuesday

afternoon my history professor <u>announces</u> that a rough outline for
₅

our semester report was due that Friday. <u>Fortunatly,</u> I had already
₆

done some <u>reading and</u> I had checked my proposed topic with her
₇

the week before. <u>Therefore, on the way home in the car that evening</u>
₈

I planned the entire history report in my mind. Then all I had to do

when I got home was quickly jot it down before I forgot it. <u>When I

handed the professor the outline at 8:30 Wednesday morning.</u> She
₉

asked me <u>"if I had stayed up all night working on it."</u> She was amazed
₁₀

when I told her that I owed it all to commuting.

1. _____   3. _____   5. _____   7. _____   9. _____

2. _____   4. _____   6. _____   8. _____   10. _____

Identify the ten sentence-skills mistakes at the underlined spots in the student paper that follows. From the box below, choose the letter that describes each mistake and write that letter in the space provided. (The same kind of mistake may appear more than once.) Then, in the spaces between the lines, edit and correct each mistake.

a. fragment	f. misplaced modifier
b. run-on	g. homonym mistake
c. mistake in subject–verb agreement	h. apostrophe error
d. missing comma	i. cliché
e. missing capital letters	

The Appalachian Trail, also known as the <u>A.T. runs</u> along the
¹
Appalachian mountain range from Maine to Georgia. The trail is

over 2,100 miles long and passes <u>threw</u> fourteen <u>states there</u> are
²   ³
four main types of hikers on the trail. "Thru-hikers" hike the entire trail

in one continuous journey that often takes six months. "Flip-floppers"

complete the entire trail in one journey <u>to avoid crowds and weather,</u>
⁴
<u>in discontinuous sections.</u> "Section-hikers" hike different sections and

complete the entire trail over several <u>year's</u>. "Day-hikers" hike short
⁵
parts of the trail with <u>know</u> attempt to complete the entire trail. The
⁶
majority of the two to three million visitors to the A.T. each year

are day-hikers; however, about 2,000 people a year attempt to

<u>"thru-hike." Averaging</u> only 250 successful hikers <u>who feel like they</u>
⁷   ⁸
<u>are on top of the world.</u> To keep the trail clean and healthy for all the

visitors, thousands of volunteers, along with the <u>national park service</u> and
⁹
USDA Forest Service, <u>spends</u> over 200,000 hours a year maintaining
¹⁰
the trail.

1. _____   3. _____   5. _____   7. _____   9. _____

2. _____   4. _____   6. _____   8. _____   10. _____

EDITING TEST 8

Each numbered box in the application below contains a sentence-skills mistake. Identify each of the ten mistakes. As you find each, write the type of mistake you found in the space provided. Then correct it next to your answer. The first one has been done for you.

1. missing comma: August 15, 2013   6. _____

_____   _____

2. _____   7. _____

_____   _____

3. _____   8. _____

_____   _____

4. _____   9. _____

_____   _____

(Work)

5. _____   10. _____

_____   _____

DT Food Services Ltd. • Employment Application		1. Date of Application *August 15 2013*	
Social Security # 123-45-6789	Last Name *Lee-Thomas*	First Name *Leona*	Middle Initial *F.*
Address (Street number and name) *550 Tenth Avenue*		2. City, State, and Zip Code *carson city, NV 89706*	
3. Desired Position *"Food Server"*	4. Date Available to Start *Tomorow*	Home Phone	Business Phone

EDUCATION

Schools	Name and Location	Dates Attended (mo/yr) From: To:	Grad?	Major/Minor Course Work	Type of Degree
High School	5. *Kennedy High school*	*9/90 to 6/94*	YES *X* NO		
College or University	*Washoe Community College*	*9/94 to 6/95*	YES NO *X*		
Other Training or Education	6. *Coarse in typing*		YES *X* NO		

WORK HISTORY (include volunteer experience. Use additional sheets if necessary.)

7. Current or Last Employer: *Grocery outlet*		8. Address: *120 South Carson Street* *Carson City NV 89706*	
9. Job Title: *Sales' Clerk*		Supervisor's Name and Title *Julie Leroy, Manager*	Telephone Number
Dates Employed (mo/yr-mo/yr) *10/10 to present*	Starting Salary *$7.00/hour*	Ending or Current Salary *$8.50/hour*	Reason for Leaving
10. List major duties in order of their importance in the job: *I operate the cash register. Also stock shelves.*			

Each underlined area in the cover letter below contains a sentence-skills mistake. Identify the mistake and write its item number in the appropriate space in the box below. Then correct the mistake in the space above each error.

Missing colon: _____	Homonym mistake: _____, _____
Missing apostrophe: _____	Dangling modifier: _____
Dropped verb ending: _____	Fragment: _____
Missing word: _____	Run-on: _____
Missing comma: _____	

Karen Sanchez

Personnel Officer

Buy Adventures

Tampa, FL 33619

¹Dear Ms. <u>Sanchez</u>

²I am replying to your ad in last <u>Sundays</u> newspaper that indicated an opening in Bay Adventures for a recreational activities coordinator. ³<u>Athletic and outgoing</u>, the position seems ideal for me.

⁴,⁵I <u>spend</u> the past two years working at an after-school program <u>wear</u> I developed fun activities for children in grades K-6. My job required me to think of creative yet safe ways to promote physical fitness. ⁶<u>And encourage teamwork and cooperation among the kids.</u>

⁷Also, I took several physical education classes <u>at University of Tampa.</u> ⁸<u>I learned about sports psychology, I even took a class on exercise techniques.</u> Right now, I hope to apply what I have learned, which is why I am very interested in your job.

Please feel free to call me for an interview. ⁹Thank you for <u>you're</u> consideration.

¹⁰<u>Sincerely</u>

Mark Rankins

EDITING TEST 10

Each underlined area in the cover letter below contains a sentence-skills mistake. Identify the mistake and write its item number in the appropriate space in the box below. Then correct the mistake in the space above each error.

Missing period: _____	Spelling error: _____
Homonym mistake: _____	Slang: _____
Faulty parallelism: _____	Fragment: _____, _____
Run-on: _____	Apostrophe mistake: _____
Missing colon: _____	

August, 28, 2013

¹<u>Mr Gordan</u> Hebling

Western Savings Bank

122 Mijo Way

Tucson, AZ 85706

²Dear Mr. <u>Hebling</u>

   ³I attended a career fair last week at the Tucson Convention Center and discovered that <u>you're</u> company is hiring part-time and relief tellers. ⁴A <u>guy</u> I spoke to told me that I would be ideal for the position because of my experience working as a cashier.

   I currently work as a cashier at an electronics <u>store. ⁵But would like to start a career in banking</u>. My job requires me to be responsible and accurate. ⁶I understand the importance of customer service and <u>communicating good</u>.

   ⁷<u>In addition to my work experience</u>. ⁸<u>I am able to use the 10-key by touch, I have used several computer systems</u>. ^{9,10}If I am hired, I can work at various banks because I have a valid <u>drivers' lisense</u> and my own car.

   Please feel free to call me at (520) 222-2222. I hope that I will have an opportunity to talk with you in person.

Sincerely,

Monique Williamson

Each underlined area in the résumé excerpt below contains a sentence-skills mistake. Identify the mistake and write its item number in the appropriate space in the box below. Then correct the mistake in the space above each error.

Missing capital letter: _____, _____	Inconsistent verb tense: _____
Dangling modifier: _____	Run-on: _____
Faulty parallelism: _____	Apostrophe mistake: _____
Fragment: _____, _____	Missing comma: _____

Alyssa Leong

[1]597 <u>bagley</u> Street

[2]<u>Torrance CA</u> 90501

Phone: (310) 555-5555 aleong@xyz.net

Objective

I hope to find a position as a certified nurse assistant at a nursing facility that will offer me rewarding work, [3]<u>hours that are full time</u>, and medical benefits.

Summary of Qualifications

[4]<u>Caring</u>, competent, and <u>hard working</u>, my experience caring for people is present. [5]<u>Having volunteered at an adult residential care home for two years.</u> I am aware of the responsibilities for providing basic care. [6]<u>At the care home.</u> [7]I helped staff members and sometimes fed, bathed, and <u>dress</u> clients. [8]My <u>supervisors'</u> encouraged me to enroll in a certified nursing assistant program. [9]<u>In 2008, I completed a six-month training, I also received my CNA certification</u>.

Education

2010	Certified Nursing Assistant Program	Los Angeles Adult Community School
2008	Diploma	Roosevelt High School

Work History

9/2008–6/2010   Volunteer [10]<u>South central adult residential Care Home</u>

- Assisted clients with personal hygiene and recreational activities
- Provided companionship

EDITING TEST 12

Each numbered line in the résumé below contains a sentence-skills mistake. Identify the mistake and write its item number in the appropriate space in the box below. Then correct the mistake in the space above each error.

Missing capital letter: _____, _____	Homonym mistake: _____
Spelling error: _____	Missing -s ending: _____, _____
Missing comma: _____	Apostrophe error: _____, _____
Inconsistent verb tense: _____	

Kalani Bowers

¹203 Mahogany avenue   •   ²St. Louis MO 63103   •   (314) *777-7777*
•   kalanib@xxx.mail

OBJECTIVE

³I wish to find a full-time sales position with an oportunity for advancement and personal growth.

WORK HISTORY

Dave's TV & Appliance, St. Louis, MO

2004 to present

Inventory Clerk

• ⁴Used a computer system to catalog and monitor inventory (electronics and appliance)

• ⁵Conducted quarterly physical inventories'

CPK Trading Company, St. Louis, MO

2001 to 2004

Data Entry Clerk

• ⁶Processed payments and invoice

• ⁷Maintain and audited numerous databases

• ⁸Entered daily sales receipts for too branch locations

• ⁹Generated reports' and memoranda

EDUCATION

Diploma, St. Anthony's High School, Columbia, MO (2001)

SPECIAL SKILLS

• Experienced with Windows, Word, and Excel

• ¹⁰c.p.r. Certified

ESL Pointers

This section covers rules that most native speakers of English take for granted but that are useful for speakers of English as a second language (ESL).

Articles with Count and Noncount Nouns

Articles are noun markers—they signal that a noun will follow. (A noun is a word used to name something—a person, place, thing, or idea.) The indefinite articles are *a* and *an*. (Use *a* before a word that begins with a consonant sound: **a** car, **a** piano, **a** uniform—the *u* in *uniform* sounds like the consonant *y* plus *u*. Use *an* before a word beginning with a vowel sound: **an** egg, **an** office, **an** honor—the *h* in *honor* is silent.) The definite article is *the*. An article may immediately precede a noun: **a** smile, **the** reason. Or it may be separated from the noun by modifiers: **a** slight smile, **the** very best reason.

To know whether to use an article with a noun and which article to use, you must recognize count and noncount nouns.

Count nouns name people, places, things, or ideas that can be counted and made into plurals, such as *teacher, restroom,* and *joke (one teacher, two restrooms, three jokes).*

Noncount nouns refer to things or ideas that cannot be counted, such as *flour, history,* and *truth*. The box on the next page lists and illustrates common types of noncount nouns.

> ## TIP
> There are various other noun markers besides articles, including quantity words (*some, several, a lot of*), numerals (*one, ten, 120*), demonstrative adjectives (*this, these*), possessive adjectives (*my, your, our*), and possessive nouns (*Jaime's, the school's*).

Common Noncount Nouns

Abstractions and emotions: anger, bravery, health, pride, truth

Activities: baseball, jogging, reading, teaching, travel

Foods: bread, broccoli, chocolate, cheese, flour

Gases and vapors: air, helium, oxygen, smoke, steam

Languages and areas of study: Korean, Spanish, algebra, history, physics

Liquids: blood, gasoline, lemonade, tea, water

Materials that come in bulk form: aluminum, cloth, dust, sand, soap

Natural occurrences: magnetism, moonlight, rain, snow, thunder

Other things that cannot be counted: clothing, furniture, homework, machinery, money, news, transportation, vocabulary, work

---

The quantity of a noncount noun can be expressed with a word or words called a **qualifier**, such as *some, a lot of, a unit of,* and so on. (In the following two examples, the qualifiers are shown in *italic* type, and the noncount nouns are shown in **boldface** type.)

Please have *some* **patience**.

We need to buy *two bags of* **flour** today.

Some words can be either count or noncount nouns, depending on whether they refer to one or more individual items or to something in general.

Certain **cheeses** give some people a headache.
(This sentence refers to individual cheeses; *cheese* in this case is a count noun.)

Cheese is made in almost every country where milk is produced.
(This sentence refers to cheese in general; in this case, *cheese* is a noncount noun.)

Using *a* or *an* with Nonspecific Singular Count Nouns

Use *a* or *an* with singular nouns that are nonspecific. A noun is nonspecific when the reader doesn't know its specific identity.

A left-hander faces special challenges with right-handed tools.
(The sentence refers to any left-hander, not a specific one.)

Today, our cat proudly brought **a** baby bird into the house.
(The reader isn't familiar with the bird. This is the first time it is mentioned.)

Using *the* with Specific Nouns

In general, use *the* with all specific nouns—specific singular, plural, and noncount nouns. Certain conditions make a noun specific and therefore require the article *the*.

A noun is specific in the following cases:

- When it has already been mentioned once

    Today, our cat proudly brought a baby bird into the house.
    Luckily, **the** bird was still alive.
    (*The* is used with the second mention of *bird*.)

- When it is identified by a word or phrase in the sentence

    The pockets in the boy's pants are often filled with sand and dirt.
    (*Pockets* is identified by the words *in the boy's pants*.)

- When its identity is suggested by the general context

    At Willy's Diner last night, **the** service was terrible and **the** food
    was worse.
    (The reader can conclude that the service and food being
    discussed were at Willy's Diner.)

- When it is unique

    There will be an eclipse of **the** moon tonight.
    (Earth has only one moon.)

- When it is preceded by a superlative adjective (*best, biggest, wisest*)

    The best way to store broccoli is to refrigerate it in an open
    plastic bag.

Omitting Articles

Omit articles with nonspecific plurals and noncount nouns. Plurals and
noncount nouns are nonspecific when they refer to something in general.

Pockets didn't exist until the end of the 1700s.

Service is as important as **food** to a restaurant's success.

Iris serves her children homemade **lemonade**.

Using *the* with Proper Nouns

Proper nouns name particular people, places, things, or ideas and are
always capitalized. Most proper nouns do not require articles; those that
do, however, require *the*. Following are general guidelines about when and
when not to use *the*.

1. Do not use *the* for most singular proper nouns, including names of
    the following:

    - *People and animals* (Benjamin Franklin, Fido)

    - *Continents, states, cities, streets, and parks* (North America,
      Illinois, Chicago, First Avenue, Washington Square)

    - *Most countries* (France, Mexico, Russia)

    - *Individual bodies of water, islands, and mountains* (Lake Erie, Long
      Island, Mount Everest)

2. Use *the* for the following types of proper nouns:

- *Plural proper nouns* (the Turners, the United States, the Great Lakes, the Rocky Mountains)

- *Names of large geographic areas, deserts, oceans, seas, and rivers* (the South, the Gobi Desert, the Atlantic Ocean, the Black Sea, the Mississippi River)

- *Names with the format* the _____ of _____ (the Fourth of July, the People's Republic of China, the University of California)

ACTIVITY 1 Underline the correct form of the noun in parentheses.

1. (A library, Library) is a valuable addition to a town.

2. This morning, the mail carrier brought me (a letter, the letter) from my cousin.

3. As I read (a letter, the letter), I began to laugh at what my cousin wrote.

4. Every night we have to do lots of (homework, homeworks).

5. We are going to visit our friends in (the Oregon, Oregon) next week.

6. Children should treat their parents with (the respect, respect).

7. The soldiers in battle showed a great deal of (courage, courages).

8. A famous sight in Arizona is (Grand Canyon, the Grand Canyon).

9. My son would like to eat (the spaghetti, spaghetti) at every meal.

10. It is dangerous to stare directly at (the sun, sun).

ACTIVITY 2 Underline the correct form of the noun in parentheses.

1. Yesterday morning, I drove to (the shopping mall, a shopping mall) to buy a new DVD player.

2. When I was in San Antonio, I wanted to find (a shopping mall, the shopping mall) so that I could buy souvenirs.

3. (The news report, News report) included a special story about the hurricane's aftermath.

4. The archaeologists handled their artifacts with (the care, care).

5. I plan to attend technical school in (the Orlando, Orlando), Florida.

6. To be successful in an online class, you need to have (self-discipline, self-disciplines).

7. The flight to Vietnam required that we fly over (Pacific Ocean, the Pacific Ocean).

8. When the police officer signaled for Travis to pull over, he was overcome with (anxiety, anxieties).

9. (The human body, Human body) is composed of mostly water.

10. (The New York City, New York City) is the most densely populated city in the United States.

Subjects and Verbs

Avoiding Repeated Subjects

In English, a particular subject can be used only once in a clause. Don't repeat a subject in the same clause by following a noun with a pronoun.

> Incorrect: The *manager he* asked Dmitri to lock up tonight.
>
> Correct: The **manager** asked Dmitri to lock up tonight.
>
> Correct: **He** asked Dmitri to lock up tonight.

Even when the subject and verb are separated by a long word group, the subject cannot be repeated in the same clause.

> Incorrect: The *girl* who danced with you *she* is my cousin.
>
> Correct: The **girl** who danced with you **is** my cousin.

Including Pronoun Subjects and Linking Verbs

Some languages may omit a pronoun as a subject, but in English, every clause other than a command must have a subject. In a command, the subject *you* is understood: (**You**) Hand in your papers now.

> Incorrect: The Grand Canyon is in Arizona. *Is* 217 miles long.
>
> Correct: The Grand Canyon is in Arizona. **It is** 217 miles long.

Every English clause must also have a verb, even when the meaning of the clause is clear without the verb.

> Incorrect: Angelita's piano teacher very patient.
>
> Correct: Angelita's piano teacher **is** very patient.

Including *There* and *Here* at the Beginning of Clauses

Some English sentences begin with *there* or *here* plus a linking verb (usually a form of *to be: is, are,* and so on). In such sentences, the verb comes before the subject.

> **There are** masks in every culture on Earth.
>
> The subject is the plural noun *masks,* so the plural verb *are* is used.
>
> **Here is** your driver's license.
>
> The subject is the singular noun *license,* so the singular verb *is* is used.

In sentences like those, remember not to omit *there* or *here*.

> Incorrect: *Are* several chickens in the Bensons' yard.
>
> Correct: **There are** several chickens in the Bensons' yard.

> **TIP**   The topic of subjects and verbs is covered more comprehensively in Chapter 21, "Subjects and Verbs," and Chapter 26, "Subject-Verb Agreement."

Not Using the Progressive Tense of Certain Verbs

The progressive tenses are made up of forms of *be* plus the *-ing* form of the main verb. They express actions or conditions still in progress at a particular time.

> George **will be taking** classes this summer.

However, verbs for mental states, the senses, possession, and inclusion are normally not used in the progressive tense.

> Incorrect: All during the movie they *were hearing* whispers behind them.
> Correct: All during the movie they **heard** whispers behind them.
> Incorrect: That box *is containing* a surprise for Pedro.
> Correct: That box **contains** a surprise for Pedro.

Common verbs not generally used in the progressive tense are listed in the following box.

**Common Verbs Not Generally
Used in the Progressive**

Thoughts, attitudes, and desires: agree, believe, imagine, know, like, love, prefer, think, understand, want, wish

Sense perceptions: hear, see, smell, taste

Appearances: appear, seem

Possession: belong, have, own, possess

Inclusion: contain, include

Using Only Transitive Verbs for the Passive Voice

Only transitive verbs—verbs that need direct objects to complete their meaning—can have a passive form (one in which the subject receives the action instead of performing it). Intransitive verbs cannot be used in the passive voice.

> Incorrect: If you don't fix those brakes, an accident *may be happened.* (*Happen* is an intransitive verb—no object is needed to complete its meaning.)
> Correct: If you don't fix those brakes, an accident **may happen**.

If you aren't sure whether a verb is transitive or intransitive, check your dictionary. Transitive verbs are indicated with an abbreviation such as *tr. v.* or *v. t.* Intransitive verbs are indicated with an abbreviation such as *intr. v.* or *v. i.*

Using Gerunds and Infinitives after Verbs

A gerund is the *-ing* form of a verb that is used as a noun: For Walter, **eating** is a daylong activity. An infinitive is *to* plus the basic form of the verb (the form in which the verb is listed in the dictionary): **to eat**. The infinitive can function as an adverb, an adjective, or a noun. Some verbs can be followed by only a gerund or only an infinitive; other verbs can be followed by either. Examples are given in the following lists. There are many others; watch for them in your reading.

Verb + gerund (admit + stealing)
Verb + preposition + gerund (apologize + for + yelling)

Some verbs can be followed by a gerund but not by an infinitive. In many cases, there is a preposition (such as *for, in,* or *of*) between the verb and the gerund. Following are some verbs and verb/preposition combinations that can be followed by gerunds but not by infinitives:

admit	deny	look forward to
apologize for	discuss	postpone
appreciate	dislike	practice
approve of	enjoy	suspect of
avoid	feel like	talk about
be used to	finish	thank for
believe in	insist on	think about

Incorrect: He must *avoid to jog* until his knee heals.
Correct: He must **avoid jogging** until his knee heals.
Incorrect: The instructor *apologized for to be* late to class.
Correct: The instructor **apologized for being** late to class.

Verb + infinitive (agree + to leave)

Following are common verbs that can be followed by an infinitive but not by a gerund:

agree	decide	plan
arrange	have	refuse
claim	manage	wait

Incorrect: The children *want going* to the beach.
Correct: The children **want to go** to the beach.

Verb + noun or pronoun + infinitive (cause + them + to flee)

Below are common verbs that are followed first by a noun or pronoun and then by an infinitive (not a gerund):

cause	force	remind
command	persuade	warn

Incorrect: The coach *persuaded Yasmin studying* harder.
Correct: The coach **persuaded Yasmin to study** harder.

Following are common verbs that can be followed either by an infinitive alone or by a noun or pronoun and an infinitive:

ask	need	want
expect	promise	would like

Dena asked to have a day off next week.

Her boss asked her to work on Saturday.

Verb + gerund or infinitive (begin + packing or begin + to pack)

Following are verbs that can be followed by either a gerund or an infinitive:

begin	hate	prefer
continue	love	start

The meaning of each of the above verbs remains the same or almost the same whether a gerund or an infinitive is used.

Faith hates **being** late.

Faith hates **to be** late.

With the verbs below, the gerunds and the infinitives have very different meanings.

forget	remember	stop

Esta **stopped to call** home.
(She interrupted something to call home.)

Esta **stopped calling** home.
(She discontinued calling home.)

> # TIP
> The topic of verbs is covered more comprehensively in Chapter 25, "Regular and Irregular Verbs," Chapter 26, "Subject-Verb Agreement," and Chapter 27, "Additional Information about Verbs."

ACTIVITY 3

Underline the correct form in parentheses.

1. The doctor (asked me, she asked me) if I smoked.

2. The coffee is very fresh. (Is, It is) strong and delicious.

3. (Are mice, There are mice) living in our kitchen.

4. The box (is containing, contains) a beautiful necklace.

5. Unless you take your foot off the brake, the car will not (be gone, go).

6. Most basketball players (very tall, are very tall).

7. Many people (enjoy to spend, enjoy spending) a day in the city.

8. The teacher (plans taking, plans to take) us on a field trip tomorrow.

9. Some old men in my neighborhood (play cards, they play cards) every afternoon.

10. When I am happy, I feel like (to sing, singing).

Underline the correct form in parentheses. | **ACTIVITY 4**

1. My friends (are, they are) like family to me.

2. My apartment is over thirty years old, but (is, it is) a relatively clean, safe building.

3. (Was brandy, There was brandy) added to the chocolate Bundt cake.

4. Nilva (owns, is owning) two dogs: a rottweiler and a German shepherd.

5. The exam will not (be covered, cover) the last four chapters in the textbook.

6. After a year-long deployment in Iraq, Jesse (very homesick, was very homesick).

7. I need (to eat, eating) on a schedule because of my diabetes.

8. Trina (wants to be studying, wants to study) at least three hours a day.

9. Derek's scooter (stalled, it stalled) at the intersection during a rainstorm.

10. If I go to the club with my friends, I will feel like (to smoke, smoking).

Adjectives

Following the Order of Adjectives in English

Adjectives modify nouns and pronouns. In English, an adjective usually comes directly before the word it describes or after a linking verb (a form of *be* or a "sense" verb such as *look*, *seem*, and *taste*), in which case it modifies the subject. In each of the following two sentences, the adjective is **bold-faced** and the noun it describes is *italicized*.

That is a **false** *story*.

The *story* is **false.**

When more than one adjective modifies the same noun, the adjectives are usually stated in a certain order, though there are often exceptions. Following is the typical order of English adjectives:

Typical Order of Adjectives in a Series

1. **Article or other noun marker:** a, an, the, Lee's, this, three, your

2. **Opinion adjective:** dull, handsome, unfair, useful

3. **Size:** big, huge, little, tiny

---

continued

> 4. **Shape:** long, short, round, square
>
> 5. **Age:** ancient, medieval, old, new, young
>
> 6. **Color:** blue, green, scarlet, white
>
> 7. **Nationality:** Italian, Korean, Mexican, Vietnamese
>
> 8. **Religion:** Buddhist, Catholic, Jewish, Muslim
>
> 9. **Material:** cardboard, gold, marble, silk
>
> 10. **Noun used as an adjective:** house (as in *house call*), tea (as in *tea bag*), wall (as in *wall hanging*)

Here are some examples of the above order:

a long cotton scarf

the beautiful little silver cup

your new black evening gown

Ana's sweet Mexican grandmother

In general, use no more than two or three adjectives after the article or another noun marker. Numerous adjectives in a series can be awkward: **the beautiful big new blue cotton** sweater.

Using the Present and Past Participles as Adjectives

The present participle ends in *-ing*. Past participles of regular verbs end in *-ed* or *-d*; a list of the past participles of many common irregular verbs appears on pages 428–430. Both types of participles may be used as adjectives. A participle used as an adjective may precede the word it describes: That was an **exciting** *ball game*. It may also follow a linking verb and describe the subject of the sentence: The *ball game* was **exciting.**

While both present and past participles of a particular verb may be used as adjectives, their meanings differ. Use the present participle to describe whoever or whatever causes a feeling: an **embarrassing** *incident* (the incident is what causes the embarrassment). Use the past participle to describe whoever or whatever experiences the feeling: the **embarrassed** *parents* (the parents are the ones who are embarrassed).

The long day of holiday shopping was **tiring.**

The shoppers were **tired.**

Following are pairs of present and past participles with similar distinctions:

annoying / annoyed	depressing / depressed	fascinating / fascinated
boring / bored	exciting / excited	frightening / frightened
confusing / confused	exhausting / exhausted	surprising / surprised

TIP The topic of adjectives is covered more comprehensively in Chapter 30, "Adjectives and Adverbs."

Underline the correct form in parentheses.

ACTIVITY 5

1. The Johnsons live in a (stone big, big stone) house.

2. Mr. Kim runs a (popular Korean, Korean popular) restaurant.

3. For her party, the little girl asked if her mother would buy her a (beautiful long velvet, beautiful velvet long) dress.

4. When their son didn't come home by bedtime, Mr. and Mrs. Singh became (worried, worrying).

5. In the center of the city is a church with (three enormous colorful stained-glass, three stained-glass colorful enormous) windows.

Underline the correct form in parentheses.

ACTIVITY 6

1. The candies came in a (little red cardboard, cardboard red little) box.

2. The creek is spanned by (an old wooden, a wooden old) bridge.

3. A gunshot left (a tiny round, a round tiny) hole in the car's rear wind shield.

4. Many people find public speaking a (terrifying, terrified) experience.

5. The museum acquired (an ancient marble, a marble ancient) statue from Greece.

Prepositions Used for Time and Place

The use of prepositions in English is often idiomatic—a word that means "peculiar to a certain language"—and there are many exceptions to general rules. Therefore, correct preposition use must be learned gradually through experience. Following is a chart showing how three of the most common prepositions are used in some customary references to time and place:

USE OF *ON*, *IN*, AND *AT* TO REFER TO TIME AND PLACE

Time

On *a specific day:* on Monday, on January 1, on your anniversary

In *a part of a day:* in the morning, in the daytime (but at night)

In *a month or a year:* in December, in 1776

In *a period of time:* in an hour, in a few days, in a while

At *a specific time:* at 10:00 A.M., at midnight, at sunset, at dinnertime

Place

On *a surface:* on the desk, on the counter, on a ceiling

In *a place that is enclosed:* in my room, in the office, in the box

At *a specific location:* at the mall, at his house, at the ballpark

ACTIVITY 7	Underline the correct preposition in parentheses.

1. Can you baby-sit for my children (on, at) Thursday?
2. Please come to my office (on, at) 3:00.
3. You will find some paper clips (in, on) the desk drawer.
4. Miguel will begin his new job (in, at) two weeks.
5. A fight broke out between two groups of friends (on, at) the park.

ACTIVITY 8	Underline the correct preposition in parentheses.

1. My grandmother always bakes me chocolate chip cookies (on, at) my birthday.
2. The customers (at, in) the showroom still need to be helped.
3. Miki wants to meet (on, at) the movie theater on Friday night.
4. The unemployment office isn't open (in, on) Dr. Martin Luther King, Jr. Day.
5. My parents were divorced (in, at) 1986, the year after my younger brother was born.

REVIEW TEST 1	

Underline the correct form in parentheses.

1. Rebecca was caught in the (rain, rains) without an umbrella during her lunch hour.
2. As the waiter handed me the menu, he said, "(Are, Here are) the daily specials."
3. The ending of the mystery novel was very (disturbed, disturbing).
4. My neighbors are noisy during the day, but at least they are quiet (at, in) night.
5. (The children, Children) at the clinic needed their immunizations.
6. After the storm, the sky was filled with (small black, black small) bugs.
7. My sister and I (are usually disagreeing, usually disagree) with each other.
8. My daughter's birthday falls (in, on) Leap Day, which is February 29.
9. I was asked to (think about to running, think about running) for city council.
10. Whenever I eat Oreos, I need to drink (milk, milks).

Underline the correct form in parentheses.

1. Volunteers who gave (bloods, blood) were served coffee and cookies afterward.

2. (Were, There were) only two donuts left in the box.

3. The instructions for the new computer were very (confused, confusing).

4. The snow began to fall (in, at) dawn and continued all day.

5. I stopped at a newsstand to buy (the magazine, a magazine) to read on the train.

6. A (large hairy, hairy large) spider crawled across the basement floor.

7. Susan agreed (marrying, to marry) her boyfriend but then changed her mind.

8. In the United States, Halloween is celebrated (on, in) October 31.

9. After we finished dinner, we (decided to go, decided to be going) to the movies.

10. Most (homes, home) in that neighborhood were affected by the blackout.

SECTION IV: WORD USE EDITING TEST I

There are 15 incorrect words or phrases in the following paragraph. Rewrite the paragraph to correct word-use problems in the margins and between the lines.

Young people today have quiet a few advantages beyond what they're parents and grandparents had. Beside computers and cell phones, they have a hole shelf full of gadgets that make there life's easier. For example, to brake up the monotony of waiting in a doctor's office, at a bus stop, or in a long line at the grocery store, they plug in their iPods and listen to the latest tunes, for ours if they have to. In addition, they have an easier time communicating with friends then there parents did. When they are not able to hang out with the guys, they simply transmit them a e-mail or text message. Last but not least, technology has made it possible for them to download hundreds of hot songs and videos, so finding an endless supply of entertainment is a breeze.

SECTION IV: WORD USE EDITING TEST II

Rewrite the following paragraph to correct word-use problems in the margins and between the lines.

Alan Paton (1903–1988), who's novels zeroed in on the struggle for human and civil rights in South Africa, was that country's finest author and writer. Paton opposed the political system known as apartheid, the principle purpose of which was to keep the races apart and separate. More importantly, it also denied basic liberties to blacks and other nonwhites in the country of South Africa. Time and time again, Paton was hassled by the cops. The reason for this was because he wanted to ditch the whole apartheid system. The guys in charge of the country even busted the Liberal Party, which Paton had

continued

established in 1953 to oppose the Nationalist Party. The Nationalists favored and supported apartheid. The government also confiscated Paton's passport and tried to shut him up. But that was easier said then done. Paton's message about the evils of apartheid got out through his novels, the most famous of which is *Cry, the Beloved Country* (1948). Paton's believe in racial equality among people of different races contributed to the eventual abolishment of apartheid in 1995.

As you are reading the following essay written by Reynaldo for a nutrition class, think about what advice you would offer him as he prepares to write his final draft. Does his essay cover all four bases of effective writing? To be sure, use the checklist that follows.

A Balanced Diet

[1]The human body works twenty-four hours a day. [2]It's always building and repairing, it's always feeding and cleansing itself. [3]It's goal is to be ready for any movement, breath, and how you think. [4]A person's quality of life depends on how well his or her body works. [5]How well the body works depends on how much energy it gets. [6]Energy comes from the food that is eaten. [7]Food contains nutrients that a body needs for growth and energy.

[8]People who eat a balenced diet give their body the six essential nutrients it needs: minerals, water, carbohydrates, fats, proteins, and vitamins. [9]Minerals are nutrients that build bones and teeth. [10]Minerals also form red blood cells and other substances. [11] water aids digestion and waste removal. [12]Carbohydrates is the body's main source of energy. [13]Two carbohydrates are sugars from foods such as fruits and vegetables and starches found in rice, potatoes, and bread. [14]Fats help build cell membranes. [15]Proteins repair and grow body tissues. [16]Finally, vitamins help the body use carbohydrates fats, and proteins.

[17]Everyone should follow the nutritional food pyramid created by the United States department of Agriculture (USDA). [18]This pyramid showing the daily number of servings a person should eat from five food groups plus fats and oils. [19]The food pyramid has six levels. [20]The first and largest part of the pyramid contained the bread, cereal, rice, and pasta group from which the body needs six ounces every day. [21]The next two levels are vegetables and then fruits. [22]The USDA recommends two and a half cups of vegetables and two cups

continued

of fruits. [23]The next part of the pyramid is the smallest level. [24]It contains fats, oils, and sweets. [25]These foods have few nutrients, so people should eat them sparingly. [26]The final two levels are the milk, yogurt, and cheese group and the meat, poultry, fish, dry beans, eggs, and nuts group. [27] They need three cups of the milk group and five and a half ounces of meat and beans. [28]These recommended daily amounts are based on a 2,000-calorie diet.

A WRITER'S CHECKLIST

Unity

✔ Is there a clear thesis statement? _____ If so, write it below:

_____

✔ Is all the material on target in support of the thesis statement? _____

✔ Can you find any problems with unity in any of the supporting paragraphs? _____.

Support

✔ Is additional specific evidence needed anywhere in the essay? _____

Coherence

✔ Does Reynaldo use transitions and other connective devices in the second supporting paragraph? _____ If yes, list them here:

_____   _____   _____   _____

Sentence Skills

✔ Can you identify the ten sentence-skills mistakes in the essay? Write the sentence number of each mistake in the space provided:

run-on _____	mistake in subject–verb agreement _____
faulty parallelism _____	incorrect apostrophe _____
missing comma _____	pronoun mistake _____
spelling mistake _____	inconsistent verb tense _____
sentence fragment _____	capitalization mistake _____

Introduction and Conclusion

✔ Does Reynaldo provide a satisfying conclusion, one that brings his essay to a natural and graceful end? _____ If not, what advice would you offer Reynaldo regarding his conclusion? _____

_____

_____

 Collaborative Activity

Together with your group or class, edit and correct each sentence-skills mistake in Reynaldo's essay.

CORRECTION SYMBOLS

Here is a list of symbols the instructor may use when marking papers. The numbers in parentheses refer to the pages that explain the skill involved.

Agr	Correct the mistake in agreement of subject and verb (434–438) or pronoun and the word the pronoun refers to (443–447).
Apos	Correct the apostrophe mistake (485–490).
Bal	Balance the parts of the sentence so they have the same (parallel) form (100–102).
Cap	Correct the mistake in capital letters (472–478).
Coh	Revise to improve coherence (85–99; 130–136).
Comma	Add a comma (498–505).
CS	Correct the comma splice (415–425).
DM	Correct the dangling modifier (460–463).
Det	Support or develop the topic more fully by adding details (71–81).
Frag	Attach the fragment to a sentence or make it a sentence (403–414).
lc	Use a lowercase (small) letter rather than a capital (472–478).
MM	Correct the misplaced modifier (459–460; 463–468).
¶	Indent for a new paragraph.
No ¶	Do not indent for a new paragraph.
Pro	Correct the pronoun mistake (443–447).
Quot	Correct the mistake in quotation marks (491–497).
R-O	Correct the run-on (415–425).
Sp	Correct the spelling error (512–516).
Trans	Supply or improve a transition (90–96).
Und Ital	Underline italics (494–495).
Verb	Correct the verb or verb form (426–433; 439–442).
Wordy	Omit needless words (107–109).
WC	Replace the word marked with a more accurate one (word choice).
?	Write the illegible word clearly.
/	Eliminate the word, letter, or punctuation mark so slashed.
^	Add the omitted word or words.
; / : / - / —	Add semicolon (506), colon (506), hyphen (508), or dash (507).
( )	Add parentheses (507–508).
✓	You have something fine or good here: an expression, a detail, an idea.

Readings for Writers

Introduction to
the Readings

Twenty Reading
Selections

Reading
Comprehension
Chart

EXPLORING WRITING PROMPT:
*Do you agree with writer Amy Tan (The Joy Luck Club) about the power of language? What are some other ways
in which language can be powerful? Can you think of a student paragraph or essay in this book, a fellow student's
writing, or a professional reading that affected you in such a way? What was it about the writing that made it
powerful?*

"I spend a great deal of my time thinking about the power of language—the way it can evoke an emotion, a visual image, a complex idea, or a simple truth."

Amy Tan, "Mother Tongue"

Introduction to the Readings

The twenty reading selections in Part Six will help you find topics for writing. These selections deal in various ways with interesting, often thought-provoking concerns or experiences of contemporary life. Subjects of the essays include the value of expressing appreciation; the shame of poverty; ways in which technology is hurting us; practical advice on surviving the first year of college; cyberbullying; ways the media influence our attitudes; and the shocks and challenges of everyday life. The varied subjects should inspire lively class discussions as well as serious individual thought. The selections should also provide a continuing source of high-interest material for a wide range of writing assignments.

The selections serve another purpose as well. They will help develop reading skills, with direct benefits to you as a writer. One benefit is that, through close reading, you will learn how to recognize the thesis in a selection and to identify and evaluate the supporting material that develops the thesis. In your own writing, you will aim to achieve the same essential structure: an overall thesis followed by detailed, valid support for that thesis. A second benefit is that close reading will also help you explore a selection and its possibilities thoroughly. The more you understand about what is said in a piece, the more ideas and feelings you may have about writing on an assigned topic or a related topic of your own. A third benefit of close reading is that you will become more aware of authors' stylistic devices—for example, their introductions and conclusions, their ways of presenting and developing a point, their use of transitions, their choice of language to achieve a particular tone. Recognizing these devices in other people's writing will help you enlarge your own range of ideas and writing techniques.

The Format of Each Selection

Each selection begins with a short overview that gives helpful background information as well as a brief idea of the topic of the reading. The selection is followed by three sets of questions:

- First, there are ten "Reading Comprehension" questions to help you measure your understanding of the material. These questions involve several important reading skills: understanding vocabulary in context, recognizing a subject or topic, determining a thesis or main idea, identifying key supporting points, and making inferences. Answering the questions will enable you and your instructor to check your basic understanding of a selection quickly. More significantly, as you move from one selection to the next, you will sharpen your reading skills as well as strengthen your thinking skills—two key factors in making you a better writer.

- Following the comprehension questions are questions on "Structure and Technique" that focus on aspects of a writer's craft, and questions on "Critical Reading and Discussion" that involve you in reading carefully and thinking actively about a writer's ideas.

- Finally, several writing assignments accompany each selection (one for a paragraph and two for essays). The assignments range from personal narratives to expository and persuasive paragraphs and essays about issues in the world at large. Many assignments provide detailed guidelines on how to proceed, including suggestions for prewriting and appropriate methods of development. When writing your paragraph and essay responses to the readings, you will have opportunities to apply all the methods of development presented in Parts 3 and 4 of this book.

How to Read Well: Four General Steps

Skillful reading is an important part of becoming a skillful writer. Following is a series of four steps that will make you a better reader—both of the selections here and in your reading at large.

1. Concentrate as You Read

To improve your concentration, follow these tips:

- First, read in a place where you can be quiet and alone. Don't choose a spot where there is a TV or stereo on or where friends or family are talking nearby.

- Next, sit upright when you read. If your body is in a completely relaxed position, sprawled across a bed or nestled in an easy chair, your mind is also going to be completely relaxed. The light muscular tension that comes from sitting in a straight chair promotes concentration and keeps your mind ready to work.

- Third, consider using your index finger (or a pen) as a pacer while you read. Lightly underline each line of print with your index finger as you read down a page. Hold your hand slightly above the page and move your finger at a speed that is a little too fast for comfort. This pacing with your index finger, like sitting upright in a chair, creates a slight physical tension that will keep your body and mind focused and alert.

2. Skim Material before You Read It

In skimming, you spend about two minutes rapidly surveying a selection, looking for important points and skipping secondary material. Follow this sequence when skimming:

- Begin by reading the overview that precedes the selection.

- Then study the title of the selection for a few moments. A good title is the shortest possible summary of a selection; it often tells you in several words—or even a single word—just what a selection is about. For example, the title "Shame" suggests that you're going to read about a deeply embarrassing condition or incident in a person's life.

- Next, form a question (or questions) based on the title. For instance, for the selection titled "Shame," you might ask, "What exactly is the shame?" "What caused the shame?" "What is the result of the shame?" Using a title to form questions is often a key to locating a writer's thesis, your next concern in skimming.

- Read the first and last couple of paragraphs in the selection. Very often a writer's thesis, *if* it is directly stated, will appear in one of these places and will relate to the title.

- Finally, look quickly at the rest of the selection for other clues to important points. Are there any subheads you can relate in some way to the title? Are there any words the author has decided to emphasize by setting them off in *italic* or **boldface** type? Are there any major lists of items signaled by words such as *first, second, also, another,* and so on?

3. Read the Selection Straight Through with a Pen in Hand

Read the selection without slowing down or turning back; just aim to understand as much as you can the first time through. This is the time to read for the overall content. During your second reading of the selection, write a check or star beside answers to basic questions you formed from the title, and beside other ideas that seem important. Number lists of important points: 1, 2, 3, ... Circle words you don't understand. Write question marks in the margins next to passages that are unclear and that you will want to reread.

4. Work with the Material

Go back and reread passages that were not clear the first time through. Look up words that block your understanding of ideas and write their meanings in the margin. Also, reread carefully the areas you identified as most important; doing so will enlarge your understanding of the material. Now that you have a sense of the whole, prepare a short written outline of the selection by answering these questions:

- What is the thesis?

- What key points support the thesis?

- What seem to be other important ideas in the selection?

By working with the material in this way, you will significantly increase your understanding of a selection. Effective reading, just like effective writing, does not happen all at once. Rather, it must be worked on. Often you begin with a general impression of what something means, and then, by working at it, you move to a deeper level of understanding.

How to Answer the Comprehension Questions: Specific Hints

The ten reading comprehension questions that follow each selection involve several important reading skills:

- Understanding vocabulary in context
- Summarizing the selection in a title
- Determining the main idea
- Recognizing key supporting details
- Making inferences

The following hints will help you apply each of these reading skills:

- *Vocabulary in context.* To decide on the meaning of an unfamiliar word, consider its context. Ask yourself, "Are there any clues in the sentence that suggest what this word means?"

- *Subject or title.* Remember that the title should accurately describe the *entire* selection. It should be neither too broad nor too narrow for the material in the selection. It should answer the question "What is this about?" as specifically as possible. Note that you may at times find it easier to answer the title question *after* the main-idea question.

- *Main idea.* Choose the statement that you think best expresses the main idea—also known as the *central point* or *thesis*—of the entire selection. Remember that the title will often help you focus on the main idea. Then ask yourself, "Does most of the material in the selection support this statement?" If you can answer "yes," you have found the thesis.

- *Key details.* If you were asked to give a two-minute summary of a selection, the key, or major, details are the ones you would include in that summary. To determine the key details, ask yourself, "What are the major supporting points for the thesis?"

- *Inferences.* Answer these questions by drawing upon the evidence presented in the selection and your own common sense. Ask yourself, "What reasonable judgments can I make on the basis of the information in the selection?"

On page 693 is a chart on which you can keep track of your performance as you answer the ten comprehension questions for each selection. The chart will help you identify reading skills you may need to strengthen.

Shame

Dick Gregory

PREVIEW

In this selection, Dick Gregory—the comedian and social critic—narrates two painful experiences from his boyhood. Although the incidents show graphically what it can be like to grow up black and poor, the essay also deals with universal emotions: shame, embarrassment, and the burning desire to hold on to one's self-respect.

I never learned hate at home, or shame. I had to go to school for that. I was 1 about seven years old when I got my first big lesson. I was in love with a little girl named Helene Tucker, a light-complexioned little girl with pigtails and nice manners. She was always clean and she was smart in school. I think I went to school then mostly to look at her. I brushed my hair and even got me a little old handkerchief. It was a lady's handkerchief, but I didn't want Helene to see me wipe my nose on my hand. The pipes were frozen again, there was no water in the house, but I washed my socks and shirt every night. I'd get a pot, and go over to Mister Ben's grocery store, and stick my pot down into his soda machine. Scoop out some chopped ice. By evening the ice melted to water for washing. I got sick a lot that winter because the fire would go out at night before the clothes were dry. In the morning I'd put them on, wet or dry, because they were the only clothes I had.

Everybody's got a Helene Tucker, a symbol of everything you want. I 2 loved her for her goodness, her cleanness, her popularity. She'd walk down my street and my brothers and sisters would yell, "Here comes Helene," and I'd rub my tennis sneakers on the back of my pants and wish my hair wasn't so nappy and the white folks' shirt fit me better. I'd run out on the street. If I knew my place and didn't come too close, she'd wink at me and say hello. That was a good feeling. Sometimes I'd follow her all the way home, and shovel the snow off her walk and try to make friends with her Momma and her aunts. I'd drop money on her stoop late at night on my way back from shining shoes in the taverns. And she had a Daddy, and he had a good job. He was a paper hanger.

I guess I would have gotten over Helene by summertime, but some- 3 thing happened in that classroom that made her face hang in front of me for the next twenty-two years. When I played the drums in high school it was for Helene and when I broke track records in college it was for Helene and when I started standing behind microphones and heard applause I wished Helene could hear it, too. It wasn't until I was twenty-nine years old and married and making money that I finally got her out of my system. Helene was sitting in that classroom when I learned to be ashamed of myself.

It was on a Thursday. I was sitting in the back of the room, in a seat with 4 a chalk circle drawn around it. The idiot's seat, the troublemaker's seat.

The teacher thought I was stupid. Couldn't spell, couldn't read, 5 couldn't do arithmetic. Just stupid. Teachers were never interested in finding out that you couldn't concentrate because you were so hungry, because you hadn't had any breakfast. All you could think about was noontime, would it ever come? Maybe you could sneak into the cloakroom and steal a bite of some kid's lunch out of a coat pocket. A bite of something. Paste. You can't really make a meal of paste, or put it on bread for a sandwich, but sometimes I'd scoop a few spoonfuls out of the big paste jar in the back of the room. Pregnant people get strange tastes. I was pregnant with poverty. Pregnant with dirt and pregnant with smells that made people turn away, pregnant with cold and pregnant with shoes that were never bought for me, pregnant with five other people in my bed and no Daddy in the next room, and pregnant with hunger. Paste doesn't taste too bad when you're hungry.

The teacher thought I was a troublemaker. All she saw from the front of 6 the room was a little black boy who squirmed in his idiot's seat and made noises and poked the kids around him. I guess she couldn't see a kid who made noises because he wanted someone to know he was there.

It was on a Thursday, the day before the Negro payday. The eagle 7 always flew on Friday. The teacher was asking each student how much his father would give to the Community Chest. On Friday night, each kid would get the money from his father, and on Monday he would bring it to the school. I decided I was going to buy a Daddy right then. I had money in my pocket from shining shoes and selling papers, and whatever Helene Tucker pledged for her Daddy I was going to top it. And I'd hand the money right in. I wasn't going to wait until Monday to buy me a Daddy.

I was shaking, scared to death. The teacher opened her book and started 8 calling out names alphabetically.

"Helene Tucker?"   9

"My Daddy said he'd give two dollars and fifty cents."   10

"That's very nice, Helene. Very, very nice indeed."   11

That made me feel pretty good. It wouldn't take too much to top that. 12 I had almost three dollars in dimes and quarters in my pocket. I stuck my hand in my pocket and held on to the money, waiting for her to call my name. But the teacher closed her book after she called everybody else in the class.

I stood up and raised my hand.   13

"What is it now?"   14

"You forgot me?"   15

She turned toward the blackboard. "I don't have time to be playing 16 with you, Richard."

"My Daddy said he'd . . ."   17

"Sit down, Richard, you're disturbing the class."   18

"My Daddy said he'd give … fifteen dollars."   19

She turned around and looked mad. "We are collecting this money for 20 you and your kind, Richard Gregory. If your Daddy can give fifteen dollars you have no business being on relief."

"I got it right now, I got it right now, my Daddy gave it to me to turn in 21 today, my Daddy said …"

"And furthermore," she said, looking right at me, her nostrils getting 22 big and her lips getting thin and her eyes opening wide, "we know you don't have a Daddy."

Helene Tucker turned around, her eyes full of tears. She felt sorry for 23 me. Then I couldn't see her too well because I was crying, too.

"Sit down, Richard."   24

And I always thought the teacher kind of liked me. She always picked 25 me to wash the blackboard on Friday, after school. That was a big thrill; it made me feel important. If I didn't wash it, come Monday the school might not function right.

"Where are you going, Richard!"   26

I walked out of school that day, and for a long time I didn't go back 27 very often. There was shame there.

Now there was shame everywhere. It seemed like the whole world had 28 been inside that classroom, everyone had heard what the teacher had said, everyone had turned around and felt sorry for me. There was shame in going to the Worthy Boys Annual Christmas Dinner for you and your kind, because everybody knew what a worthy boy was. Why couldn't they just call it the Boys Annual Dinner—why'd they have to give it a name? There was shame in wearing the brown and orange and white plaid mackinaw[1] the welfare gave to three thousand boys. Why'd it have to be the same for everybody so when you walked down the street the people could see you were on relief? It was a nice warm mackinaw and it had a hood, and my Momma beat me and called me a little rat when she found out I stuffed it in the bottom of a pail full of garbage way over on Cottage Street. There was shame in running over to Mister Ben's at the end of the day and asking for his rotten peaches, there was shame in asking Mrs. Simmons for a spoonful of sugar, there was shame in running out to meet the relief truck. I hated that truck, full of food for you and your kind. I ran into the house and hid when it came. And then I started to sneak through alleys, to take the long way home so the people going into White's Eat Shop wouldn't see me. Yeah, the whole world heard the teacher that day—we all know you don't have a Daddy.

It lasted for a while, this kind of numbness. I spent a lot of time feeling 29 sorry for myself. And then one day I met this wino in a restaurant. I'd been out hustling all day, shining shoes, selling newspapers, and I had googobs of money in my pocket. Bought me a bowl of chili for fifteen cents, and a cheeseburger for fifteen cents, and a Pepsi for five cents, and a piece of chocolate cake for ten cents. That was a good meal. I was eating when this old wino came in. I love winos because they never hurt anyone but themselves.

The old wino sat down at the counter and ordered twenty-six cents 30 worth of food. He ate it like he really enjoyed it. When the owner, Mister Williams, asked him to pay the check, the old wino didn't lie or go through his pocket like he suddenly found a hole.

[1]*mackinaw:* a short, heavy woolen coat, usually plaid and double-breasted.

He just said: "Don't have no money."   31

The owner yelled: "Why in hell did you come in here and eat my food 32 if you don't have no money? That food cost me money."

Mister Williams jumped over the counter and knocked the wino off 33 his stool and beat him over the head with a pop bottle. Then he stepped back and watched the wino bleed. Then he kicked him. And he kicked him again.

I looked at the wino with blood all over his face and I went over. "Leave 34 him alone, Mister Williams. I'll pay the twenty-six cents."

The wino got up, slowly, pulling himself up to the stool, then up to the 35 counter, holding on for a minute until his legs stopped shaking so bad. He looked at me with pure hate. "Keep your twenty-six cents. You don't have to pay, not now. I just finished paying for it."

He started to walk out, and as he passed me, he reached down and 36 touched my shoulder. "Thanks, sonny, but it's too late now. Why didn't you pay it before?"

I was pretty sick about that. I waited too long to help another man.   37

READING COMPREHENSION

1. The words *pregnant with* in "pregnant with poverty" (paragraph 5) mean

   a. full of.

   b. empty of.

   c. sick of.

   d. satisfied with.

2. The word *hustling* in "I'd been out hustling all day" (paragraph 29) means

   a. learning.

   b. stealing.

   c. making friends.

   d. working hard.

3. Which of the following would be a good alternative title for this selection?

   a. Helene Tucker

   b. The Pain of Being Poor

   c. Losing a Father

   d. Mr. Williams and the Wino

4. Which sentence best expresses the main idea of the selection?

   a. Richard felt that being poor was humiliating.

   b. Richard liked Helene Tucker very much.

   c. Richard had to work hard as a child.

   d. The wino refused Richard's money.

5. The teacher disliked Richard because he
   a. was dirty.
   b. liked Helene.
   c. was a troublemaker.
   d. ate paste.

6. *True or False?* _____ Helene Tucker felt sorry for Richard when the teacher embarrassed him.

7. Richard had trouble concentrating and learning in school because he was
   a. poor and hungry.
   b. distracted by Helene.
   c. lonely.
   d. unable to read.

8. Gregory implies that in his youth, he
   a. was not intelligent.
   b. was proud.
   c. had many friends.
   d. and Helene became friends.

9. The author implies that
   a. Mr. Williams felt sorry for the wino.
   b. Richard's teacher was insensitive.
   c. Richard liked people to feel sorry for him.
   d. Richard's father was dead.

10. The author implies that
    a. the mackinaws were poorly made.
    b. Helene was a sensitive girl.
    c. Helene disliked Richard.
    d. the wino was ashamed of his poverty.

STRUCTURE AND TECHNIQUE

1. In paragraphs 1 and 2, Gregory mentions several steps he took to impress Helene Tucker. What were they? Why does he include them in his essay?

2. A metaphor is a suggested comparison. What metaphor does Gregory use in paragraph 5, and what is its purpose? What metaphor does he use in the second sentence of paragraph 7, and what does it mean?

3. In narrating the incidents in the classroom and in the restaurant, Gregory chooses to provide actual dialogue rather than merely to tell what happened. Why?

4. At the end of the essay, Gregory shifts his focus from the classroom to the scene involving the wino at the restaurant. What is the connection between this closing scene and the rest of the essay?

CRITICAL READING AND DISCUSSION

1. When Gregory writes, "I never learned hate at home, or shame. I had to go to school for that" (paragraph 1), he is using irony—an inconsistency between what is expected and what actually occurs. What does he mean by these two statements? What is the effect of his irony?

2. What are Gregory's feelings about his teacher? What were your feelings about her as you read this essay? What could the teacher have done or said that would *not* have made Gregory feel ashamed?

3. Gregory shows how a childhood incident taught him shame. What other important lessons does Gregory learn in this essay? Explain.

4. At the end of his essay, Gregory says, "I waited too long to help another man." Why do you think he waited so long to assist the wino? What are some reasons people do not always help others who are in need (for example, ignoring a homeless person seated on the sidewalk)?

WRITING ASSIGNMENTS

Assignment 1: Writing a Paragraph

At some time in your life, you probably had an experience like Dick Gregory's in "Shame"—something that happened in a classroom, a group of friends or peers, or a family situation that proved to be both embarrassing and educational. At the time, the experience hurt you very much, but you learned from it. Write a narrative paragraph in which you retell this experience. Try to include vivid details and plenty of conversation so that the incident will come to life.

Assignment 2: Writing an Essay

Dick Gregory tells us in "Shame" that he was ashamed of his poverty and of being on welfare—to the point that he threw away the warm hooded mackinaw he had been given simply because it was obvious proof that he and his family were on relief. Do you think Gregory was justified in feeling so ashamed of his situation? How about other people who are on welfare? Are they justified if they feel ashamed? Choose either of the following thesis statements and develop it in an essay of several paragraphs:

People on welfare are justified in feeling ashamed.

People on welfare should not feel ashamed.

Then develop your thesis by thinking of several reasons to support the statement you have chosen. You might think along the following lines:

Availability of jobs

Education or lack of education

Number of young children at home requiring care

Illness, physical disability

Psychological factors—depression, work habits, expectations, mental illness

Society's attitude toward people on welfare

Assignment 3: Writing an Essay

Write an essay about three basic things that people must have in order to feel self-respect. In your thesis statement, name these three necessities and state that a person must possess them in order to feel self-respect. Here are some ideas to consider:

A certain number of material possessions

A job

A loving family or a special person

A clear conscience

A feeling of belonging

Freedom from addictions

In your supporting paragraphs, discuss the factors you have chosen, showing specifically why each is so important. In order to avoid falling into the trap of writing generalities, you may want to give examples of people who lack these necessities and show how such people lose self-respect. Your examples may be drawn from personal experience, or they may be hypothetical.

The Professor Is a Dropout

Beth Johnson

PREVIEW

After being mistakenly labeled "retarded" and humiliated into dropping out of first grade, Lupe Quintanilla knew she wanted nothing more to do with formal education. Life as a wife and mother would satisfy her . . . and it did, until she saw her own children being pushed aside as "slow learners." Driven to help them succeed, Lupe took steps that dramatically changed her life.

Guadalupe Quintanilla is an assistant professor at the University of 1 Houston. She is president of her own communications company. She trains law enforcement officers all over the country. She was nominated to serve as the U.S. Attorney General. She's been a representative to the United Nations.

That's a pretty impressive string of accomplishments. It's all the more 2 impressive when you consider this: "Lupe" Quintanilla is a first-grade dropout. Her school records state that she is retarded, that her IQ is so low she can't learn much of anything.

How did Lupe Quintanilla, "retarded" nonlearner, become 3 Dr. Quintanilla, respected educator? Her remarkable journey began in the town of Nogales, Mexico, just below the Arizona border. That's where Lupe first lived with her grandparents. (Her parents had divorced.) Then an uncle who had just finished medical school made her grandparents a generous offer. If they wanted to live with him, he would support the family as he began his medical practice.

Lupe, her grandparents, and her uncle all moved hundreds of miles to 4 a town in southern Mexico that didn't even have paved roads, let alone any schools. There, Lupe grew up helping her grandfather run his little pharmacy and her grandmother keep house. She remembers the time happily. "My grandparents were wonderful," she said. "Oh, my grandfather was stern, authoritarian, as Mexican culture demanded, but they were also very kind to me." When the chores were done, her grandfather taught Lupe to read and write Spanish and do basic arithmetic.

When Lupe was 12, her grandfather became blind. The family left 5 Mexico and went to Brownsville, Texas, with the hope that doctors there could restore his sight. Once they arrived in Brownsville, Lupe was enrolled in school. Although she understood no English, she was given an IQ test in that language. Not surprisingly, she didn't do very well.

Lupe even remembers her score. "I scored a sixty-four, which classified 6 me as seriously retarded, not even teachable," she said. "I was put into first grade with a class of six-year-olds. My duties were to take the little kids to the bathroom and to cut out pictures." The classroom activities were a total mystery to Lupe—they were all conducted in English. And she was humiliated by the other children, who teased her for being "so much older and so much dumber" than they were.

After four months in first grade, an incident occurred that Lupe still 7 does not fully understand. As she stood in the doorway of the classroom waiting to escort a little girl to the bathroom, a man approached her. He asked her, in Spanish, how to find the principal's office. Lupe was delighted. "Finally someone in this school had spoken to me with words I could understand, in the language of my soul, the language of my grandmother," she said. Eagerly, she answered his question in Spanish. Instantly her teacher swooped down on her, grabbing her arm and scolding her. She pulled Lupe along to the principal's office. There, the teacher and the principal both shouted at her, obviously very angry. Lupe was frightened and embarrassed, but also bewildered. She didn't understand a word they were saying.

"Why were they so angry? I don't know," said Lupe. "Was it because 8 I spoke Spanish at school? Or that I spoke to the man at all? I really don't know. All I know is how humiliated I was."

When she got home that day, she cried miserably, begging her grand- 9 father not to make her return to school. Finally he agreed.

From that time on, Lupe stayed at home, serving as her blind grand- 10 father's "eyes." She was a fluent reader in Spanish, and the older man loved to have her read newspapers, poetry, and novels aloud to him for hours.

Lupe's own love of reading flourished during these years. Her vocab- 11 ulary was enriched and her imagination fired by the novels she read— novels which she learned later were classics of Spanish literature. She read *Don Quixote*, the famous story of the noble, impractical knight who fought against windmills. She read thrilling accounts of the Mexican revolution. She read *La Prensa*, the local Spanish-language paper, and *Selecciones*, the Spanish-language version of *Reader's Digest*.

When she was just 16, Lupe married a young Mexican-American dental technician. Within five years, she had given birth to her three children, Victor, Mario, and Martha. Lupe's grandparents lived with the young family. Lupe was quite happy with her life. "I cooked, sewed, cleaned, and cared for everybody," she said. "I listened to my grandmother when she told me what made a good wife. In the morning I would actually put on my husband's shoes and tie the laces—anything to make his life easier. Living with my grandparents for so long, I was one generation behind in my ideas of what a woman could do and be." 12

Lupe's contentment ended when her children started school. When they brought home their report cards, she struggled to understand them. She could read enough English to know that what they said was not good. Her children had been put into a group called "Yellow Birds." It was a group for slow learners. 13

At night in bed, Lupe cried and blamed herself. It was obvious—not only was she retarded, but her children had taken after her. Now they, too, would never be able to learn like other children. 14

But in time, a thought began to break through Lupe's despair: Her children didn't seem like slow learners to her. At home, they learned everything she taught them, quickly and easily. She read to them constantly, from the books that she herself had loved as a child. *Aesop's Fables* and stories from *1,001 Arabian Nights* were family favorites. The children filled the house with the sounds of the songs, prayers, games, and rhymes they had learned from their parents and grandparents. They were smart children, eager to learn. They learned quickly—in Spanish. 15

A radical idea began to form in Lupe's mind. Maybe the school was wrong about her children. And if the school system could be wrong about her children—maybe it had been wrong about her, too. 16

Lupe visited her children's school, a daring action for her. "Many Hispanic parents would not dream of going to the classroom," she said. "In Hispanic culture, the teacher is regarded as a third parent, as an ultimate authority. To question her would seem most disrespectful, as though you were saying that she didn't know her job." That was one reason Lupe's grandparents had not interfered when Lupe was classified as retarded. "Anglo teachers often misunderstand Hispanic parents, believing that they aren't concerned about their children's education because they don't come visit the schools," Lupe said. "It's not a lack of concern at all. It's a mark of respect for the teacher's authority." 17

At her children's school. Lupe spoke to three different teachers. Two of them told her the same thing: "Your children are just slow. Sorry, but they can't learn." A third offered a glimmer of hope. He said, "They don't know how to function in English. It's possible that if you spoke English at home they would be able to do better." 18

Lupe pounced on that idea. "Where can I learn English?" she asked. The teacher shrugged. At that time there were no local English-language programs for adults. Finally he suggested that Lupe visit the local high school. Maybe she would be permitted to sit in the back of a classroom and pick up some English that way. 19

Lupe made an appointment with a counselor at the high school. But when the two women met, the counselor shook her head. "Your test scores 20 show that you are retarded," she told Lupe. "You'd just be taking space in the classroom away from someone who could learn."

Lupe's next stop was the hospital where she had served for years as 21 a volunteer. Could she sit in on some of the nursing classes held there? No, she was told, not without a diploma. Still undeterred, she went on to Texas Southmost College in Brownsville. Could she sit in on a class? No; no high-school diploma. Finally she went to the telephone company, where she knew operators were being trained. Could she listen in on the classes? No, only high-school graduates were permitted.

That day, leaving the telephone company. Lupe felt she had hit bot- 22 tom. She had been terrified in the first place to try to find an English class. Meeting with rejection after rejection nearly destroyed what little self-confidence she had. She walked home in the rain, crying. "I felt like a big barrier had fallen across my path," she said. "I couldn't go over it; I couldn't go under it; I couldn't go around it."

But the next day Lupe woke with fresh determination. "I was moti- 23 vated by love of my kids," she said. "I was not going to quit." She got up; made breakfast for her kids, husband, and grandparents; saw her children and husband off for the day; and started out again. "I remember walking to the bus stop, past a dog that always scared me to death, and heading back to the college. The lady I spoke to said, 'I told you, we can't do anything for you without a high-school degree.' But as I left the building, I went up to the first Spanish-speaking student I saw. His name was Gabito. I said, 'Who really makes the decisions around here?' He said, 'The registrar.'" Since she hadn't had any luck in the office building, Lupe decided to take a more direct approach. She asked Gabito to point out the registrar's car in the parking lot. For the next two hours she waited beside it until its owner showed up.

Lupe surrounded by her children: Martha, Victor, and Mario.

Impressed by Lupe's persistence, the registrar listened to her story. But 24 instead of giving her permission to sit in on a class and learn more English, he insisted that she sign up for a full college load. Before she knew it, she was enrolled in four classes: basic math, basic English, psychology, and typing. The registrar's parting words to her were, "Don't come back if you don't make it through."

With that "encouragement," Lupe began a semester that was part 25 nightmare, part dream come true. Every day she got her husband and children off to school, took the bus to campus, came home to make lunch for her husband and grandparents, went back to campus, and was home in time to greet Victor, Mario, and Martha when they got home from school. In the evenings she cooked, cleaned, did laundry, and got the children to bed. Then she would study, often until three in the morning.

"Sometimes in class I would feel sick with the stress of it," she said. 26 "I'd go to the bathroom and talk to myself in the mirror. Sometimes I'd say, 'What are you doing here? Why don't you go home and watch *I Love Lucy?*' "

But she didn't go home. Instead, she studied furiously, using her 27 Spanish-English dictionary, constantly making lists of new words she wanted to understand. "I still do that today," she said. "When I come across a word I don't know, I write it down, look it up, and write sentences using it until I own that word."

Although so much of the language and subject matter was new to Lupe, one part of the college experience was not. That was the key skill of reading, a skill Lupe possessed. As she struggled with English, she found the reading speed, comprehension, and vocabulary that she had developed in Spanish carrying over into her new language. "Reading," she said, "reading was the vehicle. Although I didn't know it at the time, when I was a girl learning to love to read, I was laying the foundation for academic success." 28

She gives credit, too, to her Hispanic fellow students. "At first, they didn't know what to make of me. They were eighteen years old, and at that time it was very unfashionable for an older person to be in college. But once they decided I wasn't a 'plant' from the administration, they were my greatest help." The younger students spent hours helping Lupe, explaining unfamiliar words and terms, coaching her, and answering her questions. 29

That first semester passed in a fog of exhaustion. Many mornings, Lupe doubted she could get out of bed, much less care for her family and tackle her classes. But when she thought of her children and what was at stake for them, she forced herself on. She remembers well what those days were like. "Just a day at a time. That was all I could think about. I could make myself get up one more day, study one more day, cook and clean one more day. And those days eventually turned into a semester." 30

To her own amazement perhaps as much as anyone's, Lupe discovered that she was far from retarded. Although she sweated blood over many assignments, she completed them. She turned them in on time. And, remarkably, she made the dean's list her very first semester. 31

After that, there was no stopping Lupe Quintanilla. She soon realized that the associate's degree offered by Texas Southmost College would not satisfy her. Continuing her Monday, Wednesday, and Friday schedule at Southmost, she enrolled for Tuesday and Thursday courses at Pan American University, a school 140 miles from Brownsville. Within three years, she had earned both her junior college degree and a bachelor's degree in biology. She then won a fellowship that took her to graduate school at the University of Houston, where she earned a master's degree in Spanish literature. When she graduated, the university offered her a job as director of the Mexican-American studies program. While in that position, she earned a doctoral degree in education. 32

How did she do it all? Lupe herself isn't sure. "I hardly know. When I think back to those years, it seems like a life that someone else lived." It was a rich and exciting but also very challenging period for Lupe and her family. On the one hand, Lupe was motivated by the desire to set an example for her children, to prove to them that they could succeed in the English-speaking academic world. On the other hand, she worried about neglecting her family. She tried hard to attend important activities, such as parents' meetings at school and her children's sporting events. But things didn't always work out. Lupe still remembers attending a baseball game that her older son, Victor, was playing in. When Victor came to bat, he hit a home run. But as the crowd cheered and Victor glanced proudly over at his mother in the stands, he saw she was studying a textbook. "I hadn't seen 33 the home run," Lupe admitted. "That sort of thing was hard for everyone to take."

Although Lupe worried that her children would resent her busy sched- 34 ule, she also saw her success reflected in them as they blossomed in school. She forced herself to speak English at home, and their language skills improved quickly. She read to them in English instead of Spanish—gulping down her pride as their pronunciation became better than hers and they began correcting her. (Once the children were in high school and fluent in English, Lupe switched back to Spanish at home, so that the children would be fully comfortable in both languages.) "I saw the change in them almost immediately," she said. "After I helped them with their homework, they would see me pulling out my own books and going to work. In the morning, I would show them the papers I had written. As I gained confidence, so did they." By the next year, the children had been promoted out of the Yellow Birds.

Even though Victor, Mario, and Martha all did well academically, Lupe 35 realized she could not assume that they would face no more obstacles in school. When Mario was in high school, for instance, he wanted to sign up for a debate class. Instead, he was assigned to woodworking. She visited the school to ask why. Mario's teacher told her, "He's good with his hands. He'll be a great carpenter, and that's a good thing for a Mexican to be." Controlling her temper, Lupe responded, "I'm glad you think he's good with his hands. He'll be a great physician someday, and he is going to be in the debate class."

Two members of the Houston police department learn job-specific Spanish phrases from Lupe. Lupe also trains the officers in cultural awareness.

Today, Lupe Quintanilla teaches at the University of Houston, where 36 she has developed several dozen courses concerning Hispanic literature and culture. Her cross-cultural training for law enforcement officers, which helps bring police and firefighters and local Hispanic communities closer together, is renowned throughout the country. Former President Ronald Reagan named her to a national board that keeps the White House informed of new programs in law enforcement. She has received numerous awards for teaching excellence, and there is even a scholarship named in her honor. Her name appears in the Hispanic Hall of Fame, and she has been co-chair of the White House Commission on Hispanic Education.

The love of reading that her grandfather instilled in Lupe is still alive. 37 She thinks of him every year when she introduces to her students one of his favorite poets, Amado Nervo. She requires them to memorize these lines from one of Nervo's poems: "When I got to the end of my long journey in life, I realized that I was the architect of my own destiny." Of these lines, Lupe says, "That is something that I deeply believe, and I want my students to learn it before the end of their long journey. We create our own destiny."

Her love of reading and learning has helped Lupe create a distinguished 38 destiny. But none of the honors she has received means more to her than the success of her own children, the reason she made that frightening journey to seek classes in English years ago. Today Mario is a physician. Victor and Martha are lawyers, both having earned doctor of law degrees. And so today, Lupe likes to say, "When someone calls the house and asks for 'Dr. Quintanilla,' I have to ask, 'Which one?' There are four of us—one retarded and three slow learners."

READING COMPREHENSION

1. The word *flourished* in "Lupe's own love of reading flourished during these years. Her vocabulary was enriched and her imagination fired by the novels she read" (paragraph 11) means
   a. grew.
   b. stood still.
   c. was lost.
   d. remained.

2. The word *instilled* in "The love of reading that her grandfather instilled in Lupe is still alive" (paragraph 37) means
   a. frightened.
   b. established.
   c. forced.
   d. forgot.

3. Which of the following would be a good alternative title for this selection?
   a. Difficulties Facing Spanish-Speaking Students
   b. Unfair Labeling
   c. Balancing School and Family
   d. A Courageous Mother's Triumph

4. Which sentence best expresses the main idea of the selection?
   a. Lupe, a first-grade dropout, eventually earned a doctoral degree and created a professional career.
   b. Lupe Quintanilla's experience proves that the educational system must be set up to accommodate non-English-speaking children.
   c. Through hard work and persistence combined with a love of reading and learning, Lupe has created a distinguished career and helped her children become professionals.
   d. In school, Spanish-speaking students may experience obstacles as they aim for professional careers.

5. Lupe realized that her children were not retarded when
   a. they got good grades at school.
   b. she saw how quickly they learned at home.
   c. they were put in the group called "Yellow Birds."
   d. they read newspapers, poetry, and novels to her.

6. Lupe's training for law enforcement officers
   a. teaches them to speak Spanish.
   b. teaches Hispanic literature and culture.
   c. offers a scholarship named in her honor.
   d. brings police, firefighters, and local Hispanic communities together.

7. According to Lupe, Hispanic parents rarely visit their children's schools because they
   a. do not consider schoolwork important.
   b. think doing so would be disrespectful to the teacher.
   c. are ashamed of their English language skills.
   d. are usually working during school visitation hours.

8. "Once they arrived in Brownsville, Lupe was enrolled in school. Although she understood no English, she was given an IQ test in that language. Not surprisingly, she didn't do very well" (paragraph 5). From these sentences, we might conclude that
   a. an IQ test in a language that the person tested doesn't know is useless.
   b. although Lupe was not very intelligent at first, she became more intelligent once she learned English.
   c. Lupe really did know English.
   d. there are no IQ tests in Spanish.

9. We might conclude from the reading that
   a. a school system's judgment about an individual is always accurate.
   b. it is often better for a child to stay home rather than attend school.
   c. by paying attention and speaking up, parents may remove obstacles to their children's education.
   d. working parents should accept the fact that they cannot attend important events in their children's lives.

10. The last line of the reading suggests that
    a. retarded people can become successful professionals.
    b. people should not blindly accept other people's opinions of them.
    c. Lupe's children are smarter than she is.
    d. all of the above.

STRUCTURE AND TECHNIQUE

1. Johnson begins the essay by listing Lupe Quintanilla's accomplishments, then revealing that Quintanilla was once classified as retarded. What introductory technique is Johnson employing? Why is it effective here?

2. Paragraphs 3–11 are devoted to the first fifteen years of Lupe's life. But the next decade or so is covered in only two paragraphs (12–13). Why might Johnson have presented Lupe's earlier life in so much more detail? Do you agree with her decision?

3. In paragraph 2, Johnson writes that "[Lupe's] school records state that she is retarded. . . ." But in the next sentence, she writes, "How did Lupe Quintanilla, 'retarded' nonlearner, become Dr. Quintanilla, respected educator?" Why does Johnson put the word "retarded" in quotation marks in the second sentence, but not in the first? What is she implying? Can you find another place where Johnson makes similar use of quotation marks?

4. At one point, Johnson switches from the topic of Lupe's success in college to the topic of the challenges that continued to face her children in school. In what paragraph does she make that switch? What transitional words does she use to alert the reader to her new direction?

CRITICAL READING AND DISCUSSION

1. In the course of the essay, what characteristics and attitudes does Lupe suggest are typical of Hispanic culture? Does she seem sympathetic, critical, or neutral about those qualities or attitudes? How has she dealt with cultural expectations in her own life?

2. How has Lupe handled the question of what language to use with her children? If you grew up in a two-language household, how did your family deal with the issue? How would you approach the issue with children of your own?

3. Do you think Lupe's grandfather was right in allowing her to quit school? What factors do you imagine might have gone into his decision?

4. Lupe credits her fellow Hispanic students with giving her valuable support in college. Is there anyone in your life—a teacher, family member, or friend—who has helped you through challenging times in your education? Explain what obstacles you faced and how this person helped you overcome them.

WRITING ASSIGNMENTS

Assignment 1: Writing a Paragraph

Write a paragraph that takes as its topic sentence one of the following statements:

Schools need to be prepared to help non-English-speaking students catch up with other students at their grade level.

The responsibility for catching non-English-speaking students up to their grade level rests solely with the students and their families.

Support your topic sentence with several points.

Assignment 2: Writing an Essay

Lupe Quintanilla is an outstanding example of someone who has taken charge of her life. She has been, to echo the poet whose work she teaches, the architect of her own destiny. Choose a person you know who, in your opinion, has done a fine job of taking charge of his or her own destiny. Write an essay about this person. You might describe three areas of life in which the person has taken control. Alternatively, you might narrate three incidents from the person's life that illustrate his or her admirable self-determination.

Assignment 3: Writing an Essay

Lupe had to struggle in order to balance her school responsibilities with her duties as a wife and mother. Write an essay in which you identify aspects of your life that you need to juggle along with your responsibilities as a student. They may include a job, a spouse or significant other, children, housekeeping duties, pets, extracurricular activities, a difficult living situation, or anything else that poses a challenge to your academics. Provide vivid, real-life illustrations of how each of those responsibilities sometimes conflicts with your studies.

Superman and Me

Sherman Alexie

PREVIEW

Sherman Alexie is a Spokane/Coeur d'Alene Indian who grew up on the Spokane reservation in Washington state. He has written numerous books, including *The Lone Ranger and Tonto Fistfight in Heaven* (1993), *Flight* (2007), and *The Absolute True Diary of a Part-Time Indian* (2007, 2009), and has received the National Book Award for Young People's Literature, the PEN/Faulkner Award for Fiction, a Sundance Film Festival Audience Award, and the Washington State Governor's Writers Award. This essay, filled with the humor and struggle often found in much of Alexie's work, was originally published in the *Los Angeles Times* as part of a series called "The Joy of Reading and Writing."

I learned to read with a Superman comic book. Simple enough, I suppose. 1 I cannot recall which particular Superman comic book I read, nor can I remember which villain he fought in that issue. I cannot remember the plot, nor the means by which I obtained the comic book. What I can remember is this: I was 3 years old, a Spokane Indian boy living with his family on the Spokane Indian Reservation in eastern Washington state. We were poor by most standards, but one of my parents usually managed to find some minimum-wage job or another, which made us middle-class by reservation standards. I had a brother and three sisters. We lived on a combination of irregular paychecks, hope, fear and government surplus food.

My father, who is one of the few Indians who went to Catholic school on 2 purpose, was an avid reader of westerns, spy thrillers, murder mysteries, gangster epics, basketball player biographies and anything else he could find. He bought his books by the pound at Dutch's Pawn Shop, Goodwill, Salvation Army and Value Village. When he had extra money, he bought new novels at supermarkets, convenience stores and hospital gift shops. Our house was filled with books. They were stacked in crazy piles in the bathroom, bedrooms and living room. In a fit of unemployment-inspired creative energy, my father built a set of bookshelves and soon filled them with a random assortment of books about the Kennedy assassination, Watergate, the Vietnam War and the entire 23-book series of the Apache westerns. My father loved books, and since I loved my father with an aching devotion, I decided to love books as well.

I can remember picking up my father's books before I could read. 3 The words themselves were mostly foreign, but I still remember the exact moment when I first understood, with a sudden clarity, the purpose of a paragraph. I didn't have the vocabulary to say "paragraph," but I realized that a paragraph was a fence that held words. The words inside a paragraph worked together for a common purpose. They had some specific reason for being inside the same fence. This knowledge delighted me. I began to think of everything in terms of paragraphs. Our reservation was a small paragraph within the United States. My family's house was a paragraph, distinct from the other paragraphs of the LeBrets to the north, the Fords to our south and the Tribal School to the west. Inside our house, each family member existed as a separate paragraph but still had genetics and common experiences to link us. Now, using this logic, I can see my changed family as an essay of seven paragraphs: mother, father, older brother, the deceased sister, my younger twin sisters and our adopted little brother.

At the same time I was seeing the world in paragraphs, I also picked up 4 that Superman comic book. Each panel, complete with picture, dialogue and narrative was a three-dimensional paragraph. In one panel, Superman breaks through a door. His suit is red, blue and yellow. The brown door shatters into many pieces. I look at the narrative above the picture. I cannot read the words, but I assume it tells me that "Superman is breaking down the door." Aloud, I pretend to read the words and say, "Superman is breaking down the door." Words, dialogue, also float out of Superman's mouth. Because he is breaking down the door, I assume he says, "I am breaking down the door." Once again, I pretend to read the words and say aloud, "I am breaking down the door." In this way, I learned to read.

This might be an interesting story all by itself. A little Indian boy teaches 5 himself to read at an early age and advances quickly. He reads *Grapes of Wrath* in kindergarten when other children are struggling through *Dick and Jane*. If he'd been anything but an Indian boy living on the reservation, he might have been called a prodigy. But he is an Indian boy living on the reservation and is simply an oddity. He grows into a man who often speaks of his childhood in the third person, as if it will somehow dull the pain and make him sound more modest about his talents.

A smart Indian is a dangerous person, widely feared and ridiculed by 6 Indians and non-Indians alike. I fought with my classmates on a daily basis. They wanted me to stay quiet when the non-Indian teacher asked for answers, for volunteers, for help. We were Indian children who were expected to be stupid. Most lived up to those expectations inside the classroom but subverted them on the outside. They struggled with basic reading in school but could remember how to sing a few dozen powwow songs. They were monosyllabic in front of their non-Indian teachers but could tell complicated stories and jokes at the dinner table. They submissively ducked their heads when confronted by a non-Indian adult but would slug it out with the Indian bully who was 10 years older. As Indian children, we were expected to fail in the non-Indian world. Those who failed were ceremonially accepted by other Indians and appropriately pitied by non-Indians.

I refused to fail. I was smart. I was arrogant. I was lucky. I read books 7 late into the night, until I could barely keep my eyes open. I read books at recess, then during lunch, and in the few minutes left after I had finished my classroom assignments. I read books in the car when my family traveled to powwows or basketball games. In shopping malls, I ran to the bookstores and read bits and pieces of as many books as I could. I read the books my father brought home from the pawnshops and secondhand. I read the books I borrowed from the library. I read the backs of cereal boxes. I read the newspaper. I read the bulletins posted on the walls of the school, the clinic, the tribal offices, the post office. I read junk mail. I read auto-repair manuals. I read magazines. I read anything that had words and paragraphs. I read with equal parts joy and desperation. I loved those books, but I also knew that love had only one purpose. I was trying to save my life.

Despite all the books I read, I am still surprised I became a writer. I was 8 going to be a pediatrician. These days, I write novels, short stories, and poems. I visit schools and teach creative writing to Indian kids. In all my years in the reservation school system, I was never taught how to write poetry, short stories or novels. I was certainly never taught that Indians wrote poetry, short stories and novels. Writing was something beyond Indians. I cannot recall a single time that a guest teacher visited the reservation. There must have been visiting teachers. Who were they? Where are they now? Do they exist? I visit the schools as often as possible. The Indian kids crowd the classroom. Many are writing their own poems, short stories and novels. They have read my books. They have read many other books. They look at me with bright eyes and arrogant wonder. They are trying to save their lives. Then there are the sullen and already defeated Indian kids who sit in the back rows and ignore me with theatrical precision. The pages of their notebooks are empty. They carry neither pencil nor pen. They stare out the window. They refuse and resist. "Books," I say to them. "Books," I say. I throw my weight against their locked doors. The door holds. I am smart. I am arrogant. I am lucky. I am trying to save our lives.

READING COMPREHENSION

1. The word *prodigy* in ". . . he might have been called a prodigy" (paragraph 5) means
   a. a bully.
   b. a highly talented child or youth.
   c. a show-off.
   d. an extraordinary event.

2. The word *subverted* in ". . . but subverted them on the outside" (paragraph 6) means
   a. strengthened.
   b. supported.
   c. avoided.
   d. undermined.

3. Which of the following would be a good alternative title for this selection?
   a. Superman vs. The Lone Ranger
   b. Reading Saved My Life
   c. Suffering in School
   d. Life on a Reservation

4. Which sentence best expresses the main idea of the selection?

   a. Alexie thought learning to read was fun.

   b. Alexie was poor and grew up on an Indian reservation.

   c. Alexie realized that learning to read could save his life.

   d. The Superman comic books tell a great story.

5. Why did Alexie decide to start reading?

   a. He had nothing better to do.

   b. He was struggling in school.

   c. He wanted to connect with his father.

   d. He wanted to impress his teacher.

6. Alexie realized that a "paragraph was a fence that held words." What did he mean by this?

   a. All the words in a paragraph had a common purpose.

   b. The words in a paragraph couldn't go anywhere.

   c. Paragraphs are like islands.

   d. Paragraphs should be distinct from each other.

7. *True or False?* _____ The other children in his classes were impressed with Alexie's intelligence.

8. *True or False?* _____ The teachers who taught on the reservation had high hopes for the children.

9. Why does Alexie believe he didn't fail like other kids?

   a. He was arrogant and lucky.

   b. He was richer than other kids.

   c. The teachers liked him.

   d. The school wanted him to graduate.

10. According to Alexie, why does he visit classrooms and "throw [his] weight against their locked doors"?

    a. He is tired of people locking doors on the reservations.

    b. The classrooms need to open up.

    c. He is trying to save lives on the reservation.

    d. He likes showing off how well he has done.

STRUCTURE AND TECHNIQUE

1. Which pattern of development—exemplification, narration, or description—does Alexie use in most of his essay? Explain.

2. Many of Alexie's sentences are longer and more complicated, but in two paragraphs (7 and 8), he uses a series of short brief sentences that repeat words. What do you think is the purpose of these shorter sentences? Why do you think he repeats the sentences, but changes the verb tense?

3. A title can offer interesting insights into an essay, especially if the title acquires unexpected meanings. Before reading this essay, to what did you think the title "Superman and Me" might refer? What additional meanings do you think Alexie intended?

CRITICAL READING AND DISCUSSION

1. Alexie's father loved to read. Do you think he believed that if Alexie learned to read his life would be better? Why or why not?

2. In the third paragraph, Alexie compares his reservation to a "small paragraph within the United States." Why do you think his understanding of the purpose of a paragraph spanned to reservation life?

3. Alexie credits learning and loving to read, in addition to his arrogance and luck, for saving his life. Do you think reading truly made a difference to his life? Explain.

4. Alexie has written many novels, short stories, poems, and even films, but he says he was never taught how to write. If he didn't need to be taught, why do you think he is so purposeful in visiting schools, talking about reading and writing, and helping students find their own voices in their writing?

WRITING ASSIGNMENTS

Assignment 1: Writing a Paragraph

In his essay, Alexie explains that reading the Superman comic helped him understand storytelling. Write a paragraph that explains how something you read helped you understand something new.

Assignment 2: Writing an Essay

Alexie writes about how reading influenced his life. Write an essay that reflects on someone or some book that has strongly influenced your life. You may want to focus on a book you read that changed your thinking, or you may want to focus on a teacher who either positively or negatively influenced your attitude toward reading, writing, or school. You will want to provide vivid details to help support your point and help the reader understand why this person/book has had so much influence on your life.

Assignment 3: Writing an Essay

Alexie alludes to the stereotypes of American Indians and how difficult it was to overcome those stereotypes. In his essay, he says that a "smart Indian is a dangerous person." He is obviously very smart, talented, and successful, yet he doesn't seem dangerous. In this essay, you are to choose a stereotype and argue why it is incorrect. Incorporate anecdotes, research, and any other information you can find to support your thesis.

Prison Studies

Malcolm X

PREVIEW

"Prison Studies" is an autobiographical account of the life of Malcolm X while in prison. He discusses in the article how he learns how to read and what prompted him to do so. He describes his painstaking goal toward literacy and the prison culture. He talks about how certain prison men had power and influence because of the manner in which they expressed themselves. He embarks on a journey of literacy not only for himself, but he later finds that his calling is to help his people, African American people, through the knowledge he gained while incarcerated. "Prison Studies" is an example of how a misguided young criminal turns his life around, joins a new religion, and emerges from prison with a higher purpose.

Many who today hear me somewhere in person, or on television, or those 1 who read something I've said, will think I went to school far beyond the eighth grade. This impression is due entirely to my prison studies.

It had really begun back in the Charlestown Prison, when Bimbi first 2 made me feel envy of his stock of knowledge. Bimbi had always taken charge of any conversation he was in, and I had tried to emulate[1] him. But every book I picked up had few sentences which didn't contain anywhere from one to nearly all of the words that might as well have been in Chinese. When I just skipped those words, of course, I really ended up with little idea of what the book said. So I had come to the Norfolk Prison Colony still going through only book-reading motions. Pretty soon, I would have quit even these motions, unless I had received the motivation that I did.

I saw that the best thing I could do was get hold of a dictionary—to 3 study, to learn some words. I was lucky enough to reason also that I should try to improve my penmanship. It was sad. I couldn't even write in a straight line. It was both ideas together that moved me to request a dictionary along with some tablets and pencils from the Norfolk Prison Colony school.

I spent two days just riffling uncertainly through the dictionary's pages. 4 I'd never realized so many words existed. I didn't know which words I needed to learn. Finally, to start some kind of action, I began copying.

In my slow, painstaking, ragged handwriting, I copied into my tablet 5 everything printed on that first page, down to the punctuation marks.

I believe it took me a day. Then, aloud, I read back, to myself, every- 6 thing I'd written on the tablet. Over and over, aloud, to myself, I read my own handwriting.

I woke up the next morning, thinking about those words—immensely 7 proud to realize that not only had I written so much at one time, but I'd written words that I never knew were in the world. Moreover, with a little effort, I also could remember what many of these words meant. I reviewed

[1]*emulate:* imitate, especially from respect.

the words whose meanings I didn't remember. Funny thing, from the dictionary first page right now, that "aardvark" springs to my mind. The dictionary had a picture of it, a long-tailed, long-eared, burrowing African mammal, which lives off termites caught by sticking out its tongue as an anteater does for ants.

I was so fascinated that I went on—I copied the dictionary's next page. 8 And the same experience came when I studied that. With every succeeding page, I also learned of people and places and events from history. Actually the dictionary is like a miniature encyclopedia. Finally the dictionary's A section had filled a whole tablet—and I went on into the B's. That was the way I started copying what eventually became the entire dictionary. It went a lot faster after so much practice helped me to pick up handwriting speed. Between what I wrote in my tablet, and writing letters, during the rest of my time in prison I would guess I wrote a million words.

I suppose it was inevitable that as my word-base broadened, I could for 9 the first time pick up a book and read and now begin to understand what the book was saying. Anyone who has read a great deal can imagine the new world that opened. Let me tell you something; from then until I left that prison, in every free moment I had, if I was not reading in the library, I was reading on my bunk. You couldn't have gotten me out of books with a wedge. Between Mr. Muhammad's teachings, my correspondence, my visitors—usually Ella and Reginald—and my reading of books, months passed without my even thinking about being imprisoned. In fact, up to then, I never had been so truly free in my life. . . .

As you can imagine, especially in a prison where there was heavy em- 10 phasis on rehabilitation, an inmate[2] was smiled upon if he demonstrated an unusually intense interest in books. There was a sizable number of well-read inmates, especially the popular debaters. Some were said by many to be practically walking encyclopedias. They were almost celebrities. No university would ask any student to devour literature as I did when this new world opened to me, of being able to read and *understand*.

I read more in my room than in the library itself. An inmate who was 11 known to read a lot could check out more than the permitted maximum number of books, I preferred reading in the total isolation of my own room.

When I had progressed to really serious reading, every night at about 12 ten P.M. I would be outraged with the "lights out." It always seemed to catch me right in the middle of something engrossing.

Fortunately, right outside my door was a corridor light that cast a glow 13 into my room. The glow was enough to read by, once my eyes adjusted to it. So when "lights out" came, I would sit on the floor where I could continue reading in that glow.

At one-hour intervals the night guards paced past every room. Each 14 time I heard the approaching footsteps, I jumped into bed and feigned sleep. And as soon as the guard passed, I got back out of bed onto the floor area of that light-glow, where I would read for another fifty-eight minutes—until the guard approached again. That went on until three or four every morning. Three or four hours of sleep a night was enough for me. Often in the years in the streets I had slept less than that.

---

[2]*inmate*: prisoner.

I have often reflected upon the new vistas[3] that reading opened to me. 15 I knew right there in prison that reading had changed forever the course of my life. As I see it today, the ability to read awoke inside me some long dormant craving to be mentally alive. I certainly wasn't seeking any degree, the way a college confers[4] a status symbol upon its students. My homemade education gave me, with every additional book that I read, a little bit more sensitivity to the deafness, dumbness, and blindness that was afflicting the black race in America. Not long ago, an English writer telephoned me from London, asking questions. One was, "What's your alma mater[5]?" I told him, "Books." You will never catch me with a free fifteen minutes in which I'm not studying something I feel might be able to help the black man. . . .

Every time I catch a plane, I have with me a book that I want to read— 16 and that's a lot of books these days. If I weren't out here every day battling the white man, I could spend the rest of my life reading, just satisfying my curiosity—because you can hardly mention anything I'm not curious about. I don't think anybody ever got more out of going to prison than I did. In fact, prison enabled me to study far more intensively than I would have if my life had gone differently and I had attended some college. I imagine that one of the biggest troubles with colleges is there are too many distractions, too much panty-raiding, fraternities, and boola-boola and all of that. Where else but in prison could I have attacked my ignorance by being able to study intensely sometimes as much as fifteen hours a day?

READING COMPREHENSION

1. The word *outraged* in paragraph 12 in "I would be outraged with the 'lights out' " most closely means

   a. secretly happy.

   b. excited.

   c. extremely upset.

   d. insecure.

2. The author implies in paragraph 15 that reading opened new *vistas* for him; he meant that reading gave him

   a. a new worldview.

   b. an access code to the prison libraries.

   c. outdoor exercise sessions.

   d. a historical overview of the black experience.

3. The word *confers* in paragraph 15 most closely means

   a. to bestow or give ceremoniously.

   b. mental overview.

   c. to imitate.

   d. to motivate.

[3]*vistas*: mental overviews.

[4]*confers*: bestows, gives ceremoniously.

[5]*alma mater*: the college that one has attended.

4. Which of the following would be a good alternative title for the selection?
   a. Being Black in America's Prisons
   b. A Young Prisoner's Journey
   c. Malcolm's Journey into Literacy
   d. Malcolm X's Time in Prison

5. Which of the following sentences best expresses the main idea of the selection?
   a. One's race in America determines many things.
   b. Malcolm's journey through literacy opened new worlds for him.
   c. Prison life in America offered many challenges.
   d. Prison life closely mirrors life in society.

6. The reading selection identifies the process by which Malcolm started his journey into reading. Who inspired him to begin his quest into the world of words?
   a. the prison guards
   b. his prison mates
   c. Bimbi, the eloquent prisoner and walking encyclopedia
   d. friends from his early years

7. Malcolm explains that prisoners who showed an interest in reading were
   a. beaten severely.
   b. laughed at for trying to act white.
   c. encouraged to check out books.
   d. distracted by other prisoners.

8. The author states that even after he left prison it was difficult to find him without a book. What was the only thing that kept him away from reading?
   a. his family life
   b. his work obligations
   c. his battling the white man
   d. his legal history

9. Malcolm criticizes colleges and universities because he believes
   a. there aren't enough libraries available to students.
   b. students have too many distractions to concentrate on their studies.
   c. fraternities and sororities do not accept black students.
   d. higher education should be free in America.

10. Malcolm feels that his time in prison and his education while in prison
    a. were invaluable to him.
    b. were a waste of time.
    c. could have been better spent in society.
    d. changed his accent.

STRUCTURE AND TECHNIQUE

1. The article is written in a format not unlike a journal entry or reading someone's diary. How does this style add to the story Malcolm X is trying to relay? Is it an effective way to bring the reader into the author's world? If so, how? If not, why not?

2. Malcolm's excerpt is brief, and yet the reader feels as if he or she has spent a longer amount of time with him. Malcolm condenses his experiences in a very concise manner and leaves nothing out. Do you believe the technique of using smaller paragraphs, sometimes one sentence long, was effective? How did this technique enhance the reading of the excerpt?

3. *Prison Studies* uses the personal pronoun "I" numerous times. How did this affect the reading of the passage? Did it make it come across as authentic or made up? How does the use of the personal pronoun "I" so frequently add to the urgency for knowledge Malcolm may have felt as a prisoner?

4. How do you believe his narrative could have been improved? Could he have used more examples about his life in prison? Most of his narration centers around his reading of books. How does this affect the overall story?

CRITICAL READING AND DISCUSSION

1. You might expect a journal about a man imprisoned to be dark and gloomy. But Malcolm X recounts his life in prison and uses a different tone. How does Malcolm feel about his experience in prison? Was he bitter and desolate? Or was he so engrossed in his new world to hardly notice anything else around him? What examples are given in the excerpt that make you believe this?

2. Do you think that Malcolm X's experience in prison would have been different if he had not "found" books and reading? How do you believe his views and life were shaped by his having been imprisoned? Explain.

3. Malcolm X uses sharp, direct language to convey his message of thirst for knowledge. What personality traits of his are evident in the manner in which he expressed himself in the passage? What examples can you point out that shed light on his personality?

4. What importance did being imprisoned and having discovered the world within the prison walls make in Malcolm's life? Do you believe if he had been in society he would have started to read and gotten as far as he did? If so, why? If not, then why not?

WRITING ASSIGNMENTS

Assignment 1: Writing a Paragraph

In his autobiography, Malcolm X refers to his time in prison as a period in which he "found" literacy and, in a way, himself. In the negative environment he found himself in, he was still able to make the best of his incarceration. His prison time became a blessing in disguise. Did you ever have to go through what initially appeared to be a negative situation, and it later turned out to be the best thing that could have happened to you? Under what circumstances did you find yourself? How long did this period last and what lessons did you learn from the experience?

Write a paragraph about a time you received a blessing in disguise. Make sure you address the questions listed above.

Assignment 2: Writing an Essay

Often individuals find themselves trapped in circumstances beyond their control. Can you think of a time when you felt that you had no way out but you made the best out of it? Did you grow up in a neighborhood that was dangerous or not very sanitary and/or safe? How did you cope with living under these conditions? How did you get out? Or plan to get out? What changes, if any, did you have to make in yourself?

Write an essay about "Changes I Would Like to Make in Myself." These could be physical or abstract changes. Physical changes could be wanting to lose ten pounds, having plastic surgery, or beginning an exercise or weight lifting routine. Abstract changes could include attitude changes or behavioral changes, like stop procrastinating, stop lying so much, and so on.

Assignment 3: Writing an Essay

The other prisoners, especially the ones who loved reading and debating, had a great influence on Malcolm while he was in prison. Who were they and how did they influence him to want to become literate? Do you know of someone who motivated you to become and do your best? How did this person influence your decisions? What qualities did this person or persons possess that had you wanting to emulate them?

Write an essay about a person who positively influenced your life. How is your life different and better now that you underwent this change in your life? What lessons did you learn from the experience? Explain the circumstances that surrounded you before you decided to make a change.

Straw into Gold: The Metamorphosis of the Everyday

Sandra Cisneros

PREVIEW

Sandra Cisneros was born in Chicago, Illinois in 1954. She received a BA from Loyola University in Chicago and an MFA from the University of Iowa. She has worked with high school dropouts, has taught creative writing, and has been a visiting writer at numerous universities, including University of California, Berkeley. She has written numerous books of poetry, a children's book, and two novels. She has received several awards and grants including a MacArthur Foundation Fellowship and two National Endowment of the Arts Fellowships.

When I was living in an artists' colony in the south of France, some fellow 1
Latin-Americans who taught at the university in Aix-en-Provence invited
me to share a home-cooked meal with them. I had been living abroad almost a year then on an NEA grant, subsisting mainly on French bread and
lentils so that my money could last longer. So when the invitation to dinner
arrived, I accepted without hesitation. Especially since they had promised
Mexican food.

What I didn't realize when they made this invitation was that I was 2
supposed to be involved in preparing the meal. I guess they assumed I
knew how to cook Mexican food because I am Mexican. They wanted specifically tortillas, though I'd never made a tortilla in my life.

It's true I had witnessed my mother rolling the little armies of dough 3
into perfect circles, but my mother's family is from Guanajuato; they are
provincianos, country folk. They only know how to make flour tortillas.
My father's family, on the other hand, is chilango from Mexico City. We
ate corn tortillas but we didn't make them. Someone was sent to the corner
tortilleria to buy some. I'd never seen anybody make corn tortillas. Ever.

Somehow my Latino hosts had gotten a hold of a packet of corn flour, 4
and this is what they tossed my way with orders to produce tortillas. Así
como sea. Any ol' way, they said and went back to their cooking.

Why did I feel like the woman in the fairy tale who was locked in a 5
room and ordered to spin straw into gold? I had the same sick feeling when
I was required to write my critical essay for the MFA exam—the only piece
of noncreative writing necessary in order to get my graduate degree. How
was I to start? There were rules involved here, unlike writing a poem or
story, which I did intuitively. There was a step by step process needed and
I had better know it. I felt as if making tortillas—or writing a critical paper,
for that matter—were tasks so impossible I wanted to break down into
tears.

Somehow though, I managed to make tortillas—crooked and burnt, 6
but edible nonetheless. My hosts were absolutely ignorant when it came
to Mexican food; they thought my tortillas were delicious. (I'm glad my
mama wasn't there.) Thinking back and looking at an old photograph documenting the three of us consuming those lopsided circles I am amazed.
Just as I am amazed I could finish my MFA exam.

I've managed to do a lot of things in my life I didn't think I was capable 7
of and which many others didn't think I was capable of either. Especially
because I am a woman, a Latina, an only daughter in a family of six men.
My father would've liked to have seen me married long ago. In our culture
men and women don't leave their father's house except by way of marriage. I crossed my father's threshold with nothing carrying me but my
own two feet. A woman whom no one came for and no one chased away.

To make matters worse, I left before any of my six brothers had ven- 8
tured away from home. I broke a terrible taboo. Somehow, looking back
at photos of myself as a child, I wonder if I was aware of having begun
already my own quiet war.

I like to think that somehow my family, my Mexicanness, my poverty, 9
all had something to do with shaping me into a writer. I like to think my
parents were preparing me all along for my life as an artist even though
they didn't know it. From my father I inherited a love of wandering. He

was born in Mexico City but as a young man he traveled into the U.S. vagabonding. He eventually was drafted and thus became a citizen. Some of the stories he has told about his first months in the U.S. with little or no English surface in my stories in *The House on Mango Street* as well as others I have in mind to write in the future. From him I inherited a sappy heart. (He still cries when he watches Mexican soaps—especially if they deal with children who have forsaken their parents.)

My mother was born like me—in Chicago but of Mexican descent. It 10 would be her tough street-wise voice that would haunt all my stories and poems. An amazing woman who loves to draw and read books and can sing an opera. A smart cookie.

When I was a little girl we traveled to Mexico City so much I thought 11 my grandparents' house on La Fortuna, number 12, was home. It was the only constant in our nomadic ramblings from one Chicago flat to another. The house on Destiny Street, number 12, in the colonia Tepeyac would be perhaps the only home I knew, and that nostalgia for a home would be a theme that would obsess me.

My brothers also figured greatly in my art. Especially the older two; I 12 grew up in their shadows. Henry, the second oldest and my favorite, appears often in poems I have written and in stories which at times only borrow his nickname, Kiki. He played a major role in my childhood. We were bunk-bed mates. We were co-conspirators. We were pals. Until my oldest brother came back from studying in Mexico and left me odd woman out for always.

What would my teachers say if they knew I was a writer now? Who 13 would've guessed it? I wasn't a very bright student. I didn't much like school because we moved so much and I was always new and funny looking. In my fifth-grade report card I have nothing but an avalanche of C's and D's, but I don't remember being that stupid. I was good at art and I read plenty of library books and Kiki laughed at all my jokes. At home I was fine, but at school I never opened my mouth except when the teacher called on me.

When I think of how I see myself it would have to be at age eleven. 14 I know I'm thirty-two on the outside, but inside I'm eleven. I'm the girl in the picture with skinny arms and a crumpled skirt and crooked hair. I didn't like school because all they saw was the outside me. School was lots of rules and sitting with your hands folded and being very afraid all the time. I liked looking out the window and thinking. I liked staring at the girl across the way writing her name over and over again in red ink. I wondered why the boy with the dirty collar in front of me didn't have a mama who took better care of him.

I think my mama and papa did the best they could to keep us warm 15 and clean and never hungry. We had birthday and graduation parties and things like that, but there was another hunger that had to be fed. There was a hunger I didn't even have a name for. Was this when I began writing?

In 1966 we moved into a house, a real one, our first real home. This 16 meant we didn't have to change schools and be the new kids on the block every couple of years. We could make friends and not be afraid we'd have to say goodbye to them and start all over. My brothers and the flock of boys they brought home would become important characters eventually for my stories—Louie and his cousins, Meme Ortiz and his dog with two names, one in English and one in Spanish.

My mother flourished in her own home. She took books out of the library and taught herself to garden—to grow flowers so envied we had to put a lock on the gate to keep out the midnight flower thieves. My mother has never quit gardening. 17

This was the period in my life, that slippery age when you are both child and woman and neither, I was to record in *The House on Mango Street*. I was still shy. I was a girl who couldn't come out of her shell. 18

How was I to know I would be recording and documenting the women who sat their sadness on an elbow and stared out a window? It would be the city streets of Chicago I would later record, as seen through a child's eyes. 19

I've done all kinds of things I didn't think I could do since then. I've gone to a prestigious university, studied with famous writers, and taken an MFA degree. I've taught poetry in schools in Illinois and Texas. I've gotten an NEA grant and run away with it as far as my courage would take me. I've seen the bleached and bitter mountains of the Peloponnesus. I've lived on an island. I've been to Venice twice. I've lived in Yugoslavia. I've been to the famous Nice flower market behind the opera house. I've lived in a village in the pre-Alps and witnessed the daily parade of promenaders. 20

I've moved since Europe to the strange and wonderful country of Texas, land of polaroid-blue skies and big bugs. I met a mayor with my last name. I met famous Chicana and Chicano artists and writers and políticos. 21

Texas is another chapter in my life. It brought with it the Dobie-Paisano Fellowship, a six-month residency on a 265-acre ranch. But most important, Texas brought Mexico back to me. 22

In the days when I would sit at my favorite people-watching spot, the snakey Woolworth's counter across the street from the Alamo (the Woolworth's which has since been torn down to make way for progress), I couldn't think of anything else I'd rather be than a writer. I've traveled and lectured from Cape Cod to San Francisco, to Spain, Yugoslavia, Greece, Mexico, France, Italy, and now today to Texas. Along the way there has been straw for the taking. With a little imagination, it can be spun into gold. 23

READING COMPREHENSION

1. The word *intuitively* in ". . . rules involved here, unlike writing a poem or story, which I did intuitively" (paragraph 5) means
   a. something that requires practice.
   b. something that comes naturally.
   c. something that follows specific rules.
   d. something that takes time.

2. The word *nostalgia* in ". . . and that nostalgia for a home would be a theme" (paragraph 11) means
   a. homesickness.
   b. contentment.
   c. bittersweet longing or desire.
   d. feeling of serenity.

3. The word *prestigious* in ". . . I've gone to a prestigious university" (paragraph 20) means
   a. having a distinguished reputation.
   b. having a fraudulent reputation.
   c. inexpensive.
   d. public.

4. Which of the following would be a good alternative title for this selection?
   a. Corn Tortillas
   b. My House on Mango Street
   c. Growing Up in Chicago
   d. Becoming a Writer

5. Which sentence best expresses the main idea of the selection?
   a. Cisneros really enjoys making Mexican food and eating with friends.
   b. Cisneros has lived in a lot of places.
   c. Cisneros's journey to become a writer has not been easy.
   d. Cisneros's favorite story is Rumpelstiltskin.

6. Cisneros compares writing the critical essay for her MFA exam to
   a. writing a novel.
   b. painting a house.
   c. living in a new country.
   d. making corn tortillas.

7. Cisneros's father didn't want her to become a writer. What would he have preferred?
   a. He would have liked to have seen her married.
   b. He would have liked to have seen her move to Mexico.
   c. He wanted her to become a doctor.
   d. He wanted her to live with her parents.

8. Cisneros knew only one house that she considered home as she grew up. What house was this?
   a. the house on Mango Street
   b. the house in Spain
   c. her grandparents' house in Mexico
   d. her grandparents' house in Texas

9. What did Cisneros inherit from her father?
   a. a sappy heart
   b. a diamond necklace
   c. her writing ability
   d. a love of gardening

10. *True or False?* _____ Cisneros believes her teachers would be very surprised that she is a writer.

STRUCTURE AND TECHNIQUE

1. Cisneros begins her essay with an anecdote. Why do you think she begins her essay this way? Do you find it effective?

2. Cisneros makes several references to things she has done that seem to amaze her. Go through the essay and find some of these references and mark the language that lets the reader know she is amazed that she has accomplished these things.

3. Cisneros writes, "I know I'm thirty-two on the outside, but inside I'm eleven." What is her purpose in writing this statement?

4. Cisneros's essay is filled with adjectives like "crooked and burnt, but edible" and "tough street-wise voice." Go through the essay and mark some of your favorite adjectives and be prepared to discuss why these adjectives held particular interest for you.

CRITICAL READING AND DISCUSSION

1. Why did making corn tortillas seem to be an impossible task for Cisneros?

2. What types of experiences did Cisneros have at school? Are her experiences similar to or different from your own experiences?

3. In paragraph 8, Cisneros mentions that she broke a taboo. What taboo did she break, and why does she write about it?

4. The title of Cisneros's essay references the story "Rumpelstiltskin," a story about a young woman who has to spin straw into gold or die. Why do you think she titles her essay this way? Do you think it is an appropriate title?

5. Using Cisneros's essay as support, what type of writer do you think she has become?

WRITING ASSIGNMENTS

Assignment 1: Writing a Paragraph

If you were given an opportunity to have dinner with Sandra Cisneros, would you? Use the essay to support your answer of why or why not.

Assignment 2: Writing an Essay

Cisneros writes that her parents didn't want her to be a writer, but she can't think of anything else she would rather be. Think of something you wanted to do in high school, like joining the football team or being in the school play, that your parents didn't want you to do, but that you persuaded them to allow you to join. Write an essay that tells what you wanted to do, why your parents didn't want you to participate, how you persuaded your parents, and the outcome of your participation.

Assignment 3: Writing an Essay

Cisneros writes about growing up and the experiences that influenced her as a writer. Think of moments that have been influential in your life. Write an essay that illustrates how these moments have shaped you into the person you are.

Mother Tongue
Amy Tan

PREVIEW

Amy Tan is a well-known author who was born in California to Chinese immigrants. Much of her work focuses on the Chinese immigrant experience, American-Chinese culture, and mother-daughter relationships. She has written numerous books that include *The Joy Luck Club*, *The Bonesetter's Daughter*, and *Saving Fish from Drowning*. She has also won an Emmy for her animated series, *Sagwa*. This article, in which Tan discusses the different types of English she grew up with, first appeared in *The Threepenny Review* in 1990.

I am not a scholar of English or literature. I cannot give you much more 1 than personal opinions on the English language and its variations in this country or others.

I am a writer. And by that definition, I am someone who has always 2 loved language. I am fascinated by language in daily life. I spend a great deal of my time thinking about the power of language—the way it can evoke an emotion, a visual image, a complex idea, or a simple truth. Language is the tool of my trade. And I use them all—all the Englishes I grew up with.

Recently, I was made keenly aware of the different Englishes I do use. 3 I was giving a talk to a large group of people, the same talk I had already given to half a dozen other groups. The nature of the talk was about my writing, my life, and my book, *The Joy Luck Club*. The talk was going along well enough, until I remembered one major difference that made the whole talk sound wrong. My mother was in the room. And it was perhaps the first time she had heard me give a lengthy speech, using the kind of English I have never used with her. I was saying things like, "The intersection of memory upon imagination" and "There is an aspect of my fiction that relates to thus-and-thus"—a speech filled with carefully wrought grammatical phrases, burdened, it suddenly seemed to me, with nominalized forms, past perfect tenses, conditional phrases, all the forms of standard English that I had learned in school and through books, the forms of English I did not use at home with my mother.

Just last week, I was walking down the street with my mother, and I 4 again found myself conscious of the English I was using, the English I do use with her. We were talking about the price of new and used furniture and I heard myself saying this: "Not waste money that way." My husband was with us as well, and he didn't notice any switch in my English. And then I realized why. It's because over the twenty years we've been together I've often used that same kind of English with him, and sometimes he even uses it with me. It has become our language of intimacy, a different sort of English that relates to family talk, the language I grew up with.

So you'll have some idea of what this family talk I heard sounds like, 5 I'll quote what my mother said during a recent conversation which I videotaped and then transcribed. During this conversation, my mother was talking about a political gangster in Shanghai who had the same last name as her family's, Du, and how the gangster in his early years wanted to be adopted by her family, which was rich by comparison. Later, the gangster became more powerful, far richer than my mother's family, and one day showed up at my mother's wedding to pay his respects. Here's what she said in part:

"Du Yusong having business like fruit stand. Like off the street kind. 6 He is Du like Du Zong—but not Tsung-ming Island people. The local people call putong, the river east side, he belong to that side local people. That man want to ask Du Zong father take him in like become own family. Du Zong father wasn't look down on him, but didn't take seriously, until that man big like become a mafia. Now important person, very hard to inviting him. Chinese way, came only to show respect, don't stay for dinner. Respect for making big celebration, he shows up. Mean gives lots of respect. Chinese custom. Chinese social life that way. If too important won't have to stay too long. He come to my wedding. I didn't see, I heard it. I gone to boy's side, they have YMCA dinner. Chinese age I was nineteen."

You should know that my mother's expressive command of English 7 belies how much she actually understands. She reads the Forbes report, listens to *Wall Street Week*, converses daily with her stockbroker, reads all of Shirley MacLaine's books with ease—all kinds of things I can't begin to understand. Yet some of my friends tell me they understand 50 percent of what my mother says. Some say they understand 80 to 90 percent. Some say they understand none of it, as if she were speaking pure Chinese. But to me, my mother's English is perfectly clear, perfectly natural. It's my mother tongue. Her language, as I hear it, is vivid, direct, full of observation and imagery. That was the language that helped shape the way I saw things, expressed things, made sense of the world.

Lately, I've been giving more thought to the kind of English my mother 8 speaks. Like others, I have described it to people as "broken" or "fractured" English. But I wince when I say that. It has always bothered me that I can think of no way to describe it other than "broken," as if it were damaged and needed to be fixed, as if it lacked a certain wholeness and soundness. I've heard other terms used, "limited English," for example. But they seem just as bad, as if everything is limited, including people's perceptions of the limited English speaker.

I know this for a fact, because when I was growing up, my mother's 9 "limited" English limited my perception of her. I was ashamed of her English. I believed that her English reflected the quality of what she had to say. That is, because she expressed them imperfectly her thoughts were imperfect. And I had plenty of empirical evidence to support me: the fact that people in department stores, at banks, and at restaurants did not take her seriously, did not give her good service, pretended not to understand her, or even acted as if they did not hear her.

My mother has long realized the limitations of her English as well. 10 When I was fifteen, she used to have me call people on the phone to pretend I was she. In this guise, I was forced to ask for information or even to complain and yell at people who had been rude to her. One time it was a call to her stockbroker in New York. She had cashed out her small portfolio and it just so happened we were going to go to New York the next week, our very first trip outside California. I had to get on the phone and say in an adolescent voice that was not very convincing, "This is Mrs. Tan."

And my mother was standing in the back whispering loudly, "Why he 11 don't send me check, already two weeks late. So mad he lie to me, losing me money."

And then I said in perfect English, "Yes, I'm getting rather concerned. 12 You had agreed to send the check two weeks ago, but it hasn't arrived."

Then she began to talk more loudly. "What he want, I come to New 13 York tell him front of his boss, you cheating me?" And I was trying to calm her down, make her be quiet, while telling the stockbroker, "I can't tolerate any more excuses. If I don't receive the check immediately, I am going to have to speak to your manager when I'm in New York next week." And sure enough, the following week there we were in front of this astonished stockbroker, and I was sitting there red-faced and quiet, and my mother, the real Mrs. Tan, was shouting at his boss in her impeccable broken English.

We used a similar routine just five days ago, for a situation that was far 14 less humorous. My mother had gone to the hospital for an appointment, to find out about a benign brain tumor a CAT scan had revealed a month ago. She said she had spoken very good English, her best English, no mistakes. Still, she said, the hospital did not apologize when they said they had lost the CAT scan and she had come for nothing. She said they did not seem to have any sympathy when she told them she was anxious to know the exact diagnosis, since her husband and son had both died of brain tumors. She said they would not give her any more information until the next time and she would have to make another appointment for that. So she said she would not leave until the doctor called her daughter. She wouldn't budge. And when the doctor finally called her daughter, me, who spoke in perfect English—lo and behold—we had assurances the CAT scan would be found, promises that a conference call on Monday would be held, and apologies for any suffering my mother had gone through for a most regrettable mistake.

I think my mother's English almost had an effect on limiting my pos- 15 sibilities in life as well. Sociologists and linguists probably will tell you that a person's developing language skills are more influenced by peers. But I do think that the language spoken in the family, especially in immigrant families which are more insular, plays a large role in shaping the language of the child. And I believe that it affected my results on achievement tests, I.Q. tests, and the SAT. While my English skills were never judged as poor, compared to math, English could not be considered my strong suit. In grade school I did moderately well, getting perhaps B's, sometimes B-pluses, in English and scoring perhaps in the sixtieth or seventieth percentile on achievement tests. But those scores were not good enough to override the opinion that my true abilities lay in math and science, because in those areas I achieved A's and scored in the ninetieth percentile or higher.

This was understandable. Math is precise; there is only one correct an- 16 swer. Whereas, for me at least, the answers on English tests were always a judgment call, a matter of opinion and personal experience. Those tests were constructed around items like fill-in-the-blank sentence completion, such as, "Even though Tom was _____, Mary thought he was _____." And the correct answer always seemed to be the most bland combinations of thoughts, for example, "Even though Tom was shy, Mary thought he was charming," with the grammatical structure "even though" limiting the correct answer to some sort of semantic opposites, so you wouldn't get answers like, "Even though Tom was foolish, Mary thought he was ridicu- lous." Well, according to my mother, there were very few limitations as to what Tom could have been and what Mary might have thought of him. So I never did well on tests like that.

The same was true with word analogies, pairs of words in which you 17 were supposed to find some sort of logical, semantic relationship—for ex- ample, "Sunset is to nightfall as _____ is to _____." And here you would be presented with a list of four possible pairs, one of which showed the same kind of relationship: red is to stoplight, bus is to arrival, chills is to fever, yawn is to boring: Well, I could never think that way. I knew what the tests were asking, but I could not block out of my mind the images already created by the first pair, "sunset is to nightfall"—and I would see a burst of colors against a darkening sky, the moon rising, the lowering of a curtain of stars. And all the other pairs of words—red, bus, stoplight, boring—just threw up a mass of confusing images, making it impossible for me to sort out something as logical as saying: "A sunset precedes nightfall" is the same as "a chill precedes a fever." The only way I would have gotten that answer right would have been to imagine an associative situation, for ex- ample, my being disobedient and staying out past sunset, catching a chill at night, which turns into feverish pneumonia as punishment, which in- deed did happen to me.

I have been thinking about all this lately, about my mother's English, 18 about achievement tests. Because lately I've been asked, as a writer, why there are not more Asian Americans represented in American literature. Why are there few Asian Americans enrolled in creative writing programs? Why do so many Chinese students go into engineering? Well, these are broad sociological questions I can't begin to answer. But I have noticed in surveys—in fact, just last week—that Asian students, as a whole, always do significantly better on math achievement tests than in English. And this makes me think that there are other Asian-American students whose English spoken in the home might also be described as "broken" or "lim- ited." And perhaps they also have teachers who are steering them away from writing and into math and science, which is what happened to me.

Fortunately, I happen to be rebellious in nature and enjoy the challenge 19 of disproving assumptions made about me. I became an English major my first year in college, after being enrolled as pre-med. I started writing non- fiction as a freelancer the week after I was told by my former boss that writing was my worst skill and I should hone my talents toward account management.

But it wasn't until 1985 that I finally began to write fiction. And at first 20 I wrote using what I thought to be wittily crafted sentences, sentences that would finally prove I had mastery over the English language. Here's an example from the first draft of a story that later made its way into *The Joy Luck Club*, but without this line: "That was my mental quandary in its nascent state." A terrible line, which I can barely pronounce.

Fortunately, for reasons I wont get into today, I later decided I should 21 envision a reader for the stories I would write. And the reader I decided upon was my mother, because these were stories about mothers. So with this reader in mind—and in fact she did read my early drafts—I began to write stories using all the Englishes I grew up with: the English I spoke to my mother, which for lack of a better term might be described as "simple"; the English she used with me, which for lack of a better term might be described as "broken"; my translation of her Chinese, which could certainly be described as "watered down"; and what I imagined to be her translation of her Chinese if she could speak in perfect English, her internal language, and for that I sought to preserve the essence, but neither an English nor a Chinese structure. I wanted to capture what language ability tests can never reveal: her intent, her passion, her imagery, the rhythms of her speech and the nature of her thoughts.

Apart from what any critic had to say about my writing, I knew I had 22 succeeded where it counted when my mother finished reading my book and gave me her verdict: "So easy to read."

READING COMPREHENSION

1. The word *burdened* in "… a speech filled with carefully wrought grammatical phrases, burdened, it suddenly seemed to me" (paragraph 3) means

   a. aided and helped.

   b. that which is carried.

   c. weighed down with duty.

   d. weight of a ship's cargo.

2. The word *empirical* in ". . . I had plenty of empirical evidence to support me" (paragraph 9) means

   a. provable through the scientific method.

   b. provable through observation and experience.

   c. secondhand proof.

   d. factual data gathered through Internet research.

3. The word *assurances* in ". . . we had assurances the CAT scan would be found" (paragraph 14) means

   a. promises or guarantees.

   b. self-confidence.

   c. presumptuous boldness.

   d. uncertainties.

4. The word *assumptions* in ". . . the challenge of disproving assumptions about me" (paragraph 19) means
   a. arrogance or forwardness.
   b. beliefs or opinions taken for granted.
   c. transfer of mortgages.
   d. taking a new position.

5. Which of the following would be a good alternative title for this selection?
   a. Four Englishes
   b. My Mother's Tumor
   c. Misunderstood
   d. Agony in School

6. Which sentence best expresses the main idea of the selection?
   a. Amy Tan credits her mother for her love of reading and writing.
   b. Amy Tan believes there are specific reasons that Asian-American students are really good at math.
   c. Amy Tan believes that writers should use long, intricate sentences in their writings.
   d. Amy Tan explains that she grew up with several different "Englishes" that influenced her as a writer.

7. Tan said she first noticed she spoke different Englishes when
   a. her mother pointed it out.
   b. her first book was published.
   c. her husband pointed it out at a conference.
   d. she was speaking to a large group of people.

8. Tan's mother understood English better than she spoke it. Which of the following is NOT an example that Tan uses to illustrate this claim?
   a. Her mother read the Forbes report.
   b. Her mother read Shirley MacLaine's books.
   c. Her mother went to movies regularly.
   d. Her mother listened to *Wall Street Week*.

9. When Tan was young, she was ashamed of her mother because
   a. her mother was very loud and drew a lot of attention from strangers.
   b. she believed her quality of English reflected the quality of what she had to say.
   c. her mother was very uneducated and couldn't understand simple things.
   d. doctors always treated her mother as if she were a child.

10. *True or False?* _____ Tan pretended to be her mother on certain occasions because her English was stronger than her mother's.

11. *True or False?* _____ Tan believes that many teachers underestimate the talents of Asian-American students.

12. The most important opinion regarding Tan's first book, *The Joy Luck Club*, was given by

   a. Tan's agent.

   b. the critics.

   c. Tan's mother.

   d. Tan's husband.

STRUCTURE AND TECHNIQUE

1. Tan begins her essay with some very pointed statements. She first states, "I am not a scholar of English or literature." She then states, "I am a writer." These statements seem to contradict each other. Why do you think Tan uses these statements in the beginning of her essay? Do you think it is an effective way to begin the essay?

2. Paragraph 6 is a transcription of a story Tan's mother told. It is written verbatim, word for word, and Tan has not corrected the English. Why does Tan include this paragraph in this essay? Why does Tan follow this paragraph with a paragraph about what her mother reads, listens to, and talks about?

3. Tan offers several examples of people treating her mother poorly because of her "broken English." Find two and discuss why you feel Tan used these examples.

4. At the end of the essay, Tan's mother says that *The Joy Luck Club* is "so easy to read." Why is this praise more important than what the critics say? What does it say about Tan's writing ability?

CRITICAL READING AND DISCUSSION

1. As a young child, how did Tan feel about her mother's English? As she grew older, what changed?

2. Tan often had to pretend to be her mother while on the phone. Why did she have to do this, and what did it say about the people to whom she was speaking?

3. Tan writes that she consistently scored higher in math on achievement tests, yet she became a writer. Why did she pursue writing instead of math?

4. In paragraphs 15–18, Tan addresses the assumption that Asian Americans should continue to be pushed into math. Why does she believe that teachers and counselors push these students in this direction?

WRITING ASSIGNMENTS

Assignment 1: Writing a Paragraph

Tan states that she scored better on the math portion of achievement tests, mostly because there is only one correct answer for each problem, and she saw the answers on English tests as judgment calls. In paragraphs 16 and 17,

Tan supports her claim by providing very specific examples. Write a paragraph in which you discuss a subject that you weren't very good at in high school. Support your topic sentence with details that demonstrate why you struggled with this subject.

Assignment 2: Writing an Essay

Tan's essay focuses on the different types of English she grew up speaking. She credits her ability to write stories with her experiences. For this assignment, you will need to think about the different ways you speak. Think about how you speak to your parents differently than you speak to your friends or teachers. Write an essay discussing the different "Englishes" you use with different audiences. As you plan your essay, you may want to think about what might happen if you use the wrong "English" at the wrong time and how your audience might respond. You may want to incorporate some dialogue to demonstrate your different "Englishes."

Assignment 3: Writing an Essay

As Tan details the treatment her mother received from people outside of the family, she raises an important issue. Many people are treated poorly because of their dress, speech, race, or gender. For this assignment, you can choose one of two approaches. The first option is to write an essay about a time you witnessed someone being treated poorly and what you did. The second option is to write a persuasive essay that offers ways people can help eliminate such behavior.

What's Wrong with Schools?

Casey Banas

PREVIEW

A teacher pretends to be a student and sits in on several classes. What does she find in the typical class? Boredom. Routine. Apathy. Manipulation. Discouragement. If this depressing list sounds familiar, you will be interested in the following analysis of why classes often seem to be more about killing time than about learning.

Ellen Glanz lied to her teacher about why she hadn't done her homework; 1 but, of course, many students have lied to their teachers. The difference is that Ellen Glanz was a twenty-eight-year-old high school social studies teacher who was a student for six months to improve her teaching by gaining a fresh perspective of her school.

She found many classes boring, students doing as little as necessary to 2 pass tests and get good grades, students using ruses to avoid assignments, and students manipulating teachers to do the work for them. She concluded that many students are turned off because they have little power and responsibility for their own education.

Ellen Glanz found herself doing the same things as the students. There 3 was the day when Glanz wanted to join her husband in helping friends celebrate the purchase of a house, but she had homework for a math class. For the first time, she knew how teenagers feel when they think something is more important than homework.

She found a way out and confided: "I considered my options: Confess 4 openly to the teacher, copy someone else's sheet, or make up an excuse." Glanz chose the third option—the one most widely used—and told the teacher that the pages needed to complete the assignment had been ripped from the book. The teacher accepted the story, never checking the book. In class, nobody else did the homework; and student after student mumbled responses when called on.

"Finally," Glanz said, "the teacher, thinking that the assignment must 5 have been difficult, went over each question at the board while students copied the problems at their seats. The teacher had 'covered' the material and the students had listened to the explanation. But had anything been learned? I don't think so."

Glanz found this kind of thing common. "In many cases," she said, 6 "people simply didn't do the work assignment, but copied from someone else or manipulated the teacher into doing the work for them."

"The system encourages incredible passivity," Glanz said. "In most 7 classes one sits and listens. A teacher, whose role is activity, simply cannot understand the passivity of the student's role," she said. "When I taught," Glanz recalled, "my mind was going constantly—figuring out how to best present an idea, thinking about whom to call on, whom to draw out, whom to shut up; how to get students involved, how to make my point clearer, how to respond; when to be funny, when serious. As a student, I experienced little of this. Everything was done to me."

Class methods promote the feeling that students have little control 8 over or responsibility for their own education because the agenda is the teacher's, Glanz said. The teacher is convinced the subject matter is worth knowing, but the student may not agree. Many students, Glanz said, are not convinced they need to know what teachers teach; but they believe good grades are needed to get into college.

Students, obsessed with getting good grades to help qualify for the col- 9 lege of their choice, believe the primary responsibility for their achievement rests with the teacher, Glanz said. "It was his responsibility to teach well rather than their responsibility to learn carefully."

Teachers were regarded by students, Glanz said, not as "people," but 10 as "role-players" who dispensed information needed to pass a test. "I often heard students describing teachers as drips, bores, and numerous varieties of idiots," she said. "Yet I knew that many of the same people had traveled the world over, conducted fascinating experiments or learned three languages, or were accomplished musicians, artists, or athletes."

But the sad reality, Glanz said, is the failure of teachers to recognize 11 their tremendous communications gap with students. Some students, she explained, believe that effort has little value. After seeing political corruption they conclude that honesty takes a back seat to getting ahead any way one can, she said. "I sometimes estimated that half to two-thirds of a class cheated on a given test," Glanz said. "Worse, I've encountered students who feel no remorse about cheating but are annoyed that a teacher has confronted them on their actions."

Glanz has since returned to teaching at Lincoln-Sudbury. Before her 12 stint as a student, she would worry that perhaps she was demanding too much. "Now I know I should have demanded more," she said. Before, she was quick to accept the excuses of students who came to class unprepared. Now she says, "You are responsible for learning it." But a crackdown is only a small part of the solution.

The larger issue, Glanz said, is that educators must recognize that 13 teachers and students, though physically in the same school, are in separate worlds and have an ongoing power struggle. "A first step toward ending this battle is to convince students that what we attempt to teach them is genuinely worth knowing," Glanz said. "We must be sure, ourselves, that what we are teaching is worth knowing." No longer, she emphasized, do students assume that "teacher knows best."

READING COMPREHENSION

1. The word *ruses* in "students using ruses to avoid assignments" (paragraph 2) means

   a. questions.

   b. sicknesses.

   c. parents.

   d. tricks.

2. The word *agenda* in "the agenda is the teacher's" (paragraph 8) means

 a. program.

 b. boredom.

 c. happiness.

 d. book.

3. Which of the following would be a good alternative title for this selection?

 a. How to Get Good Grades

 b. Why Students Dislike School

 c. Cheating in Our School System

 d. Students Who Manipulate Teachers

4. Which sentence best expresses the main idea of the selection?

 a. Ellen Glanz is a burned-out teacher.

 b. Ellen Glanz lied to her math teacher.

 c. Students need good grades to get into college.

 d. Teachers and students feel differently about schooling.

5. How much of a class, according to the author's estimate, would often cheat on a test?

 a. one-quarter or less

 b. one-half

 c. one-half to two-thirds

 d. almost everyone

6. *True or False?* _____ As a result of her experience, Glanz now accepts more of her students' excuses.

7. Glanz found that the school system encourages an incredible amount of

 a. enthusiasm.

 b. passivity.

 c. violence.

 d. creativity.

8. The author implies that

 a. few students cheat on tests.

 b. most students enjoy schoolwork.

 c. classroom teaching methods should be changed.

 d. Glanz had a lazy math teacher.

9. The author implies that

 a. Glanz should not have become a student again.

 b. Glanz is a better teacher than she was before.

 c. Glanz later told her math teacher that she lied.

 d. social studies is an unimportant subject.

10. The author implies that

    a. most students who cheat on tests are caught by their teachers.

    b. most teachers demand too little of their students.

    c. students who get good grades in high school also do so in college.

    d. students never question what teachers say.

RESPONDING TO IMAGES

What would you do if you caught one of your classmates copying your answers during a test?

STRUCTURE AND TECHNIQUE

1. Which method of introduction—broad-to-narrow, anecdote, or questions—does Banas use in his essay? Why do you think he chose this approach?

2. List the time transitions that Banas uses in paragraph 12. How do they help Banas make his point?

3. Throughout "Why Are Students Turned Off?" Banas shifts between summarizing Ellen Glanz's words and quoting Glanz directly. Find an instance in the essay in which both direct and indirect quotations are used in the same paragraph. What does Banas gain or lose from using this technique? (Refer to pages 493–494 for definitions and examples of direct and indirect quotations.)

4. Parallel structures are often used to emphasize similar information. They can create a smooth, readable style. For example, note the series of *-ing* verbs in the following sentence from paragraph 2: ". . . students **doing** as little as necessary to pass tests and get good grades, students **using** ruses to avoid assignments, and students **manipulating** teachers to do the work for them." Find two other uses of parallelism, one in paragraph 4 and one in paragraph 7.

CRITICAL READING AND DISCUSSION

1. After reading this essay, what do you think Glanz's attitude is? Is she pro- or anti-teacher? Pro- or anti-student? Provide evidence for your position.

2. Banas suggests that many students are in school to get good grades—not to learn. Explain whether or not you agree with this assessment. Do you find that getting a good grade isn't always the same as really learning?

3. The author ends with Glanz's view of "the larger issue": "We must be sure, ourselves, that what we are teaching is worth knowing." What was taught in your high school classes that you feel is worth knowing or not worth knowing? Explain why. Also, what is being taught in your college classes that you feel is worth knowing or not worth knowing, and why?

4. Much of this essay contrasts the behavior of students with that of teachers. In what ways does Glanz see their behavior and views differing? What do you think each group should be doing differently?

WRITING ASSIGNMENTS

Assignment 1: Writing a Paragraph

Glanz says that students like to describe their teachers as "drips, bores, and numerous varieties of idiots." Write a description of one of your high school teachers or college instructors who either *does* or *does not* fit that description. Show, in your paragraph, that your teacher or instructor was weak, boring, and idiotic—or just the opposite (dynamic, creative, and bright). In either case, your focus should be on providing specific details that *enable your readers to see for themselves* that your topic sentence is valid.

Assignment 2: Writing an Essay

Play the role of student observer in one of your college classes. Then write an essay with *either* of the following theses:

In my _____ class, students are turned off.

In my _____ class, students are active and interested.

In each supporting paragraph, state and detail one reason why the atmosphere in that particular class is either boring or interesting. You might want to consider areas such as these:

Instructor: presentation, tone of voice, level of interest and enthusiasm, teaching aids used, ability to handle questions, sense of humor, and so on

Students: level of enthusiasm, participation in class, attitude (as shown by body language and other actions), and so on

Other factors: conditions of classroom, length of class period, noise level in classroom, and so on

Assignment 3: Writing an Essay

How does the classroom situation Ellen Glanz describes compare with a classroom situation with which you are familiar—either one from the high school you attended or one from the school in which you are presently enrolled? Select one class you were or are a part of, and write an essay in which you compare or contrast your class with the ones Ellen Glanz describes. Here are some areas you might wish to include in your essay:

> How interesting the class was
>
> How many of the students did their assignments
>
> What the teaching methods were
>
> How much was actually learned
>
> How active the teacher or instructor was
>
> How passive the students were
>
> What the students thought of the teacher or instructor

Choose any three of the above areas or three other areas. Then decide which method of development you will use: *one side at a time* or *point by point* (see pages 200–202).

Propaganda Techniques in Today's Advertising

Ann McClintock

PREVIEW

Advertisers want your business, and they will use a variety of clever ad slogans to get it. If you've ever responded to ads, you have been swayed by the effective use of propaganda. You may associate the word *propaganda* with the tactics used by strong-arm governments. But Ann McClintock provides evidence that we are the targets of propaganda every day and that it shapes many of our opinions and decisions.

Americans, adults and children alike, are being seduced. They are being brainwashed. And few of us protest. Why? Because the seducers and the brainwashers are the advertisers we willingly invite into our homes. We are victims, content—even eager—to be victimized. We read advertisers' propaganda messages in newspapers and magazines; we watch their alluring images on television. We absorb their messages and images into our subconscious. We all do it—even those of us who claim to see through advertisers' tricks and therefore feel immune to advertising's charm. Advertisers lean heavily on propaganda to sell products, whether the "products" are a brand of toothpaste, a candidate for office, or a particular political viewpoint.

Propaganda is a systematic effort to influence people's opinions, to win 2 them over to a certain view or side. Propaganda is not necessarily concerned with what is true or false, good or bad. Propagandists simply want people to believe the messages being sent. Often, propagandists will use outright lies or more subtle deceptions to sway people's opinions. In a propaganda war, any tactic is considered fair.

When we hear the word "propaganda," we usually think of a foreign 3 menace: anti-American radio programs broadcast by a totalitarian regime or brainwashing tactics practiced on hostages. Although propaganda may seem relevant only in the political arena, the concept can be applied fruitfully to the way products and ideas are sold in advertising. Indeed, the vast majority of us are targets in advertisers' propaganda war. Every day, we are bombarded with slogans, print and Internet pop-up ads, commercials, packaging claims, billboards, trademarks, logos, and designer brands—all forms of propaganda. One study reports that each of us, during an average day, is exposed to over *five hundred* advertising claims of various types. This saturation may even increase in the future, since current trends include ads on movie screens, shopping carts, videocassettes, and even public television.

What kind of propaganda techniques do advertisers use? There are 4 seven basic types:

1. **Name Calling.** Name calling is a propaganda tactic in which negatively 5 charged names are hurled against the opposing side or competitor. By using such names, propagandists try to arouse feelings of mistrust, fear, and hate in their audiences. For example, a political advertisement may label an opposing candidate a "loser," "fence-sitter," or "warmonger." Depending on the advertiser's target market, labels such as "a friend of big business" or "a dues-paying member of the party in power" can be the epithets that damage an opponent. Ads for products may also use name calling. An American manufacturer may refer, for instance, to a "foreign car" in its commercial—not an "imported" one. The label of foreignness will have unpleasant connotations in many people's minds. A childhood rhyme claims that "names can never hurt me," but name calling is an effective way to damage the opposition, whether it is another car maker or a congressional candidate.

2. **Glittering Generalities.** Using glittering generalities is the opposite 6 of name calling. In this case, advertisers surround their products with attractive—and slippery—words and phrases. They use vague terms that are difficult to define and that may have different meanings to different people: *freedom, democratic, all-American, progressive, Christian,* and *justice.* Many such words have strong affirmative overtones. This kind of language stirs positive feelings in people, feelings that may spill over to the product or idea being pitched. As with name calling, the emotional response may overwhelm logic. Target audiences accept the product without thinking very much about what the glittering generalities mean—or whether they even apply to the product. After all, how can anyone oppose "truth, justice, and the American way"?

The ads for politicians and political causes often use glittering 7 generalities because such "buzzwords" can influence votes. Election

mind. Many people are simply swayed by the distorted claim that the candidate is "waffling" on the issue.

Advertisers often stack the cards in favor of the products they are 19 pushing. They may, for instance, use what are called "weasel words." These are small words that usually slip right past us, but that make the difference between reality and illusion. The weasel words are underlined in the following claims:

"Helps control dandruff symptoms." (The audience usually interprets this as stops dandruff.)

"Most dentists surveyed recommend sugarless gum for their patients who chew gum." (We hear the "most dentists" and "for their patients," but we don't think about how many were surveyed or whether or not the dentists first recommended that the patients not chew gum at all.)

"Sticker price $1,000 lower than most comparable cars." (How many is "most"? What car does the advertiser consider "comparable"?)

Advertisers also use a card stacking trick when they make an unfin- 20 ished claim. For example, they will say that their product has "twice as much pain reliever." We are left with a favorable impression. We don't usually ask, "Twice as much pain reliever as what?" Or advertisers may make extremely vague claims that sound alluring but have no substance: Toyota's "Oh, what a feeling!"; Vantage cigarettes' "the taste of success"; "The spirit of Marlboro"; Coke's "the real thing." Another way to stack the cards in favor of a certain product is to use scientific-sounding claims that are not supported by sound research. When Ford claimed that its LTD model was "400% quieter," many people assumed that its LTD must be quieter than all other cars. When taken to court, however, Ford admitted that the phrase referred to the difference between the noise level inside and outside the LTD. Other scientific-sounding claims use mysterious ingredients that are never explained as selling points: Retsyn, "special whitening agents," "the ingredient doctors recommend."

7. **Bandwagon.** In the bandwagon technique, advertisers pressure, 21 "Everyone's doing it. Why don't you?" This kind of propaganda often succeeds because many people have a deep desire not to be different. Political ads tell us to vote for the "winning candidate." The advertisers know we tend to feel comfortable doing what others do; we want to be on the winning team. Or ads show a series of people proclaiming, "I'm voting for the senator. I don't know why anyone wouldn't." Again, the audience feels under pressure to conform.

In the marketplace, the bandwagon approach lures buyers. Ads tell us 22 that "nobody doesn't like Sara Lee" (the message is that you must be weird if you don't). They tell us that "most people prefer Brand X two to one over other leading brands" (to be like the majority, we should buy Brand X). If we don't drink Pepsi, we're left out of "the Pepsi generation." To take part in "America's favorite health kick," the National Dairy Council asks us, "Got Milk?" And Honda motorcycle ads, praising the virtues of being a follower, tell us, "Follow the leader. He's on a Honda."

Why do these propaganda techniques work? Why do so many of us buy 23 the products, viewpoints, and candidates urged on us by propaganda messages? They work because they appeal to our emotions, not to our minds. Often, in fact, they capitalize on our prejudices and biases. For example, if we are convinced that environmentalists are radicals who want to destroy America's record of industrial growth and progress, then we will applaud the candidate who refers to them as "treehuggers." Clear thinking requires hard work: analyzing a claim, researching the facts, examining both sides of an issue, using logic to see the flaws in an argument. Many of us would rather let the propagandists do our thinking for us.

Because propaganda is so effective, it is important to detect it and un- 24 derstand how it is used. We may conclude, after close examination, that some propaganda sends a truthful, worthwhile message. Some advertising, for instance, urges us not to drive drunk, to become volunteers, to contribute to charity. Even so, we must be aware that propaganda is being used. Otherwise, we have consented to handing over to others our independence of thought and action.

READING COMPREHENSION

1. The word *epithets* in "labels such as 'a friend of big business' or 'a dues-paying member of the party in power' can be the epithets that damage an opponent" (paragraph 5) means

   a. courtesies.

   b. descriptive labels.

   c. assurances.

   d. delays.

2. The words *capitalizes on* in "the testimonial capitalizes on the admiration people have for a celebrity" (paragraph 12) mean

   a. reports about.

   b. ignores.

   c. cuts back on.

   d. takes advantage of.

3. Which of the following would be a good alternative title for this selection?

   a. The World of Advertising

   b. Common Persuasion Techniques in Advertising

   c. Propaganda in Politics

   d. Common Advertising Techniques on Television

4. Which sentence best expresses the main idea of the selection?

   a. Americans may be exposed daily to over five hundred advertising claims of some sort.

   b. The testimonial takes advantage of the admiration people have for celebrities, even though they have no expertise on the product being sold.

   c. People should detect and understand common propaganda techniques, which appeal to the emotions rather than to logic.

   d. Americans need to understand that advertising, a huge industry, affects their lives in numerous ways.

5. The propaganda technique in which a product is associated with a symbol or image most people admire and respect is

   a. glittering generalities.

   b. transfer.

   c. testimonials.

   d. bandwagon.

6. The technique in which evidence is withheld or distorted is called

   a. glittering generalities.

   b. bandwagon.

   c. plain folks.

   d. card stacking.

7. The technique that makes a political candidate seem to be just like the people an ad is aimed at is

   a. glittering generalities.

   b. bandwagon.

   c. plain folks.

   d. card stacking.

8. A way to avoid being taken in by propaganda is to use

   a. our emotions.

   b. name calling.

   c. clear thinking.

   d. our subconscious.

9. The author implies in paragraph 16 that

   a. most Americans do not frequently call their grandmothers.

   b. multinational corporations do not have the same values as average citizens.

   c. Bob Evans is an American celebrity.

   d. executives at AT&T and Ford are hardworking and honest.

10. From paragraphs 23 and 24, we can conclude that the author feels

   a. we are unlikely to analyze advertising logically unless we recognize it as propaganda.

   b. propaganda should not be allowed.

   c. if we don't want to hand over to others our independence, we should ignore all propaganda.

   d. we should not support the "products, viewpoints, and candidates urged on us by propaganda messages."

STRUCTURE AND TECHNIQUE

1. In paragraph 1, McClintock's choice of words reveals her attitudes toward both propagandists and the public. What specific words reveal her attitudes, and what attitudes do they represent?

2. What key term does McClintock define in paragraph 2? Why does she define it here? Where else in the essay does she use the technique of definition?

3. McClintock uses parentheses in two lists, the ones in paragraphs 7 and 19. What purpose do these parentheses serve?

4. McClintock provides abundant examples throughout her essay. Why does she provide so many examples? What does she accomplish with this technique?

CRITICAL READING AND DISCUSSION

1. Some of the propaganda techniques listed in the selection have contrasting appeals. How do name-calling and glittering generalities contrast with each other? Testimonials and plain folks?

2. Why are ads that use the bandwagon approach so effective? What ads have you seen recently that use that approach?

3. The author states, "Americans, adults and children alike, are being seduced." What might be the differences between the ways adults and children react to the seductions of advertising?

4. McClintock states, "We are victims, content—even eager—to be victimized" (paragraph 1). Do you agree? Is this article likely to change how you view ads in the future? Why or why not?

RESPONDING TO IMAGES

What propaganda technique (or techniques) does this advertisement use? Is it effective? Why or why not?

WRITING ASSIGNMENTS

Assignment 1: Writing a Paragraph

Imagine that you work for an ad agency and have been asked to come up with a campaign for a new product (for example, a car, a perfume, a detergent, jeans, beer, a toothpaste, a deodorant, or an appliance). Write a paragraph in which you describe the propaganda technique(s) that might be used to sell the product and how these claims could persuade the public to buy. Be specific about the general look, the character, and the wording of your ad and about how it fits in with the technique(s) you suggest.

Assignment 2: Writing an Essay

Analyze three ads currently appearing on television or in print. Show that each ad uses one or more of the propaganda techniques McClintock discusses. Be specific about product names, what the ad looks like, kinds of characters in the ad, and so on. Don't forget that all your specific details should back up your point that each ad uses a certain propaganda technique (or techniques) to sell a product. Your thesis will make some overall statement about the three ads, such as either of these:

> Beer advertisements use a variety of propaganda techniques.
>
> Glittering generalities are used to sell very different types of products.

Assignment 3: Writing an Essay

Do some informal "market research" on why people buy the products they do. Begin by asking at least ten people why they bought a particular brand-name item. You might question them about something they're wearing (designer jeans, for example). Or you might ask them what toothpaste they use, what car they drive, what pain reliever they take, or what chicken they eat—or ask about any other product people use. Take notes on the reasons people give for their purchases.

Then write an essay with the thesis "My research suggests that people often buy products for three reasons." Include in your introductory paragraph your plan of development—a list of the three reasons that were mentioned most often by the people you interviewed. Develop your supporting paragraphs with examples drawn from the interviews. As part of your support, use quotations from the people you spoke with.

This Is How We Live

Ellen DeGeneres

PREVIEW

Ellen DeGeneres is a popular comedian and host of her own television talk show, *The Ellen DeGeneres Show*, which has won several Emmy Awards. Her first book, *My Point . . . And I Do Have One* (1995), appeared on the *New*

York Times bestseller list for several months. "This Is How We Live" presents the funny side of the technologies we use every day. It first appeared in *The Funny Thing Is . . .* , a book by DeGeneres, published in 2003.

Everyone likes to talk about how advancements in technology will change 1 the way we live forever. Frankly, I think modern technology is hurting us. I really do.

If you want to know the truth, I blame the microwave for most of our 2 problems. Anything that gets food that hot without fire is from the devil. If you don't believe me, put a Hot Pocket in your microwave for three or four minutes, then pop that thing in your mouth. If that's not Hell, my friend, I don't know what is.

Modern life requires hardly any physical activity. We just push a but- 3 ton and stand there. Take the car window. Someone decided that having to crank the window down yourself was too hard. "I don't want to churn butter, I just want fresh air!" So we got a button to do it.

We're just so lazy. We used to have breath mints. Now we have breath 4 strips that just dissolve on our tongue. Can we not *suck* anymore?

Yes, we're lazy. Yet we also can't seem to sit still. So we've started mak- 5 ing things like GO-GURT. That's yogurt for people on the go. Let me ask you, was there a big mobility problem with yogurt before? How time-consuming was it, really?

"Hello? . . . Oh, hi, Tom . . . Oh, I've been *dying* to see that movie . . . 6 Umm, no . . . I just opened up some yogurt . . . Yeah, I'm in for the night . . . No, not even later—it's the kind with fruit on the bottom. Well, have fun. Thanks anyway."

And people are eating power bars all the time. Power bars were made 7 for mountain-climbing expeditions and hiking, not really made to be eaten in the car on the way to the mall. Is it really that much faster and more convenient? It takes longer to chew one bite of those things than it takes to make an entire sandwich. I don't know what they're made from, but you could insulate a house with that stuff.

There are certain things that they're coming up with that I just don't 8 think we need. Top of the list is that moving sidewalk you find in airports. It's like a little ride in the middle of nowhere, but I don't know what function it really serves. I mean, it's fun because it moves, so if you walk while you're on it you're almost like the Bionic Woman, just flying past the people trudgin[1] beside you on the ground. But you know how hard it is to adjust to walking again once you get off that thing? And what about those people who get on there and just stand? I guess we have to thank God they found the moving sidewalk. Without it, I don't know how they'd get anywhere.

You'd think with all these innovations that are speeding things up for 9 us and moving us along, people would be early—or at least on time— when they're going places. But somehow, everybody's still always late. And people always say the same thing when they finally show up after

[1]*trudging:* walking slowly with a lot of effort.

you've been waiting for them. "Oh, sorry. Traffic." "Really? How do you think I got here? Helicoptered in? I *allow* for it."

How else does technology torture us? Well, try opening up a brand-new CD. What has happened to the packaging of CDs? These are angry, angry people, these CD packagers. "Open here," it says. Is that sarcasm?[2] Are they mocking me? The plastic they use is so thick, it's like government plastic—civilians can't buy this stuff. And you can't get through it without slashing it with a knife or scissors or something. In fact, I find you need a sharp pair of scissors to get into just about anything these days. Have you tried to open a package of scissors lately? You need *scissors* to get into scissors. And what if you're buying scissors for the first time? I mean, how can you possibly get in there? Talk about a catch-22.[3]

Batteries are also packaged as though the manufacturers never want you to get to them. What could possibly happen to batteries that they need to be packaged like that? On the other hand, take a good look at a package of lightbulbs. Thin, thin, thin cardboard that's open on both ends. What are *those* packagers thinking? "Oh, the lightbulbs? They'll be fine."

It's hard to get into anything, even toilet paper. What has happened to toilet paper in public bathrooms? It's not even one-ply anymore, is it? It's a sheer suggestion of toilet paper. It's an *innuendo*.[4] It's like prosciutto, it's so thin. And if you're in a public bathroom and it's a brand-new roll that hasn't gotten started yet, just try to find the start of that toilet paper roll. First you turn it slowly. You think, *surely I've gone around once or twice by now.* Then you go fast. Maybe the wind will open up the first flap. Then you turn it the other way, thinking maybe you're going in the wrong direction. And back to the slow again. And then you find it, and it's glued down. So then you try to pull it apart but only a quarter of an inch separates and the rest stays glued. So you're pulling and pulling and soon you've got a five-foot-long quarter-of-an-inch strip. I don't want a streamer, I want toilet paper! So now one side is fully intact and you've got a groove cut out on the other side. Then you use your finger to try to even it out, but you never get it exactly even, so then you finally just claw at it like a wild animal. "Jesus, I just want toilet paper!"

On the other hand, some things that don't need to be made easier are being made easier. They're making these automated toilets that flush entirely on their own schedule. Sometimes they just go off randomly. You're still sitting down and suddenly it just flushes. "How *dare* you! I'll decide when I'm done!" And then other times it won't go off when you want it to. You stand up and stare at the toilet. Sometimes you have to fake it out. You sit back down . . . stand up! Sit down . . . stand up! Then you try tiptoeing away as if you're leaving. Nothing works.

Then, when you go to wash your hands, you don't have any control of that either. The faucet has to see your hands first so it can decide how much water it's going to give you. It gives out only a certain amount of water. You don't know how much you're getting, so you're like a little raccoon under there, rubbing your little paws together. It gives you some, then it

---

[2]*sarcasm:* use of irony to mock.

[3]*catch-22:* impossible situation.

[4]*innuendo:* hint or reference.

decides *that's enough*, and it's not. So you have to pull out and pretend like you are a new set of hands going back in again. Same thing happens with the dryer—you don't have any control. You have to put your hands under the vent to get the air to come out. It's all to avoid germs, which is great, fantastic. Good for the health of the world. Then you walk over to that disease-ridden door handle, open it up, and head to the bowl of mixed nuts you're sharing at the bar.

Technology has done one beautiful thing for us. It's called the cell 15 phone. There is now not one place in the world where a cell phone is not going off. And every cell phone now has its own little song! Good thing we got rid of those obnoxious rings, isn't it?

When you're on a cell phone, you can't ever have a full conversation. 16 Usually the reception is terrible, and somehow it's only bad on your side. The person talking to you has no idea that you have bad reception. They're rambling on and on and you've got your finger jammed in your ear. You're shushing people on the street, ducking behind a Dumpster, putting your head between your knees, just so you can hear about your friend's new haircut. "What about the bangs? Are they shorter? Are the bangs shorter? THE BANGS!!"

At least if there's static you have some clue that you may get cut off. 17 There's nothing worse than when you have crystal-clear reception and you've been rambling on for who knows how long, only to find out that the connection cut out who knows how long ago. Then you get paranoid. You're scared to talk too long ever again. Next time you're on the phone you become obsessed with checking. "So we were going to go to the cheese shop. . . . *Hello?* Okay . . . And we knew we were having white wine. . . . *Still there?* All right. And I thought, what kind of cheese would go with . . . ? *Did I lose you?* Okay . . . And I like Muenster. . . ."

Even if you're on a regular phone at home, you'll be interrupted some- 18 how. You'll be interrupted by call-waiting most likely. Call-waiting was invented as a convenience, but let's face it—it's really turned into a mini People's Choice awards. You find out right away who wins or loses. You're having a pleasant conversation with someone you think is a good friend, and you hear the click, and you're confident that they're going to come back to you. Then they come back and say, "I've got to take this other call." And you know what that means. They just said to the other person, "Let me get rid of this other call." That's what you just became: a call to get rid of. Then you learn to trick them the next time, when they say they've got to check on the other call. "Hey, when you come back, remind me to tell you something that somebody said about you! . . . *Hello?*"

Of course, you don't have to pick up call-waiting. You can get voice mail. 19 Voice mail will pick it up for you. My favorite voice mail is the one where you insert your name into a robotic message, and you end up sounding more like a robot than the robot itself. "Your call has been forwarded to an automatic voice message system. El-len is not available." Is that how I say my name? Like HAL from *2001: A Space Odyssey?* "Yeah, I'd like to make reservations for dinner tonight, there's four of us, and the name is El-len."

Phones have gone through such an evolution. Now we have this wire- 20 less technology that lets us talk to anybody, anywhere, anytime. Think about how far phones have come. You'll remember there was a time when there was one phone in the house, when cord was just being invented. There was a shortage of cord back then. Maybe you had a foot or two from the wall to the phone. Back then, when you said you were on the phone, you were *on the phone*.

Then the kitchen wall phone came along, usually a lovely mustard or 21 an avocado green. It had a ninety-foot-long cord that allowed you to walk all around the house, clearing tables, wrapping around dogs, so that by the time you hung up the phone, it had become this tangled wire of cord confusion. But what was fun about it was that every once in a while you would hold the phone upside down by the cord and let that thing spin and spin, around and around, till it found its center. Good times.

One surefire sign that things are going the wrong way? Now we have 22 the hands-free phone so you can concentrate on the thing you're really supposed to be doing. My thought is this: Chances are, if you need both of your hands to do something, your brain should be in on it too.

READING COMPREHENSION

1. The word *innovations* in "You'd think with all these innovations that are speeding this up for us and moving us along, people would be early—or at least on time—when they're going places" (paragraph 9) means
   a. traditions.
   b. inventions.
   c. rules.
   d. vehicles.

2. The word *paranoid* in "Then you get paranoid. You're scared to talk too long ever again" (paragraph 17) means
   a. annoyed.
   b. careful.
   c. fearful.
   d. trusting.

3. Which of the following best captures the main idea of the essay?
   a. Technology makes life more convenient.
   b. Technology means progress.
   c. Technology comes with both advantages and disadvantages.
   d. Technology is doing more harm than good.

4. Which of the following would make the best alternative title for this selection?
   a. The Horrors of Technology
   b. Technology: What's the Point?
   c. Technology and You
   d. Our Technological World

5. Which of the following is the topic sentence of paragraph 8?

   a. Top of the list is that moving sidewalk you find in airports.

   b. I guess we have to thank God they found the moving sidewalk.

   c. There are certain things that they're coming up with that I just don't think we need.

   d. Without it, I don't know how they'd get anywhere.

6. The author objects to packages in which CDs are sold because

   a. they contribute to our excess garbage problem and damage the environment.

   b. they increase the product's price.

   c. they are hard to open.

   d. they make scissors dull when you try to cut them open.

7. According to DeGeneres, packaging for light bulbs needs to be

   a. more colorful.

   b. less colorful.

   c. easier to open.

   d. more sturdy.

8. We can infer from paragraph 14 that DeGeneres finds public restrooms

   a. frustrating.

   b. useful.

   c. unnecessary.

   d. convenient.

9. What does DeGeneres think about the songs now used as ring tones in cell phones (paragraph 15)?

   a. She approves of them.

   b. They are silly.

   c. Cell phone companies should offer more choices.

   d. They are too loud.

10. *True or False?* _____ The author sees nothing beneficial in the way telephones have evolved.

STRUCTURE AND TECHNIQUE

1. Why does the author begin her essay by mentioning the microwave?

2. The essay is divided into three parts. Identify the sentences that introduce parts two and three.

3. One reason the essay's discussion of telephones keeps our attention is that DeGeneres uses so many lively examples to get her point across. Make a list of the examples that explain the advantages, the disadvantages, and the evolution of the telephone.

4. How would you describe the author's tone—her attitude toward her subject? Does she ever seem to be ironic—to be "pulling our leg"?

CRITICAL READING AND DISCUSSION

1. Why does DeGeneres say that the microwave is an invention of the devil?

2. Name four inventions that the author thinks we can live without. Do you agree with her opinion in each case? Why or why not?

3. DeGeneres refers to *2001: A Space Odyssey* in paragraph 19. What was that movie about? Who was Hal? Look up the movie on the Internet if necessary.

4. Why, according to this essay, can't you "ever have a full conversation" when you're on a cell phone (paragraph 16)?

WRITING ASSIGNMENTS

Assignment 1: Writing a Paragraph

"We're just so lazy," DeGeneres tells us in paragraph 4. To support her point, she mentions automatic windows and breath strips as examples of inventions that eliminate work that was not laborious. Can you think of one or two more such inventions? A good topic sentence for such a paragraph might go like this:

> We're so lazy that we had to invent the electric toothbrush to clean our teeth.
>
> We're so lazy that we had to invent an electric shoe shining kit.
>
> We're so lazy that we had to invent an electric pepper grinder.

Assignment 2: Writing an Essay

DeGeneres mentions various aspects and uses of the cell phone. But she really only scratches the surface. Write an essay in which you explain how the cell phone and any other communication or entertainment device makes an impact on your life. Begin by discussing various ways in which you use your cell phone. Then talk about your laptop computer, iPod, or CD/DVD player. In your introductory paragraph include a thesis statement that goes something like this:

> Portable electronic devices do more than just keep us in touch with others.

End your essay by thinking about the kinds of functions future portable electronic inventions might allow us to perform. In other words, engage in a little creative thinking. What important personal, academic, or business needs would you like such devices to fill?

Assignment 3: Writing an Essay

DeGeneres focuses on the tortures that sometimes accompany our use of electronic devices. Think of one or more electronic devices or services that have changed your life and the lives of others in the past decade. The digital camera, the fax machine, the telephone answering machine, the

GPS navigation device, the laptop computer, the iPod, the Internet, or the cell phone might be interesting topics to think about. Are they unqualified blessings? Or do they have negative aspects as well? Write an essay in which you address these questions in regard to one or more electronic devices or services that you know a lot about. You might begin with a thesis like one of these:

1. The Internet is a wonderful tool, but in the wrong hands it can be a horror.

2. Modern technological devices—like cell phones, GPS devices, and fax machines—sometimes make life simpler, but sometimes they make it more complicated.

3. Shopping online is time saving and convenient, but engaging in this activity sometimes enables thieves to steal one's identity.

Draw information from your own experience, but you might also want to interview friends and classmates to gather more information for your essay.

Advice to Youth

Mark Twain

PREVIEW

Mark Twain, born Samuel Langhorne Clemens, is one of America's most famous authors. Best known for the controversial book, *The Adventures of Huckleberry Finn*, Twain wrote dozens of novels, nonfiction pieces, short stories, and essays. Twain did not plan on becoming a writer, but through his many adventures and failures, he found an outlet for his voice and humor. In this essay, Twain uses satire to advise and lecture about morality.

Being told I would be expected to talk here, I inquired what sort of talk 1 I ought to make. They said it should be something suitable to youth—something didactic, instructive, or something in the nature of good advice. Very well. I have a few things in my mind which I have often longed to say for the instruction of the young; for it is in one's tender early years that such things will best take root and be most enduring and most valuable. First, then. I will say to you my young friends—and I say it beseechingly, urgingly—

Always obey your parents, when they are present. This is the best policy 2 in the long run, because if you don't, they will make you. Most parents think they know better than you do, and you can generally make more by humoring that superstition than you can by acting on your own better judgment.

Be respectful to your superiors, if you have any, also to strangers, and 3 sometimes to others. If a person offend you, and you are in doubt as to whether it was intentional or not, do not resort to extreme measures; simply watch your chance and hit him with a brick. That will be sufficient. If you shall find that he had not intended any offense, come out frankly and confess yourself in the wrong when you struck him; acknowledge it like a man and say you didn't mean to. Yes, always avoid violence; in this age of charity and kindliness, the time has gone by for such things. Leave dynamite to the low and unrefined.

Go to bed early, get up early—this is wise. Some authorities say get up 4 with the sun; some say get up with one thing, others with another. But a lark is really the best thing to get up with. It gives you a splendid reputation with everybody to know that you get up with the lark; and if you get the right kind of lark, and work at him right, you can easily train him to get up at half past nine, every time—it's no trick at all.

Now as to the matter of lying. You want to be very careful about lying; 5 otherwise you are nearly sure to get caught. Once caught, you can never again be in the eyes to the good and the pure, what you were before. Many a young person has injured himself permanently through a single clumsy and ill finished lie, the result of carelessness born of incomplete training. Some authorities hold that the young ought not to lie at all. That of course, is putting it rather stronger than necessary; still while I cannot go quite so far as that, I do maintain, and I believe I am right, that the young ought to be temperate in the use of this great art until practice and experience shall give them that confidence, elegance, and precision which alone can make the accomplishment graceful and profitable. Patience, diligence, painstaking attention to detail—these are requirements; these in time, will make the student perfect; upon these only, may he rely as the sure foundation for future eminence. Think what tedious years of study, thought, practice, experience, went to the equipment of that peerless old master who was able to impose upon the whole world the lofty and sounding maxim that "Truth is mighty and will prevail"—the most majestic compound fracture of fact which any of woman born has yet achieved. For the history of our race, and each individual's experience, are sewn thick with evidences that a truth is not hard to kill, and that a lie well told is immortal. There is in Boston a monument of the man who discovered anesthesia; many people are aware, in these latter days, that that man didn't discover it at all, but stole the discovery from another man. Is this truth mighty, and will it prevail? Ah no, my hearers, the monument is made of hardy material, but the lie it tells will outlast it a million years. An awkward, feeble, leaky lie is a thing which you ought to make it your unceasing study to avoid; such a lie as that has no more real permanence than an average truth. Why, you might as well tell the truth at once and be done with it. A feeble, stupid, preposterous lie will not live two years—except it be a slander upon somebody. It is indestructible, then of course, but that is no merit of yours. A final word: begin your practice of this gracious and beautiful art early—begin now. If I had begun earlier, I could have learned how.

Never handle firearms carelessly. The sorrow and suffering that have 6 been caused through the innocent but heedless handling of firearms by the young! Only four days ago, right in the next farm house to the one where I am spending the summer, a grandmother, old and gray and sweet, one of the loveliest spirits in the land, was sitting at her work, when her young grandson crept in and got down an old, battered, rusty gun which had not been touched for many years and was supposed not to be loaded, and pointed it at her, laughing and threatening to shoot. In her fright she ran screaming and pleading toward the door on the other side of the room; but as she passed him he placed the gun almost against her very breast and pulled the trigger! He had supposed it was not loaded. And he was right—it wasn't. So there wasn't any harm done. It is the only case of that kind I ever heard of. Therefore, just the same, don't you meddle with old unloaded firearms; they are the most deadly and unerring things that have ever been created by man. You don't have to take any pains at all with them; you don't have to have a rest, you don't have to have any sights on the gun, you don't have to take aim, even. No, you just pick out a relative and bang away, and you are sure to get him. A youth who can't hit a cathedral at thirty yards with a Gatling gun in three quarters of an hour, can take up an old empty musket and bag his grandmother every time, at a hundred. Think what Waterloo would have been if one of the armies had been boys armed with old muskets supposed not to be loaded, and the other army had been composed of their female relations. The very thought of it make one shudder.

There are many sorts of books; but good ones are the sort for the young 7 to read. Remember that. They are a great, an inestimable, and unspeakable means of improvement. Therefore be careful in your selection, my young friends; be very careful; confine yourselves exclusively to Robertson's *Sermons*, Baxter's *Saint's Rest*, *The Innocents Abroad*, and works of that kind.

But I have said enough. I hope you will treasure up the instructions 8 which I have given you, and make them a guide to your feet and a light to your understanding. Build your character thoughtfully and painstakingly upon these precepts, and by and by, when you have got it built, you will be surprised and gratified to see how nicely and sharply it resembles everybody else's.

READING COMPREHENSION

1. The word *didactic* in ". . . something suitable to youth—something didactic" (paragraph 1) means
   a. intended to teach a moral lesson.
   b. intended to help with pronunciation.
   c. youthful and fun.
   d. intended to entertain.

2. The word *superstition* in ". . . by humoring that superstition" (paragraph 2) most closely refers to
   a. custom.
   b. belief not based on reason or knowledge.
   c. act or ritual derived from custom.
   d. fact.

3. The word *inestimable* in ". . . a great, an inestimable, and unspeakable means of improvement" (paragraph 7) most closely means
   a. too large to be counted.
   b. valuable beyond measure.
   c. very limited.
   d. very predictable.

4. What would be the best alternative title for this selection?

    a. Do as I Say, Not as I Do

    b. Lying Is the Best Way to Get What You Want

    c. What Not to Do

    d. Adventures of Twain

5. Which statement below represents the main idea of the selection?

    a. Think for yourself.

    b. Don't question advice; follow it!

    c. Morality requires obedience.

    d. Parents are always correct.

6. Why, according to Twain, should people be careful of lying?

    a. It is morally wrong.

    b. It can be very difficult.

    c. It is an art that needs to be practiced.

    d. It can hurt a person's reputation.

7. True or False? _____ Twain believes that firearms are OK, as long as they are handled correctly.

8. True or False? _____ Twain is a great liar and believes that everyone should learn how to properly tell lies.

9. If Twain's style could be described with one word, which one would it be?

    a. funny

    b. serious

    c. depressing

    d. sarcastic

10. Which of the following subjects was not covered in "Advice to Youth"?

    a. respect

    b. reading

    c. study habits

    d. guns

STRUCTURE AND TECHNIQUE

1. Twain employs the technique of satire, using ridicule to expose or denounce something, in this essay. Although it seems he is giving bad advice, he is actually giving good advice. Why do you think he uses satire instead of writing plainly and in a straightforward manner?

2. Twain breaks up his essay into six very specific rules; do you think he left out any rules? Explain.

3. Do you think Twain's speech would have been more effective if he had not used satire? Explain.

CRITICAL READING AND DISCUSSION

1. In paragraph 3, Twain discusses the idea of being respectful to superiors and strangers and ends the paragraph with the idea that violence is "unrefined." Do you agree or disagree? Explain.

2. In paragraph 4, Twain is actually addressing the old saying, "The early bird gets the worm." Do you think that people who get up earlier are more productive and morally upright? Why do you think this saying became so popular?

3. According to this essay, lying is an art, to be practiced from an early age. What does modern society say about lying?

4. Twain is an author and essayist, yet one of his shortest paragraphs gives advice about reading, and he suggests staying confined to a very short list of books. Without knowing any details about these books, what do you think Twain is actually warning his listeners about?

WRITING ASSIGNMENTS

Assignment 1: Writing a Paragraph

Write a paragraph that discusses what audience you believe Twain was addressing in this speech, what event was being held, and why he had been asked to speak. Use evidence from the text—vocabulary and advice—to support your claim.

Assignment 2: Writing an Essay

Write an essay that instructs a group of people about how to do something. Imagine you are giving a commencement address or speaking at an elementary school. Topics for your essay could be teaching a group of younger children how to behave; a group of high school freshmen how to succeed in high school; or a group of college students how to make and keep friends. Incorporating humor into your essay can help you make your point, but don't focus so much on the humor that the message is lost. If you choose to mimic Twain's style, you may want to include statements like "always talk behind people's backs" or "never read the directions on a test," but remember to use support for the opposite idea. (For example, describe what happens if someone doesn't read the directions.)

Assignment 3: Writing an Essay

Write an essay about advice you have been given while growing up. You should create a thesis statement that tells whether the advice you have been given is either good or bad. Use the rest of your essay to support your thesis by offering examples of the advice and how it did or did not help you.

Start by Sitting Together

Randy Pausch

PREVIEW

Randy Pausch was a computer science professor at Carnegie Mellon University. Several months before he died of liver cancer, Pausch was asked to deliver what is called the Last Lecture, in which professors whose teaching career is ending are invited to talk about what is most important to them about teaching and life. Because he knew he was dying and wanted to leave behind more than just one lecture, Pausch asked Jeffrey Zaslow, who had attended his lecture, to help him write a book continuing what he had begun to talk about. Each day, while Pausch rode his bicycle for exercise, he spoke with Zaslow through his cell-phone headpiece, discussing ideas and insights that Zaslow would later put into a book called *The Last Lecture*. "Start by Sitting Together" is a chapter from that book.

When I have to work with other people, I try to imagine us sitting together 1 with a deck of cards. My impulse is always to put all my cards on the table, face up, and to say to the group, "OK, what can we collectively make of this hand?"

Being able to work well in a group is a vital and necessary skill in both 2 the work world and in families. As a way to teach this, I'd always put my students into teams to work on projects.

Over the years, improving group dynamics[1] became a bit of an obses- 3 sion for me. On the first day of each semester, I'd break my class into about a dozen four-person groups. Then, on the second day of class, I'd give them a one-page handout I'd written titled "Tips for Working Successfully in a Group." We'd go over it, line by line. Some students found my tips to be beneath them. They rolled their eyes. They assumed they knew how to play well with others: They had learned it in kindergarten. They didn't need my rudimentary[2] little pointers.

But the most self-aware students embraced the advice. They sensed 4 that I was trying to teach them the fundamentals. It was a little like Coach Graham coming to practice without a football. Among my tips:

Meet people properly: It all starts with the introduction. Exchange 5 contact information. Make sure you can pronounce everyone's names.

Find things you have in common: You can almost always find some- 6 thing in common with another person, and from there, it's much easier to address issues where you have differences. Sports cut across boundaries of race and wealth. And if nothing else, we all have the weather in common.

Try for optimal meeting conditions: Make sure no one is hungry, cold 7 or tired. Meet over a meal if you can; food *softens* a meeting. That's why they "do lunch" in Hollywood.

Let everyone talk: Don't finish someone's sentences. And talking 8 louder or faster doesn't make your idea any better.

[1]*dynamics:* relationships.
[2]*rudimentary:* basic or elementary.

Check egos at the door: When you discuss ideas, label them and write 9
them down. The label should be descriptive of the idea, not the originator:
"the bridge story" not "Jane's story."

Praise each other: Find something nice to say, even if it's a stretch. The 10
worst ideas can have silver linings if you look hard enough.

Phrase alternatives as questions: Instead of "I think we should do A, 11
not B," try "What if we did A, instead of B?" That allows people to offer
comments rather than defend one choice.

At the end of my little lesson, I told my students I'd found a good way 12
to take attendance. "It's easier for me if I just call you by group," I'd say.
"Group One raise your hands . . . Group Two? . . ."

As I called off each group, hands would go up. "Did anybody notice 13
anything about this?" I'd ask. No one had an answer. So I'd call off the
groups again. "Group One? . . . Group Two? . . . Group Three? . . ." All
around the room, hands shot up again.

Sometimes, you have to resort to cheesy theatrics to break through to 14
students, especially on issues where they think they know everything. So
here's what I did:

I kept going with my attendance drill until finally my voice was raised. 15
"Why on earth are all of you still sitting with your friends?" I'd ask. "Why
aren't you sitting with the people in your group?"

Some knew my irritation was for effect, but everyone took me seriously. 16
"I'm going to walk out of this room," I said, "and I'll be back in sixty seconds.
When I return, I expect you to be sitting with your groups! Does everyone
understand?" I'd waltz out and I'd hear the panic in the room, as students
gathered up their book bags and reshuffled themselves into groups.

When I returned, I explained that my tips for working in groups were 17
not meant to insult their intelligence or maturity. I just wanted to show
them that they had missed something simple—the fact that they needed to
sit with their partners—and so they could certainly benefit from reviewing
the rest of the basics.

At the next class, and for the rest of the semester, my students (no dum- 18
mies), always sat with their groups.

READING COMPREHENSION QUESTIONS

1. The word *obsession* in "Over the years, improving group dynamics became a bit of an obsession for me" (paragraph 3) means

   a. chore.

   b. constant desire.

   c. pleasure.

   d. habit.

2. The word *cheesy* in "Sometimes, you have to resort to cheesy theatrics
   to break through to students, especially on issues where they think they
   know everything" (paragraph 14) means

   a. tacky.

   b. dramatic.

   c. eloquent.

   d. expressive.

3. Which of the following might work as an alternative title to this selection?

   a. How to Work as a Group

   b. Motivating Students

   c. Group Learning: Getting Students to Take an Active Role

   d. Group Dynamics

4. Which of the following is the purpose of this selection?

   a. to teach students the fundamentals of working together

   b. to teach students the benefits of group study

   c. to teach teachers how to use learning groups

   d. to stress the importance of sitting together in a learning group

5. In this essay, the instructor displayed irritation over the fact that students were not sitting with their groups in order to show them

   a. how immature they were.

   b. that they had missed a basic principle about working in groups.

   c. that they needed to learn a lot more about how groups work.

   d. that they lacked motivation.

6. *True or False?* _____ According to this essay, it is not important for students to learn the names of other group members.

7. *True or False?* _____ Sometimes it is important for individual members to claim credit for an idea the group adopts.

8. The author implies that talking louder and faster than others will

   a. enable you to contribute more effectively in a group.

   b. impress other members of the group.

   c. not convince others that what you have to say is worth listening to.

   d. improve your grade.

9. The purpose of the instructor's attendance drill was to

   a. make taking attendance easier.

   b. make it easier to remember the students' names.

   c. remind students of the principles behind how groups work.

   d. avoid embarrassing quieter students.

10. We can infer that, when the instructor resorted to "cheesy theatrics,"

   a. the students got offended.

   b. most of the students realized that he wasn't really irritated.

   c. some students understood the reason for his reaction.

   d. the students reacted calmly to his instructions.

STRUCTURE AND TECHNIQUE

1. If this essay explains how to get students to work well in groups, why did the author use the title "Start by Sitting Together"? How does this title relate to the rest of the essay?

2. Why doesn't Pausch end the essay after listing the last piece of advice in paragraph 11? What does he accomplish by telling us about the attendance drill?

3. The best writing most often comes from authors who really believe in the importance of their subject. How do we know this is true of Pausch?

4. Consider the advice the author gives his students about writing in groups. Then consider the "cheesy theatrics" he tells us about in paragraphs 14–17. What do they tell us about his personality?

CRITICAL READING AND DISCUSSION

1. Who do you think Coach Graham is (paragraph 4)? Why does the author compare his teaching to the coach's coming to practice without a football?

2. Why do some students roll their eyes when the author gives the class tips on working in groups?

3. What does Pausch mean when, in paragraph 7, he says "That's why they 'do lunch' in Hollywood"?

4. What does "check egos at the door" mean (paragraph 9)? How might this advice apply to your life as a student? As a member of an athletic team or a student organization? Of a team at work? Of a family?

WRITING ASSIGNMENTS

Assignment 1: Writing a Paragraph

The author writes about using a trick to get his students to understand the importance of following certain basic advice for working in groups. The trick worked! Think of a time when a teacher used a particular method, procedure, assignment, or trick to get you and/or your classmates to learn something important or difficult. Write a paragraph in which you explain this trick, method, or assignment. As a topic sentence, you might choose something like this:

> I'll never forget the memory device Mr. Morales used to help us learn to solve tricky algebra problems.

Assignment 2: Writing an Essay

One of the best pieces of advice the author offers has to do with checking our "egos at the door." Write an essay in which you discuss this topic more fully. Rely on your own experience and interview others to gather facts and insights about the effects that not curbing one's ego has on the dynamics of a group like a class, a work crew, an athletic team, a student organization, or any other similar group.

Your purpose in this assignment is to show how an individual's concern about and focus on himself or herself can interfere with a group's progress or sometimes even wreck the project altogether.

You can approach this as a narrative. For example, try relating an experience or series of experiences in which one or more people's egos got in the way of attaining a common goal or of maintaining group harmony. Remember, however, that you are trying to show the relationship between causes and effects here. So, make certain that you clearly show what happened as a direct result of someone's not checking her or his ego at the door.

Assignment 3: Writing an Essay

"Start by Sitting Together" deals with working within groups in a classroom. However, the advice presented can be applied to any functioning group. Take your own family, a club, a religious group you belong to, or the cast of a high school or college play, for example. How about the basketball or hockey team you play on?

Write an essay in which you analyze and evaluate the workings of a group of which you are a member. Do you think that it functions well—as well as it could? If your assessment is positive, explain the group's success by discussing how it adheres to the rules listed in Pausch's essay. For example, Pausch says that praising each other is a positive step in achieving common goals. Do members of your group do this? If so, write about specific times when praising each other's work helped the group to get on with its work, to solve a difficult problem, or simply to inspire confidence in everyone.

If you think your group can function better, explain how specific pieces of Pausch's advice might help in certain situations. For example, think of a time when letting everyone talk might have prevented a rowdy argument that destroyed the group's focus and prevented further progress. Or recall a meeting of the group, a game, or some other event when one or two members forgot to check their egos at the door. How did things end up?

You can write about one occurrence or several. Either way, just remember to fill your paper with as much specific detail as you can. Also, don't forget to make specific reference to Pausch's essay. Quote from it directly or paraphrase his ideas in your own words, making sure to indicate paragraph numbers and to use quotation marks when necessary.

Inaugural Address

John F. Kennedy

PREVIEW

This is the speech delivered by John Fitzgerald Kennedy to his fellow Americans after taking the oath of office as the thirty-fifth president of the United States on January 20, 1961. In his first speech as president, he attempts to summarize the enormous task confronting not just him, but everyone striving for freedom and world peace. President Kennedy evokes an urgency when addressing the various problems confronting the United States, and yet he also engages the rest of the world through his speech. In particular, he calls on the world's leaders to aim for a higher purpose of their own lands and people, while at the same time asking the American people to join him in participating in the transformation of the United States.

Vice President Johnson, Mr. Speaker, Mr. Chief Justice, President 1
Eisenhower, Vice President Nixon, President Truman, reverend clergy,
fellow citizens, we observe today not a victory of party, but a celebration of freedom—symbolizing an end, as well as a beginning—signifying
renewal, as well as change. For I have sworn before you and Almighty
God the same solemn oath our forebears prescribed nearly a century and
three quarters ago.

The world is very different now. For man holds in his mortal hands the 2
power to abolish all forms of human poverty and all forms of human life.
And yet the same revolutionary beliefs for which our forebears fought are
still at issue around the globe—the belief that the rights of man come not
from the generosity of the state, but from the hand of God.

We dare not forget today that we are the heirs of that first revolution. 3
Let the word go forth from this time and place, to friend and foe alike,
that the torch has been passed to a new generation of Americans, born
in this century, tempered[1] by war, disciplined by a hard and bitter peace,
proud of our ancient heritage and unwilling to witness or permit the slow
undoing of those human rights to which this Nation has always been
committed, and to which we are committed today at home and around
the world.

Let every nation know, whether it wishes us well or ill, that we shall 4
pay any price, bear any burden, meet any hardship, support any friend,
oppose any foe, to assure the survival and the success of liberty.

This much we pledge and more.   5

To those old allies whose cultural and spiritual origins we share, we 6
pledge the loyalty of faithful friends. United, there is little we cannot do in
a host of cooperative ventures.[2] Divided, there is little we can do—for we
dare not meet a powerful challenge at odds and split asunder.

To those new States whom we welcome to the ranks of the free, we 7
pledge our word that one form of colonial control shall not have passed
away merely to be replaced by a far more iron tyranny. We shall not always
expect to find them supporting our view. But we shall always hope to find
them strongly supporting their own freedom—and to remember that, in
the past, those who foolishly sought power by riding the back of the tiger
ended up inside.

To those peoples in the huts and villages across the globe struggling to 8
break the bonds of mass misery, we pledge our best efforts to help them
help themselves, for whatever period is required, not because the Communists may be doing it, not because we seek their votes, but because it is
right. If a free society cannot help the many who are poor, it cannot save the
few who are rich.

To our sister republics south of our border, we offer a special 9
pledge—to convert our good words into good deeds in a new alliance for
progress—to assist free men and free governments in casting off the chains
of poverty. But this peaceful revolution of hope cannot become the prey of
hostile powers. Let all our neighbors know that we shall join with them to

---

[1]*tempered:* strengthened.

[2]*ventures:* undertaking that is of uncertain outcome.

oppose aggression or subversion[3] anywhere in the Americas. And let every other power know that this Hemisphere intends to remain the master of its own house.

To that world assembly of sovereign states, the United Nations, our last 10 best hope in an age where the instruments of war have far outpaced the instruments of peace, we renew our pledge of support—to prevent it from becoming merely a forum for invective—to strengthen its shield of the new and the weak and to enlarge the area in which its writ may run.

Finally, to those nations who would make themselves our adversary, 11 we offer not a pledge but a request—that both sides begin anew the quest for peace, before the dark powers of destruction unleashed by science engulf all humanity in planned or accidental self-destruction.

We dare not tempt them with weakness. For only when our arms are 12 sufficient beyond doubt can we be certain beyond doubt that they will never be employed.

But neither can two great and powerful groups of nations take comfort 13 from our present course—both sides overburdened by the cost of modern weapons, both rightly alarmed by the steady spread of the deadly atom, yet both racing to alter that uncertain balance of terror that stays the hand of mankind's final war.

So let us begin anew, remembering on both sides that civility is not a 14 sign of weakness, and sincerity is always subject to proof. Let us never negotiate out of fear. But let us never fear to negotiate.

Let both sides explore what problems unite us instead of belaboring 15 those problems which divide us.

Let both sides, for the first time, formulate serious and precise propos- 16 als for the inspection and control of arms and bring the absolute power to destroy other nations under the absolute control of all nations.

Let both sides seek to invoke the wonders of science instead of its ter- 17 rors. Together let us explore the stars, conquer the deserts, eradicate[4] disease, tap the ocean depths, and encourage the arts and commerce.

Let both sides unite to heed in all corners of the earth the command of 18 Isaiah—to "undo the heavy burdens . . . and let the oppressed go free."

And if a beachhead[5] of cooperation may push back the jungle of sus- 19 picion, let both sides join in creating a new endeavor, not a new balance of power, but a new world of law, where the strong are just and the weak secure and the peace preserved.

All this will not be finished in the first 100 days. Nor will it be finished 20 in the first 1,000 days, nor in the life of this administration, nor even perhaps in our lifetime on this planet. But let us begin.

In your hands, my fellow citizens, more than mine, will rest the final 21 success or failure of our course. Since this country was founded, each generation of Americans has been summoned to give testimony to its national loyalty. The graves of young Americans who answered the call to service surround the globe.

[3]*subversion:* attempt to overthrow or undermine the government.
[4]*eradicate:* get rid of.
[5]*beachhead:* an initial accomplishment that opens the way for further developments.

Now the trumpet summons us again—not as a call to bear arms, though 22 arms we need—not as a call to battle, though embattled we are—but a call to bear the burden of a long twilight struggle, year in and year out, "rejoicing in hope, patient in tribulation"—a struggle against the common enemies of man: tyranny, poverty, disease, and war itself.

Can we forge against these enemies a grand and global alliance, North 23 and South, East and West, that can assure a more fruitful life for all mankind? Will you join in that historic effort?

In the long history of the world, only a few generations have been 24 granted the role of defending freedom in its hour of maximum danger. I do not shrink from this responsibility—I welcome it. I do not believe that any of us would exchange places with any other people or any other generation. The energy, the faith, the devotion which we bring to this endeavor will light our country and all who serve it—and the glow from that fire can truly light the world.

And so, my fellow Americans: ask not what your country can do for 25 you—ask what you can do for your country.

My fellow citizens of the world: ask not what America will do for you, 26 but what together we can do for the freedom of man.

Finally, whether you are citizens of America or citizens of the world, 27 ask of us here the same high standards of strength and sacrifice which we ask of you. With a good conscience our only sure reward, with history the final judge of our deeds, let us go forth to lead the land we love, asking His blessing and His help, but knowing that here on earth God's work must truly be our own.

READING COMPREHENSION

1. In paragraph 10, President Kennedy uses the word *invective*. This most closely means
   a. abuse or insult.
   b. barrier.
   c. inclusion.
   d. communication.

2. In paragraph 15, he uses the term *belaboring*. This most closely means
   a. not using.
   b. designing.
   c. discriminating.
   d. overemphasizing.

3. What would be a good alternate title for this selection?
   a. Let Freedom Ring
   b. JFK: Our Youngest President
   c. JFK Addresses the Nation for the First Time as President
   d. America's First Catholic President

4. What is the main idea of this selection?

   a. President Kennedy addresses the nation with a call to service.

   b. President Kennedy wants to help the world become one.

   c. The world reaches out to America for help and support.

   d. President Kennedy addresses world leaders to come together.

5. In paragraph 4, President Kennedy states to nations that wish us well or ill, that we (the United States) would pay any price for the following

   a. our standing in the world.

   b. our monetary value.

   c. our survival and success of liberty.

   d. our land.

6. How does President Kennedy suggest we explore the wonders of science?

   a. tap the ocean depths

   b. eradicate disease

   c. explore the stars

   d. all of the above

7. In his speech, President Kennedy refers to all of the following except this common enemy of man

   a. money

   b. disease

   c. war

   d. tyranny

8. President Kennedy states that world peace lies not in his hands but in those of

   a. United Nations representatives.

   b. his Cabinet members.

   c. smaller nations.

   d. his fellow citizens.

9. Who is President Kennedy speaking to when he says "ask not what your country can do for you—ask what you can do for your country"?

   a. fellow citizens of the world

   b. fellow Americans

   c. Communists

   d. the United Nations

10. Which of the following adjectives describes President Kennedy's speech?

   a. dull

   b. long

   c. inspiring

   d. terrifying

STRUCTURE AND TECHNIQUE

1. President Kennedy's address is brief in nature yet contains his principal message as the thesis statement. Where is this thesis statement located? How does he support the thesis in his address? What examples or rationales does he provide?

2. The president uses the word "Let" many times during the address. How does the use of this word affect his message? What does he wish to accomplish with its use?

3. In paragraph 23, President Kennedy asks two questions: "Can we forge against . . . for all mankind? Will you join in that historic effort?" What roles do these questions play at the end of the address? Why do you believe he left these questions for last? Would their placement at the beginning of the address have been as successful? If so, why? If not, why not?

4. In paragraph 25 he makes his famous "ask not" quote. Why does he include this statement at the end of his speech? Would the statement have worked elsewhere in the speech? What does the statement mean to you?

CRITICAL READING AND DISCUSSION

1. The presidential inaugural address begins with an acknowledgement that the world has changed and that change is required to move forward. In addition, President Kennedy refers to America's forefathers and their contributions to the American cause. How does invoking the forefathers' efforts apply to the subsequent efforts Kennedy will ask of the American people? Where in the passage is this call to action made? Is this effective?

2. President Kennedy begins some of his paragraphs with "To____." He is asking specific groups to work cooperatively with him. What does invoking each group do to the address? How would the different groups react if they had not been mentioned? Why do you believe the president felt it was necessary to call special attention to these individual groups?

3. Once President Kennedy completes his request of support from the various groups mentioned, he begins to suggest the path America as a nation should take. He lists four requests. What are they and what do they represent to him, the nation, and the world?

WRITING ASSIGNMENTS

Assignment 1: Writing a Paragraph

Write a paragraph about the current president of the United States. Describe his personality and what you like or dislike about him. How does he rate compared to other presidents? Do you relate to his view of the world? What do you admire about him? What decisions has he made that you agree or disagree with?

Assignment 2: Writing an Essay

Historically, President Kennedy was considered a good leader. Even though he died young, many feel admiration and respect for his vision. What do you believe makes for a good leader of the United States? What are some of the qualities an American president should possess?

Write an essay about your ideal American president. This is a descriptive essay where you may use vivid details to support your points.

Assignment 3: Writing an Essay

Write an essay in which you contrast a good president and a bad president. Make a list of the qualities that make one excellent and the other ineffective or worse. Focus on three pairs of contrasting qualities, using either a one-side-at-a-time or a point-by-point method of development (see pages 200–202).

Neat People vs. Sloppy People

Suzanne Britt

PREVIEW

This amusing article written by Suzanne Britt depicts the virtues of sloppy people, while expressing that neat people are not kind people at all. She uses various methods and circumstances to give us the reasons she believes neat people are uncaring and ruthless with very few feelings. On the other hand, she claims sloppy people are kind-hearted perfectionists who are misunderstood. They are visionaries within a world that does not understand their creative minds and higher purpose.

I've finally figured out the difference between neat people and sloppy peo- 1 ple. The distinction is, as always, moral. Neat people are lazier and meaner than sloppy people.

Sloppy people, you see, are not really sloppy. Their sloppiness is merely 2 the unfortunate consequence of their extreme moral rectitude.[1] Sloppy people carry in their mind's eye a heavenly vision, a precise plan, that is so stupendous, so perfect, it can't be achieved in this world or the next.

Sloppy people live in Never-Never Land. Someday is their métier.[2] 3 Someday they are planning to alphabetize all their books and set up home catalogs. Someday they will go through their wardrobes and mark certain items for tentative mending, and certain items for passing on to relatives of similar shape and size. Someday sloppy people will make family scrapbooks into which they will put newspaper clippings, postcards, locks of hair, and the dried corsage from their senior prom. Someday they will file everything on the surface of their desks, including the cash receipts from coffee purchases at the snack shop. Someday they will sit down and read all the back issues of *The New Yorker*.

For all these noble reasons and more, sloppy people never get neat. They 4 aim too high and wide. They save everything, planning someday to file,

[1]*rectitude:* honesty and correct moral behavior.
[2]*métier:* specialty.

order, and straighten out the world. But while these ambitious plans take clearer and clearer shape in their heads, the books spill from the shelves onto the floor, the clothes pile up in the hamper and closet, the family mementos accumulate in every drawer, the surface of the desk is buried under mounds of paper, and the unread magazines threaten to reach the ceiling.

Sloppy people can't bear to part with anything. They give loving attention to every detail. When sloppy people say they're going to tackle the surface of the desk, they really mean it. Not a paper will go unturned; not a rubber band will go unboxed. Four hours or two weeks into the excavation, the desk looks exactly the same, primarily because the sloppy person is meticulously[3] creating new piles of papers with new headings and scrupulously stopping to read all the old book catalogs before he throws them away. A neat person would just bulldoze the desk.   5

Neat people are bums and clods at heart. They have cavalier[4] attitudes toward possessions, including family heirlooms. Everything is just another dustcatcher to them. If anything collects dust, it's got to go and that's that. Neat people will toy with the idea of throwing the children out of the house just to cut down on the clutter.   6

Neat people don't care about process. They like results. What they want to do is get the whole thing over with so they can sit down and watch the rasslin'[5] on TV. Neat people operate on two unvarying principles: Never handle any item twice, and throw everything away.   7

The only thing messy in the neat person's house is the trash can. The minute something comes to a neat person's hand, he will look at it, try to decide if it has immediate use and, finding none, throw it in the trash.   8

Neat people are especially vicious with mail. They never go through their mail unless they are standing directly over a trash can. If the trash can is beside the mailbox, even better. All ads, catalogs, pleas for charitable contributions, church bulletins and money-saving coupons go straight into the trash can without being opened. All letters from home, postcards from Europe, bills and paychecks are opened, immediately responded to, then dropped in the trash can. Neat people keep their receipts only for tax purposes. That's it. No sentimental salvaging of birthday cards or the last letter a dying relative ever wrote. Into the trash it goes.   9

Neat people place neatness above everything, even economics. They are incredibly wasteful. Neat people throw away several toys every time they walk through the den. I knew a neat person once who threw away a perfectly good dish drainer because it had mold on it. The drainer was too much trouble to wash. And neat people sell their furniture when they move. They will sell a La-Z-Boy recliner while you are reclining in it.   10

Neat people are no good to borrow from. Neat people buy everything in expensive little single portions. They get their flour and sugar in two-pound bags. They wouldn't consider clipping a coupon, saving a leftover, reusing plastic nondairy whipped cream containers or rinsing off tin foil and draping it over the unmoldy dish drainer. You can never borrow a neat person's newspaper to see what's playing at the movies. Neat people have the paper all wadded up and in the trash by 7:05 A.M.   11

---

[3]*meticulously:* carefully, precisely.

[4]*cavalier:* careless.

[5]*rasslin':* Southern style of professional wrestling.

Neat people cut a clean swath through the organic as well as the inor- 12
ganic world. People, animals, and things are all one to them. They are so
insensitive. After they've finished with the pantry, the medicine cabinet,
and the attic, they will throw out the red geranium (too many leaves), sell
the dog (too many fleas), and send the children off to boarding school (too
many scuffmarks on the hardwood floors).

READING COMPREHENSION

1. The word *heirlooms* in paragraph 6 refers to
   a. family vacations.
   b. pictures of the family.
   c. objects reflecting the family history.
   d. another name for neat people.

2. In paragraph 3, the word *tentative* can be defined as
   a. clearly stated.
   b. thoroughly investigated.
   c. intensely disliked.
   d. possible.

3. Which of the following would be a good alternate title for the selection?
   a. A Sloppy Person's Manifesto
   b. The Virtues of Being Neat
   c. Household Duties and Internal Conflicts
   d. Sloppy vs. Mean People: A Personal Analysis

4. Which of the following sentences best expresses the main idea of the
   selection?
   a. Sloppy and neat people vary in many ways.
   b. There are three major differences between neat and sloppy people.
   c. There are many reasons why neat people are mean.
   d. Sloppy people have a lot of emotional baggage.

5. The author suggests that there are many reasons sloppy people never
   get neat; they include all of these except
   a. they aim too high and wide.
   b. they save everything.
   c. they are attached to sentimental mementos.
   d. they go through their closets and give away clothing.

6. According to the author, neat people do all of these except
   a. spend lots of money on expensive things.
   b. go through their mail next to the trash can.
   c. keep all receipts for three years.
   d. throw away toys and clothes easily.

7. Neat people do not care about their family, pets, or friends because they

   a. are insensitive.

   b. are thrifty with their purchases.

   c. love to invite people over to their homes.

   d. do not take organization seriously.

8. In the selection, author Suzanne Britt makes a distinction between neat and sloppy people and concludes that

   a. sloppy people are meaner than neat people.

   b. neat people have a lot of things stocked up in their spaces.

   c. neat people prefer their children to messes.

   d. sloppy people are nicer than neat people.

9. According to Britt, neat people

   a. are very conservative about their money and expenses.

   b. value order over sentimentality.

   c. hate all who are not like them.

   d. don't understand what sloppy people are thinking.

10. We can conclude that Suzanne Britt is

    a. a neat person.

    b. a sloppy person.

    c. a little of both.

    d. neither neat nor sloppy.

STRUCTURE AND TECHNIQUE

1. "Neat People vs. Sloppy People" is written in a form that most closely resembles which pattern of development (narration, exemplification, comparison/contrast, description, or process)? Explain.

2. The effectiveness of the article can be attributed to the format the author used to explain her point of view. In your opinion, how does Suzanne Britt support her thesis statement that neat people are meaner and uncaring and that sloppy people are better individuals? Explain.

3. The article is almost written as if it were a list of attributes. Few examples are given about sloppy people while most examples are about the negative aspects of neat people. Do you think this made for an effective article? Do you think it was too one-sided and not enough examples were given about sloppy people?

4. Throughout the article, Britt alternates between neat and sloppy people, but at no point does she point out the positive attributes that neat people could possibly have. Does this style weaken her argument in any way? If yes, why? If not, why not?

CRITICAL READING AND DISCUSSION

1. According to Britt, who is a more decent person, a neat or sloppy person? What examples does she give that make you believe this is so?

2. In paragraph 7, Britt mentions that neat people don't care about process. Do you believe this is true? Are there any aspects of neat people that you believe are process-oriented? What are some examples that you can think of where being neat is more desirable than being sloppy?

3. What does Britt mean in paragraph 12 when she writes that "neat people cut a clean swath through the organic as well as the inorganic world"? Explain what she meant by inorganic.

4. In paragraph 6 Britt uses the term *cavalier* to express the attitudes of neat people towards family and possessions. How do you interpret the word *cavalier* in this passage? How does the use of this word to describe their attitudes affect the tone of the article? Does it reinforce the author's main idea, or does it take away from it?

WRITING ASSIGNMENTS

Assignment 1: Writing a Paragraph

Suzanne Britt talks about the differences between neat and sloppy people.

Write a paragraph about the differences between two siblings or friends. For example, one can be outgoing and the other introverted. What types of problems can occur in a family with different views on cleanliness and appropriation of chores? You can also write about a time you had to compromise to get along with someone who had different habits than you, a roommate, for example.

Assignment 2: Writing an Essay

According to Britt, neat people are inherently mean people as well. In her opinion, they may even give priority to order and simplicity over a creative environment. She claims that sloppy people are nicer and have more creativity.

Write an essay about a person you believe to be either a "neat freak" or a "sloppy couch potato." You can divide the essay into sections, dedicating body paragraphs to physical attributes and then behavioral differences. Mention if this individual is a part of your family, yourself, or a friend. Does Britt's analysis apply to the person you describe?

Assignment 3: Writing an Essay

In the article, Suzanne Britt talks mostly about the negative qualities of neat people. When she describes sloppy people she uses details and examples that praise the sloppy person's behavior. The article is written so that the reader comes away with a skewed view of neat people. What are some of the negative qualities of sloppy people? What are some of the obstacles and conflicts that sloppy people could encounter?

Consider including aspects such as what might happen to people who are chronically unprepared or disorganized—for instance, losing job opportunities or missing appointments.

Petophilia

Jon Katz

PREVIEW

"Petophilia" is an article written to discuss some recent findings about pets and their owners. The article's author, Jon Katz, discusses not only the different types of dog lovers he encountered in his research, but also the types of love these owners exhibit toward their pets, specifically dogs. He makes a reference to how pet ownership has taken a new role in American life, in particular, in the lives of single Americans. He discusses the various roles pets play in their owners' lives and how these same pets are being used as a substitute for human interaction and connectivity.

I encountered Sam, a 34-year-old investment banker, and his dog, Namath, when Sam responded to a column I wrote. He told me he loves his dog "to death," so much that it sometimes unnerves him. Sam and Namath, a German shepherd/husky mix adopted three years ago from a shelter in Brooklyn, jog together, play Frisbee, take long hikes in the Catskills. Sam was planning a Caribbean vacation last year but decided instead to rent a cabin in New Hampshire so that Namath could come along. "I have to say it was great, one of the best times I've ever had," he reported. He's considering leaving New York City so that Namath can have more space to run. 1

Human companionship? Sometimes Sam dates, but he's increasingly inclined to stay home with Namath, who's more fun to be with than most of his dates, he says. He's rarely more content than when he and Namath are relaxing on the sofa with a bowl of popcorn, watching ESPN. "There is nothing I wouldn't do for him, nothing he wouldn't do for me," Sam says. "We understand each other." 2

A few weeks ago I also heard from a married California couple in their late 20s who doubt they'll have children "because we are so content" with one another and their two Rottweilers. "We could not love any children more than we love our dogs, to be honest," the husband explained. "We see the dogs as the glue that helps keep our relationship strong." 3

And Jane, whom I've known for years, is a former computer programmer who just sold her suburban Boston home and moved to a ranch house on five acres in upstate New York with her seven golden retrievers—all rescued dogs with cancer, heart disease, or bone disease. She intends, she says, "to spend the rest of my life with these dogs. I want to take care of them and make them happy. Often in my life I've felt let down by people, but never by my dogs." 4

I've been living with my border collies on a farm this winter and spring. There have been moments—I think of one bitter, black winter night when the dogs and I sat huddled together in front of a wood stove while the wind wailed outside—that I, too, felt that love beyond words, pure and powerful. 5

Dog love can be comic or disturbing, painful or uplifting, neurotic,[1] joy- 6 ful, all of the above. Since the dog cannot put any limits on it, dog love can be boundless, sometimes growing beyond our intentions.

For everyone—dog owners and non-dog owners alike—loving human 7 beings is difficult, unpredictable, and often disappointing. Dog love is safer, perhaps more satisfying: Dogs can't betray us, undermine us, tell us they're angry or bored. Dogs can't leave.

Our voiceless companions, dogs are a blank canvas on which we can 8 paint anything we wish. When it comes to love, that's a powerful tempta- tion. Are dog and human love compatible? Dog love can lead human be- ings away from one another and from the painstaking work of coming to terms with our own species. But dogs can teach wounded people how to trust and love again. They can ease loneliness, buffer[2] pain.

Behavioral research suggests that men and women love dogs equally, 9 but often in different ways. Men usually love dogs because they don't talk, which makes them the perfect pals. A guy can have an intense relationship, like Samuel does with Namath, and never have to discuss it. Women are more likely to see dogs as emotionally complex creatures; it's disturbingly common to hear them say their dogs understand their moods better than their boy- friends; that their dogs know when they're upset, but their husbands don't.

There are various kinds of dog love. Some I've noticed: 10

Partner love: Working dogs—herders, hunters, bomb sniffers, agility 11 and obedience performers, search and rescue dogs, therapy dogs—have a particular kind of connection with their owners and handlers, forged by years of training and working together. My border collie Rose and I have spent months together herding sheep. We anticipate each other, communi- cate without words. We are almost telepathic.[3]

Victim love: Dog rescuers—those tens of thousands of people, over- 12 whelmingly female, who scour[4] animal shelters for dogs in trouble—see a lot of ugly human behavior and its consequences, too much, sometimes. The bonds between rescued dogs and those who heal and adopt them are among the strongest of human-animal attachments. This love often taps into the owner's own anger, painful history, and sense of victimization—as well as her need to nurture and heal, and to be nurtured and healed.

Surrogate[5] love: Certain people treat their dogs like family members 13 rather than pets—substitutes for the children or spouses they don't have or don't like. Such owners lavish all the toys, food, activities, and affection on their dog that they would customarily give children. But the dogs don't talk back, drink and smoke pot in the basement, or discover and point out our stupidity and failings. In surrogate love, unlike partner or victim love, the dog can sometimes be a one-for-one replacement for a human.

The intensity of dog love can sometimes be disturbing. People and 14 dogs have been boon companions for thousands of years, but these con- temporary kinds of dog love are new. A recent Yankelovich study for

[1]*neurotic:* unstable, crazy.

[2]*buffer:* lessen the shock of.

[3]*telepathic:* ability to communicate without using words or other physical signs.

[4]*scour:* thoroughly search.

[5]*surrogate:* taking the place of somebody else.

American Demographics found that nearly a third of respondents—and half of all single people—said that of everyone in their lives, they relied most on pets for companionship and affection. Distressingly often, owners have confessed to me that they could survive the loss of a companion or spouse, but they're not sure how they could live without their dog.

I've become a dog-love rationalist: Love them all you want, but main- 15 tain some perspective on what they are and where your love comes from.

A couple of years back, a University of Kentucky psychiatrist who stud- 16 ies human-animal bonds sent me a classic work, *Twins*, by the late British analyst and author Dorothy Burlingham. Burlingham wrote about the power of fantasies in very young children, especially during moments when they are lonely or frightened. A child, she wrote, may take "an imaginary animal as his intimate and beloved companion; subsequently he is never separated from his animal friend. This animal offers the child what he is searching for: faithful love and unswerving[6] devotion. The two share everything, good and bad experiences, and complete understanding of each other; either speech is not necessary, or they have a secret language; the understanding between them goes beyond the realm of consciousness."

This yearning, then, is part of many of our lives from our earliest years. 17 What begins as a potent, comforting fantasy later ripens. Dogs now at our sides, we escape from loneliness and solitude, find "faithful love and unswerving devotion." We feel, rightly or not, as if we share complete understanding; certainly we have a secret language. Our love goes beyond the words we have. We finally find our intimate and beloved companions.

READING COMPREHENSION

1. The word *neurotic* in paragraph 6 can most closely be defined as
   a. unpredictable.
   b. confusing.
   c. extremely active.
   d. romantic.

2. Which of the following sentences best describes the main idea of the selection?
   a. Dogs play an integral role in the lives of many Americans.
   b. Pets understand their human companions better than other humans can.
   c. In modern society, many find themselves satisfied with the love and companionship offered by dogs.
   d. There are differences between cat and dog lovers.

3. What would be a good alternative title for this selection?
   a. Hopelessly Addicted to Dogs
   b. Dogs and Their Loyal Owners
   c. Pets in America
   d. Three Things I Love About Dogs

[6]*unswerving:* steady and unchanging.

4. Name one of the ways listed in the article that dogs can be of help to humans.
    a. Dogs can help the blind.
    b. Dogs can be a companion to children.
    c. Dogs can teach the wounded to love and trust again.
    d. Dogs can assist the learning impaired.

5. Of the types of love listed in the article, which one refers to the type of love that taps into the owner's own inner anger?
    a. partner love
    b. victim love
    c. surrogate love
    d. romantic love

6. Which type of love serves as a replacement for the children or spouses that owners don't have or like?
    a. partner love
    b. surrogate love
    c. romantic love
    d. victim love

7. Which one of the following groups loves dogs for the canine's ability to emotionally understand them?
    a. men
    b. children
    c. women
    d. the elderly

8. According to the article, which one of the following groups most relies on pets' companionship and affection?
    a. children
    b. single people
    c. married couples
    d. the elderly

9. Name one of the ways dogs are more reliable than humans.
    a. Dogs are messy and unpredictable.
    b. Dogs don't betray humans.
    c. Dogs can sense danger.
    d. Dogs make humans happy.

10. The British psychiatrist mentioned in the article makes reference to a childhood yearning for faithful love and unswerving devotion as the reason why
    a. adults feel the way they do about dogs.
    b. adults love their dogs more than dogs love their owners.
    c. dogs remain at our sides through emotional turmoil.
    d. single people have a secret language with their dogs.

STRUCTURE AND TECHNIQUE

1. The article begins with five examples of individuals who have dogs and a summary of the owners and their pets' lives together. Each focuses on the role the pet plays in the relationship. The author ends his examples using himself as a dog lover and how he experienced a form of bond once. Do you believe this method is effective in introducing the author's main idea? If so, why? If not, why not?

2. The author continues his article with research findings that lend support to his main idea that human beings have created an unusual bond and relationship with their dogs. He lists three types of dog love that have been researched. How does listing research affect his article? How convincing do you believe he would have been if he had not used the scientific research in the field?

3. The author's main idea seems clear in his use of examples. However, do you believe his argument would have been stronger if he had used historical information to perhaps explain the role dogs have played in American society? How are dogs viewed differently than other pets in America?

4. The author ends the article with research on childhood attachments and fantasies. He discusses how our attachment to dogs is an extension of a bond previously held. Do you agree with this view? Why or why not? Does using this example lead to a natural and convincing end to his article? If so, how? If not, why not?

CRITICAL READING AND DISCUSSION

1. How does the author explain society's new role for the dog? Do you agree that dogs have become like humans in this society? What examples can you name of people acting as if their dogs are just as valuable, if not more so, than human beings? Why do you think this has occurred?

2. If you have a pet, can you identify, using the types of love described in the article, which type of love you hold for your pet? The pet does not necessarily have to be a dog, but can you describe the role the pet plays in your home and life?

3. The article states that men and women love their dogs in different ways. Do you believe this assertion? If so, why? If not, why not? How does this difference, then, affect interpersonal relationships between men and women? Can the knowledge of this difference be used in other circumstances?

4. The author warns us that the intensity of dog love can sometimes be disturbing. How does he make his case for this assertion? Do you agree with his point of view? If so, why? If not, why not?

WRITING ASSIGNMENTS

Assignment 1: Writing a Paragraph

Write a paragraph about a pet in your family. If you currently don't have one, you can talk about your first one. What breed was it? Was the pet bought or was it a stray? What activities did you do together? Did you feel a special bond? Be sure to describe its physical appearance and personalities. Did the pet's personality mimic your own? There's a saying that owners and their pets look similar. Is/was this the case with your pet?

If you do not or have never had a pet, write a paragraph about what your ideal pet would be like. Refer to the questions above.

Assignment 2: Writing an Essay

Write an essay about a treasured object you never wish to lose. It could be a family heirloom (a bible, jewelry such as a ring or necklace, a toy or doll, a letter written by someone special, etc.). What does this object mean to you, and how did you acquire it? Write a descriptive essay about your object. Be sure to use the five senses to describe your object.

Assignment 3: Writing an Essay

Write an essay that contrasts cat and dog lovers. What are the major differences between these types of pets and their owners? You may use examples of individuals you know to make your argument vivid and specific.

How to Make It in College, Now That You're Here

Brian O'Keeney

PREVIEW

The author of this selection presents a compact guide to being a successful student. He will show you how to pass tests, how to avoid becoming a student zombie, how to find time to fit in everything you want to do, and how to deal with personal problems while keeping up with your studies. These and other helpful tips have been culled from the author's own experience and his candid interviews with fellow students.

Today is your first day on campus. You were a high school senior three 1 months ago. Or maybe you've been at home with your children for the last ten years. Or maybe you work full time and you're coming to school to start the process that leads to a better job. Whatever your background is, you're probably not too concerned today with staying in college. After all, you just got over the hurdle (and the paperwork) of applying to this place and organizing your life so that you could attend. And today, you're confused and tired. Everything is a hassle, from finding the classrooms to standing in line at the bookstore. But read my advice anyway. And if you don't read it today, clip and save this article. You might want to look at it a little further down the road.

By the way, if this isn't your very first day, don't skip this article. Maybe 2 you haven't been doing as well in your studies as you'd hoped. Or perhaps you've had problems juggling your work schedule, your class schedule, and your social life. If so, read on. You're about to get the inside story on making it in college. On the basis of my own experience as a final-year student, and after dozens of interviews with successful students, I've worked out a no-fail system for coping with college. These are the inside tips every student needs to do well in school. I've put myself in your place, and I'm going to answer the questions that will cross (or have already crossed) your mind during your stay here.

What's the Secret of Getting Good Grades?

It all comes down to getting those grades, doesn't it? After all, you came 3 here for some reason, and you're going to need passing grades to get the credits or degree you want. Many of us never did much studying in high school; most of the learning we did took place in the classroom. College, however, is a lot different. You're really on your own when it comes to passing courses. In fact, sometimes you'll feel as if nobody cares if you

3. "To Do" List. This is the secret that, more than any other, got me through 18 college. Once a week (or every day if you want to), write a list of what you have to do. Write down everything from "write English paper" to "buy cold cuts for lunch." The best thing about a "to do" list is that it seems to tame all those stray "I have to" thoughts that nag at your mind. Just making the list seems to make the tasks "doable." After you finish something on the list, cross it off. Don't be compulsive about finishing everything; you're not Superman or Wonder Woman. Get the important things done first. The secondary things you don't finish can simply be moved to your next "to do" list.

What Can I Do If Personal Problems Get in the Way of My Studies?

One student, Roger, told me this story: 19

> Everything was going OK for me until the middle of the spring semester. I went through a terrible time when I broke up with my girlfriend and started seeing her best friend. I was trying to deal with my ex-girlfriend's hurt and anger, my new girlfriend's guilt, and my own worries and anxieties at the same time. In addition to this, my mother was sick and on a medication that made her really irritable. I hated to go home because the atmosphere was so uncomfortable. Soon, I started missing classes because I couldn't deal with the academic pressures as well as my own personal problems. It seemed easier to hang around my girlfriend's apartment than to face all my problems at home and at school.

Another student, Marian, told me;   20

> I'd been married for eight years and the relationship wasn't going too well. I saw the handwriting on the wall, and I decided to prepare for the future. I enrolled in college, because I knew I'd need a decent job to support myself. Well, my husband had a fit because I was going to school. We were arguing a lot anyway, and he made it almost impossible for me to study at home. I think he was angry and almost jealous because I was drawing away from him. It got so bad that I thought about quitting college for a while. I wasn't getting any support at home, and it was just too hard to go on.

Personal troubles like these are overwhelming when you're going 21 through them. School seems like the least important thing in your life. The two students above are perfect examples of this. But if you think about it, quitting or failing school would be the worst thing for these two students. Roger's problems, at least with his girlfriends, would simmer down eventually, and then he'd regret having left school. Marian had to finish college if she wanted to be able to live independently. Sometimes, you've just got to hang tough.

But what do you do while you're trying to live through a lousy time? 22 First of all, do something difficult. Ask yourself, honestly, if you're exaggerating small problems as an excuse to avoid classes and studying.

It takes strength to admit this, but there's no sense in kidding yourself. If your problems are serious, and real, try to make some human contacts at school. Lots of students hide inside a miserable shell made of their own troubles and feel isolated and lonely. Believe me, there are plenty of students with problems. Not everyone is getting A's and having a fabulous social and home life at the same time. As you go through the term, you'll pick up some vibrations about the students in your classes. Perhaps someone strikes you as a compatible person. Why not speak to that person after class? Share a cup of coffee in the cafeteria or walk to the parking lot together. You're not looking for a best friend or the love of your life. You just want to build a little network of support for yourself. Sharing your difficulties, questions, and complaints with a friendly person on campus can make a world of difference in how you feel.

Finally, if your problems are overwhelming, get some professional 23 help. Why do you think colleges spend countless dollars on counseling departments and campus psychiatric services? More than ever, students all over the country are taking advantage of the help offered by support groups and therapy sessions. There's no shame attached to asking for help, either; in fact, almost 40 percent of college students (according to one survey) will use counseling services during their time in school. Just walk into a student center or counseling office and ask for an appointment. You wouldn't think twice about asking a dentist to help you get rid of your toothache. Counselors are paid—and want—to help you with your problems.

Why Do Some People Make It and Some Drop Out?

Anyone who spends at least one semester in college notices that some 24 students give up on their classes. The person who sits behind you in accounting, for example, begins to miss a lot of class meetings and eventually vanishes. Or another student comes to class without the assignment, doodles in a notebook during the lecture, and leaves during the break. What's the difference between students like this and the ones who succeed in school? My survey may be nonscientific, but everyone I asked said the same thing: attitude. A positive attitude is the key to everything else—good study habits, smart time scheduling, and coping with personal difficulties.

What does "a positive attitude" mean? Well, for one thing, it means 25 avoiding the zombie syndrome. It means not only showing up for your classes, but also doing something while you're there. Really listen. Take notes. Ask a question if you want to. Don't just walk into a class, put your mind in neutral, and drift away to never-never land.

Having a positive attitude goes deeper than this, though. It means 26 being mature about college as an institution. Too many students approach college classes like six-year-olds who expect first grade to be as much fun as *Sesame Street*. First grade, as we all know, isn't as much fun as *Sesame Street*. And college classes can sometimes be downright dull.

If you let a boring class discourage you so much that you want to leave school, you'll lose in the long run. Look at your priorities. You want a degree, or a certificate, or a career. If you have to, you can make it through a less-than-interesting class in order to achieve what you want. Get whatever you can out of every class. But if you simply can't stand a certain class, be determined to fulfill its requirements and be done with it once and for all.

After the initial high of starting school, you have to settle in for the   27
long haul. If you follow the advice here, you'll be prepared to face the academic crunch. You'll also live through the semester without giving up your family, your job, or *Monday Night Football*. Finally, going to college can be an exciting time. You do learn. And when you learn things, the world becomes a more interesting place.

READING COMPREHENSION

1. The word *queasy* in "with a queasy stomach" (paragraph 3) means
   a. strong.
   b. healthy.
   c. full.
   d. nervous.

2. The word *tactics* in "try these three tactics" (paragraph 14) means
   a. proofs.
   b. problems.
   c. methods.
   d. questions.

3. Which of the following would be a good alternative title for this selection?
   a. Your First Day on Campus
   b. Coping with College
   c. How to Budget Your Time
   d. The Benefits of College Skills Courses

4. Which sentence expresses the main idea of the selection?
   a. In high school, most of us did little homework.
   b. You should give yourself rewards for studying well.
   c. Sometimes personal problems interfere with studying.
   d. You can succeed in college by following certain guidelines.

5. According to the author, "making it" in college means
   a. studying whenever you have any free time.
   b. getting a degree by barely passing your courses.
   c. quitting school until you solve your personal problems.
   d. getting good grades without making your life miserable.

6. If your personal problems seem overwhelming, you should
   a. drop out for a while.
   b. exaggerate them to teachers.
   c. avoid talking about them.
   d. get help from a professional.

7. Which of the following is *not* described by the author as a means of time control?
   a. monthly calendar
   b. to-do list
   c. study schedule
   d. flexible job hours

8. We can infer that the writer of this essay
   a. cares about college students and their success.
   b. dropped out of college.
   c. is very disorganized.
   d. is an A student.

9. From the selection we can conclude that
   a. college textbooks are very expensive.
   b. it is a good practice to write notes in your textbook.
   c. taking notes on your reading takes too much time.
   d. a student should never mark up an expensive book.

10. The author implies that
    a. fewer people than before are attending college.
    b. most college students experience no problems during their first year.
    c. all college students experience overwhelming problems.
    d. coping with college is difficult.

STRUCTURE AND TECHNIQUE

1. O'Keeney uses a highly structured format in his essay. What are some of the features of this format? Why do you think O'Keeney structured his essay in this way?

2. Does the author clearly state his thesis? If so, where is it stated, and how?

3. What method of introduction does the author use in the section on personal problems (starting with paragraph 19)? What is the value of using this method?

4. Throughout his essay, O'Keeney addresses his audience in the second person—using the word *you*. How does such a technique advance his main point?

CRITICAL READING AND DISCUSSION

1. What, according to O'Keeney, is the secret of getting good grades? Have you used any of O'Keeney's study methods? If so, how useful do you think they have been for you? Are there any that you haven't used, but might try? Explain your answer.

2. What does O'Keeney recommend students do in order to manage their time and responsibilities more effectively? Which of these suggestions are you most likely to use? Which are you least likely to use? Why?

3. What is the secret the author says got him through college? What do you think is the most helpful or important suggestion the author makes in the selection? Give reasons for your choice.

4. Do you agree with the author that Roger and Marian should stay in school? Are there any situations in which it would be better for students to quit school or leave, at least temporarily? Explain, giving examples to support your answer.

RESPONDING TO IMAGES

What tips from O'Keeney's essay might the student in this photograph find beneficial?

WRITING ASSIGNMENTS

Assignment 1: Writing a Paragraph

Write a paragraph contrasting college *as you thought it would be* with college *as it is*. You can organize the paragraph by focusing on three specific things that are different from what you expected. Or you can cover three areas of difference. For instance, you may decide to contrast your expectations about (1) a college dorm room, (2) your roommate, and (3) dining-hall food with reality. Or you could contrast your expectations about (1) fellow students, (2) college professors, and (3) college courses with reality.

Refer to the section in Chapter 11 on methods of developing comparison and contrast paragraphs to review point-by-point and one-side-at-a-time development. Be sure to make an outline of your paragraph before you begin to write.

Assignment 2: Writing an Essay

Write a letter to Roger or Marian, giving advice on how to deal with the personal problem mentioned in the article. You could recommend any or all of the following:

Face the problem realistically. (By doing what?)

Make other contacts at school. (How? Where?)

See a counselor. (Where? What should this person be told?)

Realize that the problem is not so serious. (Why not?)

Ignore the problem. (How? By doing what instead?)

In your introductory paragraph, explain why you are writing the letter. Include a thesis statement that says what plan of action you are recommending. Then, in the rest of the letter, explain the plan of action in detail.

Assignment 3: Writing an Essay

Write an essay similar to the one you've just read that explains how to succeed in some other field—for example, a job, a sport, marriage, child rearing. First, brainstorm three or four problem areas a newcomer to this experience might encounter. Then, under each area you have listed, jot down some helpful hints and techniques for overcoming these problems. For example, a process paper on "How to Succeed as a Waitress" might describe the following problem areas in this kind of job:

Developing a good memory

Learning to do tasks quickly

Coping with troublesome customers

Each supporting paragraph in this paper would discuss specific techniques for dealing with these problems. Be sure that the advice you give is detailed and specific enough to really help a person in such a situation.

You may find it helpful to look over the essay that emphasizes process in Chapter 18 (page 324).

In Praise of the F Word

Mary Sherry

PREVIEW

What does it take to get by in high school? Too little, according to the author, a teacher in an "educational-repair shop." In this article, which originally appeared in *Newsweek*, Mary Sherry describes the ways she sees students being cheated by their schools and proposes a remedy you may find surprising.

Tens of thousands of eighteen-year-olds will graduate this year and be 1 handed meaningless diplomas. These diplomas won't look any different from those awarded to their luckier classmates. Their validity will be questioned only when their employers discover that these graduates are semiliterate.

Eventually a fortunate few will find their way into educational-repair 2 shops—adult-literacy programs, such as the one where I teach basic grammar and writing. There, high school graduates and high school dropouts pursuing graduate-equivalency certificates will learn the skills they should have learned in school. They will also discover that they have been cheated by our educational system.

As I teach, I learn a lot about our schools. Early in each session I ask my 3 students to write about an unpleasant experience they had in school. No writer's block here! "I wish someone had made me stop doing drugs and made me study." "I liked to party, and no one seemed to care." "I was a good kid and didn't cause any trouble, so they just passed me along even though I didn't read well and couldn't write." And so on.

I am your basic do-gooder, and prior to teaching this class I blamed 4 the poor academic skills our kids have today on drugs, divorce, and other impediments to the concentration necessary for doing well in school. But, as I rediscover each time I walk into the classroom, before a teacher can expect students to concentrate, he has to get their attention, no matter what distractions may be at hand. There are many ways to do this, and they have much to do with teaching style. However, if style alone won't do it, there is another way to show who holds the winning hand in the classroom. That is to reveal the trump card[1] of failure.

I will never forget a teacher who played that card to get the at- 5 tention of one of my children. Our youngest, a world-class charmer, did little to develop his intellectual talents but always got by—until Mrs. Stifter.

Our son was a high school senior when he had her for English. "He sits 6 in the back of the room talking to his friends," she told me. "Why don't you move him to the front row?" I urged, believing the embarrassment

---

[1]*trump card:* in bridge, a card of the suit that ranks highest; thus, something powerful, often held in reserve to be used at the right moment.

would get him to settle down. Mrs. Stifter looked at me steely-eyed over her glasses. "I don't move seniors," she said. "I flunk them." I was flustered. Our son's academic life flashed before my eyes. No teacher had ever threatened him with that before. I regained my composure and managed to say that I thought she was right. By the time I got home I was feeling pretty good about this. It was a radical approach for these times, but, well, why not? "She's going to flunk you," I told my son. I did not discuss it any further. Suddenly English became a priority in his life. He finished out the semester with an A.

I know one example doesn't make a case, but at night I see a parade of 7 students who are angry and resentful for having been passed along until they could no longer even pretend to keep up. Of average intelligence or better, they eventually quit school, concluding that they were too dumb to finish. "I should have been held back," is a comment I hear frequently. Even sadder are those students who are high school graduates who say to me after a few weeks of class, "I don't know how I ever got a high school diploma."

Passing students who have not mastered the work cheats them and 8 the employers who expect graduates to have basic skills. We excuse this dishonest behavior by saying kids can't learn if they come from terrible environments. No one seems to stop to think that—no matter what environments they come from—most kids don't put school first on their list unless they perceive that something is at stake. They'd rather be sailing.

Many students I see at night could give expert testimony on unemploy- 9 ment, chemical dependency, and abusive relationships. In spite of these difficulties, they have decided to make education a priority. They are motivated by the desire for a better job or the need to hang on to the one they've got. They have a healthy fear of failure.

People of all ages can rise above their problems, but they need to have 10 a reason to do so. Young people generally don't have the maturity to value education in the same way my adult students value it. But fear of failure, whether economic or academic, can motivate both.

Flunking as a regular policy has just as much merit today as it did two 11 generations ago. We must review the threat of flunking and see it as it really is—a positive teaching tool. It is an expression of confidence by both teachers and parents that the students have the ability to learn the material presented to them. However, making it work again would take a dedicated, caring conspiracy between teachers and parents. It would mean facing the tough reality that passing kids who haven't learned the material—while it might save them grief for the short term— dooms them to long-term illiteracy. It would mean that teachers would have to follow through on their threats, and parents would have to stand behind them, knowing their children's best interests are indeed at stake. This means no more doing Scott's assignments for him because he might fail. No more passing Jodi because she's such a nice kid.

This is a policy that worked in the past and can work today. A wise 12 teacher, with the support of his parents, gave our son the opportunity to succeed—or fail. It's time we returned this choice to all students.

READING COMPREHENSION

1. The word *validity* in "[The diplomas'] validity will be questioned only when . . . employers discover that these graduates are semiliterate" (paragraph 1) means

   a. soundness.

   b. dates.

   c. age.

   d. supply.

2. The word *impediments* in "I blamed the poor academic skills our kids have today on drugs, divorce, and other impediments to concentration" (paragraph 4) means

   a. questions.

   b. paths.

   c. skills.

   d. obstacles.

3. Which of the following would be a good alternative title for this selection?

   a. Learning to Concentrate in School

   b. Teaching English Skills

   c. A Useful Tool for Motivating Students

   d. Adult-Literacy Programs

4. Which sentence best expresses the main idea of the selection?

   a. Many adults cannot read or write well.

   b. English skills can be learned through adult-literacy programs.

   c. Schools should include flunking students as part of their regular policy.

   d. Before students will concentrate, the teacher must get their attention.

5. Sherry's night students are

   a. usually unemployed.

   b. poor students.

   c. motivated to learn.

   d. doing drugs.

6. According to the author, many students who get "passed along"

   a. are lucky.

   b. never find a job.

   c. don't get into trouble.

   d. eventually feel angry and resentful.

7. Sherry feels that to succeed, flunking students as a regular policy requires

    a. adult-literacy programs.

    b. graduate-equivalency certificates.

    c. the total cooperation of teachers and parents.

    d. a strong teaching style.

8. The author implies that our present educational system is

    a. the best in the world.

    b. doing the best that it can.

    c. very short of teachers.

    d. not demanding enough of students.

9. *True or False?* _____ Sherry implies that high school students often don't realize the value of academic skills.

10. From the selection, we may conclude that the author based her opinion on

    a. statistics.

    b. educational research.

    c. her personal and professional experiences.

    d. expert professional testimony.

STRUCTURE AND TECHNIQUE

1. In current vocabulary, "the F word" usually refers to something other than "fail." Why do you think Mary Sherry used the term in her title, rather than simply using "fail" or "failure"? What effect does her title have on the reader?

2. In which paragraph does the author first mention her thesis? What is her main method of development, and how is it related to that thesis? Where does she use narration to support her thesis?

3. What contrast transition is used in the first sentence of paragraph 10? What ideas are being contrasted within that sentence?

4. In paragraph 11, how many times does Sherry use "mean" or "means"? What might her purpose be for repeating this word so frequently?

CRITICAL READING AND DISCUSSION

1. Sherry writes that "before a teacher can expect students to concentrate, he has to get their attention, no matter what distractions may be at hand" (paragraph 4). What examples of distractions does Sherry mention? Find several in her essay. Can you think of others—perhaps ones that existed in your own high school?

2. What does Sherry mean by calling the program she teaches in an "educational-repair shop"? What does the term tell us about Sherry's attitude toward high schools?

3. Sherry writes, "Young people generally don't have the maturity to value education in the same way my adult students value it." Do you agree or disagree? Support your view with details and observations from your own experience.

4. Do you feel your high school teachers made an honest effort to give you the skills you need—and to make you aware of the importance of those skills? If not, what should your school have done that it did not do?

WRITING ASSIGNMENTS

Assignment 1: Writing a Paragraph

Write a paragraph that has as its topic sentence one of the following statements:

> Students have no one to blame but themselves if they leave school without having learned basic skills.

> When students graduate or quit school lacking basic skills, they are the victims of an inadequate educational system.

> Flunking students has more disadvantages than advantages.

Support your topic sentence with several points.

Assignment 2: Writing an Essay

Sherry proposes using "flunking as a regular policy" as a way to encourage students to work harder. What else might school systems do to help students? Write an essay in which you suggest a few policies for our public schools and give the reasons you think those changes will be beneficial. Following are some policies you may wish to consider:

> More writing in all classes

> Shorter summer vacations

> Less emphasis on memorization and more on thinking skills

> A language requirement

> A daily quiet reading session in elementary grades

Assignment 3: Writing an Essay

Here are two letters sent to *Newsweek* by teachers in response to Sherry's article:

Letter 1

Mary Sherry's essay advocating the use of flunking as a teaching tool was well intentioned but naive. In the first place, my local school district—and I doubt it's unique—discourages the practice by compiling teachers' failure rates for comparison. (Would you want to rank first?) More important, though, F's don't even register on many kids' Richter scales. When your spirit has been numbed—as some of my students' spirits have—by physical, sexual, and psychological abuse, it's hard to notice an F. Walk a mile in one of my kids' shoes. Real fear has little to do with school.

Kay Keglovits
Arlington, Texas

Letter 2

Sherry is right: flunking poor students makes sense. But, as she notes, "making it work again would take a dedicated, caring conspiracy between teachers and parents." I once failed a high school junior for the year. I received a furious call from the student's mother. I was called to a meeting with the school superintendent, the principal, the mother, and the student. There it was decided that I would tutor the student for four months so that the F could be replaced with a passing grade. This was a total sham; the student did nothing during this remedial work, but she was given a passing grade. No wonder education is in the condition that we find it today.

Arthur J. Hochhalter
Minot, North Dakota

These letters suggest that if schools want to try flunking as a regular policy, they will have to plan carefully. Write an essay in which you discuss ways to make failing poor students work as a regular policy. Your thesis statement can be something like this: "In order for a policy of flunking to work, certain policies and attitudes would need to be changed in many schools." As support in your essay, use the ideas in these letters, Sherry's ideas, and any other ideas you have heard or thought of. Describe your supporting ideas in detail and explain why each is necessary or useful.

Is Sex All That Matters?

Joyce Garity

PREVIEW

From the skimpy clothing in ads to the suggestive themes in many of today's TV comedies, our young people are bombarded with sexuality. How does the constant stream of sexual images influence their behavior and dreams? In considering that question, social worker Joyce Garity focuses on one young woman named Elaine, alone and pregnant with her second child.

A few years ago, a young girl lived with me, my husband, and our chil- 1 dren for several months. The circumstances of Elaine's coming to us don't matter here; suffice it to say that she was troubled and nearly alone in the world. She was also pregnant—hugely, clumsily pregnant with her second child. Elaine was seventeen. Her pregnancy, she said, was an accident; she also said she wasn't sure who had fathered her child. There had been several sex partners and no contraception. Yet, she repeated blandly, gazing at me with clear blue eyes, the pregnancy was an accident, and one she would certainly never repeat.

Eventually I asked Elaine, after we had grown to know each other well 2 enough for such conversations, why neither she nor her lovers had used birth control. She blushed—porcelain-skinned girl with one child in foster care and another swelling the bib of her fashionably faded overalls— stammered, and blushed some more. Birth control, she finally got out, was "embarrassing." It wasn't "romantic." You couldn't be really passionate, she explained, and worry about birth control at the same time.

I haven't seen Elaine for quite a long time. I think about her often, 3 though. I think of her as I page through teen fashion magazines in the salon where I have my hair cut. Although mainstream and relatively wholesome, these magazines trumpet sexuality page after leering page. On the inside front cover, an advertisement for Guess jeans features junior fashion models in snug denim dresses, their legs bared to just below the crotch. An advertisement for Liz Claiborne fragrances shows a barely clad young couple sprawled on a bed, him painting her toenails. An advertisement for Obsession cologne displays a waif-thin girl draped stomach-down across a couch, naked, her startled expression suggesting helplessness in the face of an unseen yet approaching threat.

I think of Elaine because I know she would love these ads. "They're 4 so beautiful," she would croon, and of course they are. The faces and bodies they show are lovely. The lighting is superb. The hair and makeup are faultless. In the Claiborne ad, the laughing girl whose toenails are being painted by her handsome lover is obviously having the time of her life. She stretches luxuriously on a bed heaped with clean white linen and fluffy pillows. Beyond the sheer blowing curtains of her room, we can glimpse a graceful wrought-iron balcony. Looking at the ad, Elaine could only want to be her. Any girl would want to be her. Heck, I want to be her.

But my momentary desire to move into the Claiborne picture, to trade 5 lives with the exquisite young creature pictured there, is just that—momentary. I've lived long enough to know that what I see is a marketing invention. A moment after the photo session was over, the beautiful room was dismantled, and the models moved on to their next job. Later, the technicians took over the task of doctoring the photograph until it reached full-blown fantasy proportions.

Not so Elaine. After months of living together and countless hours 6 of watching her yearn after magazine images, soap-opera heroines, and rock goddesses, I have a pretty good idea of why she looks at ads like Claiborne's. She sees the way life—her life—is supposed to be. She sees a world characterized by sexual spontaneity, playfulness, and abandon. She sees people who don't worry about such unsexy details as birth control. Nor, apparently, do they spend much time thinking about such pedestrian topics as commitment or whether they should act on their sexual impulses. Their clean sunlit rooms are never invaded by the fear of AIDS, of unwanted pregnancy, of shattered lives. For all her apparent lack of defense, the girl on the couch in the Obsession ad will surely never experience the brutality of rape.

Years of exposure to this media-invented, sex-saturated universe have 7 done their work on Elaine. She is, I'm sure, completely unaware of the irony in her situation: She melts over images from a sexual Shangri-la,[1] never realizing that her attempts to mirror those images left her pregnant, abandoned, living in the spare bedroom of a stranger's house, relying on charity for rides to the welfare office and supervised visits with her toddler daughter.

Of course, Elaine is not the first to be suckered by the cynical practice 8 of using sex to sell underwear, rock groups, or sneakers. Using sex as a sales tool is hardly new. At the beginning of this century, British actress Lily Langtry shocked her contemporaries by posing, clothed somewhat scantily, with a bar of Pear's soap. The advertisers have always known that the masses are susceptible to the notion that a particular product will make them more sexually attractive. In the past, however, ads used euphemisms, claiming that certain products would make people "more lovable" or "more popular." What is a recent development is the abandonment of any such polite double-talk. Advertising today leaves no question about what is being sold along with the roasted peanuts or artificial sweetener. "Tell us about your first time," coyly invites the innuendo[2]-filled magazine advertisement for Campari liquor. A billboard for Levi's shows two jeans-clad young men on the beach, hoisting a girl in the air. The boys' perfect, tan bodies are matched by hers, although we see a lot more of hers: bare midriff, short shorts, cleavage. She caresses their hair; they stroke her legs. A jolly fantasy where sex exists without consequences.

But this fantasy is a lie—one which preys on young people. Studies 9 show that by the age of twenty, 75 percent of Americans have lost their virginity. In many high schools—and an increasing number of junior highs—virginity is regarded as an embarrassing vestige of childhood, to be disposed of as quickly as possible. Young people are immersed from their earliest days in a culture that parades sexuality at every turn and makes heroes of the advocates of sexual excess. Girls, from toddlerhood on up, shop in stores packed with clothing once thought suitable only for street-walkers—lace leggings, crop tops, and wedge-heeled boots. Parents drop their children off at concerts featuring simulated on-stage masturbation or pretended acts of copulation. Young boys idolize sports stars like the late Wilt Chamberlain, who claimed to have bedded 20,000 women. And when the "Spur Posse," eight California high school athletes, were charged with systematically raping girls as young as ten as part of a "scoring" ritual, the beefy young jocks were rewarded with a publicity tour of talk shows, while one father boasted to reporters about his son's "manhood."

---

[1]*Shangri-la:* an imaginary paradise on earth (the name of a beautiful faraway place in the novel *Lost Horizon*).

[2]*innuendo:* subtle suggestion.

In a late, lame attempt to counterbalance this sexual overload, most 10 schools offer sex education as part of their curriculums. (In 1993, forty-seven states recommended or required such courses.) But sex ed classes are heavy on the mechanics of fertilization and birth control—sperm, eggs, and condoms—and light on any discussion of sexuality as only one part of a well-balanced life. There is passing reference to abstinence as a method of contraception, but little discussion of abstinence as an emotionally or spiritually satisfying option. Promiscuity is discussed for its role in spreading sexually transmitted diseases. But the concept of rejecting casual sex in favor of reserving sex for an emotionally intimate, exclusive, trusting relationship—much less any mention of waiting until marriage—is foreign to most public school settings. "Love and stuff like that really wasn't discussed" is the way one Spur Posse member remembers his high school sex education class.

Surely teenagers need the factual information provided by sex educa- 11 tion courses. But where is "love and stuff like that" talked about? Where can they turn for a more balanced view of sexuality? Who is telling young people like Elaine, my former houseguest, that sex is not an adequate basis for a healthy, respectful relationship? Along with warnings to keep condoms on hand, is anyone teaching kids that they have a right to be valued for something other than their sexuality? Madison Avenue, Hollywood, and the TV, music, and fashion industries won't tell them that. Who will?

No one has told Elaine—at least, not in a way she comprehends. I 12 haven't seen her for a long time, but I hear of her occasionally. The baby boy she bore while living in my house is in a foster home, a few miles from his older half-sister, who is also in foster care. Elaine herself is working in a local convenience store—and she is pregnant again. This time, I understand, she is carrying twins.

READING COMPREHENSION

1. The word *dismantled* in "A moment after the photo session was over, the beautiful room was dismantled, and the models moved on to their next job" (paragraph 5) means

   a. used.

   b. photographed.

   c. taken apart.

   d. perfected.

2. The word *vestige* in "In many high schools—and an increasing number of junior highs—virginity is regarded as an embarrassing vestige of childhood" (paragraph 9) means

   a. reversal.

   b. activity.

   c. remainder.

   d. error.

3. Which of the following would be a good alternative title for this selection?

   a. Teens and Birth Control

b. The Use of Sex to Sell Products

c. An Unbalanced View of Sexuality

d. The Advantages of Casual Sex

4. Which sentence best expresses the main idea of the selection?

   a. Sexual images have helped our society become more open and understanding about a natural part of life.

   b. We live in a society ruled by Madison Avenue, Hollywood, and the TV, music, and fashion industries.

   c. Sex education courses, required in most states, have not done enough to teach our children about sexuality and responsible behavior.

   d. Nothing, not even sex education, is counteracting the numerous sexual images in our society that encourage irresponsible, casual sex.

5. According to the author, Elaine probably likes to look at sexy magazine ads because

   a. she doesn't have high moral standards.

   b. she wishes she could afford the products being advertised.

   c. they portray the kind of life she'd like to lead.

   d. they remind her of her life before she had children.

6. In contrast to Elaine, the author

   a. understands that most ads portray an unreal world.

   b. finds ads like the Claiborne ad distasteful.

   c. never looks at fashion magazines.

   d. does not have children.

7. Elaine

   a. wanted to become pregnant.

   b. thinks birth control isn't romantic.

   c. never finished high school.

   d. has a healthy fear of AIDS.

8. We can conclude the author believes that

   a. sex is a private matter that should not be discussed.

   b. many young people view sex as an adequate basis for a relationship.

   c. Madison Avenue, Hollywood, and the TV, music, and fashion industries have completely destroyed all morality in America.

   d. virginity is an embarrassing vestige of childhood.

9. The author implies that

   a. sexy ads should be illegal.

   b. schools should teach contraception at an earlier age.

   c. sex should be reserved for an exclusive, loving relationship.

   d. casual sex is sometimes, though not always, a good idea.

10. The author suggests that sex education classes
    a. are a major cause of casual, unprotected sex.
    b. should include the role of sex in a meaningful relationship.
    c. should not include the mechanics of fertilization and birth control.
    d. have taken over a role that rightfully belongs to parents.

STRUCTURE AND TECHNIQUE

1. To support her views about sexuality in popular culture, Garity presents the case of Elaine. Why has the author chosen to focus so much of her essay on Elaine? What would have been lost if Garity had omitted Elaine?

2. List the details that Garity provides as she describes the Claiborne ad. Why does she go to such lengths to describe it? Why might she think it important for the reader to see it so clearly?

3. Garity uses a number of examples to support her claim about the prevalence of sex in popular culture. Cite some of these examples and explain how they support her argument.

4. Throughout paragraph 11, Garity poses a series of questions. What does she gain by using this technique?

CRITICAL READING AND DISCUSSION

1. How do you think Garity felt about Elaine? Affectionate? Scornful? Resentful? Disapproving? Pitying? Explain your answer, pointing out evidence from Garity's text.

2. In paragraph 7, the author says that Elaine is "completely unaware of the irony in her situation." In an ironic situation, there is an inconsistency between what might be expected and what actually happens. What about Elaine's situation is ironic?

3. The author lists numerous examples to illustrate and support her claim that "young people are immersed from their earliest days in a culture that parades sexuality at every turn and makes heroes of advocates of sexual excess." What examples can you think of to add to her list? Describe and explain them.

4. In arguing against the emphasis on sexuality in our culture, Garity focuses on potential dangers to young women. How do you think this highly sexualized culture affects young men? Are they also at risk? Explain.

WRITING ASSIGNMENTS

Assignment 1: Writing a Paragraph

Garity accuses the advertising, film, TV, music, and fashion industries of contributing to our sex-saturated society by parading "sexuality at every turn." Choose one industry from that list, and write your own paragraph about how it portrays sexuality.

There is more than one way you can approach this assignment. In a paragraph on the fashion industry, for instance, you could focus on types of clothing being promoted, ads in print, and ads on TV. In a paragraph on the music industry, you might discuss three musicians and how their lyrics and their performances promote a particular view of sex. Whatever your choice, include specific, colorful descriptions, as Garity does when discussing ads and fashions. (See, for example, paragraphs 3 and 8.)

Assignment 2: Writing an Essay

Garity suggests that sex education courses should include more than the "mechanics of fertilization and birth control" (paragraph 10). Write an essay describing several ways you feel sex education classes could incorporate "love and stuff like that." Begin by selecting three general approaches that could be used in a sex education class to get students to think about what a rich, balanced romantic relationship is made of. For example, you might focus on three of the following:

> Discussion of what students seek in a relationship
>
> Discussion of a fictional relationship, such as that of Romeo and Juliet or two characters on a TV show
>
> Discussion of the lyrics of a popular song
>
> Bringing into class a psychologist who deals with problems in relationships
>
> Bringing into class one or more couples who have been together for many years

Discuss each method you choose in a separate paragraph. Describe in detail how the method would work, using hypothetical examples to illustrate your points.

Assignment 3: Writing an Essay

Advertisements represent many elements of our society. Choose an element other than sexuality, and analyze the way ads of any kind (in magazines and newspapers, on billboards and buses, on TV and radio and the Internet) portray that subject. Following are some areas of our lives that are commonly represented in ads:

> Family life
>
> Women's roles
>
> Men's roles
>
> Possessions
>
> Looks
>
> Health

In analyzing an ad, consider what images and words are used, how they are intended to appeal to the audience, and what values they promote. Use the conclusion you come to as the thesis of your essay. For example, an essay on men's roles might make this point: "Many of today's TV ads promote participation of fathers in domestic activities."

Support your conclusion with colorful descriptions of several ads. Make your descriptions detailed enough so that your readers can "see" the elements of ads you refer to. Be sure to focus on the parts of the ads that support the point you are trying to make. You could organize your essay by devoting a paragraph each to three significant ads. Or you could devote each support paragraph to one of several important points about the subject you've chosen. For instance, an essay about fathers helping at home might discuss child care, cleaning, and cooking. A paragraph on each of those topics might refer to two or more ads.

How Can Cyberbullies Be Stopped?

Social Networking Web Sites and Other Technologies
Enable Schoolyard Bullies to Pack a Bigger Punch

Thomas J. Billitteri

PREVIEW

Thomas J. Billitteri is a journalist who has worked for the *Dallas Times Herald* and for *Florida Trend*, a business magazine. He has also written for a number of other publications including the *St. Petersburg Times* and *News Observer.com*. Billitteri is the author of two books for young adults: *Alternative Medicine* and *The Gault Case: Legal Rights for Young Adults*. Cyberbullying, the harassing of people through electronic communications devices, is a growing problem among people today. This article appeared in a local North Carolina newspaper on July 20, 2008.

The episodes are hurtful, ugly—and sometimes deadly. In Lakeland, Fla., 1 a group of teenagers records the beating of another teen. The local sheriff says the attack was in retaliation for online trash-talking by the victim.

At a high school near Pittsburgh, an anonymous e-mail list features sex- 2 ually explicit rankings of 25 female students, names and photos included.

In suburban Dardenne Prairie, Mo., near St. Louis, 13-year-old Megan 3 Meier hangs herself after receiving cruel messages on the social-networking site MySpace.

In Essex Junction, Vt., 13-year-old Ryan Patrick Halligan kills himself 4 after months of harassment, including instant messages calling him gay.

The cases, albeit[1] extreme, highlight what school officials, child psychol- 5 ogists, legal experts and government researchers argue is a fast-spreading epidemic of "cyberbullying"—the use of the Internet, cell phones and other digital technology to harass, intimidate, threaten, mock and defame.[2]

Studies show cyberbullying affects millions of adolescents and young 6 adults. The Centers for Disease Control and Prevention last year labeled "electronic aggression"—its term for cyberbullying—an emerging public-health problem.

[1]*albeit*: although.
[2]*defame*: attack someone's reputation.

A reliable profile of cyberbullying, a relatively new phenomenon, is dif- 7 ficult to construct. Studies leave little doubt, however, that cyberbullying is growing.

Some cyberbullies are angry loners, sometimes seeking revenge for 8 having been bullied themselves. But experts say it is common for online abusers to be popular students who are trying to strengthen their place in the social hierarchy.

"It's not really the schoolyard thug character" in some cases, said 9 Nancy Willard, executive director of the Center for Safe and Responsible Internet Use, a research and professional development organization in Eugene, Ore. "It's the in-crowd kids bullying those who don't rank high enough."

What fuels cyberbullying is "status in schools—popularity, hierar- 10 chies, who's cool, who's not," said Danah Boyd, a fellow at the Berkman Center for Internet and Society at Harvard Law School who studies teens' behavior on MySpace, Facebook and other social-networking sites.

Of course, bullying itself is nothing new. What's new is the 11 technology.

More than 90 percent of teens are online. More than half of online teens 12 have profiles on social-networking sites.

The sites allow people to post personal facts, photos, gossip and other 13 information for others to read. Social scientists say such sites can serve a useful, and even vital, purpose by helping adolescents build friendships, learn tolerance for others' views and form a sense of self-identity. But critics say the sites have the potential to be incubators[3] for abuse, magnets for sexual predators and embarrassing archives[4] of a student's immature behavior that college admissions officials or employers may wind up seeing.

The rise of Web sites brimming with the minutiae[5] of teen antics and 14 angst has helped to create a rich climate for mayhem.[6] Locker-room photos snapped with cell phones and broadcast on the Internet, fake profiles created on social-networking sites, salacious[7] rumors spread in chat rooms, threats zapped across town in instant messages.

States Step In

Cyberbullying has impelled lawmakers, especially at the state level, to 15 either pass anti-bullying laws that encompass cyberbullying or add cyberbullying to existing statutes. Some laws are propelled by a mix of concern about electronic bullying and online sexual predators.

But using laws and courts to stop cyberbullying has been tricky and 16 sometimes controversial. "There's a big conflict in knowing where to draw the line between things that are rude and things that are illegal,"

[3]*incubators:* places to aid the development of.
[4]*archives:* collections.
[5]*minutiae:* particulars.
[6]*mayhem:* chaos.
[7]*salacious:* sexually explicit.

said Parry Aftab, an Internet privacy and security lawyer who is executive director of wiredsafety.org, an Internet safety group in Irvington-on-Hudson, N.Y.

But the law on that question can be confusing, and the U.S. Supreme 17 Court has yet to decide a case involving student Internet speech. Trying to regulate what students do or say on their home computers or in text messages sent from the local mall could wind up trampling students' constitutional rights or the rights of parents to direct their children's upbringing as they see fit, say free-speech advocates.

Still, many lawmakers are moving to add provisions to existing anti- 18 bullying laws or writing new codes. Iowa, Maryland, Minnesota, New Jersey and Oregon have passed cyberbullying laws recently, and a number of other states are considering such statutes.

"Those who bully and harass stand in the way of learning and 19 threaten the safety of our children," said Matt Blunt, the Republican governor of Missouri, after the state Senate passed a cyberbullying bill in March.

Legislators are overreacting, said the Berkman Center's Boyd. "These 20 laws aren't doing anything. What we desperately need is education and discussion," along with greater attention from parents and other adults to the heavy pressures and expectations weighing on adolescents.

Off School Grounds

Perhaps the most nettlesome circumstance is cyberbullying that is trans- 21 mitted at home or the local mall or skating rink, but that nonetheless causes disruption at school.

"There's always the legal discussion of 'If it doesn't happen at school, 22 can a district take action?'" said Joe Wehrli, policy services director for the Oregon School Boards Association. "If a student is harassed for three hours at night on the Web and they come to school and have to sit in the same classroom with the student that's the bully, there is an effect on education, and in that way, there is a direct link to schools."

But free-speech advocates say educators sometimes punish students 23 whose speech is protected by the First Amendment.

"Off-campus behavior that is not connected to the school in any way— 24 no use of school computers, no transmission of messages in school—is not within the purview[8] of school officials," said Joan Bertin, executive director of the National Coalition Against Censorship, an advocacy group in New York. "It may have some play-out within school, but the actual speech took place in a protected zone. The school can't go after the speech, but it can go after the behavior that occurs on campus" as a result of the speech.

An exception would be speech that constitutes a true threat, Bertin 25 said, but true threats must meet a high standard. "A kid e-mailing another kid saying, 'I'm going to knock your brains out' or 'I wish this teacher were dead'—these are not, in my opinion, true threats."

---

[8]*purview:* scope or range.

Teachers and Parents

Willard, at the Center for Safe and Responsible Internet Use, advises edu- 26
cators to step in even when cyberbullying occurs away from school if the
clear potential exists that it would affect students and the educational climate. Even so, she said, administrators' actions are important.

"They may impose discipline if . . . they're protecting the school's abil- 27
ity to deliver instruction, the security of students coming to school and [to
avert] violence," she said.

When juveniles do commit serious online abuses, the question often 28
arises: Where were the parents?

Shouldn't they be held accountable, or at least share the blame?   29

"The question isn't 'should,' the question is 'can,' and the answer 30
is 'yes,'" Willard said. Under parental-liability[9] statutes or parental-
negligence standards, parents may be held liable for the harm caused by
their children, she said.

In the civil-litigation system, "financial consequences for cyberbul- 31
lying are now serious enough to make even the most lenient parent of
a bully sit up and take notice," Millie Anne Cavanaugh, a family law
attorney in Los Angeles, wrote recently on the Web site of a group that
provides programs for troubled adolescents. "In addition to liability
against the cyberbully himself on theories such as defamation, invasion
of privacy, disclosure of private information and intentional infliction
of emotional distress, parents could now [be] held accountable for their
child's cyberbullying if they failed to properly supervise the child's online activity."

Susan Limber, a Clemson University psychologist who studies bully- 32
ing, said many adolescents in focus groups say parents and teachers don't
seem to talk enough with them about online behavior. "Kids on the one
hand say parents should be a little more involved," Limber said. "But as
one kid said, they want supervision, not 'snoopervision.'"

In other words, Limber said, "They want appropriate rules, but they 33
don't want parents poking into every last e-mail or text message. But that's
a fine line."

Parents can have an especially difficult time keeping track of what ado- 34
lescents are posting on social-networking sites. Some child advocates say
parents should create their own accounts so they can monitor what their
children are doing on the sites.

"Putting something on the Internet is a whole lot different than whis- 35
pering it on the playground," said Witold "Vic" Walczak, legal director of
the ACLU in Pennsylvania.

Many parents and other responsible adults often neglect to impart that 36
message to youngsters.

Weiss, of Operation Respect, said engaging adolescents in "conversa- 37
tion around moral issues" like cyberbullying "is really important for kids"
but that many adults—teachers among them—don't know how to do so.

"We're not having this conversation enough," he said. "If we did, it 38
would be the strongest thing we could do."

[9]*liability:* legal responsibility.

READING COMPREHENSION

1. The word *angst* in "The rise of Web sites brimming with the minutiae of teen antics and angst has helped to create a rich climate for mayhem: locker-room photos snapped with cell phones and broadcast on the Internet, fake profiles created on social-networking sites. . . ." (paragraph 14) means

   a. suffering.

   b. anger.

   c. tricks.

   d. practical jokes.

2. The word *nettlesome* in "Perhaps the most nettlesome circumstance is cyberbullying that is transmitted at home or the local mall or skating rink, but that nonetheless causes disruption at school" (paragraph 21) means

   a. annoying.

   b. strange.

   c. promising.

   d. unusual.

3. Which of the following best expresses the main idea of this selection?

   a. Cyberbullying cannot be stopped.

   b. Cyberbullies need our help.

   c. Cyberbullying is a difficult problem that is growing among adolescents.

   d. People convicted of cyberbullying and their parents should be prosecuted.

4. Which of the following is *not* one of the aims of a cyberbully?

   a. to spread false rumors about classmates

   b. to post inappropriate photos of people on the Internet

   c. to steal money from their classmates' bank accounts

   d. to intimidate people

5. *True or False?* _____ Teachers and parents don't spend enough time educating young people about the dangers of cyberbullying.

6. Free-speech advocates are concerned that trying to regulate student speech over the Internet or cell phones may limit

   a. the right to free speech for all people.

   b. the creativity of adolescents.

   c. the security of Internet and cell phone conversations.

   d. the rights of parents to set their own rules for their children.

7. One reason that parents should be concerned if their child is a cyberbully is that

   a. they could be tried and imprisoned for the child's actions.

   b. they might have to pay significant financial penalties for their child's actions.

   c. their child might be going through significant emotional stress.

   d. they will be shunned by other people in the community.

8. If cyberbullying occurs off campus, a school cannot punish the student unless

   a. the message contains nudity.

   b. the message is untrue.

   c. the message libels someone or falsely accuses someone of a crime.

   d. the message contains a real threat.

9. We can infer from what Billitteri says that a cyberbully

   a. is not someone who wants to cause physical harm.

   b. is an athlete.

   c. beats people up after school.

   d. is popular among his or her classmates.

10. According to Matt Blunt, cyberbullying

   a. interferes with free speech.

   b. disturbs the peace.

   c. makes educating young people more difficult.

   d. affects the emotional health of our children.

STRUCTURE AND TECHNIQUE

1. Is this selection aimed at teenagers who are cyberbullies or who may be the victims of cyberbullies? If not, what other kind of reader might this essay be aimed at? How do you know?

2. Where in this essay does the author use definition? Where does he explain causes and effects? Where does he use examples and comparison/contrast?

3. One of the reasons that this essay is easy to follow is that Billitteri uses a number of transitions to lead the reader from one idea to the next. Find a few places where he uses such transitions. Also, explain how the author's use of transitions makes this essay easier to read.

4. Is Billitteri's conclusion appropriate? What is he asking us to do in this conclusion? Does his message here fit with his thesis and with what he said earlier in the essay?

5. This essay is very persuasive. Where does the author use information from professional or academic studies and from experts to support his point?

CRITICAL READING AND DISCUSSION

1. What sentence most clearly states the author's main point?

2. How does the author define cyberbullying, and what are some of the characteristics of the people who practice it?

3. Bullying has been around for a very long time, says Billitteri. What has made cyberbullying so popular—so much of a problem these days?

4. Why is it so hard to write and enforce laws against cyberbullying?

5. What can adults do to curtail the spread of cyberbullying?

WRITING ASSIGNMENTS

Assignment 1: Writing a Paragraph

Cyberbullying is only one way modern electronic technology can be abused. Can you name another? For example, doesn't talking on a cell phone while driving pose a driving hazard? Don't people who invent and spread computer viruses deserve punishment? What about students who forget to turn their cell phones off in class or who text their friends while the instructor is trying to get an important point across? And what should be done about telemarketers who disturb our quiet and even our sleep?

Write a paragraph in which you describe the abuse of a modern technological device, explain what harm it does, and suggest ways in which it can be stopped.

Assignment 2: Writing an Essay

In this essay, cyberbullying is defined as an emerging health problem that is getting out of control. Read this essay again; then go online and do some more research about this activity. (You may refer to Chapter 20 for tips on researching.) What makes cyberbullying a health problem? In other words, in what ways does the practice threaten the health of young people?

Take notes on the ways in which cyberbullying threatens the physical, emotional, and/or moral health of young people. Also, find information to explain why a young person might be enticed into becoming a cyberbully.

Read over your notes and add to them if necessary. Next, construct an informal outline from your notes and use it as the basis of an essay that does two things:

1. Shows that cyberbullying is a symptom of moral decay in our society.

2. Explains the physical or emotional damage that it can inflict on both the victims of cyberbullying and on the bullies themselves.

You can conclude your essay in several ways. One of the most effective ways might be to explain what you think we should do to stop or curtail cyberbullying.

Assignment 3: Writing an Essay

Most young people have no fear of death because they seldom remember that, like everyone else, they too shall die. Teenagers especially engage in behavior that is risky and that is liable to result in permanent physical or emotional damage or even in death.

Perhaps you know people who are taking drugs, who smoke cigarettes, who drink too much, who drive recklessly, who have unprotected sex, who follow harmful diets, who engage in dangerous sports, or who are involved in some other such habit or activity. Write an essay in which you present the case of a person who engages in an activity you believe to be potentially harmful. In each case, explain what makes your subject do what he or she does. Then, explain why this activity is so harmful or dangerous, being as detailed as you can when you discuss the short-term and long-term risks of his or her behavior. If necessary, do some research online or in the library to gather more information about the causes and outcomes of the behavior in which your subject is engaging. (Refer to Chapter 20 for tips on how to research and cite your resources.)

Conclude your essay by discussing measures that the subject in question might take to break a harmful habit or to stop engaging in a dangerous activity. Again, you might want to rely on research to gather information for this part of your essay.

Why Profiling Won't Work

William Raspberry

PREVIEW

This article, published in the *Washington Post* on August 22, 2005, discusses the complex maneuvering authorities must do in order to keep the American public safe from terrorists. William Raspberry adeptly covers the intricate balance between profiling individuals who appear to be terrorists and ordinary American citizens. Mistakes are made by using stereotypes about certain individuals. He provides examples of how Americans can be mistaken for terrorists since America is composed of various ethnic and racial groups, and that by limiting the profile to Arab-looking male individuals, the authorities are most likely bypassing the true terrorists, who may come in different forms the next time an attempt is made.

The Transportation Security Administration, having rendered cockpit 1 crews less vulnerable to hijackers by strengthening the cockpit doors, is now (1) reviewing its list of items passengers may not bring aboard, (2) proposing to minimize the number of passengers who have to be patted down at checkpoints and (3) taking another look at the rule that requires most passengers to remove their shoes.

These are encouraging moves toward common sense.   2

This isn't: A gaggle[1] of voices is proposing—almost as though re- 3 sponding to the same memo from some malign Mr. Big—that the TSA replace its present policy of random searches with massive racial and ethnic profiling.

---

[1]*gaggle:* loud group.

After all, they argue, weren't the Sept. 11 terrorists all young Muslim 4 men? Isn't it likely that the next terrorist attack will be carried out by young Muslim men? So why waste time screening white-haired grandmothers and blue-suited white guys? Much more efficient to tap the shoulder of any young man who looks Muslim—a category that covers not just Arabs but also Asians, Africans and, increasingly, African Americans.

It must have been just such sweet reason that led to the internment[2] of 5 thousands of Japanese Americans during World War II. Even Andrew C. McCarthy of the Foundation for the Defense of Democracies—and one of the advocates of profiling—acknowledges that the Japanese internments were excessive. But only, he says in the current issue of *National Review*, because "they included American citizens of Japanese descent;[3] there was nothing objectionable in principle about holding Japanese, German, or Italian nationals."

That distinction doesn't hold up in the case of airport profiling, since 6 there's no way visually to distinguish between a Saudi citizen and an Arab American. The profilers wouldn't even try.

Actually, anyone who's ever been inconvenienced by security checks— 7 whether as trivial as having to give up a fingernail clipper or as serious as having to take a later flight—will see some merit in the case for profiling. Can't they see that I'm just a guy trying to get from here to there, while that fellow over there looks like he could be a hijacker?

One trouble with that line is that the obviously innocent tend to look 8 a lot like ourselves, while the clearly suspect tend to look like the other fellow. Which is why so many Middle Eastern–looking men (and Sikhs) were stopped and frisked in the days just after Sept. 11—and why at least one member of President Bush's Secret Service detail was thrown off an airliner.

The other, more serious problem is that the pro-profilers are fighting 9 the last war. If someone had stopped 19 young Muslim men from boarding four jetliners four years ago, Sept. 11 wouldn't have happened. Therefore, security requires that we make it difficult for young Muslim men to board jetliners. It's as though white people come in all sizes, ages and predispositions,[4] while young Arab men are fungible.[5]

Random checks at least have the virtue of rendering us all equal. I can 10 talk with any fellow passenger about the absurdity of having to remove my loafers, because that fellow passenger has been similarly inconvenienced. But with whom does a young Arab (or Turk or dreadlocked college student) share his humiliation?

And make no mistake, it is humiliating. Stop me once because someone 11 fitting my description or driving a car like mine is a suspect in a crime and I shrug and comply. Stop me repeatedly because of how I look and I respond with less and less grace.

[2]*internment:* confinement.
[3]*descent:* nationality.
[4]*predispositions:* tendencies.
[5]*fungible:* identical, interchangeable.

Am I arguing against all efforts to protect America from terrorism? Of course not. But since Americans look all sorts of ways, a more sensible way of deciding who gets extra attention is behavior. 12

The profilers say this is just political correctness gone mad. McCarthy puts it bluntly: "Until we stop pretending not to see what the terrorists who are attacking us look like, we may as well give them an engraved invitation to strike again." 13

Well, we do know what they look like. They look like the 19 hijackers of Sept. 11, but they also look like Richard "Shoe Bomber" Reid, John Walker Lindh, Jose Padilla and—don't forget—Timothy McVeigh. 14

Profile that. 15

READING COMPREHENSION

1. The word *profiling* in the article is used to describe
   a. the manner in which certain individuals stand when being stared at.
   b. the process by which terrorists escape detection at U.S. airports.
   c. the process by which law enforcement look for physical looks and behavior to target possible terrorists.
   d. the process by which terrorists spot undercover law enforcement officers in U.S. airports.

2. In paragraph 3, the word *gaggle* in "A gaggle of voices is proposing . . ." most closely means
   a. a low sound.
   b. an indistinct whisper.
   c. a group.
   d. childlike.

3. Which of the following could be an alternate title for the article?
   a. Educating Americans about Terrorism
   b. Profiling for Potential Terrorists
   c. Profiling Efforts in American Airports
   d. Profiling Efforts of TSA Officers

4. Which of the following sentences best expresses the main idea of this selection?
   a. Profiling efforts in American airports are inconvenient.
   b. American-born terrorists look just like the rest of us.
   c. Because Americans are so diverse, a better system of profiling is needed.
   d. Profiling efforts are highly ineffectual.

5. As stated in the article, one way the Transportation Security Administration now protects passengers from terrorism is by
   a. reviewing its list of items passengers cannot bring on board.
   b. deciding which flights would most likely contain terrorists.

    c. training TSA personnel in martial arts.

    d. teaching modern Arabic to its officers.

6. Although the author finds some profiling activities useless, he does see the merits of

    a. monitoring all passports and IDs.

    b. electronic surveillance through the airport.

    c. random checks.

    d. sniffing dogs in U.S. airports.

7. The author suggests that profiling doesn't work because

    a. there is no way to tell terrorists from nonterrorists.

    b. it's a racist practice.

    c. Americans mostly look all the same.

    d. terrorists can use disguises.

8. Which way does the author suggest would be a better determinant of possible terrorist identification?

    a. the person's accent

    b. the person's country of origin

    c. the person's physical description

    d. the person's behavior

9. *True or False?* _____ William Raspberry believes that all efforts to protect America are useless.

10. We can conclude that William Raspberry cares about his country, but simply

    a. is reprimanding the TSA for its behavior.

    b. is criticizing U.S. policies towards terrorists.

    c. dislikes being inconvenienced at airports.

    d. is shedding light on ineffectual profiling practices.

STRUCTURE AND TECHNIQUE

1. Raspberry uses a highly structured format for his article. What are some of the features of this format? Why do you think Raspberry structured his article in this way?

2. Does the author clearly state his main idea, or thesis, about the article? If so, where is it stated and how?

3. Raspberry uses a very familiar tone in his article, but one can clearly infer that Raspberry has had instances when he has been profiled. Can you locate areas within the article where Raspberry's opinion borders on narration?

CRITICAL READING AND DISCUSSION

1. Raspberry begins his article describing how America is not new to the concept of profiling. He uses the example of the treatment received by

Japanese Americans during World War II. How does beginning the article with a retrospective of a previous American practice affect your views on current profiling efforts? Do you believe these efforts are fair or effective? Explain.

2. The article refers mostly to airport profiling, using the 911 attacks as a basis for the modern practice. Raspberry does not agree with the practice for various reasons. What were some of those reasons and do you agree with all of them, some of them, or none of them?

3. After having read the article, do you believe that airport profiling plays a significant role in preventing future terrorist acts? If so, why? If not, why not? What does Raspberry mean by saying that random checks would render all of us equal?

WRITING ASSIGNMENTS

Assignment 1: Writing a Paragraph

Write a paragraph about a time you were mistaken for someone else. For instance, have your looks ever been compared to a celebrity or famous person? How did you feel after the incident? Were you flattered, annoyed, upset? How about the person who mistook you for someone else? Did they explain why they thought you were someone else?

Assignment 2: Writing an Essay

Profiling, in a way, is the process whereby someone accuses you of doing something or being about to do something. Therefore, it is a form of prejudice. Write an essay explaining a time you were accused of something you didn't do. What were the circumstances for the accusation? Were you accused of having stolen an item in a store? Or a school test from the teacher's desk?

Assignment 3: Writing an Essay

More often than not, certain minority groups in America are profiled more than others. Write an essay that emphasizes narration about a time you were or felt discriminated against. You can discuss a job opportunity or a promotion at work that you were not given. Perhaps you can talk about a time you felt uncomfortable in a certain surrounding, and felt that your race or ethnicity was the reason for the suspicion. For example, some individuals are sometimes followed around in stores for fear that they may steal something.

Here's to Your Health

Joan Dunayer

PREVIEW

Joan Dunayer contrasts the glamorous "myth" about alcohol, as presented in advertising and popular culture, with the reality—which is often far less appealing. After reading her essay, you will be more aware of how we are encouraged to think of alcohol as being tied to happiness and success. You may also become a more critical observer of images presented by advertisers.

As the only freshman on his high school's varsity wrestling team, Tod was 1 anxious to fit in with his older teammates. One night after a match, he was offered a tequila bottle on the ride home. Tod felt he had to accept, or he would seem like a sissy. He took a swallow, and every time the bottle was passed back to him, he took another swallow. After seven swallows, he passed out. His terrified teammates carried him into his home, and his mother then rushed him to the hospital. After his stomach was pumped, Tod learned that his blood alcohol level had been so high that he was lucky not to be in a coma or dead.

Unfortunately, drinking is not unusual among high-school students 2 or, for that matter, in any other segment of our society. And that's no accident. There are numerous influences in our society urging people to drink, not the least of which is advertising. Who can recall a televised baseball or basketball game without a beer commercial? Furthermore, alcohol ads appear with pounding frequency in magazines, on billboards, and in college newspapers. According to industry estimates, brewers spend more than $600 million a year on radio and TV commercials and another $90 million on print ads. In addition, the liquor industry spends about $230 million a year on print advertising, and since 1966 it has greatly expanded its presence on cable and independent broadcast stations. Just recently, NBC became the first network station to accept hard liquor ads for broadcast.

To top it all off, this aggressive advertising of alcohol fosters a harmful 3 myth about drinking.

Part of the myth is that liquor signals professional success. In a slick 4 men's magazine, one full-page ad for Scotch whiskey shows two men seated in an elegant restaurant. Both are in their thirties, perfectly groomed, and wearing expensive-looking gray suits. The windows are draped with velvet, the table with spotless white linen. Each place-setting consists of a long-stemmed water goblet, silver utensils, and thick silver plates. On each plate is a half-empty cocktail glass. The two men are grinning and shaking hands, as if they've just concluded a business deal. The caption reads, "The taste of success."

Contrary to what the liquor company would have us believe, drink- 5 ing is more closely related to lack of success than to achievement. Among students, the heaviest drinkers have the lowest grades. In the work force, alcoholics are frequently late or absent, tend to perform poorly, and often get fired. Although alcohol abuse occurs in all economic classes, it remains most prevalent among the poor.

Another part of the alcohol myth is that drinking makes you more at- 6 tractive to the opposite sex. "Hot, hot, hot," one commercial's soundtrack begins, as the camera scans a crowd of college-age beachgoers. Next it follows the curve of a woman's leg up to her bare hip and lingers there. She is young, beautiful, wearing a bikini. A young guy, carrying an ice chest, positions himself near to where she sits. He is tan, muscular. She doesn't show much interest—until he opens the chest and takes out a beer. Now she smiles over at him. He raises his eyebrows and, invitingly, holds up another can. She joins him. This beer, the song concludes, "attracts like no other."

Beer doesn't make anyone sexier. Like all alcohol, it lowers the levels 7 of male hormones in men and of female hormones in women—even when taken in small amounts. In substantial amounts, alcohol can cause infertility in women and impotence in men. Some alcoholic men even develop enlarged breasts.

The alcohol myth also creates the illusion that beer and athletics are 8 a perfect combination. One billboard features three high-action images: a sprinter running at top speed, a surfer riding a wave, and a basketball player leaping to make a dunk shot. A particular light beer, the billboard promises, "won't slow you down."

"Slow you down" is exactly what alcohol does. Drinking plays a role 9 in over six million injuries each year—not counting automobile accidents. Even in small amounts, alcohol dulls the brain, reducing muscle coordination and slowing reaction time. It also interferes with the ability to focus the eyes and adjust to a sudden change in brightness—such as the flash of a car's headlights. Drinking and driving, responsible for over half of all automobile deaths, is the leading cause of death among teenagers. Continued alcohol abuse can physically change the brain, permanently impairing learning and memory. Long-term drinking is related to malnutrition, weakening of the bones, and ulcers. It increases the risk of liver failure, heart disease, and stomach cancer.

Finally, according to the myth, alcohol is the magic ingredient for social 10 success. Hundreds of TV and radio ads have echoed this message in recent years. In one commercial, for instance, an overweight man sits alone in his drab living room. He reaches into a cooler, pulls out a bottle of beer, and twists off the bottle cap. Instantly dance music erupts, and dozens of attractive young adults appear in a shower of party streamers and confetti. "Where the party begins," a voice says. The once lonely man, now a popular guy with lots of male and female friends, has found the answer to his social problems—beer.

Relationships based on alcohol are unlikely to lead to social success and 11 true friendships. Indeed, studies show that when alcohol becomes the center of a social gathering, it may lead to public drunkenness and violence. The ad's image of the man's new friends ignores an undeniable reality: that alcohol ruins—not creates—relationships. In addition to fighting and simple assault, drinking is linked to two-thirds of domestic violence incidents. Rather than leading to healthy social connections, alcohol leads to loneliness, despair, and mental illness. Over a fourth of the patients in state and county mental hospitals have alcohol problems; more than half of all violent crimes are alcohol-related; the rate of suicide among alcoholics is fifteen times higher than among the general population.

Advertisers would have us believe the myth that alcohol is part of being 12 successful, sexy, healthy, and happy; but those who have suffered from it—directly or indirectly—know otherwise. For alcohol's victims, "Here's to your health" rings with a terrible irony when it is accompanied by the clink of liquor glasses.

READING COMPREHENSION

1. The word *impairing* in "Continued alcohol abuse can physically change the brain, permanently impairing learning and memory" (paragraph 9) means

   a. postponing.

   b. doubling.

   c. damaging.

   d. teaching.

2. The word *fosters* in "this aggressive advertising of alcohol fosters a harmful myth about drinking" (paragraph 3) means

   a. avoids.

   b. delays.

   c. promotes.

   d. discourages.

3. Which one of the following would be a good alternative title for this selection?

   a. The Taste of Success

   b. Alcohol and Your Social Life

   c. Too Much Tequila

   d. Alcohol: Image and Reality

4. Which sentence best expresses the main idea of the selection?

   a. Sports and alcohol don't mix.

   b. The media and our culture promote false images about success and happiness.

   c. The media and our culture promote false beliefs about alcohol.

   d. Liquor companies should not be allowed to use misleading ads.

5. According to the selection, drinking can

   a. actually unify a family.

   b. lower hormone levels.

   c. temporarily improve performance in sports.

   d. increase the likelihood of pregnancy.

6. *True or False?* _____ Alcohol abuse is most severe among middle-class people.

7. *True or False?* _____ The leading cause of death among teenagers is drinking and driving.

8. From the first paragraph of the essay, we can conclude that
   a. even one encounter with alcohol can lead to death.
   b. tequila is the worst type of alcohol to drink.
   c. wrestlers tend to drink more than other athletes.
   d. by the time students reach high school, peer pressure doesn't influence them.

9. *True or False?* _____ The author implies that one or two drinks a day are probably harmless.

10. The author implies that heavy drinking can lead to
    a. poor grades.
    b. getting fired.
    c. heart disease.
    d. all of the above.

STRUCTURE AND TECHNIQUE

1. What method of introduction does Dunayer use? What effect do you think she hoped to achieve with this introduction?

2. Dunayer begins her criticism of alcohol with "Part of the myth is . . . ." (See the first sentence of paragraph 4.) What additional transitions does she use to introduce each of the three other parts of the myth (in the first sentences of paragraphs 6, 8, and 10)? What is gained by the use of these transitions?

3. The body of Dunayer's essay is made up of four pairs of paragraphs (paragraphs 4 and 5; 6 and 7; 8 and 9; 10 and 11). What is the relationship between the paragraphs in each pair? In which of the two paragraphs does Dunayer present her own perspective? Why do you think she puts her own perspective in that paragraph?

4. In her essay, Dunayer provides vivid descriptions of alcohol advertisements, particularly in paragraphs 4 and 6. What vivid details does she provide? How do these details support her main point?

CRITICAL READING AND DISCUSSION

1. Dunayer presents and then rebuts four "myths" about alcohol. What are these four myths? According to Dunayer, what is the reality behind each myth?

2. Dunayer concludes, "'Here's to your health' rings with a terrible irony when it is accompanied by the clink of liquor glasses" (paragraph 12). What is the "terrible irony" she refers to? How does this irony—already signaled in her essay's title—relate to her main point?

3. Do you think Dunayer's essay is one-sided or balanced? Explain. What additional points could be used to support her point or to rebut it?

4. Advertisers often create myths or use false ideas to get people to buy their products. Besides alcohol ads, what are some other examples of manipulative or deceptive advertising? Do you think advertisers should be permitted to use such tactics to sell products?

RESPONDING TO IMAGES

Describe and analyze the accompanying billboard advertisement for vodka. Argue whether the ad is socially responsible or irresponsible in the way that it portrays drinking.

WRITING ASSIGNMENTS

Assignment 1: Writing a Paragraph

Write a paragraph about what you consider responsible or irresponsible advertising for some product or service. Cigarettes, weight loss, and cosmetics are possibilities to consider.

Assignment 2: Writing an Essay

If you have a friend, relative, or classmate who drinks a lot, write a letter warning him or her about the dangers of alcohol. If appropriate, use information from Dunayer's essay. Remember that since your purpose is to get someone you care about to control or break a dangerous habit, you should make your writing very personal. Don't bother explaining how alcoholism affects people in general. Instead, focus directly on what you see it doing to your reader.

Divide your argument into at least three supporting paragraphs. You might, for instance, talk about how your reader is jeopardizing his or her relationship with three of the following: family, friends, boss and coworkers, instructors and classmates.

Assignment 3: Writing an Essay

Dunayer describes how alcohol advertisements promote false beliefs, such as the idea that alcohol will make you successful. Imagine that you work for a public service ad agency given the job of presenting the negative side of alcohol. What images would you choose to include in your ads?

Write a report to your boss in which you propose in detail three anti-alcohol ads. Choose from among the following:

Ad counteracting the idea that alcohol leads to success

Ad counteracting the idea that alcohol is sexy

Ad counteracting the idea that alcohol goes well with athletics

Ad counteracting the idea that alcohol makes for happy families

READING COMPREHENSION CHART

Write an X through the numbers of any questions you missed while answering the comprehension questions for each selection in Part 6, Readings for Writers. Then write in your comprehension score. If you repeatedly miss questions in any particular skill, the chart will make that clear. Then you can pay special attention to that skill in the future.

Selection	Vocabulary in Context	Title and Main Idea	Key Details	Inferences	Comprehension Score
Gregory	1 2	3 4	5 6 7	8 9 10	%
Johnson	1 2	3 4	5 6 7	8 9 10	%
Alexie	1 2	3 4	5	6 7 8 9 10	%
Malcolm X	1 2 3	4 5	6 7 8	9 10	%
Cisneros	1 2 3	4 5	6 7	8 9 10	%
Tan	1 2 3 4	5 6	7 8	9 10 11 12	%
Banas	1 2	3 4	5 6 7	8 9 10	%
McClintock	1 2	3 4	5 6 7 8	9 10	%
DeGeneres	1 2	3 4	5 6 7	8 9 10	%
Twain	1 2 3	4 5	6	7 8 9 10	%
Pausch	1 2	3 4	5 6 7	8 9 10	%
Kennedy	1 2	3 4	5 6 7	8 9 10	%
Britt	1 2	3 4	5 6 7	8 9 10	%
Katz	1	2 3	4 5 6 7	8 9 10	%
O'Keeney	1 2	3 4	5 6 7	8 9 10	%
Sherry	1 2	3 4	5 6 7	8 9 10	%
Garity	1 2	3 4	5 6 7	8 9 10	%
Billitteri	1 2	3	4 5 6 7 8	9 10	%
Raspberry	1 2	3 4	5 6 7	8 9 10	%
Dunayer	1 2	3 4	5 6 7	8 9 10	%

Writing a Formal E-mail

E-mail

Like all writing, e-mails need to account for their audience. E-mails sent to friends can be casual in tone and language, but e-mails sent to employees or bosses should be formal in tone, language, and format. A sample formal e-mail follows:

TO: Tom Jones
Subject: Paper Usage at Acme Widgets, Inc.
Attachment: 2012 HR Paper Report

Dear Mr. Jones:

  I submit to you the paper usage in the Human Resources Department at Acme Widgets, Inc. for the year 2013. You will find that we used 500 reams of paper, up 100 reams from 2012. This increased paper usage cost the company an additional $1,000. Additional details can be found in the attached report.

  I would like to meet with you to discuss actions that can be taken to reduce our paper usage in the future. Please let me know your earliest available time, and I will bring my ideas.

Sincerely,
Jane Smith
Manager, Human Resources
Acme Widgets, Incorporated
600 South Smith Road
New York, NY 62210
(555) 555-5555
jane.smith@gmail.com

Points to Note about Formal E-mails

Your formal e-mail should have the following features:

1. A very specific subject-related title in the subject header.
2. Formal formatting, which includes using the word *dear*, addressing the person by his or her full name or title, and using a colon at the end of the greeting.
3. A concise, detailed message that includes necessary information.
4. Attachments if necessary.
5. A formal closing that uses words like *sincerely* or *cordially*.
6. A "signature" that includes address, phone number, and e-mail address.

Transition Words and Phrases

Addition Signals

also	for one thing	moreover
and	furthermore	next
another	in addition	one
finally	indeed	second
first	last	the third reason
first of all	last of all	to begin with

Time Signals

after	later	third
as	next	when
before	meanwhile	while
finally	second	
first	then	

Space Signals

above	in back	next to
across	in front	on the opposite side
behind	near	to the left
below	nearby	to the right

Change-of-Direction Signals

although	instead	otherwise
but	nevertheless	still
however	on the contrary	yet
in contrast	on the other hand	

Illustration Signals

as an illustration	for instance	specifically
for example	once	such as

Conclusion Signals

as a result	in summary	therefore
consequently	last of all	thus
finally	then	to conclude

CREDITS

Photo Credits

Part 1 Opener: © The McGraw-Hill Companies, Inc./ Jill Braaten, Photographer; Chapter 1 Opener: © Digital Vision/Getty Images; Chapter 2 Opener: © Digital Vision/Getty Images; Part 2 Opener: © Lars A. Niki; Chapter 3 Opener: © BananaStock/PunchStock; Chapter 4 Opener: © Dynamic Graphics/JupiterImages; Chapter 5 Opener: Courtesy of Ad Busters; Part 3 Opener: © Masterfile; Chapter 6 Opener: Photo by Trae Patton © NBC/Courtesy Everett Collection; Chapter 7 Opener: © Jeff Gross/Getty Images; Chapter 8 Opener: © NetPhotos/Alamy; p. 176: © PRNews-Foto/Columbia Records/AP Photos; Chapter 9 Opener: AP Photo; Chatper 10 Opener: © Chao Soi Cheong/AP Photo; p. 196: © Neno Images/PhotoEdit; Chapter 11 Opener: © Digital Vision/SuperStock; p. 210: Book Design by George Karabotsos, used with permission; Chapter 12 Opener: © NASA/Getty Images; Chapter 13 Opener: © Radius Images/Jupiter Images; Chapter 14 Opener: © Bob Daemmrich/PhotoEdit; p. 243: © Mike Siluk/The Image Works; Part 4 Opener: © Scott Stulberg/Corbis; Chapter 15 Opener: © Ingram Publishing/SuperStock; Chapter 16 Opener: © Tannen Maury/epa/Corbis; Chapter 17 Opener: © BananaStock/Jupiterimages; Chapter 18 Opener (left): © Swim Ink 2, LLC/Corbis; Chapter 18 Opener (right): © US DOD/Alamy; p. 333: © ABC/Photofest; Chapter 19 Opener: © Frederick Bass/Getty Images; Chapter 20 Opener: © The McGraw-Hill Companies, Inc./Leroy Webster, photographer; p. 389: © Royalty-Free/Corbis; Part 5 Opener: © Jeff Greenberg/PhotoEdit; Section 1 Opener: © Natalie Hummel; p. 442: © Mike Greenlar/ The Post Standard/The Image Works; Chapter 30 Opener: © Image Source; Section 2 Opener: Photo illustration by David Tietz/Editorial Image, LLC; Section 2 Opener: Photo illustration by David Tietz/ Editorial Image, LLC; Section 3 Opener: © Clive Andrews; Section 4 Opener: Courtesy of James Yu; p. 516: © Dennis MacDonald/PhotoEdit; Part 6 Opener: © Joe Tabacca/AP Photo; p. 570: © Reuters NewMedia Inc./Corbis; p. 576: Courtesy of Beth Johnson; p. 579: Courtesy of John Langan; p. 581: Courtesy of John Langan; p. 585: © Globe Photos/ ZUMAPRESS.com; p. 590: © Michael Ochs Archives/ Getty Images; p. 595 (top): © Brand X Pictures; p. 595 (bottom): © Riccardo De Luca/MAXPPP/Newscom; p. 601: © imago stock&people/Newscom; p. 609: © Chicago Tribune/MCT/Landov; p. 612: © Pixtal/ AGE Fotostock; p. 621: © Lars A. Niki; p. 622: © Frank Trapper/Corbis; p. 629: Library of Congress Prints and Photographs Division [LC-USZ62-5513]; p. 638: © Corbis; p. 644: Courtesy of Suzanne Britt; p. 662: © Purestock/Alamy; p. 664: Courtesy of Mary Sherry; p. 676: Courtesy of Thomas J. Billitteri; p. 683: Courtesy of William Raspberry; p. 688: Courtesy of Joan Dunayer; p. 692: © Splash News/Corbis.

Text and Line Art Credits

From *Nigger: An Autobiography,* by Dick Gregory, copyright © 1964 by Dick Gregory Enterprises, Inc. Used by permission of Dutton, a division of Penguin Group (USA) Inc.

Beth Johnson, "The Professor Is a Dropout." Reprinted by permission of the author.

From *The Los Angeles Times,* by Sherman Alexie, April 19, 1998. Copyright © 1998 by The Los Angeles Times. All rights reserved. Used with permission of LA Times Reprints.

From *The Autobiography of Malcolm X,* by Malcolm X and Alex Haley. Copyright © 1964 by Alex Haley and Malcolm X. Copyright © 1965 by Alex Haley and Betty Shabazz. Used by permission of Random House, I11.c. and The Random House Group Ltd.

From *Literature: The American Experience,* January 1, 1996. Copyright © 1996 by Pearson Education. Reprinted by permission.

Copyright © 1990 by Amy Tan. First appeared in THE THREEPENNY REVIEW. Reprinted by permission of the author and the Sandra Dijkstra Literary Agency.

Casey Banas, "What's Wrong with Schools?" From *Chicago Tribune,* August 5, 1979. © 1979 Chicago Tribune. All rights reserved. Used by permission and protected by the Copyright Laws of the United States. The printing, copying, redistribution, or retransmission of the Material without express written permission is prohibited.

Ann McClintock, "Propaganda Techniques in Today's Advertising." Reprinted by permission of the author.

INDEX